The

S

The Garland Handbook of Southeast Asian Music

Edited by

Terry E. Miller and Sean Williams

Routledge
Taylor & Francis Group

NEW YORK AND LONDON

First published 2008
by Routledge
270 Madison Avenue
New York, NY 10016

Simultaneously published in the UK
by Routledge
2 Park Square, Milton Park
Abingdon, Oxon 0X14 4RN

Routledge is an imprint of the Taylor and Francis Group, an informa business

The Garland Handbook of Southeast Asian Music is an abridged paperback edition of *Southeast Asia*, volume 4 of *The Garland Encyclopedia of World Music*, with revised essays.

Typeset in Adobe Garamond and Gill Sans by EvS Communication Networx, Inc.
Printed in the United States of America on acid-free paper by Sheridan Books, Inc., MI

Library of Congress Cataloging in Publication Data
A catalog record for this book has been requested

ISBN 10: 0-415-96075-4 (pbk)
ISBN 10: 0-203-93144-0 (ebk)

ISBN 13: 978-0-415-96075-5 (pbk)
ISBN 13: 978-0-203-93144-8 (ebk)

TABLE OF CONTENTS

LIST OF AUDIO EXAMPLES

The following examples are included on the accompanying audio compact disc packaged with this volume. Track and CD numbers are also indicated on the pages listed below for easy reference to text discussions. Complete notes on each example can be found on pages 483–486.

Compact Disc

LIST OF CONTRIBUTORS

Corazon Canave-Dioquino
University of the Phillipines

Amy Catlin
University of California
Los Angeles, California, U.S.A.

James Chopyak
California State University
Sacramento, California, U.S.A.

David Harnish
Bowling Green State University
Bowling Green, Ohio, U.S.A.

Thomas Hudak
Arizona State University
Tempe, Arizona, U.S.A.

Karl L. Hutterer
Santa Barbara Museum of Natural History
Santa Barbara, California, U.S.A.

Margaret J. Kartomi
Monash University
Australia

Ward Keeler
University of Texas at Austin
Austin, Texas, U.S.A.

José Maceda (deceased)
University of the Philippines

Patricia Matusky
Grand Valley State University
Allendale, Michigan, U.S.A.

Terry E. Miller
Kent State University (Emeritus)
Kent, Ohio, U.S.A.

Phong T. Nguyễn
National Conservatory of Music
Hồ Chi Minh City, Vietnam

Hans Oesch (deceased)
Basel, Switzerland

Marina Roseman
Queen's University Belfast
Belfast, Norther Ireland

Sam-Ang Sam
Phnom Penh, Cambodia

Ramón P. Santos
University of the Philippines

Lee Tong Soon
Emory University
Atlanta, Georgia, U.S.A.

Endo Suanda
Bandung, Indonesia

R. Anderson Sutton
University of Wisconsin
Madison, Wisconsin, U.S.A.

Ruriko Uchida (deceased)
Tokyo, Japan

Sean Williams
The Evergreen State College
Olympia, Washington, U.S.A.

PREFACE

This volume of *The Garland Handbook of Southeast Asian Music* covers one of the most diverse places on the planet, home to hundreds of millions of people. Yet Southeast Asia is considered by some to be utterly remote and inaccessible because of its perceived physical and cultural distance from the West. Numerous images of the region may come to mind. With these conceptions shaped partly by such dramatic fictions as *The King and I* and *The Year of Living Dangerously*, partly by colonial and wartime experiences, and partly by glorious travel footage on television and in magazines, Westerners have been dazzled and confused by what Southeast Asia represents. Is it a tropical earthly paradise? A dense group of forests with landmines and former headhunters? A sweeping panorama of breathtaking terraced rice fields and volcanoes? Trance-dancing rituals, extraordinary wildlife, and incredibly crowded urban scenes? Southeast Asia is certainly all of these, but for the writers of this volume it is the music that has brought us together to explore and write about this extraordinary region.

HOW THIS HANDBOOK IS ORGANIZED

The *Handbook* includes a number of essays from the much larger *Garland Encyclopedia of World Music*, Southeast Asia volume (Routledge 1998). The editors have carefully read, reduced, and in some cases updated the articles, with the expectation that you, the reader, are looking for relevant and up-to-date information on Southeast Asian music in a concise and effective format. To that end, we have organized this *Handbook* to reflect its new focus. Part I comprises not only an introduction to the area of Southeast Asia (divided into the mainland and the islands, but unified by a number of important features), but also a series of issues and processes, such as influences from surrounding areas, religious practices, and modernization. Part II is entirely about mainland Southeast Asia, with multiple nations and ethnic groups represented. Part III divides into three sections: Indonesia, the Philippines, and Borneo. Despite our presentation of discrete articles on each modern nation, readers will nevertheless find musical traditions and instruments that cross national and cultural boundaries (changing their local spelling and often their context as well).

An important aspect of the current volume is the inclusion of Questions for Critical Thinking at the end of each major section. These questions are intended to guide not only student work in the area, but to focus attention on what issues—musical and cultural—arise when one studies the music of Southeast Asia, issues that might not occur in the study of other musics of the world.

RESOURCES FOR STUDENTS AND INSTRUCTORS

Some readers new to Southeast Asian music may be surprised to find that Western musical notation does not appear frequently in this volume. In most cases, standard notation is ill-equipped to handle the kind of tones, timbres, and musical motions that occur in Southeast Asian musics. Instead, contributors have often used local conventions to describe music (such as a numerical system for Indonesian gamelan), and these conventions are explained in each article. An accompanying compact disc offers examples of some of the music of Southeast Asia.

Also, *The Garland Handbook of Southeast Asian Music* now has a companion website, **www.routledge.com/textbooks/garlandhandbooks.**

This is provided for both teachers and students and will have multiple resources, such as quizzes, web links, and other material.

INTRODUCTION TO THE MUSIC CULTURES OF SOUTHEAST ASIA

The island of Java was one of the first sites of research by Westerners in the young field of ethnomusicology in the early twentieth century. In fact, the Javanese gamelan orchestra was at one time virtually synonymous with the relatively new field of "world music." Worldwide knowledge of Southeast Asian musical traditions had been scattered and uneven for hundreds of years, but in the 1960s and 1970s the appearance of gamelan ensembles at colleges and universities in North America and Europe made them foremost in the minds of those interested in "exotic" music. Mainland Southeast Asian musics, on the other hand, are still largely unknown in the West despite years of contact during wartime and following the exodus of more than a million refugees after 1975. Until the 1980s, only a few books and articles on Southeast Asian music were available in Western libraries. Since then, broader knowledge of and interest in Southeast Asian expressive culture have led to a large cohort of younger ethnomusicologists discovering new excitement in Southeast Asia and exploring the region far beyond the limits of what might appear in a typical college survey of world music.

Together, we (the volume's two editors) wrote many of the articles in Part I and we were lucky to find diligent, expert authors who were willing to work with us on this project. We thank them for their years of patience and good humor in their dealings with us. The Southeast Asian musicians with whom we all have lived and worked—and whose original knowledge forms the core of this volume—deserve more appreciation, acknowledgment, and celebration than any of us could begin to offer.

We would like to express our genuine and heartfelt thanks to Constance Ditzel, Lynn Goeller, and Denny Tek, who have all worked diligently to facilitate the publication of this book. We also want to thank our spouses, Sara Stone Miller and Cary Black, and Sean's daughter Morgan, who supported our long hours of work on the original volume and on the current volume, ten years later. We have done our best to prevent any errors from sneaking unnoticed into the final versions of the articles in this *Handbook*, but we recognize that a few may surface. We bear sole responsibility for these.

—TERRY E. MILLER AND SEAN WILLIAMS
2008

GUIDE TO PRONUNCIATION

Thomas John Hudak

Listed below are approximate English equivalents to the sounds that appear in the South-east Asian language terms used in this volume.

GENERAL GUIDELINES

Unless otherwise indicated, vowels and consonants in Southeast Asian languages have the following English equivalents.

Vowels

Character	Pronounced as in English…
a	father
ae, ac	bat
e	bait
i	beat
o	boat
u	boot

Consonants

The consonants *p, t,* and *k* are unaspirated stops (without a puff of air) as in the English *spill, still,* and *skill*. The consonant *c* is similar to the English sequence *t-y* in the phrase nex*t year*. The consonant cluster *ny* is similar to the English sequence *n-y* in the word ca*ny*on.

In contrast, *ph, th, ch,* and *kh* are aspirated stops (with a puff of air) as in the English *p*ill, *t*ill, *ch*ill, and *k*ill. The consonant *q* indicates a glottal stop as in the sound that appears in the middle of the English sequence *oh-oh*. Glottal stops are also indicated in some languages with a ' symbol.

For names and terms in the articles listed below, exceptions to the general guidelines can be found in the appropriate chart. In all cases, vowels precede consonants, with both in English alphabetical order.

Khmer

For Khmer names and terms that appear in the article on the music of Cambodia, the following additional equivalents are suggested.

Character	Pronounced as in English...
ai	*ai*sle
ao	g*o*
au	c*ow*
ea	b*ai*t plus the vowel in b*u*t
eu	b*u*t
ey	b*u*t plus the vowel in b*ea*t
ie	b*ea*t plus the vowel in b*u*t
oa	N*oa*h
oeu	n*ew* (with lips spread) + the vowel in b*u*t
ou	b*oo*t
uo	b*oo*t plus the vowel in b*u*t

Thailand

aw	l*a*w
oe	b*u*t
ü	n*ew* (with lips spread)
u	b*oo*t

Burma

ai	s*i*gn
au	s*ou*nd
e	b*e*t
ei	s*a*ne
o	s*a*w
ñ	(nasalizes the vowel that precedes it)
hy	*sh*ore
th	*th*aw
c̠, h̠c̠	*j*udge
k̠, h̠k̠	*g*ood
p̠	*b*ig

s	zoo
<u>t</u>	*do*

Tones (shown with vowel *a*)

a (unmarked tone)	low, level, long
à	high, long, falling toward the end
á	high, short, falling (with catch of breath)
a	high, short (with sharp catch of breath)

Laos

ae	b*a*t
aw	l*aw*
oe	b*u*t
ou	b*oo*t
ü, eu	n*ew* (with lips spread)
x	*s*ing

Vietnam

â	b*u*t
e	b*e*t
ê	b*ai*t
i, y	between b*ea*t and b*i*t
o	l*aw*
ô	n*o*
oa	*wa*nt
o	d*oe* (with lips spread)
u	n*ew* (with lips spread)
d	*z*ero
d	*d*o
gi	*z*ero
nh	ca*ny*on
ph	*f*un
r	*z*ero
x	*s*on

Tones (shown with vowel *a*)

a (unmarked)	midtone
á	high rising
à	low falling
a	falling, then rising
ã	high (with break in voice)
a	low (with break in voice)

Upland Minorities

Akha People

ö	b*ai*t (with lips rounded)
ü	b*ea*t (with lips rounded)

Hmong

Final consonants indicate tone. Double vowels are nasalized.

b	high level
j	high falling
v	midrising
[no consonant]	midlevel
s	lower midlevel
g	low breathy
m	low glottalized ending
d	low rising

Lisu People

ü	n*ew* (with lips spread)

Indigenous People of the Malay Peninsula

ɛ	b*e*t
ə	b*u*t
i	n*ew* (with lips spread)
c	l*aw*
n	ca*ny*on
ŋ	*si*ng
ʔ	oh-oh (glottal stop between syllables)

Indonesia

é	b*ai*t
è	b*e*t
eu	b*oo*k (with lips spread)
dh	*d*one

PART I

Issues and Processes in Southeast Asian Musics

Introduction to Southeast Asia as a Musical Area

Most major Southeast Asian musics bear strong similarities to one another, crossing boundaries of culture, language, and land. But although bronze gongs, xylophones, and bamboo flutes link the musics of the region, there is nevertheless a remarkable diversity of peoples and music styles. For centuries, the unique sounds and organizational systems of these musics have attracted outsiders—including dozens of scholars and the Western composers Debussy, Britten, and Reich.

Musicians of the restored court ensemble perform at the former Forbidden City in Hue, Vietnam. Photo by Terry E. Miller, 1993.

Southeast Asian Musics: An Overview

Terry E. Miller and Sean Williams

Regional Issues
Two Approaches to Listening

REGIONAL ISSUES

The subcontinent of Southeast Asia is too large to be treated holistically; therefore, it is divided here into two parts: mainland and islands. Within each division, the most obvious subdivision is the nation-state. Mainland Southeast Asia consists of seven nations (Burma, Cambodia, Laos, Malaysia, Singapore, Thailand, and Vietnam); island Southeast Asia consists of three (Brunei, Indonesia, and the Philippines). Malaysia, extending into both divisions, is treated here as part of the mainland. Papua (formerly known as Irian Jaya), the Indonesian province that occupies the western section of the island of New Guinea, is covered in the Oceania volume. And finally the large island of Borneo is divided into provinces of Indonesia and (East) Malaysia, though its inhabitants share many important cultural traits.

The national boundaries that demarcate Southeast Asia into its countries are recent and largely colonial inventions. Laos, a landlocked country, sandwiched among Vietnam, Cambodia, Thailand, Burma, and China, is a cobbled-together remnant of the spoils of war. The Republic of Indonesia came into being when a group of islanders attained self-rule over the Netherlands East Indies. The Philippines was once a group of islands united in the name of a Spanish king's son, Felipe. Few of these countries developed an indigenous national consciousness before their national creation. Indeed, even within areas that have used the same linguistic and political systems for centuries, we have no reason to assume any kind of social, political, or musical unity.

Lowland and Upland Peoples

Except for Singapore, all Southeast Asian nations have both lowland plains, usually drained by a major river, and upland areas, which may be either vast plateaus or rugged mountain ranges. Nearly every country or region discussed in this volume is tied in some way to the ocean, and some areas (especially the island regions) are frequently rattled by earthquakes and volcanic eruptions. The way the land shapes and is shaped by its inhabitants has an impact on differences in musical production. Most nonmainstream minorities live in upland areas, and most of the dominant population lives in lowlands. Since most minorities differ in language and lifestyle from the dominant people, their musics are usually so different as to bear no comparison to those of the dominant people. Thus, it makes sense to treat minority musics separately.

Regionalism

Each country of Southeast Asia displays diversity of culture and population. Each has more than one cultural region, even within the majority population. These are never completely discrete but may exhibit individuality in language (dialect or accent), central literary works, clothing, architecture, cuisine, musical instruments, and musical styles. In some countries (such as Thailand), a regional culture has been adopted as the national culture. Whether the other regional cultures are viewed as challenges to the dominant culture or as complements to it depends on the time and place.

Regionalism is most likely to be tolerated, even celebrated, in countries that have achieved stability based on the "national" culture—true of both Thailand and Indonesia. Where such a consensus has not been reached, or where the lack of mass communications allows the maintenance of regional distinctiveness, all regions may be near-equals, or even rivals; in the latter case, regionalism works against nationhood and may consequently be suppressed. Regionalism is mainly an issue within the dominant culture, leaving minority groups largely on the outside.

Urban and Rural

Asian cities reflect least the distinctiveness of "traditional" and especially regional culture. Many of the first centers of population in Southeast Asia were Hindu-Buddhist courts and commercial cities. The courts functioned as places to house the person in power with accompanying family, personnel, and regalia; the entire city would be laid out according to its relationship to the center. Many of these cities were inland. Commercial cities drew most of their population from those interested in profiting from trade; these cities tended to be located either at the crossroads of major inland trade routes or in ports. Commercial cities are laid out according to needs of access in relation to the market. Once Islam had become established in Southeast Asia, a kind of Muslim city developed, particularly in Malaysia and Indonesia; it included a large mosque located at the center of the city. Last, colonial administrative cities were created by various colonial empires, either on the foundations of other types of cities, or out of areas that appeared convenient for administration and commerce. Each Southeast Asian city reflects the kind of urban planning and centrally

Figure 2.1
Hội An, Vietnam,
one of the country's
first ports of entry,
preserves architecture
reflecting the coming of
the Chinese, Japanese,
Europeans, and other
foreigners. Photo by
Terry E. Miller, 1993.

located architecture (mosque, grand temple, government buildings, etc.) that characterize its origins; all, however, include some of the most unfortunate aspects of twentieth-century architecture as well. Cities are the most modern places in a country, and the main cities are the most internationalized. The most modern cities of Southeast Asia are Singapore, Jakarta, Kuala Lumpur, Bangkok, Manila, and Hô Chí Minh City (Saigon); the least modern include Rangoon (Yangon), Vientiane, and Phnom Penh. The largest cities often attract the regional poor, seeking opportunities. Money earned from urban wages is frequently channeled back to villages, and most urbanites maintain close ties to family and friends in villages. Cities, then, tend to develop pan-urban cultures, though pockets of regional populations sometimes maintain aspects of their culture. Urban populations have the greatest choices of musical styles, especially from the media, and are most thoroughly exposed to mass culture.

It is largely true that if you do not live in a city, you live in a village. Depending on the country's level of poverty or prosperity, village life may be slow to change (as in Borneo, Burma, certain areas of Indonesia, Laos, Cambodia, and Vietnam) or much affected by modernization (as in the Philippines, Malaysia, and Thailand). Some villagers with homes that once stood on the outskirts of Southeast Asia's cities now find themselves surrounded by factories, airports, bus terminals, and housing developments. Dispersed throughout many of the largest cities are village enclaves, complete with chickens, wells, tiny plots of cultivated land, and rural people.

The poverty of village life tends to preserve its traditionalism. At least in earlier times, village cultural life centered on cycles related to agriculture, religion, and the calendar. Songs and rituals are, or were, associated with various stages of agriculture (especially the growing of rice) and seasonal rituals and festivities. In general, musical activities ceased during the rainy season, which in Theravada Buddhist countries (Burma, Cambodia, Laos, Thailand) coincides with the Buddhist period of withdrawal, when rice requires little attention, allowing males to be ordained and to withdraw into a temple to earn spiritual merit.

 TRACK 1

Because this music originated in villages, where people must work year-round to maintain house, family, and food supply, it tends to be simpler than that found in cities, particularly in the mainland regions. Few music specialists support themselves through performance, and anyone with a modicum of talent may sing and play music. Musical instruments tend to be user friendly and simple, made from locally available materials (though exceptions occur).

The theme of courtship permeates village musics throughout Southeast Asia. Courtship was formerly ritualized and in places remains so. Males and females alternated in performing various forms of repartee, creating veritable gender wars, based on wit and double entendre. The texts of repartee transmitted rural wisdoms, reminding listeners of their history, literature, role models, religion, and sometimes even "the facts of life." In its fundamental forms, ritualized courtship could be spoken (as with Lao *phanya*), but most forms involve some kind of heightened speech or song, with or without an instrument. In some places, certain performers grew so highly skilled that they became professional or semiprofessional entertainers, and the original function of courtship metamorphosed into a paid exhibition of talent.

Classical, Folk, Popular

A tripartite division of music into classical, folk, and popular has limited validity in Southeast Asia. Each term creates dilemmas. *Classical* has connotations of sophistication, high value, being representative of the best of a culture, and expressive of political and economic power, what Milton Singer has called the Great Tradition of a culture. In Burma, Cambodia, and Thailand, scholars agree on what genres fit the classical category; for Laos, Malaysia, the Philippines, Singapore, and Vietnam, they do not. Substituting *court* for *classical*, as some writers do with Cambodian, Javanese, and Thai musics, is not necessarily better, for the music described as *court* was never restricted to a court and survives today—at least in Thailand and Cambodia—entirely outside the context of a court, even in villages.

Figure 2.2
In Yogyakarta, Java, small villages coexist with modern urban accouterments within the boundaries of the city. Photo by Sean Williams, 1989.

Regardless of the term, "classical" musics have several traits in common. Musical instruments play a prominent role. Some are complex and highly decorated, and performance on them requires advanced technical skills. The repertory is usually extensive, requiring the undivided attention of musicians who must memorize complex works, practice long hours, and play for a variety of occasions, some ceremonial, some ritualistic, some for entertainment. These musics often require enough surplus wealth to allow the musicians to give their full attention to the art of music and to be relieved of any necessity of growing their food, providing their shelter, and securing their safety. Consequently, musics called classical are often associated with an aristocracy, or at least a wealthy elite. There is also a consensus among the wealthy elite that these musics best represent the culture of the nation to the outside world, whether the citizenry commonly listens to them or not.

Such definitions create few problems in categorizing some Burmese, Thai, Cambodian, and Indonesian musics as "classical," but elsewhere the issue becomes thorny. Though Laos has a "classical" music similar to that of Thailand, it is less extensive and sophisticated. Laos arguably has a classical music, but the tradition was damaged when the Pathet Lao (a Communist party) banned such "aristocratic decadence" in 1975, and the country's poverty and lack of an aristocracy prevent this kind of music from flowering beyond a minimal level. Vietnam's imperial court is long gone, and though its music survived until the 1970s, it was never widely known or played. Today, it has been revived, but more as a symbol of the city of Huế than as a symbol of the country. Malaysia, formerly a collection of sultanates, had royal music and entertainment, but these barely survive in isolated pockets. The term *Malaysian classical music*, like *Vietnamese classical music*, has no clear meaning. The Philippines has been so deeply Christianized that its current classical music traditions are direct responses to Western European classical music; its nearest relative to other Southeast Asian classical traditions, the *kulintang*, is not locally promoted as a classical music.

For there to be folk music, there must be an identifiable group of people who constitute the folk. Urban people assume these folks are other people, usually villagers. If the term has any currency, it usually denotes the music heard in villages, frequently performed by nonspecialists, and usually associated with "functional" contexts, like rituals, festivals, and daily activities. The accessibility of bamboo for large portions of the rural Southeast Asian population has led to the prevalence of bamboo flutes, rattles, and other musical instruments. By a similar token, the need for inexpensive, easily available, lightweight instruments (such as small plucked lutes and Jew's harps) by certain inland and upland groups throughout Southeast Asia is understandable, considering the limits on resources, craftsmen, and portability. Villagers also perform on both flat and bossed gongs in what appear to be some of the most remote areas; however, the gongs and their methods of suspension tend to be less elaborate than in the courts or cities. Vocal music, wordplay, and poetic competition are strongly valued in most Southeast Asian rural traditions.

In countries such as Cambodia, Laos, and Thailand, scholars make a clear distinction between classical and folk musics, but for Vietnam, no such distinction can be made. Since Vietnam does not have an agreed-upon classical music, Vietnamese musics are usually distinguished as traditional or modernized. Vietnam has the strongest Western classical-music tradition in mainland Southeast Asia, with Malaysia and Singapore running a close second and third, and its intellectual and cultural elite has received training in Western music in the conservatories of France, the former Soviet Union, and other Eastern European states. They prefer that Vietnam be represented by modernized compositions, leaving traditional music to fend for itself. At the same time, the kinds of traditional music being used to represent the nation to the outside world—water-puppet theater and chamber music—clearly derive from village culture. Folk songs may be sung by farmers in a rough voice, but they are also played by skilled amateurs (nonprofessionals) on finely decorated instruments in formal situations.

Figure 2.3
Villagers pump water in a quiet village in northeast Thailand. Photo by Terry E. Miller, 1992.

Whether derived from traditional indigenous music or influenced by outside cultures (especially the United States, Hong Kong, India, the Middle East, and Japan), the popular-music category is the least debatable. Primarily disseminated through the media to almost all members of society, regardless of regional origin, income level, or degree of musical sophistication, this music has become predominant, or at least present, in people's lives. Not surprisingly, it is most developed in countries having the greatest wealth and urbanization—Thailand, Singapore, Malaysia, Indonesia, and the Philippines. Utilizing a creative combination of Western instrumentation and blended linguistic and musical features, it may be heard not only within the borders of such cities as Bangkok, Manila, and Singapore, but also in the remotest villages. It draws from a variety of traditions to appeal to the broadest number of listeners and therefore to become as commercially successful as possible. Vietnam's popular tradition derives from a movement to modernize the country, which led to the creation of both entertainment and revolutionary songs in Western style. Though Vietnam is considerably urbanized, it remains too poor to afford the music videos, spectacular pop concerts, compact discs, and slick nightclubs that make popular music powerful elsewhere. In other mainland Southeast Asian countries, the popular-music industry is modest, little more than a cottage industry of small shops copying small quantities of locally produced cassettes.

Networks of Power and Influence

Southeast Asian lands support millions of people, from kings and presidents to roadside vendors and beggars. Its alluvial plains and terraced hillsides are fertile ground for agriculture; indeed, most Southeast Asians are involved in agricultural endeavors. In addition to agriculture, every Southeast Asian country supports its own versions of governmental, economic, educational, religious, and legal systems. The diversity of systems within each nation reflects that nation's history, colonial ties, and current phase of modernization. What each country has in common with the others, however, is a local understanding of the concentration and dispersal of power.

In some areas of the world (particularly the West), power has often been measured by the strength of a nation's borders and that nation's ability to accumulate land. In Southeast Asia, power is usually centered in a person, a place, or an object. Strong, dynamic rulers who have gathered a large number of followers can wield power in a radiating field; those closest to the ruler have more power, while those farther away have less. Places such as Java's Borobudur or Cambodia's Angkor Vat are invested locally with the power ascribed to sacred sites which have withstood the ravages of time and wars. Important objects—including certain daggers, bronze drums, gongs, and masks—carry their own special kind of power and are believed to have an impact on people, places, and other objects.

Southeast Asian musical contexts tend to reflect the influences and behavior of persons believed to have some kind of power. Patrons of music might be responsible for owning and protecting an ensemble's musical instruments, for arranging performances, and for paying the musicians. The musical leader of an ensemble, however, might attract fellow musicians on the basis of outstanding musicianship. In Muslim countries or regions, a musician who has been to Mecca is usually considered purer and therefore more powerful than one who has not. In some cases, fame (as from a hit recording) confers power; however, it may be locally considered less enduring than power achieved through other means. As with Southeast Asian political leaders, power ascribed to particular musicians or patrons is fleeting and can shift to other people as circumstances dictate.

The traditional investment of inanimate objects with power has an impact on musical performance and functions as a determinant of musical hierarchies across Southeast Asia. This situation is more widely encountered in the islands than on the mainland. Within a typically stratified gong-chime ensemble, instrumentation usually includes one or more large gongs (or their equivalents), smaller gongs, a gong chime, multiple xylophones or metallophones, a set of drums, and stringed or wind instruments that serve an ornamental or melodic function. The gong or gong equivalent is the spiritual center of the ensemble. It acts as the periodic marker for the beginning, ending, and cyclic points within each performance. Ritual offerings, if they are made, are traditionally offered to the gong, which guides the entire ensemble. Though the gong typically has the easiest musical role to play (in terms of how it is struck during a performance), its spiritual weight is considerable. Instruments considered difficult to play may have little spiritual weight. In a musical performance, any Southeast Asian ensemble could probably do without many of the instruments that play a decorative function, but a performance without a gong or gong-functioning instrument is unthinkable.

TWO APPROACHES TO LISTENING

One can respond to music on at least two levels, sensually and intellectually. Perhaps too often pedagogues take an intellectual, cognitive approach, insisting that listeners "understand," "know," and "appreciate" the music being heard. Ultimately, this is necessary, especially if one is to teach or explain the music to someone else. Such communication also requires the use of a technical vocabulary, which, though often denoting concepts that

Figure 2.4
Java's eighth-century Borobudur temple, covered with detailed stone carvings reflects the ruler's power as deriving from the gods themselves. Photo by Sean Williams.

exist only in the mind, are customarily described in analogous terms—timbre, texture, melodic contour, and extramusicality. Even without this kind of knowledge, however, we can respond on sensual and emotional levels to the beauty and power of the music. This approach is not to be avoided if the novice listener has reservations about his or her ability to understand the sounds of these musics.

The Sensual Response

Music consists of vibrations, perceived as sound when transmitted through the ear to the brain. For sounds to be perceived as music, the listener must perceive them as an ordered process, playing out in real time. John Blacking defined music as "humanly organized sound" (1973:10). In a sense, then, music is a microcosm of order, which proceeds according to a known and perceivable plan. To go beyond this notion is to enter the realm of the intellect and its cognitive abilities—which leads to the intellectualization of music. Preceding this stage, however, is one where the listener may respond to music as a purely sensual experience, a series of sensed physical vibrations that feel good in the way a massage, a pleasant smell or taste, or a beautiful image feels good. One possibility is for the listener simply to let go, relax, and allow the vibrations to wash over without reference to cognitive knowledge. In doing so, the listener can appreciate Southeast Asian musics on one level, possibly the level on which many Southeast Asians appreciate it.

Something can be said for an analogy between cuisine and music. Each Southeast Asian music can be heard as a unique mixture of spices: some cuisines are spicier than others; some are an acquired taste. Certain musics, such as Thai classical, Javanese court gamelan, and Lao *lam*, have a smoothness and consistency quite dissimilar to the pungent flavors of Burmese *hsaìn*, Vietnamese chamber music, or Balinese gamelans. Just as some foods may not appeal to us on first tasting, some musics may not appeal on first hearing.

The Intellectual Response

Perceiving music is not only a holistic experience but also one that occurs out of sight and beyond touch—within the brain. Verbalizing music, what Charles Seeger called speech about music, partakes of an altogether different realm, language. To intellectualize about music, the listener must dissect the holism of sound systematically into constituent elements, all of which must be expressed in analogous terms or through physical demonstration. These elements of music are commonly listed as *medium* (what makes the sound), *melody* (an organized succession of tones), *rhythm* and *meter* (the organization of sounds in

Figure 2.5
An intricately crafted mother-of pearl desing on a door at Bangkok's Wut Rajabophit illustrates the Thai penchant for symmetry within a totally decorated panel, a visual analog to the construction of Thai classical music. Photo by Terry E. Miller, 1992.

time), *texture* (the relationship among the music's constituent elements), *form* (structural organization), *timbre* (qualities of sound), and *extramusicality* (nonmusical meaning). We cannot possibly discuss all these elements in all the musics covered in this volume, but we do wish to point out certain of their more obvious challenges.

In-tuneness and out-of-tuneness are culturally learned norms. Westerners, not to mention many non-Westerners, have been conditioned to accept a twelve-tone, equal-tempered system of tuning as the norm of in-tuneness. Many Southeast Asian musics, however, use systems of tuning that are neither equally tempered nor organized in twelve steps. The fixed-pitch instruments of the Thai classical ensemble are tuned to seven equidistant tones, many of them seemingly out of tune in comparison with the Western system, but non-fixed-pitch instruments (such as bowed lutes and the voice) or flexibly pitched instruments (such as the flute) diverge even more, through portamentos and subtle ornamentation. Certain intervals in many Vietnamese scales diverge from any found in the Western equal-tempered system. Indonesian gamelans are uniquely tuned in nonequidistant steps. These systems of tuning contradict the Western notion that tuning is a natural process (equal temperament aside), based on the overtone series.

If anything is challenging to listeners unfamiliar with Southeast Asian musics, it is their timbres. Western ideas of pleasant and beautiful sounds may be encountered, but a great many instruments—including the human voice—produce sounds perceived as unpleasant and even ugly by some uninitiated listeners. It is difficult to describe timbres except by analogy, and using words like *nasal*, *raspy*, *strident*, *piercing*, and *clunky* may tell more about the listener's norms than about the music. Timbre may pose the greatest challenge to people meeting Southeast Asian musics for the first time.

As quoted above, Blacking's assertion that music is "humanly organized sound" presumes that music is organized. An understanding of all the constituent elements of music does not guarantee that the listener will perceive that organization, however. Formal order, though present, is often difficult or even impossible to recognize. Without detailed analysis from a fully notated transcription or a crystal-clear oral interpretation from an insider (or at least an informed outsider), there is little chance the listener can perceive the subtle recurrence of unifying motives or a sophisticated rondolike structure.

Knowing that music is organized raises a question: how is it created? Those accustomed to European-American traditions expect to find the name of a composer specified on a notated score. But the absence of scores—and in most cases, composers' names—does not mean the absence of composers. Musicians do play compositions throughout Southeast Asia, but these works are rarely notated, are performatively flexible, and are customarily transmitted orally.

The term *improvisation* comes immediately to mind as a second possibility for creating music. In English, that term implies a process that is free, loose, and unpredictable; in a negative sense, it is something musicians do when they cannot perform a composition or have forgotten one—a strategy for getting out of trouble, or worse, "faking it." In Asia, the term is normally associated with the concept of mode. In English usage, a mode is simply a scale that is neither minor nor major, as in the ecclesiastical modes of Europe (Dorian, Mixolydian, and so on)—though major and minor are themselves modes: groupings of

timbre
The quality or character of a musical sound

half steps and whole steps in a particular order. In Asian contexts, the term denotes a complex of elements, both musical and extramusical, that are together the basis for the creation—that is, composition—of music.

These include pitch-based material, which can be ordered in ascending and descending patterns (scales); a hierarchy of tones, starting from or implying a resting point (the tonic); particular melodic and rhythmic motives appropriate to a particular mode; obligatory ornaments; cadential formulas; and a customary character or mood. Mode can govern anything from fully written composition to on-the-spot improvisation, the latter being simply a nonpermanent composition, created simultaneously with its first performance. As such, modal improvisation is not an expression of freedom, but a disciplined and bounded process. Possibly the most famous Asian modal system is embodied in the Indian terms *rag* and *rāga*.

In many traditions, mode has been a nonformalized, unarticulated, and intuitively practiced process. This is true in Lao and northeastern Thai music for the free-reed mouth organ (*khaen*). Northeastern Thai players customarily use five named modes (*lai sutsanaen, lai yai*, and so on), each preceded by the word *lai*. Though few players would explain this systematically, all will stay within a given set of constraints when spontaneously creating compositions in a given *lai*.

In the Javanese system, the term *pathet* embodies the concept of mode and governs the creation of relatively fixed compositions. Though only the skeletal structure of the composition is firmly fixed, the elements added in performance are also controlled by the conventions of a particular mode. Musicians in Java are well aware of their modal system, but Thai classical musicians, though they also operate within a modal system, are less aware of it, and do not articulate its conventions. Burma has modal systems too, and they are unusually complex because their terminologies vary according to the instrument, especially between the harp and *hsaiñ*-ensemble instruments.

Vietnam preserves Southeast Asia's fullest modal system, the *điệu* system, which governs the creation of fixed compositions and extended improvisations. Each mode consists of a set of tones, certain of which require ornamentation or vibrato. Each has a specific modal character or mood. Though ensembles play fixed compositions, each musician customarily warms up with a brief, free modal improvisation (*rao*) before all join together in playing the piece. Within the piece, each musician maintains the fixed structure but realizes the melody according to the mode and the idiom of the instrument.

Texture creates challenges equal to those of timbre. Southeast Asian ensemble musics may confront hearers with a seemingly chaotic matrix of sounds. Knowing that all performers are playing the same composition may even deepen the confusion, since it may sound more like each musician is playing a *different* composition simultaneously. These statements are more true of some Southeast Asian musics than others, but certain of them—Thai, Vietnamese, Indonesian, and especially Burmese—are particularly daunting to sort out aurally.

After listening to such an ensemble, we might draw an analogy with Southeast Asian traffic patterns. The degree of confusion varies from one city to another, and the rules of negotiation vary dramatically, but one can observe this phenomenon in virtually any Asian

mode
Fundamental guidelines for composition and improvisation
rāga
Modal system used in India

city choked with traffic—Bangkok, Hồ Chí Minh City, Manila, Jakarta. The roads have clearly painted lanes, but few drivers stay within them; they treat the lanes merely as suggestions. All manner of vehicles use every bit of pavement, even the sidewalks. The object is to arrive at a final destination, but normally this requires passing through periodic points of control—traffic signals, traffic police, and roundabouts. Between these intersections, each driver is free to use whatever space is open, weaving this way and that, cutting in, holding back, rushing ahead, to arrive at the next point of control, where all drivers must come together again before proceeding.

Much Southeast Asian ensemble music moves in this way. In Thai classical music, the composition consists of a skeletal structure whose tones regularly occur at points articulated by a pair of small cymbals (*ching*), which play two strokes, *ching* and *chap*. The *chap* falls on the last beat of each cycle, making Thai music end-accented, rather than front-accented, as is usual in Western music. These points are like the controlled intersections negotiated by Bangkok's traffic: the *chap*, at the end of each cycle, are more highly controlled moments than the other sounds. Between these points, however, individual players, working within the constraints of their own instrument's idiom, are free in most cases to vary their parts each time they play the composition. The result may sound as chaotic as Bangkok's traffic appears, but both processes have a logic of their own. And the rules vary from one city to another. Bangkok drivers would most likely get into trouble driving in Hồ Chí Minh City, where major intersections are sometimes without controls and all four directions proceed continuously. Not surprisingly, Vietnamese music is less clearly controlled, and sometimes the musicians seem to be apart in their beats.

INDIVIDUAL REGIONS

Figure 2.6
Many busy intersections in Vietnam's Hồ Chí Minh City lack traffic controls, but drivers carefully negotiate to keep all four directions flowing at once. Photo by Terry E. Miller, 1993.

These thoughts should make sense when read in conjunction with performances of various Southeast Asian musics. The following paragraphs offer more specific pointers for the most prominently known musics of each country.

Mainland Southeast Asia

Vietnam

Vietnamese music is played largely on instruments derived from China, modified to suit the Vietnamese musical aesthetic, but the two musical systems differ fundamentally. Vietnamese music is created within a modal system that allows both improvisation and composition. These modes often require ornaments or vibrato on specified tones, and indeed, one of the salient features of Vietnamese music is its ornateness.

Vietnamese chordophones have unusually high frets and loose strings, allowing for much bending of tones. Vietnamese music is also noteworthy for the syncopation of its rhythms, made all the clearer by a rhythmic instrument that marks certain beats in the cycle. In texture, there are often striking differences among instruments, in both melodic contour and rhythm. The pervasive bending of tones is especially expressive in the sadder, more minor-sounding modes, giving the music a somewhat plaintive flavor.

Thailand

Much has been said about the texture of Thai classical music and its seeming chaos upon first hearing. Though the listener may know intellectually that Thai music is actually highly organized, even square, he or she may not be able to hear the organization easily. First, one must listen for duple metrical organization, articulated by the cymbals (*ching*), with their constantly alternating *ching* and *chap* (some pieces use nothing but *ching*). One can also focus on the drums, which usually play regular cyclic patterns with little variation. These cycles provide a clear and rather rigid matrix, within which Thai composers and performers are required to play.

chordophone
Stringed instrument

One can then focus on individual instruments. Unless a *piphat* or *mahori* is clearly recorded with a microphone on the larger gong circle (which plays the fundamental form of the composition), the listener will more likely focus on the leading instruments—the higher xylophone (*ranat ek*) or the higher fiddle (*saw duang*). The fiddle tends to play a fairly clear melodic form of the work, but the xylophone plays a variation of it, usually in constantly and evenly moving octaves. This motion, however, masks the articulation of phrases, and one sometimes wonders how the player could possibly memorize this seemingly random peregrination of tones, the aural equivalent of unwinding a large ball of string. If the ensemble includes a double-reed oboe (*pi nai*), its part is usually so different from those of the rest of the ensemble, so free in rhythm, and so flexible in pitch, that the listener may wonder what it has to do with the work at all. Such are the challenges of listening to Thai classical music, especially the "high" repertory associated with ceremony. But actually, a great number of pieces are primarily organized as memorable melodic phrases; these constitute the "light classical" repertory and include some of the country's favorite pieces.

Cambodia

In comparison to the classical music of Thailand (especially the "high" repertory), Cambodian classical music seems simpler and easier to follow. This situation is due in part to less individual virtuosity and the fact that the double-reed oboe (*sralai*) plays a basic form of the melody rather than an elaborated one. Another easy way to distinguish Cambodian music from Thai is the former's tendency to unequal pairs of notes, a kind of dotted rhythm, which contrasts to the evenness of Thai rhythm.

To many, Cambodian village music, especially that for weddings (*kar*) and spirit-related ceremonies (*arakk*), is among the most attractive musics of Southeast Asia. The melodic inflections, especially those played by the reed instruments, have a bouncy, almost jazzlike feel, while the chest-resonated monochord (*khse muoy*) provides a distinctively resonant plucking sound.

Laos

The main challenge for outsiders wishing to listen to Lao (and by extension, northeast Thai) music is that the predominant genres (*khap* and *lam*) are closely bound to their lyrics. Though the melodies of *khap* and *lam* can be intriguing and the accompaniments attractive, the listener cannot fully appreciate Lao music without knowing the language and its dialects. It could be said about any music that hearing it live is better than hearing a recording, but this is especially true of Lao singing, in that the singers usually dance and often engage in suggestive horseplay.

The sound of the main Lao instrument, the *khene* free-reed mouth organ, is unusual in Asia because it produces vertical sonorities, not unlike chords. They do not function in a Western functional harmonic sense, but they do produce different degrees of tension and relaxation, providing a full-bodied, homorhythmic sound. Other instruments, including the plucked lute (*phin*) and the fiddle (*saw pip*) are rarer. The sound of the plucked lute is intriguing, especially when the player produces a succession of parallel fifths over a drone.

Regional Lao styles are distinguishable in melody and rhythm. Some, like that of the *khap ngeum*, sound rather dreamy because of their nonmetered, speechlike rhythms, but others are catchy in their rhythms, often reinforced by drums and small metal cymbals. Certain of them, especially *lam salavane* and *lam tang vay*, are so attractive that with little change they have become danceable popular types of song. In northeast Thailand, where central Thai influence is strong, the *lam* styles have been transformed into actual popular songs, accompanied by electrified local and standard rock instruments, brass instruments, and a set of drums. Indeed, since 1989, the rise

Figure 2.7
The busy tinwork on Rangoon, Burma's Sule Pagoda suggests a Burmese aesthetic that is also heard in its music. Photo by Terry E. Miller, 1994.

of *lam sing*, a popularized form of *lam*, has been setting the pace for all sorts of other genres in Thailand.

Burma

On first hearing, Burmese classical music, especially that for the *hsaìñwaìñ* ensemble, resembles utter chaos. Western students, on first hearing Burmese music, are often unable to stifle looks of amazement, laughter, or verbal comments. This is because few other musics in the world exhibit such joyfully sudden shifts in rhythm, changes of texture and timbre, and a most disjunctive melodic style. Thai and Cambodian classical musics (and their styles of dancing) could be described as smooth, continuous, and more or less relaxed, but Burmese music and dance are seemingly unpredictable, jagged, mercurial, and energetic. In this respect, the most similar (but somewhat tamer) style within Southeast Asia is the music of the Balinese *gong kebyar*.

Knowing cognitively how Burmese melody is constructed, like knowing how serial music is composed, does not necessarily mean that the listener can actually hear the process. In Thai classical music, the large gong circle plays the basic and straightforward version of the composition, as does the double-reed oboe in Cambodian classical music. These you can hear. But in Burmese music, nobody plays a coherent, intact version of any melody. Following a fixed structure that exists only in players' minds, even the lead musicians sound their instruments in an idiom comprising octave displacements, beat displacements, and other melodic "rearrangements." Perhaps a visual comparison to the formal displacements of European cubist art will help the listener discern what has happened to the composition. A good way to understand this process is to ask a Burmese musician to play a familiar Western tune, as pianist Ù Ko Ko does on a recent compact disc, when he plays "When the Saints Come Marching In" (*Piano birman/Burmese piano* 1995:17). Perhaps two valid analogies to the process of displacement would be Schönberg's concept of *Klangfarbenmelodie*, in which the listener must connect disjointed bits of melody into a continuous whole, and Seurat's technique of pointillism, in which the viewer must connect discrete dots of color into a coherent image.

When listening to Burmese music, one cannot help but be struck by the distinctiveness and unblendedness of its timbres. Most Burmese solo instruments are individualistic, even unique in Southeast Asia—the set of twenty-one tuned drums, the harp, and the piano (at least as a "traditional" instrument). The sudden shifts in the music, which to foreigners can make it seem jerky and nervous, are also seen in Burmese dance, which, like the music, is energetic and kinetically sudden; it is unlike Thai dance, which (like Thai music) is smooth and continuous. That it also has a regular, underlying structure is confirmed in a repertory that requires two small idiophones to articulate cyclic patterns—a pair of tiny cymbals and a pair of hollowed-out wooden shells, hinged at one end.

Malaysia

On hearing Malaysian traditional music for the first time (such as the music for the royal coronation played on the double-reed oboe, or the accompanying music of the *ma'yong* theater played on the spike fiddle), one might be forgiven for confusing it with music from Western Asia. The melody flows continuously, using small intervals with little phrasal articulation while remaining within a narrow range. Nor does the cyclicality of its meter set it apart from Western Asian music, for the same is true there. What announces its Southeast Asianness is the presence of hanging gongs, which play on prescribed beats in temporal cycles.

Because Malaysia was colonized by Britain and remains multiethnic (Chinese, Indian, Malay), its music is also multiethnic, and the term *Malaysian music* covers a wide variety of somewhat unrelated styles. Some of them, such as for *ronggeng*, sound quite Western; others are purely Chinese. Some were borrowed from the popular-music traditions of Southern and Western Asia. "Malaysian" music, then, is the sum of its parts, but the music of the Malay is distinctive for blending Western and Southeast Asian traits.

Island Southeast Asia

The overall sound of island Southeast Asian music is often described as sonorous, probably referring to the fact that some of the most visible and audible music from the islands is performed on resonant bronze instruments, especially gongs. Indeed, a big portion of this music is played on stratified bronze ensembles, known collectively in Indonesia as gamelan and in the southern Philippines as *kulintang*. Variations on the basic gamelan and *kulintang* formats are common throughout the island nations and Borneo, and hundreds of different names are applied to what is basically a gong-chime ensemble.

In addition to gong-chime ensembles, thousands of other genres—European-style orchestras, indigenous vocal groups, solo instrumental performances—are spread across the islands of Southeast Asia, reflecting diverse musical priorities, contexts, and influences. While focusing on the sound and structure of the gong-chime ensemble, the reader should recognize that certain features of gong-chime music are readily applicable to other regional musics.

What makes a gong-chime ensemble? The basic component is a gong chime—a rack, usually horizontal, of small, tuned, bossed kettlepots (see, for example, this book's cover photo). These pots may be laid out in a single row (as with the Filipino *kulintang* and the Balinese *trompong*), they may be arranged in double rows (as with the Javanese *bonang*), or they may be in a V- or U-shaped formation (as with the Sundanese *bonang*). Other main components of the ensemble are one or more hanging or horizontal bossed gongs, one or more drums (usually shaped like barrels, cones, or goblets), and xylophones made of wood or bamboo, or metallophones (especially bronze and iron). Many ensembles in the islands also have bamboo flutes, double-reed oboes, bowed lutes, or plucked zithers. The presence or absence of male or female singers varies according to repertorial requirements.

Gong-chime ensembles are often called stratified—a term that offers an indication of the musical texture. Within a piece of music, certain instruments have a punctuating function, said to be colotomic when they regularly mark temporal cycles. Much as a period (full stop) ends written sentences, the largest gong—or the instrument that has the function of that gong—ends musical sentences. Unlike most Western musics, island music of Southeast Asia tends to have a stronger emphasis on the last note of a four-beat pattern

gong-chime ensemble
An ensemble with a set of small kettle gongs arranged in a rack.
colotomic structure
The organization of music by periodic punctuation

rather than the first note. Smaller hanging and horizontal gongs act as commas, occurring regularly at intervals that may be divided into two or four segments. Still smaller hanging or horizontal gongs may further punctuate a musical sentence. This texture then serves as the framework for the main theme, often played by large metallophones. Other instruments—including small metallophones, gong chimes, flutes, and zithers—may serve an elaborating function, decorating the main musical theme in dense musical patterns. The drum serves not only as the timekeeper and the keeper of the tempo, but as the instrument that usually outlines the form of the piece. Therefore, a stratified gong-chime ensemble has a four-part texture: colotomic gongs, a main musical theme, elaborating instruments, and drum patterns. Some ensembles (particularly in Central Java) may also have an "inner melody" performed on the rebab, which takes precedence over the more prominently heard main musical theme (Sumarsam 1975).

Much of island Southeast Asian music is performed cyclically. In the basic form of a cycle, each time the largest gong is struck, a cycle has been completed. In some pieces, several different cycles (each requiring the striking of a large gong) may be performed for the completion of a single, large-scale cycle. Once a cycle has been played, it may be repeated with variations on the elaborating instruments, or the piece may move on to a new cycle. The length of these cycles varies widely, from perhaps ten seconds to many minutes. Individual variation from region to region and genre to genre determines the length of a cycle. What is often baffling to nonindigenous observers is the apparent lack of a sense of forward motion in this type of performance: how does the music move forward if the musicians keep repeating the same parts?

A partial answer to this question is that in many cases, the musicians use variation rather than exact repetition. The colotomic structure and the main musical theme may remain the same (at various densities), but the drummer and the musicians who play the elaborating instruments often spice up their playing with variations. The drummer may speed up or slow down the ensemble, allowing more open musical space for intricate rhythmic or melodic patterns to be performed. Small metallophones may be played in interlocking patterns or in a succession of melodic figures appropriate for certain types of performances. A player of bamboo flute or double-reed oboe may use ten or twenty cycles to complete a melody and may then use the same number of cycles each time to perform variations on the initial melody. Vocalists may perform when the colotomic instrumentation is quite sparse or (conversely) when it is dense enough to serve as a melodic outline on its own. Tension—and thus a sense of movement toward release—is created as the listeners learn to wait for the stroke of the gong at the end of each cycle. These and many more factors shape a different kind of listening experience for the uninitiated.

Island Southeast Asian music spans a continuum from note-for-note composition to improvisation. Tourists in Bali may be dazzled by promoters who claim that the intense, high-speed playing of the *gamelan gong kebyar* ensemble is "totally improvised"; however, *kebyar* musicians spend months working out intricate patterns and negotiating repertorial changes. At another extreme, a boy sprawled across the back of a water buffalo may improvise melodic figures appropriate to his culture and the capabilities of his bamboo flute without having to negotiate those patterns with anyone else.

Improvisation always occurs within certain musical contexts. In the gong-chime ensemble, neither the colotomy nor the main musical theme is improvised; however, the players of elaborating instruments and drums may choose from a variety of musical options: hundreds of short melodic phrases, ornaments, rhythmic flourishes, or minor variants. In the southern Philippines, the player of the *kulintang*, the instrument that functions as the primary carrier of the melody, works in a gradual ascending and descending progression through a series of patterns appropriate for each piece; the player has the option of repeating single patterns or groups of patterns. For solo instruments, the player's skill may be judged on the basis of improvisations, from the degree of the improvisations' appropriateness within the genre to the accuracy and fluidity of the melodic ornaments.

New listeners are also likely to notice the tonality of island Southeast Asian music. The term *pentatonic*, loosely and mistakenly applied to Asian music for decades, does not take into consideration either individual tonal variation or the concept that Asian musics do not simply lift five out of the twelve tones of the chromatic scale and use them in music. The tuning of each ensemble in island Southeast Asia is internally coherent: all the instruments in a given ensemble are tuned to match each other. However, the instruments from one ensemble generally cannot play with those of another, because they do not use any standard tuning, such as equal temperament and A=440. Though some master craftsmen may deliberately imitate either a prestigious or a commonly accepted tuning, variations in tuning between ensembles give each ensemble a unique sound and perceived temperament, such as "sweet" or "bright."

Informed Southeast Asian musicians and listeners recognize good music on the basis of the ensemble's rhythmic coherence, dynamic balance among players, improvisational virtuosity when it happens, and general appropriateness according to local modal rules, musicians' on-stage demeanor (said to be audible in their music), and seamless transitions from one section to the next. Good musicians know that if they play together long enough and listen closely to one another, all the above features will fall into place. Within the context of good music, all the joys and competitive urges that have a place in Southeast Asian society are given free rein, and informed audiences are free to appreciate musical events from the standpoints of both passion and reason.

REFERENCES

Blacking, John. 1973. *How Musical is Man?* Seattle: University of Washington Press.
Piano Birman/Burmese Piano. 1995. U Ko Ko. UM MUS/SRC UMN 203.

Southeast Asia in Prehistory

Karl L. Hutterer

Early Agricultural Communities
The Coming of Civilization
Prehistory in the Islands
Asian Art and Music in Prehistory

It has been known for more than a century that Southeast Asia has had one of the longest histories of human settlement of any part of the world. Fossils of ancient hominids (human ancestors), discovered in Java in 1891 by the Dutch physician Eugene Dubois and classified by scientists as *Homo erectus,* played an important role in the early debates over human evolution. Since then, the Javanese sites have yielded a rich series of fossils, covering much of the history of the biological evolution of humankind. That it has proven difficult to date the earliest human remains with confidence has resulted in a lively and continuing debate, which places their age anywhere from somewhat less than one million years to nearly two million years.

EARLY AGRICULTURAL COMMUNITIES

On the mainland of Southeast Asia proper, good evidence for early agricultural communities comes from well-studied sites in Thailand and in northern and central Vietnam. Though the evidence is indirect, studies of sediments containing prehistoric charcoal, pollen, and phytoliths (microscopic silica grains, found in plant structures) strongly suggest that rice cultivators were settled in the coastal area of the Gulf of Siam by at least the fifth, and maybe the sixth, millennium B.C.E. Hunters and gatherers have historically been involved in the collecting of highly prized forest products (including resins, beeswax, and aromatic woods) for the worldwide trade in exotic Southeast Asian raw materials.

The oldest direct evidence for settled agricultural villages comes from northeastern Thailand and dates back to at least 3000 B.C.E. or earlier. Most of the sites occur as low mounds, which rise from a meter to three meters above the surrounding plain and are the result of the activities of generations of early villagers. These farmers tended to settle on slightly elevated ground along the margins of floodplains. The remains of their villages include evidence of houses on stilts, cemetery areas, well-made pottery, and a variety of utilitarian and ornamental artifacts. The presence of burials and associated artifacts has helped archaeologists to define cultural sequences and has allowed them to engage in tentative studies of demography and social organization.

In the early settlement phase (dating from the beginning of the third millennium B.C.E. to about 2000 B.C.E.), the technology of these villages was typically neolithic, marked by ground and polished stone axes and pottery, most of which were decorated with cord impressions and occasionally incised designs. There is indubitable evidence of rice and domesticated animals, including pigs, cattle, and dogs. The agricultural economy was complemented by some amount of hunting and exploitation of freshwater resources (fish and shellfish). There is considerable variety in the forms of pottery vessels, including utilitarian styles and others evidently meant for ritual or other special purposes. At some sites, such as Khok Phanom Di, situated in a resource-rich estuarine environment, prehistoric villagers seem to have commanded considerable wealth.

During the second phase of settlement history, we can tentatively trace some broad social developments in northeastern Thailand. There is evidence for population growth, an expansion and intensification of agricultural systems, craft specialization (in the manufacture of pottery and bronze, the latter discussed below), some differentiation in the size and function of settlements, and distinctions in the way people were treated in burial. Together, the evidence suggests both an expansion of social systems and increasing complexity in their organization, particularly the emergence of social ranking. The second settlement phase is also associated with the appearance of bronze metallurgy, a prehistoric development often seen as a sign of social intensification.

Bronze manufacture apparently started out as a local village craft and is in evidence at most sites of that period. Recent excavations by Vincent Piggott at Non Pa Wai and other sites in central Thailand suggest that the manufacture and distribution of bronze artifacts may actually have involved a more complex system, with specialized communities smelting copper from ore and distributing it as ingots. Local artisans seem to have then remelted the copper with tin and cast it as bronze artifacts. The range of artifacts produced included axes, points of spears, fishhooks, bells, and bracelets. Many of them were cast by a fairly sophisticated process in bivalve molds made from sandstone.

Neolithic developments in northern Vietnam parallel fairly well those in northeastern Thailand. At the confluence of the Red and Black rivers, settled villages appeared toward the latter part of the third millennium B.C.E. Similar to their counterparts in Thailand, the archaeological sites form low mounds, located on slightly elevated ground along the margins of floodplains. Vietnamese archaeologists call the first phase of this development the Phùng Nguyên culture. Sites of this period are rich in stone adzes of a variety of forms, stone bracelets and other ornaments, and pottery. Many of the pots are decorated with

Issues and Processes in Southeast Asian Musics

incised parallel lines, filled with multiple impressions made by a small tool to create a typical design. Similar designs are found in sites of a comparable age in Thailand. Evidence of rice has been found in Phùng Nguyên sites. The working of bronze seems to have made its appearance toward the end of this phase, though extant bronze artifacts remain rare.

Around 1500 B.C.E, the Phùng Nguyễn culture was replaced by the Đồng Đậu culture, associated not only with a different type of pottery—vessels decorated with multiple parallel incised lines, rarely with impressions—but also with a great blossoming of the use of bronze. The bronze technology was quite similar to that of Thailand and involved the use of rather sophisticated bivalve molds. Around 1100 B.C.E, the Đồng Đậu culture was succeeded by the Gò Mun culture, which lasted until about the fifth century B.C.E.

There has been much discussion about the historical source of metallurgy in Southeast Asia. Before the excavations in Thailand and Vietnam, it had been assumed that the knowledge of metals and their manufacture had been introduced to the region in protohistoric times from China, India, or both regions. The early dates we now have for metal in Southeast Asia make this assumption more difficult to sustain, particularly since the early metal sites are not associated with other materials derived from these distant sources. Both the technology and the cultural forms it is associated with are quite different from the working of bronze and bronze artifacts found in either China or India and exhibit a strongly local character. Few archaeologists would suggest that bronze metallurgy in Southeast Asia represents an independent invention, but its historical sources remain obscure.

The introduction and spread of agriculture in island Southeast Asia is less well defined. Few sites have yielded remains of cultivated plants, so the presence of agriculture is inferred on the basis of indirect evidence, including the presence of pottery and tools interpreted to be agricultural in function. The Southeast Asian islands also lack, for the most part, excavations of permanent village settlements until a much later stage of prehistory.

THE COMING OF CIVILIZATION

The study of Southeast Asian civilizations has always been affected by the manifest dominance of religious, philosophical, and political systems derived from India and to a lesser extent, China. Until after the 1950s, when modern prehistoric research was introduced to the region, it was not unreasonable to assume that what culture historians like to call civilizations were due in Southeast Asia almost entirely to derivation from the outside. In this interpretation, Indian and Chinese systems of statecraft and administration were seen as having been superimposed on unsophisticated local societies. Though the late prehistory of Southeast Asia remains difficult to interpret in many ways, there is now ample evidence that indigenous peoples formed complex social and political systems before the rise of the earliest recognizable Hinduized states.

One of the more important technological innovations of the late settlement phase involved the addition of iron to the metallurgical repertory, probably sometime between 600 and 500 B.C.E. It appeared first in the form of such bimetallic artifacts as points of spears with forged iron blades, to which a bronze socket was cast on. Iron artifacts became

Figure 3.1
Bronze drum-gong in the collection of the Institute of Culture and Arts, Hồ Chí Minh City, Vietnam. Photo by Terry E. Miller.

more common during the later part of the phase but never replaced bronze. At about the same time, excavations at the site of Ban Don Ta Phet in western Thailand revealed, besides iron implements, a large number of bronze artifacts that stand out for their variety and technological sophistication. Most of the artifacts have a high tin content, which produces a shiny, silvery metal (the Romans called a similar bronze *speculum*), brittle and difficult to work. Extremely thin-walled and often remarkably large, vessels were first cast in a lost-wax process, then forged, and eventually finished by being polished on a lathe. Many of them are decorated with engraved geometric patterns and figurative designs. There is also excellent evidence at Ban Don Ta Phet of trade interactions with distant India and northern Vietnam.

In Vietnam, the working of bronze blossomed greatly during the Gò Mun Period (from c. 1100 to 500 B.C.E). Artifacts previously made of stone were now made of bronze, retaining their traditional forms. New types of bronze artifacts appeared and became standard items during the Đông Son Period, which followed. Pottery was more highly fired than during the previous periods, indicating improvements in manufacturing technology (and probably more sophisticated demands), and was decorated with incised curvilinear and rectangular lines.

The most spectacular items in that regard are bronze drums, cast in complex piece molds and highly decorated, both on top and on the sides (Figure 3.1). The top (tympanum) always has a star in the center, surrounded by multiple concentric circles, filled variably with geometric motifs and stylized animals, particularly common among them birds identified as cranes. On the edge of the tympanum are often four frogs, cast in the round. The side (mantle) is normally decorated, in some cases with incised scenes of boats filled with fantastically dressed humans, sometimes brandishing spears or bows and arrows. Other decorations on drums show domestic scenes, processions, and what may be interpreted as ritual performances, which appear to include mouth organs and other instruments. Much valuable information about life during the Đông Son Period can be derived from the information on the drums, though the interpretation of the scenes, often highly stylized, is open.

The information gleaned from the drums is of importance, however, because archaeological research on the Đông Son Period is deficient in two important kinds of evidence: few settlement sites are known for the period, so our knowledge almost exclusively derives from cemetery sites. Because of soil conditions, few traces of the bodies have survived with the graves, so the presence of a grave must often be inferred on the basis of clusters of artifacts. This deprives archaeologists of important evidence in the interpretation of the cemeteries. One significant settlement has been found in the site of Cổ Loa, which may furnish us with the earliest evidence of urbanism in Southeast Asia. The first phase of Cổ

Loa as a central settlement is associated with Đông Son pottery, a large bronze drum, and many other bronze artifacts and probably dates to 300 B.C.E or earlier. The area defined by the outermost of three ramparts encloses some 600 hectares, though this probably represents an expansion sometime after the Đông Son Period.

PREHISTORY IN THE ISLANDS

Turning from the Southeast Asian mainland to the islands, we find that the archaeological record for the last two or three millennia B.C.E is sparse and incoherent. We do know, however, that prehistoric communities in the islands did not share with their mainland counterparts an early involvement in bronze metallurgy. In the absence of evidence to the contrary, it appears that until the middle of the first millennium B.C.E, island societies remained organized in small, autonomous units, focused on subsistence economies based on agriculture and fishing. There was evidently a great deal of mobility among island societies during the last fifteen hundred years B.C.E, with far-flung exchange contacts, but it occurred in the context of a maritime-oriented subsistence economy.

The picture changed suddenly and drastically around 500 to 400 B.C.E, when both bronze and iron appeared simultaneously through many of the islands. In the Philippines, the source seems to have been Sa Huynh in Vietnam. This is suggested by other exchange goods and similar pottery shared with that site. In Indonesia, however, the source was more likely Đông Son, as the scattering of Đông Son drums throughout much of the archipelago suggests.

The occurrence of Đông Son drums in Indonesia raises a problem. Clearly, these artifacts must have been of enormous value, given the skill and labor invested in their manufacture and the long distance they traveled. How could small autonomous farming and fishing communities afford such treasures? Did they possess exchange goods of equal value to the Đông Sonians? Or is the currently available archaeological record greatly understating the level of development of island societies in the late first millennium B.C.E?

ASIAN ART AND MUSIC IN PREHISTORY

Even though the archaeological record remains inadequate in many respects and is full of gaps, an ever more coherent picture of the ancient cultural development of the region has emerged over the past four decades. It tells us not only about the great changes that have occurred but also of long-term cultural-historical continuities. It demonstrates clearly a strong internal dynamic, in which Southeast Asia interacted with surrounding parts of the world as a recipient of cultural innovations and as a source of demographic, social, and cultural developments. We are now able to perceive deep, indigenous roots for the Hinduized and Sinicized historical civilizations of the region.

Among the arts represented in the Đông Son and Djan record is music. Much discussion has taken place about the function and use of the drums themselves. Given the enormous effort, skill, and cost involved in their manufacture, it is logical to assume that they were made for, and closely associated with, powerful leaders. Some writers have claimed that the drums were seen as representations of the king or a paramount chief. By the same token, it is claimed that they were sacred instruments, invested with great supernatural powers.

We are fortunate in having, on the mantles of drums and in sculpted scenes, illustrations that show drums in use. Some show an individual drum under a platform in the aft section of a boat filled with warriors in ceremonial garb; in one sculpted scene on the lid of a cowrie-shell container from Yunnan, three drums are stacked on top of each other in the center of a grouping that seems to portray a human sacrifice; and several engraved scenes depict drums arrayed under a raised platform on which humans are placed with staffs, as if to play the drums. On a drum excavated at Cổ Loa, four players have their staffs alternately raised and lowered. These latter scenes are particularly interesting. While they do not exclude the possibility that bronze drums were beaten as isolated rhythmic instruments (e.g., to call people to assembly or to war), they indicate that bronze drums were used in musical ensembles. Similar to the bronze gongs in Southeast Asian ensembles, Đông Sonian drums come in a range of sizes. In 1990, Vietnamese archaeologists surveyed 115 drums found in Vietnam. The heights of the instruments ranged from 17 to 67 centimeters, and the diameters from 20 to 90 centimeters. Chinese archaeologists have studied

Figure 3.2
Drawing of the tympanum (top) of a bronze drum-gong from Vietnam. From Nguyễn Văn Huyên and Hoáng Vinh, *Những Trống Đồng Đong Son Đã Phát Hiện Ở Việt Nam* (Viện Bảo Tàng Lịch Sử, 1975), p. 279.

0   5cm

scraping marks on the inside of Dian drums and believe that they are the result of tuning. All this suggests that individual drums were manufactured to conform to a specific pitch and that several drums could be, and were, combined into ensembles. Since each drum in such an ensemble seems to have been played by an individual musician, it is tempting to infer that this involved either a simple form of ostinato or that they were used in a way akin to bell choirs (Figure 3.2).

Decorations on bronze drums show other musical instruments in use. Among them is an instrument strongly reminiscent of the contemporary Lao free-reed mouth organ (*khaen*), something that may be interpreted as hand-held cymbals similar to those now familiar from traditional Thai ensembles (*ching*), flutes, and bells. The mouth organs occur repeatedly, usually in the context of a row of dancers. Sculpted scenes from the Dian culture portray also several other instruments in action, in groups of musicians or groups of dancers and musicians. These instruments include hand-held drums and wind instruments related by Chinese archaeologists to the Chinese mouth organ (*sheng*). Examples of the latter have also been found as artifacts made of bronze in some of the Dian sites, at least one of which is shaped like a calabash and adorned with a small cattle figurine. These instruments are less reminiscent of their Han counterparts than of similar wind instruments found today among south Chinese minorities (Figure 3.3).

A full study of the musical traditions of the Đông Son and Dian cultures is yet to be carried out, but it is clear that there is a wealth of valuable archaeological information. The music of Southeast Asia appears to have ancient indigenous roots.

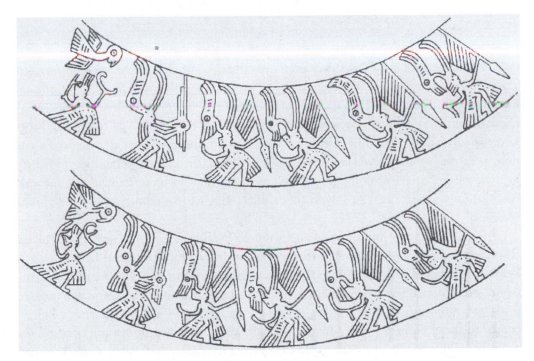

Figure 3.3
Detail of martial dances and players of free-reed mouth organs. From Nguyễn Văn Huyên and Hoáng Vinh, *Những Trồng Đồng Đong Son Đã Phát Hiện Ở Việt Nam* (Viện Bảo Tàng Lịch Sủ, 1975), p. 175.

Waves of Cultural Influence

Terry E. Miller and Sean Williams

Precontact Musical Sources
Indian Culture in Southeast Asia
Chinese Music in Southeast Asia and Its Legacy
Islam in Southeast Asia
The West

To the extent that scholars can reconstruct a chronology and a history for Southeast Asia, the process is complex. People prefer to assert their national and regional identities. Often they do not see, and sometimes they even deny, that this individuality has resulted from a process extending back into history and prehistory, in which layer after layer of outside influence transformed, and was transformed by, the cultures that received it. We cannot speak of cultural purity in any sense, and the people of Southeast Asia recognize themselves as participants in multiple levels of society: as Southeast Asians, as citizens of a nation, as carriers of a regional tradition, as groups distinct from those of another province, district, village, or even family. It is therefore appropriate to understand that Southeast Asian cultures were formed from waves of cultural influence, from both nearby and distant societies.

An examination of Southeast Asian terminology easily shows how each language has absorbed words and writing systems from others, including those of India, China, Arabia, France, the United States, and Japan. The process is obvious in the case of musical instruments. Still, though terms for instruments (and even the instruments themselves) migrate easily, the musical styles to which they contribute are too individually expressive of a given people to travel entirely intact. Anyone who dismisses Vietnamese musical instruments as simply Chinese does not understand that Vietnamese melodies, being modally based, require an entirely different approach to ornamentation and the bending of tones—which proves impossible to realize on Chinese instruments; hence, to embody the Vietnamese aesthetic, Vietnamese musicians modified Chinese-derived instruments with high frets, looser strings, and a different style of decoration.

In most Southeast Asian nations, people know that their culture has foreign origins, and they are aware of enclaves of resident foreigners, foreign invasions, and their own attraction to artistic foreignness. The Burmese repertory of classical songs includes *yòudayà*, songs said to have derived from Siamese taken to Burma after 1767, when the Siamese capital (Ayuthaya) was defeated. Many Thai classical compositions invoke one of the so-called twelve languages (*sipsawng phasa*). For example, the term *khaek* in the Thai composition "*Khaek Lopburi*" suggests a Malaysian or Indian origin, but it is actually a composition by Choi Suntarawathin. Similarly, the *jin* in "*Jin Rua*" suggests a Chinese origin, but it is by Luang Pradit Phairoh. Vietnamese in Thọ Xuân Village in Thanh Hóa Province perform masked dances invoking the Cham, the Chinese, the Dutch, and the Lao. Sundanese vocalists in West Java occasionally intersperse rhymed couplets in Dutch, Japanese, or English with classical Sundanese couplets, primarily so audiences may enjoy the exoticism of those languages. Filipinos perform elaborate song-and-dance creations, celebrating the Spanish era of the Philippines. Awareness of foreigners and foreign cultures has been a part of Southeast Asia throughout its known history. Though its peoples have not been equally affected by foreign influences, few have remained isolated from them.

PRECONTACT MUSICAL SOURCES

Southeast Asia is distinctive for the uniqueness of each culture's response to outside influences, especially from India, China, and the West. The idea of assessing the region's precontact musical resources presumes that we can isolate them, but we cannot be sure we can. Nevertheless, a discussion of possible precontact resources is reasonable. Two topics, organology and animistic rites, include aspects most likely to have predated the coming of foreign religions, languages, and instruments.

Musical Instruments

Southeast Asia, or the areas from which the peoples of Southeast Asia originated, probably gave rise to types of instruments that did not derive from donor cultures. Some are unique to the subcontinent, some exemplify universal types, and some likely became modified into instruments found elsewhere. The most difficult questions to answer are who created these instruments, where the creation occurred, and when. Since some instruments are associated with upland groups, which reflect little influence from India or China, their instruments probably represent the oldest organological layer. Many are found on both the mainland and in the islands. The direction of cultural diffusion is more likely from the former to the latter, but there is no way to determine whether this diffusion occurred during prehistoric periods (when land bridges between the areas arose), or whether it occurred by sea. Cultural diffusion may have proceeded from or through Taiwan to the Philippines as early as 3000 B.C.E.

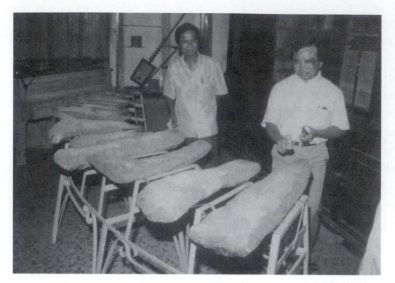

Lithophones

The oldest extant Southeast Asian musical instruments are the lithophones unearthed in Vietnam since about 1950 (Figure 4.1). Some nine or ten sets have been discovered, but they have attracted little attention from prehistoric specialists despite their having come to light over fifty years ago (Condominas 1952). Each set consists of eight to twelve narrow, variously shaped stones, each capable of producing a pitch when struck with a hammer. Since no one knows when they were made, by whom, or for what reason, it follows that we know nothing of the music played on them. They are likely associated with some phase of the Hoabinhian culture, dating from ten thousand to a few thousand years ago. Ancient lithophones are still being discovered, and copies of them are being made on which newly composed music is performed.

Figure 4.1
Lithophone discovered in Khánh So'n, a village in the central highlands of Vietnam, in September 1979; now housed at Institute of Culture and Arts, Hô Chí Minh City. Photo by Phong T. Nguyễn, 1991.

lithophone
Stone xylophone

Xylophones

Xylophones made of bamboo or hardwood, hung vertically from a post or set horizontally over a trough resonator, appear to have originated in Southeast Asia. Hanging bamboo xylophones, likely the oldest configuration, are primarily found in the mountains that straddle the borders of Vietnam, Cambodia, and Laos. Examples made of hardwood logs appear in Thailand's Kalasin Province (Figure 4.2). Others appear in the Philippines and on various Indonesian islands, where they are played in both hanging and horizontal configurations.

The classical xylophones of lowland Burma (*pa'talà*), Thailand (*ranat*), Laos (*lanat*), and Cambodia (*roneat*) consist of hardwood or bamboo keys suspended on two cords over a wooden resonator. In Indonesia, Javanese gamelans include the *gambang*, with wooden keys lying flat on the edges of a resonator. Highland groups in the Philippines use hanging bamboo or wooden keys.

Figure 4.2
The northeastern Thai vertical-log xylophone (*khaw law* also *pong lang*), Kalasin Province. Photo by Terry E. Miller, 1973.

Bronze Instruments

Bronze metallurgy in the mainland dates to the early second millennium B.C.E. or before. Bronze instruments with keys, plus bossed and flat gongs, are distinctive to

Southeast Asia. The boss, a large raised knob in the center of the gong, enables the instrument to be precisely tuned. Hanging gongs, most with bosses, are found widely in both mainland and island areas. The uplands of the mainland are distinguished for their ensembles of individually held gongs. Lowland musicians play on sets of small, horizontally mounted gongs. In the islands, the great gamelans, especially those of Java, include the largest hanging gongs in Asia, and probably in the world (Figure 4.3).

The most distinctive bronze instruments are called bronze drums, which have drum-shaped bodies with a flat bottom and top. At least 138 such instruments have been discovered since 1730 throughout Southeast Asia, including Vietnam, Yunnan Province (China), Thailand, Cambodia, Malaysia, Sumatra, Java, and some of Indonesia's lesser-known islands (including Luang, Roti, Salajar, and Sangeang). The historical specimens date to the Đông So'n Period (late fourth century B.C.E.), but such instruments are still made and are occasionally used in Thai Buddhist temples. In Vietnam, artisans stand ready to make replicas for anyone willing to pay the price. While we know little of the drums' original use, the presence of sculpted frogs along the rims suggests a connection to ceremonies of rainmaking. The tops of some drums show figures that appear to be dancing and playing mouth organs (see SOUTHEAST ASIA IN PREHISTORY).

Figure 4.3
A large hanging with boss, from Central Java. Photo by Sean Williams.

Other Widespread Instruments

At least three other instrument types appear to be indigenous: free-reed pipes and mouth organs, Jew's harps, and tube zithers. Though free-reed instruments are now used in East Asia, Europe, and the Americas, there is evidence that they spread to these areas from Southeast Asia. Within Southeast Asia, there are six types of free-reed instruments: a free-reed animal horn, a free-reed pipe with holes for fingering, a free-reed pipe and a gourd wind chest, a gourd wind-chest mouth organ, a Hmong mouth organ (Figure 4.4), and a Lao raft mouth organ. A seventh, a rounded bundle of pipes in a circular wind chest, occurs in East Asia.

Jew's harps, mostly of bamboo but some of metal, are found widely, more often than not used as disguisers of the voice (Figure 4.5). Such

Figure 4.4
A Hmong free-reed mouth organ (*qeej*) from central Laos. Photo by Terry E. Miller, 1973.

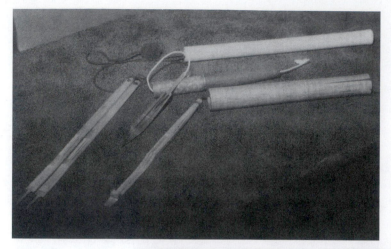

instruments are distributed worldwide and are probably a universal type, suggesting multiple points of origin. Bamboo tube zithers (Figure 4.6) are less commonly used. They are most prevalent in upland regions, and are also found throughout Borneo and among some lowland Lao. There is reason to believe that the *valiha*, the tube zither of Madagascar (now the Republic of Malagasy) came with the Malayo-Polynesian-speaking peoples who migrated there from regions of Indonesia about 500 C.E.

Figure 4.5
Jew's harps from upland Mainland Southeast Asia. The bamboo double Jew's harp (*left*) and bamboo single Jew's harp (*right*) are from Sino-Tibetan groups; the metal example (*center*) is Hmong. Photo by Terry E. Miller, 1995.

Figure 4.6
Tháo Giang, a Bahnar minority member living in Pleiku, Vietnam, plays a tube zither (*ding goong*). Photo by Terry E. Miller, 1994.

Locally Unique Instruments

Throughout the subcontinent, instruments unique to one area or people are likely of ancient origin. Some are monochords. The Vietnamese *đàn b'âu* has a single string, extending diagonally from a long, box resonator to a flexible wand at one end, allowing the player to bend the harmonics produced by plucking at the nodes. In the uplands of Vietnam, a bowed monochord stick zither (*k'ni*) is resonated through a string connecting the main string to the player's mouth. In lowland Cambodia and northern Thailand, monochordal stick zithers are resonated through a coconut shell placed on the player's chest.

The Lao, the northeastern Thai, and the Malay attach rattan-strung bows to large kites, which they fly during the cold, windy months; the air currents make the rattan vibrate, producing random successions of pitches (Figure 4.7). Many rural Southeast Asians use bamboo to create music generated by the forces of nature, such as musical irrigation tubes, aeolian flutes (played by the wind), and the like.

Animistic Rites

Foreign religions, and the cultures from which they sprang, have long been part of the cultural matrix that defines each people or country. Few of these religions are practiced in a "pure" form. The rites, practices, and beliefs associated with indigenous manifestations of animism are often absorbed into the major religions or coexist with them. Most Southeast Asians perceive no contradiction in honoring the Lord Buddha, a supreme deity, and a pantheon of spirits. Roman Catholics in Vietnam often have altars for spirits. Muslims in Indonesia maintain remnants of the old pantheon of Hindu-Buddhist gods, some of whom derived from local forms of animism. The mixing of precontact animism with later "official" religions is the norm, not the exception, in Southeast Asia. The kinds of animistic rites are legion, and we do not intend to discuss them systematically.

In many areas, particularly the upland regions of Vietnam, Cambodia, and Laos and the outer islands of Indonesia, an annual sacrifice of a buffalo is an event of major importance. Music, particularly gong ensembles with dancing, plays a major role at these festivals. In Vietnam, mediums (*ch`âu văn*), accompanied by instruments and singing, go into trance to be possessed by spirits and thereby learn information that can help solve problems. Though the current government has banned such rituals, in isolated places they continue to occur, but the music can be performed alone as well.

Figure 4.7
A musical bow (*sanu*) mounted on a homemade kite (*chula*), northeastern Thailand. Photo by Terry E. Miller, 1988.

Few upland peoples have been exposed to the major religions of their respective countries, and they continue to practice all manner of animistic rituals. The major exception is in areas where Christian missionaries have been active, but even there, old habits persist, sometimes reinterpreted into a Christian system of beliefs. In northeast Thailand and Laos, when someone is ill and does not respond to treatment by a medical doctor, spirits are suspected of having caused the illness. Among the mediums who may intercede are *mawlam phi fa*, mostly females, who sing and dance around an altar of objects considered to be attractive to spirits, accompanied by a free-reed mouth organ (*khaen*). When possessed, the mediums behave as if they are the spirits inhabiting their bodies and provide an explanation for the victim's illness (Figure 4.8). In Burma, Buddhist temples include

Figure 4.8
A curing ceremony (*lam phi fa*) is accompanied by a free-reed mouth organ (*khaen*), northeastern Thailand. Photo by Terry E. Miller, 1973.

shrines to a pantheon of thirty-seven spirits (*na'*). Of various origins, these deities are worshipped with music in a three-day ritual, *na'pwè*, which includes possession (Rodrigue 1992). In upland Malaysia, Temiar shamans go on spiritual journeys and sing dream songs—communications that tell the reasons for the community's problems (Roseman 1991).

In East Java, Muslim performers of hobbyhorse trance dancing become possessed by the spirits of horses. To the accompaniment of gongs, drums, and an oboe, they make

horselike movements and commit potentially dangerous acts, like breaking and eating glass. In the Toraja area of Sulawesi, as part of elaborate funerals sending the spirit of the deceased to the next world, Roman Catholic Torajans join in large circles and dance. They leave an effigy (*tau-tau*) to guard the grave. In east central Flores, Roman Catholic Lio people maintain dwellings to house their ancestors' bones (Figure 4.9). During seasonal agricultural festivities, they invoke these ancestors' spirits.

Figure 4.9
An east central Flores house for spirits (*left*) echoes the shape of the volcanic cone seen to the right. Photo by Cary Black.

INDIAN CULTURE IN SOUTHEAST ASIA

The term *Indo-China*, though Eurocentric in character, correctly suggests the importance of Indic and Chinese influences on Southeast Asia. Assuming that Southeast Asian cultures *are* Indic or Chinese, however, would misrepresent reality. These civilizations did indeed influence the foundations of most civilizations in Southeast Asia, but in every case, those receiving the Chinese and Indic cultures transformed them into new cultures, in which visiting Indians and Chinese would likely feel foreign. The cultural distinctiveness of every group that adopted and adapted the Indic and Chinese cultures, both historical kingdoms and contemporary nation-states, is what makes Southeast Asia one of the most colorful and attractive areas on earth.

When we speak of India and Indian culture, we must differentiate between historical and contemporary influences. There is a world of difference between the culture of a state overseen by a Hindu-Buddhist god-king residing in a great temple and the culture of recent immigrants and their entertainments, especially Indian films and the ubiquitous genre of *filmi* songs. A visitor to Bali, Burma, Malaysia, Thailand, and Vietnam therefore finds both the great Indian-style temples of antiquity and recently built Hindu temples for merchants living in the neighborhood.

The study of early Southeast Asian history is daunting because the reader must sort out a bewildering succession of vaguely located and dated Indianized kingdoms. These kingdoms were the foundations of modern Burmese, Cambodian, Javanese, and Thai civilizations. The place where this culture originated is not contemporary India, for great

Figure 4.10
Prasat Phanom Rung, the ninth-century, Indian-influenced Khmer temple on Phonom Rung Hill, Surin Province, northeastern Thailand. Photo by Terry E. Miller, 2006.

changes have occurred in both the South and the Southeast Asian subcontinents. About two thousand years ago, contact occurred primarily for two reasons—trade and religion. Some influence came to Southeast Asia indirectly, through China. Contemporary cultures of southern India more likely resemble the source than do those of northern India. Before this contact, small political entities probably dotted the landscape of Southeast Asia, ruled by local chiefs. The concept of a nation under a king descended from gods living at a temple representing a holy mountain is said to have come from India. The official religion of Southeast Asian kingdoms was usually a form of Hinduism, but Buddhism played a major role among the common people. The mixing of Buddhism and Hinduism with local forms of animism occurred widely and contributes to the individuality of Southeast Asian cultures. In fact, the magnificent Buddhist temple of Borobudur in central Java is only half an hour's drive from Prambanan, a great Hindu temple.

Over time, contacts with Indian culture and the intermarriage of culture-bearing Indians with Southeast Asians transformed all those living within the radiating power of the sacred temple of the mountain (and in the islands, that mountain is often a volcano with its own spiritual and physical power). Those at the margins, especially people living at higher elevations, were least and last affected. Southeast Asian peoples received and adapted to their own needs many aspects of Indian civilization, including religion, architecture, sculpture, decoration, literature, language, scripts, farming practices, rituals, concepts—and music.

Spiritual Matters

The essentials of this process include an understanding that Hinduism is not a unified and bounded religion but the sum of disparate parts, and when scholars invoke the gen-

Figure 4.11
A *Sukhwan* takes place around a holy-tree altar. Northeast Thailand. Photo by Terry E. Miller, 1973.

eral term *Hinduism*, they are likely referring to the systems of belief surrounding a particular deity, such as Shiva. While Hindu concepts, beliefs, and practices deeply influenced the leaders of the early Southeast Asian kingdoms, this kind of Hinduism survives only marginally on the mainland. A Brahman remains at the Thai court, responsible for rituals that maintain the kingdom's prosperity and stability. Though music is associated with these rituals, outsiders know little about it.

In areas of Thailand, Laos, and the Shan State of Burma, a *phram* (from Brahman) oversees the *sukhwan* or *bai si* ritual (Figure 4.11). In heightened speech, before an altar of ritual objects, he calls back a person's *khwan* (a timid, spiritual essence, which tends to flee during times of stress or transition), which he figuratively binds to the person by tying threads around the person's wrist. At the Cambodian court, female dancers are seen as heavenly maidens (*apsara*), who link the kingdom to the gods. Thai classical musicians must be initiated through a series of *wai khru* rituals before altars bearing masks of deified Hindu and Buddhist figures from Indian religious literature, principally the Ramayana, the great pan-Asian epic. Indeed, the literary Rama himself is seen as an incarnation of the god Vishnu.

Bali, considered by many to be an earthly paradise, is the center of Hinduism in Indonesia. An unofficial system of castes still exists, and Hindu priests preside over local religious festivals, hundreds of which require artistic performance. The image of the god-king was much more powerful and prevalent before the twentieth century arrived in Bali, but many aspects of Hinduism are accepted and practiced on the island. People make offerings at all gateways, borders, boundaries (such as crossroads, springs, doors, beaches, and volcanoes), and gateway events (such as births, deaths, and marriages). Most important, to be a Hindu in Bali means that creating art—music, dance, sculpture, or painting—is a fundamental means of practicing one's religion.

Literacy, Literature, and the Imagination

The scripts of the Balinese, the Burmese, the Javanese, the Khmer, the Lao, the Shan, and the Thai, including local variants (like Sundanese and northern [*lanna*] Thai), derive from phonetic Indic scripts, which allowed these (non-Indic) vocabularies to be written and pronounced in their own ways. The transformations, however, are of such a magnitude that readers of modern Indic scripts can discern little. With them came a great deal of vocabulary, especially from Buddhist writings in both Sanskrit and Pali.

The more Indianized the culture, the more words of Indian origin in the language. Within Southeast Asian languages, the higher ranking the class of vocabulary, the more

Indian-derived words it has. The levels of language reserved for Buddhism and for royal speech are so thoroughly Indian that learned individuals from Burma, Cambodia, and Thailand can converse using this vocabulary, though their everyday languages are quite different and mutually unintelligible. Multiple levels of language (with separate vocabularies for each level) occur in Javanese, Sundanese, and Balinese in Indonesia. Though some words are shared (or at least markedly similar) among the three areas, the least refined levels of each usually have the least in common.

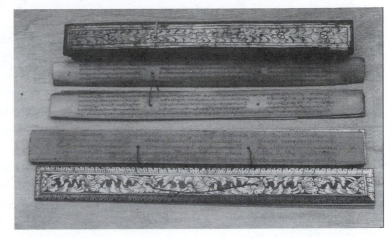

Figure 4.12
Three palm-leaf manuscripts from Thailand. Photo by Terry E. Miller.

Many early written documents were those of the court and its activities, but those with musical implications derive from religion (primarily Buddhism and Hinduism) and literature. Traditional literature and Buddhist sermons or Hindu tales and texts of chants were, and in some places continue to be, written on palm-leaf strips (Figure 4.12). Writers scratch the letters into the leaf and fill them in with carbon powder; they then bind the leaves with a cord or cords. In Thailand, these manuscripts preserve traditional stories, which serve as the foundations for preaching, solo narrative, and theater. Among them are a great number of local stories, stories of Buddha's birth (*jataka*) and the Ramayana.

Two Indian epics, the *Ramayana* and the *Mahabharata,* are central to the literature of all Indianized cultures. Since, like the (Nordic) *Ring of the Nibelungs*, the stories are long and complicated, only episodes can be told or acted at one time. Through Indianized Southeast Asia, the general population is familiar with the main characters and the basic plots. The Ramayana's monkey-general, Hanuman, is as well known to Southeast Asian children as Mickey Mouse is to Western children. Dances, human theater, shadow-puppet theater, doll-puppet theater, and the decoratve motifs that permeate society—all derive from these epics. In addition, the main characters of the stories are so well understood, that humans may formally or casually be called by the names of characters in indication of their psychological makeup.

Musical Influences

Trying to distinguish what *is* of Indian origin from what merely resembles it is the scholarly equivalent of walking in quicksand. Comparing the contemporary musical artifacts of Southeast Asia with those of India while seeking conclusions about a relational process that occurred possibly two thousand years ago can produce distorted results. Nevertheless, several topics require exploration, among them terminology, organology, musical process, and style. We must bear in mind several caveats: terms may travel apart from their objects, instruments may travel without their styles, similarities do not prove relationships, and proven relationships do not demonstrate the direction of transmission.

Terms and Their Objects

A great many Southeast Asian instruments bear Indian-derived names, but these instruments are not necessarily derived from India. Certain Indian terms are also found widely, denoting a variety of instrumental types in nearly endless verbal permutations. In Indian usage, the term *vina* merely denotes stringed instruments, but Southeast Asian usage has transformed it into *phin*, referring to the northern Thai chest-resonated stick zither (*phin nam tao*) and multistringed stick zither (*phin phia*) and to the northeastern Thai-Lao plucked lute (*phin*).

Several lutes and board zithers derive their names from a common linguistic ancestor; they include the Sundanese boat-shaped zither (*kacapi*), the central Thai long-necked lute (*krajappi*), the Cambodian long-necked lute (*chapey*), a lute in the Philippines (*kudyapi*), and various lutes in Borneo and Sumatra (including the *sapeh*, the *safe*, and the *husapi*). The north Indian term *sitār*, which names a long-necked plucked lute, becomes *siter* in central and west Java, where it denotes small board zithers.

In seeking relationships between Indian and Southeast Asian instruments, we cannot be sure similarities between contemporary specimens prove a historical connection, but a few types seem clearly of Indian origin. Southeast Asian drums with laced heads are most likely of Indian origin, especially the pairs of long drums common to Malaysia (*gendang*), Indonesia (*kendang*), Thailand (*klawng khaek*), and Cambodia (*skor khek*). The Thai term *khaek* "guest" denotes Malaysians and Indians. Indeed, these drums are somewhat similar to the Indian *tavil, pakhavaj,* and *mridanga,* and to the Sri Lankan *gata bera*.

Conical double-reed aerophones, including the Malaysian *serunai* and the Thai *pi chanai,* often bear a name related to that of the Indian *shenai*. But the Filipino *serunai* is a set of small, tuned, metal plates in a frame, on which musicians practice for playing the *kulintang*. The Sundanese and east Javanese double-reed aerophone sidesteps the *shenai* name altogether, using the term *tarompet* or *terompet* (borrowed from a Western term reflected in Dutch as *trompet* and English as *trumpet*), though the instrument is clearly not a trumpet (Figure 4.13). A more obvious relationship is seen between small Indian cymbals (*talam*) and those of the Burmese *(si),* the Thai *(ching),* the Lao *(sing),* the Khmer *(chhing),* and the Balinese *(cengceng).*

Dance

Southeast Asian dancers perform episodes from some of the same stories that Indian dancers do, and both traditions bear a major similarity: dancers tell stories gesturally; movements and poses represent encoded objects, actions, emotions, and ideas. For communication to take place, a connoisseur must know the dancer's codes, though in

aerophone
a wind instrument

Figure 4.13
An East Javanese *terompet.* Photo by Sean Williams.

many cases a singer simultaneously performs the text. Each Indianized Southeast Asian tradition of dance—Balinese, Burmese, Cham, Javanese, Khmer, Lao, Sundanese, Thai, and perhaps some in Malaysia—is distinctive, but all usually follow the same process of Indian dance, which differs strikingly from the concept of aesthetically pleasing but non-lexical movement ("pure dance") that predominates in some genres in the West.

Even in modern choreography, the reliance on Indian models is prominently in evidence. Choreographers recognize that to build bridges to their audiences, certain aspects of the dance should be based on familiar, Indianized material. The result often takes the form of a dance that reacts to or against Indian models of gestural expression and spatial orientation. In either case, the audience uses the prevailing mode of dance-based storytelling and gestures as its cultural referent.

Musical Processes

There are two basic ways of playing music or singing: to reproduce a preexisting melody, with or without ornamentation and individual or idiomatic expression; or to create a composition while playing it, by following a set of conventions collectively called mode. India has both, and so does Southeast Asia. It is also possible to play fixed compositions that have been created according to the conventions of a given mode. Mode provides a musician with tonal material, a hierarchy of tones (allowing for the creation of tension and its release), typical melodic phrases and ornaments, and an emotional character. The Indian modal system (*raga*) is widely known and even more complex.

Metrically free modal improvisation, as heard in the *alap* of an Indian raga, is not the norm in Southeast Asia, but the Vietnamese system of modes is nearly as complex as that of India. In Vietnamese chamber music, each musician usually warms up with a brief, unmetered improvisation (*rao*) before all begin the fixed composition. In addition, soloists improvise long and elaborate compositions based on modal principles. Another tradition of modal improvisation, though much simpler, is that of the northeastern Thai-Lao *khaen*, whose players improvise in two scalar systems, each having three modes.

An analysis of the musics of Burma, Cambodia, and Thailand suggests an underlying modal system, but the classical traditions are almost entirely made up of fixed compositions, capable of shifting tonal centers throughout—what Western harmonic theory calls modulation and non-Western melodic theory calls metabole. The generation of melody in Malaysia, with arabesquelike streams of melody, spinning small intervals in a seamless web, points to Western Asia origins.

The system of *pathet* in central Java denotes not just a repertory of allowable tones but also a tonal hierarchy that defines a mood, a general character, or another nonmusical element. The tonal hierarchy sets up boundaries (clear in every musician's mind) as to which melodic patterns, elaborations, and variations are appropriate. The correct performance of improvised elaborations and variations must be carried out according to the rules of individual *pathet*.

pathet
Javanese modal classification system

Indian influence is also likely where rhythmic-metrical cycles exist. The Indian system of *talas*, in which a closed cycle of beats underlies the melodic system (*raga*), is not unlike the cycles found throughout Southeast Asia, especially in classical musics. As in India,

Southeast Asian drummers know individual drumstrokes by name and initially memorize a fundamental form of the cycle (but may improvise to a limited degree on it). In Burmese, Cambodian, Lao, and Thai classical traditions, small bronze cymbals mark the cycle; in Vietnam, a slit drum or castanetlike instruments mark certain beats. Cyclic meters distinguish Vietnamese music from Chinese, placing Vietnam within the Southeast Asian musical world despite its superficial similarities to that of East Asia.

It is difficult to say that the concepts of melodic modes and metrical cycles in Southeast Asia came directly from India, since both are found elsewhere (especially in Western Asia), but the similarities make the connection compelling. Aside from the process indicated by modal and cyclic construction, however, little else about Southeast Asian musical styles points toward India.

Contemporary Indian Influence

Contemporary Indian culture exists in enclaves in Burma, East Java, Thailand, and Vietnam, and around 10 percent of the population of Malaysia is of contemporary Indian extraction. Many Indians in Burmese cities, brought there by the British during the colonial period, operate shops and restaurants. Most in Thailand migrated in order to open businesses, primarily fabric shops, but they also established temples and shrines, to which even the ethnically Thai pay homage. To our knowledge, except in Malaysia, Indian musics do not flourish within these communities, and where they do, they are not classical genres. The Malaysian *bangsawan,* a theater that mixed cultures to increase its popular appeal, traditionally had Indian elements, but modern, government-sanctioned *bangsawan* has largely been stripped of them.

Throughout Southeast Asia, theaters show Indian films, and shops sell cassettes of Indian *filmi* popular songs. The flood of popular Indian culture through films and their sound tracks has led to a spectacular local response in Indonesia. By the 1960s, Indonesian films based on Indian successes had caught the public imagination, and sound tracks featured *dangdut,* the genre that mimics the tabla, the flute, and the vocal ornamentation of *filmi.* Sung in Indonesian (more rarely in a local language), *dangdut* is the one musical genre that can be heard virtually anywhere in Indonesia. The elite consider it a music of the masses, but even the elite enjoy dancing to it when they let their guard down. Indian films and *filmi* remain popular in Indonesia, but they are outstripped by *dangdut,* with its use of the national language and Indonesian subjects.

CHINESE MUSIC IN SOUTHEAST ASIA AND ITS LEGACY

It would be hard to imagine Southeast Asia without the Chinese. The so-called Overseas Chinese vary from being unassimilated (and therefore easily noticed) to nearly assimilated. Although some Chinese had come to Southeast Asia by about 1600, most came from southern China during the nineteenth and twentieth centuries. They established businesses in the cities, major and minor. Many Southeast Asian cities retain a Chinese atmosphere, especially in their business sections. As in other parts of the world, many Chinese established restaurants, and the commercial cuisines of each country include Chinese dishes, modified to appeal to local palates. Because of success in business, the Chinese have come to dominate the economies of several countries, sparking resentment during tough times. As a result, they have been made scapegoats in times of stress and have suffered when local populations turned on them. Some fled, some suffered but survived, and some died.

Figure 4.14
A Chinese Buddhist temple to Quan Âm, the goddess of mercy, in the Chõ Lón section of Hồ Chí Minh City, Vietnam. Photo by Terry E. Miller, 1993.

Chinese influence on the cultures of Southeast Asia has been a factor for centuries, especially in Vietnam, a Chinese colony for more than a thousand years. Unlike the (mostly peaceful) relationship between India and Southeast Asia, that with China—especially for Vietnam—was violent. Many battles were fought, against both the Chinese and the Mongols, who controlled China during the Yuan Dynasty. Despite resentment toward the Chinese, the Vietnamese adopted Chinese ideographs long before converting to a romanized script, and the ability to read Chinese remains a requirement for Vietnamese scholars and religious people. The Vietnamese language is permeated with words of Chinese origin, much as Burmese, Khmer, Lao, and Thai are permeated with words of Pali and Sanskrit origin—and as English is permeated with words of Latin origin. As in these cases, it was a foreign religion—Mahayana Buddhism—that brought much Chinese culture to Vietnam (Figure 4.14).

Chinese musical influence manifests itself in two ways: through the maintenance of genuinely Chinese musical genres, and through the apparent influence of those genres on Southeast Asian musics, both in style and in organology. Indeed, some Chinese musical activities in Southeast Asia are examples of survivals, for genres played in such places as Bangkok, Ipoh (Malaysia), and Hồ Chí Minh City are often older versions of types that have changed or diminished in the People's Republic of China. The following must be considered a tentative survey, since a systematic study of Chinese musics in Southeast Asia remains to be done.

Vietnam

The Chinese are a prominent minority in lowland Vietnam, especially in the cities of the south, including those of the Mekong Delta. Visitors to these cities, especially the Chọ' Lỏ'n section of Hồ Chí Minh City, will find Chinese-descended people, spectacular temples, schools, restaurants, and shops. Today's Chinese population has little connection to the history of Chinese domination of the Vietnamese kingdoms. Of all Southeast Asian nations, Vietnam shows the most Chinese influence, modified to local tastes. The historical Vietnamese courts followed the Chinese model in both aesthetics and organization. The last series of Vietnamese emperors, the Nguyễn Dynasty, which governed in Huế from

1802 to 1945, established a "forbidden city" inside a larger walled city, the citadel. The court's musical establishment included Chinese-type ensembles, which played, at least in part, imported Chinese pieces.

Many of Vietnam's musical instruments originated in China: The *dàn tranh* zither is virtually identical to an older, sixteen-stringed *zheng*, the pear-shaped lute (*dàn tỳbà*) derives from the *pipa*, and the moon-shaped lute (*dàn nguyệt*) resembles both the *yue qin* and the *ruan*. Though these instruments appear to be Chinese, they have been modified to accommodate the Vietnamese musical system. Much of the latter requires tones outside the pentatonic tuning of the Chinese-derived instruments, plus ornaments peculiar to Vietnamese music. These can be realized only on instruments whose frets have been raised (to allow for the bending of tones) and whose strings have been made looser. These modifications make the instruments Vietnamese, not Chinese.

Today's Chinese population in Vietnam enjoys instrumental music at least as much as vocal music. It is played on familiar, unmodified instruments: a fiddle (*er hu*), a moon-shaped lute (*yue qin*), a pear-shaped lute (*pipa*), an oboe (*suona*), and various kinds of percussive instruments. Most Chinese music is played in private situations and cultural clubs, at funerals and festivals, and in theatrical performances for the linguistic communities, the Tiều (Chaozhou), the Quảng (Guangdong), and the Phuóc Kiến (Fujian). The Quảng and Tiều traditions are the most famous in Vietnam. After 1960 in Saigon, Quảng and Tiều musicians formed professional-level music clubs (*yue she*), where players rehearsed to play for fundraisers, commemorations, and funerals. Some Chinese instrumental pieces and melodies are known to Vietnamese musicians, who have adopted them into chamber music (*nhạc tài tủ*) and theater (*cải lương*). These tunes are modally classified into a Vietnamese subcategory, *hởi quảng* "Cantonese tunes." Though Vietnamese and Chinese musicians share instruments and tunes, they cannot play together because Vietnamese musicians change the character of the Chinese tunes.

Thailand

At Ayuthaya, the former Siamese capital, Chinese music and theater existed by the 1600s, for several French visitors to the court—Bouvet, Chaumont, Choisy, La Loubere, and Tachard—wrote at length about the Chinese entertainments they watched there (Miller and Chonpairot 1994: 34–40). These entertainments included both Chaozhou and Guangdong opera. By the 1800s or before, street and restaurant performances of Chinese shadow-puppet theater also occurred in Bangkok.

Modern Thai cities include people of Chinese descent; some have lived in Thailand for only a generation, others for many generations. Most, constituting the vast majority of the country's shopkeepers, operators of hotels, and restaurateurs, engage in business and professional activities. Thai cities have at least one Chinese temple, plus Chinese organizations that organize festival activities and the hiring of opera troupes. The dominant Chinese-language group in Thailand is the Chaozhou (locally pronounced Taejiu), which is spoken by people who migrated from eastern Guangdong Province in southern China. The internal business language of Thailand has been, and continues to be, Taejiu. But the Chinese-descended people have also taken Thai names, speak, read, and write Thai as their first language, and participate fully in Thai cultural life. Though the community retains Chinese music, Chinese students usually learn to play Thai classical music at school.

The Chinese temples and community organizations maintain at least three kinds of musical activity. First, numerous professional Taejiu opera troupes tour the nation's cities during most of the year, performing in eight-night runs in the traditional ritual setting, on a temporary stage facing the temple's main deity. This performance occurs around the deity's birthday. In many cities, the festival follows an all-day parade, involving student musicians playing *daluogu* instruments (drums, gongs, and cymbals) and sometimes *chuida* instruments (double reeds and side-blown flutes). The performances of operas occur each night, but during the day apprentice singers may have a chance to perform. Chaozhou opera requires a chorus of children, most of whom speak Thai-Lao as their native language. They come from the northeast and attach themselves to the opera troupe to get money. When grown up, they become the main actors and actresses; many do not speak Taejiu but can sing it. Fewer and fewer Chinese-Thai can understand Taejiu, and a simultaneous translation into Thai is sometimes read through loudspeakers (Figure 4.15).

Many temple clubs support a silk-and-bamboo (*sizhu*) club which plays traditional Taejiu music. This style is distinctive for its use of a nasal-toned, two-stringed fiddle (*tou xian*, closely resembling the Thai *saw duang*) and a tradition of patterned rhythmic variations of the tunes. Local businessmen enjoy playing this music in its traditional setting, purely for their own enjoyment (Figure 4.16). Some temples maintain Chinese-funeral musicians (*chuida* "blowing and hitting"), who use a variety of melodic instruments, led by a *suona* and accompanied by percussion. Various Taejiu instruments imported from China are available at shops in Bangkok's old Chinese section, on New Road and Yaowarat Road.

Malaysia

Malaysia is a multiethnic country whose population is 31 percent Chinese. We should expect that Chinese music and theater would be performed there, but little information has been published on the subject. Most performances occur in ritual contexts—before a deity on the deity's birthday.

Figure 4.15
A performance of Taejiu-language Chinese opera in Mahasarakham, Thailand. Photo by Terry E. Miller, 1973.

Figure 4.16
A Taejiu-speaking Chinese-Thai musician prepares for the rehearsal of a silk-and-bamboo ensemble in Khorat, Thailand. Photo by Terry E. Miller, 1988.

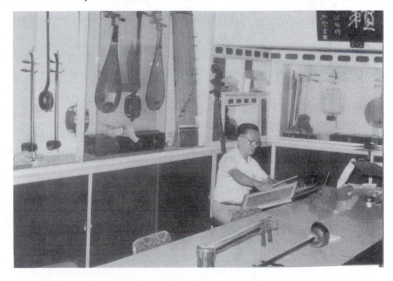

Human theater is said to be performed as it is in Thailand, and troupes from Thailand are said to perform in Malaysia. Puppet theater, however, is quite common, and has been documented. Three forms are maintained. The Hokkien-dialect glove-puppet theater was brought to Malaysia around the turn of the twentieth century. Small, boxlike stages are set up; the puppeteers sit in the lower portion, working the puppets on a small stage above their heads. Musicians play lutes, fiddles, and perhaps a flute behind them. The performances of a Hokkien marionette theater are reserved for the Jade Emperor deity. There are also Chaozhou rod puppets (Stalberg 1984).

Nothing is known to have been written in the West about Chinese music or theater in Burma, Cambodia, or Singapore. The level of activity, if there is one, is probably modest, though Singapore likely has active Chinese musicians. The Chinese do not figure in Laos at all, and many Chinese-Cambodians either fled the Khmer Rouge or died.

Indonesia

Dutch administrators brought Hokkien-speaking Chinese men (and later, Hakka and Chaozhou men) to establish commerce in Indonesia, and they offered marked political, educational, and economic advantages to men who migrated from China. These advantages bred resentment among local populations, which, in the months after the aborted coup of 1965, culminated in a large-scale massacre of at least five hundred thousand people, many of whom were Chinese-Indonesians. Though most Chinese-Indonesians are of mixed ancestry, local populations still consider them Chinese.

At least partially as a result of the troubles surrounding the massacre, public expressions of Chinese culture were minimal until the first decade of the twenty-first century. In the area around Jakarta (the national capital), local amalgams of Chinese and Indonesian music have developed. The main genre of Chinese-oriented music, *gambang kromong,* uses an eighteen-key xylophone (*gambang*), a ten-pitch gong chime (*kromong*), one or more two-stringed bowed lutes (*tehyan*), a side-blown flute (*suling*), and local percussion instruments, with singers and (for the modern repertoire only) optional Western band instruments (Yampolsky 1991). Though the ensemble once had a large number of Chinese melodies as part of its repertoire, the events of the mid-1960s have led to a gradual disappearance of these Chinese pieces and their replacement by local songs; nevertheless, the current ensemble performs at weddings and other Peranakan (mixed-blood, Chinese-Indonesian) cultural events.

During the economic crisis of the late 1990s, many Chinese-Indonesians were targeted for economically and racially based discrimination and outright violence, including some of the poorest members of Indonesian society. In addition, Chinese-Indonesian citizens were subjected by law to severe restrictions on their civil rights. As a result, many had immigrated to other countries by the turn of the twenty-first century. Since that time, legal restrictions have eased, public displays of Chinese culture have been increasing, and Chinese-oriented music (popular as well as syncretic) is beginning to emerge once more as a form of entertainment for Chinese-Indonesians: people who are neither fully Chinese nor fully Indonesian. Finally, one can find multiple variants on Cantonese-style popular music, sung in Indonesian but with occasional Cantonese words thrown in.

The Philippines

The Chinese experience in the Philippines bears a marked similarity to that of Indonesia. Chinese merchants have maintained a presence in the Philippines for hundreds of years, ever since Manila developed as a center for Asian trade before the appearance of Spanish colonists. Even today, more than half the Chinese in the Philippines live in Manila. As in Indonesia, every urban center in the Philippines has numerous Chinese residents, who involve themselves in businesses and restaurants. Chinese men came to the country from Fujian Province (southern China). They intermarried with Filipinas and converted to Roman Catholicism; however, their complete integration with the Filipinos has not occurred. At the start of Spanish rule, the Chinese were forced to live together in limited areas; once that rule was relaxed, the Chinese continued staying together. Since the twentieth century, younger generations of Chinese-Filipinos have begun to assimilate more closely with young Filipinos, and further cultural intermixing is likely.

Because Chinese expressions of cultural identity in the Philippines do not have to function in a postmassacre climate (like that of Indonesia), festive celebrations of boat races, weddings, Chinese operas, and Chinese New Year celebrations are common, accompanied by various types of music. Older Chinese immigrants still play in silk-and-bamboo ensembles. The far greater preservation of Chinese musical culture in the Philippines (especially in Manila) may reflect the government's tolerance of Chinese culture, plus the fact that many of the most important leaders of the Philippines (José Rizal and others) are or were of partly Chinese ancestry.

ISLAM IN SOUTHEAST ASIA

Islam, with roots in the Arabian peninsula of the seventh century, is based on God's teachings to the Prophet Mohammed. The basic Islamic system of beliefs includes the testimony of faith, *La ilaha illa Allah, Muhammad rasul Allah* "There is no god but God, Muhammad is the messenger of God." Being a Muslim also means believing in angels, prophets, scriptures, final judgment, divine decrees, and predestination. Muslims pray five times daily, facing the holy city of Mecca, and revere Friday as the holy day of the week. The five main elements ("pillars") of Islam include the testimony of faith (*shahada*), the ritual prayer (*salat*), alms giving (*zakat*), fasting during the holy month of Ramadan (*sawm*),

Figure 4.17
An Islamic mosque (*masjid*) in Penang, Malaysia. Photo by Terry E. Miller, 1973.

and the pilgrimage to Mecca (*hajj*). Prayers are held at local mosques; nearly every Muslim neighborhood includes a mosque, so the calls to prayer may sometimes be heard from the loudspeakers of more than thirty mosques simultaneously. Islam has two primary branches, the minority Shi'a and the majority Sunni; most of Southeast Asia's Muslims belong to the Sunni branch.

In Southeast Asia, the overwhelming majority of Muslims live in Indonesia, Malaysia, Thailand, the Philippines, and Brunei. Islam's position as the fastest-growing religion in the world is due in part to the growth rate of Southeast Asia's Muslim population. Indonesia has a majority Muslim population (about 90 percent). Though Muslims make up significant numbers in the populations of Brunei (68 percent) and Malaysia (47 percent), and lesser numbers in Thailand (4 percent) and the Philippines (4 percent), they do not comprise the entire ruling class of those nations. Islam in Southeast Asia is characterized by variety (rather than unity), because, over hundreds of years, the beliefs embraced by each ethnic group have become intertwined with Islamic beliefs.

Islam and Music

Though relations between Islamic leaders and Muslim musicians have occasionally been problematic, most Southeast Asian Muslims regularly enjoy both instrumental and vocal music. Part of the congeniality between music and Islam in Southeast Asia reflects an Islamic adaptation to local customs concerning the performance of music. Spoken and chanted words, because of their links to Muhammad's reception of the word of God, are important to Muslims; as a result, vocal music and vocalists have always been regarded more highly than instrumental music and musicians. Furthermore, female vocalists are often granted a higher social (and sometimes, economic) status than male instrumentalists. As in many areas of the world, Southeast Asian musicians are sometimes regarded by religious authorities to be just short of respectability, and as Muslims themselves, musicians must tread a fine line between perpetuating their art and following their faith.

The type of music that receives the strongest censure from Islamic authorities is popular music because of its associations with dancing and drinking. Similarly, Islam officially discourages traditional musics associated with prostitution and, sometimes, with female singer-dancers with whom male "customers" may dance publicly. Regional traditions of music, however, are accepted as part of local cultures to which Islam must adapt.

Certain instruments associated with Islam have become established in Southeast Asia. These include frame drums, huge barrel drums (used for the call to prayer), plucked lutes, and oboes (Figure 4.18). These instruments have fit in with, and become absorbed by, local traditions, but the frame drums remain closely linked with an

Figure 4.18
A huge Islamic barrel drum (*bedug*) from central Java, used to signal the call to prayer. Photo by Sean Williams.

Islamic sound when used to accompany singing. Though Islamic music is a part of Southeast Asian culture generally, it has closer associations with Mecca and the roots of Islamic culture than some of the more locally derived traditions. Like the layers of religious influence that characterize many modern Southeast Asian systems of belief, Islamic music is yet another layer that enriches the spectrum of Southeast Asian music.

Indonesia

The systems of belief of the Indonesian peoples ranged from animism to Hindu-Buddhism before the full-scale introduction of Islam (between the 1200s and the 1600s). The kingdom of Majapahit (1200s to 1500s), essentially the last Hindu-Buddhist kingdom in Java, was the first Indonesian kingdom since Srivijaya (600s to 800s) to exercise control over trade routes. This power was significant to the entry of Islam because sea trade was the primary means of early Islamic penetration into Indonesia. Though a large part of Indonesia was Hindu-Buddhist during the pre-Islamic period, not all residents of Hindu-Buddhist areas were exclusively adherents of an established religion. Locally dominant systems of belief were largely combinations of animist and Hindu beliefs. Hindu beliefs emphasized ritual actions and their correct execution, and the charismatic image of the divine ruler. These aspects of worship became important contrasts to Islam; some aided in the conversion of locals to the new religion, while others altered the new religion substantially.

The first Muslims in Indonesia were probably traders from South Asia. Opinions about the precise location of their origin differ, but the area of Gujarat (western India) is commonly believed to have been the origin of Muslim traders to Indonesia and other parts of Southeast Asia. The adaptations of Islam to local conditions and beliefs in India had helped to pave the way for its adoption in Indonesia; it was brought to Indonesia by non-Arab Muslims, and it lacked the cultural unity that characterized its later development in West Asia. Arriving in Indonesia with individual traders first, and later with Sufis (a segment of Islam that emphasizes mystical practices and adaptation to local customs), Islam was absorbed into an already highly *syncretic* culture.

syncretic
The amalgamation of different sounds, styles, or traditions

As early Muslim traders from India began to settle in Indonesia's coastal towns (especially in north Sumatra and the north coast of Java), being a Muslim gradually became advantageous. Expansions in trade, made possible by increased contact between coastal Muslims and Indian traders, led to alliances with the Javanese merchant class. Once a substantial number of Muslim traders had begun to establish themselves in coastal areas (like Aceh, Banten, and Demak), a process of gradual incorporation with local communities took place. Intermarriage was effective because it ensured a steady supply of goods to a local administrator; it also increased traders' status and elevated them to positions of greater standing in the community.

Sufism was the main means by which Islam entered Indonesia. The influence of Sufis began in the 1400s and 1500s on a nonpolitical level; an individual would gather a group of followers and teach the mysteries of inner revelation and spiritual journeying. Thus, the actual conversion of the Indonesians was hardly formal; it began as a mild overlay onto a variety of syncretic beliefs and did not undergo the far more rigid process of total acceptance that was supposed to be typical of the Arabian Peninsula.

Figure 4.19
A Javanese shadow-puppet figure (*wayang*).
Photo by Sean Williams.

A reason for Islam's success in the Indonesia has been its adaptation to local conditions. Every Indonesian is required to carry a personal identity card (*kartu tanda penduduk*, also KTP) that indicates the religion of the bearer, but the range of Islamic belief runs from fundamentalist to what some Indonesians jokingly call Muslim KTP ("I'm a Muslim only insofar as that is the religion printed on my personal identity card"). Not everyone prays five times a day, but nearly all Muslims fast during Ramadan. Some women cover all but their hands and faces, but others wear Western skirts and blouses. The flexibility of Islamic cultural practice reflects the Indonesian government's requirement of religious tolerance, written into the national constitution.

Islamic-influenced forms of music have become increasingly popular; for example, the pop genre of *qasidah*—featuring Islamic-themed texts set to synthesized dance music—is featured regularly on television videos. In addition, the wildly popular *dangdut,* derived from Indian film music, has often focused on Muslim values even as the dance moves that it accompanies can be intensely erotic. As Islam grows in cultural importance in Indonesia, people have come to use more Arabic words in daily life (not just for praying), and Arabic words or even the Arabic-accented pronunciation of Indonesian words has grown in popularity.

Muslim leaders are not necessarily synonymous with political leaders, and local attempts to agitate for the creation of an Islamic state are, for the most part, swiftly suppressed by the government. Though the majority of Indonesians are Muslims, agreement on issues is rare and further unification unlikely. In the post-9/11 world, however, Islamic political parties in Indonesia have gained considerably more power in the nation, and have been much more vocal in their demands for the curtailment of the performing arts that emphasize sensuality and sexuality.

Malaysia

The blend of Malay Muslims with Chinese and Indians in the population of Malaysia has led to a slightly different manifestation of Islam than in Indonesia, but its roots are similar. The Malay Peninsula was once called Malaya, but has been part of Malaysia since 1963, when the federation of Malaya, North Borneo, and Singapore was created (Singapore left the federation in 1965). The peninsula is quite close to the east coast of Sumatra, and the same merchants and Sufi mystics who traveled past Sumatra also stopped at Malay ports. Sea trade throughout the region was almost completely controlled by Muslims by the 1500s, and the expansion of Islam that characterized Indonesia's history during the past five centuries applies also to Malaysia.

The city of Melaka (Malacca), on Malaya's southwest coast, was a major center of trade, a base from which Muslims spread their influence along major routes. It was an extremely influential place in trade, culture, and religion, and though it fell to Portuguese rule in the early 1500s, it remained one of the most important cities in Malaysia. The presence of Sufis (who often came on board with traders) promoted the local expansion of Islam. They tended to shun politics, preferring to gather in rural schools to teach their disciples.

In the late 1800s, when the British came to govern Malaya, they did not discourage Islam. They were motivated primarily by economic and political goals. The British colonial experience in Malaya left intact the existing system of sultanates and general religious hierarchies. Because change so often begins in ports, it was appropriate that the beginnings of an Islamic reformist movement began in the Malay ports. These reformers were called the Kaum Muda (Young Group), as opposed to the Kaum Tua (Old Group) of religious conservatives, but their impact was felt much more strongly in the Dutch East Indies (soon to be Indonesia) than in Malaya. The nonreformist Muslims of the midtwentieth century formed an alliance with the Chinese and Indian residents of the country as the colonial empire collapsed, and the Alliance Party won the elections in newly independent Malaysia.

The current Malaysian Islamic community is dominated by a conservative but adaptive majority, which recognizes the need for cooperation with the other two large groups of Malay society. That Muslims in Malaysia had to avoid both a fundamentalist and a heavily reformist movement to gain cooperation from the Indian and Chinese members of society meant that nationalism had to come before Islam. Though Malaysia and Indonesia both have pluralist societies, what differentiates them is that most of Indonesia's ethnic groups are Muslims, while it is primarily the Malays of Malaysia who are Muslim and therefore more culturally unified.

The Philippines

The Philippines, because of their location as an eastern point in a square including China to the north, Borneo and Sulawesi to the south, and Vietnam to the west, are particularly well suited to trade and communication. Most of the Muslims in the Philippines live in the southernmost islands—Mindanao, Palawan, and the Sulu Archipelago, which links the Philippines to northeastern Borneo. Though there were once more Muslims in the northern islands, since the 1500s the Spanish colonial effort resulted in a concentration of the Muslim population in the south, where Muslims have always been more closely oriented culturally toward the southwest than toward the north and their Christian fellow citizens.

The spread of Islam into Sumatra and the Malay peninsula led to its eventual establishment in the Sulu Archipelago on one of the routes from Melaka. The first real stronghold of Islam in the Philippines was the Sulu sultanate, dating from the mid-1400s. By the 1500s, the area of Maguindanao (on the western part of Mindanao) had become an Islamic area. Gradually, through trade and Sufism, most of the island became Islamic. Most of the country at that time comprised autonomous societies that traded with each other but lacked a unifying force. Only in western Mindanao and Sulu, where Islam had developed a strong presence, was there any semblance of a government whose influence extended beyond its immediate area.

In 1521, when the Spanish came to colonize and convert the Filipinos to Christianity, the Islamic populations of the south were the only ones able to resist encroachment into their territory and culture. As a result, Muslims of the southern Philippines maintain a strong cultural presence, despite an overwhelmingly Christian majority and the increasing presence of Christians in Muslim areas. In the decades just after World War II, the Bangsa Moro (Muslim Nation movement) became a strong insurgent force and has grown in power.

Thailand

Thailand is mostly a Buddhist nation, but it has a small Muslim population of Malays, concentrated primarily in the southern peninsula. From the beginning, one of Thailand's main contacts with the Muslim world was through its networks of trade set up with the city of Melaka. When the Portuguese took over Melaka, trade with Muslims through that city was disrupted and replaced by Portuguese trade; however, the Muslim network continued for several more centuries, leading to the establishment of Muslim communities in various parts of the country.

The extension of Thai control onto its southern peninsula and its sharing a border with Malaysia have led to a greater concentration of Muslims in the south. Because of Muslim attempts to develop autonomously, Muslims have been at the forefront of Thai domestic difficulties during past hundred years. In the early 1900s, the southern Patani sultanate was divided so its southern half would fall under British control and become part of Malaya, while its northern half would remain in Thailand. The outlawing of Malay and Islamic organizations and special schools in the 1940s and 1950s contributed to the isolation of the Muslim population. More recent attempts by the Thai government to exercise control over the area have resulted in Muslim resistance, aided by support from Muslims in Malaysia and other nations with large Muslim communities.

Brunei

The sultanate of Brunei occupies the northeastern part of Borneo. Like Malaysia, Brunei supports a large Chinese population (25 percent). It works closely with its Chinese community, but its government is more fundamentally Islamic than that of Malaysia. Brunei was an important stopover for Muslim traders and Sufi mystics during the early days of Islamic expansion into the area. Its location enabled it to become a major trading power by the early 1500s, when it controlled all of the island of Borneo and several smaller islands. Until 1971, it was a British protectorate, but because conversion to Christianity was not a motivating factor in the establishment of political and economic control, the British did not interfere with local religion.

Brunei enjoys a high standard of living; a large proportion of its Muslim population can afford the pilgrimage to Mecca at least once a year. Because of this contact with Arab culture, the Muslims of Brunei have been closely allied with Arabic Islam. Other Muslims in island Southeast Asia (especially Indonesia) tend to regard the Muslims of Brunei as being truer to Arabic forms and perhaps practicing a purer form of Islam because of the regularity of this contact.

Mainland Southeast Asia

Though all of Southeast Asia has been influenced from time to time by foreign cultures, and much of that influence has been acculturated into the identities of individual groups or nations, Western influence is in most ways more apparent, more recent, and perhaps more disruptive. Some of that influence has been imposed from the outside, particularly through colonialism and military occupation, but much of it has come about voluntarily, even enthusiastically. During colonial times, European influence was quite strong. In the postcolonial period, but particularly during the fighting in Vietnam, U.S. influence increased dramatically. Since then, however, at least part of what appears to be Western influence has actually come from Hong Kong, Japan, Singapore, (South) Korea, and Taiwan.

The dynamics of the relationships are complex, with emotions running the gamut from love to hate. Certain countries, Burma and Singapore in particular, have sought to curb what they view as the excesses of Western culture. Others, especially the Philippines and Thailand, have been open to as much westernization as people desire. In some places, Western (mostly American) popular culture dominates the scene, and American popular music has been widely available on pirated recordings. The rise of the music industry in the urban centers of Southeast Asia is a major theme in the music histories of Indonesia, Malaysia, the Philippines, and Thailand.

Vietnam

Vietnam's culture has undergone profound influence from at least two outside cultures: China and the West. During the late 1500s and early 1600s, Westerners—Dutch, French, Italians, Portuguese, Spanish, and others—entered Vietnam through the port of Hội An, just south of Đà Nẵng. Over the centuries, the Roman Catholic Church and the efforts of its missionaries wrought many cultural changes, some of which involved music. A group of Portuguese, French, and Spanish Jesuits and at least two Vietnamese converts created the system used for romanizing the Vietnamese language, but the French more cleverly used the church as a tool in efforts to make Vietnam a protectorate during the 1800s. They did this by converting those in power and granting power to those who converted. French-style Roman Catholic music, including Gregorian chant, came to Vietnam during the 1600s, and in one form or another, it continues to be sung.

The development of French schools, a preference for all things French by the Vietnamese elite, and the return of Vietnamese teachers and performers educated in France (and elsewhere in the West) brought to Vietnam the earliest and perhaps most complete Western musical establishment. Eventually this included conservatories, orchestras, opera performances, chamber music, and active composers. After people in the north turned to Eastern Europe for help, the conservatories and universities of such countries as the former Soviet Union, Bulgaria, Romania, the former Czechoslovakia, and (East) Germany began providing both European and Vietnamese teachers to maintain Vietnam's Western music. Despite the war and the feelings many Vietnamese have about Western culture, Hanoi still has an active symphony orchestra and a conservatory devoted to Western classical music. The conservatory in Hồ Chí Minh City continues to train performers of Western classical music.

The Vietnamese have been warm to returning Westerners, particularly Americans and French, but they have not become so enamored of American popular musical culture that it is replacing Vietnamese styles. The Vietnamese remain attracted to their own kinds of popular music, including modernized folk songs (*dân ca*). As the country modernizes, however, especially in the south (Hồ Chí Minh City is fast becoming a Vietnamese Hong Kong), American influence may grow. Within a few years, the local appreciation of popular music could change drastically.

Laos

With regard to westernization, there is little to say about Laos. Though the United States once had a strong presence (which influenced the nightclub scene in Vientiane), since 1975 the combination of poverty, isolation, and political conservatism has allowed for little growth in Western culture. Aside from a few clubs where rock may be heard, the Lao have few opportunities to develop aspects of Western culture. The French school is long closed and abandoned, foreign publications are few available, and foreigners maintain a low profile.

Cambodia

Whatever impact the West had on colonial and postcolonial Cambodia vanished under the Khmer Rouge, who stripped the country of its existing culture and killed or caused to die nearly two million people. Before 1970, when Prince Sihanouk and his wife ruled in Phnom Penh, the French atmosphere of the capital included performances of both classical and light European music. The nightclub scene included popular songs and dancing. The School of Fine Arts maintained a small Western orchestra. All this has vanished, and the continuing poverty of the country has precluded the reappearance of nearly everything except popular music in Phnom Penh.

Thailand

Ironically, as Western and modern Japanese influences have increased in Thailand, so has the strength of Thai classical music, though regional musics have fared less well. Never having been colonized, the Thai have viewed the West differently from their neighbors. Though the French had tried to convert King Narai and gain influence in old Siam during the late 1600s, their plan failed, and foreigners were kept at bay until the early 1800s. Since that time, the Thai have done remarkably well at dealing with Western powers. Rather than resist westernization because of its association with colonialism, the Thai actually encouraged it after the 1932 coup d'état. The military regimes that followed encouraged the Thai to behave as they thought Westerners did—for everyone to wear shoes, for men to wear hats and ties, for husbands to kiss their wives when leaving and returning, and so on. Governments encouraged social dancing—and the cha-cha, the rumba, the tango, swing, and other dances became fashionable. The Thai created their own social dance, *ramwong*, done in a circle by men and women using simple gestures with their hands.

During the 1800s, foreign powers' brass bands made a strong impression, and from 1850 to 1900, the Thai court had its own band. Such bands became fixtures in schools and universities and continue to this day. Western classical music, however, penetrated Thailand slowly. Before about 1980, most classical music was performed by visiting Western ensembles, soloists, and members of the expatriate community. With the founding of the (semiprofessional) Bangkok Symphony Orchestra and various student orchestras, particularly at the College of Dramatic Arts and Chulalongkorn University, the country had at least a modest Western-music presence.

Western instruments—especially the piano, the violin, the guitar, and, more recently, all types of pop instruments, including synthesizers—have proven to be particularly popular in Thailand. As in the West, the children of cultured families are often expected to study piano or violin, but there is less prejudice against popular music, and many young people learn to play popular instruments. The Yamaha School in Bangkok is large and active.

The impact of the West is not so prominent in music as it is in all other aspects of modern Thai life, particularly in the cities. Not only Bangkok and Chiang Mai, the country's largest cities, but regional cities are rapidly showing evidence of affluence and modernization, some of it of Japanese origin, some American. This includes technology, popular music, fast food, films, shopping malls, lifestyles, and a preference for English. Yet much of this kind of westernization appears to be superficial, retaining a particularly Thai character.

Burma

Outside the capital (Rangoon, now called Yangon), Western influence is a nonissue. Western influence gives the capital a slightly cosmopolitan air, but it feels more like the 1940s and 1950s than the present day. Having been colonized by the British, the Burmese have little love for their former masters and their culture, but the Americans are more fondly remembered for helping liberate Burma from the Japanese during World War II. Remnants of American efforts—including old military vehicles—still serve the Burmese. Though American pop culture must pass censorship committees, young Burmese are showing a particular fondness for it, including its music, but this kind of activity maintains a low profile.

Malaysia

At least superficially, the former British colony of Malaya (including Singapore) appears to be the most deeply Westernized country in mainland Southeast Asia. This situation has affected many aspects of modern Malaysian life, from its well-organized traffic to its educational system. Musically, Malaysia reflects the multiculturality of its population, and its affluence permits the importation of foreign films, recordings, and instruments. Western classical music is taught and performed in major urban areas, and earlier types of British ballroom music have helped mold such genres of dance as *ronggeng*. Western and Western-influenced popular music is available on recordings and in live performance venues (nightclubs, dance places, etc.) in all the major cities.

Island Southeast Asia

Indonesia and the Philippines have been participants in a fairly positive relationship with the West since World War II, but that relationship was preceded centuries ago by violent conflict and colonization. The two countries differ markedly in their respective histories: Indonesia's was largely an economic colonization, but the Philippines' was religious. The lasting legacy of these forms of colonization has been the economic plundering of Indonesia and the almost complete Christianization of the Philippines.

Indonesia

European needs for Indonesian spices and the Portuguese willingness to procure those spices led to the development of routes that brought cloves, mace, nutmeg, and pepper to Europe. In 1511, the Portuguese established themselves in Melaka, a powerful center of trade, and their presence led to an almost immediate evaporation of trade from the area and the dispersal of Asian goods through other routes.

The 1700s saw the struggle for dominance in the eastern Indonesian trade in spices, as the Spanish sailed down from the Philippines to Maluku and the English set up networks at various sites throughout the archipelago. The Dutch, who eventually gained control over the area, took a colonial approach that differed from that of the Portuguese. Rather than controlling the area from the center of the spice-growing area, the Dutch established a base in Batavia (now Jakarta) in 1619 and governed parts of the archipelago for the next three centuries. The initial motivation for the Dutch had been to take over the spice trade from the Portuguese, and after several years of infighting between competing Dutch shipping companies, the United East India Company (Vereenigde Oost-Indische Compagnie, VOC) was formed. The Dutch government gave the VOC near-autonomous governing power during the early years of its operation, and the VOC established the initial Dutch foothold in the area.

In a few decades, the Dutch had begun to exercise military control over a portion of the archipelago. By about 1800, the VOC had pulled away from the spice trade to concentrate its economic efforts on the cultivation of coffee and tea in the West Javanese highlands and elsewhere.

The Dutch forged an alliance with the indigenous aristocracy, and the Javanese people were governed through paid local administrators in an effort to maintain the most visible forms of traditional rule. Those leaders then put a large amount of activity and funding into cultural development; as a result, the courtly arts (particularly on Java) flourished throughout the 1800s.

Sukarno, Indonesia's first president, had received a Dutch education and had spent several decades agitating for no less than total independence. He spent time in exile and under house arrest, as did some of his contemporaries. In 1942, when Japanese troops invaded the area and took control from the Dutch, the myth of European superiority was irrevocably shattered. Though the Dutch tried to regain control of Indonesia after World War II, Sukarno rose to prominence again and proclaimed the independence of Indonesia on 17 August 1945. Since that time, the Dutch presence and their influences have receded considerably, having been replaced by a powerful sense of Indonesian nationalism and patriotism.

Although one can find Western classical music groups in Jakarta and other large cities in Indonesia, the strongest musical influence is in the arena of popular music. Every type of Western popular genre has its adherents in Indonesia, from light pop to hard rock to house to rap and hip-hop. Nightclubs throughout the downtown regions of the nation's largest cities are populated with pretty female singers crooning Western love ballads in English, usually to the accompaniment of a synthesizer and occasionally a drum set. Many tourist hotels and restaurants include a duo or trio of balladeers who hover over guests, performing hits ("Unchained Melody" and "Guantanamera" place rather high on the rotation of songs). Indonesia also is home to jazz musicians, bluegrass musicians, Christian choirs, and other nonlocal musical creations.

The Philippines

The Treaty of Tordesillas, signed in 1494, divided parts of the world into what would become Portuguese and Spanish territory, leaving the Philippines to Spain. The first colonizers arrived in the Philippines led by Ferdinand Magellan, who, though Portuguese, was funded by the Spanish. He left Spain with five ships in 1519 and arrived in the Philippines two years later. Though he did not survive to return to Spain, eighteen of his original 264 men did. Later explorers named the islands of Leyte and Samar Las Islas Felipinas after Felipe, son and heir apparent of Spain's King Charles I; by the end of the 1500s, Spanish navigators were calling the entire island chain the Philippines.

The first Western cultural influences came initially from Central America, because most sixteenth-century expeditions originated in Mexico, funded by Spain. Until Mexican independence (1821), the viceroy of Mexico was the chief administrator of the Philippines. Therefore, though the Spanish were officially in control of the Philippines, the nature of this relationship was such that the Spanish profited from one of their colonies through its control by another of their colonies. The economic balance among Spain, Mexico, and the Philippines was strictly maintained by the Spanish, and Manila became an outlet for trade goods purchased from other Asian countries.

In addition to functioning as a center of trade, the Philippines became the most Roman Catholic nation in Asia. Once military control was established, friars became the emblems of Spanish power in many small towns. Because religious colonization was more important to the Spanish than political rule, most of the Philippines' indigenous cultural traditions were either eradicated or subsumed within Roman Catholicism. By the twentieth century, only the southernmost islands and inland highlands remained non-Christian. Throughout its history in the Philippines, the Roman Catholic Church has been a center of power and influence, and its occasional clashes with the state have led to the continuing affirmation of separation between the two.

The Philippines became a U.S. possession in 1898, when the U.S. Asiatic fleet smashed the Spanish navy in the Philippines. Several years of an extremely bloody insurrection followed as the Americans established military control before setting up a civilian government and eventually a commonwealth. In addition to the establishment of a democracy, the strongest and most enduring influence from the American colonization of the Philippines was the establishment of a widespread system of free education, with instruction in English. Through its policy of education, the language, values, and culture of the United States were broadly infused into the heartland of the Philippines. By the time the Philippines achieved independence (1946), the nation's people were a blend of a Malay foundation overlaid with Mexican Catholicism and American language and culture.

Implications for Musical Development

The colonial legacy of the Dutch, the Portuguese, the Spanish, and the Americans has had a strong impact on the musical cultures of the main archipelagos of Southeast Asia. In Indonesia, the Dutch approach—selecting local administrators to force economic cooperation from the people—led to the infusion of financial resources into the performing arts; many local administrators could afford to keep entire staffs of performers on hand to increase the local perception of power. Because the Dutch had no intention of eradicating traditional culture in the name of Christianization, the performing arts were allowed to thrive and expand in many cultural centers. The declaration of Indonesian independence led to the immediate disappearance of funding for these arts, causing a reshuffling of personnel and genres as priorities shifted.

In the Philippines, the primary intent of the Spanish was to Christianize the population, establishing a foothold for Spanish trade in the area. As friars and their schools developed into centers of power, local musical traditions faded, to be replaced by Spanish religious musical traditions. As reflections of a pre-Christian culture, indigenous traditions were no longer perceived as relevant. The eventual result of this was the virtual disappearance of all pre-Christian musical traditions in Roman Catholic areas. In contrast, Filipino Muslim and tribal peoples have continued to maintain unique forms of cultural expression.

In both island nations, current local traditions vie for economic standing with internationally marketed popular music and its local practitioners. Many of the articles in this volume include a discussion of how the dichotomy between local and international cultures affects the traditional performing arts, and some authors acknowledge that the rise of locally produced popular music has been an important step in the drive for modernization. In both Indonesia and the Philippines, however, the undercurrent of the colonial legacy remains an indelible part of national consciousness.

REFERENCES

Condominas, Georges. 1952. "Le lithophone préhistorique de Ndut Lieng Krak." *Bulletin de l'École Française d'Extrême-Orient* 45:359–392.

Miller, Terry E., and Jarernchai Chonpairot. 1994. "A History of Siamese Music Reconstructed from Western Documents, 1505–1932." *Crossroads: An Interdisciplinary Journal of Southeast Asian Studies* 8(2):1–192.

Rodrigue, Yves. 1992. *Nat-Pwe*. Garthmore, Scotland: Paul Strachan-Kiscadale.

Roseman, Marina. 1991. *Healing Sounds from the Malaysian Rainforest: Temiar Music and Medicine*. Berkeley: University of California Press.

Stalberg, Roberta Helmer. 1984. *China's Puppets*. San Francisco: China Books.

Yampolsky, Philip. 1991. *Music of Indonesia 3: Music from the Outskirts of Jakarta: Gambang Kromong*. Washington, D.C.: Smithsonian/Folkways SFCD 40057. Liner notes.

Culture, Politics, and War

Terry E. Miller and Sean Williams

Mainland Southeast Asia
Island Southeast Asia

Art, particularly music, is rarely isolated from its time and place. Affected by events, it often reflects events in turn. When a revolution or a war breaks out, musicians can be deeply affected, and often, with other members of the population, they suffer injuries, lose their means of support, and even die.

Official controls over the arts have existed to some degree over long periods of time throughout most of the world, but the twentieth century saw unprecedented attempts to control or inhibit the arts. Because music has communicative potential, particularly in narrative and theatrical genres, people in power often try to harness it for their own ends. Their efforts include manipulating the messages of music to influence people. Because singers can deliver messages efficiently to a broad spectrum of people, governments often want to use them for state purposes, but when they give voice to dissent, governments may subject them to censorship.

Even during peaceful times, music may be affected by developments in national cultural policies. The role that governments play in developing, controlling, and manipulating the arts is in some instances beneficial but in others detrimental. The following article provides an overview of important political events and issues embedded in Southeast Asian musics.

Vietnam

As many have said, "Vietnam is a country, not a war," but for much of the world, especially the United States, Vietnam is synonymous with memories of a demoralizing military excursion, which scarred many people's memories. Americans easily forget that the suffering and disruption in Vietnam was many times greater than that experienced in the West. Without attempting a history of the war, an explication of its roots and causes, or psychoanalysis of its legacy, we intend to explore selected themes: the disruption of culture, music, and theater as propaganda, the creation of a musical diaspora, and the legacy of gradual political change, changes in cultural policies, economic development, and globalization.

Colonialism brought European influence and the eventual founding of conservatories with European-trained instructors [see VIETNAM: Modernization], but the traditional musical arts flourished or declined with the many wars that permeate the country's history. After independence (1954), Vietnam divided into the People's Democratic Republic of Vietnam (the communist north) under Hồ Chí Minh and the Republic of Vietnam (the American-supported south) under a succession of presidents and generals. In both parts, music and theater served as weapons of propaganda and patriotism. The north followed the models of Russian socialist realism and Chinese revolutionism; efforts in the south were less systematic and ideological. In both parts of Vietnam, many songs with political texts urged people to resist the enemy (for a wartime account, see Brandon 1967).

In the south, musical life continued as best it could in both the cities and the countryside controlled by the government and the areas controlled by the National Liberation Front. In the latter areas, traveling troupes (*đoàn văn công*) performed on movable stages set up at night. From powerful secret transmitters, they broadcast songs, music, and theater, mostly with patriotic themes, urging people to overthrow the government. Many artists were arrested. Some were killed by napalm bombs. Some died in prison, including in the infamous "tiger cages" on Côn Son Island. U.S. air strikes in the north killed some of Vietnam's most expert performers and composers. Many of those in the north and the revolutionary zones of the south who survived continued to perform. One of them, composer Trần Hoàn, became Minister of Culture and Information until his passing in 2003.

Though Saigon was relatively secure, random rocket attacks could and did kill musicians, actors, and actresses, with other members of the general population. In 1970, a rocket fell into a prominent theater during a *cái lương* performance, destroying the building and killing members of the cast and people in the audience. As the Republic of Vietnam approached its collapse (on 29 April 1975), thousands of people fled the country. These included some of the country's most prominent singers, actors, actresses, and musicians. Most resettled in France and the United States, where, over time, they built a Vietnamese music industry, which continues to this day to produce large numbers of compact discs and music videos, primarily of popular songs, but also of *cái lương*, especially from California.

The current cultural policies of the Socialist Republic of Vietnam, formulated and executed from the Ministry of Culture and Information in Hanoi, have been selectively

kind to the tradi-
tional arts. Though
certain genres, par-
ticularly those of the
south, have not re-
ceived governmen-
tal support, some
important genres
have been revived
and restored to high
artistic levels. These
include the *chèo*, the
tuồng, and water-

Figure 5.1
The government-
sponsored Đam San
ensemble of Pleiku,
Vietnam, performs
cải biên for a visiting
delegation on modified
minority instruments.
Photo by Terry E. Miller,
1994.

puppet theaters, certain genres of folk song, and many ritual activities, for which the government has supported groups in purchasing instruments, costumes, and props. Though
officials of the Information and Culture Service maintain a certain control over cultural
activities under their purview, the traditional arts were generally allowed to flourish or
decline on their own.

During the 1990s a major controversy over control and representation erupted over
a type of modernized "ethnic" (or "neotraditional") music, *nhạc dân tộc cải biên* (Figure
5.1), created by Soviet-bloc trained composers at the Hanoi Conservatory along socialist
models [see VIETNAM: Modernization]. Using modified instruments of both the lowland
Viet and various central highland groups, *cải biên* became a site of contention regarding
both modernization and control, for the questions it raised included, who decides what
"traditional" is to mean in modern Vietnam and what kind of music should represent the
national culture to the outside world? Although the conservatories no longer insist on
representing Vietnam's "traditional" music with *cải biên*, and have allowed the old forms
to be taught again, they continue to teach this new music and offer it to tourists otherwise
unaware of its original purpose.

Following reunification, Vietnam's leaders slowly loosened restrictions on economic
development and tourism, allowing more and more foreign culture into Vietnam. By the
late 1990s the government no longer used music as propaganda, permitted the singing
and broadcast of pre-1975 popular songs, and has generally allowed music to develop
according to capitalistic principles. With the war long forgotten by a population largely
born after the war, today the country's various musics—traditional, Western classical, neotraditional, and popular—must negotiate the vagaries of public preference in their quest
to survive and thrive.

Laos

During the fighting in Vietnam, Laos suffered far more than most outsiders realized. In-
credible numbers of bombs were dropped over wide areas, particularly in the south, along
the Hồ Chí Minh Trail. In some provinces, virtually every permanent building was destroyed, cluster bombs were spread over the countryside (where they continue to maim

and kill), and many people, including musicians, died. During the war, the United States Information Service supported teams of northeastern Thai traditional singers (*mawlam*), who traveled widely in Laos singing anticommunist themes.

After 1975, when the Pathet Lao (communists) gradually gained complete power, what remained of the classical, courtly arts (music, theater, dance) in Luang Phrabang and Vientiane was disavowed because of its connection to the former regime and the aristocracy. Many traditional singers, including some of the country's most prominent singers, fled to the West. Those who remained were sent to "seminars" (reeducation camps), and their talents were harnessed to spread the news and views of the country's political establishment. In the later 1980s, the School of Fine Arts was reestablished in Vientiane, and ironically, the classical arts were used once again to represent Lao culture to the outside world. Though the government continued to control access to traditional musicians and limited their opportunities to perform until well into the 1990s, these restrictions, including those on travel, have been lifted, leaving the traditional arts to survive largely on their own.

Burma

Burma, officially the Union of Myanmar since 1989, is administered by a military junta that came to power after the failed revolution and elections of 1988 and 1989. With complete control of the media and all cultural activities, the generals have tried to keep Western influence to a minimum while supporting the traditional Burman arts. All newly composed music, all imported music, and all publications must pass through censorship committees; foreign observers, noting young Burmans' preference for everything from heavy metal to America's latest crooners, can rest assured that every song has been inspected by the government and is clean of antistate messages. The Ministry of Education founded secondary-level Schools of Music in Rangoon (now Yangon) and Mandalay, and in 1993 founded the University of Culture, a four-year college-level institution that teaches traditional Burman music, dance, theater, painting, and sculpture. Currently Burma remains under extremely tight control, and the education system has nearly ceased to function.

While the Burman arts are maintained in traditional fashion, those of the National Brethren—the non-Burman states, such as Shan State and Kachin State—have been manipulated for political purposes. Many of these states have been in longstanding rebellion against the central government and do not wish to be part of a united Myanmar. In the states themselves, traditional forms of dance and music continue to thrive, but the forms depicted in the media deliver messages of national unity through multiethnic collective dances, accompanied by popularized renditions of the original music. In this way, many otherwise traditional dances receive overt political interpretations in televised broadcasts.

Cambodia

The people of Cambodia suffered a worse fate than any other people in Southeast Asia during the twentieth century. The film *The Killing Fields* (1984) has confronted something of the horrors that befell the Cambodian people when the Khmer Rouge conquered the nation (in 1975) after the fall of the American-supported government of Lon Nol. The Khmer Rouge sought to reinvent Cambodian civilization on a simple agrarian model. To do that, they determined to destroy all sophisticated aspects of the culture, including most forms of music, theater, and dance. Some artists managed to flee the country, but a high percentage of the nation's cultural carriers were killed. Most musical instruments were destroyed, the National Library was stripped and its contents destroyed, and the National Museum's treasures were damaged or destroyed. An invasion by the Vietnamese army in 1979 stopped the Khmer Rouge from finishing the eradication of Cambodian culture.

During the reign of terror, artists were forced to create and stage spectacles glorifying the Khmer Rouge. Even after 1979, the new government adopted this form of theater for its own glory (Figure 5.2). During the later 1980s, with help from nongovernmental organizations and at least one foreign government (Australia), efforts were made to rebuild the School of Fine Arts and to reassemble the troupes of dancers and musicians who had once been connected with the palace of Prince (later King) Sihanouk. The arts have been so important in restoring the Cambodian people's spirits that they have received an unusually high priority. During the 1990s, the government has sent troupes of dancers and musicians—even actors and puppeteers—on worldwide tours, demonstrating the resilience of Cambodian culture.

Since 1979 the country has undergone a spotty transformation, with pockets of development and prosperity (e.g., around the Angkorean temples near Siem Reap and in Phnom Penh) surrounded by continuing poverty, endemic corruption, human slavery, and foreign exploitation, especially in rural areas. The Khmer musical arts are now on their own and struggling. Visitors to tourist sites are likely to hear wedding music ensembles of musicians blinded or maimed by the continuing and widespread problem of landmines. Large restaurants offer programs of music and dance to tourists.

Figure 5.2
A tableau from a grand historical pageant held to celebrate the tenth anniversary of the overthrow of the Khmer Rouge, at Phnom Penh's National Theater in December 1989. Photo by Terry E. Miller.

Thailand

War has not been an issue in Thai life since 1767, the light bombing of Bangkok during World War II notwithstanding. Cultural politics has played a role in the national development of music and theater but not more than in most countries. In 1865, King Mongkut (Rama IV) of Siam, fearing the loss of "Siamese" culture to a growing preference for Lao (northeastern region) music, banned the performance of Lao music and dance in central Siam. The greatest interference in the arts occurred after the 1932 coup d'état, when a succession of military governments suppressed Thai classical music, preferring a policy of westernization. These governments encouraged Thai musicians to play classical music on Western instruments, and *ramwong*, a genre of Western-influenced social dance, came into being. The suppression of classical music declined during the 1950s and was ended in the 1960s. During the 1930s and early 1940s, some Thai musicians, fearing the loss of the classical repertory, began transcribing the music into staff notation. By 1941, some 475 pieces had been transcribed into parts or full scores. This collection of manuscripts was largely lost in a fire on 9 September 1960, but David Morton, then a student from the University of California at Los Angeles doing research on his dissertation, had microfilmed most of it. Some compositions were later published by the Fine Arts Department, and today there is an ongoing project to publish the entire manuscript collection.

Since the 1980s, the Thai Ministry of Education has supported a growing number of music departments in the nation's system of education, and Thai students at all levels are exposed to classical and regional musics. More recently the newly founded Ministry of Culture has provided some venues for the traditional arts. Despite pressures from Thailand's increasing affluence, modernization, and urbanization, the classical arts are thriving, thanks largely to the education system [see THE IMPACT OF MODERNIZATION ON TRADITIONAL MUSICS].

Malaysia

A modernized, multiethnic state, Malaysia presents a useful example of how a well-meaning government has sought to establish a national culture that aims at simultaneously unifying the country's ethnic groups and assuring the preeminence of the Malay (over the Chinese and Indian) segments of the population. As traditional contexts and patronage for such traditional arts as shadow theater (*wayang kulit*) and human theater (*ma'yong*) have changed, these genres have been restored to their allegedly original state and purged of modernisms and commercialisms. This process is most clearly documented in Tan Sooi Beng's study of *bangsawan* (1993), a formerly commercial and eclectic genre, restored to supposedly traditional Malay purity.

ISLAND SOUTHEAST ASIA

Indonesia

The Indonesian government has played a strong and consistent role in the music industry. Some of the most prominent performers are linked closely to the government, either by having a position in the military or civil service as their primary means of employment or by being married or otherwise related to someone who does. The civil service is the largest employer of Indonesians, and most major political decisions by governmental leaders trickle down to the lives of civil servants and their families. Therefore, when the government makes a decision about the use or misuse of the performing arts, that decision almost immediately has an impact on even the lowliest musicians, dancers, and actors.

Indonesia's climate of religious tolerance (as set forth in Pancasila, its five principles for government) and its national motto (Unity in Diversity) allow for a broad range of performing arts and for the fostering of local traditions that do not have to follow nationalist models. Most people in power in Jakarta are Muslims, and the potential conflicts between Islam and music are well known [see WAVES OF CULTURAL INFLUENCE: ISLAM], but few expect the Hindu Balinese to give up their blend of music, dance, and theater to conform to some kind of nationalist vision of the performing arts. Furthermore, the government recognizes that fostering diversity in the performing arts (through sponsorship of competitions) leads to local pride, believed to support general patriotism.

One of the strongest tools used by the government to control the performing arts is a national ban, or at least a national chill, on particular songs, dances, or artists. The government does not impose bans lightly. To ensure that the Indonesian performing arts reflect local pride and are neither offensive nor a potential embarrassment to Indonesian national consciousness and development, a body of consultants reads lyrics and studies danced and staged performances.

No one in Indonesia (including the members of the government) is fooled into believing that banning or disapproving performances will lead to total compliance and the creation of strictly patriotic arts. The government recognizes the potential danger of political unrest, should such a harsh climate prevail. Although the Indonesian government is famous around the world for its restrictions on some of its greatest literary artists, cartoonists, and playwrights, performers are given much greater leeway to express themselves. Partly to maintain a peaceful climate and partly to occasionally jerk the reins, the government usually resorts to concerned disapproval of a song, style, dance, or performer, expressed in speeches, which are then widely cited in newspaper and magazine articles. The ways in which artists respond (through the use of metaphor, modification, or outright rebellion) keep the relationship between culture and politics a source for endless debates among performers, politicians, and the media.

One of the largest perceived threats to the performing arts appeared in February 2006, when a group of legislators proposed that the Indonesian performing arts be restricted so that suggestive dancing and exposed body parts (shoulders, stomachs, backs, limbs) be kept covered, in keeping with the precepts of Islam. The bill covered other expressive arts (photographs, paintings, and poetry) as well. The *dangdut* artist Inul Daratista, whose eroticized dance style has led to significant media attention domestically and abroad, was widely perceived to be one of the targets of the legislation. The proposed legislation met with significant protests, not only from those performing artists whose traditions include bare shoulders (e.g., the Balinese) or "suggestive" dancing, but also from some of the most outspoken writers, journalists, and intellectuals in the nation. A large outcry arose from scholars of Indonesian performing arts from around the world as well. A somewhat less restrictive bill has been continually under debate since 2006, but artists are wary of the curtailment of their freedoms, not by higher-ups in the national government directly, but through the influence of religious fundamentalists.

The Philippines

Warfare has played an important role in the traditional musics of the southern Philippines, especially on Mindanao, where Muslim-oriented insurgents have fought the government since the 1970s. Though the insurgents are not known to have harnessed traditional music extensively for political purposes, the areas of the island under their domination have been virtually off limits to researchers. The affected musical traditions include some of the *kulintang* traditions, particularly of the Maranao branch.

The insurgency is located in a non-Christian region of an overwhelmingly Christianized nation, so not just Muslims but Muslim performing artists (as bearers of Muslim culture) are suspect. Musicians in the Maranao region sometimes face official intimidation and harassment because of the musicians' public performances, and the families of musicians who have traveled abroad may face ill-treatment because of local assumptions about the channeling of foreign funds to the Muslim rebels. Public adherence to Islam and the performance of music enjoyed by Muslims provide the Philippine government with fodder for suspicion, surveillance, and persecution.

In recent years, many Filipino artists have chosen to voice their political views through rap, rock, and singer-songwriter performance. These artists are not limited to the Muslim southern parts of the country; indeed, many of the most current artists are from Manila or its environs (and some are returnees from the United States). The tendency for Filipino artists to take what they like from non-Filipino traditions and rework it in a local style applies to all contemporary popular music, with political, social, and environmental causes forming a subset of a larger musical sphere.

REFERENCES

Brandon, James R. 1967. *Theatre in Southeast Asia*. Cambridge, MA: Harvard University Press.
Tan Sooi Beng. 1993. *Bangsawan: A Social and Stylistic History of Popular Malay Opera*. Singapore: Oxford University Press.

The Impact of Modernization on Traditional Musics

Terry E. Miller and Sean Williams

Loss of Traditional Contexts
Revival Movements
Compositional Innovations
Tourism

It has been widely believed that, at least until the twentieth century, the rate of musical change in Asia has been extremely slow. Western music histories have tended to place non-Western music at the beginning of a chronological history in the "Ancient and Oriental" category, assuming that even living "Oriental" music had changed little since "Ancient" times. But even from current knowledge of Asian musical histories (knowledge that remains limited in important ways), we can surmise that change was always a factor, and when calamity struck, as when a population was carried off to a conqueror's kingdom, radical change could and did occur. From a closer perspective, however, we can see that indisputably from 1900 to the present has been an age of nearly cataclysmic change, much of it stimulated by contact with the West. These factors may be considered under the heading of modernization.

LOSS OF TRADITIONAL CONTEXTS

Just as species of plants and animals disappear when their habitats are disrupted or vanish, musics require a habitat for their continued existence. As with species of flora and fauna, some musical genres are hardier than others, more able to cope with changes; but the most vulnerable of them simply vanish. Musics performed in concert settings for attentive audiences are less likely to perish in the face of modernization than musics closely linked to functions that may disappear, such as agricultural practices, rituals, and festivals.

Whether musics survive the loss of their contexts also depends to some extent on general attitudes toward tradition, preservationism, and national or local identity. Prosperity and modernization do not necessarily degrade traditional musics, but poverty tends to preserve old ways by limiting options. Nothing destroys cultural habitats more quickly or thoroughly than factional violence, revolution, and war, processes that Southeast Asia has experienced on a grand scale. The following paragraphs provide case studies illustrating particular kinds of challenges to traditional musics.

Changes in Agricultural Practices

Throughout Southeast Asia, numerous musical genres, mostly vocal, are (or were) associated with the stages of growing rice. In Thailand, these songs were categorized as local songs (*phleng phün ban*, also *phleng phün müang*). Before the arrival of modern agricultural practices (which, through mechanization, required fewer workers), members of village communities worked together in the fields. During breaks in work, in the heat of the day or after work, they enjoyed engaging in vocal repartee, pitting the best male singers against the best female singers in a contest of wits; allied onlookers often provided choral responses. In musical terms, this repartee blended antiphonal and responsorial patterns. The songs differed in text and melody according to the stage of work—transplanting, cutting rice, threshing, husking, or raking. Few musical instruments were involved; most were markers of rhythm (Figure 6.1).

As Thailand prospered after World War II, its financial wealth was first concentrated in the cities, especially Bangkok. Over time, the government constructed a fine system of highways, electrified villages, beamed radio and television into the country's remotest corners, and encouraged farmers to use gasoline-powered tractors instead of water buffaloes. People no longer worked the fields communally.

In Indonesia (especially on Java), traditional music associated with growing rice included the use of tuned bamboo rattles (*angklung*), whose sound was pleasing to the goddess of rice, Dewi Sri; she would reward the villagers with the blessing of rain. The rituals traditionally used to perpetuate the agricultural cycle and the *angklung* music that went with the rituals have mostly been

Figure 6.1
A remote *lao thüng* village in Salavane Province, Laos, is largely insulated from all aspects of modernization, especially because of poverty. Photo by Terry E. Miller, 1991.

abandoned, replaced by chemical pesticides, fertilizers, and government-dictated plans for irrigating, planting, and harvesting.

Urbanization

During the twentieth century, some Southeast Asian cities—Bangkok, Jakarta, Manila, and Saigon—grew into megacities. As rapidly growing populations in the provinces ran out of land to divide or found few local opportunities, heavy migrations to the cities occurred. Cities have the best and worst of what the world offers, including everything modern. Peoples from various areas are mixed together, and rural identities give way to urban ones.

Musics formerly heard in distant villages are drowned out by new sounds, especially those of the media, but sometimes this situation in turn gives rise to new and vibrant types. In Thailand, where vast numbers of young men and women from the north, northeast, and south have migrated to Bangkok, the areas are remembered in *phleng luk thung*—pop songs, to be sure, but hybridizations, blending regional instruments and stylistic traits into modern urban sounds, which blare from shops, cars, and corners. Music videos invoke objectified images of rural life: fishing nets, farmer hats, agricultural tools, costumes, and behaviors. The modern city gives rise to modern musics.

In Manila, the primary urban center of the Philippines, migrants find their way into an intensely heterogeneous society with a broad overlay of Spanish colonial and American popular culture. Regional and rural traits that make rural migrants stand out (and thus be less employable) are quickly abandoned. In the coastal cities of Borneo, discoveries of oil have led to the creation of large company towns, complete with discos and modern conveniences. In this kind of urban climate, options for the perpetuation of local Dayak culture are nonexistent.

Loss of Regionality

Before Southeast Asia had modern nation-states, it had courts, surrounded by towns and villages. In the distance were other power centers, but no precise boundary between them existed. Isolation, preserved by poor or nonexistent roads, little communication, and linguistic differences, meant that regionalism continued to be a factor, even after nation-states had established boundaries and had begun building pan-national cultures. Regionalism remains most pronounced in the least wealthy—therefore least modernized—nations, particularly Burma, Laos, and Vietnam. Though Vietnam was reunified in 1975, regional differences among the south, the center, and the north remain strong. Throughout Southeast Asia, one should (and in some cases, must) go to a particular region to hear its music in context.

Regionalism in Thailand, among the most modernized of Southeast Asian nations, has undergone drastic change since the early 1970s. Then, the regional cultures were looked down upon. An educated northeasterner would prefer to behave as a (central) Thai. The study of northeastern music and theater was considered of little value. Each region's people nursed stereotypes about the peoples of the other regions. Ironically, as they weakened,

Figure 6.2
The modern urbanite has access to every form of modernization at Bangkok's six-story Mah Boon Krong Shopping Center. Photo by Terry E. Miller, 1988.

they became more attractive. As the nation became more tightly unified and fears of regional secessions receded, the Thai could celebrate the colorfulness of the north, northeast, and south. In the north, where regionalism has become especially weak, civil servants wear local clothing styles on Fridays, but little local architecture survives. On Thai television, troupes of supposedly regional performers act like rustics, wearing mannered farmers' clothes, but play modernized versions of the old music. The homogenization of Thai culture is proceeding rapidly because there are national media, a national network of roads, a unified group of universities, national newspapers, and the requirement that all government business be transacted in (central) Thai (Figure 6.2).

The Philippines is one of the most modernized of the Southeast Asian countries; its literacy rate is extremely high, and an educated populace speaks several international languages, including English, in some of the remotest villages. An advanced network of communication and transportation, aided by a growing economy, has led to a countrywide push to leave the excesses of the previous eras behind, in a general effort toward prosperity and unity. Any celebration of regional culture has been replaced by generic images of rural life (water buffaloes, rice terraces, and so on), which result in the simultaneous distancing and romanticizing of the regions' peoples into an exotic rural "other," to which few want to belong.

Changes in Patronage

The classical arts, because of their complexity and expense, have depended most on the patronage of the wealthy and powerful. Local aristocracies, including the courts of kings and extended royal families, formerly made classical music and theater possible in Burma, Cambodia, Indonesia, Laos, Malaysia, Thailand, and Vietnam. Before achieving independence from the Dutch (who heavily subsidized the aristocracy), many court musicians in Java could count on lifetime employment; after independence, many had to leave their positions and seek nonmusical employment in the cities just to support themselves and their families. Today, only Cambodia retains a king and palace, and Malaysia rotates a kingship among the surviving sultans. Since independence, central Java's sultans have retained a revered status but little genuine political power.

In all these countries, including Cambodia and Malaysia, the classical arts are patronized by a government-supported system of education. Schools operate differently from the old court music establishments, with fixed schedules, credit classes, and the codification of the arts through textbooks and collective instruction.

Wars

Wars have always been part of human life, and wars have always affected the arts. Since the 1960s, however, several events have shaken Southeast Asia to its core. The massacre of thousands of Chinese Indonesians in 1965 was a stunning assertion of "nationalism" by a population dealing with the aftermath of a military coup. The reign of terror of the Khmer Rouge, from 1975 to 1979, nearly obliterated the entire Khmer culture. At least two million people perished, including a high percentage of the country's artists, dancers, actors and actresses, makers of instruments, and musicians. Enemies had formerly come from without, but in 1975, enemies came from within, perpetrating another twentieth-century holocaust.

Warfare in Vietnam, which raged after World War II, when the Viet Minh challenged the French, resulting in a protracted conflict involving the United States, severely disrupted the arts. Partisans and ideologues harnessed the arts for political purposes, and many individual tragedies occurred. In Laos, provinces were bombed back into prehistory, and with the destruction of towns and villages went the loss of many musicians' lives. The modernizations of warfare enhanced human efficiency in disrupting human life [see Culture, Politics, and War].

REVIVAL MOVEMENTS

Warfare and revolution have been extremely damaging to traditional music systems of mainland Southeast Asia. This effect was especially strong in Cambodia and Vietnam. During the reign of terror (1975–1979), the Khmer Rouge might have succeeded in eradicating Cambodian culture had the Vietnamese not invaded. By the mid-1980s, after liberated areas had been stabilized and survivors had begun to enjoy a somewhat normal life, the first moves were made to restore music and dance. A high percentage of the nation's musicians and dancers had been killed or had fled abroad. Those who remained began reviving these arts. By 1989, the tenth anniversary of the Vietnamese invasion, young troupes from the reestablished Royal University of Fine Arts could again dance in the yet unrestored dance pavilion of the palace in Phnom Penh. Within a few years, troupes of dancers, musicians, and shadow puppeteers began touring the United States and Europe. Though these institutions have been revived, their fixture hangs on the country's ability to overcome continuing political chaos, corruption, crime, and a lingering Khmer Rouge.

During the war in Vietnam, Hanoi was heavily damaged, and many of its artists were killed by American bombs, but since 1975 the government has restored, through official support, many of the nation's most important performance genres, including water-puppet theater, *chèo* and *tuồng* theaters, and many local traditions of ritual and chamber music.

COMPOSITIONAL INNOVATIONS

Figure 6.3
The National Conservatory of Music of Hồ Chí Minh City, Vietnam, formerly the Saigon Conservatory. Photo by Terry E. Miller, 2007.

The idea of traditional composition mainly pertains to the still-evolving classical musics of Southeast Asia, the most fertile fields being Burma and Thailand in mainland Southeast Asia and Java and Bali in island Southeast Asia. New compositions divide into two types: those using traditional instruments and procedures and those adding non-indigenous instruments and using Western compositional devices. The latter are easy to recognize. The former are often indistinguishable from older-stratum compositions. In Cambodia and Laos, conservation (rather than innovation) has been the goal.

The idea of traditionality appears to leave little room for composers, but composers, whether known or unknown, have always existed. Perhaps the greatest difference between composers in the West and those of much of Southeast Asia is that the former write their music into notation, impose their personalities and visions on their works, and receive social acclaim from the popular appreciation of those works. From the 1600s through the 1800s, European composers allowed their contemporaries to complete their compositions in performance, especially through a kind of stylistic improvisation, but this trait has always been part of traditional Asian composition. It is not necessarily true, however, for "modern" Asian composers, trained in Western-style music.

Most Southeast Asian composers remain anonymous—a situation not difficult to understand since few compositions are written down and those that are usually are notated in a minimalist, skeletal fashion. Indigenous notations other than staff notation occur in Burma, Indonesia, the Philippines, Thailand, and Vietnam; but it is rare to see musicians performing from notation. The role of the traditional composer is more to provide a distinctive framework to be fleshed out by musicians.

Fundamentally in Southeast Asia, musicians have had two ways to make music: by playing preexisting melodies or compositions and by simultaneously composing and performing according to the requirements of a modal system. Modal systems are found to lesser and greater extents in most Southeast Asian countries, especially in Vietnam, northeast Thailand, Laos, and Indonesia. Even where composition occurs, it is often governed by a modal system. When musicians perform preexisting compositions, they may often realize their own version of the melody within the confines of several variables, including the modal system, the idiom of their instrument, the style of their school, and perhaps their regional idiosyncrasies.

Innovative Composers in Mainland Southeast Asia

Contemporary compositional innovations are quite limited within mainland Southeast Asia. Innovations are most likely to occur in places where modernization in the arts is advanced, where musicians have obtained compositional training outside of Southeast Asia, and where a musical establishment can perform new kinds of works. Burma has innovative traditional composers who write for the nation's premier ensembles, but the country has remained too poor and isolated to develop a modernistic stream of composition. Laos, with its small population and lack of wealth, has given rise to little in the way of modern composition, other than a few popular songs. Cambodia, too, has seen little innovative composition, though one native-born Cambodian, Chinary Ung, having left his country for training in the West, has written many modern compositions, few having anything to do with Cambodia. Vietnam, with a longer tradition of Western conservatories, has European-trained composers writing traditional symphonies, concertos, and operas in conservative European styles, but the expatriate composer P.Q. Phan writes in an avant-garde style. Only Singapore and Thailand have produced composers seeking ways to join their Asian musical heritage with Western techniques and styles (Ryker 1991). Vietnam has produced a socialist-inspired modern music that purports to be traditional.

Thailand

A clear distinction cannot be made between "modern" and "traditional" composition in Thailand. Rather, they are two ends of a continuum. Though all Thai classical music is composed, the names of composers from before the early 1800s are rarely known. Except for the most serious of *naphat* compositions (which must be played exactly as taught), performers have latitude in realizing a composition according to their instrumental idioms and their abilities. What the composer created was a title and a skeletal structure, which he transmitted orally to other musicians, who preserved the composition in their memories. Composers sometimes added to existing compositions; sectional composition, especially those called *phleng thao* (in three tempo levels), have sometimes resulted from the work of two or more composers.

From the mid-1800s at the latest, the names of composers are known, and it is possible to compile lists of works for most composers, though the dates of composition are missing, and there never were manuscripts. Most composers served the court as performers and composers, not unlike the situation in Europe before about 1800, when J. S. Bach, Telemann, and Haydn, for example, were both performers and composers. Some Thai composers—again as in old Europe—were members of the royal family. Most of their works are perceived as "traditional" and "classical" works, but some are modern or Western. Prince Nakorn Sawan (1881–1944), whose full royal name was Chao Fa Grom Pra Nakorn Sawanworapinit, composed the famous traditional piece "Khaek mon bang khun phrom" and wrote the Mekla waltzes, said to be the first original Thai work for symphony orchestra. Prince Narit (1863–1947), composer of several of Thailand's most beloved compositions (including "Khamen sai yok" and "Phraya sok"), also created the *Cinderella Suite*, based on a Western story. The nation's most celebrated composer, Luang Pradit Phairoh (1881–1954), creator of much of today's standard repertory, was not an innovator in the Western sense.

The most clearly innovative composers are mostly young and active. They include Boonyong Gatekong (b. 1920), Panya Roongrüang (b. 1947), Dnu Huntrakul (b. 1950), and Somtow Sucharitkul (b. 1952). Other than Boonyong, who is mostly traditional in orientation, most composers combine in some way both Thai and Western instruments, with or without the use of Thai melodies. Ironically, Thailand's most famous modern composer is the American-born and educated Bruce Gaston (b. 1946), who has lived in Thailand since the 1970s. A member of the traditional ensemble Fong Naam, he composes in a fresh, modern idiom, blending Thai traits with Western classical, jazz, and popular styles, played by a mixture of Thai and Western instruments. One of his works, the *Chao Phraya* Concerto, created jointly with Boonyong, requires prepared and electronically extended piano, Thai ensemble, four Western ensembles, and electronics. Panya Roongrüang has composed extensive works combining vast numbers of Thai and Western instruments. His melodic material is borrowed from both Thai and Western sources, and many of his compositional practices derive from Thai traditions. His works include the extensive *Chao Phraya Suite*, unrelated to Gaston's work.

Burma

In Burma, new compositions for the classical *hsaìñwaìñ* ensemble continue to be composed and performed. Many are notated in a skeletal form for each instrumentalist. Newer compositions tend to be virtuosic, displaying subtlety of orchestration through the use of individual instruments and contrasted groups. Because they are played entirely on Burmese instruments, most outsiders assume they are traditional rather than modern; indeed, they are both.

Singapore

Music in Singapore, since 1965 an independent, business-oriented city-state, is almost entirely the result of the city's most prevalent traits: modernization and multiculturalism. Having been a British colony, Singapore experienced Westernization to a greater degree than any other place in Southeast Asia except the lowland Philippines. Consequently, several modern musical institutions were founded after World War II, including choirs, orchestras, theaters, and schools. Support for the arts is modest, but private and public funds allow composers to create new works, though they must earn their livings in other areas, principally teaching. Among the most active composers are Samuel Ting Chu San, Shen Ping Kwang, Kam Kee Yong, Bernard Tan, and Leong Yoon Pin. Some composers are seeking to bring together the musics of Singapore's disparate communities by combining sounds derived from the city's Malay, Chinese, and Indian heritages.

Vietnam

The term *nhạc dân tộc cải biên* "modernized music" denotes a new genre of composition in Vietnam. It originated during the 1950s among conservatory musicians trained at institutions in the former Soviet bloc (particularly Russia, Bulgaria, Romania, and the former East Germany), where socialist aesthetics held sway. They brought back a socialist vision of folkloric music remarkably congruous with revolutionary compositions being created in China before and during the Cultural Revolution (1966–1976). During the 1970s and 1980s, *cải biên* became the official music used by the government to represent Vietnam, both to the outside world and within Vietnam.

Cải biên is played on a combination of modernized instruments of Vietnamese, upland, and Western origin, some of which have been electrified and all of which have been given chromatic, equal–tempered tunings to facilitate virtuosity, harmony, changes of key, and colorful orchestrations. Even the prehistoric lithophone has been copied, and new works have been written for it. The performers dress in various kinds of nativistic costume, affect joyous, peasantlike attitudes, and consciously show off their skills through programmatic compositions created primarily at the Hanoi Conservatory.

Cải biên offers audiences an exciting repertory of composed, programmatically titled, harmonically based, virtuosic music, often with voice and dance, blending traits from late nineteenth century Eastern European romanticism with newer kinds of Asian and Western popular music. Although one cannot object to the composer's right to create such a music, problems occur when this music is represented to both the Vietnamese and the outside world as traditional, while the older and still living types are excluded from both the conservatory and the media. With official encouragement, ethnomusicologically ignorant recording teams from Europe, the United States, and Japan have recorded albums of such compositions, which they have disseminated on compact discs as traditional. Cultural officials have preferred to send *cải biên* troupes on international tours because nonspecialized audiences find the music attractive. The conservatory has preferred to teach this kind of notated music because it fits the institution better than traditional music transmitted from master to disciple, because traditional musicians do not have advanced degrees, and because it better realizes the government's goals of modernizing Vietnam along socialist models.

Musical Composition in Island Southeast Asia

Indonesia

Composing in the court and aristocratic ensembles of Indonesia has taken two main approaches. In the older approach, a composer creates a main melody and a title, and the musicians of the traditional ensemble realize the composition for the composer. In the newer approach, all parts may be written out (or no indication of form may be given at all), and various blends of styles may be used. Most new compositions in Indonesia (often called *kreasi baru* "new creations") have come out of the institutions of music training, but some composers have developed new works outside institutional contexts. Both faculty and students at institutions are expected to develop new creations, using both traditional and nontraditional forms and instruments. These creations are performed at the school, for a largely school audience; not many of the older, more conservative musicians from the community attend. New creations are almost always reviewed in local newspapers and discussed eagerly by younger musicians. Occasionally an innovation catches on outside the academy, and in some areas of composition, such as regional pop music, new compositions establish entirely new genres.

In Java, composers in all the major cities (including Jakarta, Bandung, Surakarta, Yogyakarta, Surabaya, Semarang, and Banyumas) are working to expand the boundaries of traditional Javanese and Sundanese musics. The central Javanese composers Hardjo-soebroto, Martopangrawit, Nartosabdho, and Wasitodiningrat worked primarily within the traditional compositional style, creating the main musical themes and vocal lines for gamelan performances but also adding to and modifying earlier works. Groundbreaking Sundanese composers Nano Suratno, Ismet Ruchimat, Gugum Gumbira and Ubun Ku-barsah create new works constantly, for performance and further development, both inside and outside the Sundanese academic world.

The Balinese composer Lotring was one of the first early twentieth-century innovators to expand Balinese ideas about the creation of new forms and new works. He used approaches such as selecting melodies and rhythms and recontextualizing them in different genres, switching systems of tuning, or simply opening up the boundaries between genres (Tenzer 1991:55). Since his work in the 1920s and 1930s, hundreds of Balinese composers have followed his lead, and the current climate of competition-driven composition has caused composers to create at a dizzying pace.

Perhaps the most exciting aspect of modern composition in Indonesia has been the passion that it generates among musicians and other composers. While many composers would be delighted for their compositions to become commercially successful, many new compositions generate lively debate, discussions in the newspapers, late-night conversations among musicians, new recordings, and eagerly anticipated experimentation with genres, instruments, and ideas. That new composition should be so thoroughly accepted and supported among contemporary musicians may come as a surprise to Western audiences, who tend to regard new compositions warily, if they are regarded at all.

The Philippines

Because since the twentieth century the Philippines has had a strong Western orientation, compositional trends in the West have been reflected in the Philippines. Many foreign composers and performers visited the Philippines, either as guest faculty at local institutions or as performers for the musical societies that are a part of Filipino life [see THE PHILIPPINES: ART MUSIC OF THE PHILIPPINES IN THE TWENTIETH CENTURY]. Many composers in the early twentieth century used Western forms to highlight Filipino melodies, as in Antonino Buenaventura's works; others created musical theater based on local themes, such as Juan Abad's "*Mabuhay Ang Pilipinas*" ("Long Live the Philippines"). Since the late twentieth century, Francisco Feliciano, Bayani de León, José Maceda, Ramón Santos, and others have run the gamut of compositions, from the Western classical idiom (concertos, choral and orchestral works) to works as much outside the boundaries of traditional Western forms as any being produced in the United States or Europe.

TOURISM

Tourism for much of the non-Western world has been a two-edged sword: one side provides jobs and hard currency; the other brings great numbers of visitors, some of whom behave insensitively and through their patronage encourage seamy activities, including prostitution, drugs, and gambling. In parts of Southeast Asia, tourism is so important that it is responsible for at least part of the country's prosperity. Two Southeast Asian countries—Thailand and Indonesia, especially Bali—have been havens for tourists. Malaysia, the Philippines, and Vietnam are attracting fewer visitors. Cambodia, Laos, and Burma attract few, for various reasons. In each case, tourists can expect to see so-called cultural shows, offered by hotels, restaurants, or government agencies. What is shown, how it is shown, and why it is shown are all issues begging for discussion.

For most non-Southeast Asians (not just Westerners, but even East Asians), the lands and peoples of Southeast Asia are exotic. Travel posters and books play up the bright colors of markets, clothes, temples, and palaces, all inhabited by attractive, smiling natives. Travel videos provide clips of endless festivals, parades, displays of tropical fruit, wild animals, and performances, especially dance. Rarely do they show the musicians, and often they substitute newly composed, inoffensive music for the original music, fearing, one assumes, that the real sounds, possibly too harsh or strange, would repel the potential visitor. The countries most successful at tourism have done so in part by offering themselves as exotic—a treat for visitors' eyes, palates, and video cameras (Figure 6.4). Bangkok, one of the most Westernized of Southeast Asian cities, recently advertised itself as "the most exotic destination in Asia." Once the visitors arrive, those representing travel companies, ministries of tourism, and "culture centers" usually know what to do to start the artesian well of money flowing.

Though the locals appreciate the flood of foreign currencies, they are often less pleased with the visitors' behavior. For most visitors, two weeks in a Southeast Asian paradise represent a deserved vacation, a relief from the workplace and from a colder climate. Being on holiday, they dress down. But in the local world, whose inhabitants dress conservatively in business or work clothes or school uniforms, the visitors' individualistic outfits, odd hairstyles, skimpy clothing, piercings or tattoos and rubber sandals make *them*, rather than the locals, seem exotic. Tourists' encounters with the genuine—a great temple,

Figure 6.4
Dancers and musicians perform for tourists in a Bangkok restaurant that offers a Thai meal followed by demonstrations of music, dancing, fighting with swords, and boxing. Photo by Terry E. Miller, 1988.

Figure 6.5
A Western tourist photographs dancers of the sacred rejang in Tenganan, Bali. In earlier times, outsiders were often prohibited from watching such ritual performances. Today, even the most sacred rituals are flooded with domestic and international tourists and representatives of the media. Photo by Tom Ballinger, 1984.

a great palace—may become problematic. At Bangkok's Temple of the Emerald Buddha and former palace, incorrectly dressed visitors are now given makeshift skirts and shoes to wear rather than be turned away (the former practice). In Bali, visitors are requested to wear narrow scarves around their waists when entering temples; menstruating women or people with wounds are requested not to enter at all (Figure 6.5).

Experiencing traditional culture on its own terms and in its original context is, as any researcher knows, a challenge that can be overcome only through diplomacy, development of an effective network of friends, and discretion. There is no way for daily busloads of visitors to have this kind of experience. Therefore, it has proven better to offer such parties more or less genuine experiences in controlled atmospheres, some of which *are* genuine (as in the Imperial Palace in Huế, Vietnam) and some of which are ersatz (Thailand's Rose Garden). For visitors to Thailand who cannot make the a trip to the country's important historical sites, the Ancient City (an open-air museum-park) offers scaled down reproductions of the great temples and palaces from Ayuthaya, Sukhothai, and elsewhere. Visitors to Jakarta are advised to go to Taman Mini, an amusement park with life-size representations of the people, art, architecture, clothing, and other cultural artifacts from each of the country's many provinces.

A question planners have to face in each country is this: do you give visitors what *they* want to see, do you give them what *you* want them to see, or do you give them what you *think* they want to see? Most officials and travel agents have discovered that audiences want a variety of brief, visually exotic presentations that will fill their photo albums and video anthologies. Full-length theatrical performances, long instrumental suites, text-dominated vocal genres, and context-dependent genres (such as ritual music) are avoided. Few visitors have a solid foundation in the country's history and culture (despite the availability of better and better travel guides) and most of those on vacation really do not come to be educated. The answer: provide entertainment (Figure 6.6).

The most usual venues for such entertainment are hotels, restaurants, and historical sites. The best shows present meritorious artists, even faculty and students of nearby educational institutions, in the performance of serious musical and theatrical segments.

The worst employ a troupe of mediocre performers who try to be everybody, from dancing farmers to courtly musicians.

Visitors to Hanoi are offered nightly performances of Vietnam's water-puppet theater in a comfortable venue with live, traditional music. Visitors see and hear only a series of vignettes rather than complete stories, but the performances are genuine and tastefully done. Similarly, visitors to the Forbidden City within the Citadel of Huế hear restored court music played by surviving masters and a new generation of

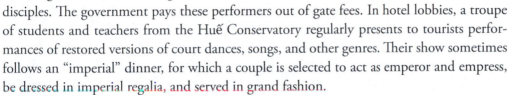

disciples. The government pays these performers out of gate fees. In hotel lobbies, a troupe of students and teachers from the Huế Conservatory regularly presents to tourists performances of restored versions of court dances, songs, and other genres. Their show sometimes follows an "imperial" dinner, for which a couple is selected to act as emperor and empress, be dressed in imperial regalia, and served in grand fashion.

At the Inya Lake Hotel or at open-air restaurants around that lake in Rangoon, Burma (or Yangon, Myanmar, as it is now called), foreigners can nightly see variety shows of Burmese instrumental pieces, dances, and marionette plays, with athletic displays, folkloric performances, and popular songs. Many of the performers are moonlighting professionals.

Most of the dancers and players in Bangkok's restaurants are faculty and students from the country's most prestigious institutions. While in Vientiane, visitors may enjoy a sukiyaki dinner across the street from the Lan Xang Hotel while listening to Lao classical music played by faculty members from the School of Fine Arts.

In areas like Borneo and the farthest reaches of eastern Indonesia, the traditional performing arts have begun to be encouraged and supported by local governments in an effort to attract cultural tourism. On Biak, tourists from Honolulu used to stagger off an airplane at 4:30 A.M., go through immigration and customs, and view an early-morning staged performance of "local

Figure 6.6
Neighborhood children provide Sudanese and diatonic Western music on angklung, and dance jaipongan for tourists at Saung Angklung, on the outskirts of Bandung, West Java. Photo by Cary Black, 1988.

Figure 6.7
Members of the K'por minority welcome guests to a specially built "traditional" house in which tourist shows take place in their village near Dalat, Vietnam, in the Central Highlands. Photo by Terry E. Miller, 2007

traditions" before their plane took off again for Bali. The performance was entirely out of context, but the musicians got paid. In both central Java and Bali (Sanger 1988), the tourist machine is well run, and visitors can always expect to see excellent performances every night and sometimes during the day. Bandung, the Sundanese regional capital, has begun to feature tourist performances at restaurants and hotels, but most of the best music and dance occurs for private events only.

In the Philippines, performances of local traditions, particularly in upland areas, have increased as tourism has become a part of the local economy. To attract more tourists than neighboring communities, villagers stage decontextualized performances of local music and dance at guest houses, where the proprietors speak fluent English and serve American-style meals.

In virtually all cases, someone has to decide "*what* is displayed, *how* it's packaged, and *who* controls the representation" (Sarkissian 1994:34). This statement suggests that messages delivered through performances can be, and almost invariably are, manipulated. Sarkissian has studied the cultural show offered to visitors to Melaka (Malacca), Malaysia, a city conquered in 1511 by Portuguese sailors, some of whom stayed on and married into the local population. Working from the thesis that "tourist performances become cultural texts, constructions, stories people *choose* to tell about themselves," Sarkissian demonstrates how, with government encouragement, the State Economic Development Corporation of Melaka has turned imaginatively recreated but ersatz performances of Portuguese folk art into a local cash crop. Evidently, visitors are happy to accept the premise that old Portuguese culture survived in Melaka and that the performers are simply behaving as they normally do; indeed, they do behave that way, every Saturday evening.

During the fighting in Vietnam, U.S. soldiers on leave in Bangkok (and the usual civilian tourists) visited one of Thailand's first "cultural centers," Thailand in Miniature or Timland, a theme park offering a one-stop look at the farming of rich soil, animal husbandry, boxing, music, dance, fighting with swords, making lacquerware, weaving, and other types of crafts. Thirty years later, such parks are far more sophisticated, and even include a recreated "floating market" to replace the real one that used to flourish in Thonburi, across the river from Bangkok proper.

Guidebook series, including the *Rough Guide*, the *Lonely Planet*, and *Insight*, cater to a class of visitors who dislike people who buy package tours, stay in expensive hotels, and eat at American fast-food outlets. Wearing cutoffs and backpacks, guidebook-toting visitors walk around Asian cities and trek through the countryside, camera (if any) hidden away. Some seek music, theater, and dance on its own terms. But can they find it? If they arrive at the right time (not, for example, during the rainy season, when outdoor performances cease), they may encounter it at a temple fair, at a New Year's street celebration, in association with a ritual (the *phleng korat* singing in Khorat, Thailand, near the shrine to Khun Ying Mo), or in an ordinary public theater. A local radio station may be a surprise setting for a performance of high-quality traditional music (Figure 6.8). But finding it will not be easy, especially if they do not know the local language.

Visitors who do find such performances, however, will be rewarded with exceptional experiences, in which they themselves may become a focus of attention. Other members of the audience may be so impressed that they seek someone who speaks English or French or German or Japanese to interpret for them. Visitors may be offered an opportunity to go backstage, to meet the performers, and to make friends who will lead them to fur-

Figure 6.8
At the national radio studio in Denpasar, Bali, the hosts of a popular program invite listeners to phone in their favorite traditional songs or poems to share with an island-wide audience. New poetry is also welcomed, and the hosts and other listeners comment on—and critique—the correct use of melodies and prosody. Photo by Richard Wallis, 1995.

ther (and usually less obvious) performances. Visitors may learn of Bangkok Bank's Friday afternoon performances of traditional theater or music at one of its branches, of chanting for a special Buddhist ritual, or of a local temple fair where several traditional theatrical troupes are to compete.

Even casual visitors with limited funds and a nonrenewable short-term visa can experience the genuine. But this outcome requires a flexibility that package tours' schedules usually preclude. The best recommendation may be to travel alone; people will be curious and likelier to strike up a conversation than if they observe visitors busily photographing them. If you must take a tour, go in the smallest group possible (no more than five people) with someone comfortable in the local language. But the first job of those people interested in directly and intimately experiencing the performing arts of Southeast Asia is, of course, to get themselves to Southeast Asia.

REFERENCES

Ryker, Harrison, ed. 1991. *New Music in the Orient*. Buren, Netherlands: Frits Knuf.
Sanger, Annette. 1988. "Blessing or Blight? The Effects of Touristic Dance-Drama on Village-Life in Singapadu, Bali." In *Come Mek Me Hol' Yu Han': The Impact of Tourism on Traditional Music*, ed. Adrienne L. Kaeppler, 89–104. Kingston: Jamaica Memory Bank.
Sarkissian, Margaret. 1994. "'Whose Tradition?' Tourism as a Catalyst in the Creation of a Modern Malaysian 'Tradition'." *Nhac Viet* 3(1–2):31–46.
Tenzer, Michael. 1991. *Balinese Music*. Singapore: Periplus Editions.

Questions for Critical Thinking:

Issues and Processes in Southeast Asian Musics

Southeast Asian Musics: an Overview

1. What are some of the factors that led to the creation of nation-states and their boundaries, and do national divisions determine musical divisions?
2. What are some essential differences between rural/village musics and urban/court musics? Why does their location make such a difference?
3. What roles do wealth or power have in the creation and development of music?
4. What do you find to be the greatest challenges in listening to Southeast Asian musics?
5. How are Southeast Asian musics organized differently from the musics you know?

Southeast Asia in Prehistory

1. Is a bronze drum actually a drum? What constitutes a drum?
2. Is there any known relationship between living musics today and prehistoric musics?
3. Are bronze drums the only musical instruments ancient Southeast Asians had access to? Why or why not?
4. How did technological developments have an impact on musical developments in prehistoric Southeast Asia?
5. What are some of the challenges to reconstructing a history of Southeast Asian music from the earliest periods?

Waves of Cultural Influence

1. How does the music of precontact Southeast Asia differ from music of the postcontact era?
2. When and why did Indian music come to Southeast Asia, and what are some aspects of its musical legacy?
3. Why did Chinese music survive intact in mainland Southeast Asia to such a degree?
4. How do approaches to music differ between Hindu-Buddhists and Muslims?
5. What is the legacy of European colonialism on Southeast Asian music?

The Impact of Modernization

1. Why would the loss of a music context affect the survival of the music?
2. How has music changed as a result of the shift from patronage by the court to patronage by the national government?
3. Why is Southeast Asian music politically charged?
4. What were some of the effects of the wars and revolutions that occurred in twentieth-century Southeast Asia?
5. What kinds of innovations have contemporary Southeast Asian composers developed?

PART II

Mainland Southeast Asia

Introduction to the Musics of Mainland Southeast Asia

Terry E. Miller

Nation-states do not necessarily define human cultural groups, but by virtue of their individual histories they deeply affect all ethnic groups living within their borders. Because of the vagaries of history (wars, colonialism, migrations), linguistic groups rarely live simply and cleanly within current, internationally recognized boundaries. Though the majority of lowland Khmer-speakers live within the borders of Cambodia, significant populations live in Thailand and Vietnam. To a great extent, those outside Cambodia have long been disconnected from mainstream Cambodia and were therefore unaffected by the Khmer Rouge, who devastated Cambodia's culture from 1975 to 1979.

Articles focused on nation-states do not tell the entire story of the musics heard within the national borders. In every case, the nation-state is a complex of linguistic and ethnic groups and cultures. Such terms as *Thai music, Lao music,* and *Burmese music* are as problematic as the term *African music:* no one type of music is Thai, Lao, Burmese, or African. Rather, there are *musics* (plural) in Thailand, Laos, Burma, and Africa. At least in mainland Southeast Asia, terms like *Thai, Lao,* and *Burmese* denote the more or less unified majority, mainstream cultures of their nation-states whose musics tend to dominate because of their numbers, their visibility, and their variety.

The deeper one digs into the musical cultures of the countries described in this volume, the more complex matters become. From a distance, each country may appear homogenous, unified, and susceptible to the handy reductionism required in encyclopedias. On closer examination, however, each country is complex. Each has cultural regions, minority ethnic groups, and numerous historical strata, some ancient, some modern. From

The blind *khaen* player Thawng-khun Sia-run performs in an obscure northeastern Thai village as neighbors watch. Photo by Terry E. Miller, 1973.

the (emic) viewpoint of the indigenous population, further subdivisions within each cultural region may extend down to the village level, and although these may numb outsiders trying to make sense of a more generalized experience, they may have great significance to insiders. Just as some Western observers may view each album produced by a given band as virtually a style period, so might the people of northeast Thailand distinguish among provinces and among districts of each province. From the viewpoint of Western pedagogues, a seminar on the string quartets of Beethoven makes perfect sense, but a seminar on the *phleng thao* of the Thai composer Luang Pradit Phairoh is overly specialized; in Thailand, however, the reverse may be true. Any study of music—particularly one intended for readers living outside the cultures under study—must have a clear sense of how "deep" one is to descend into the bottomless realm of difference.

In this section, we have striven to provide a basic musical ethnology of each nation-state, and although, since the mid-1970s, ethnomusicology has moved away from descriptive methodologies toward theoretically based ones, we have concluded that a descriptive foundation—a musical road map—must be comprehended before one can delve into the diverse and often thorny issues of interpretation. Interpretive theories, especially of the school of deconstructionism, can be heavily subjective and therefore susceptible to challenge and revision. We are hopeful that the following articles will be more stable and less trendy.

The lengths of the articles reflect several factors, especially proportion of population and current knowledge. Burma, for example, is geographically larger than Thailand but receives far less space. The reader must understand that Thailand has been continuously open to researchers who may travel anywhere within the country and that several scholars specialize in that country's music—but until the 1990s, Burma was virtually closed to researchers. It has a far less developed infrastructure (inhibiting travel within the country), and no ethnomusicologists known to us have specialized in Burma alone. All authors have agreed that the space given them is inadequate; all could have written much more.

The following articles, then, reflect the current state of knowledge, but even as this volume goes to press, the nation-states covered in this section (actually, the topics of the entire volume) continue to be actively researched, in many cases by the authors who have written here. New researchers have established themselves since 1989 to 1990, when the volume was commissioned.

This volume appears at an auspicious time for research in mainland Southeast Asia. In 1994, Burma began allowing visitors to stay for a full month, rather than a single week. The same year, Laos suspended its restrictions on internal travel, though obtaining a visa still poses a challenge. Thailand, Singapore, and Malaysia remain open, as they have been. Though parts of Cambodia are still off limits and dangerous, researchers travel freely to and from Phnom Penh. Since 1993, Vietnam has given researchers relative freedom to seek out music and theater, and since 1994, people of all nationalities have again been permitted to visit its central highlands. The articles that follow, then, represent the state of knowledge at the beginning, rather than the end, of what promises to be the most productive period of musical research in Southeast Asian history.

The Khmer People of Cambodia

Sam-Ang Sam

INTRODUCTION

The word *Khmer* designates the majority ethnic group in the Kingdom of Cambodia—a people more commonly called Cambodians. In the Khmer language, the nation was traditionally called Kampuchea, but because of the Khmer Rouge reign of terror from 1975 to 1979, when the country was called Democratic Kampuchea, that term gained such notoriety that the word *Kampuchea* is now avoided. During the years of Khmer Rouge rule, the Khmer people suffered famine, mass killings, loss, separation, distrust, disgrace, and shame. In Southeast Asia, no other country's culture has suffered so extensively, its people's psyches been so deeply scarred, and the lives of so many of its musicians, makers of instruments, and dancers wasted.

Cambodia occupies an area of 181,040 square kilometers, about the same size as the state of Washington. Today's Cambodia, with official boundaries created during colonialism, belies the fact that lowland Khmer live across its borders in Vietnam and Thailand, and that upland Khmer live across the border in Laos and Vietnam. With the exception of the mountainous areas along the Lao and Vietnamese borders, most of Cambodia is flat, dominated by extensive forests and open plains, where wet-rice cultivation is the norm. The country is drained by two major rivers. The mighty Maekhong (also spelled Mekong), more than a kilometer wide at the capital, Phnom Penh, flows from southern Laos through Cambodia on the way to its delta in Vietnam, where it divides into nine branches. Starting from the Great Lake in western Cambodia, the Tonle Sap River flows southeast to join the Maekhong at Phnom Penh, where the Basak River adds to the flow. Cambodia is a land whose culture is closely related to the water on which its people depend.

Cambodia's 2006 estimated population of 13,881,427 has grown rapidly since 1979 when the Khmer Rouge, accused of murdering or starving more than two million people, were overthrown. The birthrate has declined from 2.87 percent in the 1990s to 1.78 percent in the early twenty-first century, while life expectancy has increased only slightly to 57 for males and 61 for females because medical care remains minimal for most Khmer. Ninety percent of the population is ethnically Khmer (lowland and upland); Vietnamese constitute about 5 percent and Chinese about 1 percent.

The Khmer absorbed many aspects of Indic culture, including the Hindu-based concept of the *deva raja* "god king" and the great temple as a symbolic holy mountain. Though Khmer kingdoms waxed and waned and were eventually eclipsed, the Khmer penchant for building stone temples throughout their kingdoms left monuments by which today's people can sense the power and cosmic order of their ancient forebears. King Jayavarman II (802–830) revived Khmer power and built the foundation of the Angkorean Empire, founding three capitals (Indrapura, Hariharalaya, and Mahendraparvata), whose archaeological remains reveal much about his times.

Cambodia became a great empire; the temples of Angkor, an archaeological treasure replete with detailed bas-reliefs showing many aspects of the culture (including musical instruments), remain monuments to Khmer culture. After the death of Suryavarman II (1113–1150), who built Angkor Vat, Cambodia lapsed into chaos until Jayavarman VII (1181–1218) ordered the construction of a new city. He was a Buddhist, and for a time Buddhism became the dominant religion in Cambodia. As a state religion, however, it was adapted to suit the *deva raja* practice, with a *Buddha raja* being substituted for the former Hindu–derived *Shiva raja* or *Vishnu raja*.

The Siamese Tai became increasingly powerful in the valley of the Chao Phraya River. In 1238, they captured Sukhothai and soon established a powerful, independent kingdom. The rise of the Tai kingdoms of Sukhothai (1238) and Ayuthaya (1350) resulted in almost ceaseless wars with the Khmer, leading to the destruction of Angkor in 1431 when, through the treachery of two Buddhist monks, the force of Ayuthaya captured Angkor itself. The Tai are said to have carried off ninety thousand prisoners, many of whom were likely dancers and musicians (Blanchard 1958:27). The period after 1432, with the Khmer people bereft of their treasures, documents, and human bearers of culture, was one of precipitous decline. In 1434, King Ponhea Yat made Phnom Penh his capital, and Angko was abandoned to the jungle. During the following century, King Ang Chan (1516–1566) transferred the capital to Lungvek (Lovek), but it was captured in 1594 by the Siamese. To stem Siamese and Vietnamese aggression, Cambodia appealed to France for protection in 1863 and became a French protectorate in 1864. During the 1880s, with southern Vietnam and Laos, Cambodia was drawn into the French-controlled Indochinese Union. For nearly a century, the French exploited Cambodia commercially and exercised power over Khmer politics, economics, and society.

During the second half of the twentieth century, the political situation in Cambodia became chaotic. King Norodom Sihanouk proclaimed Cambodia's independence in 1949 and ruled the country until 18 March 1970, when he was overthrown by General Lon Nol, who established the Khmer Republic. On 17 April 1975, the Khmer Rouge, led by Pol Pot (alias Saloth Sar), came to power and virtually destroyed the health, morality, education, physical environment, and culture of the Khmer people. On 7 January 1979, Khmer forces under Heng Samrin, augmented by Vietnamese forces, ousted the Khmer Rouge. After more than ten years of painfully slow rebuilding with only meager outside help, United Nations intervention resulted in the Paris Peace Accord (23 October 1992), which created the conditions for general elections, leading to the formation of the country's current government and the restoration of Prince Sihanouk to power as king in 1993. Now in ill health, he has been succeeded by his son.

MUSIC IN CAMBODIA

A distinction must be made between "music in Cambodia" and "Khmer music." The former embraces all ethnic groups within the national boundaries, and the latter is limited to the majority, lowland Khmer. The northern provinces of Rattanakiri and Mundulkiri include hilly plateaus, home to the Pnong (Phnorng), an upland Mon Khmer-speaking group, and in the southwest, along the Koulen and Cardamom ranges live the Kuoy (Kui), Por, Samre, and other upland Mon–Khmer speakers, whose musical expression emphasizes gong ensembles, drum ensembles, and free-reed mouth organs with gourd wind chests. In the west, around the Great Lake (Tonle Sap) live Chăm, Chinese, Vietnamese, and other lowland minorities, but if these groups maintain their traditional musics, they are all but invisible.

Khmer civilization reached its peak from the ninth to the fifteenth centuries. The great temple-city of Angkor marked the apex of Khmer glory. In it stand gigantic masterpieces symbolizing the union of celestial and earthly beings. Carved on the walls of the great temples are figures of celestial dancers (*apsara*) along with musical instruments: angular harp (*pinn*), circular frame gongs (*korng vung*), suspended barrel drums (*skor yol*), small cymbals (*chhing*), chest-resonated monochord (*sadev*), and a quadruple-reed oboe (*sralai*) (Figure 8.1). These are believed to have developed into *the pinn peat,* the ensemble now used to accompany court dances, masked plays, shadow plays, and religious ceremonies. Among Khmer ensembles, the *pinn peat* is the most important legacy of the period of Angkor.

Figure 8.1
Two Khmer instruments as depicted in a late-twelfth-century relief from the Bayon at Angkor Vat: (left) chest-resonated stick zither (*khse muoy*) and (right) the extinct curved harp (*pinn*). Photo by Terry E. Miller, 2007.

In 1431, Angkor was looted by conquering Siamese armies, abandoned, and overrun by vegetation. The Khmer king and his court fled, and the capital was moved to Lungvek. Once again, in 1594, Lungvek was sacked by the Siamese. Little is known of music during this period, the most obscure in Khmer history. This second eradication shocked and weakened the Khmer. Music and its functions were deeply affected, and a new style of melancholic and emotional music is said to have emerged. The period from 1796 to 1859 saw a renaissance of Khmer music. King Angkor Duong, the greatest of the monarchs of this period, ascended the throne in 1841 in the capital, Oudong. Under his rule, Khmer music and other forms of art were revived and began to flourish again.

For Khmer traditional arts, the twentieth century has been a period of conservation, preservation, and revival. Forms of art surviving from the past were carefully conserved under the eyes of traditional masters. At the beginning of the century foreign influences resulted in new forms of art. Chinese theater is now presented in a modified Khmer form, *basakk*. Islamic-influenced theater appears in a modified form, *yike*. As in the early period, we see the modification of imported forms into Khmer style. Costumes, languages, performing styles, décor, song, and music of the Chinese and the Muslims were Khmerized to suit local needs and tastes.

MUSICAL INSTRUMENTS

Classification

Khmer organology follows a single-step scheme. At the most general level, Khmer musicians use a tripartite division: *kroeung damm* "percussion instruments," *kroeung khse* "stringed instruments," and *kroeung phlomm* "wind instruments." The Khmer system of classification derives from the verb that denotes the action of making the sound. In Khmer, *leng* "to play" applies to all instruments. Each division is associated with a more specific verb, like *damm* "to hit, to strike" for idiophones and membranophones, *kaut* "to bow" or *denh* "to pluck" for chordophones, and *phlomm* "to blow" for aerophones. *Kroeung damm* include both idiophones and membranophones. Since both groups are struck, both involve the same verb—*damm*.

The Khmer system was created to serve neither organology nor museology but only for the practical making of Khmer music. Thus, it derives from the culture, from within, instead of from without. Both music theory and practice, including ideas of organology, are passed subconsciously in an unsystematic way from master to pupil during music lessons and performances.

In functional terms, the Khmer conceive of instruments as being primarily religious or secular. Playing techniques are associated with music and therefore affect musical style—which leads to other kinds of classifications. The following kinds of description summarize this sort of thinking.

1. Physical materials and playing characteristics
2. Role, such as leading (*ek*)
3. Musical style, such as running (*roneat rut*)
4. Ensemble context, such as *arakk, kar, pinn peat, mohori*
5. Controlling action, such as mouth with aerophone and Jew's harp
6. Size, such as *tauch* and *thomm*
7. Status, such as court and folk
8. System of beliefs, such as religious or otherwise sacred, or secular

The musical instruments of Cambodia are made from clay, hide, bamboo, gourd, other plants, silk, horn, wood, iron, copper, brass, and bronze. Instruments are arranged below according to the Sachs-Hornbostel system of classification.

mohori
Court ensemble for entertainment music
chrieng chapey
Narrative accompanied by long-necked lute (*chapey*)
chapey dang veng
Long-necked lute with two to four strings

Idiophones

Concussion Idiophones

The term *chhing* is likely onomatopoeic for the sound a pair of thick, bowl-shaped cymbals produces. Made of a bronze alloy of iron, copper, and gold, each measures about 5 centimeters in diameter. They are joined by a cord that passes through a small hole at the apex of each. The *chhing* and *chhepp* strokes mark unaccented (O) and accented (+) beats respectively during performance, and consequently the *chhing* functions as the timekeeper of entertainment theater and dance ensembles.

The *chhap* is a pair of cymbals larger in diameter but thinner than *chhing*.
The *krapp* is a pair of clappers made of bamboo or hardwood in different sizes and shapes.

Struck Idiophones

Roneat is a generic term in Khmer referring to xylophones or metallophones-idiophones, with bars of bamboo, wood, or metal. The name *roneat* derives from *roneap* "bamboo strips." Khmer xylophones have bars suspended with cords over trough-shaped and boat-shaped resonators, evidently indigenous to mainland Southeast Asia. Miller and Chonpairot (1981) have documented the known histories and speculated on the origins of three such instruments: the Burmese *pa'tala,* the Thai *ranat,* and the Cambodian *roneat.*

Khmer xylophones have bamboo or wooden bars strung together along two cords running through holes in each bar and suspended on two hooks on the upper ends of the resonator. The maker takes care to ensure that the bars are spaced so they can vibrate freely.

Figure 8.2
An informal ensemble, consisting of xylophone (*roneat ek*), metallophone (*roneat dek*), two gong circles (*korng vung touch, korng vung thomm*), and two drums (*skor thomm, sam-pho*), plays at Tonle Bati Temple, south of Phnom Penh. Photo by Terry E. Miller, 1988.

Each bar is tuned by attaching to the ends of its underside some *pramor,* a mixture of lead, beeswax, and rosin *(mrum, sab).* Khmer musicians practice both "rough" and "fine" tunings. The former aims merely at finding approximate pitches; the latter finely adjusts the required pitches. Khmer musicians prefer to fine tune their xylophones with lumps of *pramor,* which also keep the sound from ringing too long.

Roneat ek (combining *roneat* "xylophone" and *ek* "one, first, leader" to mean "first xylophone" or "leading xylophone") is also known as *roneat rut* "running xylophone." Its role is to start a piece and to cue the others, but contrary to what many Khmer musicians think, it does not play the melodic line. Instead, it plays variations of the melody, whose actual form is realized by a vocalist or oboist. Its twenty-one hardwood or bamboo bars provide a three-octave range, but because it is played in octaves (between the left and right hands), its working range is only two octaves. The resonator of the *roneat ek,* about 115 centimeters long and about 5 centimeters high, sits on a raised square base 14 centimeters high. Its bars are cut equally in width, in different lengths and thicknesses. Thicker bars produce lower pitches; thinner ones produce higher pitches. The player beats the bars with two mallets having thick disk heads. For indoor performances, soft mallets are used; but at outdoor performances, hard mallets are used (Figure 8.2).

Roneat thung is better called *roneat thomm* "large xylophone" because its resonator and bars are larger and longer than those of the *roneat ek,* and its range is lower. The rectangular trough resonator, about 125 centimeters long, is supported on four short legs. The ends of both *roneat ek* and *roneat dek* are flat and straight, but those of the *roneat thung* are curved slightly outward. The *roneat thung* has sixteen bamboo or wooden bars. Only soft mallets are used to play the *roneat thung,* either indoors or outdoors. The handles of those mallets are about the same length as those of the *roneat ek,* but their disks are larger and thicker. The range of the *roneat thung* partially overlaps that of the *roneat ek,* their highest notes being an octave apart. Because of differences in style, the sixteen bars of the instrument permit a range of music of over two octaves, a range greater than that of the *roneat ek.* The role assigned to the *roneat thung* is to counter the melody, especially in rhythm. The *roneat thung* plays a line almost identical to that of the *korng thomm,* but in a vivacious, funny, comic fashion *(lak).*

The *roneat dek* is the higher-pitched metallophone, whose origin remains obscure. For Thailand, Morton concluded that metallophones had appeared in the mid-1800s, perhaps modeled after the Javanese *saron* and *gender* (1974:62, 190). The *roneat dek* has twenty-one bronze bars. Because of their weight, the bars cannot be suspended on cords but are laid in stepwise order on pads over a rectangular trough resonator. In shape and size, the bars resemble those of the *roneat ek,* but they are tuned by scraping or filing away part of

chhing
Small, thick metal cymbals connected by a cord
chhap
Medium-size cymbals, thinner than *chhing*
krapp
Pair of bamboo wooden clappers
roneat ek
Higher-pitched xylophone, with twenty-one keys

the metal. The player uses a pair of mallets similar to those of the *roneat ek* but with disks of wood or the hide of a buffalo. The style of playing is identical to that of the *roneat ek.*

The Khmer word *korng* "gong" is generic for all gongs, whether flat or bossed, single or in a set, suspended on cords from hooks, or placed over a frame. Their history can be traced in part from the epigraphy and iconography of the Founan-Chenla and Angkor periods, for many can be seen in carvings on the walls of ancient Khmer temples. Among the minority ethnic groups inhabiting the highlands, several types of *korng* predominate.

The Khmer have two sets of bossed gongs—*korng vung tauch* and *korng vung thomm*—arranged on circular frames, both used in the *pinn peat.* The individual bossed gongs differ in size and are made of bronze. Each is suspended horizontally from leather thongs passing through holes in the metal and placed over a rattan frame about 30 centimeters above the floor. The gongs are arranged with the lowest pitch to the player's left and the highest to the right; the player sits in the middle of the frame. Each gong is tuned to its required pitch using *pramor*, a mixture of mud and lead (*samna phuok*), rice chaff (*kantuok*), and beeswax (*kramuon khmum*) slightly different from that used to tune xylophones. This material is applied to the underside of the boss. For this application, the gong must be untied and turned over and its boss must be heated; when cool, it can be tied back into the frame and played. The player of a *korng* uses two mallets to strike each gong on the boss. There are two types of mallets, soft and hard. Soft mallets are for indoor use; hard mallets, for outdoor use.

The *korng vung tauch*, or simply *korng tauch*, is the smaller (higher-pitched) set of gongs, the ovular frame of which measures about 110 centimeters from left to right. The number of bossed gongs varies with some having sixteen, some eighteen, and some twenty-one. The *korng tauch* is normally used only in the *pinn peat vung thomm* (*pinn peat* of greater instrumentation), which needs two *korng*. As with the *roneat ek*, the *korng tauch* plays melodic variations in continuous notes divided between both hands.

Korng vung thomm or *korng thomm* denotes the larger and lower-pitched circle of gongs, similar to the *korng tauch* but larger in size, both gongs and frame. The latter measures about 1.2 meters from side to side. Since *korng tauch* and *korng thomm* overlap in range, identical pitches are normally identical in size. The *korng thomm* plays a line almost identical to that of the *roneat thung*, but it is steadier, with less syncopation.

The *korng mong* is a single, suspended bossed gong played with a padded stick, larger in size than those used in circular frames. It has several uses, as in the *korng skor* and *chhai-yaim* ensembles that are used in temples to signal mealtimes and to call a gathering for a temple ritual. In the *korng skor*, this gong informs friends and relatives in the village that an ill person is about to die; consequently, using it in the wedding ensemble is taboo.

The *khmuoh* is a flat gong played with a closed fist, open palm, or padded stick. It is primarily used in wedding ceremonies to signal the arrival of the bride and the bride-groom, but it is also part of the *basakk* theater ensemble.

Plucked Idiophone

The *angkuoch*, also called *kangkuoch,* is a Jew's harp similar to other such instruments found in Southeast Asia and Oceania. In Cambodia, it has long been used by keepers of cattle and others, both as a solo instrument and sometimes to accompany a vocalist. In the Sachs-Hornbostel system, it is classed as a plucked linguaphone within the idiophone category, but in Khmer thinking it is a wind instrument because Khmer musicians use the verb *phlomm* "to blow" to describe its playing action. The Khmer *angkuoch* is usually made of bamboo or iron. When made of iron, it has an outer frame (commonly 10 to 15 centimeters long by 1 centimeter wide) in which a movable vibrating tongue, wider towards the attached end, is curved upward at the free end. The frame follows the outline of the tongue. Those of bamboo are similar, but the tongue does not curve.

The player holds the *angkuoch* firmly, usually in the left hand between the thumb and the index finger, and sets part of the frame between the lips, keeping the jaw somewhat open to allow the oral cavity to amplify and modify select overtones among the vibrations of the device. The right index finger sets the tongue into vibration with soft, backward strokes. Various pitches can be obtained by altering the shape of the oral cavity and by inhaling and exhaling to change timbres. Traditionally, Jew's harps served as disguisers of the voice for courting couples to communicate and serenade one another privately.

Membranophones

Drums

In Khmer, drums are classed as struck instruments (*kroeung damm*). The Khmer use drums merely to accompany singing and dance and do not attribute to them any magical, spiritual, or ritual significance. *Skor* is a generic term denoting practically all membranophones, including those listed here without the prefix *skor*.

The *skor arakk,* also known as *skor dey* "clay drum" or *skor dai* "hand-held drum," is a single-headed goblet-shaped drum, its body made of baked clay or wood and its resonator of snakeskin, lizardskin, or calfskin. The *skor arakk* is made in different sizes, according to its use. Traditionally, it is used in the *arakk* (spirit ceremony) ensemble, from which the instrument takes its name, but it can also be found in the ensembles for *kar* "weddings," *mohori* "entertainment," and *ayai* "alternate singing."

Skor thomm "big drum" denotes a pair of large barrel drums, the largest Khmer membranophones. They are played for a great variety of occasions, from informal gatherings to formal dances. According to carvings on Angkorean temples, these drums were used in military ensembles and were likely called military drums (*skor toap*). They were used to encourage and signal troops, telling them when to march, rest, retreat, or mount an assault (Pich 1970:29). The *skor thomm* had a prominent function in traditional Khmer society, being found in pagodas, district headquarters, and schools. In pagodas, they announced times for prayer and eating; in district headquarters, they called people to come to meetings; in schools, they signaled class times, recesses, and dismissals.

Skor thomm are made of a light but strong wood, such as *chreh*, *koki*, or *tnaot*. First, the log is cut into a piece about 50 centimeters long, which is then carved with a slight bulge at the center and a slight taper at both ends. The heads are normally of oxhide, but buffalo hide is also used; both skins require treatment before use. The fresh hide is boiled in water with salt, betel, and citron to remove the hair, to make the hide soft and strong, and to prevent stretching. Then the maker of the drum covers the ends of the body with the treated

angkuoch
Jew's harp of bamboo or iron
kroeung damm
Khmer
classification term for percussion instruments
skor arakk
Single-headed goblet-shaped drum of clay or wood
skor thomm
Pair of large barrel drums
skor chhaiyaim
Long, vase-shaped single-headed drums

hide while it is wet, secures it with pegs or nails, and lets it sit for at least two weeks (or sometimes more than a month) before it can be played. The finished drum must be able to produce two untuned sounds: a low tone (*toung*) and a high tone (*ting*). Khmer musicians refer to this duality as *chhloeuy knea* "to answer each other." Finally, a metal ring about 3 centimeters in diameter is screwed into the body at the center of the bulge so the drum can be hooked to a wooden stand while being played. Normally, *skor thomm* are played in a pair with two unpadded wooden sticks, each about 35 centimeters long; the drums are tilted obliquely against stands, leaving only one head playable and the other vibrating freely (Figure 8.3).

Figure 8.3
A display of Cambodian gong circle, xylophone, and drums. Photo by Terry E. Miller, 1991.

Skor chhaiyaim are long, vase-shaped drums, used mainly in the *chhaiyaim* ensemble, associated with religious and traditional ceremonies such as the flower ceremony (*bonn phka*) and the fundraising ceremony (*bonn kathinn*). According to older musicians, such ensembles have been maintained in Khmer villages for many centuries. In performance, drummers wear clown masks to create a comic atmosphere, enlivening the celebration. Each of the four drums that make up an ensemble is supported on the players' shoulders by strips of cloth, and the single heads are beaten with the hands. The four drums are also grouped into two sets, one pair producing a higher tone and the other pair a lower tone. To adjust the pitch, tuning paste is placed on the center of the head.

The *skor yike* is a large frame drum with a head of crocodile skin, a *tunsang* (a kind of large lizard), or an ox. Eight drums, seven of the same size and the larger, conical *skor chey* "victory drum" (played by the troupe's leader, the teacher), make up the *yike* ensemble. Casually playing and stacking them are forbidden.

The *skor klang khek* are long, two-headed drums in conical shape with heavy leather lacing. Since they are regarded as suspended drums, they are also called *skor yol* "suspended." When associated with the funeral ensemble (*klang chhnakk*), the number of drums per ensemble varies according to the rank of the deceased. A king's funeral requires sixteen drums (eight of gold and eight of silver), plus three oboes; for commoners, three drums and one oboe suffice. The ensemble most often plays the piece "Klang Yaun." Today, this ensemble is preserved only in the royal palace in Phnom Penh.

The *sampho* is a two-headed barrel drum with a bulge near the center, tapering to each head. Its body, made of any of several kinds of wood (*khnaor, kakoh, raing,* or *beng*), is hollowed from a solid piece of wood, and its ends are covered with the hide of a calf tightened with gut, or sometimes with rattan strips. For easy carrying, a rattan or gut handle is woven into the top of the bulge, and the drum is permanently attached to a wooden stand in a horizontal position. The *sampho* has a length of about 49 centimeters and a height (including its permanently attached stand) of 50 centimeters. At the center bulge, the drum is about 35 centimeters in diameter: the larger head 28 centimeters and the smaller head 25.

The most important drum in Khmer music, the *sampho* is closely associated with the *pinn peat*, in fact as its leader. It is equally important for accompanying the solo playing of an oboe in freestyle-boxing pieces and "*Salauma*," a tune used for the actions of fighting. The *sampho* has a variety of rhythmic patterns appropriate to its function. When used in an ensemble without dancing, it plays a fixed eight-beat cycle in *muoy choan* (the first-level rhythmic pattern) or a sixteen-beat cycle in *pi choan* (the second-level rhythmic pattern). When accompanying a dance or a *sbek* (shadow-play) performance, it uses a special pattern (*laim* "dance"), specific to the piece it accompanies.

Beyond its leading role and uniquely among Khmer instruments, the *sampho* is considered by Khmer musicians to be sacred and spiritual. According to Khmer belief, the membranes can be attached only on a Thursday that is a *guru* day. As part of this process, a ceremony is conducted and offerings are made to Preah Pisnukar, a spiritual architect and god of construction, asking for blessing and good sound (Pich 1970:30). Known for centuries from its carved depictions at various Angkorean temples, it maintains both ritualistic and entertainment roles to this day.

The player uses both hands to strike the heads of a *sampho*. Because the drum must produce both lower and higher tones, one head is larger than the other. The heads, their centers painted black, are tuned with a paste (*bay sampho* "rice for *sampho*"), which is a mixture of cooked rice mashed with ashes from burned branches of palm or coconut midribs, but new bread will also do. The thicker and heavier the paste, the slower the vibration of the parchment and the deeper the tone. The *sampho* controls the tempo and regulates the preestablished rhythmic cycles. Therefore, it is considered the leading instrument in the *pinn peat* and the instrument of the teacher (*krou*). Surprisingly, many Khmer musicians regard it as a simple instrument, easy to play, and thus neglect it.

The *thaun* is a single-headed, goblet-shaped drum similar to the *skor arakk,* but it has a shallower head area and a slimmer body. Like the *skor arakk,* its body is made of clay or wood, and its head is made of calf, goatskin, or snakeskin, laced to the body by leather thongs, rattan strips, or nylon cord. Its primary use is in *mohori,* where it is paired with the *rumanea*. In performance, the player lays the drum horizontally on his lap and strikes it softly with bare right-hand fingers, playing an interlocking pattern with the *rumanea*.

The *rumanea* is a single-headed, shallow, wooden frame drum with a calfskin membrane nailed to the body. Like the *thaun*, with which it is paired, its primary use is in the *mohori*. The player holds it vertically on his left leg, with the *thaun* on the lap, and strikes its head softly with bare left-hand fingers.

Mirliton

The mirliton (*slekk*) is the leaf of a tree. The player selects a leaf that is stiff and thick enough to vibrate freely—especially the leaves of *lumpuoh*, *puoch*, or *kravann* trees. The player picks a leaf, folds it along its length, places it between his lips, and blows over the folded edge. Such temporary instruments can be used in the wedding ensemble (*vung phleng kar*), but they are most often played solo.

Chordophones

Harp

The *pinn*, an angular harp prominent in Cambodia during the Angkor period, is known only from carvings on the walls of several temples around Angkor. It is not known today, nor has it been revived; nevertheless, the Khmer court-music ensemble (*pinn peat*) takes its name from it. The word *pinn* is likely related to the Sanskrit *vīnā*, which may have derived from the Egyptian *vin* (Sachs 1940:224).

Zithers

Khmer musicians consider the *khse muoy* (also *say diev*, both terms meaning "string one" or "one string") one of the oldest musical instruments in Cambodia. The resonator is half of a round, dried gourd, the open side of which is placed against the player's chest. The body-fingerboard, a stick about 90 centimeters long, is securely attached with wire to the round side of the gourd. A single string of steel or brass runs along the fingerboard from a carving at the lower end to a tuning peg at the upper end. To pluck the string, the player wears a metal or bronze plectrum on the index finger, or more frequently, on the middle finger. The *khse muoy* is used mainly in traditional *arakk* and *kar* ensembles.

The *krapeu*, also known as *takhe*, *takkhe*, and *charakhe*, is a three-stringed zither. This instrument is zoomorphic, constructed in an abstract shape of a crocodile (*krapeu*). The other terms suggest a Thai origin, for in Thai *charakhe* means "crocodile," but whether *takhe* and *takkhe* mean the same or refer to a large lizard called *thukay* is uncertain. Beneath the resonator box are three or five legs to raise the instrument off the floor and permit its sound to project. Along the neck are twelve high, graduated frets of ivory, bone, bamboo, or wood. There are three strings, the highest one (*khse ek*) made of gut or nylon, the middle one (*khse kor*) also made of gut or nylon, and the lowest (*khse bantor*) made of metal. The melody, restricted to the upper two strings, is played by a plectrum made of ivory, bone, animal horn, or wood, tied to the player's index or middle finger. The third (lowest) string serves as a drone (Figure 8.4).

The *khimm* is a small hammered zither with two rows of bridges, played with two lightweight beaters. It is believed that the Khmer *khimm* was brought to Cambodia by the Chaozhou Chinese, who used it in their theater ensembles. In Cambodia, it was modified for use in the Khmer *basakk* theater. The *basakk* ensemble uses two sizes of *khimm*: high pitched (*khimm tauch*) and low pitched (*khimm thomm*). While the former plays the melody line, the latter plays a partly harmonic bass version. It is also commonly used in the *mohori* and *kar* ensembles.

Figure 8.4
A zither (*krapeu*), one of a handful of palace instruments that survived the Khmer Rouge reign of terror. Photo by Terry E. Miller, 1988.

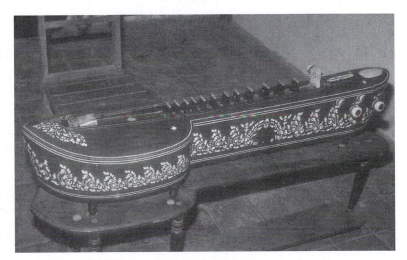

Lutes

The term *tror* is generic for bowed lutes, including spike fiddles. Some types of *tror* may derive from Chinese bowed lutes (*hu*), which came to Cambodia at the turn of the twentieth century with the Chinese theater called *hi* (Pich 1970:21). Khmer musicians have adopted and modified them into Khmer instruments and use them in several ensembles, including the *arakk*, the *kar,* the *mohori*, the *yike*, the *ayai*, and the *basakk.*

The *tror Khmer*, also known as *tror khse bey* "three-stringed fiddle," is among the oldest of Khmer musical instruments. Its body is made from the dried shell of a coconut, cut in thirds and covered with a snakeskin resonator. It is smaller than its nearest relative, the Thai *saw sam sai*; the Javanese *rebab*'s body is wood not coconut. The *tror Khmer* is used principally in the *arakk* and *kar* ensembles. Its bow is detached, in contrast to two-stringed Khmer fiddles, which place the hairs of the bow between their strings. The bow (*chhak*) is made of bamboo or wood, with horsehair or nylon (*say*). Like Western players of stringed instruments, Khmer musicians put rosin on their bows. The tuning of this instrument (from low to high) is A–D–G (approximate tempered pitches).

The *tror chhe*, also known as *tror ek*, is a two-stringed fiddle with the hairs of the bow passing between the strings. Its cylindrical resonator is made of bamboo, wood, or ivory, with a snakeskin resonator on the front. The two strings (*khse ek* "higher" and *khse kor* "lower") are made of metal and tuned in a perfect fifth (D–A). Among the fiddles, the *tror chhe* is the highest in pitch. Its name is thought to be onomatopoeic.

The *tror so tauch* is a two-stringed fiddle similar to the *tror chhe*, but larger and tuned G–D. It is used in the *arakk*, the *kar*, the *mohori*, and the *ayai* ensembles as the lead instrument.

The *tror so thomm* is still larger than the *tror so tauch*, and its tuning is D–A. Its use is similar to that of the *tror so tauch*, except that it does not play a leading role.

The *tror ou* is a low-pitched, two-stringed fiddle that differs from the previous three in that its strings are made of gut, nylon, or metal, its resonator is the shell of coconut, with a calfskin resonator, and it is tuned C–G. Some resonator boxes have beautiful designs carved into the back.

The *tror ou chamhieng* is a two-stringed fiddle with a turtleshell body. This instrument is used exclusively by Cham people living in Cambodia.

The *chapey dang veng* is a lute with a long neck which curves backward at the top. The body of the resonator (*snauk*) is made of a specific wood called *raing,* the fingerboard (*dang*) is made of *krasaing*, the resonator cover (*santeah*) is a piece of wood called *khtum*, the bridge (*kingkuok*) is of *thnung*, and the frets are carved from bone. There are either two strings or two courses of two strings, each made of gut or nylon. The Khmer terminology regarding this instrument is (Figure 8.5):

Snauk raing	The resonator box made of *raing,*
dang krasaing	the fingerboard made *of krasaing*
santeah khtum	the piece of thin wood made *of khtum*
kingkuok thnung	the bridge made of *thnung*
khtung chha-oeung	the frets made of bones

Though the *chapey dang veng* is used in the older forms of the *arakk* and *kar*, it is most commonly used in epic singing (*chrieng chapey*), in which the singer accompanies himself on this instrument.

Aerophones

Flutes

The *khloy* is an end-blown duct flute made of bamboo, wood, plastic, or metal, used in the *mohori* and *kar* or as a solo instrument. It has two sizes: smaller, higher-pitched (*khloy ek*) and larger, lower-pitched (*khloy thomm*).

Figure 8.5
A student at the Royal University of Fine Arts plays the long-necked lute (*chapey dang veng*). Photo by Terry E. Miller, 1988.

Each normally has six holes for fingers and one hole for a thumb, but some have seven holes for fingers and others have no hole for a thumb. A hole drilled between the highest hole and the duct opening may be covered with a membrane made of rice paper or bamboo inner skin. When used, it provides a bright, slightly buzzy timbre. Most Khmer players of aerophones, including those who play the *khloy*, master circular breathing, which enables them to produce a continuously flowing melody. Students learn this technique early in their study, soon after acquiring their instruments.

Reed Instruments

The *sneng* is an aerophone made of the horn of a buffalo or an ox. Though found in different sizes, most are about 39 centimeters long. The horn is open at both ends, which serve as holes for fingering. At about the middle concave side of the horn is a rectangular hole, over which a bamboo free reed is placed and sealed with a black insect wax. The player inhales and exhales into this hole. The *sneng* plays two notes a perfect fourth apart—the smallest range of all Khmer wind instruments. It is used by keepers of cattle, firewood collectors, and bee collectors, especially to signal the time for a meal or for returning to the village. It is most commonly used both during elephant-hunting expeditions and for the *arakk* ceremony, playing the piece "*Bangkauk Sneng*," which invites a spirit to come and preside at the ceremony.

The *ploy*, also called *m'baut*, is a free-reed mouth organ with a gourd wind chest, found among upland Mon-Khmer speakers in Boutoy District, Mondulkiri Province, and among the Por and Kuoy in Kampong Chhnang, Pursat, and Siem Reap provinces. The number of bamboo pipes varies from five to seven. Each pipe, which pierces the bottom of a dried gourd wind chest, has one hole for fingers and a free reed, and sounds when a player inhales or exhales through the hole for blowing and covers the hole for fingering. Similar instruments are found in the mountains straddling the borders of Cambodia, Laos, and Vietnam.

The *pey pork* is a side-blown pipe with a bronze free reed placed over a hole about 2 centimeters from the upper end. The tube is of wood or bamboo (*pork*); the term *pey* denotes several types of reed instruments. The player places the mouth over the section with the reed and holds the instrument almost horizontally. The seven holes for fingers and the one hole for a thumb produce seven pitches with a range of slightly more than an octave. The *pey pork* is used in the *arakk* ensemble to play, among others, the piece *"Surin"* to invite a spirit to come to the ceremony. It is mostly used as a solo instrument or to accompany a vocalist.

The *ken*, a free-reed mouth organ in raft form closely associated with lowland Lao speakers in Laos and northeast Thailand, is also found in northwestern Cambodia, an area once part of the Lao principality of Champassak [see LAOS and THAILAND]. In Cambodia, the *ken* is used to accompany a regional folk dance called by the same name.

The *pey prabauh* (also known as *pey a*) has a wood or bamboo body about 30 centimeters long. The double reed (*loam, andat*), nearly 8 centimeters long and positioned into the upper end of the body, is made of an aquatic plant called *prabauh*, from which the instrument takes its name. At the base, the reed is rounded to fit into the body, and at the upper end (where it is played), it is shaved thin to vibrate. Along the body are one membrane-covered hole and seven holes for fingering. The *pey prabauh* is principally used in the *arakk* and *kar* ensembles, where it functions as the standard by which the other instruments are tuned. In structure, it resembles the Chinese *guan*, the Korean *piri*, and the Japanese *hichiriki* (Figure 8.6).

Figure 8.6
A Royal University of Fine Arts student plays a double-reed pipe (*pey prabauh*). Photo by Terry E. Miller, 1988.

The *sralai* is a quadruple-reed oboe with a slightly bulging wooden body. Early iconographical evidence of it is seen in bas-relief carvings at Angkor. It is of central importance in *pinn peat*, the ensemble that accompanies court dances, masked plays, shadow plays, religious ceremonies, and boxing matches. It comes in two sizes: small (*sralai tauch*) and large (*sralai thomm*). There is also a *sralai* with a flared bell (*sralai klang khek*), of Javanese origin.

The body is made of various hardwoods (*kakaor, beng, neang nuon*) or ivory. The maker is conscientious about the wood he uses. When cutting a tree, he carefully distinguishes the top from the bottom, because constructing an instrument upside down would make it hard to blow; the upper end (with the reed) must be the top end of the tree. The bodies are also carved with a bulge at the center and slight flaring at both ends. The inside is hollowed in a slightly conical shape. Sixteen pairs of rings are carved around the bulge, between which six holes for fingering are bored—four in one group on the upper end, two in another on the lower end—separated by a noticeable space. These rings add beauty and help prevent the fingers from slipping. The space between the two groups of holes also serves as a standard of measurement for the length of the reed. The *sralai tauch* varies in length from 31 to 33 centimeters, each end having a diameter of about 3 to 4 centimeters. The length of the *sralai thomm* varies from 40 to 42 centimeters, each end having a diameter of about 4 centimeters.

The reed has two parts: the tube and the tongues. The tube, made of bronze, brass, or sometimes silver, is tapered so that the end that fits into the top of the oboe is a little larger than the other end, to which the tongues are fastened. This lower (larger) end is also wound with thread for a tight fit when inserted into the instrument. The reed is made of the leaf of a palm, cut into four small tongues and fastened to the tube with thread. The length of the *sralai tauch* reed is about 5.5 centimeters, and the length of the *sralai thomm* reed is about 7 centimeters. When played, the entire reed (tube and tongue) is placed in the mouth, with the lips resting against the oboe.

A complete *pinn peat* includes both a *sralai tauch* and a *sralai thomm*. This orchestration is more common in villages and at the Royal University of Fine Arts for accompanying masked plays and shadow plays; at the palace, only the *sralai thomm* is used, sometimes replaced by a duct flute.

Sralai klang khek means "oboe used in the *klang khek* [funeral] ensemble," but it is also called Javanese oboe (*sralai chvea*) and Javanese wind instrument (*pey chvea*). Its body, made of either wood or ivory, is carved from one or two pieces. The reed resembles those of the *sralai tauch* and the *sralai thomm*, and there are seven holes for fingers and one for a thumb. The *sralai klang khek* is most often used in funeral and boxing ensembles.

Trumpets

The conch (*saing*) is perhaps the oldest wind instrument in Cambodia. Used only by Brahmin priests, it served at certain court functions to signal the sovereign's arrival. In Thailand, "Brahmin priests still serve…at certain court functions and are a curious survival in a Buddhist court. They originally came to Ayuthaya from Angkor after the Thai conquest of the Khmer capital, and the Ayuthayan kings, seeking to take over the mantle of the Khmer empire and legitimize their claims to power, took over the rites as well" (Smithies 1971:72). The *saing* produces a single pitch.

SYSTEM OF TUNING

Khmer tuning is done according to aesthetic preference, but basing the intervals on the ensemble aerophone is widely practiced. When this changes, so does the tuning. Though Khmer musicians tune their instruments by ear, the concept of perfect fifth and octave

sralai klang khek
Small wood or ivory double reed with flared bell

saing
Conch shell trumpet

Angkor Vat
Temple-city in Cambodia, center of ancient Khmer civilization

is constant. Pitches between these are adjusted to suit the overall context of the music being played. Some musicians continue to retune their instruments time and time again before concerts, after trying out a given piece. In short, one leader's xylophone will likely exhibit a tuning different from another's. Each leader imposes his or her tuning on the ensemble. Khmer vocalists also do not sing equidistant intervals. As a result, traditional Khmer music has been played on Western instruments with a degree of satisfaction, using a modern music ensemble called modern *mohori* (*mohori samai*). Except for the *thaun-rumanea* pair of drums, this ensemble uses all Western instruments (flute, violin, banjo, mandolin, guitar, accordion, organ, and violoncello) to play traditional Khmer music. Of these instruments, only the violin and violoncello allow for the use of a non-Western tuning pattern.

SCALE, KEY, MODE

Scale

The term *scale* normally denotes the presentation of the tonal material of a composition or group of related compositions in ascending and descending order. These pitches are drawn from the total system of tuning and are consequently fewer in number. On the concept of scale, there are no written sources by Khmer musicians. Not surprisingly, then, there is no Khmer term for *scale*. Surviving music reveals that there are two scales in Khmer music: one pentatonic (or more precisely, anhemitonic pentatonic, consisting of five pitches devoid of semitones) and one heptatonic (having seven pitches with approximate semitones and tones).

Key

The word *key* as applied to Khmer music refers to centering music on a given xylophone or metallophone bar, a given gong, or a given aerophone fingering, not to the concept of key in the Western sense. The Western pitch G, used as the normal "key" of the *pinn peat*, refers to bar 6 on the *roneat* and gong 6 on the *korng* (counting from top to bottom, highest to lowest). In the *mohori* ensemble, the general pitch is C. Consequently, Khmer musicians of a given ensemble play pieces only at the designated level. Since there are only two types of Khmer scales, there are only two distinct intervallic structures. That of the pentatonic is M2–M2–m3–M2–m3, and that of the heptatonic is M2–M2–m2–M2–M2–M2–m2.

Partly because all *pinn peat* music is played in what sounds like the G scale, Khmer pieces sound the same to many listeners. However, some pieces, such as *"Lo"* and *"Rev"* switch tonal levels, or (to use harmonic language) modulate. There is no standard pitch in Cambodia, so instruments are not necessarily built at the same level. The notated "key" of G, the central pitch *of pinn peat* music, is referenced to a certain bar of the xylophone or the gong, or to the fingering on an aerophone, not to Western pitch standards (Figure 8.7).

Figure 8.7
The beginning of "*Lo*," in which a metabole occurs from the first scale (G–A–B–D–E) up a fourth to a second scale (C–D–E–G–A).

Metabole

Mode

Whereas the term *scale* is a conceptual abstraction or reduction based on analysis, the term *mode* or *melody type* denotes a complex of traits related not only to melody but to actual practice. Mode is the basis for melodic composition, improvisation, and embellishment, consisting of such factors as tonal material, a hierarchy of tones, and typical melodic movement and phrasing. It may include extramusical aspects relative to proper performance context, time, mood, or (as with the Indian raga) even magical powers. As with scale, there is no Khmer term for mode, and Khmer musicians do not verbalize it; yet the concept exists, though transmitted in a nonsystematic manner.

The basis of Khmer modes apparently lies in a set of five, six, or seven tones in a hierarchical system of tonal relationships. The modes neither have names nor convey articulated feelings (like the modes of, for example, Burma, India, Indonesia, Korea, Thailand, and Vietnam). Khmer modes are based on the same set of tones but with different finals. The hierarchy in Khmer mode correlates points of rest, final tone, tones at the endings of cycles and phrases, and cadential resolutions, all essential to the identification of mode because they govern the basic structure of a piece.

Mode in *pinn peat* music is difficult to separate from scale, whose central tone is the constant G, to which all finals (including G itself) relate. Mode, therefore, is recognizable according to its final in relationship to the principal tone of the scale. Because modes are based on different finals, they manifest different intervallic structures; each set of intervals is distinctive to a particular mode. Five modes are generated from the pentatonic scale (G-A-B-D-E), and seven are generated from the heptatonic scale (G-A-B-C-D-E-F), each with a different final. Thus, it is theoretically possible to have altogether twelve modes, but in practice there are fewer. The most common mode is G-A-B-D-E, but D-E-G-A-B, A-B-D-E-G-A, and D-E-F-G-A-B are also frequently encountered.

Khmer musicians do not find it necessary to talk about their music. For them it is more important to play well and have a large repertoire. Knowing how to start and end a piece properly (with regard to pitch, ambitus, and level) is much more important than knowing what the scale or mode is. When Khmer musicians are learning a piece, their teachers tell them exactly how to play it, and they do not ask why. They trust their teachers to have the requisite knowledge and experience. The "traditional" way is right, provided one has been properly taught; one need not theorize beyond that.

TEXTURE

Khmer music is melodically based and does not depend on vertical sonorities. Its texture is usually regarded by ethnomusicologists as heterophonic, or as Hood (1982) and Morton (1976) prefer to call it, polyphonically stratified. The linear character of the melody flows according to the scale and mode, but each composed melody has its individual character.

Though specific compositions can be reduced to a generic version (as is presented, for example, in a single-line transcription), in fact, an abstract and underlying structure known to the musicians is more important. Each instrumentalist or vocalist has a characteristic way of realizing this structure, creating a different idiomatic version. Depending on the instrument, the idiom of this structure has specific patterns and a greater or lesser density according to the degree of ornamentation. The development of an intricate melodic line through variation technique not only avoids repetition and monotony but allows players to exhibit their skills by improvising. Beginning players, though, play simpler versions than experienced players.

In a solo rendition, the texture of Khmer music is monophonic, though in the case of xylophones and gong circles numerous octaves, fourths, and fifths produce polyphony that differs completely in function from Western harmony. When many musicians play together, the texture results from the simultaneity of many distinct versions of the same melody. More than one pitch occurs at any given moment, but these sonorities result more from chance and instrumental idioms than from an intention to play polyphonically (Figure 8.8).

BEATS, RHYTHMS, CYCLES

Khmer compositions are in duple meter, customarily transcribed as 2/4 or 4/4 time. In notation using staffs, accented or strong beats occur at the beginning of a measure. In Western music, phrases can begin either on a downbeat or on an upbeat that leads to a downbeat; thereafter, the same pattern of hierarchical accents (main beat, secondary beat, interior beats, and so on) repeats itself to the end of the phrase or piece. Khmer music, however, is organized in rhythmic or metrical cycles, the last stroke of which is the strongest. These cycles coincide in length with melodic phrases—meaning that Khmer music, like Thai music, appears to be accented at the ends of phrases. Because a melodic phrase ends on a strong beat, the phrase must begin on a weak beat, similar to an upbeat in Western music. This requirement can be easily seen in transcriptions on staffs.

Within the four-stroke cycle, stronger beats are articulated by the *chhep* stroke (symbolized as +), played on the small cymbals, and weaker beats on the *chhing* stroke (indicated by o): o + o +. Parallel to both melodic phrase and *chhing* cycle is a cyclic pattern of drumming. The final beat of a cycle does not always coincide with a stressed drumstroke.

Figure 8.8
The first four measures of "Chinaroeur" as performed by a singer, with six possible instrumental variations.

O = *chhing*
+ = *chhep*

As in many other Asian musics, Khmer drumstrokes are onomatopoeic: sounds verbalized as *choeung, chapp, ting, tup, teung,* and *theung* are obtained by striking the head of the drum at different places and with different strokes, closed or open. Though the last stroke of the cycle is the most stressed and the melodic tone at that point the most important structurally, musicians do not accentuate this fact by playing louder or harder. Drums also serve as leaders in Khmer music ensembles, setting tempi and keeping time. Yet to many Khmer musicians, drums are only supportive of other pitched instruments and are therefore secondary. Consequently, few Khmer musicians make the drum their main instrument of study.

It is important to understand that the tones falling at the end of each cycle, that is, on its strongest beat, together constitute the skeletal or abstract form of a melody, and pitches falling on secondary beats begin to flesh out the melody. The final beats are also important to the texture, for here all instruments reunite on a unison or an octave. Between these points, musicians have great latitude to fill in according to the scale or mode and the idiom of the instrument (Figures 8.9).

Oral tradition, in the Khmer musical context, lends itself to flexibility, variability, and embellishment. Musicians in an ensemble have in mind a collective melody, which no one person plays, more like the generic melody mentioned above than the abstracted one based on skeletal tones. The collective melody serves as a guideline for the musicians to follow from beginning to end, and it holds them together as an ensemble. An analogy would be the network of roads on a map, potentially directing a band of travelers to a

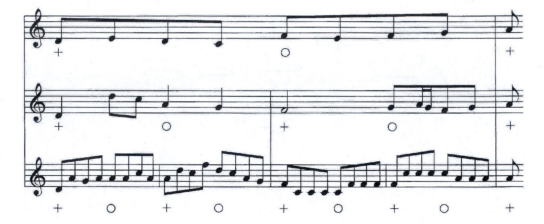

Figure 8.9
The first two measures of each tempo of "*Chvea Srok Mon*," showing melodic relationships.

common destination. Each traveler is free to choose a route, but because musical playing in ensembles is a collective process, the musicians—the travelers—must periodically meet at agreed-on locations before taking off again. In this manner, the travelers keep together as a band. Only with the collective melody can a Khmer ensemble realize the common goal of playing a composition.

LEVELS OF TEMPO

Khmer music has three lengths of cycles, each having four strokes on the *chhing*. The first level (*muoy choan*) is half the length of the second (*pi choan*), which in turn is half the length of the third (*bey choan*). If a first-level phrase lasts four measures, a second-level phrase lasts eight, and a third-level phrase lasts sixteen (Figure 8.10).

The drum or drums appropriate to a particular ensemble or genre execute a specific pattern associated with the prescribed metrical level (*choan*). There are two classes of rhythmic patterns for the *sampho*, probably the most important drum in the *pinn peat*: (1) patterns associated with the three tempo levels, and (2) pieces and unique patterns known as

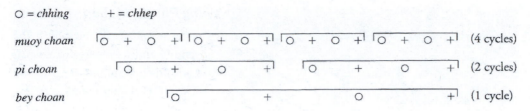

muoy choan   O + O + | O + O + | O + O + | O + O + | (4 cycles)

pi choan   O + O + | O + O + | (2 cycles)

bey choan   O + O + | (1 cycle)

O = *chhing*   + = *chhep*

Figure 8.10
The *chhing* strokes for the three levels of tempo: *muoy choan, pi choan*, and *bey choan*.

music for drumming (*phleng skor*) or music for dancing (*phleng laim*), usually used with dance and theater pieces.

COURT MUSIC, DANCE, AND THEATER

Until Western ideas and practices came to Cambodia, music graced nonmusical contexts, be they spiritual or nuptial ceremonies, boxing, the shaving of hair, or ordination. It was seldom that music, with the exception of *mohori*, was rendered merely the sake of listening. Music was intended primarily to accompany dance and the performances and national and religious ceremonies.

Ensembles and Genres

Vung Phleng Pinn Peat

The *vung phleng pinn peat* is the main court ensemble. Besides playing music alone, it accompanies court dance, masked plays, shadow plays, and religious ceremonies. Out of the traditional context (as in concert halls), it can perform alone, without an extramusical context. It is thought to be more than one thousand years old because reliefs of its instruments—oboes, gongs, cymbals, and drums—were carved in stone at Angkor Thom.

Considered to have the loudest sonorities of all Khmer ensembles, its full instrumentation includes two oboes (*sralai tauch* and *sralai thomm*), two xylophones (*roneat ek* and *roneat thung*), one metallophone (*roneat dek*), two gong circles (*korng tauch* and *korng thomm*), one pair of small cymbals (*chhing*), two drums (*skor thomm* and *sampho*), and vocalists (*naek chrieng*). A small *pinn peat* consists only of the low-pitched oboe, the high-pitched xylophone, the low-pitched circular frame gong, one drum, one pair of small cymbals, and vocalists (Figure 8.11).

The *pinn peat* repertoire is called drum music or dance music. It also includes action tunes: each tune, with its prescribed drum pattern, accompanies a particular action on stage, executed by a dancer, an actor or actress, or a puppeteer. "*Punhea Doeur*" is for a human march; "*Prathomm*" is for monkey actions; "*Krao Nak*" is for monkeys marching into battle; "*Krao Nai*" is for demons going into battle; "*Phlekk* is for the movements of birds; "*Lo*" is for floating on water; "*Cheut Chapp*" is for combat; and "*Aut*" is for expressing grief. When there is no action (as in religious ceremonies), the repertoire is treated the same as when it is used for dance or theater performances. Because this ensemble is the basis for Khmer classical music, its repertoire and traits are discussed at greater length elsewhere in this article.

Figure 8.11
In the foreground, a *pinn peat* with two female singers accompanies dance in the smaller dance pavilion at the palace. Photo by Terry E. Miller, 1988.

Vung Phleng Mohori

The term *mohori* denotes both the ensemble and its repertoire. Its origin and history are unclear. Morton (1976:102) documented the existence of a Thai cognate, *mahori*, at least as early as the Ayuthaya Period (1300s to 1700s), though Prince Damrong (1931:3) had asserted that the Thai *mahori* was of Khmer origin. The Khmer word *mohori*, more generally, is the name of a bird. With reference to music, it denotes a large ensemble composed of many kinds of instruments, but today it is applied more specifically to a small ensemble of wind, stringed, and percussion instruments, whose ideal instrumentation is high-pitched xylophone (*roneat ek*), low-pitched xylophone (*roneat thung*), duct or fipple flute (*khloy*), high-pitched two-stringed fiddle (*tror chhe*), medium-high-pitched two-stringed fiddle *(tror so tauch),* medium-low-pitched two-stringed fiddle (*tror so thomm*), low-pitched two-stringed fiddle (*tror ou*), three-stringed zither (*krapeu*), hammered dulcimer (*khimm*), small cymbals (*chhing*), and two-piece set of drums (*thaun-rumanea*). In practice the instrumentation varies from ensemble to ensemble, depending on patronage and ownership. Sixteen instruments constituted the *mohori* of the Royal Palace in Phnom Penh: *roneat ek, roneat thung, korng tauch, korng thomm, tror Khmer, tror ou, tror chhe, khloy, skor arakk, chapey dang veng, krapeu ek, krapeu thung* (now obsolete), *thaun, krapp, chhing, and rumanea* (Pich 1970:4) (Figure 8.12).

Other Khmer music ensembles such as the *arakk, kar,* and *pinn peat* function in religious contexts, but the *mohori* functions in secular contexts. It is played at banquets, accompanies a *mohori* play, and performs for folk dances of recent origin—the bamboo clappers' dance (*robaim krapp*), the pestle dance (*robaim angre*), and the harvest dance (*robaim chraut srauv*). It may also be heard in the evening after dinner, merely for entertainment and self-enjoyment. The usual performance pattern in *mohori* music calls for the vocalist and ensemble to alternate performing each section. The vocalist, accompanied only by drums (*thaun-rumanea*) and cymbals (*chhing*), sings one or two verses, followed by the ensemble playing the same sections of music.

Repertoire

To perform a piece properly, musicians must understand it thoroughly. They must know the nature and style of the piece and the instrument (usual range and style), to which they must apply their own skill and creativity. A musician shows his skill by playing his instrument stylistically, providing proper octave displacements conforming to its range in the realization of a melody, and interpreting the piece according to its proper character and sentiment.

A special trait of Khmer music centers on the notion of *bamphley*, "to cheat, to alter, to change." At the general level, it denotes an action by which a person (magician, goldsmith, seller of meat) cheats his audience or customers. The action of *bamphley* is to make things appear different from their original forms. In music, *bamphley* denotes the action of embellishing a melodic line. A given piece is not rendered the same each time it is played; it can be heard in renditions from the simplest to the most complex. The embellishment stamps the quality of performance as excellent or mediocre. Many factors contribute to the variations within a rendition: (1) a piece, particularly a short one, is usually repeated several times, and to avoid monotony, the players provide embellishment; (2) musicians have great freedom to interpret their lines; and (3) musicians' creativity and inspiration are different every time they play.

Figure 8.12
A *mohori* ensemble. Photo by Sam-Ang Sam.

Court Dance

Dance has been associated with the court of Cambodia for more than a thousand years. An ancient inscription of Vat Kdey Trap (a temple in Ba Phnom, a historical city southeast of Phnom Penh) of the Chenla period (500s–800s), mentioned the first offering of a dozen sacred dancers to the local sanctuary (Groslier 1965:283). Images of these sacred dancers (*apsara*) were first carved on the walls of Phnom Bakheng Temple during the reign of King Yasovarman (887–900).

Dancers strive to realize the concept of extreme curvilinear lines in the hands, arms, torso, and feet—the ultimate goal of Khmer court dance. *Chha banhchauh*, or the "mother of postures," constitutes the 4,500 gestures of pure dance. They are the basis and foundation of all Khmer dance and performing arts involving postures, movements, and gestures (Figure 8.13).

Figure 8.13
A court dance is performed in the smaller dance pavilion of the palace. Photo by Terry E. Miller, 1988.

There are three types of dance in the court form: pure dance, thematic dance, and dance-drama. Pure dances are composed of those movements in the "mother of postures" or "dance alphabets" that serve as the basis and foundation of Khmer dance. Pure dance movements are also seen in the transitional dance phrases when dances are accompanied by instrumental music. In the performance of court dance, dancers act out plots using the *kbach* language of dance (a system of gestures that denote meanings), all articulated by the chorus during vocal renditions. The performance thus comprises the alternation of vocal and instrumental performances.

The *Reamker* (*Fame of Preah Ream*), the Khmer version of the Indian epic *Ramayana*, has long been the principal theme for court dance. It permeates Khmer culture. The culture's classic story, it has served as a main theme for the visual and performing arts in Cambodia for centuries. Its story concerns conflicts between good and evil, involving heroes and heroines. Its monkeys and demons have divine powers that allow them to fly, lift mountains, and so on. Its main characters include Preah Ream, heir to the throne of Ayuthaya, husband of Sita and brother of Preah Leak; Reap, King of Lanka, a demon; Hanuman, the white monkey; and Sita, Preah Ream's wife.

Khmer court dance, a compound art, includes dance, mime, song, and music. Music is fixed to fit formalized movements and gestures, which depict each type of action; for example, crying, walking, and flying. Dance is traditionally accompanied by a *pinn peat*. A chorus sings texts that tell the story while dancers express the plot through movements and gestures. The *pinn peat* music sets the tone and mood and provides appropriate background sonorities for the dance, while the chorus reinforces and echoes dance movements, gestures, and dramatic expressions. They unveil the story through texts, describing what is seen on stage. In the time of King Sisowath, there were twenty-four singers plus two first female singers and two readers (Thiounn 1930:51).

The *pinn peat* provides support for court dance by introducing new actions and connecting them; it signals changes of scenes and ends them; it projects the rhythmic patterns for the dancers' footwork. When the music slows down, it gives dancers a feeling of relaxation, and when it accelerates and increases in intensity to the climax, it sharpens the dancers' actions. This is because the *pinn peat* is the one element that links the dance performance by providing cues. *Pinn peat* music also evokes a specific value, feeling, and atmosphere, be it a royal cortège, a march of a demonic army to the palace, a battlefield scene, a happy return of the monkey army, or whether a character is in grief or joy. All this can be recognized through the music in the *phleng laim* or *phleng skor* repertoire, pieces associated with specific actions, scenes, or emotions. Each instrument, particularly the drums (*sampho, skor thomm*), provides detailed dynamics and nuances for the dance.

MASKED PLAY

Masked-play performances are seasonal, ritualistic, and associated with village beliefs. They were typically performed at night during the Khmer New Year (13–15 April) or during the day of the ceremony to worship spirits (*pithi sampeah krou*), to attract rain, or to save villagers from illness. The *Reamker* traditionally served as the only story on which masked-play performances are based, but in the 1980s new themes were created by faculty of the Royal University of Fine Arts, the Department of Arts and Performing Arts, and the provincial troupe of Kampong Thom Province. Only episodes based on fortunate themes were selected for performance. Perceiving the *Reamker* as an interplay between real life and spiritual life, villagers refused to perform scenes of separation or death, fearing this would attract bad luck. The deaths of secondary characters, however, were tolerated. Often seen performed, for example, is the death of Kumphakar, whose defeat signifies the liberation of water from the sky, which had been blocked by the gigantic demon's body. Time and time again, the presentations of masked play develop the same theme, stressing the battle between good and evil. After many years, the episode of Kumphakar remains the favorite, since it plays a role in agrarian rites, especially ones appealing for rain during a drought. Accompaniment for the masked play is provided by a *pinn peat*. In contrast to the court ensemble, which primarily accompanies court dance, the village *pinn peat* accompanies village plays for religious ceremonies and the masked play or *lkhaon khaol*.

SHADOW PLAY

Before movies, television, and videos, the Khmer watched and enjoyed shadow plays. With the advent of modern forms of entertainment, these plays have declined in popularity, becoming a nearly forgotten art. Occasional performances are offered in theater contexts for tourists or on international festival stages by members of the Royal University of Fine Arts and the Departments of Arts and Performing Arts. The all-night performances of the past have given way to presentations lasting thirty minutes or less. There are two kinds of shadow plays in Cambodia: small shadow plays (*sbek tauch* "small leather") and large shadow plays (*sbek thomm* "large leather"), also called *ayang*.

Figure 8.14
Large shadow puppet (*sbek thomm*). Courtesy of Sam-Ang Sam.

Small Shadow Plays

In performance, the puppets for these shadow plays are placed between a light and the back of a white cloth. They have articulated arms and jaws. Accompaniment is provided by a *pinn peat*.

Large Shadow Plays

The large shadow play is a compound art, having dance, mime, song, music, and narration. The puppets may be as tall as 2 meters and weigh as much as 7 kilograms each. They are translucent and do not have articulated arms or jaws. Each is mounted on two sticks and handled by a male puppeteer, who also dances. Puppeteers hold the puppets firmly against a white screen lit by the flame of torches or burning coconut shells (Figure 8.14).

Ceremonial Music

Home and family remain important anchors in the lives of the Khmer people. Most ceremonies that mark Khmer life's passages—birth, the shaving of hair, marriage, illness, death—take place in a home. Seasonal celebrations held in the temple include annual temple festivals; the Rains Retreat, during which young Khmer may take vows to be monks and novices for a brief period; commemorations of the Buddha's birth and death; and the anniversary of the Buddha's first teachings. Temple fairs are among the most exciting events in traditional Cambodia, occasions to meet friends and community members, taste different foods, see many kinds of entertainments, purchase art objects and souvenirs, and feel fully a part of the Khmer culture.

The temple (*vat*), a place where monks live, study, and conduct Buddhist rituals, remains central to traditional Khmer society. It is also an educational center for villages. Funerals are held in it. Most rituals and festivals include music, especially funerals for an important personage, when performances of dances, masked plays, and shadow plays are usually included.

Spirit-Worship Ceremony (*arakk*)

Arakk is a ceremony for the worship of spirits, during which a medium attains trance to identify the cause of an illness. In the 1200s, there were "sorcerers who practiced their arts on the Cambodians" (Zhou Daguan, 1967:35). This ceremony remains prevalent in Cambodia because most people live in rural or remote areas, where hospitals and modern medicines are scarce. Consequently, people rely heavily on traditional healing methods, which use roots, leaves, tree bark, and fruits as medicines, with the intervention of mediums. In Khmer animism, people believe their happiness is determined by the spirits that live around them. Therefore, when a villager becomes ill, people believe the spirits are angry. In this situation, to heal the ill person, friends and relatives invite a medium to go into trance to tell the cause of the illness. Such a ceremony is known to be *banhchaul roup* "enter to body" or *banhchaul arakk* "enter the guardian" (Figure 8.15).

The ceremony is preceded by consultation with a village elder, someone who has knowledge of the existence of spirits and their powers. Then there is a search for the right medium. Mediums may be male or female, and they are already known in the community. In many cases, mediumship is hereditary. Finally, an *arakk* ensemble is engaged and the required offering objects secured. With the preparations completed and the arrival of the predetermined date, the ill person is brought to the place where

Figure 8.15
A spirit-ceremony ensemble (*vung phleng arakk*). Photo by Sam-Ang Sam.

the ceremony is to be performed. Then the spirit ensemble (*vung phleng arakk*) begins to perform for the medium and the spirits.

The spirit ensemble consists of a musical bow (*khse muoy*), a three-stringed fiddle (*tror Khmer, tror khse bey*), a long-necked lute (*chapey dang veng*), a double-reed pipe (*pey prabauh*), goblet drums (*skor arakk, skor dai*), small cymbals (*chhing*), and vocalists (*neak chrieng*). Outside an ensemble situation, two other instruments, a single free-reed pipe (*pey pork*) and an animal horn (*sneng*), can serve as solo instruments during the opening ceremony and invitation of the great teacher (*krou thomm*) named Samdech Preah Krou or Samdech Poan. After the interrogation, when the causes of the illnesses are known, the ensemble plays the piece "*Ke*" and offerings are made, thanking the spirits and closing the ceremony.

Wedding Ceremony (*kar*)

Weddings are exciting and important events in Khmer life. Each couple expects to be married only once in a lifetime. The traditional Khmer wedding originally lasted seven days and seven nights. Later, it was reduced to three days and three nights. Today, because of limited family financial resources and time, it is conducted within a single day and night. A long and elaborate wedding is now perceived as wasteful and impractical (Figure 8.16).

Courtship usually begins when a young man, using metaphors derived from nature (sky, moon, trees, birds, animals), makes remarks on a young girl's beauty. As in traditional Khmer society generally, it is unseemly to speak of love directly. As the relationship develops, the prospective marriage will be the subject of gossip among friends, relatives, and neighbors. This ultimately leads to formal negotiations and an engagement. The future in-laws investigate each other's families before making a serious commitment. They might consult an astrologer to read dates and signs of birth, luck, and the fortune of the prospective couple.

The *vung phleng kar,* the most popular of all Khmer music ensembles, can be found in virtually every village, town, and city in Cambodia, and even in Khmer refugee communities in the United States. Playing in this ensemble was formerly reserved for old, serious male musicians; young musicians were not allowed to play this music because the Khmer

Figure 8.16
A wedding ensemble (*vung phleng kar*). Photo by Sam-Ang Sam.

perceived wedding ceremonies and music as bestowing a blessing. Those who practiced the tradition closely even went so far as to hire only old musicians who were not blind or handicapped (Pich 1970:6). The original instrumentation was a leaf (*slekk*), a double-reed pipe (*pey prabaub*, which served as a tuning standard for the ensemble), a musical bow (*khse muoy*), a three-stringed fiddle (*tror Khmer*), a long-necked lute (*chapey dang veng*), small cymbals (*chhing*), goblet drums (*skor arakk*), and a vocalist (*neak chrieng*). Today such ensembles are commonly seen

around the temples of Angkor playing for tourists; most of the musicians are victims of landmines (Figure 8.16).

Funerals

Funerals are the saddest of all ceremonies. In the Khmer tradition, a death is announced to relatives, friends, and neighbors of the departing member of the family and community through the playing of music, and music permeates the funeral rituals. A funeral ceremony is divided into phases: predeath, precremation, procession to the crematory, the cremation, and the postceremony or death anniversary. Each phase of the funeral and its rite requires an appropriate funeral ensemble.

Traditionally, after a person dies, the corpse is kept in the house for one, two, or three days—a decision that reflects the financial resources of the family. If the deceased is a head monk, his corpse could be kept for three to six months before the cremation ceremony is performed. For a king, it could be six months to a year. If the death was caused by a contagious disease, the corpse would be kept at the temple for a shorter period of time to prevent the disease from spreading to other members of the family or community.

The *klang chhnakk*, sometimes incorrectly called *vung phleng klang khek*, is used when the corpse is kept at home or in the temple, during the procession when the corpse is carried to the crematorium, or during the cremation. Formerly, the ensemble performed on the backs of elephants as a military band to encourage the army in battle. In the ensemble's name, *klang* means "drum" and *chhnakk* is a derivation of *chhneah* meaning "victory." Thus, *klang chhnakk* or *klang chhneah* means "victory drum." Though other instruments are now added, the term means "ensemble of victory drums." The instrumentation of this ensemble includes *sralai klang khek*, *skor klang khek thnakk*, and two *skor sangna* (Figure 8.17).

Figure 8.17
A funeral ensemble.
Photo by Sam-Ang Sam.

Other Festivals

In Cambodia, ceremonies called *bonn* take place year-round, but only some require a musical ensemble. When music is required, it functions as a background by creating an appropriate ambience. Among the ceremonies using music are the flower ceremony (*bonn phka*), the fundraising ceremony (*bonn kathinn*), the ancestral or soul-day ceremony (*bonn phchum benn*), the boat-rowing ceremony (*bonn omm touk*, more commonly known as the festival of water), and the New Year's ceremony (*bonn chaul chhnaim*).

Theater

Lkhaon is a generic term referring primarily to theater or play. Over time, several types of theater—including *lkhaon yike*, *lkhaon basakk*, *lkhaon mohori*, *lkhaon ape*, *lkhaon pramotey*, and *lkhaon niyeay* (spoken)—

were found in Cambodia. Khmer court dance (*lkhaon kbach* "theater of movements," from *lkhaon* "theater" and *kbach* "movements") is also classified as a type of theater. Today in Cambodia, such theater performances are virtually nonexistent, with the exception of occasional performances offered by theater groups of the Royal University of Fine Arts and the Department of Arts and Performing Arts. This decline is due partly to the impact of video productions that are easily available at minimal cost. Consequently, these theater genres face extinction.

Yike

Yike theater consists of dancing, acting, miming, narration, songs, and music. By the end of the 1800s, it had attained great popularity and was performed in every province across the country. It used to be performed in the palace for the king, his family, and their guests. Today, it has lost its prestige and royal patronage, and is confined to villages and the Royal University of Fine Arts.

The scenery, props, and décor are largely symbolic. At first, a bedlike riser was placed on stage to symbolize a house, a palace, a mountain, or a forest, depending on the situation. Later, a door was added to symbolize the house, or a pillar for a palace—as seen, for example, in *Turn Teav* (a story like that of Romeo and Juliet). Performances at the Royal University of Fine Arts include moving clouds, flowing streams of water, waves, rain, and lightning. Lighting has also evolved, starting with torches, then using fish-oil lamps (*changkieng thma sa-oy*), petroleum lamps (*maing song*), and finally modern lighting. King Norodom introduced a style of scenery that mixed Khmer and Western conventions, representing, for example, a mountain or forest, or simply a cloudy sky. Traditionally, a *yike* performance lasted all night. University performances, however, last only two hours, presenting only the key elements of the plot.

Yike music emphasizes drumming, singing, and dancing over speaking. Each ensemble uses two to thirteen drums. Over time, it was found that the vocalists sang more in tune when accompanied by melodic instruments, and at some point two such instruments made their way into the ensemble—the *tror ou chamhieng* (half of the shell of a coconut, low-pitched, two-stringed fiddle) and later, the shawm.

Yike traditionally performed *jataka* (Buddha birth stories). Later, popular themes joined the repertoire. Scenes and stories are performed by three roles: a narrator, clowns, and dancers, all using singing. Performances begin with an invocation (*hom rong*) because Khmer performers believe ghosts, spirits, and witches live around the stage. Thus, it is natural for them to invite the supernaturals to come and bless the stage, the performers, and the performance.

Basakk

Lkhaon basakk remains a popular form of theater in Cambodia. It owes its origin to a type of Chinese theater called *hi* (*xi* in Mandarin), which was introduced in 1930 to the Basakk River region, from which it takes its name (Jacq-Hergoualc'h 1982:10). Chinese influence is obvious in the music, songs, musical instruments (especial the cymbals and woodblocks),

lkhaon
Generic term referring primarily to theater or play
yike
Village theater genre of Cham origin
tror ou
Two-stringed fiddle with coconut resonator

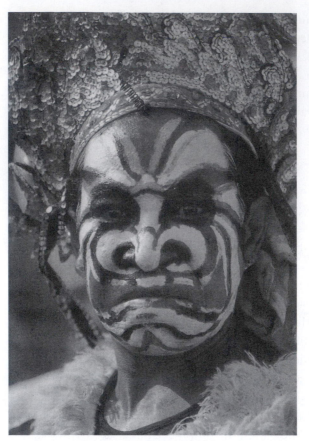

costumes, makeup, and acrobatics. In *basakk*, the actors and actresses improvise their roles according to a scenario under the guidance of a director who knows the story well. The musical ensemble comprises *tror ou chamhieng, khimm tauch, khimm thomm, pann, lo,* and *khmuoh.* The stories include *Tipp Sangvar* (a name), *Rattanavung* (a name), and *Kandanh Panhchapoar* (Five-Colored "Dreadlocks") (Figure 8.18).

Functional Repertoires

Narrative (**chrieng chapey**)

Chrieng chapey is a male-dominated, vocal, narrative-entertainment genre. In earlier times, it was performed from dusk to dawn, yet kept the audience laughing throughout the night. *Chrieng chapey* is performed by a male vocalist who accompanies himself on a long-necked lute (*chapey dang veng*). The words *chrieng chapey* mean literally "sing the lute" (*chrieng* "to sing" and *chapey* "lute"). Before 1975, the vocalist drew his repertoire from popular legends, such as *Preah Chinavung* and *Hang Yunn,* but more contemporary events—such as describing Khmer Rouge atrocities, liberation from the Khmer Rouge, and so on—have been added (Figure 8.19).

Figure 8.18
A painted-face character from a *basakk* theater performance. Photo by Sam-Ang Sam.

Figure 8.19
At the Central Market in Phnom Penh, a singer of epics sits on the street, playing a *chapey* (long-necked plucked lute). Photo by Sam-Ang Sam.

Repartee (**ayai**)

Ayai is a kind of repartee singing, usually the alternation of a man and a woman, accompanied by an ensemble of the same name. Vocalists perform for hours, improvising on short, topical themes, which are sometimes discussed and agreed on before the performance, but are otherwise created spontaneously in performance. Singers of *ayai* perform an unaccompanied line of text, immediately followed by a small ensemble of strings and a flute playing standard patterns. This art requires talent, fast thinking, a good voice, some acting ability, and mastery of Khmer poetry. Sung phrases conform to set poetic meters, often in a twenty-eight-syllable stanza, consisting of four phrases of seven syllables each. Intellectuals and the elite consider *ayai* to be a low-class entertainment for peasants. This attitude is partly due to the bawdiness of the language. In traditional Cambodia, polite young women were not allowed to watch such a performance.

Boxing (**pradall**)

Boxing is considered the number-one sport in Cambodia, soccer being second. Though the boxers wear gloves, some matches result in death. Khmer freestyle boxing is normally accompanied by the music ensemble called *vung phleng pradall* or *vungphleng klang khek*, consisting of an oboe (*sralai klang khek*), drums (*skor klang khek* or *sampho*), and small cymbals (*chhing*). The music is unique and can be immediately recognized by any Khmer familiar with boxing. The music is in two parts: for the invocation and for the fight. The former invokes a spirit (*krou* "teacher") to concentrate the boxers' minds and to give them confidence. Music for the first part is played slowly in *rubato* style; the oboe plays the melody, accompanied by a *sampho* playing strokes at important structural points in the melody. The second part is faster and in meter. As the rounds progress, the music accelerates, stopping only at the end of a round or when a boxer is knocked out. During an exciting fight, the audience joins in by clapping their hands in rhythm with the *sampho*.

Folk Dance

Because written documents pertaining to Khmer dance are lacking, the origin of Khmer folk dance is obscure. Some masters of dance believe that folk dances are as old as the Khmer people. Khmer folk dance is solely of peasant origin and use and is considered a part of the peasants' lives. It has its deepest roots and flourishes among the rural people, who dance on the village common or on a rough stage built under the spreading trees and shielded by their shade, creating a beautiful setting. In villages, there is a spirit of intimate understanding and candor among both performers and spectators.

Nature has been a major inspiration for folk dances, coupled with customs, traditions, and beliefs, all of which are interrelated. Dance is not merely an optional luxury; it is a way of life. The subjects of Khmer folk dance are various, indicating how important a role dance plays in the social, religious, and sociological life of the people.

Various types of folk dance are intended to satisfy a need for security and happiness through their relationship to belief, tradition, and recreation. The religious form of dance emerges from the customs and beliefs that give value to miracles, nature, the soul, witchcraft, and animism. The traditional form emerges from traditions practiced by peasants and farmers. This kind of art is usually performed during traditional ceremonies and is best represented by the *trott*, a dance performed during the Khmer New Year in April, marking the transition from the old year to the new. Recreational forms of dancing are sometimes

Figure 8.20
The Cambodian "fishing dance." Photo by Sam-Ang Sam.

called peasant's art or people's art. After the harvest, peasants gather to perform village dances that express their spontaneous joyfulness after the completion of their work, as exemplified by the *krapp* and the pestle dances. The most popular folk dances are those of more recent origin. They include the coconut-shell dance (*robaim tralaok*), the bamboo-clapper dance (*robaim krapp*), the pestle dance (*robaim angre*), and the cardamom-picking dance (*robaim beh kravanh*) (Figure 8.20).

The musical accompaniment for folk dance varies. Drums and oboe are used to accompany *robaim veay kuoy*, but a gong ensemble accompanies the Sacrifice of Buffalo. For ambience and effect, the large frame drum often replaces the goblet drum. One can observe such a situation in the fishing dance (*robaim nesat*), the crossbow dance (*robaim sna*), and the Cham dance (*robaim cham*).

Solo Instrumental Music

Though practically any instrument can be used for playing solo, only a few instruments in Cambodia are considered solo instruments. Such instruments, tending to have timbres and intensities that are incompatible with other instruments in an ensemble, include the conch (*saing*), the Jew's harp (*angkuoch*), the leaf (*slekk*), the single free-reed pipe (*pey pork*), the free-reed horn (*sneng*), and the chest-resonated monochord (*say diev*).

The *slekk* is merely a leaf from a tree, of which the most favored are *lumpuoh, puoch*, and *kravann*. One can simply pluck the leaf from a tree and play. The player places the leaf against the lower lip by folding the leaf to curve upward. Blowing the air out against the folded end makes the leaf vibrate against the upper lip, creating the sound. Different pitches can be obtained in the same way as in whistling. In a normal context, players of leaves are not necessarily considered musicians. People play leaves while walking to the rice fields and while watching their cattle. Besides its principal function as a solo instrument, the leaf is sometimes heard (but rarely) in the wedding ensemble.

Another solo instrument is a bamboo Jew's harp (*angkuoch, kangkuoch*). It is restricted to solo playing because it is too soft to be heard in an ensemble. Today it is no longer popular, and few people know how to play it. People often say its main function is to serenade a lover, usually a man courting his girlfriend. In practical courtship today, men and women speak to one another directly because it takes too much time to fall in love with one another using the *angkuoch* as a disguiser of speech. Using such an instrument, the man must first get the woman's attention to listen to his Jew's harp; second, she has to figure out what he is saying through it.

The free-reed horn (*sneng*) is made of a buffalo horn or oxhorn open at both ends. On one side of it, a small, rectangular hole is carved, and over it a bamboo free-reed is placed.

The instrument produces only three pitches (E, G, A, or ascending intervals of a minor third and major second). Among Khmer aerophones, this has the smallest range. It was used in an elephant-hunting expedition by hunters to attract wild elephants. The most commonly heard piece played on the free-reed horn is *"Bangkauk Sneng."* In the deep forests while a hunter approaches wild elephants, he plays the instrument, whose seemingly magical sounds are thought to have a powerful effect on elephants. On hearing such a sound, elephants turn and charge at it, giving the hunter an opportunity to catch and tame them. Besides its function in hunting elephants, *"Bangkauk Sneng"* is played in the *arakk* ceremony to invite a spirit to possess a tranced medium.

The conch shell (*saing*), devoid of any holes for fingering, is a solo instrument used only by Brahmin priests in religious events, such as the ancestral-worship ceremony and the plowing ceremony, and to signal the sovereign's arrival. It produces only one tone.

The free-reed pipe with fingering holes (*pey pork*) is normally a solo instrument because of its timbre, though it was formerly a member of the wedding ensemble. The most commonly heard pieces played on it are *"Surin," "Banloeu Prev Vedl,"* and *"Thngai Trang Kro-luoch."* When accompanying a vocalist, the pipe plays whatever the vocalist chooses to sing.

The chest-resonated monochord (*say diev*) appears in the bas-relief carvings on the walls of Cambodia's temples at Angkor and is considered to be among the oldest Khmer musical instruments. Because of the slightness of its volume, it has more commonly served as a solo instrument or to accompany a vocalist, though it formerly appeared in the wedding ensemble.

MUSIC IN KHMER RELIGIOUS CONTEXTS

The state religion of Cambodia is Theravada Buddhism, to which most of the population subscribes. Buddhists believe that life is a series of cycles of death and rebirth, during which the individual passes through a succession of incarnations. Depending on the person's conduct in previous lives, a new incarnation may be of a higher or lower status. Buddhists strive to perfect their souls to be released from the cycle of death and rebirth and attain the state of enlightenment (*nirvana*).

Though Buddhist scriptures, classical literature, epics, fables, books of games, and dance manuals all may be written in prose, most are written in verse. For dance and theater, poetic writings are adapted and set to song and music. The category of religious music embraces primarily chanting of the Buddhist scriptures and reciting poems rendered by monks and laypeople at the temple or at home. Ordinary chanting (*saut thoar*) is rendered simply by monks and laypeople, within a narrow range and in an intertwined texture, which seems chaotic on first hearing. The texts of the chants, usually in Pali (the sacred language of Theravada Buddhism), are rarely understood by either the practitioners or the listeners. This fact has led to debates over whether Khmer should become the language of Cambodian Buddhism so that all may understand. Some monks have offered chanting in Khmer, but it is not widely accepted.

Another category of Buddhist performance, the recitation of poems (*smaut*), is distinguished in style from both chanting and singing. *Smaut* occupies a position between chanting and singing, but unlike the former may be accompanied by a solo instrument such as a free-reed pipe, a duct flute, or a fiddle. For the Khmer, *smaut* is both powerful and didactic, even entertaining. It sets the mood and creates a religious atmosphere. It usually appears at various points in the sequence of a ritual. For example, a kind of *smaut* called *saraphanh* is associated with festivals celebrating the birth, death, and rebirth of the Buddha.

Musically, the distinctions among chanting (*saut thoa*), reciting (*smaut*), and singing (*chrieng*) are not well expressed in the English terms. Khmer recitation is actually considered sweet, melodious, and musical, but it differs from song because it is in the rhythm of speech (also called rubato style) rather than strict pulsation or meter. Consequently it is considered a separate category from both chant and song.

FOREIGN AND MODERN MUSIC

Popular Music in Cambodia

Popular music in Cambodia has its roots in the songs brought by French colonialists during the nineteenth and early twentieth centuries. In addition, many wealthy Khmer sent their children to France, where they heard European popular songs. By the 1950s, Khmer forms of popular music had developed, partly from songs believed to have been introduced by Filipinos, for the genre was first called "music from Manila" (*phleng Manil*). This genre, which rose in the 1950s, peaked in the mid-1960s to the mid-1970s, particularly with the nationally recognized figure Sin Sisamouth, the so-called Cambodian Elvis. Popular music in Cambodia virtually disappeared from 1975 to 1979. The Khmer Rouge, believing it symbolized the decadence of urban residents, intellectuals, aristocrats, and the capitalistic and domineering classes of society, killed most pop-song writers, composers, and singers active before 1975.

Popular music, a product of the city, is heard mostly at nightclubs, private parties, weddings, sporting events, social dances, and in restaurants. At home, people in all levels of society listen to it on radio and cassettes, and occasionally on television. Since the early 1980s, Khmer music videos have become popular. Even members of the royal family were known to listen to popular music, and King Sihanouk formerly played pop songs on the saxophone. Sometimes Khmer court dancers and musicians played backup music for pop singers. Though classical music is revered as the national music, most prefer to listen to popular music. Even so, pop musicians have a low social status, and popular music is not considered a serious career and is not studied formally. Indeed, it is put in the same category with alcohol, illegal drugs, and illicit sex.

During the period of the monarchy (before 1970), most songs dealt with themes of love. From 1970 to 1975, the period of the republic, themes of revolution critical of the monarchy appeared. From 1975 to 1979, there were no popular songs, but after the expulsion of the Khmer Rouge, themes of revolution, heroism, and liberation came to dominate. Even current hits continue these themes, plus those of separation and sadness, because too much has happened for most people to think again about love.

Khmer popular bands, *mohori samai* "modern *mohori*," use only Western instruments. Earlier, these included banjo, metal flute, cello, violin, and accordion, but more recently, so-called standard bands are made up of electric lead guitar, rhythm guitar, electric bass, keyboards, and a drum set (the standard sets used in bands in the West, but smaller).

Pop songs are classified by their rhythms and styles of dancing. *Roam vung* is a dance in a circle, *roam kbach* is a dance that echoes gestures from temple dances, *saravane* derives from southern Laos, and *laim leav* is also derived from Lao singing. The *roam vung* is danced by a couple around a table covered with flowers. Khmer versions of the bolero, the cha-cha, and swing use Western rhythms. Khmer can hear pirated cassettes and compact discs of American pop stars singing hard rock and heavy metal, but Khmer bands do not yet play these styles. Among the best-liked Western artists were Carlos Santana, the Beatles, and the Rolling Stones.

About 90 percent of pop songs follow a fixed melodic format, basically ABCB. Two stanzas (A and B) are sung, followed by a refrain (C), then by a third stanza using the same melody as B. All the known lyricists are men; women only sing. Sometimes Khmer pop singers borrow Western songs but substitute pertinent Khmer lyrics. At parties made up of guests of mixed ages, musicians play many kinds of songs to please everybody, some Western, some Khmer or Lao. Usually slow songs are followed by fast ones. The most popular rhythms danced to include the rumba, the bossa nova, the waltz, and the foxtrot. Even though the music is popular, musicians seldom earn much money; further, they must avoid overtly political lyrics, especially those critical of the regime, or face jail.

The traditional Khmer arts used to be performed for recreation, entertainment, custom, and tradition. Today, they are more likely to serve politics or tourists. New themes have been created to suit the political policies of the régime in power. Political leaders, usually with little knowledge of the arts, have used them as vehicles to assure their ascendancy.

The Khmer have one of the oldest and richest traditional cultures in Southeast Asia. With the introduction of Western culture to Cambodia, traditional cultural practices have gradually diminished as the Khmer came to see the older cultural patterns as useless and a waste of time. Traditional ceremonies, entertainments, festivals, and games were simplified, shortened, and even eliminated. Some genres, including *Ikhaon ape, Ikhaon pramotey*, and *sbek poar*, exist only in peoples' memories. Though urban residents describe *arakk* ceremonies as superstitious and regard them as things of the past, for many living in the countryside they remain part of life. Wood and stone guardians and other images connected with spirit worship and ceremony are still found throughout Cambodia, and belief in them remains alive among Khmer living outside the country.

The mass media are largely responsible for the growth of popular music and the fading away of traditional music. This change coincides with the increasing neglect of Khmer musicians and the populace. With the explosion of technology and the increased importation of Western culture, particularly rock, fewer and fewer youngsters in Cambodia understand, appreciate, or practice their traditional culture. Poor economic conditions have also contributed to the decline of traditional culture.

In modern Khmer society, traditional music has a minor place in concert halls, during dance and theatrical performances, and in a few ceremonies. The duration of Khmer

sralai
Quadruple-reed aerophone with bulging shape
khloy
End-blown duct flute of bamboo
kantrüm
Village Khmer ensemble in northeast Thailand

weddings, which formerly lasted seven days and nights, has been reduced to barely one day. In the past, music was played almost continuously, but now it has been cut to a few hours or a single morning. Not surprisingly, many old Khmer musicians have given up playing music since the rewards are meager, and they have had to choose more lucrative professions to support their families, which naturally takes precedence over the preservation of traditions. Traditional musicians have an even lower status than pop musicians, who themselves are paid badly.

There may be no other country in the world whose people have more strongly attached their lives to the arts as symbols of their soul and identity. Among the refugee communities in the United States, the Hmong are known for their needlework and the Vietnamese for their popular music, but the Khmer are known for their commitment and dedication to the classical performing arts. Reflecting this image, Khmer refugees have worked to rebuild their culture for almost two decades, both in refugee camps and after 1975, when resettled in the United States and France. Such rebuilding has largely depended on a handful of devoted artists. In new Western environments and settings, where they find no Khmer monasteries, temples, palaces, schools, and universities (sites that once passed on the knowledge of the traditional arts), Khmer artists have had to find other methods, often at their own expense, to see that their arts, which are so dear to them, survive.

REFERENCES

Blanchard, Wendell, ed. 1958. *Thailand: Its People, Its Society, Its Culture*. New Haven, CT: HRAF.

Chonpairot, Jarernchai. 1981. "The Diffusion of the Vina in Southeast Asia." In *Proceedings of the Saint Thyagaraja Music Festivals: Cleveland, Ohio, 1978–81,* ed. T. Temple Tuttle, 98–108. Cleveland: Greater Cleveland Ethnographic Museum.

His Royal Highness Prince Damrong (Rajanubhap). 1931. *Siamese Musical Instruments.* 2nd ed. Bangkok: The Royal Institute.

Groslier, Bernard-Philippe. 1965. "Danse et musique sous les rois d'Angkor." *Felicitation Volumes of Southeast Asian Studies* 2:283–292.

Hood, Mantle. 1982. *The Ethnomusicologist.* 2nd ed. Kent, OH: Kent State University Press.

Jacq-Hergoualc'h, Michel. 1982. "Le Roman source d'inscription de la peinture khmère à la fin du XIXᵉ et au debut du XXᵉ siècle." *Bulletin de l'École Française d'Extrême-Orient* 126:3–10.

Morton, David. 1974. "Vocal Tones in Traditional Thai Music." *Selected Reports in Ethnomusicology* 2(l):89–99.

———. 1976. *The Traditional Music of Thai.* Berkeley: University of California Press.

Pich, Sal. 1970. *Lumnoam Sangkhep ney Phle Khmer* (A Brief Survey on Khmer Music). Phnom Penh: Éditions de l'Institut Bouddhique.

Sachs, Curt. 1940. *The History of Musical Instruments.* New York: Norton.

Smithies, Michael. 1971. "*Likay*: A Note on the Origin, Form, and Future of Siamese Folk Opera." *Journal of the Siam Society* 59:33–64.

Thiounn, Samdech Chaufea. 1930. *Danses cambodgiennes.* Phnom Penh: Bibliothèque Royale Cambodge.

Zhou Daguan. 1967. *Notes on the Customs of Cambodia,* trans. from French of Paul Pelliot by J. Gillman D'arcy Paul. Bangkok: Social Science Association Press.

Thailand

Terry E. Miller

HISTORY

Delimiting a discussion of "Thai music" to the peoples living within the borders of the Kingdom of Thailand masks the true extent of the "Tai people," a variety of linguistically related groups found in northern Vietnam, southwestern China, throughout Laos, and in northern Burma. While the majority of people living in present-day Thailand are described as "Siamese Thai," to distinguish them from the "Laotian Thai" living in the northeastern region, the Thai population, and as a result Thai culture, is made more complex by the fact that a great many other ethnic groups long ago blended together, including Chinese,

Khmer, and Mon. In addition, there are several non-Thai ethnic groups living within Thailand including Khmer in the lower northeast, small groups of Mon-Khmer in the upper northeast, Malay in the deep south, and a variety of upland minorities in the north.

Thailand today is comprised of 76 provinces with a total population of 64.6 million (July, 2006). Bangkok (Krungthep Mahanakhon ["City of Angels"]), with a population of approximately 10 million, dominates the country, while Khon Kaen, Nakhon Ratchasima, and Chiangmai are the next largest cities. The great central plain is drained by the country's most important river, the Chao Phraya, which empties into the Gulf of Siam just below Bangkok.

The first historical Tai kingdoms were at Chiangmai and Sukhothai in modern-day Thailand, both founded in the 1200s. Ayuthaya, founded in 1350, gradually eclipsed the others. This period saw the final destruction of the Khmer Kingdom at Angkor by Ayuthaya in 1431, the golden age of the Tai court culture and penetration by Europeans in the 1600s. The French, among others, had designs on the Kingdom of Siam (as they had on other areas of Southeast Asia), but plans to convert the king to Roman Catholicism and gain control of his kingdom came to naught: Siam remained a neutral, independent buffer state between the later British colonies of Burma and Malaya and the French Indochinese colonies (Laos Cambodia, Vietnam). The Burmese destroyed Ayuthaya in 1767, but the Siamese reestablished a court at Thon Buri (opposite modern Bangkok) the same year, and moved the capital to Bangkok in 1782.

The current era, called Rattanakosin, has maintained unity through a succession of nine kings, each called Rama, of the Chakri dynasty. Westernization began during the reigns of King Mongkut (Rama IV, ruled 1851–1868) and King Chulalongkorn (Rama V, ruled 1868–1910). A bloodless coup d'état in 1932 ended the absolute monarchy, and in 1939 the name of the country was changed to Prathet Thai (Land of the Free), westernized as Thailand. The current monarch is His Majesty Bhumibol Adulyadej (Rama IX), who ascended the throne in 1946 and is now the world's longest reigning monarch.

THE FOUR CULTURAL REGIONS

The Thai understand their country as having four cultural regions: center, south, north, and northeast. Each is distinguished from the other in dialect, diet, housing, decorative motifs, literature, and especially music. Though the dialects are interrelated, people from one region tend to have trouble understanding people from another. This is especially true with regard to the texts of songs. The language of the Siamese Tai in central Thailand, known commonly as Thai, has become the official language of the country; it is the language of the national media, officialdom, and school.

Central Thailand consists of a vast plain emanating north from the capital, Bangkok, with the Chao Phraya River at its center. Besides Bangkok, central Thailand's thirty-five provinces include the ancient cities of Ayuthaya, Lopburi, Sukhothai, and Nakhon Pathom. Prominent among its musics are the classical court tradition, various repartee songs, and theatrical genres (*lakhawn chatri* and *li-ke*).

Southern Thailand's fourteen provinces occupy the peninsula extending along the Burmese border to the Malaysian border. The southernmost provinces, Yala and Narathiwat, were originally Malay sultanates, and consequently the typically southern Thai culture is mostly found farther north, especially in Nakhon Si Thammarat and Phatthalung provinces. The two most prominent musical genres of this region are shadow-puppet theater (*nang talung*) and human theater (*manora*).

Northern Thailand, consisting of the nine provinces in the northwestern bulge bordering Laos and Burma, centers on Chiangmai. In addition to the Thai population, these provinces are home to significant numbers of upland peoples unrelated to the Thai linguistically and whose music is treated elsewhere in this volume [see MUSIC OF UPLAND MINORITIES IN BURMA, LAOS, AND THAILAND]. Northern Thai music is distinct for one ensemble (*salaw süng pi*), the fingernail dance, and the candle dance.

Northeastern Thailand's eighteen provinces are on the Korat Plateau, extending to the Maekhong River, bordering Laos and Cambodia. Culturally diverse, this region includes the Korat Tai (around the city of Nakhon Ratchasima, known also as Khorat), the Khmer-dominated provinces along the Cambodian border, and the mainstream culture of the remaining provinces, known among the Thai as Isan (a Pali-Sanskrit word meaning "northeast"), whose culture is essentially the same as that of the lowland Lao in Laos. Around Khorat, where the language is closer to Siamese Tai than to Laotian Tai, the main musical genres are *li-ke* and a kind of repartee-song. In the three provinces bordering Cambodia, the main language is Khmer, and the distinctive musical genres are one traditional ensemble (*kantrüm*), a narrative type, and two classically based ensembles. The most distinctive Isan genres are highly developed forms of repartee called *lam*, accompanied by the region's most famous instrument, the *khaen*, a free-reed mouth organ. In Laos, lowland Lao music is closely related to the music of northeast Thailand.

VILLAGE AND COURT

In Thailand, as in most Southeast Asian countries, a basic distinction is to be made between village and court. Traditions of the latter were originally associated with the ruling elite, their ceremonies, and their entertainments, while those of the former were part of rural life and closely associated with a cycle of festivals related to agriculture and Buddhism. Village traditions in Thailand are often based on the idea of repartee, a stylized courtship ritual between male and female singers.

With the increasing importance of modern urban life centered in Bangkok, a more fundamental distinction is to be made between traditional musics (both court and village) and modern music—primarily popular songs, disseminated both live and through the media. In spite of the growth of popular culture, classical music, dance, and theater remain strong because of their importance for Thai identity—internally, externally, and for rituals and other formal events. At the same time, these classical arts, formerly reserved for the aristocracy, are now primarily transmitted through both private and public schools and universities, allowing anyone, regardless of background, access to them. The educational system has become the bastion of Thai classical music, a place where anyone, even villagers from a poor province, can study with traditional masters. Musical study leading to college and university degrees is a recent development, thanks to a growing appreciation of the arts as a legitimate academic area.

Nevertheless, it would be difficult to argue that classical music plays more than a minor role in the musical life of the modern Thai. Increasingly affluent and rapidly growing, Bangkok's population primarily listens to various kinds of popular music, some more Thai in style than others, heard through the media (radio and television), on inexpensive cassette tapes, compact discs, and music video compact discs (VCDs), and in live performances. The people of smaller cities and villages tend to follow Bangkok's lead, though in the less developed areas of the kingdom, nonclassical traditional musics remain important.

GENERAL OBSERVATIONS ON THAI CLASSICAL MUSIC

Some classical musicians have achieved a certain prominence as soloists, but Thai music is primarily ensemble-oriented—unlike, for example, Indian music, where star soloists predominate. Since little improvisation beyond idiomatic ornamentation occurs in the music, master performers are respected more for their extensive repertories, subtle ornamentation, and lineage than for virtuoso techniques. This is not to say that solo playing is not cultivated—a few flashy musicians have brought solo playing to an extremely high level—but that this aspect is secondary to the ensemble, in which the individual's sound is subordinated to the mixture.

The traditional mode of training was time consuming but thorough. The student may have lived in the home of the master, spending many hours a day in study and supervised practice. Masters taught everything by rote, showing students a phrase at a time and asking them to repeat it. As each phrase was mastered, the piece was repeatedly played from the beginning to that point. Gradually, entire pieces were learned. Neither notation nor note taking was permitted; discussion and questions were unusual. Over time, the student's repertoire increased. Even today, these methods prevail among traditional masters and in the College of Dramatic Arts and its branches. Even young musicians can play hours of difficult music entirely from memory. Nevertheless, as the pace of Thai life has quickened, less and less time remains for this sort of teaching. In Bangkok, students may have to settle for carefully scheduled lessons once or twice a week.

Notation is a recent phenomenon, from about the third decade of the twentieth century. Though the Fine Arts Department has published classical music transcribed into staff notation, the notations used by Thai students are much simpler, being either tablature or pitch notation, the latter indicated either by arabic numerals or Thai initials of the solfège system. Students learning string music are the most likely to use notation, and most of the published collections are either generic or for these instruments.

Musicians observe obligatory conventions of etiquette. It is customary to remove one's shoes when entering a home or a temple; students also do so in many public-school classrooms. Since Thai instruments are played on the floor, the removal of shoes before entering an instrument room is requisite. Instruments must be treated with respect, and consequently rough treatment—especially stepping over them—is forbidden. Students were traditionally required to keep their heads below their master's, even to the point of crawling into the room. Today, that custom is not strictly followed, but it is still polite to keep one's head below the heads of important people. Before playing, students will fold their hands in the praying position (*wai*) and perform a brief *wai khru* ritual in remembrance of their teacher and their teacher's lineage. Before public performances, entire ensembles or dramatic troupes perform more elaborate rituals.

IDIOPHONES

Concussion Idiophones

Ching. Two identical bronze cymbals with thick walls and the shape of a shallow teacup are joined with a cord which passes through a hole in the center of each. The name of the instrument is onomatopoetic, describing the undamped sound produced when the cymbals are struck together; the damped sound is described as *chap*. The function of the instrument is to provide an audible beat, marking the accented and unaccented beats in accompanying both instrumental and vocal music.

Chap. Onomatopoetic in name, the *chap* cymbals are also of bronze, flatter and thinner than the *ching*. Two sizes are distinguished: the *chap lek* "small *chap*," measuring 12 to 14 centimeters in diameter, and the *chap yai* "large *chap*," about 23 to 26 centimeters in diameter.

Krap "castanets." Again onomatopoetic for its *krap-krap-krap* sound, three specific types of *krap* "castanets" are distinguished: *krap khu*, *krap phuang*, and *krap sepha*. The *krap khu* "pair of castanets" is rarely heard and consists of either two pieces of a bamboo tube split lengthwise, or two pieces of wood carved like bamboo halves. The *krap phuang* "cluster castanets" is a bundle of five thin pieces of hardwood or ivory 21 to 22 centimeters long, alternating with six sheets of brass enclosed in two flared wooden or ivory end pieces. Finally, the recitation castanets (*krap sepha*) consist of two polished hardwood bars 18 to 21 centimeters long (Figure 9.1).

ching
Pair of small, thick metal cymbals connected by a cord
chap
Medium-size cymbals, connected by a cord, flatter and thinner than the ching
krap
Several kinds of percussion idiophones

Figure 9.1
Thai percussion: (from left to right, top to bottom) *thon, rammana, chap lek, krap,* and *ching.* Photo by Terry E. Miller, 2005.

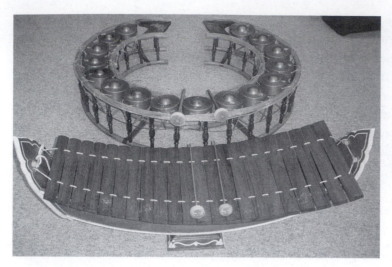

Figure 9.2
Ranat ek xylophone (front) and *khawng wong yai* gong circle (rear) Photo by Terry E. Miller, 2005

ranat ek
Higher xylophone, with twenty-one keys
ranat thum
Lower-pitched xylophone, with seventeen or eighteen keys

Struck Idiophones

Bar Idiophones

Ranat ek. The foremost xylophone, *ra-nat ek* "first" or "principal," is distinctive to mainland Southeast Asia. As described by Dhanit,

The present model of the *rana-t ay-k* [*ranat ek*] has twenty-one keys. The lowest-toned key is 38 centimeters long, 5 centimeters wide and 1.5 centimeters thick. The keys decrease in size and become thicker as the tones become higher. The highest-toned key is 30 centimeters long. The keys are hung on a cord which passes through holes at each of the nodes of the keys—7 to 9 centimeters in from the end of each key. This "keyboard" is suspended over a boat-shaped body from metal hooks on the end pieces—two on each end. The distance between the two end pieces is 120 centimeters. (Dhanit 1987:17)

Ranat thum. Larger and lower in range than the *ranat ek,* the *ranat thum* measures 126 centimeters along the keyboard, with the seventeen or eighteen keys ranging in size from 42 by 6 centimeters at the lower end to 35.5 by 5 centimeters at the upper. Unlike the *ranat ek*'s curved wooden resonator supported on a square base, the *ranat thum*'s resonator is parallel to the floor, supported on four feet. The idiom is quite unlike that of the *ranat ek*; broken octaves and syncopated rhythms—considered playful by the Thai—predominate. This instrument acts as a foil to the *ranat ek*, playing around the main notes of the melody rather than reinforcing them.

Khawng wong yai. Meaning "gongs in a circle" (*wong*), this instrument is of two sizes, larger (*yai*) and smaller (*lek*). A smaller version of the *khawng wong yai*, made for the *mahori* ensemble, is softer in tone to balance the strings. The instrument consists of sixteen brass-bossed gongs horizontally mounted on an oval rattan frame. The player enters the frame through the rear gap; sitting cross-legged, he strikes the boss with a pair of disc mallets, the soft ones of wood covered with cloth, the hard ones of untanned buffalo hide. The musical function of the *khawng wong yai* is to play the *luk khawng*, the least dense version of the melody, sometimes conceived as the basic form of the melody, and students customarily begin with this instrument. The idiom consists primarily of octaves, fourths, fifths, and single-note playing (Figure 9.2).

Khawng wong lek. For the smaller oval, eighteen gongs vary in diameter from 13 centimeters on the player's far left to 9.5 centimeters on the right and have a range one octave above that of the *khawng wong yai*. Unlike the *khawng wong yai*, the part played by the smaller instrument is denser, more melodic and active, exhibiting many stereotyped ornamental figures. Consequently, only advanced performers play it.

Khawng mawn. So similar and yet so different, the *khawng mawn* consists of fifteen or sixteen gongs mounted in a beautifully carved wooden frame shaped like the letter U with a single pedestal. The largest gongs are to the player's left, and a humanlike figure, a god's face (*na phra*), is carved on the frame (Figure 9.3).

Membranophones

Single-headed drums

Thon or thap. This inverted-vase or goblet-shaped drum, with body of clay or (less commonly) wood, is related in shape to drums from North Africa and Western Asia, like the Arabic *darabuka* and the Persian *dombak.* The head, directly laced to a metal ring at the waist of the body, cannot be tuned. These are used with central Thai classical ensembles to accompany certain kinds of songs. The *thon mahori* is slightly larger with a clay body and a head of any of various materials (calfskin, goatskin, snakeskin). The body is sometimes highly decorated with gold, silver, lacquer, mother-of-pearl, or pieces of colored glass. Both types are played by the right hand, leaving the left available to influence the tone by covering the open end.

Rammana. This is a shallow, conical, wooden drum with a single head of calfskin tacked directly to the body—a method of fastening that suggests a Chinese origin, though the Chinese are not known to have had a drum of this type. This drum is used with the *thon* in *mahori* and *khrüang sai.*

Figure 9.3
Khawng mawn gong rack (front) with *ranat ek* and *ranat thum* xylophones in rear. Photo by Terry E. Miller, 2007.

Double-Headed Drums

Klawng that. The largest Thai classical drum, used as a pair, is the *klawng that, klawng* being a generic term for drum and *that* the specific type. Each of its heads, measuring some 46 centimeters in diameter, is attached firmly to the wooden body with metal tacks, or less commonly with pegs of wood, ivory, or bone. Barrow-shaped, the body is a hollowed-out piece of hardwood.

Taphon. The *taphon* is the most significant drum because it is considered quasi-sacred and must therefore be kept in a high place. An asymmetrical barrel drum with the larger head (25 centimeters in diameter) to the player's left and the smaller head (22 centimeters) to the right, it is played with the hands.

Klawng khaek. The modifier *khaek* suggests vaguely an Indian, Muslim, or (according to Dhanit) Javanese origin. Indeed, nearly identical drums are found in Malaysia (*gendang*) and Java (*kendhang*), and the Indian *mridangam* is similar. The Thai *klawng khaek* is a pair of drums with carved wooden bodies, 58 centimeters long, nearly conical in shape, but having a slight bulge near the larger head. The *klawng khaek* are sometimes used in *piphat* for informal occasions and more routinely in *mahori.* With the conical double-reed aerophone (*pi chawa*), however, they are requisite in the accompaniment to Thai boxing (Figure 9.4).

Boeng mang kawk. In *piphat mawn*, an observer is likely to encounter *boeng mang kawk*, a set of seven *boeng mang*, hung vertically in a semicircular wooden frame about

Figure 9.4
A military procession in the murals at Wat Phra Keo, Bangkok (early 1800s). Left to right (lower row): *klawng chana, pi chawa, klawng yao, trae ngawn*, and *sang*; (upper row) *trae ngawn* and *sang*. Photo by Terry E. Miller, 1988.

116 centimeters wide and 66 centimeters high. The heads are tuned with rice and ash to produce the seven tones of the tuning system, and each drum is played with the hands by a person seated on a stool or chair within the frame.

Aerophones

Flutes

Khlui. The *khlui*, a vertical block flute, has six to seven holes for fingering on the upper side and a hole for the thumb on the lower (with the opening for the duct). Instruments made of bamboo have a pierced node about 2.5 centimeters from the lower end, but *khlui* are also made of hardwood and plastic; formerly, some were made of ivory. The *khlui* is made in three sizes: *khlui lip* (36 centimeters long, 2 centimeters in diameter, pitched in d), *khlui phiang aw* (45 centimeters long, 4 centimeters diameter, pitched in c), and *khlui u* (60 centimeters long, 4.5 centimeters diameter, pitched in G). The *khlui u* has only six holes for fingering on top. The pitch of each instrument matches one of the modes or scales, and depending on the "key" of the piece and the ensemble, players choose a particular instrument.

Reeds

Pi. The double reed (*pi*) is distinctive in shape and peculiar to Thailand and Cambodia (where it is known as *sralai*). Externally the carved wooden body flares slightly at the ends, while the middle bulges with fourteen pairs of lathed rings. Six holes for fingering on the

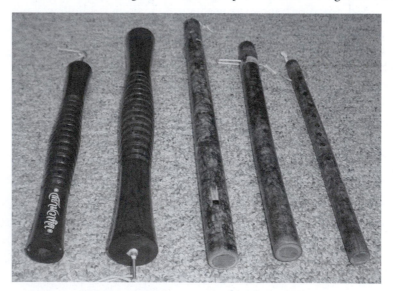

Figure 9.5
Thai aerophones: (from left to right) *pi nawk, pi nai* quadruple reeds, *khlui oo, khlui phiang aw*, and *khlui lip* fipple flutes. Photo by Terry E. Miller, 2005.

top and a single hole for the thumb on the bottom are within these rings. The bore is slightly conical. A metal tube (*kam phuat*) is placed into the upper end, sealed into the *pi* with cotton thread. Onto this tube are tied four small palmyra-palm-leaf pieces in two double layers; when played, they are turned vertically (sometimes horizontally) within the player's oral cavity, not held between the lips. The *pi* idiom, with its flexible pitch, sliding between fixed pitches, and flowing rhythm, contrasts markedly with the other instruments of the ensemble, all having fixed pitch and played with attention to the beat (Figure 9.5).

Pi chawa. The *pi chawa*, ostensibly from Java (*Chawa*), is a conical wooden tube, again with seven upper and one lower holes for fingering, is 27 centimeters long; with the wooden bell (7 to 8 centimeters in diameter), it measures 38 to 39 centimeters long. This instrument is associated with the *klawng khaek*. Formerly used in royal and military processions, it is now heard primarily as accompaniment to boxing, in certain funeral ensembles, and for episodes from the *Inao* story in *lakhawn* drama.

Pi mawn. The largest of the three conical *pi*, that of the Mawn (Mon) has a wooden body 50 centimeters long and a metal flared bell another 23 centimeters long, joined loosely to the body with cord.

Chordophones

Lutes

Krajappi. The *krajappi*, a plucked lute, is flamboyant, but is now rarely seen, and measures 180 centimeters from top to bottom. The somewhat oval, flat body is 44 centimeters long, 40 centimeters wide, and 7 centimeters thick; the tapered neck, which curves back beyond the tuning pegs, is 138 centimeters long. Four gut strings, attached to four lateral pegs, run over eleven frets on the neck and over a wooden bridge and are attached to a tailpiece. The player plucks the strings with a plectrum of horn, bone, or tortoiseshell.

Saw sam sai. The name of the instrument literally means bowed lute or fiddle (*saw*) with three (*sam*) strings (*sai*). Elegantly rounded and triangular, its body consists of the lower half of a special coconut with three bulges and the opening covered with a goat or calfskin resonator. Wooden and fretless, the neck is 24 centimeters long and has three lateral tuning pegs; the portion below the body measures 19.5 centimeters and tapers into a metal spike. Three gut strings, tuned A–d–g, are anchored through a hole in the hollow lower piece, run over an arched ivory or plastic bridge, disappear through a hole into the neck just below the tuning pegs, and fasten inside. A separate, S-shaped, wooden bow stick 86 centimeters long has horsehair tied at the tip and extends to the handle. Seated on the floor with legs to the left, the player turns the fiddle on its spike, resting the neck of the instrument on his shoulder, holding the bow underhanded and stationary.

Saw duang. The higher pitched of the Thai two-stringed fiddles, the *saw duang* has a cylindrical body of wood (sometimes ivory) 13 centimeters long and 7 centimeters in diameter. A wooden neck 70 centimeters long pierces the body near the python or boa resonator, while the rear is left open. The two strings, tuned g and d', are attached to the slightly protruding neck below the body and run over a small bamboo bridge to two rear pegs near the top. A loop of string, about two-thirds up the neck, pulls the strings toward a fretless neck, defining the playing area and putting the requisite tension on the string. The bow hairs, passing between the strings, are pulled against the lower string and pushed against the upper, while the left hand touches the strings without pulling them against the neck.

Saw u. The lower-pitched two-stringed bowed lute consists of a large, round coconut, one side of which has been cut away and covered with goat or calfskin, 13 to 15 centimeters wide. The rear portion has holes to let the sound out, with a carving, usually of Hanuman, the white monkey of the Ramayana story. As with the *saw duang*, the two gut strings, tuned c and g, are attached at the lower end to the base of a neck 80 centimeters long and pass over a bridge of tightly rolled cloth to two rear pegs; similarly, a cord loop pulls the strings toward the neck, and the bow hairs pass between the strings.

Zithers

Ja-khe. The name of the Thai zither is derived from *jarakhe* "crocodile" and likely relates to the Mon equivalent, *mi gyaung*, also meaning crocodile, which has realistic zoological features; the Thai *ja-khe* has only the abstract animal form. Although played on the floor like a zither, it is arguably a lute, since the body and neck are differentiated. The *ja-khe* measures 130 to 132 centimeters long, divided into a "head" portion (52 centimeters long, 28 centimeters wide, 9 to 12 centimeters deep) and a "tail" portion (81 centimeters long, 11.5 centimeters wide). The entire body is supported by five legs, 8 centimeters high. Along the neck of the hardwood body are eleven high frets graduated from 2 centimeters in height near the center to 3.5 centimeters in height at the three lateral tuning pegs. There are three strings, tuned C–G–c, but most playing occurs on the upper two. The player fastens a 5- to 6-centimeter-long ivory or bone plectrum to the right index finger by wrapping the plectrum's silk cord around the finger and bracing it with the thumb and middle finger (Figure 9.6).

Khim. Ironically, the *khim*, a hammered dulcimer, is probably the most popular of Thai instruments but also the most clearly of recent and Chinese origin. Derived from the Chaozhou Chinese *yang qin*, the *khim* is a small, butterfly-shaped (trapezoidal) dulcimer, 86 centimeters on the longer side, 56 centimeters on the shorter, and 34 centimeters wide. It has two sets of bridges and fourteen courses of strings, some with four strings, some only three. Used primarily for solo playing and much favored by female players, the *khim* can also be added to the *khrüang sai* and the *mahori* ensembles.

Figure 9.6
Students at Chulalongkorn University, Bangkok, have a group lesson: left to right, *ja-khe, ranat thum, saw duang.* The teacher is at the far right. Photo by Terry E. Miller, 1988.

ENSEMBLES

In importance, the ensemble far outweighs the instrumental solo and is at least the equal of the vocalist. A singer, though crucial in telling a story in drama or conveying the words of nontheatrical songs, is rarely accompanied by an ensemble but alternates with it. Over time, the names and instrumentation of most ensembles have been standardized, but an observer is as likely to encounter ensembles that in some way violate the published standards as to find ones in rigid conformity. Each ensemble includes at least one aerophone (a flute or a double reed), which determines the pitch in which the music is played. Here, the standard contemporary ensembles will be described first, followed by a discussion of what is known of their history.

Thai ensembles perform seated on the floor, players sitting cross-legged or with legs to the left. Positions for each instrument are fairly standard, but when accompanying theater (where space is limited), musicians may seat themselves differently. Except for some student ensembles using stringed instruments, musicians play from memory, not notation. Men traditionally wear high-collared, white, military-style jackets (after British colonial styles) and wraparound trousers (*jong kraben*). Women often wear colorful wraparound trousers, a tight-fitting top, and a large sash over the left shoulder.

Piphat

Earlier called *phinphat* (the equivalent Khmer ensemble is still called *pinn peat*), the *piphat* is the most important ensemble of Thailand. Traditionally, all players were male, and the ensemble accompanied masked plays (*khon*), nonmasked dance plays (*lakhawn*), epic narratives (*sepha*), and various rituals or ceremonies. The inclusion of the *pi* quadruple reed is what normally makes this ensemble distinctive, but variants use other aerophones. The standard *piphat* uses hard mallets (*mai khaeng*) and is configured in three sizes; four other types are also called *piphat*.

Piphat Khrüang Ha

Literally "five instruments," this ensemble actually includes six if both drum and cymbals are counted separately (Figure 9.7): one *pi nai,* one *ranat ek,* one *khawng wong yai,* one *taphon,* one pair of *ching,* and one set of *klawng that.*

Piphat Khrüang Khu

Literally "pairs of instruments," this ensemble includes nine instruments with an optional tenth: two *pi* (*pi nai* and *pi nawk*, though today the latter, being nearly obsolete, is replaced with a second *pi nai*), one *taphon,* one pair of *ching,* two *ranat* (*ranat ek and ranat thum*), two *khawng wong* (*khawng wong yai* and *khawng wong lek*), one pair of *klawng that,* and (optionally) one *mong.*

Piphat Khrüang Yai

Literally "large [group of] instruments," this ensemble includes thirteen instruments, with another optional one: two *pi* (as above),

Figure 9.7
A *piphat khrüang ha* with *ranat thum* added in performance at the Siam Society, Bangkok. Left to right: *khawng wong yai, taphon, ranat ek, pi nai,* and *ranat thum.* Photo by Terry E. Miller, 1972.

two *ranat* (as above), two metallophones, *ranat ek lek* and *ranat thum lek,* two *khawng wong* (as above), one *taphon,* one pair of *ching,* one pair of *chap lek,* optionally, one pair of *chap yai,* one *mong,* and one pair of *klawng that.*

Piphat Mai Nuam

Literally "soft mallets" (opposed to the above, presumed to be *mai khaeng* "hard mallets"), this ensemble is a softer-sounding ensemble. In it, the fipple flute (*khlui phiang aw*) replaces the *pi,* and a coconut-body fiddle (*saw u*) is added.

Piphat Mawn

The *piphat* of the Mon people of western Thailand and Burma, this ensemble is actually played by Thai. The repertory, primarily pieces in *mawn* (Mon) accent, is most often heard at funerals.

Mahori

The word *mahori* originally meant "instrumental music" but later came to denote an ensemble that specifically includes melodic idiophones, chordophones, and a flute. The three-stringed fiddle (*saw sam sai*) is the leader of the *mahori,* the only ensemble in which it plays. Earlier, the main function of the *mahori* had been entertainment, but later it replaced the *piphat* in accompanying *lakhawn,* a genre of dance-drama (Figure 9.8).

Mahori Boran

The "old ensemble," this consisted of four instruments: one *saw sam sai,* one *krajappi,* one *thon,* and one *krap phuang.*

Mahori Khrüang Hok

The six-instrument *mahori* (with seven instruments in all) includes the instruments of the *mahori boran,* plus three more: one *khlui,* one pair of *ching,* and one *rammana.*

Mahori Wong Lek

The "small ensemble," using nine instruments, is in contemporary use (Figure 9.8): one *ranat ek* (*mahori* size for this and all melodic idiophones), one *khawng wong yai,* one *saw sam sai,* one *saw duang,* one *saw u,* one *ja-khe,* one *khlui phiang aw,* one pair of drums (*thon and rammana*), and one pair of *ching.*

Mahori Khrüang Khu

Literally "instruments in pairs," this ensemble uses nine paired instruments and one *mong*: two *ranat* (*ek* and *thum*), two *khawng wong* (*yai* and *lek*), two *saw sam sai,* two *ja-khe,* two *saw duang,* two *saw u,* two *khlui* (*phiang aw* and *lip*), one pair of drums (*thon* and *rammana*), one pair of *chap lek,* and one *mong.*

Mahori Khrüang Yai

Literally "large [number of] instruments," this ensemble includes all instruments in the ensemble above, plus the following: two metallophones (*ranat ek lek* and *ranat thum lek*), one pair of *chap yai*, and one additional *khlui* (*khlui u*).

Khrüang Sai

This is a string ensemble (*khrüang* "instruments," *sai* "string"). Its history is unknown, but its lineage appears fairly recent, possibly from only the twentieth century. Its function is not clearly defined since it has not been closely associated with either theater or dance. Its basic instrumentation is fixed, consisting of the two-stringed bowed lutes and zither plus flute, but instruments of diverse origin have been included at times (Figure 9.9).

Khrüang Sai Khrüang Lek or Khrüang Sai Wong Lek

A small ensemble (Figure 9.9), this consists of: one *saw duang*, one *saw u*, one *ja-khe*, one *khlui phiang aw,* one pair of drums (*thon* and *rummana*), and one pair of *ching*.

Khrüang Sai Khrüang Khu

An ensemble in pairs, this includes: two *saw duang*, two *saw u*, two *ja-khe*, two *khlui* (*khlui phiang aw* and *khlui lip*), one pair of drums (*thon* and *rummana*), one pair of *ching*, one pair of *chap lek,* and one *mong*.

Khrüang Sai Pi Chawa

Having some characteristics of the *khrüang sai*, this ensemble can also be seen as an expanded *klawng khaek* ensemble that accompanies boxing: one *saw duang,* one *saw u,* one *ja-khe,* one *pi chawa,* one *khlui phiang aw,* one pair of *ching,* and one pair of *klawng khaek.*

CONTEXTS FOR CLASSICAL MUSIC

Though Thai widely acknowledge the importance of classical music, both as a symbol of their culture and as an art expressive of what it means to be Thai, few actually choose to listen to it. Opportunities to hear it remain scarce, and with few economic incentives to encourage its study and practice, this situation is not likely to change. Alas, classical music better represents the past than the present and its status is reinforced by the apparent lack of development in the tradition since the early 1900s. Thai classical music is more a museum piece, maintained as a living specimen in what David Morton (1976) has called a hothouse environment than a vital part of modern Thai life. It was not always so. Though during its heyday classical music was largely for the aristocracy, it was also cultivated locally for important community and Buddhist rituals.

Historical Contexts

Most early European sources mention Thai making music as part of court activities, though accounts as to what ensembles or instruments were used remain vague. According to early documents, music accompanied the activities of the king (and likely other noblemen) throughout the day and wherever he went. When the king traveled by land his subjects were forbidden to gaze on his person, and a group of musicians that preceded the procession warned them he was coming. A Mr. Glanius, writing in 1682, notes:

> All along the way nothing is to be heard but Fifes, Drums, Flutes, and other instruments, which make a passable Harmony…. His Majesty's subjects were permitted to see his person only during the *kathin* procession in October, when all lay people, including the royal family, were expected to take gifts and new robes to Buddhist monks. When the King proceeded by water, several boats of musicians followed. (p. 112)

Coronation ceremonies were occasions for much music, but before the 1800s few foreigners actually saw these. In 1851, at the coronation of King Mongkut, after the chief astrologer performed the naming ceremony, "priests or astrologers" blew conchs "and beat gongs and drums" (Bowring 1969[1857]:424). Likewise, the funeral of the king and likely of other dignitaries was occasion for music. Mendes Pinto, who likely witnessed the funeral of King Yot Fa in 1548 in Ayuthaya, wrote that the burning of the king's body "was accompanied with so horrible a din of cries, great Ordnance, Harquebuses, Drums, Bells, Cornets, and other different kinds of noyse, as it was impossible to hear it without trembling" (1663:276).

Contemporary Contexts

After the coup of 1932, not only was the court-music establishment disbanded and its musicians sent out to fend for themselves, but the nonroyal leadership, favoring Western manners and customs, discouraged and even forbade the performance of traditional classical music. Officials encouraged the performance of classical music or Western instruments, and the Fine Arts Department, newly founded to oversee cultural matters, created a Western orchestra.

Though the College of Dramatic Arts, a division of the Fine Arts Department continued to teach and produce both classical music and theater, performances were presented only periodically in the National Theater. Music was not considered an acceptable academic area in Thai higher education until the 1970s. Gradually music has become an acceptable major, and now it is possible not only to study music at many Thai universities and colleges, but to choose a major in Western or Thai classical music. Consequently, universities and other educational institutions have become the primary haven for classical music in Thailand, just as they are in the West for its classical music. In sum, Thai classical music continues to thrive within the educational system, appeals to a moderately large audience, and maintains a high standard of skill, representing a remarkable comeback from the late 1930s, when all seemed about to be lost.

Classical music is also found outside academia. There are numerous private ensembles that meet in the homes of masters and perform for special occasions little known to the general public. Ensembles are also sometimes hired to play for temple fairs, the Western New Year, and other festive occasions. Several Buddhist temples in Bangkok specialize in funerals, and there an observer is likely to encounter a *piphat mawn* performing throughout the day as a background to funerals and processions. A ubiquitous and all-too-predictable venue for classical music is the tourist restaurants in Bangkok and theme parks outside. The typical show, lasting about thirty minutes, includes scenes from masked drama and dance-drama (both accompanied by an ensemble that is rarely "pure"), followed by simulations of boxing and sword fighting, accompanied by at least an imitation of the *klawng khaek* boxing ensemble. The instrumentalists may play alone during dinner.

Khon

Khon, the masked drama based entirely on the Thai version of the Indian epic *Ramayana* (Thai *Ramakian*), almost certainly derived from the large shadow-puppet theater. In the latter genre, male puppeteers dance beneath their puppets in front of a cloth screen. It is widely believed that later the puppets were discarded, and *khon* evolved as an independent human genre. After 1932, *khon* was maintained exclusively by the Fine Arts Department, with occasional presentations at the National Theater, but since the 1980s *khon* performances by students at both secondary and baccalaureate institutions have become usual.

Originally played by an all-male cast, *khon* was later influenced by the *lakhawn* dance-drama and began to include female performers. Gradually, the divine human roles shed their masks in favor of makeup, leaving only demons and simians wearing them. Masked

khon
Classical masked theater, based entirely on *Ramayana*
lakhawn
Various types of dance-drama
Ramakian
The Thai version of the Indian *Ramayana* epic
nang yai
Classical large shadow-puppet theater

Figure 9.10
Several members of the monkey army, led by Hanuman (second from right), appear in a *khon* performance of part of the *Ramakian* in Roi-et. Photo by Terry E. Miller, 1988.

or not, the actors neither speak nor recite, leaving this function to the reciter (*khon puk*), seated offstage.

Because a complete performance of the *Ramakian* (Figure 9.10) would last many days, episodes called *chüt* lasting a few hours are normally given. The term *chüt,* meaning "set," derives from the practice in *nang yai* of collecting a set of puppets for a given scene. Performances were formerly given in the open air on the ground, but when on a stage, it was open on three sides with the ensemble and reciter in front or to one side. Accompanying *khon* is the *piphat* with hard mallets (*mai khaeng*). The player of the *ra-nat* is the melodic leader, but the *taphon* must carefully coordinate with the dancers. The melodic members of the ensemble, silent during dialogue and recitation, accompany stage action, drawing from a repertoire of tunes appropriate to a specific action (*pleng naphat*), such as fighting, making love, or fleeing. In addition, there are pieces for processions. The performance may be preceded by a group of instrumental pieces in the form of an overture (*homrong*).

Nang Yai

There are two kinds of shadow-puppet theater in Thailand today: small puppets with articulated limbs (called *nang talung* in the south, *nang bra mo tai* in the northeast); and, in central Thailand, the large puppets (*nang yai*), related to the classical *khon* and accompanied by the same *piphat* and repertoire.

Cut from cowhide, the puppets measure from 100 to 200 centimeters high and 50 to 150 wide; most require the hide of a single cow, but some require those of two cows. Rather than represent a single character, each is a tableau showing one or more characters, with its scenic context, in a particular pose or scene (like "Duel between the white monkey and the black monkey" and "Hanuman wrecking Totsagan's garden"). Each puppet is supported by two (rarely one) wooden poles protruding to 30 to 60 centimeters below. These are held in performance by a male manipulator, who, while displaying a puppet, moves gracefully, as if dancing.

In performance (Figure 9.11), a screen of white cloth about 16 meters long and 6 meters high with decoration around its border is stretched across the stage, and a bonfire (now electric lights) is prepared behind it. According to some early Siamese documents, performances also used to occur during late afternoons and early evenings before the screen, but without the fire. The manipulators assemble puppets in sets (*chüt*), as a performance requires from one hundred to three hundred puppets. The story is told by offstage reciters in a kind of heightened speech. The instrumental ensemble accompanies periods of action by playing standard action tunes while the manipulators move in time with the music. Though *nang yai*, like *khon*, plays the story of Rama exclusively now, during the late 1700s and early 1800s it also presented adaptations of the story of *Inao*.

Today in Thailand, only three troupes still perform *nang yai*, and only three complete sets of puppets exist (a fourth collection, of two hundred, is in the Ledermuseum in Offenbach, Germany). The Fine Arts Department troupe rarely performs, and the other two, both based at Buddhist temples, have few opportunities to perform.

Lakhawn

The term *lakhawn* is usually glossed "dance-drama," but with various modifiers it refers to specific genres, each associated with a particular region and audience. It is distinguished from *khon* by its emphasis on singing and graceful dance. Two possible origins for *lakhawn* can be posited, one from southern Thailand, another from the Khmer after the fall of Angkor Vat; both may have contributed to the resulting genres that attained their peak of development in the years before 1932. While the Khmer retain elaborate and graceful dances obviously similar in style to those of Thailand, we cannot be sure of the relationship five hundred years ago. There is more concrete evidence that central Thai *lakhawn* was influenced by troupes from the south playing a genre of theater called *manora*, *nora*, or *manora chatri*. These terms derive from a *jataka* story, *Suton Manora* (Sanskrit *Sudhana Manohara*), the most important story played. Prince Damrong writes that during the 1800s numerous *manora* troupes were brought to Bangkok to settle and perform, but he also claims that *manora* occurred as early as the funeral of the father of King Rama I. These southern troupes gradually changed in language, manners, and music to suit the central Thai taste and came to be called *lakhawn hatri*.

In addition to *lakhawn chatri*, there were two other types, *lakhawn nawk* and *lakhaum nai*. *Nawk* is interpreted by various writers to mean one of two things: "outside," as in "outside the court," that is, of the common people, and "countryside," as in ban *nawk* "rural villages," meaning that *lakhawn nawk* came from rural regions, perhaps the south. *Nai* means "inside," as in "inside the palace," and may be a shortened form of *lakhawn nang nai* "dance-drama of the inside ladies." In the beginning, *lakhawn nawk* was played exclusively by males and *lakhawn nai* by females.

Traditional *lakhawn* was played before a plain curtain, with only a bench for a prop, everything being symbolic. There were no scene divisions. Actors and actress had exposed faces, except for certain special characters, such as animals. But during the reign of Rama V, a period of Westernization, dramas came to be divided into scenes, and scenery was introduced. The stories played by both kinds of *lakhawn* were varied but made little use of the *Ramakian*. Traditional stories included *Khun Chang Khun Phaen* and *Khrai Thawng*,

Figure 9.11
In a mural painting at Wat Phra Keo, Bangkok (early 1800s), a *nang yai* performance is accompanied by a small *piphat* ensemble. Photo by Terry E. Miller, 1988.

Figure 9.12
Lakhawn chatri performed in a ritual context near the great Phra Pathom Chedi temple in Nakhon Pathom, west of Bangkok. Photo by Terry E. Miller, 1973.

set by old Siam's best dramatists. During the reign of King Boromokot (1733–1758), at the end of the Ayuthaya Period, Javanese *Panji* stories became popular at the court and were staged as plays in *lakhawn* style under the Thai name *Inao*.

The hard-mallet ensemble originally accompanied both *nawk* and *nai*, but at some point the soft-mallet ensemble replaced it. Eventually, the *mahori* sometimes replaced the *piphat*. Both dance and singing were important, the dances being set to specific pieces (*phleng*). For stage action, there was additional use of the action tunes used in *khon*. The vocal parts were performed by an offstage chorus, since the actors or actresses could not manage it while acting; they could, however, speak during dialogue.

Performances outside the control of the Fine Arts Department exist, but terminology is confusing. The original *lakhawn nawk* is said to have died out shortly after World War II. People widely believe, too, that it combined with the southern genre *li-ke* to create the modern folk-theatrical form of that name. *Li-ke* as a central Thai village genre is widespread. At certain temples, however, theatrical performances variously called *lakhawn chatri*, *lakhawn rawng*, and simply *lakhawn* still occur. All are associated with Buddhist temples or Hindu shrines and therefore have a religious function. On a permanent stage within the grounds of Bangkok's *lak müang*, a Hindu-derived shrine for the pillar considered the exact center of the city, a theatrical genre called *lakhawn rawng* is performed daily. Citizens come to the *lak müang* asking for help, for lucky lottery numbers, for a mate, for children, and so forth. If they are successful, one of the possible responses is to sponsor a segment of a *lakhawn* performance. The audience consists of rougher sorts who come and go while the stories are performed by troupes of modest talent. Dialogue, action, singing, and dancing occur, all accompanied by a small hard-mallet ensemble (usually without a *pi nai*). Similar kinds of theater occur at certain Buddhist temples, like the Phra Pathom Chedi in Nakhon Pathom (Figure 9.12).

Hün

Seldom seen and never widespread, *hün krabawk* is nevertheless a theater of Thailand's only remaining non-shadow-type puppets. Evidence that rod-type puppets with moveable arms manipulated from below were once somewhat common is found in the National Museum. Of greater certainty is that in Sukhotai in 1892, a prince observed bamboo-rod puppets said to have been copied from puppets brought from Hainan Island, off the southeastern coast of China. He brought one back to Bangkok, where it was copied, and the first *hün* troupe was founded in 1893, with another in 1899. Evidently iron sticks, used to move the arms, were added only in 1899. One troupe remains, performing a variety of stories, including Sunthon Phu's classic *Phra Aphai Mani* and the Indian epic *Ramakian*.

The complete ensemble, if used, is said to be a soft-mallet *piphat* ensemble with *khlui* and *saw u*, but a smaller ensemble is also possible. The story is told by a group of some six or seven women reciting the words while each keeps an audible beat with a pair of long concussion sticks (*krap khu*). Action is accompanied by the ensemble using standard action tunes (Figure 9.13).

Figure 9.13
Rod puppets in a performance of *hun krabawk* with the troupe's address below; note the European figure in the middle. Photo by Terry E. Miller, 1973.

Wai Khru

The ritual of *wai khru* (*khru*, from the Indian *guru*), which greets or honors teachers, is of fundamental importance in Thai culture. Through it, those who learn any art, both nonmusical (like boxing) and musical (including making instruments, dance, singing, and instrumental performance), establish a lifetime relationship through their teachers to their teachers' teachers, finally to the Hindu-Buddhist cosmology, which oversees these arts. Indeed, even teachers in public schools and university professors are so honored. Of greatest importance in this pantheon are the *thewada* or *deva* who created music and transmitted it to humans. Rituals are held on Thursday, because each day is associated with a planet, and Thursday is reserved for Phin Pharyhatsa-baudii, the Thai equivalent to Jupiter, but Sunday is also acceptable.

Wai khru are of many levels and types. When a student is accepted by a teacher, whether privately or in a formal school, the student is expected to perform a beginning-level ceremony, which requires only modest offerings—candles, cloth, incense, flowers, and coins. High-level ceremonies take place before a multilevel altar, on which are placed the masks of the gods and certain main characters of the *Ramakian*. Various offerings—rice, candles, cigarettes, whiskey, a boiled chicken, an egg, a pig's head—are also placed there, each with its own significance (the pig's head, for example, is for the demon king Totsagan). The student is led in repeating lines in Pali, the sacred language of Theravada Buddhism. The *wai khru* concludes with a ritual first lesson, when the student is taught (in the case of *piphat*) the first few notes of the piece "*Phleng Tra*."

In addition to the ritual objects, the best musical instruments available are displayed at the altar. In a ceremony that can last up to three hours, a hard-mallet *piphat* ensemble performs high-level compositions (*phleng naphat*) in alternation with a ritualist, who chants auspicious texts in Pali. Each piece has a function, marking a ritual event in the process. Toward the end, female dancers perform before the altar to honor teachers of dance.

Sepha

A nearly extinct narrative genre now revived at Chulalongkorn University, *sepha* existed to tell just one story, that of *Khun Chang Khun Phaen*, Mr. Chang and Mr. Phaen. The story is believed to be based on fact—that its hero, Khun Phaen, was born in 1485, had

wai khru
Ritual ceremony to honor one's teacher
sepha
Narrative genre accompanied with *krap*
thet mahachat
Preaching/chanting the story of Prince Wetsandon, the Buddha-to-be
tham khwan
Ceremony to restore a person's spiritual essence

five wives, and was sent by King Ramadhipati II of Ayuthaya (1491–1529) to lead a punitive force against the king of Chiangmai, a rival. *Sepha* was performed as entertainment for guests at various occasions, like housewarmings and birthdays, but especially tonsure ceremonies. More reciters, either male or female, were invited to tell in heightened speech (*khap*) the story of Mr. Phaen, each accompanying himself or herself with two pairs of wooden castanets (*krap sepha*). Each reciter played a role, or if there were too few reciters, each played more than one role, as in old-fashioned radio plays. Because the recitation was tiring, both to the performers and audience, it was customary to interrupt the recitation with music played by a *piphat*. Later, as the genre died out, the *piphat* retained for solo performance the repertory associated with *sepha* but without the recitation. This repertoire is of the type most commonly heard in live performance and on recordings outside the theater.

Thet Mahachat

Thet is a verb meaning "to preach" in heightened speech, and *mahachat* means "the great birth"—the human, penultimate life of the Lord Buddha, just preceding his enlightenment. *Chat* is short for *chatok*, or the story of Buddha's birth, from the Pali *jataka*. It is customary in central Thailand to recite the life of Prince Wetsanton, the Buddha-to-be (*bodhisattva* in the Mahayana tradition), as an exemplary life to be copied. Taking place in October, before the rice is harvested, the festival is held in the preaching hall (*sala*) of the local temple (*wat*), beginning early in the morning and lasting until midnight. The original text was entirely in Pali; it is now customarily recited in Thai, with some Pali stanzas interspersed throughout, but these cannot be understood by most laity. At the end of each chapter and before the following one, a hard-mallet *piphat* ensemble customarily plays from a standard repertoire. Those who know the pieces can detect which chapter is about to start, even from a distance. Today, such complete performances are rare.

Tham Khwan

The ceremony to call back and bind the spiritual essence *khwan*, symbolized in the tying of threads around the wrist (which has Hindu roots), pervades Buddhist Thailand. Though rare in southern and central regions, in contrast to the north and northeast, the central *tham khwan* included a *piphat* to perform music at auspicious moments. Since the ceremony could be performed for commoners and royalty alike, the musicians could also vary from local village musicians to those of the court.

THE STRUCTURE OF THAI MUSIC

Pitch Materials

Controversy swirls around the problem of Thai tunings, specifically whether the tones of the Thai system are equidistant or not. The issue, however, is primarily limited to instruments with fixed pitches, the *ranat* and the *khawng wong*, which have seven bars or gongs per octave. The voice, aerophones, and most chordophones make use of intonations between those of the fixed-pitch instruments, and these are difficult to accommodate in any system; indeed, the gliding commonly played on these suggests a continuum of sound, rather than a series of specific levels of pitch. Thai equidistance, like that of the West, may represent a practical compromise over the more flexible and complex system that is reality. Neither Western nor Thai string ensembles necessarily play in equidistance, since it, certainly for the West, would produce undesired beats in polyphony. Consequently, any discussion of equidistance and nonequidistance concerns only certain members of the Thai instrumentarium.

The earliest scientific measurements of pitch made on Thai instruments were done in 1885 by the English phonologist Alexander J. Ellis (1885). When musicians from Siam arrived with their instruments Ellis carefully measured their *ranat ek* and *ranat ek lek* and found intervals on the first varying from 127 to 219 cents and on the second varying from 160 to 200 cents. The newly arrived instruments had lost bits of the lead-and-beeswax mixture normally used to weight the bars and gongs. The same problem may well hold true for contemporary instruments, just as an exacting measurement of most pianos sitting around a Western conservatory would reveal deviations from equidistance. Thai tuners, like many tuners of pianos, set the temperament by ear, not with a mathematically calibrated machine. One tuner's in-tuneness may vary from another's. Furthermore, instruments are not continuously checked and retuned. Thai musicians tolerate a certain deviance from the ideal before feeling the need to correct the situation. Consequently, there is truth to the assertion, which has become the conventional wisdom of Thai music, that the system of tuning consists of seven equidistant pitches—but it is also true that in reality it is not exactly so.

Traditional teachers of *piphat* instruments do not use any notation in transmitting the music to their students, but teach by rote, note by note. Sometimes the initial Thai letters for the Western *do–re–mi* system are written with chalk on the keys (a system to be explained shortly), but references to Western letters are not part of the system. And yet, Thai have been transcribing classical music into Western staff notation since the 1930s, not for pedagogical purposes, but for publication and analytical study. A project to preserve Thai music in transcription (begun in the 1930s, but never completed) made use of staff notation. The relationships among the notational systems used in Thailand (staff, solfège, and cipher), the variables of ensemble type and aerophone, are quite complex.

Unlike in the West, which acknowledges one standard pitch (A=440 hertz), in Thailand the standard is more variable. A xylophone from one ensemble placed in another ensemble may or may not be in tune in the new setting, for ensembles are tuned together rather than to a national standard. Compared to Western pitch, then, the fourth bar, notated as B(flat) for *piphat* and tuned at approximately 262 hertz, is roughly equivalent to C.

Scale

As seen on fixed-pitch instruments, the Thai system of tuning has seven tones in the octave, functionally equidistant, though the voice and nonfixed-pitch instruments use tones beyond these seven. The term *scale* denotes an abstract series of tones derived from the system of tuning, presented in ascending order and forming the basis of a given composition

Figure 9.14
Example of metabole in a Thai classical melody.

or class of compositions. In Thai music, five fundamental tones, forming a pentatonic scale, are the basis of most compositions. The pattern is three consecutive tones, a skipped tone, two consecutive tones, and a skipped tone, or, 1–2–3–5–6. Many compositions, however, use six or seven tones. Morton offers two reasons for these seemingly extra scalar entities: their use as passing notes on weak beats, and their use during a temporary shift of tonal center Exceptions occur. Compositions in the *mawn* or *khaek* accents routinely use six fundamental tones (Figure 9.14).

Mode

The closest Thai equivalent to "mode" is *thang*, a term that can mean different things in different contexts: the melodic idiom of a particular instrument, as *thang ranat ek*, as opposed to *thang saw duang*; the overall style of a particular teacher or school, as *thang Luang Pradit Phairoh*; a national melodic style, as *thang mawn* (Mon) and *thang khaek* (Indian or Malay), plus the drum patterns associated with them; the pitch level of a composition as played on instruments. The last usage relates most closely to mode. Each of the seven fixed pitches has a name, and each can be pitch 1 for a scale, conceived either as seven successive pitches or as a pentatonic scale in the 1–2–3–5–6 pattern. The following summarizes the essentials of the system of *thang* based on *piphat*-pitch names.

Thang nai is notated as G, the fourth gong on the lower gong circle and second bar of the upper xylophone and is the pitch of the *pi nai*. Consequently it serves for all ensembles and theatrical genres requiring the hard-mallet ensembles: *lakhawn nai, lakhawn nawk, khon*, and *nang yai*.

Thang klang is notated as A, the fifth gong and the third bar, and is the pitch of the *pi klang*, now virtually obsolete.

Thang phiang aw bon is notated as B-flat, the sixth gong and fourth bar, and is the pitch of the *khlui phiang aw*. Consequently this mode is the pitch level of the soft-mallet *piphat* ensemble, the *mahori*, and the *khrüang sai*, ensembles that use *khlui phiang aw*, though in staff notation the tone C serves for the latter two. It is also the pitch level for the standard hard-mallet *mawn* ensemble.

Thang kruat or *thang nawk* is notated as C, the seventh gong and fifth bar, and is the pitch level of the (little-used) *pi nawk*.

Thang klang haep is notated as D, the first gong and sixth bar, but exists more in theory than in reality.

Thang chawa is notated as E-flat, the second gong and seventh bar, but is rare.

Thang phiang aw lang is notated as F, the third gong and first bar, and is the pitch level of the now rare *khlui u* (notated, however, as G). It is the pitch level for numerous ensembles. At written F, it is used by *piphat mai nuam* and *piphat dük-damban*, ensembles that use *khlui*, and by *piphat mawn mai khaeng*.

Colotomy

The concepts of meter, rhythm, and tempo are not clearly demarcated in Thai: the word *jangwa* serves in various contexts for all three. The term *jangwa saman* "general rhythm" refers to the feeling of beat, even the pulses of the heart.

Rhythmic density is articulated in Thai classical music by a small pair of brass cymbals (*ching*), which provide an audible beat throughout a given composition. The rhythm defined by the *ching* is called *jangwa ching*. The *ching* play two strokes: an undamped, unaccented stroke, sounding *ching*; and a damped, accented stroke, sounding *chap*. The symbol "+" in notation indicates *chap*, and "o" indicate *ching*. In a high percentage of Thai compositions, *ching* and *chap* alternate, with *chap* always at the end—meaning that Thai music is both duple in meter and accented at the end.

Furthermore, the *ching* pattern is conceived in cycles of four strokes, which parallel the cycles of drumstrokes (*nathap*). The four-stroke cycle ends on the second *chap*, which has greater importance than the first; coinciding with an important structural melodic pitch, *siang tok*, it serves as the cycle marker. In Thai notational systems, *ching* and *chap* fall before the bar. Modifying staff notation to have the accent before the bar has proved extremely confusing, and consequently, when Thai music is so written, the accent falls after the bar as in Western music.

Three rhythmic densities (or tempo levels, *chan*) are common in Thai music: *chan dio* "first level," *sawng chan* "second level," and *sam chan* "third level." The third level is the least dense (the strokes are farthest apart), and the first is the most dense (the strokes are closest together). The relationship among them is proportional: a pattern in the second level takes half as much time as one in the third level, and a pattern in the first level takes half the time of the second (Figure 9.15).

There is a third rhythmic concept, *jangwa nathap*, patterns related to drums in the *thap* (or *thon*) category. The strokes made by Thai drums, like those of many other Asian

nathap
Cycle of drum strokes

natthap propkai
Longer set of three drum cycle patterns

nathap sawngmai
Shorter set of three drum cycle patterns

klawng khaek
Two-headed conical drums; ensemble for boxing and theater

thon
Wood or clay single-headed, goblet-shaped drum

rammana
Wooden frame drum with single head

○ = *ching* stroke + = *chap* stroke ⊕ = final stroke (*siang tok*)

sam chan	○	+	○	⊕	(1 cycle)
sawng chan	○ +	○ ⊕	○ +	○ ⊕	(2 cycles)
chan dio	○ + ○ ⊕	○ + ○ ⊕	○ + ○ ⊕	○ + ○ ⊕	(4 cycles)

Figure 9.15
Patterns for *ching* in the three *chan*. A circle indicates *ching*, a cross indicates *chap*, and a circle and a cross together indicate *siang tok*, the final and more accented *chap* stroke.

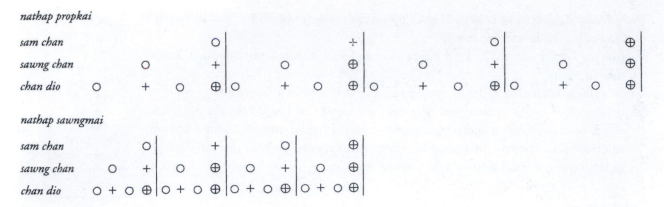

Figure 9.16
Ching stroke patterns in each *chan* for *propkai* and *sawng mai* systems.

drums, bear names. Paralleling a given *ching* is a pattern that can be articulated on drums through these strokes. The words vary from drum to drum—and to a limited extent from teacher to teacher and school to school. Generally speaking, there are two major sets of drum patterns. Discussion is limited to the sets *nathap propkai* and *nathap sawngmai*. Each is a set of three patterns, one for each of the three rhythmic densities (*chan*). A *propkai* pattern takes twice the time of its equivalent pattern in *sawngmai*; if the former's third level takes eight measures in notation, the latter's third level takes four. Figure 9.16 shows each of these with the appropriate *ching*. Which pattern occurs in a particular composition is a matter of custom, not choice. These patterns, with predictable phrase lengths, duple meter, and symmetry, reveal the classicality of Thai music, its restraint and balance—traits that harmonize with other kinds of traditional Thai behavior.

The drums used to play the standard cycles include the *taphon*, the *sawng na*, the *klawng khaek*, and the *thon rammana* (a pair, one laced and the other tacked). A second category of drums, usually defined as having tacked heads rather than lacing (though the *thon* is an exception to the rule), is called *mai klawng*. Drums of this category, played with sticks, produce patterns particular to specific pieces.

The following strokes constitute the basic vocabulary of the *klawng khaek* and the *thon rammana*. The former have a total of four heads, but the latter have only two. The *thon* is the wife (*mia*) and the *rammana* the husband (*phu*). With the *klawng khaek*, the wife has a slightly lower pitch than the husband.

Thang: an undamped stroke on the center of the wife drum's head by closed right-hand fingers.
Ting: same as the preceding, but on the husband drum's head.
Ja: an undamped stroke on the wife drum's rim by two or three left-hand fingers.
Jo: same as the preceding, but on the husband drum's rim.

Besides these standard sets, individual pieces have many special patterns (*nathap phiset*), which can be categorized into three groups. First are patterns for the action-related tunes of the masked theater and dance-drama, some of which have complex, changing tempos. They are called *nathap taphon klawng* since they are played on the *taphon* and the *klawng that*. Second are national patterns for language-tune pieces (*phleng pasah*), such as specific *nathap* for Burmese, Lao, Cambodian, Malay, Mon, and Chinese compositions. Last are *nathap* for dances that require the expression of specific moods.

Because constant repetition of the same pattern would become boring for both players and listeners, drummers play variants of the basic patterns, but these do not deviate much in style or brilliance from the basic patterns. The Thai drummer is a timekeeper, reinforcing the cycle in subservience to melodic instruments; virtuoso display, as heard among Indian tabla drummers, is unknown in Thai music.

Excepting the idiom of the *ranat thum* (lower xylophone) and solo work on the *ranat ek*, the rhythms of Thai music are simple, compared to those of India and Vietnam. Three characteristics account for most rhythmic activity in melody. First, continuous notes (notated as quarters, eighths, or sixteenths) are common, especially in motif-constructed melodies, music for *piphat*, and versions for particular instruments, especially *ranat ek*. Second, unequal patterns—notated as dotted, but realized in a proportion closer to 2/1 than 3/1—characterize certain instruments, such as the *ja-khe*. Third, syncopation occurs mainly in certain stereotyped and idiomatic ornaments on specific instruments, such as the *sabat* (slide) on *ranat thum* or *khawng wong lek*, but the *ranat thum* allows extraordinarily complex improvisation, which defies transcription. Syncopation can also occur in certain polyphonic passages, discussed below under the heading of texture.

The changes in rhythmic density as articulated by the *ching* are not to be confused with the concept of tempo. A *piphat* playing *sepha*-repertoire music—played alone, originally to permit the reciter time to rest—may be inclined to play as fast as the skills of the leader (*ranat ek*) allow, but music of *lakhawn* will usually be played more slowly, to fit the character of the dance. A solo *ranat ek* will usually play rapidly, but a solo *khlui* or *saw* will play more slowly, to allow more extensive and subtle ornamentation. The vocal section of a composition is usually sung more slowly than the instrumental section is played. The tempo will slow at the end of a section that leads back to the singer, as it will from the fast to the slow sections in a solo piece—a phenomenon called *thawt*. The concept of accelerating tempo has no term but is expressed as *reo khün*; there is some tendency to accelerate tempos in instrumental music, especially in the three-part *phleng thao*, which successively presents the basic melody in each of the three rhythmic densities.

MELODY

Thai classical music is based on melody, but melody is manifested not in an abstract ideal form (*thang phün* or *thang kep*) but in many individual realizations according to the idiom of the instrument or voice realizing the melody (*thang khrüang*). Morton's analysis shows that, broadly speaking, Thai melody has two possible characters: motivic and lyrical. Older compositions, especially for *piphat*, tend to be motivically constructed; they are difficult for beginners and outsiders to remember and recognize. Consequently, theatrical music (such as action tunes) and the longer suites appropriate to ceremonial occasions show a motivically based melodic style. The individual, idiomatic realizations of the melody tend to be quite diverse. Newer compositions, especially those identified with the *sepha* tradition, are distinguished by long, flowing phrases. They are more easily remembered, and individual idiomatic realizations tend to resemble each other closely. Lyrical melodies lend themselves to generic presentation, whereas motivic melodies can be reduced only to structural abstractions.

Thai melodies tend to be far more conjunct than disjunct. Gaps appear between pitches 3 and 5 and between 6 and upper octave 1, but these do not violate the contiguous pattern of the pentatonic scale. Intervals larger than a Thai fourth (as between pitches 2 and 5) occur infrequently. However, both abstract and idiomatic realizations may exhibit intervals of a sixth, a seventh, or an octave, but these primarily result from octave displacements required by limitations of instrumental range (in idiomatic versions) and avoidance of extreme ranges (in abstract versions). Figure 9.17 shows a conjunct version of the beginning of "*Kamen Sai Yok*" ("Sai Yok Waterfall," in Cambodian accent).

The regular and symmetrical phrases seen earlier in the colotomic structure are also characteristic of the melodic structure. The clarity with which the resulting phrases are articulated, however, varies; motivic melodies, being based on short units, have less feeling for phrase than do lyrical ones. Some lyrical melodies have phrases that in an abstract version would end with long, sustained pitches. Thai music, like Western classical music of the Baroque period, prefers restlessness over repose, and instrumentalists normally play stereotyped filler material (*luk thao*) in place of these long notes.

A discussion of fundamental structure and ornamentation inevitably leads to the matter of idiom (*thang*), and idiom begs the question of texture. Each instrument has a unique character in its realization of a melody, for even lyrical melodies are based on a series of structural pitches that fall on the strokes of the *ching*. Further, there is a hierarchy of structural pitches, with pitches coinciding with *chap* being more important than those with the *ching*, and the second *chap* in the cycle is more important than the first. The individual instrumental realizations can be so different from each other that the relationships are obscured, but they nevertheless exist in the structural pitches or skeletal melody.

Thang depends on two variables: the instrument and the teacher (or school). Additionally, the melodic idiom taught to beginners is simpler than that of advanced players, and ensemble idioms are simpler than solo idioms. A catalogue of all possible characteristics available to a soloist on each instrument would constitute a small book, but the basic traits, taught to ensemble players of modest skill, are fewer.

The most demanding idiom is found in solo playing (*thang dio*), but solo performance is secondary to ensemble performance. Besides extremely fast tempos, solos include the most advanced techniques, greater rhythmic variety and complexity, and a high density of notes. Accompaniment is usually limited to drum(s) and *ching*.

Figure 9.17
"*Kamen Sai Yok*," first section, in generic form.

Defining the texture of Thai classical music leads through arguments over whether "polyphonic stratification" or "heterophony" is the better descriptor. Those who see a closer relationship with other so-called gong-chime cultures of Southeast Asia, particularly Java and Bali, argue for the former term. But categorizing Thai music as part of the Southeast Asian gong-chime culture seems too simple, for only the hard-mallet *piphat* ensemble, including one aerophone and two wooden and melodic idiophones, comes close to being a gong-chime ensemble. A direct relationship between island Southeast Asia and Thailand (and by extension Burma, Cambodia, and Laos) cannot be assumed, despite historical contact, for neither xylophones nor tuned gongs are peculiar to either region, and both are used by the least developed and least influenced peoples of mainland Southeast Asia. Ensembles with strings are clearly not gong-chime.

Piphat music of theater and ceremony tends to be motivic and the differences in idioms among the instruments rather great; but *piphat* music in *sepha* style tends to be more lyrical, with slighter differences among the instruments. The former is comparable to polyphonic stratification, and the latter is comparable to heterophony. Beyond that, Thai music exhibits passages that are nearly polyphonic, not the result of chance combinations but stemming from compositional processes (discussed below). Broadly speaking, then, the texture of Thai classical ensemble music is heterophonic in that each musician realizes the preexisting melodic structure in the idiom peculiar to his or her instrument or voice (Figure 9.18).

Figure 9.18
The idioms (*thang*) of *piphat* instruments, from a Fine Arts Department score for the beginning of "*Sathukan*," from the Evening *Prelude* or *Homrong yen*.

The underlying structure of any melody, motivic or lyrical, is defined by the pitches that fall on the strokes of the *ching*, with the hierarchy from most important to less important being from the final *chap*, to the secondary *chap*, to the *ching*, to beats between these strokes. These pitches unify the often radically different realizations based on instrumental idiom, vocal-textual realization, and rhythmic-density level. Formal analysis of motivic compositions without first isolating these pitches is difficult, but with lyrical melodies it is much easier to recognize the recurrences of tuneful phrases.

Thai composers, unlike their Western counterparts, work easily within the bounds of tradition, creating new works from an old mold rather than establishing personal identities through stylistic uniqueness. Tradition offers Thai composers many conventions, which they rarely violate, giving a certain unity to Thai classical music as a whole. Formal organization is usually bounded by established colotomic structure, with its regularity of phrase length, balancing of symmetrical phrases, and duple meter. Greater degrees of freedom, with phrases of flexible length and nonmetered passages are mostly restricted to *phleng naphat*, both high *naphat* and action tunes.

Many compositions are constructed of two or more sections (*thawn*). Typically, the vocal version is performed first and only once, immediately followed by the instrumental version, which repeats. The instruments customarily overlap the last several beats with the vocalist and then continue into the next vocal phrase. If the text has more than one stanza, the pattern repeats. Instrumental tempos are usually faster than vocal tempos. Sections are usually related motivically, but by and large, multisectional compositions are through-composed. Though binary compositions maintain unity, ternary compositions do not exhibit ABA form. The same rhythmic density (*chan*) is maintained throughout a section and often throughout a piece. Works entirely in the second or third level of density are common, but works entirely in the first level are not known to exist. A few works are composed to begin in the third level and go without break into the second. Works having all three levels, pieces called *phleng thao*, are more fully described below.

A major factor in Thai melody is unity, achieved at the level of motive in some compositions and at the level of phrase in others. It is achieved by many devices, among them immediate repetition, the return of earlier material in later parts of a composition (especially a return to the opening material at the conclusion), melodic sequence, and motivic unity. Many compositions end with a coda (*luk mot*), appended to the main composition and normally unrelated to it melodically. Codas tend to be drawn from a preexisting group, are often performed contrapuntally with a divided ensemble, accelerate to the fastest tempo of the piece, and end on a pitch other than pitch 1, 3, or 5 of the pentatonic scale (usually pitch 2). Further, the coda's final pitch must coincide with the end of a rhythmic cycle and its *chap*. Sometimes an ensemble appends an additional section comprised of solo versions of a short composition unrelated to the main one, this being called a *hang khrüang* (instrumental tail).

EXTRAMUSICAL RELATIONSHIPS

Functional compositions, such as those for theater, have extramusical relationships. Most other works have titles that suggest some kind of programmatic relationship, though some compositions (such as *tayoi*) appear to be abstract. The meanings of the titles may be expressed in the vocal text, when there is one. For example, the title of the well-known "*Khamen Sai Yok*," composed by His Royal Highness Prince Narit in 1888, mentions a place in Kanchanaburi Province (the *Sai Yok* waterfall) and describes the beauty of the scenery of the area, the animals, their sounds, and the sounds of water. The extended instrumental work "*Khlün Kratop Fang*" ('Sounds of the Surf'), by King Prajadhipok, attempts to depict in music the ebb and flow of the waves. The king used much divided-ensemble back-and-forth answering, with passages of counterpoint and even hocket to simulate the action of the waves. A great many Thai compositions allude to animals: "*Aiyaret*" ("Elephant"), "*Jarakay Hang Yao*" ("Long-Tailed Crocodile"), "*Nok Khao Khamae*" ("White Cambodian Dove"). The last includes the sounds of a bird (usually played on the *khlui*), but few such compositions depict their titles realistically.

IMPROVISATION

Impromptu composition simultaneous with performance, as in India (*raga*) or Vietnam (*rao*), does not exist in Thai classical music. Students are taught by rote to play specific versions (*thang khru*) of particular pieces. In certain kinds of repertoire, especially high *naphat* compositions, the version learned cannot be varied, but in most other literature a certain amount of flexibility in performance regarding the details of instrumental idiom (*thang khrüang*) is permissible, especially as the player gains experience and maturity. Though Morton has argued that a sense of modality exists in Thai music, it exists for the purpose of creating new compositions worked out in advance rather than in live performance. Thus, Thai musical improvisation exists only in idiomatic realizations, which might better be described as improvisatory rather than improvisations.

COMPOSERS AND REPERTOIRE

Thai classical music is a composed tradition, but the place of the composer and the method of transmission are different from those of the Western tradition. Most Thai compositions from the 1800s and 1900s are attributed to known composers, and those from earlier times are considered anonymous. Composition continues. But Thai composers normally write nothing on paper: they compose elaborate tunes and structures in their heads. The fleshing out of the composition occurs in performance, when the composer, acting as teacher, orally transmits the composition to other players. Sometimes the composer teaches each instrumental part by rote, sometimes by playing the *luk khawng* version on the *khawng wong yai* from which other players derive their own parts according

ประเทศไทย THAILAND

26 AUG. 1981

1.25 บาท BAHT

LUANG PRADIT PHAIROH'S CENTENARY

Figure 9.19
Thailand's most famous composer, Luang Pradit Phairoh, appearing on a postage stamp on the occasion of his centenary, 1981.

to the idioms of their individual instruments. As a consequence, the process of realizing a composition into sound is shared among all players of the ensemble. The stylistic details are flexible, and patterns of individual ownership and copyright have not developed.

The names of Thai composers are potentially confusing. Since 1913, Thai have been required to have surnames, but it remains customary both to address and alphabetize people by their given names. Most Thai also have informal names, and these are sometimes part of the name by which a composer is known. Further, from the time of Rama V and Rama VI, Thai kings have bestowed both ranked titles and honorific names on notable citizens—recognition confined to the individual, not passed to the next generation. King Rama VI also bestowed these on musicians and dance-drama actors, though he at first excluded women from the system. The most famous of these titled musicians (Figure 9.19) is also Thailand's most famous composer, usually known as Luang Pradit Phairoh (1881–1954). His given name was Sorn (Arrow), and his family name Silapabanleng (Performing Arts), but Rama VI conferred on him both the title Luang (approximately "Sir") and honorific name Pradit Phairoh ("Beautifully Creative"). Other musicians received names meaning, for example, "Recite Sweet Words," "Be Adroit at Music," and "Beautiful-Sounding Fiddle." Musicians not having such titles and names are normally addressed as teacher (*khri*) or professor (*ajan*).

Some composers were royalty. King Prajadhipok (Rama VII, ruled 1925–1935) composed "*Khlün Kratop Fang*" ("Sounds of the Surf"), "*Ratri Pra Dap Dao*" ("Starlit Night"), and *Khamen La Aw Awng* ("Refined One"). Prince Narit composed Thailand's most famous composition, "*Khamen Sai Yok*" ("Sai Yok Waterfall"), in 1888. Others were commoners too young to have received honorific names from Rama VI. The most famous of them was Nai ("Mr.") Montri Tramote (d. 1995) of the Fine Arts Department, who besides being a prolific composer (including "*Som Sawng Saeng*" ["Moonlight"] and "*Kaek Doi Maw*" ["Indian Beats the Pot"]) was Thailand's foremost music historian. He and others composed additional variations (rhythmic densities) to preexisting anonymous works.

1. *Naphat.* Considered the most serious of all Thai musics, *phleng naphat* are the instrumental compositions associated with both theater and ritual ceremony. Because they are so important, musicians may not change even a single note from what the teacher transmitted. *Naphat* are of two types: ordinary and high, differentiated according to the kind of role whose action they accompany—ordinary ones for human or unimportant persons, high ones for gods and royalty. Because in the masked theater, the large shadow puppet theater, and dance-drama they accompany specific characters, actions, and situations, they are often called "action tunes" and have been compared to Wagnerian Leitmotifs. These actions include military marching, traveling, fighting, changing bodies, drinking, eating, sleeping, and greeting or inviting. In addition these compositions comprise the suites played in conjunction with rituals, the so-called "Overtures" for, for example, the "teacher greeting ceremony" (*wai khru*).

2. *Phleng rüang.* Though *rüang* means "story," a *phleng rüang* is a suite of pieces not linked to a story. These pieces consist of three types of compositions in their most complete form: *phleng cha* (slow pieces) in *sam chan, phleng sawng mai* (medium-tempo pieces) in *sawng chan,* and *phleng reo* (fast pieces) in *chan dio.* Each group is organized into a section under its own title. There is also a special category of ceremonial or ritual suites called *phleng ruang pitikan,* which includes *Homrong yen* (published by the Fine Arts Department as the "*Evening Prelude*") with twelve pieces, the *Homrong chao* ("*Morning Prelude*") with five pieces, the *Homrong klang wan* ("*Afternoon Prelude*") with fourteen pieces, the *Homrong thet* ("*Preaching Prelude*") with six pieces, the *Ritual to Call Back the Spiritual Essence*") The first piece of these ceremonial suites is "*Sathukan,*" meaning a Buddhist greeting, which is also the first serious piece a *piphat* musician learns.

3. *Homrong. Homrong* literally means "overture," but some works so designated are actually suites. One group precedes theatrical performances, another musical performance. The *Homrong sepha* suite formerly preceded a performance of the *sepha* narrative genre. Overtures for the masked theater (*khon*), called *homrong kan sadaeng,* are the most important.

4. *Phleng tap.* Shorter suites, consisting mostly of melodious compositions, are called *phleng tap.* There are two kinds, though, depending on whether the suite is purely instrumental or interspersed with singing. The former, called *tap phleng,* bring together several pieces, either in the same "key" (*thang*) or in the same tempo level. For the latter, called *tap ruang,* the music does not need to be unified—and may even include *naphat* pieces—but they are used within a sung story, such as the *Ramakian.*

5. *Phleng thao.* Perhaps the most intriguing in structure are *the phleng thao,* from a term meaning "a set in graduated sizes" (e.g., of bowls). In music, it refers to a composition played continuously in three rhythmic densities, *sam chan* (third), *sawng chan* (second), and *chan dio* (first), with or without singing. They originated during the mid-1800s and reached their zenith during the first three decades of the twentieth century. When royalty visited other royalty, they often took with them their musicians, who engaged in friendly contests with the host's musicians. Playing special and clever arrangements of known

tunes, each ensemble tried to stump the other, for failure to detect the tune embedded in the new arrangements meant loss of face.

The *phleng thao* grew out of the practice of taking a melody and both expanding and contracting it. The original melody was in *sawng chan*, the augmentation in *sam chan*, and the diminution in *chan dio*. The structural pitches occurring on the *ching* and *chap* strokes were preserved in the longer and shorter versions, but in the former extra filler notes had to be added and in the latter notes were removed (Figure 9.20).

6. *Phleng yai.* The *phleng yai* category, meaning "great pieces," includes extended ensemble compositions requiring solid memories and playing skills adequate to negotiate as many compositional devices, many of them polyphonic, as the composer can muster.

7. *Phleng dio.* Works for solo instruments are called *phleng dio.* They are created to show off a performer's skills and memory, but they also allow the performer to exhibit both virtuosic and subtle playing. A melody will be presented in at least two forms, *thang wan* "sweet version" (also called *thang ot*) and *thang kep* "fast, continuous version" (also called *thang phün*).

8. *Phleng la.* These are special pieces to end a concert, since *la* means "goodbye." Indeed, the ceremonial suites and overtures usually end with the *phleng naphat* "*La*."

9. *Phleng kret.* Miscellaneous pieces, including portions of longer works and suites played separately, are called *phleng kret.* Mostly they are in the *sawng chan* tempo level, but some have been extended to *sam chan.* Among the former compositions are three especially well known examples, with singing sections. "*Lao Kum Hawm*" has three sections. The other two, "*Lao Duang Düan*" ("The Moon, in Lao accent") and "*Lao Dumnün Sai*" ("Walking on the Sand, in Lao accent"), are shorter.

A class of compositions has titles that begin with a descriptor of culture: *Khamen* "Khmer," as in "*Khamen Sai Yok*," and *Lao*, as in "*Lao Siang Thian*." These works are considered to have a national accent (*samniang*), and it has long been customary to play many of them as a suite, *Awk Pasa* ("Out of Language," or "Language Suite"). The original tune for a composition so designated may or may not have come from the culture denoted but is at least considered to be in the style of that culture. The most common tunes are "*Lao*," "*Khamen*" (Cambodian), "*Khaek*" (Muslim, Malay, or Indian), "*Mawn*" (Mon), "*Khaek-Mawn*," "*Jin*" (China), and "*Phama*" (Burma), but others are possible, including "*Jawa*" (Java), "*Yipun*" (Japan), "*Farang*" (Western), and "*Yuan*" (Vietnam). The "exotic" quality

Figure 9.20
Lao Siang Thian Thao, *sawng chan*, the first line of *sam chan*, *sawng chan*, and *chan dio*, section 2 compared, with structural pitches (G-D) circled.

of each composition is made clear through the use of specific percussion, often from the culture invoked, and a specific drum pattern.

10. *Phleng hang khrüang*. Literally an "instrumental tail," these are short, sometimes playful pieces, mostly in *chan dio*. They can be attached to longer pieces as a kind of coda. Coming at the end of a long, serious work, they are like a sweet dessert. They also permit the ensemble, or individual members, to exhibit their skills in solo renditions.

For non-Thai, the vocal sections of Thai classical compositions are perhaps the hardest parts to understand, for the words are strung out in long melismas, the intonation is complex (using portamento and pitch levels quite outside those of the xylophones and gong circles), and the timbre is nasal, totally unlike vocal timbres in the West. Singers normally begin the composition, accompanied only by *ching* and drum(s). During the last few beats of the section, the leader of the ensemble parallels the singer and then, joined by the rest of the ensemble, launches into the instrumental version of the same section, usually at a faster tempo. The vocal versions are generated from the same set of structural pitches as the instrumental versions, but the melodic result is usually quite different.

NOTATION

Thai music, especially *piphat* music, is normally taught orally through rote memory, but the use of notation has become common with the two-stringed fiddles (*saw duang* and *saw u*), the *ja-khe*, and the *khim*. Sometimes notation is used to convey a generic version of a melody and to require individual instruments to convert it to their idioms. Besides staff notation, Thai musicians have used two kinds of notation—tablature and pitch notation. For the latter, they use two symbolic schemes (numbers and solfège), but for tablature, they use only numbers.

All Thai notations exhibit a convention that confuses anyone accustomed to staff notation: the accented beat (downbeat in Western terms), coinciding with the *ching* strokes, falls just before the bar. Within a measure there are four beats, usually transcribed as four sixteenth notes. Two eighth notes would normally require hyphens between the pitch numbers, and a dotted eighth would require three hyphens, but many versions leave these out. Seeing only two numbers, the user assumes they are even eighth notes; a single number indicates a full quarter note.

To use these notations, the player must know the conventions that are implied but not indicated. How does the notation relate to the pitches of the instrument? Where is 1 or *do*? Tablatures do not indicate pitch, but the player must know the tuning of the instrument, plus how the numbers relate to the frets or holes for fingering. Such notations have been used since only the 1940s.

1. Solfège notation (Figure 9.21). The initial letters of the Western *do-re-mi* syllables written in Thai constitute a kind of pitch notation.
2. Number notation (pitch). Used generically, this notation works similarly to solfège, in that the numbers 1 to 7 indicate the seven pitches of the fixed-tuning system.

Figure 9.21
An example of Thai solfège notation.

3. Number notation (tablature). Tablatures must distinguish strings, frets, or fingers. In the case of two-stringed-fiddle notations, a horizontal line separates the lower and upper strings, and 0 indicates the open string, 1 the first finger, and so on (Figure 9.22).

THAI MUSIC HISTORY

Reconstructing Thai music history is particularly challenging for three reasons: few documents have survived the ravages of time, insects, weather, and war; the scholarly study of Thai music, particularly its history, is a recent phenomenon in Thailand, and few have attacked the problem; and there are problems in dating many of the surviving documents, particularly iconographical evidence.

Traditional Thai musicians share a kind of oral history that challenges the modern scholar who insists on documentation. For them, truth remains in the beholder's eye. Promising but admittedly ethnocentric sources of information have been the written reports of European and American travelers, emissaries, missionaries, and others who observed Siamese music firsthand, going back to the 1500s (Miller and Chonpairot 1994).

Written Sources

The earliest known document concerning Thai music is a fourteenth-century Buddhist cosmology, *Trai Phum Phra Rüang* (also spelled *Traiphum P'a Rüang*), rewritten from an Indian document entitled *Traibhumikatha* in 1345 by Lu T'ai (also called Payah Lithai and Lidaiya). Included in the list are human and earthly instruments, but none of them

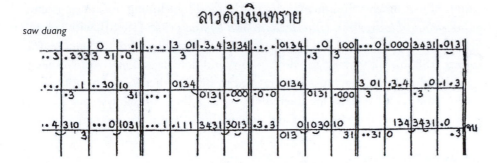

ลาวดำเนินทราย

saw duang

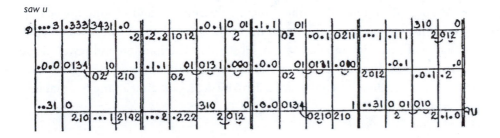

saw u

Figure 9.22
Examples of *saw duang* and *saw u* notations.

can be related to present-day instruments, except possibly the *saw pung daw*, which some Thai believe refers to the *saw sam sai*.

The earliest European account with mentions of music was written in 1505 by the Bolognese traveler Ludovico di Varthema, but since he visited Tenasserim, now in Burma, its value is limited. The greatest number of useful sources stem from France's effort, between 1662 and 1688, to convert Pra Narai, King of Siam (at Ayuthaya), to Roman Catholicism and thereby attain control over his kingdom. The most detailed accounts of music and instruments were written by Nicolas Gervaise and Simon de La Loubere; the former includes an attempt to transcribe a Siamese melody, and the latter includes both a song and drawings of several instruments.

Between 1810 and 1920, an increasing number of visitors, more of them ambassadors than missionaries, visited Bangkok, and many of them published books with chapters or sections on music. Oddly, some of the most biased and ethnocentric descriptions of Thai culture come from this period. An exception to this trend was Anna Harriette Léonowens' *The English Governess at the Siamese Court* (1870), the basis for Margaret London's *Anna and the King of Siam* (1944), in turn the basis for Rodgers and Hammerstein's Broadway musical *The King and I* (1951)—a piece still banned in Thailand because of its allegedly barbaric treatment of King Mongkut (Rama IV) and his son Chulalongkorn (Rama V).

By about 1900, detailed, scholarly treatments of Thai music and theater had begun to appear, most of them written by European scholars who had worked with Siamese musicians visiting Europe for various expositions. Exceptionally detailed was the work of the Italian Col. G. E. Gerini, who published a fine book on Thai arts and crafts in 1912. A visit by Siamese musicians to the London Inventions Exposition in 1885 led to three important studies: A. J. Ellis's "On the Musical Scales of Various Nations" (1885a), detailing the tunings of instruments from many parts of the world, including Siam, using cents; A. J. Hipkins's *Musical Instruments Historic, Rare, and Unique* (1945 [1888]), with color illustrations of several instruments; and Frederick Verney's pamphlet *Notes on Siamese Musical Instruments* (1885b), with systematic descriptions and drawings of many instruments. In 1900, a delegation of Siamese musicians traveled to Berlin, where Carl Stumpf and Erich M. von Hornbostel made what are likely the first recordings of Siamese music; most of their cylinders survived the world wars and remain in the Berlin Phonogram Archive.

Iconographic Sources

The interior walls of numerous Thai temples of the eighteenth and nineteenth centuries and later are covered with murals, some depicting instruments and making music in processions, ensembles, theater, and rituals, all in the midst of scenes depicting the life of the Buddha or one of many jataka tales. When substantial deterioration and restoration has taken place, common because Thai murals are painted on dry plaster, it is difficult to ascertain whether the scenes of music making actually depict the time of the original murals or are re-imaginings.

The Modern Period

In many ways, Thai classical music remains extremely conservative, and though innovation occurs, its scale is small compared to the modernization that has occurred in China, Indonesia, and Malaysia. Is Thai music a museum piece? Composition continues, though most new works deviate little from tradition. Works that combine Thai and Western instruments have been created. Popular songs have been developed from the classical tradition, using the same melodies, but this is a new development, quite apart from classical music.

From the 1930s to the 1950s, the government severely suppressed classical music, and rural genres were disappearing on their own. Since the 1960s, remarkably, classical music has become stronger, even as the popular-music industry has grown. The greatest growth has come in educational programs. In many schools, Thai music remains extracurricular, but the founding of the regional *nathasin* (high schools for the arts) throughout Thailand has led to an unprecedented growth in the teaching of music, both of classical and regional genres, and degree-granting programs in both Thai and Western music have become strong in several universities and colleges.

Though few Thai choose to listen to classical music (preferring, instead the sounds of popular culture emanating from radios and televisions), people acknowledge the propriety of having classical music in conjunction with ceremonies and rituals and representing their culture to the outside world.

The Place of Buddhism in Thai Music

The importance of Buddhism in the traditional musical life of Thailand cannot be overstated. Besides the significance of chant itself, the temple is the focus of festivities where musical and theatrical events take place, the source of the literacy that serves as the basis for theatrical and narrative stories, and sometimes the patron of musical ensembles. The calendar of Buddhist festivals parallels the agricultural cycle, providing regular activities that require music; Buddhist rites themselves also provide opportunities for making and hearing music.

Buddhism and Hinduism both entered the area of Thailand over a period of several hundred years, beginning about five hundred years after the passing of the Lord Buddha (543 B.C.E.). The magnificent *chedi* at Nakhon Pathom, west of Bangkok, whose original Dvaravadi structure is believed to date from about 500 C.E. (it is now covered with a 115-meter high structure built by King Rama IV in 1860), and is thought to be the oldest Buddhist structure in Thailand.

Buddhism can be viewed in two ways: first, as a philosophy of life based on the doctrine of the Buddha; second, as a syncretistic popular religion practiced by ordinary people more attuned to its festivities and social activities than to its deeper meaning, and who see no contradiction in also maintaining traditional animistic practices.

The temple or monastery (*wat*) is the focus of the Buddhist life and associated secular social activities, not the least of which are music and theater. The compound of any fairly important monastery will include most of the following structures: a *chedi* (stupa), a high, pointed or rounded structure built over sacred objects, such as a bone, a hair, or a tooth of the Lord Buddha; a *wihan* (Pali *vihara*), a hall for preaching; an *ubasot* or *bot*, for rites of the *sangha*; a *sala*, a public hall for preaching; *kuthi*, dormitories for monks; an open tower housing a large metal bell or a large, barrel-shaped drum for signaling, or both instruments; and a sacred bodhi tree (*Ficus religiosa*). Both the *wihan* and the *bot* have images of Buddha, in front of which chanting takes place. Most ceremonies and chanting open to the laity occur in the *wihan* or *sala*.

Occasions for Chanting

Certain Buddhist festivals can be the cause of musical performances, both on the temple grounds and elsewhere. The following are among the most likely to include music.

1. *Songkran*, the traditional new year, on 13 April, celebrating the end of the dry season and the imminent return of the rains.
2. *Awk phansa*, the end of the Buddhist Rains Retreat (*khao phansa*), occurs in October on the fifteenth day of the waxing moon. This three-month period, when agricultural work is heavy and musical performances are avoided, ends with relief, merrymaking, and making music.
3. *Kathin*, between the full moons of October and November, centers around the community's gift of new robes and other gifts to the monks. The procession will likely include dancers and musicians (such as a *klawng yao* drum ensemble), and theatrical troupes may be hired to entertain at night.
4. *Loi kratong*, the festival of lights, occurs on the full moon of November, when villages and towns organize parades culminating with the launching of tiny, candle filled boats, and large, electrically lighted floats on rivers, canals, and lakes.
5. Temple fairs, intended to raise money to help maintain buildings or build new ones, usually occur during the dry months (November to March).

6. Music may occur in conjunction with other occasions, such as ordinations, marriages, funerals, the king's birthday (5 December), New Year's Day (1 January), and so forth.

Monks and Their Activities

Chanting is the responsibility of both monks and novices, led by the abbot, but since the repertoire of chants takes time to learn and the minimum period one may retreat to the temple is one week, many will learn only some chants or parts of them. The sacred texts were traditionally written on long strips of dried palm leaf using a sharp stylus, the letters filled with lampblack and the leaves joined with cords at two points. Today, texts are more likely to be read from printed palm leaves or modern books.

Routines of Chanting

Chanting takes place both inside and outside the temple compound, both in the presence of lay persons and in private, both collectively and individually. The daily routine is altered both during the penitential season and on holy days (*wan phra*), which occur four times a month when the laity bring food to the temple, hear the chanting of the sacred canon and hymns, and hear blessing chants.

Ordinary texts are found in the *Jet tumnan* and *Sip sawng tam nan*, published as book collections. Ideally, each monastery is to have both services; in reality, many have only the evening service, and some observe that only occasionally outside the penitential (*khao phansa*) period. During the three months of withdrawal, a great deal more chanting takes place than usual, with extra services at 4 A.M. and 9 A.M., in the early afternoon and just before sunset (Figure 9.23).

Types of Chant

Chanting texts privately by the *sangha* is simply called *suat*, and other types are reserved for the laity's hearing, specifically chants for general and meritorious use (*suat hai ngan mongkon*), and chants for funerals (*suat hai upamongkon*, also *awa-mongkon*). Pali is understood only by educated monks who have spent years studying it. There are also chants for ordination (*suat nak*), for the robe-giving festival (*suat kathin*), and for miscellaneous occasions. During services, the abbot selects the texts to be chanted, cueing the chapter with the first words. Certain chants are in responsorial form. All, including the abbot, face the image of Buddha, kneeling.

Learning the chants first requires the monk or novice to memorize the texts, a process accomplished over time. Inexperienced

Figure 9.23
Monks chant the afternoon service (*tham wat yen*) at a temple in Roi-et, Thailand. Photo by Terry E. Miller, 1988.

members are permitted to use their copies of the *Jet tam nan* when no laity are present but must chant from memory when they are. The pitch level is set by the abbot, and no instruments of any kind are customarily used, excepting the temple drum (or bell) and a large hanging bossed gong, which on special occasions in major temples marks important points in the text.

The available body of recorded chants demonstrates two melodic tendencies—one in which a reciting pitch alternates with a pitch either a tone or a semitone below and the reciting pitch alternates with a lower fourth. The following scale patterns, expressed in pitch letters, summarize the scalar formations found thus far (reciting pitch italicized):

Group I	Group II
1. F–*G*	1. D–*G*
2. F–*G*–A	2. D–*G*–A
3. F–*G*–B-flat	3. D–*G*–B
4. F–*G*–A–B–flat	

Chants using scales in Group I have been found to be more common than those of Group II. The text *Namo tatsa phakhawato arahato samma samphutthatsa* "We worship the Blessed One, Arahat, Supreme Lord Buddha," is chanted thrice; this text occurs frequently in all services.

Preaching (**thet**)

Preaching normally occurs on holy days, when the laity gathers with lighted candles and incense to hear a learned monk, seated in a large, wooden chair. The people sit before him, legs to their left, hands folded in front of them. In times past, sermons were written in Pali on palm leaves in one of the learned alphabets. Few understood the words, but their efficacy was realized simply by being transformed into sound. In delivery, preaching has two basic styles. Ordinary theological sermons (*thet thammada*) are chanted primarily on a single pitch, with inflections down one pitch and up a minor third, similar to Pali chant. A second category, story-sermons (*thet nitan*), have greater appeal to listeners because they are in the regional vernacular and are often the same stories seen on stage. Story sermons are delivered in a more melodic fashion than ordinary sermons, but like chant, they hover around a reciting pitch.

The preaching of the story of Prince Wetsandon occurs during a multiday festival from late October to early November in central Thailand and in late February to early March in the northeast. Read from palm-leaf manuscripts written in Thai letters but having dialectal differences according to region, the story is divided into thirteen chapters (*kan*), fourteen in the northeast. Traditionally, the central Thai *thambun mahachat* required a classical *piphat* ensemble to play between each chapter. The northeastern version omits the music but includes four sections unknown to the central Thai, two telling the story of the travels of Pra Malai (who visited heaven and hell and returned to tell mortals about them), and two stories that serve as introductory and concluding chapters. The northeast also has *thet lae*, preaching in which monks deliver *klawn-type* poetry in a highly melodic fashion, simi-

Figure 9.24
A talented monk (in raised chair) chants *thet lae at a kathin* festival in Barabu. Photo by Terry E. Miller, 1973.

Figure 9.25
The temple's abbot ties a string on the wrist of a newly promoted monk in northeast Thailand. Photo by Terry E. Miller, 1974.

lar to singing, but not so designated because of the traditional proscription on monks' singing (Figure 9.24).

The Sukhwan Ritual

The Thai and the Lao have a Hindu-derived ritual intended to preserve or restore the health of a person undergoing life changes or a rite of passage. It is properly called *sukhwan* or *tham khwan* in Thai and *sukhuan* in Lao, though when performed for monks it is called *ba si* or *bai si*. Its purpose is to retain or call back the *khwan*, variously glossed as "psyche," "morale," and "spiritual essence." The *khwan* is said to be a timid spirit, inclined to flee at times of stress, danger, and important changes of status, or even during a long trip. Its loss may cause afflictions and misfortunes, and its flight must be checked before the crisis if possible.

The ritualist who summons the *khwan* is a *maw khwan* or *phram*, the latter term derived from Brahman. This person is typically an older and respected male, a householder, formerly a Buddhist monk, and literate in learned scripts. The *phram*'s texts are traditionally written—actually incised—in one of the learned alphabets on palm-leaf strips. The ceremony may be performed in the temple meeting hall (*sala*), in a home, outdoors, or wherever necessary and appropriate. The *phram* and other participants seat themselves around ritual offerings intended to attract the *khwan*. A conical tiered altar object (*pha khwan*) is decorated and surrounded by other offerings, including boiled eggs, bananas, flowers, candles, money, lumps of glutinous rice, and lengths of string. At the conclusion of the chanting, the *phram* begins tying strings around the participants' wrists, including onlookers if they desire. The tying of the string symbolically binds the *khwan* back into the person (Figure 9.25).

REGIONAL THAI CULTURE

Historically, the Kingdom of Siam only gradually became modern Thailand as it expanded into areas formerly under Khmer, Lao, Malay, Mon, and (in northern Thailand) Tai control. Borders were loosely defined, and these outlying areas acknowledged allegiance to the court in Bangkok more than they were administered directly. Until railways and highways were built to the south, north, and northeast, these re-

gions were quite isolated from central Thailand (the original Kingdom of Siam) and consequently developed and long maintained distinct cultural patterns.

In each region, people spoke the local languages at home, but had to use central Thai, the official language, in school and in government business. During the 1960s and 1970s, the highway system began to reach formerly remote areas, the media (both radio and television) began penetrating into every electrified town and village, and increasingly urban centers became more uniform, more central Thai. At the same time, great numbers of people from the regions migrated to Bangkok seeking work, and they brought back home the wonders of modern Bangkok whenever possible.

Old central Thai culture, which was found in villages, declined dramatically, even during the middle years of the twentieth century. Communal farming changed to individual work, leaving most genres of folksong without a context. That same process affected the other regions more slowly. Popular music of many kinds has become dominant, not only because the media are filled with it, but because young people, having more money than their elders, hired the *luk thung* (the so-called country songs) troupes they preferred over *like* theater or *mawlam* song troupes their parents preferred.

Even the northeast, the most conservative and least developed economically, succumbed. The decline of the local language, *phasa isan* "northeastern language," is so sharp that classes in it are now offered in a few schools. Genres traditionally sung in it cannot survive in a world where few understand it. Consequently, these genres are gradually changing over to central Thai lyrics. Depictions of *isan* culture have become stereotyped, even when done by northeasterners. Before people were conscious of regional culture, performers dressed variously in central Thai, Western, or local styles, but today they wear the most obvious and colorful local styles available.

Central Thailand

Central Thai village life, like village life throughout Thailand and Southeast Asia generally, is centered on agriculture, wet rice being the main crop. The communal aspects of farming have all but disappeared since the 1940s. Consequently, village song is largely a matter of history, and the few remaining performers are elderly.

Village Songs

The term denoting these songs is *phleng pün ban* "songs of the village." When roads were poor or nonexistent, groups of villages tended to be isolated from each other, giving rise to endless variants in terminology, melody, and practices. Certain traits underlie virtually all of them, however.

1. Most songs alternate male and female singers (repartee) and soloist and a chorus of onlookers (call and response).
2. Songs are sung without melodic instrumental accompaniment; some genres use simple idiophones.
3. Two types of poems occur: improvised poems and memorized traditional poems.

4. Improvised texts use the vernacular with many double entendres.
5. Whether the words are serious or not, the manner of performance and attitude are lighthearted.
6. Sexuality, normally repressed in ordinary conversation, is given free reign, both in direct and indirect statements.
7. All aspects, textual and melodic, are orally transmitted.
8. Melodies coincide in length with the lines of the poetry, realize the lexical tones of the words, and rarely exceed a single octave in range. Styles of ornamentation vary from place to place. The scales used are typically pentatonic, but often concentrate on three pitches.
9. Rhythm and meter vary on a continuum from free-speech rhythm to strict metrical organization, always duple.

Songs occurred in conjunction with both agricultural and festival cycles. Most were sung in conjunction with harvesting and threshing, which occur in December and January, and at festivals occurring during the last three months and first month of the year, though certain songs associated with specific ceremonies could be sung any time. The nearly universal format is courtship—genuine in an informal context, feigned in a formal one. Following the *wai khru*, the contents progress from a call to an answer (*bot krün*) to a greeting (*bot pra*) to various kinds of courtship poetry, much of it heavily laden with insults and mockery, sexual and otherwise, thinly disguised under a surface meaning; in short, it is a verbal war of the sexes.

Some specific types are distinguished by name. The following are considered the most important and were, at least in the past, pervasive.

1. *Phleng phuang malai* "garland songs" are sung in a circle with males and females separated, sometimes accompanied by hand clapping.
2. *Phleng rüa* "boat songs," now extinct, were sung during the high-water season (October and November) in the late afternoon and evening, when boatloads of men and women gathered at a quiet spot on a river or canal.
3. *Phleng lamtat* "cutting songs" are sung throughout the year. They survive through professional singing groups, hired to entertain. The singers divide into two groups of two or three persons each according to sex, and all wear costumes consisting of traditional wraparound trousers (*jong kra-ben*) and a colorful old style shirt. Accompaniment is provided by a group of three or four persons playing a large, flat drum with a single tacked head (*rammana lam tat*, as distinguished from the smaller, classical *rammana*), *ching*, *chap*, and *krap*. Performances last from dusk until dawn.
4. *Phleng propkai* or *phleng top bai*, similar to *phleng phuang malai*, are sung at Buddhist festivals, ordinations, and other occasions.
5. *Phleng choi* are thought to have originated in *phleng propkai* too, but serve for the most intense competition and are sung at a faster tempo, with clapping as the only accompaniment.

6. *Phleng khorat* are sung in and around the city of Nakhon Ratchasima (commonly called Khorat) by pairs of unaccompanied singers. Today, they are primarily heard in the city near the shrine to Khun Ying Mo, the legendary female figure who once defended the city against Lao invaders (Figure 9.26).

7. *Phleng kio khao* "rice-cutting songs" were sung in the fields, both during work and especially during breaks.

8. *Phleng i-saeo* are similar to *phleng lamtat* but are faster and require greater skill at improvising poems.

Figure 9.26
Phleng khorat performed near the shrine of Khun Ying Mo in Nakhon Ratchasima Province (Khorat). Photo by Terry E. Miller, 1988.

9. *Phleng hae nangmaeo* "procession carrying a female cat" is a rainmaking song sung after the *songkran* festival in April if the rains have not started. Sung during a procession in which a cat is carried on a stretcher, the singers—often drunk—plead for rain, and beat drums and gongs.

10. *Phleng songfang*, associated with dehusking the rice during harvest, were sung for relaxation in the threshing area.

11. *Phleng phanfang* were sung when the rice straw was separated from the grain.

12. *Phleng song khaw lam phuan* were sung when the chaff was removed from the grain.

13. *Phleng chak kradan* were sung when the grains of rice were raked into piles with a long board.

14. *Phleng rabam* or *phleng rabam ban rai* suggests an association with dance, and some simple gestures are part of most performances.

15. *Phleng ram pha khao san* originated in Patum-thani province and were sung by groups of women in boats

16. *Phleng den kam ram kio* originated from cutting rice.

17. *Phleng phitsathan* were associated with courting while gathering flowers for a Buddhist temple.

Li-ke

Among ordinary Thai, both in the cities and villages, especially in central Thailand, but also in other regions, *li-ke*, a kind of theater, retains enormous popularity. Inexpensive to hire, troupes often perform at temple fairs or in conjunction with other festivities, such as an ordination, on the temple grounds, in the street, or even to attract people for the opening of a new market. *Li-ke* is sometimes seen on television, heard on radio, and is easily available on inexpensive CDs.

Li-ke performances take place on temporary stages erected for the occasion, with or without seats for the audience. A series of scenic drop cloths provided highly stereotyped locales, separating the actors on stage from those in waiting. Behind the scenes, the

Figure 9.27
Li-ke on a temporary stage in the street in Mahasarakham; the musicians are on a raised, enclosed platform on stage right. Photo by Terry E. Miller, 1992.

personnel get in costume, apply makeup, and perform a *wai khru* before their performance. A small ensemble is seated on stage left or right. The audience, far from being passive, responds audibly to what is happening on stage, interacting with the comedians. Enamored members of the audience may interrupt the performance to place garlands and large-denomination bills on handsome actors and beautiful actresses. Each member plays a stock role: leading male, leading female, second male, second female, parent, king, queen, antagonist, comedian. Their costumes are fanciful, intended to suggest the royalty of most characters (Figure 9.27).

Musical accompaniment is provided by classical instruments, as few as a *ranat ek*, drums (such as *taphon*), and metal idiophones (*ching*, *chap*, and others) for small troupes, or a small *piphat*, usually without *pi nai*, for more formal ones. The actors and actresses speak dialogue and declaim poetry in a form of heightened speech closer to chant than to song. As in village songs, the vocal timbre is quite nasal. The stories played in *li-ke* run the gamut from famous classical stories in nineteenth-century literature (such as *Khun Chang Khun Phaen*) to newly created stories based on highly conventional themes. Plots are created in an improvised fashion, from a scenario rather than a script but using many previously memorized blocks of dialogue and poetry.

Long-Drum Ensembles

The drums called *klawng yao* "long drum" or *klawng hang* "tail drum" are typically found in ensembles marching in all kinds of processions associated with festivities, religious and secular. The members of the troupe include drummers (usually male) and dancers (usually female). Serious troupes strive for consistency of costume. They usually consist of people from a particular village, school, or some other organization.

The *klawng yao*, carved of hardwood, has a single head. Its upper 40 percent is shaped like a deep kettle, the head attached with leather thongs or cord to a ring at the bottom of a rounded body. The head, with a black circle painted on it, must be tuned with lumps of rice and ash so that all drums in the group have the same pitch. The lower 60 percent of the body is narrow, in a slight hourglass shape. The player uses his hands to strike the head; but if inclined to virtuosity, he may use his fists, elbows, knees, heels, or head. A great number of cyclic patterns are possible, some involving much syncopation, but a regular pulse is normally maintained by the *khawng mong* gong and the *krap* clapper.

Southern Thailand

The neatly drawn border between Thailand and Malaysia masks the history of the peninsula, for the Thai province of Pattani was once a center of Malay civilization. The prov-

li-ke
Central Thai theater for the common people
klawng yao
Long, single-headed village drums

inces bordering Malaysia have a substantial Muslim population, and for years there has been a low level insurgency which flares up sometimes, as it has since 2004. The south is distinctive for its architecture, dress (men often cover their heads and wear sarongs), diet, language, and arts. Buddhism is the dominant religion, but the southernmost provinces have many mosques. Unlike the north, which has a developed tradition of instrumental music and little theater, the south is known primarily for its theatrical genres, both human and puppet.

Musical Instruments

The southern instrumentarium is limited, and most types are found elsewhere in Thailand, albeit sometimes with a different name, but a few are distinctive to the region.

1. *Pi ka law* or *pi haw*, a conical double reed with a wooden body about 33 centimeters long, has seven holes for fingering and one for the thumb.
2. *Pi nai*, the classical Thai double reed, is used for both human and puppet theater.
3. *Saw* fiddles, the classical Thai *saw duang* and *saw u*, sometimes now replace the double reed in theatrical performances.
4. *Khawng khu*, a pair of bossed metal gongs, are usually tuned a third apart and suspended horizontally in a small wooden box, each struck with a padded stick.
5. *Krap, krap phuang*, or *krap chak*, a vertical stack of six to ten thin pieces of hardwood, 1 by 23 by 4 centimeters, strung together and mounted on a thick wooden base, which has a vertical rod piercing each piece.
6. *Klawng nang* or *klawng chatri*, a pair of small barrel drums, each with two tacked heads 20 centimeters in diameter and 25 centimeters high. Tilted forward by an X-shaped stand of crossed sticks, the drums are struck with two sticks.
7. *Thap* or *thon chatri*, a hardwood, goblet-shaped drum, has a single head, similar to the central Thai *thon*.

Genres

Only three genres, two major and one minor, are found in the south, but the former two are distinctive and in the minds of many Thai symbolize the arts of the region.

Human Theater (**manora**)

The term *manora*, usually shortened to *nora*, refers to a famous story of Indian origin. Manora, a heavenly bird-maiden, comes to the earthly plane and marries a human prince, Suthon (in Sanskrit, Sudhana). They become separated, and Suthon seeks to travel to her realm to regain her.

Nora is often described as dance-drama, but the emphasis is on dance rather than on drama. The main characters are dancers, considered to be heavenly birdlike creatures (*kinnara*), and the costume includes wings and a tail. The comedian, however, is called a hunter (*phran*), for the third character in the *manora* story was Bun, a hunter. A full performance includes several hours of dancing and singing interspersed with rhyming comic verse in southern dialect accompanied by instruments. The play took place only after this routine.

Traditional *nora* troupes were quite small and until the early 1900s were all-male, with female roles taken by boys; females are now standard members of the troupe. There were three basic characters: a hero, a heroine, and a comedian, plus a troupe leader, helpers, and musicians, about twelve in all. Life in the troupe was tiring, for performances lasted from evening until perhaps 4 A.M., and soon the troupe had to pack up for the trip to the next venue. Performances also occurred as fulfillments of vows made to a spirit asked for a favor—a custom called *kae bon*. The *nora* troupes that migrated to Bangkok in the 1800s and evidently merged with central Thai *lakhawn nawk* to form *lakhawn chatri* were often hired to fulfill vows. At the *lak müang* shrines in Bangkok and sometimes at major temples in Nakhon Pathom and Petchaburi, this custom continues. These *lakhawn chatri* troupes, however, are now accompanied by a small *piphat* and sing in Central Thai.

The ensemble depends on three primary instruments, the double reed (*pi chawa*) for melody, and the gong pair (*khawng khu*) and drum (*klawng chatri*) for rhythm. In modern performances, a bowed lute (*saw duang* or *saw u*) may substitute for the double reed. The music that accompanies dance is drawn from a repertoire of more or less fixed tunes and rhythmic patterns realized on the drum(s), while the gong pair maintains a rapid pulse by alternating tones. Some recitation is delivered in speech rhythm over the regular instrumental pulse, but the usual declamatory style is in duple meter with much syncopation.

Shadow-Puppet Theater (**nang talung**)

The word *nang* "leather" denotes the puppets. The modifier *talung* refers to the southern Thai city of Pattalung in the center of an important area for shadow theater. Shadow-puppet theaters are temporary structures set up on the grounds of temples, schools, or governmental offices. A wooden platform is built on four wooden posts between 2 and 2.5 meters off the ground (some are now built on oil drums), with additional posts supporting full side walls, a half back wall (over which people climb to enter and leave), and a roof that slants downward from front to back. The front is partially covered with a tightly stretched, thin, white cloth, 2 meters high and 4 meters wide. Into a freshly cut banana stalk, placed horizontally behind and below the screen, are stuck the puppets' bamboo spines. Formerly, light was provided by a kerosene lamp, but with electricity (provided until recent years by portable generators), a lamp is substituted (Figure 9.28)

The personnel inside this space include the master puppeteer (*nai nang* "leather man"), his assistant or apprentice, and five or six musicians, all of whom sit on the floor. The instruments used in shadow-puppet theater are essentially the same as in *nora*, but the *ching* is quite prominent. Dialogue is spoken; only invocations are chanted. Action is accompanied by fixed melodies appropriate to specific actions. To attract an audience, in place of the original overture (*homrong*), popular music may precede the performance, and instruments other than the traditional ones, such as a trap set or congas, may be added.

Made of calfskin, shadow puppets are of two types: a thicker set in vivid colors for daytime use without a screen; and a thinner set, formerly in subdued earth tones, now in vividly painted colors, which allow the light to pass through. Nearly two-dimensional,

manora
Type of southern Thai theater named for the leading character
nang talung
Southern Thai shadow-puppet theater

each side-view figure is attached to a thin bamboo spine about 28 centimeters long. The figures vary in size, with main characters (such as Rama) measuring around 20 centimeters high and 7 wide. A full set numbers between 150 and two hundred, but only forty or fifty are used during any given performance. Characters are both traditional and modern (for modern stories), dressed in the latest fashions with prominent hairdos, jewelry, and watches. Each character has one movable arm, attached to a separate and thinner stick, but comic characters, invariably painted black, may have two movable arms, a moveable jaw, and visible genitals.

Figure 9.28
Shadow puppet (*nang talung*) performance of Ramakian, with Hanuman (the sacred monkey general) and a monkey soldier on left and Phra Ram (protagonist) on right. Photo by Terry E. Miller, 2007.

A nighttime performance typically begins about 9 P.M., after people have returned from the fields, bathed, and eaten. It lasts until midnight, when a temple drum signals a break of one hour. About 1 A.M., it resumes, and proceeds until dawn.

Northern Thailand

The nine provinces that comprise the northern bulge of the kingdom border Laos on the north and east and Burma on the west—an area which includes the Golden Triangle, so named for its production of opium. Lowland culture centers around Thailand's third largest city, Chiangmai, but numerous upland ethnic groups unrelated to the Thai live in the hills and mountains of the north. Northern Thai culture is distinct from that of central Thailand in many ways, including dialect, script, literature, diet, architecture, and the arts. Whereas the epic story forming the cultural foundation of central Thailand is the *Ramakian*, in the north the analogous foundation is *Phra Law.*

Northern Thai music is distinguished by the use of certain instruments unique to the region, the extensive and distinctive ornamentation of melody, and the heterophonic texture of ensemble music.

Musical Instruments

1. *Pi chum*, a bamboo pipe with metal free reed and seven holes for fingering. Placing the mouth over the reed (mounted on the side near the upper end) and holding the instrument almost horizontally, the player exhales, ideally using circular breathing. There are four sizes, called (from largest to smallest) *pi mae*, *pi klang*, *pi koi*, and *pi tat*, which together form an ensemble to accompany singing.
2. *Süng*, a hardwood or teak plucked lute, about 80 centimeters long, with a round body, a fretted neck, and four metal strings in two courses, tuned in either a fourth or a fifth, plucked with a piece of animal horn.
3. *Salaw* or *thalaw*, a bowed lute with a coconut resonator on a spike, three strings, forward tuning pegs, and a separate bow. *Salaw* are made in three sizes.

Figure 9.29
The longest Thai drums, *klawng ae*, on carriages in Chiangmai. Photo by Terry E. Miller, 1973.

4. *Phin pia*, a chest-resonated stick zither with a half gourd or coconut-shell resonator, with two or four strings. The stick measures nearly one meter, but the tuning pegs are about 18 centimeters long. Traditionally, the player used it to accompany his singing as he walked to court his girl friend.

5. *Teng thing*, a two-headed asymmetrical barrel drum with lacing mounted horizontally on a stand, similar to a *taphon*. The name is onomatopoetic, after its strokes.

6. *Klawng düng nong* or *klawng ae*, a long single-headed wooden drum with a slightly waisted body. The upper 40 percent includes the head, with leather lacing fastened to a ring; the lower 60 percent has a series of turned rings. Some measure up to 4.5 meters in length and are mounted on a two-wheeled cart (Figure 9.29).

7. Cymbals. There are two sizes of cymbals: the *sa-wae* and the *sa-wa*.

Ensembles

A small number of ensembles have names and are more or less standardized.

1. *Salaw süng pi*, being the names of the three instruments—fiddle, lute, free-reed pipe—that comprise the ensemble. It is also known as *penja duriyang* "five instruments"—*pi mae*, *pi klang*, *pi koi*, *salaw*, *süng*—and is used for festive occasions, dances, and processions (Figure 9.30).

2. *Wong dontri lanna wong yai* "large northern ensemble" consists of three *süng*, three *salaw*, a drum, wood castanets, *khlui*, *ching*, and *pi chum*.

3. *Pi chum* may have three, four, or five members. The basic ensemble uses *mae*, *klang*, and *koi*, the medium adds the *tat*. The *pi chum* ensemble primarily accompanies the singing of *saw*.

The occasions for music included courting, weddings, housewarmings, ordinations, processions, the *loi krathong* festival, the *thet mahachat* festival (reading of the life of Prince Wetsandon), and funerals. Many of these contexts have become rare, or have disappeared or changed over to mediated music, but the percussion ensembles primarily associated with temples are likely to be used now and then at temples preserving them.

Genres

1. *Khao* denotes a narrative genre, the heightened-speech reading of long stories from palm-leaf manuscripts, some of northern origin, others widely known, such as the

story of Prince Wetsandon. The melody of *khao* derives from the lexical tones of the text, articulated to seven distinct scalar tones spanning an octave.

2. *Saw*. A repartee genre with at least one male and one female singer, *saw* is performed from about 10 A.M. to 5 P.M. A stage singer is called *chang saw*, meaning someone skilled at performing *saw*. The texts, partly memorized and partly extemporized, are sung to standard melodies adapted for the particular texts. Although the topics may be local and satirical, even bawdy, they also include discussions of ethics, history, and episodes about folk heroes drawn from northern epics. At least twelve melodies, most of them from a specific

Figure 9.30
A traditional northern Thai ensemble plays in a shrine. Photo by Terry E. Miller, 1994.

area, are identified by name. Pentatonic, the melody is supported by an accompaniment of densely woven heterophony typically played by a *pi chum* ensemble, with or without other instruments.

3. *Saw lakhawn* or *lakhawn saw*. The only type of theater found in northern Thailand, *saw lakhawn* is played from a scenario much like that of central Thai *li-ke*, and the troupe consists of stock character roles:

4. *Joi*. Until the midtwentieth century, courtship required the male to visit his lover at her home, engage in ritual dialogue based on poetry called *aeo sao*, and sing terse poetry, both serious and risqué called *joi* (less commonly *saw siang yao* "*saw* with melismas" or *ram lam nam* "singing a story with dance").

5. *Fawn phi* "spirit dance," a communal spirit ceremony done once a year in April or May, is organized around a small building filled with hanging pieces of multicolored cloth. During the day, music is provided by an ensemble, and participants eat, drink, and become possessed as they bury their faces in a piece of hanging cloth and swing from it. Around 5 P.M., diviners kill a chicken and predict the future according to how the entrails fall.

6. Dance. The north is famous for the grace of its dances and martial displays, also called dances. The former, performed in pairs, are typically accompanied by an ensemble of drums, gongs, cymbals, and double reed. The most important dances follow.

Fawn thian "candle dance" was originally sacred in character but has lost this quality. Each dancer has a lighted candle in each hand.

Fawn lep "fingernail dance" is danced usually during the daytime for festivals and ceremonies. Each dancer wears 15-centimeter-long brass fingernails on the four fingers of each hand.

Fawn ngio "Shan dance" derives from dances of the Tai-Yai (or Shan) and includes the use of scarves.

Fawn man kam boe or *man mui chiang ta* "butterfly dance" mixes aspects of northern and central Thai and Burmese dances.

Fawn man mong khon also mixes aspects of northern, central, and Burmese dancing. It is distinguished by a faster tempo, a distinctive costume, and a unique hairdo.

Fawn dap "sword dance" can be danced by men or women, each holding a sword, at times gripped by their teeth. Accompaniment consists of drums, gongs, and medium-sized cymbals.

Fawn joeng 'combat dance' is only for men. Bare-handedly wielding swords, they display combat ability.

Musical Style

Instrumental melody varies in idiom, with some (like *khlui* and *salaw*) using extensive ornamentation. The most complex melodies are those realized on *pi chawa*, where intonations outside the basic seven and portamento make analysis difficult. Most melodies are fundamentally fixed, especially those played by ensembles, but variation bordering on simple improvisation occurs in solo playing. When two or more instruments play together, heterophonic texture occurs (Figure 9.31).

Northeastern Thailand

Eighteen provinces make up the northeastern region, *phak isan*. Covering 170,226 square kilometers and constituting fully one-third of Thailand's territory, this area borders Cambodia on the south and Laos on the east and north, primarily following the Maekhong River. Geographically, the region is a plateau, which receives less rainfall than the rest of the country, resulting in frequent droughts and greater poverty than elsewhere. Three separate cultural subgroups are distinguished in the northeast. The majority are Lao-speakers who occupy fourteen provinces. Three provinces are home to a majority of Khmer-

Figure 9.31
Two northern Thai melodies.

speakers. Lastly, Nakhon Ratchasima province is the center of the Thai-Korat population, whose language is close to central Thai.

Musical Instruments

Northeastern instruments remain rich and largely distinct from those of the rest of Thailand, but one instrument, the free-reed mouth organ (*khaen*), is preeminent. Consequently, the *khaen* will be treated separately from the following list of instruments.

1. *Phin* (also *süng*). The term *phin* denotes a plucked lute. The body of the instrument is made of wood, but the shape of the resonator varies widely: round, oval, rectangular, or waisted (imitating a guitar). The instrument has two to four metal strings (three being most common), which pass over a series of frets to lateral tuning pegs. A standard three-stringed instrument has at least four commonly used tunings: (1) "big mode" (*lai nyai*), A–e–a; (2) "small mode" (*lai noi*), A–d–a; (3) "head-falls-off-the-pillow mode" (*hua tok mawn*, A–a–a; and (4) "old-time-*lam-ploen*-theater mode" (*lam ploen samai boran*), A–a–é. The player plucks the strings with a small piece of horn held in the right hand. The *phin* can be played alone or in combination with the *khaen* and percussive instruments. During the past thirty years, electrified *phin* have become common (Figure 9.32).

2. *Saw pip* or *saw krabawng*. *Saw* denotes a bowed lute, and *pip* or *krabawng* denote metal cans. The *saw pip* is thus a homemade bowed lute with a body made from a discarded metal container, square or cylindrical, such as for kerosene, Hall's lozenges, or Ovaltine. Two metal strings run over a bridge along a stick neck to two rear tuning pegs. The strings are tuned in a fourth or a fifth. Unlike the *khaen* and the *phin*, the *saw pip* is of recent origin, probably during the 1930s (Figure 9.33).

3. *Sanu* or *tanu*. This is a musical bow with a strip of rattan, palm leaf, or plastic held by pieces of rope or cord. The bow, which may vary widely in size, is attached with cord to a large traditional kite (*wao*) and launched during the windy season (November to January), usually at night. The wind vibrates the strip, causing random pitches to sound. Changes in wind speed alter the pitches and create rhythms, resulting in a kind of melody that may vary in range up to a fifth or more.

4. *Phin hai*. Developed in 1979, the *phin hai* consists of two or three graduated sizes of ceramic jars (similar to pickle crocks) with a thick rubber band stretched over the open top of each. The player strikes the rubber band with the hand, producing low pitches, which function rhythmically rather than melodically.

5. *Wot*. The *wot* consists of six to nine bamboo tubes about 7 to 18 centimeters long, clustered around a tapering piece of bamboo 28 centimeters long. Each tube is closed at the tail end and cut off at an angle at the upper (which is open), with a rounded

Figure 9.32
A *klawng yao* ensemble prepares to parade at a Roi-et temple following the abbot's birthday observation; note the electrified *phin*, with its amplifier and speakers on the cart. Photo by Terry E. Miller, 1994.

Figure 9.33
Thawng-khun Sia-run plays a *saw pip* made from a Hall's lozenge can. Photo by Terry E. Miller, 1973.

lump of beeswax or, more commonly, *khisut* (a black insect product, pliable in warm weather), to guide the air over the ends of the tube. Originally a toy spun at the end of a rope, it was adopted as a musical instrument in the 1970s.

7. *Pi luk khaen* "reed child mouth organ." This is a Phuthai free-reed pipe with five holes for fingering. A tiny metal free reed near the upper end is covered by the player's mouth. The instrument can be played alone or in small ensembles that accompany both dancing and singing.

8. *Hun* (in Korat, *hia*). This is the northeastern Jew's harp. Made of bamboo and measuring 12 to 15 centimeters long and about 1.5 to 2 centimeters wide, it has an end section with a vibrating tongue. It is played alone, and its "music" is more rhythmic than melodic.

9. *Pong lang* or *khaw law*. The original *khaw law* was a simple vertical xylophone with at least seven and sometimes as many as fourteen logs, which were hung from a tree or post and struck with beaters. The term *khaw law* derives from a village headman's signal box, which consisted of a single log or section of bamboo. The term *pong lang*, which actually denotes a large metal bell mounted in a wooden frame and strapped to the back of a lead cow, derives from "*Pong Lang*," the title of a piece of programmatic music played on both the *khaen* and *khaw law*—a piece that imitates the rhythm of the *pong lang* bell as the cow sways from side to side. The instrument consists of twelve solid, hardwood logs of graduated length, strung on two strands of rope (with knots holding the logs in place), with the longest log hung at the top of a frame and the lower end hooked to the base. The center portion of each log is shaved thinner, both front and back, for tuning and resonance. Tuned pentatonically (A–c–d–f–g–a–c'–d'–f'–g'–a'–c"), it is often played by two musicians, one seated on the left (playing melody with two beaters), one seated on the right (playing drones with one or two beaters).

10. *klawng seng, klawng jing,* or *klawng toe*. Primarily associated with the Phuthai, these pairs of two-headed, conical drums, made of hollowed tree trunks covered with cowhide and secured with leather straps between heads, are used both in processions and to accompany dancing. They are also used at festivals, especially in contests (*jing*) during the rocket festival (*bun bang fai*). Two drummers, each beating a pair of suspended drums with hardwood sticks covered with lead sheeting, compete to attain the higher pitch and louder volume (Figure 9.34).

11. *Klawng yao* or *klawng hang*. The single-headed long drums of the northeast are essentially the same as those of central Thai village music.

Genres

Among Lao-speakers in the northeast, the primary kind of music is vocal, called *lam*, that refers to singing in which a flexible melody is coordinated with the lexical tones of the poetry. A skilled person is called *maw*, and consequently a singer is a *mawlam*, though the term has come to denote singing or a genre of singing; the latter usage may be shortened to simply *lam*. Most kinds of *lam* are accompanied by a *khaen*, with or without other instruments.

Change has probably always been a factor in the northeast, but since 1974 the degree of change in traditional music and theater has been breathtaking. At first the popular songs of the *phleng luk thung* variety—which not only express the feelings and culture of each region but sometimes do it with the instruments and idioms—came from all four regions; but over time, those from the northeast prevailed, and others fell into obscurity. The region's population is significant and growing, and with many migrant workers from the northeast living in Bangkok, the market for up-to-date songs was expanding. *Luk thung* shows, supported by the younger generation (with its relative wealth, earned in the big city), became so popular in the 1980s that they threatened to eclipse traditional singing and theater. By the end of that decade, the *mawlam* began fighting fire with fire, developing a new kind of *lam* for the 1990s—*lam sing*. Traditional in format, its contents accommodated the times by blending *luk thung* with traditional material, but accompanied by electrified instruments and a trap set.

Figure 9.34
Players of two pairs of *klawng jing* contest drums battle for the highest and loudest pitch in a village in Roi-et Province. Photo by Terry E. Miller, 1991.

Several nontheatrical genres of *lam* consist of male-female alternation (repartee). Though not sung or recited, courtship poetry (*phanya*) appears to be the basis for these genres. Until the period of modernization, ritual courtship was common in northeastern villages, as elsewhere in Thailand. Among the Lao, boys and girls were expected to memorize subtle poetry, replete with double entendres, to be used in the war of wits and sexuality. Questions and insults had to be answered, and someone without an appropriate poem lost face.

The stories used in theatrical genres and excerpted in nontheatrical genres derive from traditional Lao literature, originally recorded on palm-leaf strips in thick books (*nangsü phuk* "book in a pile"), using *thai noi*, the old Lao alphabet. These stories are used in vernacular Buddhist preaching (*thet nithan* "story preaching"), some of which are localized *jataka* stories. Besides entertaining, they teach people how to behave and thus serve to transmit the worldview of the Lao from generation to generation.

The **Khaen** as the Basis of a Theory of Northeastern Thai Music

The basic tuning of northeastern Thai music is fundamentally different from that of central Thailand. It has nonequidistant steps approximating the Western pattern of tones and semitones. Other instruments of fixed pitch (like the *pong lang*) follow the same system of pitches, and since the *khaen* accompanies most genres of singing, singers also sing in this intonation.

The *khaen* (also romanized *kaen, khene, ken, can,* and *khen*) is the most important instrument of northeastern Thailand and of the Lao generally. It is a free-reed bamboo mouth organ in raft form; that is, having two flat rows of pipes. *Khaen* are made in four standard sizes with regard to the number of pipes: six, fourteen, sixteen, and eighteen. The pipes, traditionally measured in a forearm's length (*sawk*), can vary from around 40 centimeters (for a small *khaen* of six pipes) to between 4 and 5 meters long. The latter are now obsolete, with the approximately 1 meter length being standard. It is not necessary for *khaen* to have any standard length because they are normally played alone and must comfortably match just one singer's voice. Numbers of pipes are distinguished by a number, but the system has one inconsistency. A *khaen* with six pipes is *khaen hok* "six *khaen*," but those with fourteen, sixteen, and eighteen pipes are called *khaen jet* "seven *khaen*," *khaen paet* "eight *khaen*," and *khaen kao* "nine *khaen*," respectively, referring to pairs of pipes. In Laos and northeast Thailand until the 1950s, the *khaen jet* was standard, but now *khaen paet* has become standard (Figure 9.35).

With the *khaen paet* a point of reference and the lowest pitch designated A (to avoid sharps and flats), an examination of the arrangement of pitches, standard for all instruments, shows no apparent logical pattern (Figure 9.36). Though the pitches occur in a series of seven, the scales of most of the repertoire are pentatonic. Because it is difficult to play more than three successive pipes, the pitches have been arranged to balance the pitches of each scale between the hands while avoiding more than three successive pipes—an arrangement comparable in concept to that of a QWERTY typewriter keyboard.

Figure 9.35
Playing the *khaen* free-reed mouth organ in a village west of Roi-et, Thailand. Photo by Terry E. Miller, 1988.

Typically, a beginner receives basic instruction informally from a friend or a relative but after that is mostly left alone to evolve a personal style based on what he hears from others. Today it is also possible to study *khaen* in a few schools, such as the *Natasin* (art high schools) of the northeast. Many players tend to be eclectic, clearly distinguishing the style of one province or generation from another. *Khaen* playing is exclusively male, except in modern schools, where some female students learn to play it.

The *khaen* consists of thin bamboo pipes (*mai ku khaen*) whose nodes are pierced with a red-hot poker. They are arranged in two parallel rows in raft form. From front to back, the tallest four pipes are nearest the player, and each succeeding pair is shorter than the preceding pair. The pipes are fitted into a hollowed-out wind chest (*tao* "breast," "gourd") carved of hardwood with a hole for blowing (*ru pao*) and sealed into place with *khisut*. The rows are separated by thin bamboo dividers at the bottom and near the top, and the pipes are tied with a natural grasslike material (*ya nang*) at the bottom, upper middle, and top. A series of holes for fingering (*ru nap*) are burned into the outside of the pipes above the wind chest, but the first pair, played by the thumbs, has its holes on the front; the last pair's holes, played by the little fingers, are lower than the rest, which are otherwise even in height.

Each pipe has a small metal free reed of copper-silver alloy (*lin khaen*) mounted over a hole (*ru lin*) cut in the pipe. Facing the outside of the instrument, these are enclosed within the wind chest and are activated into vibration only when the hole is covered. The player inhales and exhales alternately through the wind chest while holding the chest in his palms. The player tilts the instrument to the left, his lips pressed firmly to the mouthpiece.

Khaen music is improvised, based on *lai*, a simple modal system. There are five named *lai*, but an unnamed sixth mode completes the system. Several basic programmatic pieces, also improvised, are known to all players, and many others may be known locally or individually.

Two pentatonic-scale patterns form the basis of *khaen* music—and by extension, singing. No fixed term designates them, but many players understand the distinction based on the terms *san* and *yao*, associated with named types of singing. The two scalar systems are shown in Figure 9.37. For singers, there are only the scales, but for *khaen* players, there are specific modal manifestations of these scales, the *lai* mentioned above. Each *lai* begins on a different pitch, three based on the *san* pattern, three (including the unnamed one) on the *yao* pattern. They are called *lai sutsanaen* "melody of love," *lai po sai* "left-thumb mode," *lai soi* "fragmented mode," *lai yai* "big mode," and *lai noi* "little mode." Each *lai* has one or two drones, which reinforce the fundamental or starting pitch at the octave and fifth

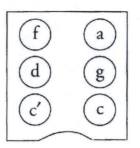
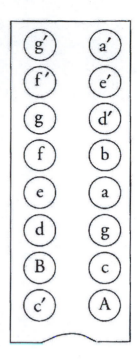

Figure 9.36
Arrangements of pitches of *khaen hok* and *khaen paet*.

g a c d e a c d e g

Figure 9.37
The *san* and *yao* scales.

(only the octave in one case), these held during play either with fingers or small pieces *of khisut.*

The basic repertoire required of a *khaen* player consists of improvisations in each of the five standard modes. Such spontaneous compositions may last from a minute to any length desired. As an accompaniment to singing, the patterns may be maintained for hours. The modes based on the *san* scalar pattern are normally in meter, but those of the *yao* pattern may be in either meter or speech rhythm. The usual metrical organization is duple.

Genres of Lam

The vocal music of the Lao in both northeast Thailand and Laos is centered on its texts, the language of which is Lao. Two activities common to human communities worldwide give rise to the various kinds of *lam*: storytelling and courtship. The telling of traditional stories, including localized *jataka* stories (Buddha birth stories from Indian literature), has been mentioned earlier. These stories were sung by *mawlam* accompanied by *khaen* and acted out and sung by troupes of humans (*lam mu* and *lam ploen*) and puppets (*nang pra mo thai*). The second pattern—courtship—ritualizes gender relationships in various kinds of repartee, which can include tender love poetry, descriptions of nature, Buddhist lessons, excerpts from old stories, challenges, insults, mockery, and sexual innuendo.

Lam phün. Already in decline in the 1940s, *lam phün* story singing required but one singer and a khaen kao (of eighteen pipes) for the performance of an epic-length tale lasting up to several nights. Most of the stories were localized jataka, such as Thao Kalaget, Thao Suriwong, and Naphak klai-kradon, but one—Wiangchan (Vientiane)—was historical, telling the story of the rise and fall of the Lao capital, Vientiane.

Lam klawn. Until its precipitous decline in the late 1980s, *lam klawn* was the most widespread and popular repartee genre in the northeast. A pair of singers—one male, one female, each accompanied by his or her own player of a *khaen*—alternated from about 9 P.M. until daybreak, feigning a developing courtship through memorized *klawn* poetry. Though the poems were memorized in advance, their order was determined by the developing conversation. Singers asked questions of each other, from the personal (How old are you? Are you married? Would you like to run away with me?) to the intellectual (questions of geography, history, Buddhism, literature, and so on). Some singers engaged in double entendre with sexual innuendo; singers could sing thoughts that ordinary people could not politely say (Figure 9.38)

The singing progressed in three stages, each distinguished by its scale, rhythmic-metrical qualities, and poetic content. *Lam klawn* began with "short" style (*lam thang san*), sung in the *san* scale, accompanied on *khaen*. After a short ABA introductory sec-

Figure 9.38
A pair of *mawlam klawn,* each with *khaen* player, perform on a temporary stage in Mahasarakham. Photo by Terry E. Miller, 1973.

tion in speech rhythm, the main poem began, using the *klawn* form, sung in duple meter. Singers took turns lasting up to thirty minutes throughout the night, until about 5 A.M. Then the *khaen* switched to a *yao*-scale mode *(lai yai* or *lai noi)*, but kept a steady beat while the singer proclaimed the poetry in speech rhythm. This section, "long" style *(lam thang yao)*, tended to be more introspective, invoking such images as the sound of thunder (which implied rain and the continuation of life), the tender side of love, and the pain of parting. After about fifteen to thirty minutes without break, the *khaen* continued in the same mode but changed to the patterns for *lam toei.* In this section, faster-paced and metrical, the poems became lighter, even humorous, bringing the performance to an end about 6 A.M., when everyone still in attendance would return home to begin a long day of work.

Performances occurred in conjunction with calendrical rites: the New Year (Thai and Western), Buddhist festivals (such as *kathin*), and rites of passage (such as ordinations). The main season for performances extended from mid-October to February or March, after which the weather became too hot and were festivals rare.

Lam sing. As late as 1989, few had heard of *lam sing,* but within a few years, it had not only eclipsed all other genres of *lam* but had become the rage all over Thailand. Though it is modernized, it retains its traditional roots in the repartee format and the use of *khaen.* Associated with motorcycle and car racing, the term *sing* implies speeding, something fast and modern. *Lam sing* is accompanied by a *khaen,* an electric *phin,* and a drum set. Musically it consists of traditional elements. However, singers incorporate *luk thung* songs into the performance, and this is what made *lam sing* so powerful: it retained the traditional repartee format and the traditional poetry but brought in a modernized accompaniment and its nemesis, the pop song, which had nearly eclipsed traditional singing. In addition, the youthful in the audience danced in styles seen in *luk thung* shows (Figure 9.39).

Luk thung popular songs were already in existence by 1970, but *lam klawn* was strong and well supported by villagers. The old pattern of youths migrating to Bangkok for work grew to a virtual exodus, since the northeast remained poor, the fields were getting overworked, families were grow-

Figure 9.39
On New Year's Eve of 1992, a pair of *mawlam sing,* accompanied by *khaen* and modern Western instruments, performs for a crowd on the village-temple grounds. Photo by Terry E. Miller.

ing rapidly, and land was insufficient for the new generation. The youth were successful in Bangkok and brought back home their newly acquired wealth and tastes. They wanted modern entertainments—and could pay for them. The result was *lam sing*.

Lam mu. Theater in northeastern Thailand dates only to the 1950s (a few claim to the 1940s), and because travel was so difficult then and isolation made it impossible for anyone to have comprehensive knowledge, reconstructing this history has proved difficult. Central Thai *li-ke*, some times performed in localized versions, provided one influence, especially for staging, costumes, and scenery; *lam phün* and Buddhist sermons provided the stories. Two kinds of theater developed: "collective" singing (*lam mu*) and "spontaneous" singing (*lam ploen*), both of which appeared soon after 1950 but in different areas.

Lam mu developed gradually by using raised wooden stages with multiple backdrops, adding lighting and amplification and adopting the latest fashions in costume alongside those of *li-ke*. Accompaniment was provided by a *khaen*, but by the 1970s a drum set was sometimes used with styles of song other than the usual *lam thang yao*. The stories performed were the same Lao epics and *jataka* stories sung by *mawlam phün*. Troupes averaged about twenty-four persons, including actors, actresses, musicians, and staff. All actors and actresses played stock roles, including leading male and female, second male and female, parents, the enemy of the leading male, comedian, servants, and miscellaneous roles. Unlike *li-ke* (which improvised on a scenario), *lam mu* was played from a fully written script, though comedians could improvise topical routines (Figure 9.40).

Between the mid-1970s and the late 1980s, *lam mu* underwent a transformation that involved greatly enlarging the troupe, adding numerous pop songs, adding Western brass and electrified stringed instruments, and especially in creating the *hang khrüang*, a troupe of young female dancers. The performance began with hours of pop songs danced by the *hang khrüang* and sung by star singers, followed only late in the night by some semblance of the story. Young people dance near the stage, sometimes getting drunk and disrupting the performance with fights.

Lam ploen. Though *lam ploen* had a separate origin from *lam mu*, they soon came to resemble each other, visually but not musically. *Lam ploen* used not only *khaen* and

Figure 9.40
A performance of *lam mu* on a temporary stage on temple grounds in Mahasarakham. Photo by Terry E. Miller, 1973.

phin but also a drum set and congas. Singing consisted of two types, a speech-rhythm introduction accompanied only by *khaen* and *phin* and the main body of the poem in meter, accompanied by all instruments, in *the yao* scale. In northeastern Thailand, *lam ploen* followed the same route as *lam mu*—expanding the troupe, adding Western instruments, electrifying instruments, and especially having a *hang khrüang* dance to *luk thung*—and as a result, these genres have become nearly indistinguishable.

Nang pra mo thai. Least known and little encountered is northeastern shadow-puppet theater. In the early 1970s, most troupes had performed a combination of central Thai music with southern Thai small puppets but using northeastern comic characters speaking the local language. Accompaniment was provided, therefore, by a homemade xylophone (*ranat ek*), a drum, and cymbals, and the main story was the epic of Rama. A few troupes performed the Lao epic *Sang Sin Sai* using all northeastern music. In 2007 a few troupes continue to perform, virtually unchanged from the 1970s.

Lam phi fa. Though most Thai are Buddhists, they see no contradiction in maintaining age-old beliefs in spirits, both natural and human-derived ones. There are many local ways to deal with the world of spirits. Only one kind involves music. It is known variously as *lam phi fa* "sky spirit," *lam phi thaen* (the sky spirit's proper name), *lam thai thüng* "group of spirits," and *lam song* "to possess, to enter." All the ritualists are women, who sing accompanied by a male *khaen* player. The ritual takes place around an altar of sacred objects intended to attract the spirits, and the female mediums seek to be visited by spirits who will reveal why the victim is ill.

POPULAR MUSIC IN THAILAND

Thailand's rapidly expanding economy has produced astounding affluence, especially in the cities, which, for sophistication, rival those of Korea, Malaysia, and Taiwan. This is especially true of Bangkok.

Perhaps because the Thai avoided colonization, they have had a long-running love affair with Western culture, originally from both Europe and the United States, later the Westernized popular culture of Hong Kong, Japan, and Taiwan as well. The development of popular music in Thailand can be traced to the introduction of Western dance music during the 1800s, especially from Great Britain and the United States.

Brass Bands

During the first half of the 1800s, Western military bands evidently accompanied some of the foreign missions sent to Bangkok. Besides playing for public ceremonies, they also played dance music for social events. By 1874, the court was supporting a military band:

> After the parade His Majesty's own brass band played for us. There were sixteen instrumentalists, led by a sergeant major, a mere youngster seven or eight years old and three feet in height; their uniform was the same as that worn by the guards. They played in remarkably good time and tune, first the "Siamese National Hymn," and, second, a very familiar western waltz. Afterwards another band of musicians, were ordered out, and they rendered a piece of dance music tolerably well. (Vincent 1874:152–153)

W. A. Graham (1912:467) said Bangkok supported several fine military bands whose performance of European tunes was quite acceptable by Western standards. Prince Krom

Phra Nakhon Sawan Waraphinit, Supreme Commander of the Siamese Navy, was thoroughly trained in European music. Not surprisingly, the most important military band was that of the Siamese navy, whose musicians learned both performance and theory, but other military units also had bands.

The military-band heritage, while continuing in its own right, was also the starting point for both classical Western music and Thai popular music. Western classical music exists in modern Thailand, but it is restricted to the Bangkok elite and the expatriate community. The Bangkok Symphony Orchestra offers a brief season of concerts, supplemented by visits from foreign ensembles. It was not until the late 1970s that music degrees became established in a few universities, offering concentrations in both Western and Thai musics.

One result of the 1932 coup was a government-sponsored preference for Western culture over Thai culture. Besides requirements to wear hats and socks, and for men to kiss their wives when leaving for work, this program included the encouragement of social (or ballroom) dancing, out of which grew *ramwong*, a circular social dance, using Thai-derived gestures of the hands, accompanied by Westernized Thai music.

In the early 1900s, military bands played arrangements of Thai classical compositions, but Western instruments (such as the pump organ, the accordion, the violin, and the piano) also joined the string ensemble (*khrüang sai*, then called *khrüang sai prasom* "mixed ensemble"). To accommodate differences in tuning and pitch, performers considered the organ's B–flat key a Thai C, but differences between the seven-tone equidistance of Thai tuning and the twelve-tone equidistance of Western tuning remained problematic. Military-derived wind ensembles played for silent movies, often using action tunes (borrowed from Thai traditional theater), but the *khrüang sai prasom* played Westernized (that is, harmonized) Thai melodies during changes of reels. Brass bands also played for ballroom dancing.

The Development of the Modern Popular Song

An important development leading to Thai popular song was the composition of new texts for Thai classical melodies, resulting in what were called *phleng thai nua tem.* Unlike classical singing (which is melismatic), this new type had one syllable per note—syllabic text setting. By the 1950s, songs using both Thai classical and newly composed melodies accompanied by Western instruments were known as city-people songs (*phleng luk krung*). Being either slow ballads or ballroom/Latin dance songs crooned by young men and women backed by a combo that might include a violin, a saxophone, a trumpet, an accordion, and an electric organ, these pieces were associated with the wealthier and most Westernized segments of Thai society and were played in clubs and restaurants as well as to accompany ballroom dancing. The "Thai classical" form of the *phleng luk krung* was created by Suntarapon, a band of the Public Relations Department, whose name became synonymous with the genre. These old-style *phleng luk krung* are still favored by a small segment of Thai society, but with the rapid increase of the population and the growing affluence of the younger generation, American and British styles of popular music have come to the fore.

In the 1960s, British musicians such as Cliff Richard and the Shadows influenced Thai pop to the point that this music was known in Thai language as *shadow*. After that, American influence became dominant. The pirating of American recordings onto cheap cassette tapes quickly spread every new development from the West. A great array of magazines focusing on popular culture in general or popular music in particular are sold to the newly affluent younger generation, and some shops offer nothing but photos and other mementos of their latest heartthrobs. The current styles are generally known as *phleng sakon* "modern songs" and represent every American style from country to rap, though usually with a Thai flavor that removes their hard edges.

Social and political unrest since the mid-1970s—related to the Communist movement, uprisings against oppressive dictators, and the mass migration of country folk to Bangkok and the resulting growth of slums—gave rise to "songs for life" (*phleng phua chiwit*), a socially conscious genre, akin to the music of American folk styles of the 1950s and 1960s. The songs composed and performed by two groups in particular—Caravan and Carabao—commented on disillusionment with contemporary Thai society, environmental issues, political matters, and materialism.

For years, to impoverished sons and daughters living in the remote provinces of the north, the south, and the northeast, Bangkok looked like a pot of gold at the end of a rainbow. There they found work as taxi drivers, maids, vendors, and in even less desirable occupations. Their musical heritage, the traditional musics of each region, became the basis for modernized songs generically known as *phleng luk thung* "country-folk songs." Looked down upon as rustics by their employers, homesick migrants could assert a kind of regional identity and pride through these songs.

Though *phleng luk thung* were created from the traditional musics of all regions, those of the northeast came to dominate. Being the poorest and most disparaged region, the northeast had the most to gain. Its people, more than others, knew both the poverty of their home villages and the urban slums in which they lived. Their songs came to have meaning for all Thai of similar experiences, and that success raised the prominence of northeastern *phleng luk thung* to a par with *phleng sakon*. As these now well-heeled youth returned to their home villages during holidays, they came to dictate musical taste, since they had the funds. With the rise of larger and larger touring *phleng luk thung* troupes and their dancing girls during the 1980s, the local traditional genres—*lam klawn* and its related theatrical genres, *lam mu* and *lam phloen*—declined or adapted to the situation by using more and more *phleng luk thung*.

Everyday life in modern Thailand is seemingly dominated by popular culture. Popular music is heard throughout the country—in hotels and restaurants, on the radio, on temporary stages in remote villages, on cassette tapes and compact discs, and in music videos on VCD. And yet when Thai represent themselves and their culture to outsiders—tourists visiting the Rose Garden southwest of Bangkok or their hosts at American universities—they universally choose Thai classical music, whether they otherwise prefer to listen to it or not. Thailand's heart may beat to the sounds of rock and modernized regional music, but its soul rejoices in its classical tradition.

REFERENCES

Bowring, John. 1969 [1857]. *The Kingdom and People of Siam*. Kuala Lumpur: Oxford University Press.

Dhanit Yupho. 1987. *Nangsü khrüang dontri thai/Book of Thai Musical Instruments*, combination reprint of Dhanit Yupho 1957 and 1971, with new illustrations. Bangkok: Fine Arts Department.

Ellis, Alexander J. 1885. "On the Musical Scales of Various Nations." *Journal of the Society of Arts* 33:485–527.

Glanius, Mr. 1682. *A New Voyage to the East-Indies*, 2nd ed. London: H. Rodes.

Graham, W[alter]. A[rmstrong]. 1912. *Siam: A Handbook of Practical, Commercial, and Political Information*. London: Alexander Moring.

Hipkins, A.J. 1945 [1888]. *Musical Instruments Historic, Rare, and Unique*. London: A. and C. Black.

La Loubere, Simon de. 1691. *Du Royaume de Siam*. Paris: Jean-Baptiste Coignard.

———. 1969 [1693]. *A New Historical Relation of the Kingdom of Siam*. Kuala Lumpur: Oxford University Press.

Landon, Margaret. 1944. *Anna and the King of Siam*. New York: John Day.

Léonowens, Anna Harriette. 1870. *The English Governess at the Siamese Court*. Boston: Fields, Osgood.

Mendes Pinto, Fernão. 1663 [1558]. *The Voyages and Adventures of Ferdinand Mendez Pinto [Peregrinação]*. Translated by H. C. Gent. London: J. Macock.

Miller, Terry E., and Jarernchai Chonpairot. 1994. "A History of Siamese Music Reconstructed from Western Documents, 1505–1932." *Crossroads* 8:1–192.

Morton, David. 1976. *The Traditional Music of Thailand*. Berkeley: University of California Press.

Rajanubhab, Damrong. H.R.H. Prince S.A.R. 1931. *Siamese Musical Instruments* (2nd ed.). Bangkok: The Royal Institute.

Verney, Frederick. 1885. *Notes on Siamese Musical Instruments*. London: William Clowes and Sons.

Vincent, Frank, Jr. 1874. *The Land of the White Elephant*. New York: Harper and Brothers.

Laos

Terry E. Miller

Nonclassical Music
Classical Music
Popular Music
Lao Music Today

Since the majority populations of both the Lao People's Democratic Republic (hereafter, Laos or PDR Laos) and northeastern Thailand are culturally related, their musics have much in common. But because of different political histories, the Lao-speakers in each area have become distinct in many ways, including in music. The Lao of Laos are economically far poorer than the Lao across the Maekhong River, whose orientation is toward Bangkok, its modernization, and its dramatic growth.

Laos is a landlocked, mostly mountainous nation of 236,800 square kilometers. It shares a long, mountainous border with Vietnam on the east, and an equally long border with Thailand on the west, south, and southeast, with the Maekhong River marking about half the boundary. Formerly, the Lao controlled part of what is now Cambodia in the south, and Lao-speakers lived there at least until 1975. In the northwest, Laos shares borders with China and Burma in an area known as the Golden Triangle.

Less than 4 percent of the land is arable, with much of the remainder in forest or meadow, mostly on hills or mountains. Consequently, Laos has always had a low population density. With an estimated 2006 population of 6.3 million, the population density is only twenty-six persons per square kilometer. Most of the nation's people live in the lowlands (primarily in the Vientiane plain), along the Maekhong River, and in isolated pockets in valleys and along tributary rivers. Because Laos became part of French Indochina in the late 1800s, its cultural-political orientation was Francophile, isolating it from its neighbor, Siam. Although musical culture in Laos remains conservative, the main factor resisting rapid modernization on the Thai model is simple poverty.

Ethnically, Laos is a multicultural mosaic, consisting of 50 percent lowland Lao and 50 percent upland Tai, Mon-Khmer, and Tibeto-Burman language groups. Theravada Buddhists, the lowland Lao remain the dominant people despite the Communist Party's claims to equality for all people. Although some upland groups are said to be Buddhist, most are animist. Buddhism appears to be weak and often mixed with animism in Laos, with limited activity at even the greatest temples. The Lao view their population in three groups: *Lao Lum*, lowland Lao; *Lao Theung*, the tribal Tai and Mon-Khmer, who dwell at lower or midelevations; and *Lao Sung*, mostly Hmong and Yao, who usually live at the highest elevations. After 1975, the new Socialist government reorganized the country into sixteen provinces (*khoueng*) and one municipality (*kampheng nakhon*), Vientiane, the capital. The nation's largest city, with a population of slightly more than half a million, Vientiane is one of the world's quietest and least densely populated capitals.

Despite an exceptionally low population density, the musics of Laos are strikingly diverse. Isolation, stemming from both linguistic and geographical barriers, preserves these differences. Musically, Laos is among the least-researched nations in the world—not surprisingly, considering its linguistic diversity, the natural inhibitors to travel and communication, underdevelopment, its being virtually closed to outsiders from 1975 until about 1990, and governmental restrictions on everyone's movements (most especially researchers') until 1994.

NONCLASSICAL MUSIC

Instrumental Music

In Laos, most classical and village instruments—those of the upland minorities excepted—have parallels in Thailand. The classical instruments differ little from those of Thailand, and village instruments have counterparts in northeastern Thailand, a culturally Lao region. The manufacture of instruments occurs on a small scale in isolated villages throughout the country (Figure 10.1).

Though fipple flutes (*khui*), plucked lutes (*phin, kachappi*), and fiddles (*so, so i*) are found here and there—more in the south than in the north—the free-reed mouth organ (*khene*) is the predominant melodic instrument in rural Laos. Whereas the instrument with sixteen pipes predominates in Thailand, the *khene chet* with fourteen tubes was usual in Laos until the late twentieth century, when sixteen became usual as well. Related to the *khene* is the single free-reed pipe with holes for fingering, used by Thai Dam (Black Tai, so called because of the prevalence of black in their clothing). It has two sizes, larger (*pi luang*) and smaller (*pi bap*).

Idiophones and membranophones are few but important. Variously shaped two-headed laced drums played with the hands are called *kong*, and the smaller and larger cymbals similar to those of classical Thai music are pronounced in the Lao manner (as *sing* and *sap*). Single-headed long drums called *kong nyao* are commonly seen in processions. An idiophone distinct to the southern Lao is a clapper-scraper (*mai ngop ngep*); the player claps together two hinged pieces of wood about 30 centimeters long while scraping teeth cut into

khene
Free-reed bamboo mouth organ, main instrument of Laos
lam
Traditional vocal genres of southern Laos
khap
Traditional vocal genres of central and northern Laos

the lower piece over a block of wood.

Tuning

The tuning of traditional Lao music, like that of northeastern Thailand, is based on the *khene*, which has seven tones per octave, in intervals that match closely those of Western diatonic tuning: A–B–c–d–e–

Figure 10.1
Three musicians from Salavane in southern Laos play music for *lam salavane* on, left to right, the *khene*, the *phin*, and the *soi*. Photo by Terry E. Miller, 1991.

f–g. Higher tones on the *khene* duplicate these at the octave. Though few players of *khene* in Laos commonly use the theoretical terms known to players in northeastern Thailand, the same principles apply. Thus, northeastern Thai theoretical terminology will serve in reference to Lao styles.

Two basic pentatonic scalar systems derive from this tuning: one, called the *san* scale, sounds major, and is expressible as starting on G (G–A–C–D–E); the other, called the *yao* (pronounced *nyao* in Lao) scale, sounds minor, and is expressible as starting on A (A–C–D–E–G). On a *khene*, the *san* scale can be played in three modes, and the *yao* scale can be played in two. In northeastern Thailand, *san* modes (with starting tone in parentheses) are called *lai sutsanaen* (G), *lai po sai* (C), and *lai soi* (D), and *yao* modes are called *lai yai* or *lai nyai* (A) and *lai noi* (D) [for a fuller explanation of *khene* music, see THAILAND: Northeastern Thailand].

Styles of Playing

As in northeastern Thailand, Lao players of *khene* sometimes play solo, but they do so less commonly and with less virtuosity than across the Maekhong. Terminology used for titles varies widely. Among Lao players, *thang* "style, way" replaces *lai,* and qualifying terms may refer to regional vocal genres (such as *thang savannakhet*), techniques (such as *thit sut noi* "to plug" [with *khisut* wax] high d' or a'), function (such as *pheng nang thiam,* for a spirit-related ceremony), or allude to extramusical images (such as *mae hang kom luk* "the widow sings a lullaby to her child"). Solo playing named after regional genres is usually an accompaniment style played alone. The titles of Lao music for the *khene* show little consistency from region to region. Players were also aware of, and often played, the styles of northeastern Thailand, including *lot fai tay long* "the train runs along the track"—clearly imported, since Laos has no railroads.

The primary function of the *khene* is to accompany singing. It is said that a fully qualified player must know thirty-two varieties of song but that knowing fifteen to eighteen is acceptable. Each regional vocal genre has a distinct accompaniment in mode, rhythm, and melodic traits, but variations among players are normal. To accommodate the tessituras of male and female voices, players must be able to accompany in at least two modes of each scale (*san* and *yao*).

Vocal Music

The names of regional vocal genres are preceded by either *khap* or *lam*, but though both denote song, neither is used in reference to singing Lao classical music or Westernized music. Most genres called *lam* or *khap* are in repartee: in a battle of the sexes, alternating male and female singers feign courtship, or even trade insults. Since a skilled practitioner is called *mo*, a singer is *mokhap* or *molam*, and a player of a *khene* is *mokhene*.

Rituals

Lam phi fa "singing [to invite the] spirit of the sky" (also called *lam phi thai* and *lam phi thaen*) occurs when a patient who does not respond to either traditional or modern medicines is thought to have become ill because spirits have been offended. Ritualists, usually older women accompanied by a *khene*, sing to invite the offended spirits to enter their bodies and reveal the cause of the illness, while the patient observes. The ritual occurs in a home around an assortment of ritual objects (*kheuang bucha*), and may last several hours.

An important ritual, practiced in many rural areas of Laos, is the sacrifice of the buffalo. Jacques Brunet (1992 [1973]) included on a compact disc an example of music from the sacrifice at Vat Phu (south of Champassak), which has a small ensemble of hand-held gongs, some beaten with the hands, some with sticks, accompanying a vocalist-ritualist. This ritual, part of the Spring Festival, is attended by both lowland Lao and uplanders from the Boloven Plateau, and entertainment music is provided by the classical *piphat* of Champassak.

Of animistic origin, the rocket festival (*pong fai*) is important in much of southern Laos and northeastern Thailand. During the hot, dry months preceding the monsoon rains—April, May, sometimes as late as June—villagers prepare long, highly decorated, powder-filled rockets (essentially phallic symbols), which they launch to break the clouds and tell the deity of the sky (*phayah thaen*) to send rain. Associated with the festival are parades, which include both dancing accompanied by long drums (*kong nyao*) and responsorial singing in the streets, often by drunken revelers begging for whiskey and money; this genre is *seung pong fai*.

Entertainment

The Lao have at least twelve named and widely acknowledged regional genres, some designated by a provincial name (such as *lam salavane*), some after a village (such as *lam tang vay*), and some after an ethnic group (such as *khap thai dam*). Five genres whose names are preceded by *khap* are found in the north, mostly in pockets separated by rugged mountains. In these areas, infrequent communication results in distinctness and specialization: singers of one *khap* genre do not normally sing any other. Seven genres with names preceded by *lam* are found in the south. Since these genres originate in the lowland areas along or near the Maekhong River and its major tributaries, intercommunication is possible. As a result, southern Lao singers usually know more than one local genre as well as *lam klawn*, a northeastern Thai genre, called *lam kawn* or *lam tat* in Laos. Besides regional genres, three other genres occur but less commonly. In *lam nithan* (also called *lam puen* and *lam leuang*), a soloist accompanied by a *khene* sings epic-length tales, especially those derived from Buddhist *sathaka* (stories of Buddha's previous births), such as *Kalaket*.

Performances of traditional music occur in conjunction with several kinds of events, including calendrical and Buddhist rites and national festivals. Among the most important are *bun song kan* "water-throwing festival" during the fifth lunar month (April), *bun bang fai* "rocket festival" during the sixth lunar month (May), *bun kathin* "festival of presenting gifts to monks" during the twelfth lunar month (November), for ordinations, temple fairs, the New Year, and certain national holidays.

The principles that govern the creation of *khap* and *lam* are virtually the same as those pertaining to northeastern Thai *lam*. Poetry is composed in four-line stanzas in *kawn* form, with a fixed lexical-tonal pattern. The coordination of melodic pattern and lexical tone is necessary for full comprehension, but in practice, singers do not rigidly apply melodic formulas: they allow musical phrases and their individuality to override total coordination.

Lao singers traditionally perform in smaller, more intimate settings than do northeastern Thai singers. As was true until the midtwentieth century in the northeast, many Lao singers still perform seated, executing the simple gestures of the dance (*fon*) from the waist up. The player of the *khene* is seated behind or to one side of the singer. Much slower than genres from across the Maekhong, Lao genres give singers time to think of variant patterns to individualize the memorized poems. The traditional singer (*molam*) holds a special position in Lao society, not as a professional but as a person knowledgeable about culture, history, behavior, Buddhism, stories, and courtship.

During the Vietnam War (which also involved Laos), the Lao army gave *molam* the rank of sergeant, to teach and entertain troops. In Vientiane, the Lao Military Radio Station broadcast *lam* of many kinds with government propaganda embedded in the texts. The use of *lam* to propagate policies in Laos goes back at least to 1957, when the United States Information Service recruited singers and players of the *khene* from northeastern Thailand to mock the Pathet Lao in the earthy images of *lam* poetry.

Regional Genres

Since Lao singers perform specific, named regional genres, each genre is distinct in some way. For the novice listener, most of the southern *lam* types may sound alike. Each type, however, is distinguished in several ways—including regional tonal inflections and subtle ways of handling text. The following descriptions focus on musical elements discernible to any sensitive listener. These include accompanimental instruments, whether accompaniment or voice is declaimed or metrical, scale or mode; typical melodic motives; and other idiosyncratic features.

Lam Sithandone

Also called *lam siphandon* "four thousand islands," this genre is most similar to Ubon-style *lam klawn* in northeastern Thailand. Only the *khene* has been found to accompany this type, playing any of the *san*-scale modes (discussed above) in a manner indistinguishable from the style of players in northeastern Thailand—that is, using a sixteen-pipe instrument and in meter. The singer, however, declaims the poetry, though brief passages become regular in accent. (Figure 10.2).

Figure 10.2
Male and female singers, accompanied by a *khene*, sing *lam sithandone* in the old recording studio of the former building of the United States Agency for International Development in Pakse, Laos. Photo by Terry E. Miller, 1991.

Lam Som

Said to be named after a river and found on and around Khong Island in the Maekhong in southern Champassak Province, *lam som* is the rarest of the Lao genres. Like *lam sithandone*, which shares the same area, *lam som* is accompanied only by a *khene*, which plays slow, metrical patterns in a variant of the *yao* scale, having a sixth tone, one just above the tonic (A–B–c–d–e–g); in northeastern Thailand, this is called *lai nyai lam phoen*, after the narrative genre it accompanied.

Lam Salavane

Salavane Province's population includes many Mon-Khmer upland groups, *Lam salavane* is a Lao-language genre, sung by both Lao and Mon-Khmer but derived from Mon-Khmer styles. Instrumental accompaniment varies from solo *khene* to an ensemble that includes

lute, fiddle, flute, drum, and other small percussive instruments, which play steadily moving metrical patterns in a *yao*-scale mode. A drummer strikes the drumhead on the first, second, fourth, and fifth beats of an eight-beat rhythmic cycle (see Figure 10.1).

The genre is further distinguished by a melismatic vocal introduction. *Lam salavane* is one of the most popular types from southern Laos. With its catchy drumming, it has often been transformed into popularized arrangements, especially in the song "*Tia long, salavane, tia long*" ("Slow Down and Relax, Salavane").

Lam ban xok. Though denoted separately, *lam ban xok* (named after a village) may either be a predecessor of *lam khon savan* or a variant of it. Accompaniment is rarely less than *khene,* drum, and small cymbals, but some recordings add an electric bass guitar. A metrical accompaniment using the *san* scale (in *lai sutsanaen* or *lai po sai* modes) supports a declaimed vocal line, which may approach regular accents. Stanzas tend to begin high and cascade to a tone one, three, or four tones above the "tonic." Functionally, *lam ban xok* is different: people do not dance to it, singers are not hired specifically to sing it, it is associated with ceremonial occasions, and it is described as serene and reserved.

Lam tang vay. The name of a village in Savannakhet Province, *tang vay* means "rattan chair" because this village is known for its rattan crafts. Originally accompanied by a free reed pipe (*pi*) or a flute (*khui*), with a gong, a drum, and sometimes a scraper (*mai ngop ngep*), it is now normally accompanied by *khene*, a lute (*kachappi*), a fiddle (*so*), and percussion. The metrical, ostinato-like accompanimental pattern, basically | AAGG | F–D– |, supports a vocalist who metrically sings eight-beat phrases, each of which tends to descend.

Lam khon savan. Derived from the name of the city Nakhon Savannakhet, *lam khon savan* is probably the most important of the southern Lao genres. Each singer opens his or her section of a round with a short introduction, followed by the long middle section made up of stanzas of *kon* poetry and a closing section consisting of three short phrases. Accompaniment is provided minimally by a *khene,* but all the instruments normally encountered in central southern. Laos may be used, including the *mai ngop ngep.* The metrical accompanying motives, sometimes ostinato-like, support a predominantly metrical vocal line, which is often distinguished by short-long patterns and syncopations, particularly at the ends of phrases. *Lam khon savan* is closely related to, and easily confused with, *lam ban xok* and *lam mahaxay* in Laos and *toei hua non tan* and *lam phanya yoi* just across the Maekhong in Thailand.

Lam mahaxay. This genre is named after the town of Mahaxay, 45 kilometers east of Thakhek, Khammouane Province, on the road to Vietnam. Because of similar accompanimental patterns and mostly metrical singing, it is easily confused with *lam khon savan.* A distinguishing feature is each phrase's scalar descent to the "tonic." The metrical accompaniment is normally an ensemble of *khene, kachappi, so, mai ngop ngep,* and other percussive instruments, using the *san* scale (Figure 10.3).

Lam phu thai. The term *Phu Thai* "Thai people" is a lowland Lao or Thai term for upland Tai-speakers, such as the Red, White, or Black Tai, who migrated from northeastern Laos and northwestern Vietnam to lowland Laos. Thus, the term refers not to a linguistically distinct Lao subgroup but to acculturated uplanders living among lowlanders. These people may practice true *phu thai* singing, but the Lao genre called *lam phu thai* is mostly sung by ethnic Lao "in the style of" the *phu Thai.* As in other central-southern Lao genres, the accompaniment can be an ensemble of *khene*, lute, fiddle, drum, and percussion, playing metrically in a *yao* scale, especially *lai not*, which allows for tones below the "tonic." The singing, however, is more declamatory than metrical.

Figure 10.3
Lam Mahaxay in repartee form accompanied by *Khene* being recorded near Thakhaek, Laos. Photo by Terry E. Miller, 2005.

Figure 10.4
Male and female singers, accompanied by *khene*, sing *khap ngeum* on a covered veranda in Tourakham Village, north of Vientiane. Photo by Terry E. Miller, 1991.

Khap ngeum. Though found in the environs north of Vientiane, especially along the Ngeum River around the town of Tourakham, the style of *khap ngeum* suggests a northern origin. The people who sing *khap ngeum* likely descend either from migrants from northeastern Laos or from conquered upland peoples brought by the lowland Lao to the vicinity of Vientiane. *Khap ngeum* is accompanied by a *khene* alone. Though the playing of the *khene* can be related to a standard mode, usually *lai noi*, neither the patterns nor the drones and sonorities are like those of ordinary *lai noi*. The accompanist plays in rapid arabesques, often trilling between two tones a third apart. The singer slowly and deliberately declaims lines of text, often separated by long pauses. Because of the slow delivery and the gaps between lines or sections, singers can more easily improvise poetry and comment on immediate events. Typically, the woman answers in *phanya* (spoken courting poetry), but today, some women sing instead (Figure 10.4).

Khap phuan. Formerly called *khap xieng khuang*, this genre is properly named after the Lao subgroup called Phuan, who dwell in the Xiengkhuang area. Living on the Plain of Jars (a cool, rainy plateau), the Phuan are roughly equivalent to the lowland Lao elsewhere. Accompaniment is provided by the *khene* in Phuan tuning. The player's metrical pattern typically lasts four beats, each somewhat accented as he plays the "tonic" and octave of a *yao*-scale mode, either *lai nyai* or *lai noi*. The male singer's melody, in meter, is simple and syllabic; the female singer's response was performed at a tempo slightly more than twice that of the male to a four-tone scale related to the "tonic," rhythm was nonmetrical.

Khap sam neua. The genre most remote from mainstream Laos originates in extreme northeastern Laos (Houaphanh Province, near the town of Sam Neua) and across the border into northwest Vietnam. Speaking a Tai language different from lowland Lao, the Neua people who inhabit this area are the singers of *khap sam neua*. The *khene* used to accompany has no more than fourteen pipes, and perhaps as few as ten. It follows the nonmetrical vocal line closely, without drones but with multiple tones.

Khap thai dam. The Thai Dam do not use the *khene* but prefer a smaller free-reed pipe (*pi bap*), or a larger one (*pi mon*). While the singer declaims the poetry to somewhat indistinct steps of the *yao* scale (such as d–f–g–a–c'–d'), the *pi* plays only five tones: four in that scale, and one not in it (c#–d–g–a–d') Their rhythmic relationship is so free that it is difficult to detect any correspondence. Portamentos occur in both voice and instrument, especially at the ends of lines (Figure 10.5).

Khap thum (luang phrabang). Historically a separate principality, later the royal capital and the location of the most important Buddhist temples of Laos, Luang Phrabang is sited at the junction of the Maekhong and Khan rivers in remote central-northern Laos. The hills and mountains that surround the city on all sides are home to numerous upland groups,

khap ngeum
Repartee song of the Ngeum River basin near Vientiane
khap phuan
Repartee song of the Phuan Lao of Xiengkhuang Province
khap sam neua
Vocal music of the upland Lao of Houaphanh Province
khap thai dam
Repartee song of the Black Thai minority

many of which migrated into the area during the last couple of centuries. Originally part of the unified Kingdom of Lanxang (Kingdom of a Million Elephants), Luang Phrabang became a separate kingdom in 1707 as a result of a civil conflict and remained independent

Figure 10.5
Male and female singers, accompanied by a free-reed pipe (*pi*), sing *khap thai dam* on an open porch in Ban Ban, a village east of Phonsavan, Xiengkhouang Province. Photo by Terry E. Miller, 1991.

of Vientiane until 1946, when King Sisavang Vong of that city became the first king of reunified (but colonized) Laos (Figure 10.6).

Stylistically, *khap thum* has little relation to the other Lao types described above but is a local counterpart to the court tradition in repartee form. Instrumental accompaniment is provided by various combinations of court/classical instruments. Some are quite close to the formal *sep noi* or *maholi*, which consists of xylophone (*lanat*), gong circle (*khong vong*), fiddles (*so i, so u*), flute (*khui*), drums, and large and small cymbals. Many of these may be omitted, and other instruments, such as the dulcimer (*khim*), may be added. The ensemble plays a composed melody in duple time, while male and female soloists alternate, singing a more or less fixed melody, different from that of the ensemble. At the end of a couplet, a chorus of hand-clapping listeners completes the line with a single-tone response. The scale is pentatonic in the form of 1–2–3–5–6, with some passing use of 4. *Khap thum* is therefore a type of song, closer to being a tune than the melodies of traditional *lam* and *khap*, which are only partially fixed. Though *khap thum* clearly has classical

Figure 10.6
Male and female singers, instrumentalists, and a chorus of onlookers enjoy an impromptu performance of *khap thum* in Luang Phrabang City. Photo by Terry E. Miller, 1991.

foundations, its style and context are casual and close in spirit to that of village *lam*. As it did not depend for survival on court functions, it persists for festive occasions among ordinary urban people. Because of its instrumentation, classical players in Vientiane perform it as a lighter alternative to classical compositions.

General Observations on Nonclassical Vocal Genres

The foregoing data reveal patterns that suggest groupings of regional genres and possible common origins for these groupings, leading to eight preliminary conclusions:

1. The *khap* genres of the north differ stylistically from the *lam* genres of the south.

2. Three *khap* genres (*ngeum, phuan, sam neua*) exhibit similarities with regard to accompanimental patterns, the *khene* used, and its relationship to the singer's melody.

3. The *lam* genres of central southern Laos (*ban xok, khon savan, mahaxay, phu thai, salavane, tang vay*) are typically accompanied by a small ensemble rather than solo *khene*, though the latter instrument alone is acceptable when other performers are unavailable. Each has distinctive melodic patterns, especially in the accompaniment, which differentiate them. *Salavane* is perhaps most different, since it is performed by acculturated Mon-Khmer, rather than lowland Lao, and *phu thai* is based on the singing of "tribal" Thai (Figure 10.7).

4. Melodies of the same central-southern Lao genres consistently exhibit descending contours, but those of the remaining two southern genres (*sithandone* and *som*) do not.

5. The latter two southernmost *lam* genres use solo *khene* accompaniment and are similar to styles in northeastern Thailand, which also use solo *khene*.

6. All southern Lao genres have metrical accompaniment, but only *tang vay, khon savan*, and to a lesser extent *mahaxay* have metrical vocal lines.

7. Southern Lao singers normally perform more than one genre, even four or five, but northern singers perform only one.

8. Two genres are radically different from all others, and point to separate origins: *khap thai dam* is more correctly "tribal" Tai rather than lowland Lao; and *khap thum* is related to court music.

Figure 10.7
Laos' most famous singer during the 1960s and 1970s, Bountong Inxichiangmai, sings *lam khon savan* accompanied by *khene* in Murfreesboro, Tennessee. Photo by Terry E. Miller, 1981.

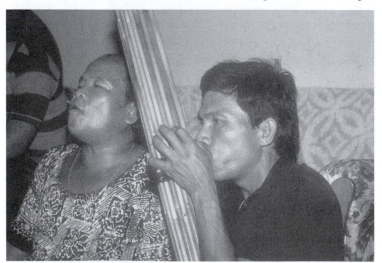

Theater

Nonclassical theater virtually did not exist in Laos until around the 1940s and 1950s, when three genres from Thailand began crossing the Maekhong, mostly to border areas. The development of these genres began with a central Thai theater called *li-ke*, which used classical instruments, heightened speech, and song, all in central Thai style, with colorful costumes, realistically painted backdrops, and spontaneous action based on a scenario rather than on a fully written script. *Li-ke* reached Laos between 1947 and 1950 from Khorat, Thailand, and the original members of that troupe were involved in founding the Natasin Fine Arts School in Vientiane in the mid-1950s.

At about the same time (from the early 1930s), a solo narrative genre accompanied by a *khene*, found both in Laos and northeastern Thailand—*lam poen*—was transformed into *lam leuang*, where the singer acted out various parts through gesture and costume. This development is said to have begun in Laos, and then became known in the northeast by about 1932. In 1952, a troupe of actors in Khon Kaen province, Thailand, began performing stories using a fully written-out script sung to Lao music, and called the genre *lam mu* "collective singing." The genre came to be known both as *lam mu* and *lam leuang*. This form, along with a second form of theater from northeast Thailand, *lam ploen*, first appeared in Laos in the mid 1960s and was performed in some southern areas. Following the end of monarchy in 1975 when the communist government began ruling Laos, little is known of theater until the 1980s when the government sponsored at least one propaganda troupe. Since the end of the 1990s, however, commercial troupes have reappeared in the south and perform regularly.

CLASSICAL MUSIC

The ensembles and theatrical genres associated with the court at Luang Phrabang and the Fine Arts School in Vientiane have long been called classical. The Lao term *peng lao deum* "Lao traditional compositions" differentiates this tradition from that of *lam*. Though similar in style and function to related traditions in Thailand and Cambodia, the Lao version, for various reasons, remained more modest, and the court context ceased to exist after 1975.

Historical relations between the courts of the Lao and the Siamese (the Tai of the Chao Phraya Valley, in present-day central Thailand) have often been difficult. The Lao and the Siamese, while historical and linguistic cousins, were also rivals. After 1828, when Bangkok's armies invaded and destroyed Vientiane and forcibly resettled much of the population in central Thailand, relations have become imbalanced in Thailand's favor, compounded when Laos became a French protectorate. Clearly, many Lao today have mixed feelings about modern Thai power, wealth, and the fact that Laos, being landlocked, depends on Thailand for access to goods and a route for exports.

Vientiane's tradition seems to have disappeared, at least temporarily, when Siamese troops sacked the city in 1828 and exiled the population to central Thailand. A classical tradition reemerged into prominence in the mid-1950s with the founding of the Natasin School (or National School of Dramatic Arts). After 1975, most of the Natasin staff was resettled in Des Moines, Iowa, but they too have failed to maintain the tradition. After 1975, the Natasin School continued with a new staff. With the exception of a few families playing classical music, the court tradition has disappeared from Luang Phrabang. The third principality was Champassak, in the deep south, whose history is interwoven with that of the Siamese. A classical ensemble descended from the court survives in a village setting there.

Classical music (*peng lao deum*) served varied purposes at the court. It provided entertainment and atmosphere at festivities and ceremonies and provided appropriate music within rituals. It accompanied theater and dance and entertained foreign guests on state occasions. Some have viewed it as the "great tradition" of the Lao, one of the highly developed court traditions of Southeast Asia, in contrast to the alleged 'little tradition' of *lam* and *khene.*

Musical Instruments

The Lao customarily divide instruments into four categories: *tit* "plucked," *si* "bowed," *ti* "beaten," and *bao* "blown." The main classical instruments are distinct from those used in *lam* (except *khap thum*), but a few overlap, such as the flute (*khui*), certain drums, and two kinds of cymbals: *sing,* the smaller type; and *sap,* the larger. All have Thai classical equivalents. The earliest physical evidence of Lao classical instruments is found on the gilded carvings in relief covering the exterior front wall of Vat Mai in Luang Phrabang, dated variously between 1796 and 1820. The ensemble of musicians includes a xylophone (*lanat*), a gong circle (*khong vong*) having at least eleven gongs, a small horizontal drum on a stand (*taphone*), a two-stringed bowed lute with coconut body (*so u*), small cymbals (*sing*), and two barrel-shaped drums played with sticks (*kong that*), plus a small mouth organ (*khene*) and a reader of a palm-leaf manuscript.

Plucked Instrument

Kachappi (Thai *krajappi*): a two-, three-, or four-stringed, fretted, plucked lute, whose body is usually rounded.

Bowed Instruments

So i (Thai *saw duang*): a two-stringed fiddle, with cylindrical body and snakeskin resonator.

So u (Thai *saw u*): a two-stringed fiddle, with coconut body and calfskin resonator.

Beaten Instruments

Lanat (Thai *ranat ek* and *ranat thum*): xylophones, the higher called *lanat ek mai* with twenty-one bars of wood or bamboo, the lower one called *lanat thum mai* with seventeen or eighteen bars of wood or bamboo.

Khong vong: gong circles, the higher called *khong vong noi* or *khong wong ek* with eighteen bossed gongs, the lower called *khong vong nyai* with sixteen gongs, suspended horizontally on leather strips in a rattan frame open at the rear (through which players must enter and exit).

Khim (Thai *khim*, from Chao-zhou Chinese *yang qin*): a dulcimer with two sets of bridges.

Kong taphone (Thai *klawng taphon*): an asymmetrical-shaped, two-headed barrel drum, mounted horizontally on a stand, and played with the hands.

Kong that (Thai *klawng that*): a pair of Chinese-style barrel drums with tacked heads, mounted obliquely on a stick frame, beaten with two sticks.

Sing (Thai *ching*): small cup-shaped metal cymbals, beaten in open (*sing*) and damped (*sap*) strokes to mark cycles in classical compositions.

Sap (Thai *chap*): thin, disklike, metal cymbals, which play syncopated patterns in opposition to the *sing*.

Blown Instruments

Pi kaeo (Thai *pi nai*): a quadruple reed instrument, carved of wood with a bulbous shape.

Khui (Thai *khlui phiang aw, khlui lip*): a fipple flute of bamboo, with seven holes for fingering and one rear hole for the thumb, made in two sizes, the larger (lower) simply *khui*, the smaller (higher) *khui lip*.

Ensembles

Two ensembles are usually named, but they had different names in Vientiane and Luang Phrabang. The ensemble associated with ritual, formal, state occasions, theater, and dance is called *piphat* in Vientiane (after Thai usage), and *sep nyai* in Luang Phrabang. It consists of one or two xylophones, gong circles, and, depending on whether hard or soft mallets are used, an oboe (hard) or flute (soft). The second ensemble is called *maholi* in Vientiane (again the same as the Thai term *mahori*), or *sep noi* in Luang Phrabang. The instrumentation of this group is quite flexible. It includes virtually any of the instruments listed above, except the oboe, in greater and smaller groupings that include the bowed strings.

REGIONAL STYLES OF CLASSICAL MUSIC

Though a unified kingdom at its founding, Lan Xang included three widely dispersed centers of power connected by the Maekhong River: Champassak in the south, Vientiane in the center, and Luang Phrabang in the north. The French reunified Laos as part of Indo-China. Three separate court-music traditions developed, all similar to each other and to those of Cambodia and Thailand. Over time, however, local idiosyncrasies developed. The court at Champassak vanished as the Thai gained power in that area, and part of its territory was ceded to Cambodia, but a classical ensemble persists in a village near Champassak. Luang Phrabang became the royal capital and the king's residence, while Vientiane became the administrative capital. After 1975, however, with the king's abdication, court music at Luang Phrabang ceased to function, and the city lost its royal status.

Luang Phrabang

Assessing how glorious the court tradition really was is difficult. Though no evidence of large-scale ensembles remains, there was classical dance, the masked drama called *khon*, and a hand-puppet theater. The latter was reported to have originated about 1930; it performed both the story of Rama and a Lao epic, *Sang Xin Xay*. The repertory is of Thai origin, since the compositions are by known composers. After the Luang Phrabang musicians fled the country, only the instruments remained. They are housed in the palace museum, silent. Classical music, however, is said to remain alive in several private homes.

Vientiane

Vientiane's tradition may be younger, having returned to prominence only in 1956 as the Natasin School (or National School of Dramatic Arts), with help from the United States

piphat/sep nyai
Lao classical ensemble with xylophones, gong circles, and oboe
maholi/sep noi
Lao classical ensemble of strings and flutes

Agency for International Development. Its purpose was to promote Lao national identity through music, dance, and theater, and one important function was performances for visiting foreign dignitaries. Its most important regular function was playing at *bun that luang*, a festival held in December at the city's most famous temple, built originally in 1566, destroyed in the later 1800s, and rebuilt with French help in the 1930s. The school officially opened in 1959 with ten teachers, trained in Bangkok from 1956 to 1959. Consequently the Vientiane tradition began largely as a copy of that of Bangkok.

As part of the school's purpose of promoting Lao nationalism, choreographers created new dances illustrating characteristic life in Laos both among the lowland Lao and upland groups—dances such as the *fon ha pla* "fishing dance," the *fon phao lao* "ethnic dance," and five "friendship dances." Instrumental teachers created ensembles that combined *khene* with other instruments for accompaniment. In 1975, most of the Natasin staff, with much of the city's population, fled to Thailand, and many musicians resettled in Des Moines, Iowa, USA.

Neither a wealthy nor a highly respected institution, the Natasin School barely survived the change to communist rule, which condemned the arts of elites and elevated those of "the people"; consequently, the friendship dances and other dances depicting the life of "the people" survived. Thai influence was eliminated, the costumes from Bangkok lost, and in 1992 the name changed to the National School of Folkloric Music and Dance. The Lao developed an elaborate, classical-derived performance from the Lao *Pha Lak Pha Lam* (but using both classical and Lao instruments) and has presented it in Thailand.

In the 1990s, the institution moved to better quarters, rebuilt its staff from former students, and has begun to be used internationally again by the Lao government to promote Lao cultural identity. According to a teacher at the school interviewed in 1991, there are ensembles of *piphat, maholi,* and *khene vong* (mouth organs), and training in *khon, lakhon* and various genres of Lao *lam*. The staff was said to include fifty-five teachers, who teach these subjects plus ballet, piano, violin, saxophone, and guitar to 150 students ranging in age from thirteen to eighteen,.

Champassak

Champassak, along the Maekhong in southern Laos, was in the 1700s and 1800s the court center of one of the three principalities that eventually combined into modern Laos. Little remains of Champassak besides village homes, old colonial buildings, and a few minor temples; but before 1975, because the Angkor-period Khmer temple called Vat Phu is located eight kilometers to the south, Champassak was the center of tourism in southern Laos. Champassak's history during the last two centuries is complicated by the fact that it was not a state (with defined boundaries) but a court center (with shifting spheres of influence), and after 1778 became more a vassal of the Thai than of the Lao. The continuing presence today of a classical instrumental ensemble made up of farmers living in surrounding villages is remarkable, but its history is difficult to ascertain. The ensemble's repertory is essentially Thai, but the last known teacher who worked with the ensemble is said to have come from Cambodia in 1967 (Figure 10.8).

The ensemble, called a *pinpat*, consists of at least seven musicians, all male, who play xylophone (*lanat ek*), gong circle (*khong vong*), oboe (*pi*), plastic soprano recorder (called *khui lip*), horizontal drum (*tapon*), a pair of barrel drums (*kong that*), and small cymbals (*sing*). The tradition continues to be passed orally from father to son, for the youngest member, who plays xylophone, learned from his father, who plays a gong circle. The ensemble plays periodically for local festivals, but the most important event of the year is the annual buffalo sacrifice, held at Vat Phu.

Figure 10.8
The *pinpat* ensemble of Champassak performs in the otherwise empty lobby of a hotel in Champassak City. Photo by Terry E. Miller, 1991.

The Lao Accent and Lao Identity

Some observers note the existence of Thai classical compositions in the Lao accent (*sam-niang lao*), all by Thai composers. Among them are some of the most famous titles in the repertoire—"*Lao siang tian,*" "*Lao duang düan,*" and "*Lao jarün sri.*" Some Lao believe these to be Lao melodies adapted by Thai composers. For evidence, they point to the thousands of Lao forcibly exiled in central Thailand after the destruction of Vientiane. Though some supposedly Lao melodies were possibly derived from the songs of the Lao, most were derived from the music of northern Thailand around Chiangmai, an area commonly called Lao by the central Thai. Nonetheless, based on this (mis)understanding, the Lao prefer to play compositions in the Lao accent.

POPULAR MUSIC

Before 1975, Vientiane was known for its nightlife, including popular types of music performed in hotels and clubs, but after the change of government in 1975, Vientiane (and all of Laos) fell on austere times. Until about 1990, there was virtually no free enterprise, and the drabness of daily life was only occasionally broken by festivities. For anyone with a radio or television, however, the Thai media were always available, and because the Thai media along the Maekhong remain stronger than the radio stations and single television station in Laos, all owned by the government, Lao popular culture is essentially borrowed Thai popular culture.

The most prevalent form of distinctly Lao popular music is modernized renditions of the traditional, regional genres, a Lao parallel to Thailand's *luk thung* songs. Some genres are more flexible in this regard than others; indeed, of the northern (*khap*) genres, only *khap thum* lends itself to this treatment. Most *lam* genres from the south work well. The change involves the use of an electric guitar, an electric *phin*, or a synthesizer with an electric bass guitar, a set of drums, and new poetry. More in the past than at present were songs in ballroom dance tempos, similar to Thailand's *luk krung* songs, accompanied by a small jazz combo.

Two factors hold back the development of popular music in Laos. First, the power of the Thai media will continue to overwhelm the minuscule Lao popular-music industry for years to come. Second, poverty makes it difficult for musicians to purchase the equipment necessary for playing popular music. Opportunities for learning how to compose, arrange, and play modern instruments are also limited.

LAO MUSIC TODAY

The fall of the coalition government in 1975, and the resulting flight of tens of thousands of ethnic Lao, Hmong, Khmu, and other minorities (first to camps in Thailand, then to permanent resettlement in the United States, France, Canada, Australia, and other countries) have created a musical diaspora. The *lam* tradition, however, was carried by some of the country's finest singers, particularly Bountong Insixiengmai (living in 1997 in Nashville, Tennessee) and his cousin Khamvong Insixiengmai (living in 1997 in Fresno, California), a recipient of a National Heritage Award from the National Endowment for the Arts in 1992.

Musicians who remained in the newly established People's Democratic Republic of Laos after 1975, especially those who specialized in *lam*, were required to work for the government and sing its messages, but the government found that *molam* were less than reliable and would return to traditional material when out of officials' earshot. Currently, musicians may be hired privately, and they have primarily returned to the traditional themes of Buddhism, love, and lore. Today in Laos, though musicians are mostly free to perform, little money is available for hiring them. Poverty prevents the radical change that is sure to come if the country achieves a measure of prosperity. The Lao hear modern popular music on Thai radio and television every day, and since many people favorably view the modernization of traditional music, only lack of money holds back conversion to electric guitars, sets of drums, and other symbols of modernization and Western freedoms.

Before a complete picture of music in Laos can be drawn, a great deal of field-work must be conducted. Even now that the government has lifted its controls on in-country travel, the remaining obstacles are formidable. There is as yet no national inventory of musicians. Consequently, researchers are uncertain where to go. With overland travel getting better but still somewhat rough, one is limited to flying to isolated airstrips serviced by Lao Aviation. Laos has a tremendous variety of ethnic groups, and until their individual musical systems, often linked with little-studied languages, can be documented in depth, our knowledge of music in Laos will remain incomplete.

REFERENCE

Brunet, Jacques. 1992 [1973]. *Laos: Traditional Music of the South.* Auvidis / UNESCO D 8042. Compact disc and commentary.

Burma

Ward Keeler

History
Types of Ensembles
Percussive Patterns
Vocal Music
Tuning
Modes
Transmission and Change

Officially called Myanmar, Burma borders five other nations: Bangladesh and India on the west, China on the north, and Thailand and Laos on the east. Burma's landmass—657,740 square kilometers—is slightly smaller than that of Texas. Of a total population of 47.3 million (2006 estimate), 68 percent are Burmese (also called Burman), 9 percent Shan, 7 percent Karen, 4 percent Rakhine, 3 percent Chinese, 2 percent Mon, 2 percent Indian, and 5 percent "other." Areas dominated by the Burmese are called provinces whereas those of the "National Brethren" are states. Burmese culture predominates in seven provincial divisions (Irrawaddy, Magwe, Mandalay, Pegu, Rangoon, Sagaing, and Tenasserim), and non-Burmese tend to dominate in seven states (Chin, Kachin, Karen, Kayah, Mon, Rakhine, and Shan). Some of these states have been in rebellion against the central government since 1948, when Burma gained independence from Britain. Consequently, research in these areas has been extremely limited. Nationwide, the predominant religion is Theravada Buddhism, but sizeable groups of Christians and Muslims exist.

In part because Westerners find Burmese music less immediately alluring than some other musical traditions of Southeast Asia, and in part because entry into Burma for Western researchers has been difficult since the early 1960s, outsiders know much less about Burmese music than about, say, Javanese, Balinese, or Thai music. Each of Burma's ethnic groups has its own language and musical traditions. The ethnic Burmans, native speakers of Burmese, have enjoyed some degree of political preeminence within a region roughly corresponding to the present nation since the days of Pagan, the kingdom that ruled from a city by the Irrawady in Upper Burma in the tenth through the twelfth centuries. This article focuses on the music of the majority Burmese, especially because there is relatively little literature on other types. Burmese music can be divided into two styles: an outdoor type and an indoor, chamber type.

HISTORY

The earliest documentary reference to Burmese music is found in China, in a Tang Dynasty chronicle. It gives an account of a troupe of musicians and dancers sent to the Chinese court by the Pyu, in Lower Burma, in the 800s. A few instruments known to have existed earlier are now either lost or no longer in widespread use. A bowed fiddle (*tayò*) has been replaced by the Western violin; how the mouth organ (*hnyìñ*) was played is no longer known; it is not even known for sure what one instrument was (its name, *sàñdeyà*, is now applied to the piano); the "crocodile-shaped zither" (*mì jaùñ*) is no longer used by Burmans, though the Mon still have such an instrument (Garfias 1985) (Figure 11.1).

It was the practice in Southeast Asia that a triumphant army did not long occupy a vanquished kingdom. Instead, conquerors physically removed many of its inhabitants, forcing them to settle in the invading army's homeland, where their labor could be put to use. Artists' labor was as likely to be exploited in this way as anyone else's. Burmese claim that many of their artistic traditions developed out of Siamese-Thai courtly arts brought to them by artists obliged to move to the Burmese capital when Ayuthaya fell to invading Burmans in 1767.

The classical repertoire continued to grow throughout the 1800s, but with the end of the era of Burmese kings in the late 1800s, the corpus of classical compositions ceased to develop further. Instead, Burmese and Western musical styles have become increasingly hybridized.

Figure 11.1
A Mon zither (*mì jaùñ*) in the shape of a crocodile. Photo by Terry E. Miller, 1994.

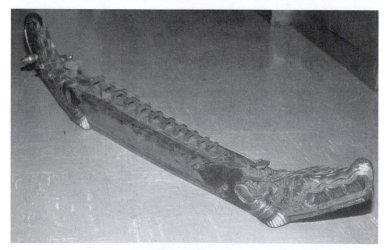

TYPES OF ENSEMBLES

The distinction between outdoor and indoor music in Burma corresponds to that between loud, vigorous music, and soft, chamber music. Outdoor ensembles come in many varieties, most named for their respective drum types. The *hsaìñwaìñ*, or simply *hsaìñ*, is the most commonly used outdoor ensemble; it consists of drums, gongs, and aerophones. A chamber-music ensemble may consist of as few as one vocalist and one instrumentalist (either a harp or a xylophone), plus the vocalist's bamboo clapper and small cymbals. During the twentieth century, and increasingly since the late 1970s, musicians often combine Burmese and Western instruments, creating a broad spectrum of musical styles, from a largely classical Burmese style that incorporates the piano and violin to a more Western popular style.

In the following, the word *hsaìñ* denotes the most common outdoor ensemble, and the phrase "chamber ensemble" denotes any configuration of instruments playing in a small group with a vocalist: the latter type usually includes a singer (or singers who take turns singing individually) accompanied by one instrumentalist—either a harpist or a xylophonist.

Hsaìñwaìñ

The most important and frequently heard ensemble in Burma is the *hsaìñwaìñ,* or simply *hsaìñ,* which includes from six to ten performers. At a minimum, it includes a drum circle, a gong circle, a bass drum, large cymbals, a smaller set of cymbals, and an oboe. The first three instruments are placed in a row in front, with the others set behind them. It can also include gong racks, a set of side drums, one or more stick-beaten drums, and a large bamboo clapper. The *hsaìñ* accompanies all types of theatrical performances, of which Burmese are great devotees, and it is also played on ritual and religious occasions, such as spirit-propitiation rites, pagoda festivals, boys' entries into a temple as novices, girls' ear-piercing ceremonies, and so on (Figure 11.2). Officials' visits take on pomp from the presence of a *hsaìñ,* as does an important funeral.

Figure 11.2
Two Burmese dancers (after Frost and Strickland 1927: between pp. 56 and 57).

Instruments of the Ensemble

Drum Circle

The *pa'waìñ* (*pa'* "drum," *waìñ* "circle, circular") consists of twenty-one tuned drums hung vertically by cords from a circular wooden frame. The frame, about a meter tall, is elaborately decorated with colored glass and gold paint. The drums, held away from the frame by cane, vary from 13 to 41 centimeters high. They have two heads, but only the upper one is struck. The *pa'waìñ* is tuned by loading the center of the head with a paste of boiled rice and ashes; the more *pa'sa* added, the lower the tone. One of the most imposing instruments in the ensemble, it is divided into eight sections, with a circumference of about five meters. The player of the drum circle, *hsaìñ hsaya* (*hsaya* "master"), sits in the middle on a small stool (Figure 11.3).

Properly called the *pa'waìñ,* the drum circle is usually called the *hsaìñ,* but in everyday speech the names of this instrument and the whole ensemble are the same. This usage attests to the importance of these drums among the several in the ensemble, as does the

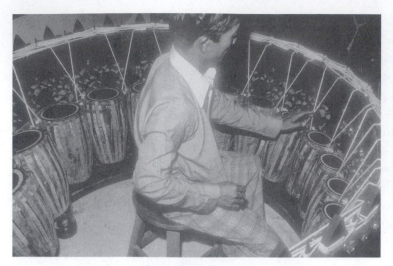

Figure 11.3
The Burmese drum circle (*pa'waìñ*) of twenty-one tuned drums. Photo by Terry E. Miller, 1994.

fact that the player of the drum circle is the troupe's leader. Most *hsaìñ* are known by the name of the drum player who is their leader: the name of the ensemble, with the drum player's name prominently displayed in gold lettering, is usually emblazoned across a cloth backdrop used in performance.

Gong Circle

The gong circle (*cìwaìñ*, *cì* "copper, bronze") consists of twenty-one small, graduated, knobbed gongs set on a circular rattan frame resembling that of the drum circle. The gongs are struck with two beaters, now made of wood with rawhide tips. To obtain the best tone, the player must strike the gongs at an angle. In the upper range (but not in the lower range), the gongs are damped with the fingers. Players tune the gongs by using beeswax to make lead filings adhere to the inside of the bosses of the gongs: the more filings added, the lower the pitch (Figure 11.4). The wooden frame is not so large as that of the drum circle: it is slightly smaller in circumference, and only about half as high. The number of gongs in the *cìwaìñ* has increased: in the early 1800s, they numbered only seventeen; by 1939, they numbered nineteen; and today, there are twenty-one.

cìwaìñ
Set of twenty-one graduated bossed gongs mounted horizontally in a circle

maùñsaìñ
Set of eighteen or nineteen bossed gongs on wooden frames in five rows

Figure 11.4
The Burmese gong circle (*cìwaìñ*). Photo by Terry E. Miller, 1994.

Gong Rack

The gong rack (*maùñsaìñ*) consists of eighteen or nineteen small, graduated, knobbed gongs, secured by cords to wooden frames divided into five rows (Figure 11.5). The gongs are flatter and larger than those of the gong circle, and their tone is lower. Their sound differs, too, because they are made of a different alloy than is used for the gongs of the gong circle. This alloy gives them a less resonant, somewhat tinny sound. All but the largest of the frames are set flat; the largest one is propped upright. The introduction of the gong rack seems to date from the 1920s or so (Becker 1980:475).

Figure 11.5
The Burmese gong rack (*maùñs̱aìñ*). Photo by Terry E. Miller, 1994.

Figure 11.6
A set of Burmese drums used to accompany dance. Photo by Terry E. Miller, 1994.

Miscellaneous Drums

The *pàmá* (*pa'* "drum," *má* "main") is the largest drum of the ensemble, a barrel drum suspended from a wooden beam, often decorated with a dragon's head, inlaid glass, and gold paint. The *sakhúñ*, another double-headed horizontal drum, rests on a rack.

The word *hcau'loùñpa'* (*hcau'* "six," *loùñ* "counting word for objects," *pa'* "drum") refers to these two drums plus smaller barrel drums, of various sizes, each standing on one drumhead (Figure 11.6). Tuning is achieved either by using paste (*pàsa*) or by tightening the drumhead to raise the pitch. The drumheads are struck by three or four fingers of either or both hands. The body of

each drum is made by hollowing out a single teak log, with one end larger than the other; the larger drumhead is struck. Strips of hide secure the drumheads to the drum, and the crisscrossing strips over the body of the drum give it a striped look.

Oboe

The multiple-reed oboe (*hnè*) is made of a conical tube of acacia or other hardwood, bored through the center. It has seven holes for fingering on its anterior side, equidistant from each other, plus a hole for the thumb on the underside, and a copper bell loosely attached to the end of the tube by means of a red cord. The bell does not amplify the sound; it appears to be primarily decorative, and the instrument can be played without one. The reeds are made of a toddy-palm leaf that has been soaked, and then smoked for months, folded, and cut so as to make six concentric layers (Figure 11.7). In performing softer music, particularly if accompanying singers, an oboist may substitute a bamboo, end-blown fipple flute (*palwei*), which has the same pitches and same fingering as the oboe. Both instruments have two-octave ranges, starting at about middle C on the larger and at the G above on the smaller.

Other Instruments

In the *hsaìñ* ensemble, small cymbals (*si*) are played with the *byau'*, a small block of wood with a slit in it, struck with a stick. *Si* and *byau'* together articulate colotomic structure. The large metal cymbals in the *hsaìñ* can be called either *yakwìñ* or *lakwìñ* (Figure 11.8). The *wale'hkou' are* large bamboo clappers, made from a section of a large type of bamboo. The *hsaìñ* ensemble includes one large, hanging, bossed gong (*maùñ*).

Relations among Instruments

The timbre of each instrument determines its role in the *hsaìñ*. The oboe, ubiquitous in all outdoor ensembles (not just the *hsaìñ*), stands out for its reediness and extremely rapid variations. It carries the melody clearly, though the complexity of its variations can obscure the melody more than a vocal part would, and its sound tends to dominate any ensemble. The drum circle and gong circle also play idiomatic variants of the melody, but because of timbre and the fact that they can sound two notes simultaneously, they do not sketch the melodic line quite so clearly. The one time the gong circle is not subordinate to the drum circle is at the outset of a performance. Tuning the drum circle is a time-consuming process, and during that time, the gong circle leads the *hsaìñ*, playing *yoùdayà* songs and other classical compositions. Indeed, the gong circle provides the standard tuning for the ensemble.

The drums of the *hsaìñ* ensemble are integrated in performance according to two principles: the larger the drum or set of drums, the deeper its pitch or pitches; and the more rarely it is struck, the more important a role it plays in maintaining the rhythmic pattern, and the less it contributes to the melodic line of the song. The largest drum, at one extreme, is the *pa' má*, and the drum with the greatest range is the drum circle (Figure 11.9).

Though certain instruments can play two notes simultaneously, Burmese musicians do not distinguish between a melodic part and a harmonizing part secondary to it. But the overall effect is not one of harmony. This kind of texture, known as heterophony, is as typical of the drum circle and gong circle in the *hsaìñ* as it is for the harp and the xylophone in chamber ensembles.

Figure 11.7
The Burmese multiple-reeded oboe (*hnè*). Photo by Terry E. Miller, 1994.

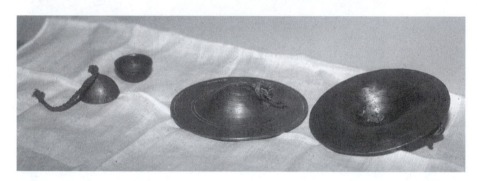

Figure 11.8
Si cymbals (left) and *yakwìñ* cymbals (right). Photo by Terry E. Miller, 1994.

Occasions for Use: Repertoire

The *hsaìñ* ensemble accompanies many kinds of performances (Figure 11.10). Increasingly, electronically amplified or acoustic Western instruments are mixed with the Burmese ensemble. One context in which no Western instruments are likely to be mixed with Burmese is the spirit-propitiation rite called *na' pwè*, for which a *hsaìñ* will be hired to accompany mediums, most of them transvestites (of either sex), who dance to invoke spirits (*na*), and then dance as the spirits take possession of them. A *na' pwè* begins, like a traditional marionette performance, as the *hsaìñ* gives a musical depiction of the threefold destruction of the world, swept by wind, fire, and flood. Then a devotee appears and sings a series of verses, dedicating offerings to the spirits and calling to witness the stage itself, the local spirit, and the people in attendance. She then sings the song of Indra, who in Burma is considered the king of the spirits. He speaks through her to say he is joining the celebration, then to say that he has enjoyed himself and is returning to his heaven. After this, the series of songs invoking individual spirits begins, lasting several hours into the night (K 1981).

A specific tune and rhythm are associated with each spirit, and people who attend *na' pwè* with any frequency know after a few moments of music which spirit is about to be invoked. As in many other contexts, the musicians will often banter with some of the people dancing. Much of this interaction consists of punning, and much is bawdy. It is unclear whether it is the ritual nature of the event that makes *na' pwè* more resistant to Western musical influence than other kinds of performances, or simply the slightly unfashionable, somewhat licentious reputation they have among Burmese who disapprove of the ritual on both theological and moral grounds.

Figure 11.9
An exceptionally ornate carved wooden stand for drums at Rangoon's University of Culture. Photo by Terry E. Miller, 1994.

Figure 11.10
A village *pwé* (after Frost and Strickland 1927: between pp. 62 and 63).

In full-scale theatrical performances (*za' pwè*), the *hsaìñ* accompanies actors as they sing, and provides a musical commentary on much of the action. Most of this music derives from the classical collection of texts, the *Maha Gitá*. The *hsaìñ* also plays an overture at the opening of the performance, interludes between scenes, and closing music at the end. When actors sing, they enter into something like a dialogue with the drum circle. The actor sings a verse of music, and then the player of the drum circle replicates as closely as possible the embellishments the actor has used. The actor then sings another verse. Musicians playing the standard repertoire can count on spectators' ability to make the appropriate associations to the music. Much of this is conventionalized, so that in scenes marked by grief, the *hsaìñ* plays a certain composition (*ngouhcìñ*); for fight scenes, another (*leìhcìñ*); for scenes of longing, yet another (*hmaìñ*), and so on. Aside from evoking specific emotions, certain compositions are appropriate to particular situations; a hero meditating in a forest calls for one tune; certain compositions are available for use when an evil king makes his entrance; and so on.

It is possible for the *hsaìñ* to play alone, especially in modern compositions. Called *bala hsaìñ* (*bala* "bare, naked"), this kind of performance is rare, but it gives players an opportunity to display their virtuosity. In this context, the player of the drum circle is not beholden to someone else—either the vocalist, a spirit medium in the *na' pwè*, or the actor in a *za' pwè*. The musicians must try to hold people's attention by their remarks and jokes, and by the speed, intricacy, and variety of their playing. Players of drum circles have been observed at such a performance playing a particular tune several times over, identifying each rendering as the way one or another famous predecessor had played it (John Okell, personal communication).

There is one exception to the rule that the player of the drum circle is the leader of the *hsaìñ*. A genre called *anyeìñ* brings together musicians, women who sing and dance, and clowns. In the days of Burmese kings, this was a royal entertainment. Now it is a popular one, less elaborate and costly than a *za' pwè*, and more easily arranged on short notice, since it involves fewer players and few or no props.

Other Outdoor Ensembles

In Burma, as in much of Southeast Asia, drums are the defining element of many ensembles: Only in the style of chamber music does the percussive pattern become so reduced as to allow the elimination of drums. In it, a vocalist articulates rhythmic structures with a wooden clapper and hand-held cymbals.

Òzi

Òzi are goblet-shaped drums, about 25 centimeters across the head. An *òzi* is made by hollowing out a single block of light wood about a meter long. It is played vertically, resting on the drummer's chest and suspended by a cord from the drummer's neck. The *òzi* is played with cymbals, bamboo clappers, and often a bamboo flute or an oboe. The drummer and others sing and dance (Figure 11.11).

Figure 11.11
A long drum (*òzi*), used in village ensembles. Photo by Terry E. Miller, 1994.

Doùpá

Doùpá are small, double-headed drums, about 75 centimeters long. Their heads, made of cowhide, are of different sizes, the right one larger than the left one, measuring about 25 and 18 centimeters in diameter respectively. *Doùpá* are played suspended horizontally across the chest, usually in an ensemble that includes large cymbals, an oboe, and large bamboo clappers.

Boúñçì

Boúñçì, like *doùpá*, are double-headed drums, and they are likewise played suspended horizontally across the chest. However, they are somewhat larger, about a meter long. They are usually played in pairs, on the occasion of rice-planting festivals, pagoda festivals, or other important events. They may be joined by an oboe, large cymbals, and large bamboo clappers, or they may play in a complete *hsaìñwaiñ*.

Byò

Unlike the drums mentioned above, all of which are struck with the hands, *byò* are stick-beaten; made of teak, they are slightly larger than *doùpá*, are played in pairs, and are accompanied by a smaller drum, *palou'tou'*. Used in any ensemble, they are usually accompanied at least by a large oboe and cymbals.

Siṭo

All the drums mentioned above are associated with rural Burma, at least in origin. *Siṭo*, however, are associated with royalty, as the name suggests (*si* "drum," *to* "royal"), and in keeping with their special status, they are Burma's largest drums. They measure close to 1.25 meters long and 50 centimeters in diameter, and are double-headed but played on one side only, struck with a stick.

Figure 11.12
The Burmese chime (*cìsi*) played in a procession at Rangoon's Shwe Dagon pagoda. Photo by Terry E. Miller, 1994.

Cisi

The Burmese *cisi* is a suspended metal chime associated with temples where it is struck in such a way that it spins while dangling from the end of a rope. When used in this way, it produces a unique wavering tone (Figure 11.12).

Sporting-Event Ensembles

Two types of Burmese sporting events may be accompanied by a small ensemble consisting of gongs, an oboe, and drums. These events are Burmese boxing and a game called *hcìñloùñ,* in which people standing in

Saùñ
Burma's arched harp, the last surviving harp in Asia
pa´talà
Xylophone with twenty-four bamboo keys suspended over a wooden resonator
sì
Two small hand-held cymbals shaped like bells
wà
Clapper of spoon-shaped bamboo pieces

a circle use their feet, heads, and torsos, but not their hands, to keep a rattan ball in the air; their aim is grace and agility.

Indoor Ensembles (Chamber Music)

The chamber ensemble, unlike the *hsaìñ,* is likely to be heard by small gatherings of people—probably musicians themselves—who enjoy its qualities. It is also heard on state-run radio and television. It affords women more opportunities for music making than the *hsaìñ.* Women may learn to play the harp, and female vocalists are probably more numerous than male. Otherwise, women can take part in musical performances only as actresses, singers, or dancers, either in *za' pwè* or *anyeíñ.* Chamber music usually combines one vocalist and one instrument, either the arched harp or the bamboo xylophone. The bamboo flute (*palwei*) can join either of these instruments. Piano and guitar are sometimes used in modern styles of chamber music.

Arched Harp

Burmese consider the arched harp (*saùñ*) their most prestigious instrument, associated with the refinement and sophistication of the old royal courts. It consists of two parts: a resonator, carved from a hollowed piece of hardwood; and the curved root of an acacia tree, set into the resonator to provide a long, graceful arch. The design gives the instrument an unusually elegant form, resembling a swan arching its neck.

The top of the resonator is covered with deerskin. The fourteen strings of the modern harp are stretched between a slightly curved bar on the resonator and the lower portion of the arch. Some of the strings are of twisted silk, and some of them are now of nylon. The strings can be tightened or loosened with tuning cords whose tassles hang down from the arch. A small wooden loop is attached to the front of the resonator to secure the harp during tuning. The instrument is covered with three coats of lacquer to conceal the seams between the various parts of the instrument, giving it a smooth, even surface. It may be decorated with gold leaf, semiprecious stones, and lacquer designs. Four holes are cut in the deerskin membrane. The moment these openings are made is considered astrologically influential over the harp's future performance. As one opens these holes, one asks spirits to take up residence in the resonator, and one must treat the instrument with the respect that heirlooms and other valuables often elicit in Southeast Asia (Williamson 1968, 1975).

The harpist sits cross-legged, with the

Figure 11.13
Daw Yi Yi Thant, an eminent singer of classical Burmese music, playing the harp at her home in Rangoon. Photo by Ward Keeler.

resonator placed on the right thigh and the arch against the left one. The right elbow rests on the top of the resonator while the thumb and index finger of the right hand pluck the strings. The left thumb presses the strings to modify the pitch (Figure 11.13).

> The history of this harp suggests development toward an ever more complex, virtuoso style, perhaps inspired by Thai musicians said to have influenced Burmese music after the fall of Ayuthaya. At present, the harpist plays in accordance with the tempo set by the hand-held cymbal and the bamboo clapper (both under the singer's control), but the harpist may either follow the vocal line or diverge from it. (Williamson 1980:482–484)

Figure 11.14
Secondary students at the Fine Arts Department school in Rangoon practice xylophone (pa'talà). Photo by Terry E. Miller, 1994.

Pa'talà

The alternative major instrument of a chamber ensemble is the bamboo xylophone (pa'talà). The term probably derives from the Mon words for a percussion instrument and a box or chest. The contemporary pa'talà consists of twenty-four bamboo bars suspended over a resonating chamber. The bars narrow progressively as one moves up the scale, toward the player's right. Twine passing through holes at either end of each bar links them. Their range covers three full diatonic octaves, plus two notes on the treble end. Makers tune each bar by shaving its underside: shaving the middle lowers the tone; shaving the ends raises it. The pa'talà is played by two padded beaters (Figure 11.14). The earliest evidence for the instrument comes from the Kalyani Inscription (1400s) and a literary reference of the 1500s. The pa'talà resembles several Southeast Asian xylophones, including the Thai *ranat* and the Khmer *roneat*.

Sì

The *sì* consists of two small, hand-held cymbals shaped like bells. Between the thumb and the forefinger of the right hand, a vocalist holds one bell steady, its mouth upturned. A string links this bell to another one of the same size and shape, held and manipulated by the other fingers of the same hand. In performance, the latter bell strikes the former at set intervals.

Figure 11.15
Two forms of Burmese clappers (wà). Photo by Terry E. Miller, 1994.

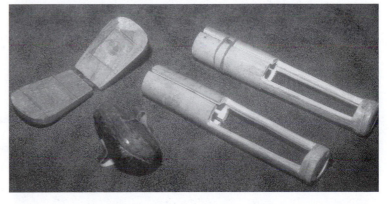

Wà

A hand-held clapper (*wà*) is made of bamboo. The vocalist holds it in the left hand, rapping it against the thigh at set intervals, in coordination with the *sì*, to control the tempo (Figure 11.15).

PERCUSSIVE PATTERNS

Burmese music typically includes a wide array of percussive instruments—drums of many shapes and sizes and gongs spanning several octaves. But the most important percussive instruments in any ensemble that includes vocalists are the diminutive cymbals (*sì*) and the bamboo clapper (*wà*), held in the singer's hands. Using these, the vocalist controls the tempo.

Most classical songs begin with a nonmetered section, which leads to a fixed meter for the greater part of the composition until a final coda, when nonmetered music returns. The meter is articulated by the *sì* and the *wà* in one of three cyclic rhythmic patterns, each with eight beats. In the following three patterns (after Becker 1980:479), x is *sì* and o is *wà*.

Phrasal beats	1	2	3	4	5	6	7	8
Pattern 1		x		o		x		o
Pattern 2		x		x				o
Pattern 3				x		x		o

A point of some confusion is whether the *wà* marks the first or the final beat of a four-beat cycle. It is agreed that it marks the strong beat, and the *sì* marks weaker beats. The first song a student learns begins with a little exercise, two lines in which one sings the words *sì* and *wà*, striking each of them in time to the appropriate word. The song is in duple time, and the first line begins with *sì*. The first line of the poem itself, however, begins on *wà*. It appears true, however, that every composition ends on *wà*, usually held off in much the same way that the final gong in a Javanese gamelan composition is briefly delayed.

Judith Becker (1969), analyzing Southeast Asian percussive patterns, has helped clarify the principles at work in Burmese music. She finds throughout Southeast Asia the pervasive use of eight-beat and sixteen-beat phrases, phrases in which odd-numbered beats are little stressed, and even-numbered beats are stressed in a hierarchical pattern that reserves the greatest emphasis for the final beat of the phrase. Both percussive patterns and melodic contours support the sense of completion at the end of eight-beat or sixteen-beat phrases.

The structure provided by these rhythmic patterns is a foil to the variations and embellishments played by members of the ensemble. Much of the artfulness of Burmese music lies in how a singer, a harpist, or another instrumentalist plays around a steady beat. A good singer should maintain an almost nonchalant air, singing variations that bear little obvious relation to the steadiness of the *sì* and the *wà*. But that nonchalance must never lead the singer to compromise a responsibility to keep the beats in good order.

VOCAL MUSIC

Burmese music is essentially vocal: most compositions are settings of poetic texts, although not always performed with a vocalist. The repertoire of songs divides up into types. The name of a type may be that of a poetic form; it may refer to the pattern of its rhythmic accompaniment; or it may refer to some circumstance, historical or cultural, connected to a set of compositions.

The Burmese musical modes and the principal types of song exemplifying them are:

1. hnyìñloùñ	coù
	bwé
	thahcìñhkañ
2. auʼ pyañ	paʼ pyoù
	lòká naʼ thañ
	leìdwei thañ gaʼ
3. pale	Yoùdayà
	talaìñ
	moñ
	bole
	thañzàñ
4. myìnzaìn	teìdaʼ
	shiʼhsebo
	deìñ than

The classical repertoire, consisting of the above types of song and called *thahcìñ cì* (*thahcìñ* "song," *cì* "great"), developed over several centuries. The earliest song, "*Bauñ Là Coù*," the sixth of a set known as the "First Thirteen *Coù* Songs," reputedly describes a king's passage up the Irrawady to Tagaung in about 1370. Two other songs in that set are also believed to have originated in the 1300s. The first five *coù* of the set, in the order in which they were eventually arranged, are believed to date from the early 1700s:

Yoùdayà songs are traditionally thought to have been brought to Burma at the time of the Burmese sack of Ayuthaya (1767), though contemporary Thai apparently hear nothing familiar in them. *Moñ* and *talaìñ* songs, far fewer, are also thought to derive from a non-Burman source—the Mon people, living in Lower Burma, Thailand, and Cambodia. *Deìñ than* songs are used in propitiating spirits (*na*); like several of the smaller groups of types of song, they are short, strophic songs whose melody changes slightly to conform to the text.

Language and Music

The language of the texts is both archaic and allusive; many Burmese have difficulty understanding the songs. Burmese who do not care for classical music cite this lack of intelligibility to explain why it bores them; aficionados, however, though they may have little more sense of the songs' meaning, are not daunted by the obscurity of the language, and are satisfied to have some minimal notion of a song's meaning.

An intriguing, but as yet too little researched, question is how the phonetic constraints of Burmese, a tonal language, are reconciled with the tonal variations of the melodic lines to which words are set. The Burmese language has only two distinct tones, but syllables are further differentiated by voice quality, duration, and the presence or absence of a final glottal stop. The result yields five possible types of syllables: high, short, "creaked" (with

a slight final glottal occlusion); high and heavy (in final position, falling); high with a full glottal stop; low, though sometimes pronounced as a rising tone; and toneless.

A related and even more difficult question is how types of syllables and their musical settings relate to each other in a series, that is, not simply the melodic handling of single syllables, but the relation between types of syllables and pitches in phrases. In speech, what indicates the tone is not the absolute pitch of any one syllable but whether it is higher or lower relative to the preceding tone. The relationship is likely to be compromised by virtually any musical phrase. How is intelligibility maintained?

What Is a Burmese Tune?

Given that there is no standard system of notation for Burmese music, and that anthologies contain only the texts of songs, the question arises of just what it means to "know" a particular composition. No single participant in an ensemble sings or plays "the song" in an isolable, repeatable form. Instead, each member of the ensemble plays variants. To uncover their basis, Williamson elicited three sung versions of a single *bwé* song, one of them with a harp accompaniment played by the singer. She then extracted an underlying, unembellished tune, which she labels the basic tune, one that only a beginner, if anyone, would ever learn. The crucial elements of this tune, she concludes, are the initial pitches and the cadential formulas for each stanza and line, and for any important part-line break in the poem (Williamson 1979).

P. A. Marano reported (1900) that Burmese favored high tenor voices in men and deep contralto voices in women. Those preferences still seem to hold, particularly in the classical repertoire. Vocal range is not much stressed, however. If a singer finds that a song is reaching beyond the limits of his or her range, sudden octave displacement up or down can be done without embarrassment.

A few songs are sung without accompaniment, a few more are sung with the *sito* ensemble, and others are sung with the various folk ensembles mentioned above; however, it was hard, already in the 1960s, to find people who could still sing such songs (K 1981). Much more common is for a singer to be accompanied by a harp, a xylophone, or sometimes a *hsaìñ* ensemble, the musicians repeating each sung verse. Burmese musicians say the accompaniment to a singer should be fairly simple. The repeat, however, affords musicians an opportunity to display their skill at improvising complex variations. In *anyeíñ*, the repeat accompanies the singer as she executes a dance, and in this, as in all contexts, the rhythms are livelier than in the initial rendition.

TUNING

The Burmese scale—or perhaps more accurately, the Burmese system of tuning—consists of seven notes to the octave. Burmese who are familiar with Western music theory often compare their scale to the C-major scale. The pitches of the scale are given one set of names for instruments in the *hsaìñ* ensemble and a different set of names for instruments in the chamber ensemble. In the case of the *hsaìñ* instruments, pitches are named after the fingering positions of the oboe. The tonic is called *thañ hmañ* (*thañ* "sound, note," *hmañ* "correct"), the note obtained by open fingering. The rest of the pitches are named not in ascending order, but in descending order, as obtained if one covers each of the seven holes of the oboe in order, proceeding from the top to the bottom of the cylinder.

The names of the tones make this model clear: the second note of the Burmese scale, called "two holes" (*hnapau*), meaning that two holes are covered, is the seventh degree; the third note, "three holes" (*thoùñpau*), corresponds to the sixth degree. Garfias suggests that the descending order is explained by the fact that Burmese melodies tend to follow a descending contour (Garfias 1975:39). The reversed order of the notes from Western practice sometimes causes confusion.

In the chamber-music ensemble, a different set of names applies. The two sets of names are as follows:

Chamber Music	Hsaìñ	Degree
Hnyìñloùñ	thañ hmañ	tonic
pale	hnapau'	seventh
duraká	thoùñpau'	sixth
pyidopyañ	leìpau'	fifth
au' pyañ	ngápau'	fourth
myìñsaìñ	hcau'pau'	third
hcau'thwenyúñ	hkuni'pau'	second

How closely the Burmese scale actually corresponds to the Western diatonic scale is somewhat vexing, however. It seems clear that in the classical tradition the seventh and third degrees were somewhat lower, and the fourth degree somewhat higher, than their Western equivalents. Because the seventh and third degrees of the Burmese scale are slightly lower than the Western ones, and the fourth degree is slightly raised, the Burmese scale gives a Westerner the impression of having equidistant intervals, much like those of Thai classical music. Garfias has warned us not to assume this to be the case, however, on the grounds Burmese musicians do not speak of equidistance as the ideal, nor do measurements demonstrate it (1980b:480).

As in Java and Bali, there seems in Burma to be a generally agreed-on tuning, with considerable tolerance for variation. The intervals among the fixed-pitch instruments need not, therefore, conform to a single standard. If a Burmese harpist and a Burmese vocalist hit slightly different pitches, the effect is not likely to be as jarring as if a Western vocalist and an instrument with sustainable notes, such as flute or piano, hit and held slightly dissimilar pitches. No indigenous Burmese instrument except the oboe and the flute can sustain notes in this way, and there is no evidence that these two instruments use a tuning distinct from a vocalist's. Burmese audiences seem to tolerate pitch discrepancies to a surprising degree.

Actually, the Burmese playing of pianos is in itself somewhat surprising to Western ears. To Burmese, notions of a harmonic accompaniment to a melodic line often matter but little; instead, one hears the piano played in much the same way as the Burmese harp or the Burmese xylophone, the two parts playing a melodic line in support of the vocalist's

Figure 11.16
Instrumental version of last *coù* song published by the Ministry of Culture in 1960 (excerpt). Provided and edited by Robert Garfias.

line but not really harmonically subordinate to it. One cannot preclude the possibility that a vocalist could maintain disparate tuning even when accompanied by the piano.

MODES

Burmese musical terminology appears to have no general word meaning mode, but there are named modes for both *hsaìn* and chamber ensembles, and the concept is basic to the process of performing traditional Burmese music. Modes are distinguished according to their fundamental pitches and the pitches receiving greater or lesser stress in a composition: there is a "hierarchy of pitch relationships" (Powers 1980:377). At the same time, modes typically have recurring melodic formulas, shorter or longer passages that musicians exploit in improvisation and that listeners recognize as specific to particular modes.

Figure 11.17
The composer U Ko Ko plays traditional accompaniments on an electric piano with a violin, also playing traditional music.
Photo by Terry E. Miller, 1994.

Although every mode is based on five tones, all seven tones are used in all the available modes. The same heptatonic series of pitches is employed, classically with the raised fourth and lowered third and seventh degrees mentioned above, in every mode. In each mode, however, at least two tones are avoided in positions of stress, and in one mode (*hkunithañci*) three tones are so avoided. Stressed positions are defined by rhythmic patterns. Cadences are particularly important to the identification of a specific mode (Figure 11.17).

Modes and the Names

Just as there are two series of names of tones, one applied to the *hsaìñ*, the other to the chamber ensemble, so there are two sets of names for the modes. Each set, furthermore, admits of certain variations. Unfortunately, the published sources do not agree on what the names of the modes are. Burmese agree that the chamber-music ensemble has seven possible modes, of which only four are commonly used. Four names of tones from the chamber-music system of tuning do double duty as the names of these most commonly used modes. They are *hnyìñloùñ, au' pyañ, palé,* and *myìñsaìñ*. The remaining three are *pyidopyañ, duraká,* and *hcau'thwenyúñ*.

The names of the nine named modes in the *hsaìñ* ensemble, their fundamental pitches, and their approximate Western equivalents, as set forth by Garfias (1975), are provided below.

Mode	Fundamental tones				
thañ you hcau'pau	I	III	IV	V	VII
	C	E	F	G	B
hkunithañci	I	III	IV	V	VII
	G	B	C	D	F
pa'saboù	I	II	III	V	VI
	C	D	E	G	A
tahcañ pou	I	III	IV	V	VI
	C	E	F	G	A

Mode		Fundamental tones				
ngàpau'		I	II	III	V	VI
		F	G	A	C	D
hsi' cì		I	II	III	V	VI
		B	C	D	F	G
ngàpau' au' pyaň		I	III	IV	V	VI
		F	A	B	C	D
Leìpau' au' pyaň		I	II	III	V	VI
		G	A	B	D	E
thaň yoù hnapau'		I	II	IV	V	VI
		B	C	E	F	G

All but two of these modes (*thaň yoù hnapau'* and *ngàpau' au' pyaň*) can be reduced to two general sets, according to what the secondary pitches (S) are and what the intervals between the primary pitches are (after Garfias 1975:44):

Type 1	1	S	3	4	5	S	7
Type 2	1	2	3	S	5	6	S

Not all modes arc equally represented in either the *hsaìň* repertory or the repertory of chamber music. The compositions most frequently played by *hsaìň* are in the modes *thaň yoù hcau'pau'*, *hkunithaňci*, *ngàpau'*, and *pa'saboù*. How the modes of chamber music relate to *hsaìň* modes is unclear. *Hnyìňloùn* in the repertory of chamber music seems to correspond to *thaň yoù* in the *hsaìň* repertory, *palè* to *pa'saboù*, and *myìňsaìň* to *ngàpau'* (Garfias 1980a:479). Garfias did not actually specify such equivalences systematically, however. Becker followed Khin Zaw's equivalences (1940), but the latter's modal names do not correspond to those of Garfias' list.

The modes imply changes in the tuning of variably pitched instruments. The drum circle and the harp must be retuned for each mode. Of twenty-one drums of the drum circle, the highest eleven are still tuned consecutively to all seven pitches of the scale, no matter what the mode. The secondary pitches in a specific mode occur in passing in the melodic variations that the drummer plays. In the lower registers, the drums are tuned to the five primary pitches of the mode, and the secondary pitches are not available. The harp's strings are tuned to the five main pitches of each mode, and the secondary tones are attained by pressing strings with the fingers of the left hand. The fixed-pitch instruments cannot simply eliminate the secondary pitches from the lower register, as the drum circle does; but in performance, players easily pass over such pitches (Garfias 1975).

Modal Melodic Units

Becker (1969) emphasized melodic formulas rather than scalar constraints. Noting that Burmese nonmusicians can distinguish the modes with ease, she attributed this facility to the recurrence of melodic patterns specific to particular modes. The existence of a store of such patterns for each mode explains musicians' fluency in creating new compositions in performance.

mode
Collection of musical elements forming the basis for improvisation and composition

fixed-pitch instruments
Instruments, such as xylophones and gong circles, whose pitch cannot be changed during performance

variable-pitch instruments
Instruments, such as fiddles and flutes, whose pitch is infinitely controllable during performance

yoùdayà
Genre of classical songs said to be derived from the Siamese at Ayuthaya

TRANSMISSION AND CHANGE

The classical music tradition in Burma is maintained in two forms, written and oral. The written portion consists of the words of about five hundred songs. These have been collected in two anthologies, *Maha Gitá* and *Gitá Withòdani*, published in editions readily available in Burma. The anthologies do not show how the texts are set to music, and the layout of the texts on the page does not suggest divisions into verses and stanzas—which readers must discern on the basis of the rhymes.

Since Burmese music does not have a consistent or a widely known system of notation, outsiders may wonder how its repertory of compositions can be transmitted from one generation to the next. The solution has been to embed the music-learning process in a larger social context and to develop a vocabulary of oral conventions by which specific musical figures could be identified. The transmission of the musical tradition in Burma has always been marked by personal relationships between musicians and their apprentices. In the past, a young musician would go to live at the home of an established master—usually the leader or manager of an orchestra—for two or three years. In accordance with patterns for acquiring any desired skill in Southeast Asia, the apprentice would be available to do odd jobs around the house, and would accompany the troupe to its performances. Occasionally, the master would give the apprentice a lesson (Okell 1964). To what extent the pattern of live-in apprenticeship applied to female students is unclear.

When a master gave a lesson, he would usually teach tryout pieces (*asàñ*), brief compositions without a fixed beat, demonstrating a particular mode's important pitches. A student's later ability to improvise correctly depended on this knowledge. Another means to ease study was the existence of three versions of a tune, graded in difficulty, from the simplest (*acè* "widely spaced"), to one of middling difficulty (*ala'* "middle"), and finally an intricately embellished version (*asei'* 'densely packed'). But probably most important was the apprentice's experience of listening to the ensemble perform. This enabled him to become familiar with tunes before learning to play them. He would eventually do so, but only after he had mastered the tune would he go to his teacher for guidance on fine points (Figure 11.18).

Beside troupes to which aspiring musicians could attach themselves, the traveling theatrical troupes, most based in Rangoon or Mandalay and managed by the male romantic lead (*mìnthà* "prince"), were important in transmitting Burmese music.

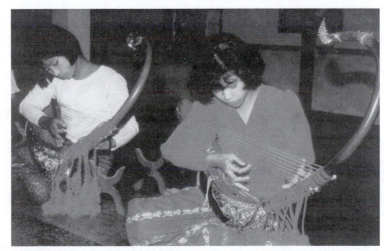

Figure 11.18 Secondary students at the Fine Arts Department school in Rangoon study the Burmese harp. Photo by Terry E. Miller, 1994.

Figure 11.19
Two marionettes displayed in the Museum of History, Rangoon. Photo by Terry E. Miller, 1994.

They visited the towns of Upper and Lower Burma, especially in the central zone, during the cool, dry months from October to April. Local musical groups then imitated their music. At the same time, audiences learned the repertoire well enough to associate many important compositions to specific contexts. Such shared associations are essential to the effectiveness of the tradition's use of evocative themes.

Such touring troupes still exist, but it is uncertain to what extent they maintain the classical repertoire. Increasingly, the parts of the performance dealing with old-style historical and religious subjects (those linked to the classical repertory), are shortened or even omitted in favor of pop-music concerts at the start of a performance and dancing in mixed style, followed by modern-dress plays. In the last, the Burmese *hsaìñ*, while still present, is largely overshadowed by Western instruments (including electric guitars, amplified violins, electronic keyboards, trumpets, snare drums) playing in alternation with or even simultaneously with the Burmese instruments. The marionette (*you'thei*) tradition, which drew on the same repertory as the traditional *za' pwè*, has not taken on these modern forms, but it has become virtually extinct (Figure 11.19).

In town, too, many people study music in private lessons rather than through apprenticeship, though lessons are more likely to be exchanged for gifts and services than for cash, which would offend the dignity of some highly regarded musicians.

The establishment of the state schools offered students an alternative way to get musical knowledge. Administered by the Fine Arts Department, a unit of the Ministry of Culture, four schools at the secondary level (two each in Rangoon and Mandalay) enroll pupils. Each city has a school of music and drama and a school of painting and sculpture, said to have opened in 1954. The school of music offers classes in Burmese music and its history, and instruction in voice, harp, piano, xylophone, and ensemble instruments. In September 1993, the department opened the University of Culture, a baccalaureate-level institution with degrees in music, theater, painting, and sculpture. Each freshman class in music would have fifty students, so after four years the university would have two hundred. Besides studying Burmese music, they would receive instruction in other world musics (Figure 11.20). At the present time the Burmese education system is said to be in disarray, and while schools are apparently "open," there may be no activity.

Pedagogy

Most students first study singing, then an instrument. The first instrument taken up is usually the bamboo xylophone. A student of either voice or xylophone begins by learning the "First Thirteen *Coù*" songs. The first three are in the "widely spaced" style; the rest are usually taught in the "middle" style (Okell 1964). The whole cycle teaches the beginner a basic vocabulary of musical phrases, which recur in other *coù* songs and other compositions.

The basic vocal line and the instrumental accompaniment of a composition are closely tied. For example, the falling third in the vocal part of the first stanza of the first *coù* imposes a specific figure on the xylophonist, a figure always associated with that vocal pattern in the repertoire. Indeed, the basic structure of the accompaniment to any song is fixed by oral tradition. Nevertheless, players have room for ornamentation, provided that they know the constraints of the meter and mode.

Since the tradition has long been transmitted orally, passed down through lines of masters and their pupils, it is not surprising that variant versions of many songs exist and that proponents of one variant or another defend them tenaciously. Given that modernity is understood by virtually all bureaucracies as equivalent to standardization, it is not surprising that the Burmese Ministry of Culture has attempted to establish "correct" versions of all songs. It remains to be seen how successful these efforts will be at eliminating rival traditions.

Figure 11.20
A teacher at the University of Culture demonstrates a horse marionette. Photo by Terry E. Miller, 1994.

Westernization, the Media, Cultural Policies

Perhaps the greatest threat to the continued transmission of Burmese music lies not in the absence of a system of written notation but in Burmese interest in Western music. That interest dates back to the nineteenth century and remained strong even in the face of official disapproval during General Ne Win's rule.

Burmese responses to Western music must be understood in the context of Burma's history, particularly in relation to colonialism, as these tinge all of Burma's problematic relations with the outside world. The Burmese mix of defensiveness, imitation, and eclecticism is no doubt common to cultural developments in many postcolonial societies. Yet Burmese responses start from Burma's own musical traditions, and so give the results a particular cast. In fact, Burmese have found several means of bridging the gap between their own and Western music. In some cases, they have chosen to use a Western instrument such as the piano to accompany classical or neoclassical Burmese songs in a way resembling that of indigenous instruments. In other cases, they have forged new styles of singing that incorporate much about Western popular music, often choosing to accompany a single song with alternating Burmese and Western instrumental backups. In these modern songs with their mélange of styles, modes are no longer consistent within a composition. Finally, since the 1980s, Western pop has appeared ready to displace Burmese music entirely from popular tastes. Actually, to call this music "Western" is tendentious. Much of the most popular music in Burma today consists of pop music sung in Burmese but with fairly generic tunes, similar to those of Thailand, Indonesia, and Hong Kong, often in ballroom dance tempos.

Another practice common throughout Southeast Asia is to take popular Western hits and dub them in national languages. Comparing a few Burmese and Indonesian versions of the same Western original suggests that Burmese renderings are more successful at maintaining a jazzy or bluesy feeling. This difference may be attributed to the greater amount of syncopation and generally freer variations in Burmese singing. Regardless of origin, all songs intended for media dissemination, private (via cassette) or public (television, radio, or public performance), must first be approved by official committees. Even songs originating in small, private studios undergo this process.

People have long decried the imminent loss of Burmese musical traditions. In a book published in 1900, the author of an appendix on Burmese music bemoaned how Western influences were driving out Burma's own music (Marano 1900). It is difficult, at this point, to determine just how many vocal and musical styles have been altered since then. In the late 1930s, an urgent appeal was made to the government to finance the recording of some of Burma's renowned older singers and musicians, lest their knowledge die with them. The establishment of state-supported art academies has encouraged the continued training of musicians and dancers schooled in the classical traditions. An unfortunate consequence of those schools' founding was that regional variations in the musical repertory were eliminated in favor of uniform teaching, and much of the dancing that students learn in the two academies is of a hybrid sort.

The state television station broadcasts brief programs of classical singing one evening a week, plus occasional dance performances. These, with performances by the two large state-supported National Cultural Troupes and a smaller one, are in some respects the purest expressions of Burmese classical musical traditions one can find in Burma. Though these troupes' performances of Burmese music, dance, and theater are quite conservative, if highly abridged, those representing the National Brethren (including Chin, Kachin, Mon, Shan) are usually considerably altered, and a patriotic message is often imposed on them (Figure 11.21).

Probably the long-term result of pop's increasing popularity in Burma will be the confinement of the classical repertoire to a tiny segment of the population devoted to its pleasures, much as has occurred with classical music in the West. Commercial recordings of classical music are already difficult to find, despite the proliferation of cassette-shops in the cities. Enthusiasts with the necessary equipment record songs off radio and television as best they can. In recent years, the government has sponsored a nationwide competition for singers of classical songs and their accompanists each November in Rangoon. In preparation, during the months prior to the competition, the country's FM radio station broadcasts performances of much of the repertoire of classical songs by established performers.

Most performances in Burma use elaborate sound systems, though of poor quality, turned to a high volume. A za'pwè troupe usually has four or five loudspeakers arrayed across the front of the stage, and the actors stand stage front and center through most

Shadow-play and dance-drama performances tell one story over successive nights. To ensure a successful performance, the first night requires a special opening ritual, the *buka panggung* "opening of the stage." For shadow plays, the puppeteer conducts the ceremony; for major dance-dramas, a traditional medium or shaman (*bomoh*) does. The puppeteer or shaman reads special prayers and presents offerings of prepared foodstuffs, including rice, eggs, and betel. Uttering special recitations to elements in the unseen world, he ritually bathes in incense the musical instruments and (for shadow plays) the puppets.

Shadow-Puppet Theater

The shadow-puppet theater (*wayang kulit*), a popular form of theater for centuries, continues to be performed. In peninsular Malaysia, it takes any of four types: *wayang kulit Jawa, wayang gedek* (or *nang talung), wayang Siam* (or *wayang Kelantan*), and *wayang melayu* (or *wayang Jawa*).

Wayang Kulit Jawa

This is the *wayang purwa* of Indonesia, performed by peoples of Javanese descent living along the southwest coastal areas in Johore (see JAVA). The languages of the stories are Malay and Javanese. The accompaniment is the Javanese gamelan, which in Malaysia consists of *saron* (*demung, barung, peking*), one or two *bonang, gambang, ketuk, kenong, kempul,* and *gong agung* (*gong kumbang*). The orchestra uses the *sléndro* system of tuning.

Wayang Gedek

The southern Thai form of shadow play, which uses leather puppets, is performed by Thai peoples living along the northern border regions of Malaysia. The Thai language, mixed with the local Malay dialect, is used to relate the stories, while the musical accompaniment comes from an ensemble of Thai fiddles, drums, knobbed gongs, and cymbals. The ensemble strikingly resembles that of the Thai *manora* dance-drama and the Malay shadow play of the northeast coast, utilizing (in the state of Kedah, for example) two goblet-shaped drums (*gedumbak*), one stick-hit barrel drum (*geduk*), one oboe (*serunai*, a quadruple-reed aerophone), a pair of finger-held cymbals (*ker-incing*), and a pair of small, knobbed gongs set in a wooden box and struck with padded beaters (Ku Zam Zam 1983).

Wayang Siam and Wayang Melayu

These forms are the indigenous types of shadow theater, with distribution in the north- and east-coast regions. As products of Malay culture, both forms are performed by Malay peoples in regional dialects. The *wayang melayu* was formerly performed in court as entertainment for aristocrats. In contrast, the more popular of these forms, the *wayang Siam*, with many regional styles, has always been performed in the rural and semiurban areas of the north, by and for the common people. It is folk theater, performed mainly for entertainment.

The *wayang Siam* and the *wayang melayu* are performed in a small, raised hut (*panggung* "stage"), of which one wall is a white screen (*kelir*). A lamp hangs before the screen,

jikay
Comic theater derived from Islamic *zikir* and southern Thai theater
manora
Southern Thai theater featuring a half-bird, half-human creature, performed in northern Malaysia

of a scene to remain near the microphones. Music ensembles, too, are highly amplified; only rehearsals and small gatherings of friends are exempt from the rule of intensely distorted sound. Popular taste seems to have grown so accustomed to this sound that it is deliberately cultivated.

Musicians in Burmese society enjoy only limited respect unless they attain unusual renown, and even then they are regarded with some suspicion by the proper denizens of society. An accomplished Burmese harpist may enjoy some measure of prestige; the members of a *hsaìn* troupe do not. The modest payment musicians receive does not, of course, explain their devotion: art and camaraderie are the only rewards they can count on. But for all the celebration of Burmese culture in the pronouncements of the state and among older people, it is unclear to what extent young people will feel moved to learn traditional musical forms.

Figure 11.21
Performance of marionette puppets in a restaurant in Rangoon that caters primarily to tourists. Photo by Max T. Miller, 1987.

REFERENCES

Becker, Judith. 1969. "Anatomy of a Mode." *Ethnomusicology* 13(2):267–279.
———. 1980. "Burma: Instrumental Ensembles." *The New Grove Dictionary of Music and Musicians*, ed. Stanley Sadie. London: Macmillan.
Garfias, Robert. 1975. "Preliminary Thoughts on Burmese Modes." *Asian Music* 7(1):39–49.
———. 1980a. "Burma: Classical Vocal Music." *The New Grove Dictionary of Music and Musicians*, ed. Stanley Sadie. London: Macmillan.
———. 1980b. "Burma: Theory." *The New Grove Dictionary of Music and Musicians*, ed. Stanley Sadie. London: Macmillan.
———. 1985. "The Development of the Modern Burmese Hsaing Ensemble." *Asian Music* 16:1–28.
K [Khin Zaw]. 1981. *Burmese Culture: General and Particular.* Rangoon: Sarpay Beikman.
Khin Zaw. 1940. "Burmese Music: a Preliminary Enquiry." *Journal of the Burma Research Society* 30(3):387–460.
Marano, P. A. 1900. "A Note on Burmese Music." In *Burma*, ed. Max Ferrar and Bertha Ferrar, appendix C. London: Sampson Low, Marston.
Okell, John. 1964. "Learning Music from a Burmese Master." *Man* 64:183.
Powers, Harold S. 1980. "Mode." *The New Grove Dictionary of Music and Musicians*, ed. Stanley Sadie. London: Macmillan.
Williamson, Muriel, ed. 1968. "The Construction and Decoration of One Burmese Harp." *Selected Reports in Ethnomusicology* 1(2):45–72.
———. 1975. "Aspects of Traditional Style Maintained in Burma's First 13 KYO Songs." *Selected Reports in Ethnomusicology* 2(2):117–163.
———. 1979. "The Basic Tune of a Late Eighteenth-Century Burmese Classical Song." *Musica Asiatica* 2:155–195.
———. 1980. "Burma: Harp." *The New Grove Dictionary of Music and Musicians*, ed. Stanley Sadie. London: Macmillan.

Peninsular Malaysia

Patricia Matusky and James Chopyak

Rural Traditions
Urban-Based Folk Music

The Federation of Malaysia consists of peninsular Malaysia and the states of Sarawak and Sabah on the north shore of Borneo [see THE INDIGENOUS PEOPLES (ORANG ASLI) OF THE MALAY PENINSULA and BORNEO]. Extending southward from the mainland of Southeast Asia and the Isthmus of Kra, the landmass of peninsular Malaysia separates the South China Sea from the Indian Ocean. Lying on a sea route from China to Europe, it has received many different peoples who have stopped to conquer, settle, and trade. The racial mixture of the country reflects continual migration to and from the peninsula.

Orang asli "original peoples" inhabit tropical forests in the interior mountains of the peninsula. Some have settled on farmlands, but most are hunter-gatherers. Near the foothills and on the coastal plains are the Malay peoples, who for centuries have inhabited and ruled the peninsula. By the second or third century, Indian traders had carried Hinduism and Mahayana Buddhism to the peninsula, overlaying with alternate beliefs the animistic practices of the Malay peoples. By the mid-1200s, Arab traders and missionaries had brought Islam to the peninsula. By 1400, the town of Malacca, on the west coast, had become an important center of government, trade, and religion.

Early in the 1500s, European colonialism began. Around 1511, Portuguese adventurers captured Malacca. In 1641, the Dutch conquered it. Finally, in 1786, the British established colonial rule throughout the peninsula, which lasted until the mid-1900s. With British colonization came migrations of southern Chinese peoples, who engaged in commerce and worked the tin mines, and of Indian peoples, who found positions in the civil service and worked on rubber and palm-oil plantations.

The nation's 2006 population was estimated at 24.3 million. In 2004 the ethnic composition of Malaysia overall was 50.4 percent Malay, 11 percent other indigenous groups, 23.7 percent Chinese, 7.1 percent Indian, and 7.8 percent other nonindigenous groups. The urban centers of the country, the largest of which lie along the west coast (with Kuala Lumpur as the federal capital) support a mixture of ethnic groups, of which Chinese and Indians form the largest segment. Malay peoples dominate federal and local governments, the agricultural areas and small towns along the east coast, and to some extent, those along the west coast.

The performing arts of each main ethnic group in the country have remained distinct and separate for the most part. The aspects of Indian music that have entered the milieu of traditional Malay musical practice stem from Indian influence during the first centuries of the Christian era. Indian musical practice has had little effect on traditional Malay rural and court musics, but North Indian styles have influenced some twentieth-century urban theatricals. Malay music shows little influence from Chinese immigrants.

RURAL TRADITIONS

The musical traditions of the rural and semiurban areas take a variety of forms, including traditional theatrical genres and other kinds of storytelling, plus music for royal ceremonies, the martial arts, life-cycle events, and religious occasions. Other important forms are music associated with traditional healing and the cultivation of rice and music for general entertainment.

Theatrical Music

Village musical-theatrical genres, including shadow plays and dance-dramas, encompass vocal and instrumental music, plot, improvised monologue and dialogue, and dance. All such genres in Malaysia have developed through an oral tradition in which knowledge passes from one generation to another by word of mouth and rote learning. No written history or theory exists, but myths and legends recount the origin of traditional theatrical genres.

The performers of theatrical instrumental music are exclusively men, who from an early age attach themselves to a particular troupe performing a specific theatrical genre. Boys aspiring to be musicians in a shadow-play troupe informally join a troupe and for several years play alongside experienced musicians. (The puppeteers and the actors of some dance-drama genres, however, undergo a formal apprenticeship.) The music of traditional Malay theatricals is usually performed by small, percussion-dominated orchestras, which typically consist of several drums, a gong chime, one or more hanging, knobbed gongs, and a single, nonpercussive melodic instrument (an aerophone or a chordophone). The orchestra plays as needed to accompany the drama. In each theatrical genre, these pieces comprise specific repertoires of music. Pieces to express mood or emotion, information, and intent are vocal numbers with instrumental accompaniment. Purely instrumental music usually accompanies dance or movement of some kind. In the shadow-puppet theater, all puppet movements require musical accompaniment—as do gestures with hands, steps, and swift strides in dance-dramas.

on which, as the puppeteer (*dalang*) relates a story, the puppets cast shadows. The puppeteer takes all roles in the story, manipulates the puppets, cues the ensemble to begin and end musical pieces, and sings the requisite vocal pieces. The ensemble—drums, gongs, cymbals, and oboe—is also in the hut, just behind the puppeteer. As in most Malay traditional theatrical forms, a single story usually takes several nights to complete. The dramatic repertoire of the *wayang Siam* comes from the oral Malay version of the *Ramayana* epic (the "root" or main story, rarely performed), the *Panji* stories, Malay folktales, and stories of local themes and events (Sweeney 1972).

Figure 12.1
The *wayang kulit* Siam stage (inside view) with the *gendang, gedumbak,* and *geduk* drums ready for performance. Photo by Patricia Matusky.

The ensemble for the *wayang Siam* is mainly percussive: pairs of *tetawak*, large, hanging, knobbed gongs, struck on the knob with a padded beater; *canang*, small, knobbed gongs, suspended horizontally in a wooden rack, struck on the knobs with padded sticks; *kesi*, small hand-held cymbals, struck together; *gedumbak* and *gendang*, double-headed, elongated barrel drums, tuned and hit with hands; *geduk*; and one *serunai* "oboe" (Figures 12.1, 12.2). Each instrument has large and small sizes, metaphorically called mother (*ibu*) and child (*anak*), respectively. The musical repertoire, involving some thirty-five pieces, provides an appropriate tune for any dramatic situation encountered in the stories.

The movements of the puppets require specific music, played by the orchestra on cue from the puppeteer. The music features a dense, highly ornamented melody, played by the oboe or sung by the puppeteer. The tuned drums provide a percussive, melodylike counterpoint, while the gong chime, hanging gongs, and cymbals mark the colotomic units of the pieces.

Dance-Drama

Traditional dance-dramas are performed primarily in the rural areas of the northwest and east-coast regions. They include *mak yong, mek mulung, hadrah, mak yong laut,* and *rodat*. In the extreme north, Thai and Thai-related forms, such as *manora* and *jikay*, are

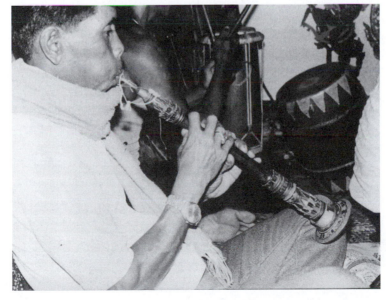

Figure 12.2
The quadruple-reed oboe (*serunai*), the main melody instrument in the *wayang kulit* Siam and *gendang silat* ensembles. Photo by Patricia Matusky.

performed by troupes of Thai and Malay peoples. The island of Penang, off the northwest coast, is home to two additional urban theatricals: *bangsawan* (an acculturated form, incorporating Indian, Western, and other elements) and *boria*.

Mak Yong

The most elaborate of the dance-dramas, and possibly the oldest, is the *mak yong*, believed to have originated in the northeast state of Kelantan and the southeastern Thai provinces of Patani and Narathiwat. Written sources suggest the *mak yong* flourished in the villages of these regions during the late 1800s. Briefly in the early 1900s, the court of the Kelantan sultanate gave this genre royal patronage.

The *mak yong* is usually performed on a roofed platform, raised a meter off the ground. The central area of the platform serves as the area for acting (*gelenggang*). The musicians sit along its northeast edge. Actresses not actively participating in the drama during the performance also sit there, serving as the chorus. The actors wear elaborate costumes, but use few props—as is typical of traditional Malay theater. The dramatic repertory of the *mak yong* consists of twelve tales, featuring the adventures of local heroes (Ghulam-Sarwar 1976). All *mak yong* stories are told through dialogue, singing, and dancing by the major roles, including the king (*pak yong*) and queen (*mak yong*), two down-servants (*peran*), and the *tok wak* (an astrologer or expert of some kind). The roles of king, queen, and retinue are always played by women; men perform only the down-servant parts (Figure 12.3).

The basic *mak yong* orchestra is a percussion-dominated ensemble consisting of two *gendang*, two *tetawak*, and a three-stringed rebab as the main melodic instrument. Just as in other traditional Malay theatrical genres, music is an integral part of the performance. Pieces in the repertoire are distinguished as either drummed pieces (*lagu paluan-paluan*) or sung pieces (*lagu nyanyian*). The drummed pieces accompany the entrance and exit of the actors from the stage and provide traveling music. More numerous are the sung pieces: music for dance. Once these pieces have ended, the clown-servants herald the beginning of the story. The musical pieces have highly florid melodic lines, either sung by one of the major characters or played on the rebab, while two drummers play interlocking rhythms on the *gendang*. The melodies and percussive patterns fit within a time-organizing gong unit, played on two *tetawak* (Matusky 1993).

Figure 12.3
From the *mak yong* theater, the salutation dance before the bowed lute (*rebab*), with the *gendang* drums and *tetawak* gongs in the background. Photo by Patricia Matusky.

Mek Mulung

The *mek mulung* theater is found only in the northwest state of Kedah. Like the *mak yong*, it features a repertoire of stories told through spoken dialogue, song, and dance. The stories of the *mek mulung* treat local events and legends, the most important of which, "The Young Demigod," carries the same title as

Figure 12.4
The *mek mulung rebana* drums, with the *serunai*, hanging gong, and *kecerek* concussion sticks (right background). Photo by Ghulam Sarwar Yousof.

the root story of the *mak yong*. Performances of *mek mulung* take place at ground level in a roofed, hutlike stage, closed only at the back wall. A small, circular area at stage center serves as the area for acting, and the musicians sit at the edge of the stage near the back wall. In contrast to the *mak yong*, men play all roles, both male and female. The costumes are plain. As in other Malay and Thai-related theatricals of Kedah and Perlis, the clowns wear red masks over the top half of their faces.

The musicians are exclusively male, and their instruments are predominantly percussive. A small oboe, the only melodic instrument in the ensemble, complements these instruments. The musicians also sing (Figure 12.4). The style of singing the *mek mulung* is predominantly syllabic, with little vocal ornamentation. The *rebana* drums, producing high and low pitches, provide accompanying rhythms in duple meter.

Hadrah and Rodat

These forms of Malay theater grew from the tradition of singing Islamic religious verses (*zikir*) in praise of God and the prophet Muhammad. The singing was, and is, accompanied by an ensemble of *rebana*, on which the singers beat rhythms. Occasionally, a full story is danced. Both the *rodat* and the *hadrah*, having lost most of their religious significance, are secular genres, performed at weddings, after harvests, and at public festivals.

Mainly all-male troupes perform *hadrah*. A performance takes place on a temporary stage, at ground level or raised, with a simple drop cloth at the rear. Typically, props are minimal. Actors in male roles wear the traditional *baju melayu* ("Malay suit": headgear, long-sleeved shirt, trousers, and a *samping* cloth, tied at the waist); those in female roles wear the Malay women's sarong and *baju kebaya* "Malay-style blouse."

At the foot of the stage, the musicians sit facing the actors, playing drums and a knobbed gong. The orchestra consists of eight or more large *rebana*, with jingles (*kerincing*) inserted in their bodies (*gendang hadrah* "*hadrah* drums"); one somewhat smaller *rebana*, with a deeper frame and no jingles (*gendang peningkah*); and one small, hanging, knobbed gong, hit on the knob with a padded beater. The drummer who directs the singing and drumming is the leader (*kalifah*). He is usually the solo vocalist. The other drummers sing the choral parts as they play.

Like the *hadrah*, the *rodat* was originally a religious event, in which verses were sung to the accompaniment of rhythms played on frame drums (see below). In the 1800s, traders from Aceh (north Sumatra) traveling to Sambas (in Borneo) and then to the east coast of the peninsula may have brought *rodat* to Terengganu. By the early 1900s, several all-male troupes performed the original style of singing the *zikir* with frame-drum accompaniment. In the 1930s, however, performances included dancing by men and transvestites. After 1945, women replaced the latter, and troupes got bigger, until a given troupe had three separate groups of performers: the male singer-dancers (*pelenggok*), the female singer-dancers (*mak inang*), and the musicians (*pen-gadis*).

The *rodat* was originally performed to celebrate Muhammad's birthday and Malay weddings. With the addition of dancing and the singing of popular Malay and Hindustani songs, and especially with the addition of women to the troupes, performances became popular at secular events, such as the harvest celebration, the sultan's birthday, and festivities for Malaysian National Day, 31 August. Performances of *rodat* take place on a simple stage at ground level, with a curtain serving as a backdrop. The *pelenggok* sit and perform on the stage in front of the curtain. Rhythmic accompaniment comes from the *tar*, small frame drums. As with their *hadrah* counterparts, jingles are set into their bodies. However, no laces are used to secure the drumhead; the skin is stretched and secured by a metal rim.

Jikay

The *jikay*, also known as *dikey* or *likey*, is believed to have originated in the late 1800s in the singing of *zikir* among the Malays living in the present-day southwest Thai provinces. After the late 1800s, it developed into secular theater with many regional styles, and it was eventually brought southward to Perlis and Kedah, and to Langkawi Island, where it is still occasionally performed. Through song, dance, and improvised dialogue, local legends are enacted, with considerable emphasis placed on slapstick comedy, song, and dance.

The opening rituals, similar to those in other forms of traditional Malay theater, are carried out before the presentation of a local story. Both men and women take the roles of stock characters. The stage is usually a raised platform with a simple drop cloth at the rear. The actors enter from behind the curtain to stage center, where the dramatic action, song, and dance take place. The musicians, an all-male group, sit downstage, facing the actors. The actors and actresses wear traditional dress, and the musicians wear normal street attire.

Like all Malay theatrical orchestras, the ensemble that accompanies the *jikay* is dominated by percussion. A complete orchestra includes *rebana* (with no jingles), in large, medium, and small sizes; one tambourine; one hanging, knobbed gong, hit with a padded beater; five or more pairs of *cerek*; one pair of *kesi*; one oboe, which may be the Malay *serunai* or the Thai *pi*; and one violin (*biola*). Smaller ensembles consist of the basic three *rebana*, two pairs of *cerek*, and a violin. The musical repertoire is small. Only a few pieces introduce an act or episode and accompany the dances. Specific pieces are used only by certain types of characters.

Manora

A dance-drama of the rural southern Thai peoples, the *manora* (*menora*) is performed by groups of Thai and Malay peoples throughout the northern Malay states, including Penang Island. Depending on the geographical area, a mixture of the local dialects and the southern Thai dialect is used. A performance may occur for special religious occasions at Thai and Chinese Buddhist temples (Tan Sooi Beng 1988), or for secular festivities, as for the sultan's birthday and state holidays.

In north Malaysia, the *manora* has a variety of regional styles. The basic features of a performance include a lengthy invocation, a dance by the main character, and a play or skit. The invocation consists of a dance of stylized poses and gestures, alternating with rhymed verses. The text, responsorially chanted by the dancer and the members of the orchestra, tells the story and recounts the genealogy of the performer's teacher. The dramatic repertoire of the *manora* involves twelve basic stories, related to a tradition of central Thai stories. These stories are performed by men and women, with one or more clowns.

The stage for the *manora* may be at ground level or on a raised platform, with a painted scene as backdrop. Action takes place in front of the backdrop. The musicians sit along one edge of the stage, facing the actors. The *manora* character wears an elaborate costume, featuring a pinnacled, crownlike headpiece; a beaded shirt; trousers; feathers from a bird's tail; bangles on the arms; long, arched, silver fingernails; and a cloth that hangs from the waist. The source of the genre can be found in southern Thai folk legends and in the *jataka* tales about the lives of the Buddha. In the *jataka* stories, the *manora* character is identified with the heavenly bird (*kinnara*) named Manohara (Ginsberg 1972:63).

Within the complex of *manora* styles of Malaysia, the eastern regional style found in Kelantan and Terengganu incorporates much use of the Malay language and a play performed in the *mak yong* style. This stylistic type, locally known as *manora-mak yong*, utilizes a fairly large orchestra, incorporating musical instruments and pieces from both genres. In the northwest regions of Malaysia, the *manora* does not incorporate other local theatrical forms, but adheres to the invocation-play or comic-skit dichotomy in a distinctly north Malaysian musical style. The play or comic skits that fill out an evening's performance invariably include male and female actors, with one or more clowns in red masks, similar to those used in the *mek mulung* and *jikay*, and in the *awang batil*. The plays or skits feature at least one well-known *manora* actor and are told in a mixture of Thai and the dialect of the audience.

Music is used in several ways. A musical piece signaling the beginning of the *manora* is characteristic of all regional styles, as is a ritual presentation of prayers and offerings. The musical pieces found in the dramatization of a story or comic skit in the second half of the performance of a *manora* usually accompany the performers' entrances and exits.

Dance

Barongan and Kuda Kepang

The dances *barongan* "demon" and *kuda kepang* "hobbyhorse" may stem from the totemistic worship of natural spirits in the ancient animistic religion of the Javanese peoples.

Both forms involve music and trance-dance. The origin myths of both forms show a fusion of animistic and Islamic elements. In the Malaysian context, stories of the worship of animal spirits are mixed with tales of Islamic prophets and the propagation of their faith. According to some legends, the *barongan* involves a tiger dancing with a peacock on its back. Hence, the most commonly used mask in Malaysia incorporates a tiger's physiognomy, with peacock feathers and other decorations. Other stories tell of an old woman who snatched the corpse of a famous Islamic warrior as she rode his horse (Mohammad Ghouse 1979:114–115).

In a village context, a performance begins with the appearance of the demon, who, using dance movements, stalks and spars with a dancer representing a prince on horseback by carrying the figure of a horse. The demon's dance is accompanied by a small ensemble: one *gendang*, a small barrel drum (*tipung*), one oboe (*selumprit*), one *mong*, and a *kenong* (a gong chime, two knobbed gongs, set on a wooden rack). The oboe carries a continuous, unbroken melodic line, while the double-headed drums provide percussive rhythms. The *kenong* and the *mong* mark the rhythmic-temporal (or colotomic) unit.

Randai

The Minangkabau peoples of West Sumatra perform this type of theater. It incorporates acting, dance, song, instrumental music, and *pencak silat*, the Malay art of self-defense (see below). Its repertory has roots in the *kaba* and the *tambo alam minangkabau*, traditions of storytelling in which poetical narration and the singing of songs were accompanied by a three-stringed rebab. Later, acting was introduced, and stories dramatized legends and historical events. A celebration of a major event to benefit a given community, such as completing the harvest or erecting a school building, provides a reason to hold a performance of a *randai*. Women play female roles in costumes appropriate to the characters. All men in the troupe wear the traditional *silat* costume: a long-sleeved shirt, loose-fitting trousers, a tied waistband, and cloth headgear. The martial arts are important in *randai*, and a performer must be highly skilled in them, for the movements of *pencak silat* are the basic gestures and footwork of the dance.

A performance can occur in any setting—from a temporary raised stage to a ground-level area outdoors; in the hall of a school or in another building. Performances feature singing and dancing in a circle (*randai*) with the audience gathered around. Once the dancers have entered the area of the stage, they sing in unison, as in a circle they perform a sequence of dance movements. The dancers' entrance to, and exit from, the performing area is accompanied by music played by a *taklempong pacik*, an ensemble consisting of five small, knobbed gongs, played by three men (Mohammad Anis 1986:25). At intermissions, music is played by a *taklempong* (or *caklempong*), a large ensemble, consisting of at least three gong chimes of different sizes, all tuned to the same diatonic scale. The melody-carrying gong chime, the *gereteh* (*gerteh*), is made up of fifteen tuned, small, knobbed gongs, in double rows in a wooden frame. The *tingkah* and *saua* each consist of eight small, knobbed gongs, in a single row on a wooden rack. All gongs are hit with a pair of sticks.

Dabus

The performance of *dabus* (among the Minangkabau in Malaysia and Sumatra called *bermain dabus, berdabus,* and *dabuih*), with roots in Sufi traditions, was believed to be a way to reach a higher state of consciousness and ultimately to attain unity with God (see INDONESIA: SUMATRA). It was brought to the peninsula from Aceh (Sumatra) by seafarers around the 1700s and also by the Minangkabau immigrants who settled in Negeri Sembilan and Malacca. *Dabus*, an Arabic word, means "iron awl with a handle." In Malaysia, it names the dance, perhaps formerly a dervish dance, performed with sharply pointed iron awls (*anak dabus*); metal rings or jingles attached to the handles sound when the dancers shake the awls. The *dabus* may be seen and heard at weddings and other life-cycle events and on national holidays (Figure 12.5).

Figure 12.5
"*Gendang keling*" drums, with the *serunai* and two hanging gongs (far left) for the *tarinai*. Photo by Patricia Matusky.

A performance takes place on a temporary stage at ground level. The group, all men, wear the *baju melayu.* In Arabic, they sing *berzanji*, verses in the *Kitab Berzanji*, the book of verses praising God and Muhammad. As they begin to sing, the dancers, each carrying an *anak dabus*, begin to dance. After reaching a trancelike state, they stab their bodies and arms with the *anak dabus* and do other extraordinary feats without physically injuring themselves. The basic ensemble consists of several small- and large-sized *rebana* and one hanging, knobbed gong. Some groups add an oboe to accompany the beginning of the singing. The patterns of drumming usually repeat in four-beat units.

Tari Inai

Formerly a court dance, the *tari inai* (*tarinai, terinai*) is associated with traditions of towns and villages in the northern states. It is performed in Perlis for weddings, circumcisions, processions, state ceremonies, and public festivities. The dance involves supple movements of the arms and hands, with the dancer sitting or standing. There is little footwork, and some pieces feature a lighted candle held in the dancers' hands. The music is played by a small ensemble, the *gendang tarinai* (also *gendang keling*). The ensemble consists of two *gendang* (struck with a straight rattan beater, or with an out-curved stick on one drumhead and the hand on the other), one or two oboes, and a pair of hanging, knobbed gongs, providing a high and a low pitch.

Stylistic Features of Theatrical Music

The ensembles for traditional Malay theater and dance are small, chamberlike orchestras. They are mainly percussive. The texture of nearly all theater musics has two or three layers of polyphonic sound: a rhythmic-temporal unit (colotomic unit, or more specifically a gong unit), a drummed pattern of rhythms, and a melodic line, voiced or instrumental. These layers, as they progress through time in a seemingly linear way, join together, and present a logical and coherent totality, by means of a repeated rhythmic-temporal unit, played by specific instruments.

Music for Storytelling

Storytelling in Malay culture includes the use of stylized language, singing, chanting, instrumental accompaniment, and sometimes drama. In past generations, professional storytellers related romances (*penglipur-lara*), often accompanying themselves instrumentally. As late as the mid-1900s, the art of storytelling was widespread in the northern Malay states and as far south as Selangor. By the 1990s, however, in both rural and urban areas, published texts, film, television, and modern drama had begun to hold greater interest, and many of the old storytellers had died, taking their art with them. Regional genres were known by specific names, derived from the main (or root) story, or from a hero in the most popular story of the genre. In the northwest states, the genres were *jubang linggang, selampit,* and *awang batil* (also *awang belanga*). The *jubang linggang* and the *selampit* involved song and recitation, without instrumental accompaniment. The *awang batil* used an overturned brass bowl (*batil*), on which the storyteller beat out short, repeated rhythms to accompany and complement his recitation. Sometimes he would wear a mask, representing the character about whom he was speaking. In Selangor, a narrative tradition known as *kaba* was performed by and for Minangkabau peoples living in the region. A three-stringed rebab may originally have accompanied the storyteller, but a violin has replaced it.

Probably the most musically complex of the extant traditions of storytelling was found in Kelantan. The storyteller (*tok selampit*) was often a blind man who sang tales (*tarikh selampit*) as he accompanied himself on a rebab. The rebab doubled or imitated the vocal part, either playing in unison with the voice or repeating the vocal melody. The parts played on the rebab were melodically dense, with considerable sixteenth- and thirty-second-note movement. The melodies were usually ornate, with many grace notes, slides, and other embellishments. In both the voice and rebab parts, the melodic range was narrow, and microtonal intervals were common. In many traditions, the music acted as a catalyst to enable the storyteller to develop his story (Sweeney 1972:60). The rebab melody in the *tarikh selampit* served to cue the storyteller for a specific starting pitch, and melodic phrases played on the rebab between the lines of sung text gave him time to collect his thoughts, prepare for the next line of text, or simply to rest.

Music for Healing

Traditional Malay medicine encompasses various kinds of ritual ceremonies intended to communicate with the world of spirits to determine whether the nature of an illness is physical or psychological. In such ceremonies, the aim is to summon and exorcise the spirits causing the illness. A ritualist serves as a medium, and a small ensemble often provides the musical component. Known by different names, healing rituals appear in different forms. The *main saba* (a curing ceremony, incorporating dance around a *saba* tree) and *main lukah* (a fishermen's curing ritual performed in Pahang) are regional types using song, dance, and drumming. The *main puteri (peteri)*, another form that extensively uses music, is found in Kelantan and Terengganu (Malm 1974).

In the *main puteri*, a medium (*tok puteri, tok teri, bomoh*) becomes possessed by the spirits causing an illness. The performance of vocal and instrumental pieces helps him enter a state of trance. A trance-dance (*tarian lupa*) is a prominent feature of the ceremony. An assistant, the *tok minduk*, plays the rebab as he converses and sings in dialogue with the medium (Figure 12.6). The orchestra used in Kelantan is larger, perhaps because of the occasional performance of the *main puteri* with the *mak yong* (resulting in a hybrid form, *main puteri-mak yong*). The contemporary *main puteri* orchestra of Kelantan includes the core *mak yong* orchestra (a rebab, a pair of *gendang*, and a pair of *tetawak*), plus two or more *canang*, a pair of *kesi*, and sometimes an oboe.

Figure 12.6
The *tok puteri* or *bomoh* (medium) offering foods to the spirits; the *gendang* and *tetawak* are in the background, and the rebab is facing the *bomoh* (*kesi* and *canang* not shown). Photo by Ghulam Sarwar Yousof.

The dialogue between the *tok minduk* and the *tok puteri* is sung in a slow tempo, with long gong units (marked by the knobbed gongs), long rhythmic patterns in the drum part, and a vocal line featuring a basically syllabic style of singing. The rebab accompanies the vocal lines of both singers by either playing heterophonically with the voice or reiterating short melodic phrases as ostinatos. The trance-dance sections feature the repetition of brief gong units and short drummed rhythms, a fast tempo, and the reiteration and emphasis of the running beat by the small gongs and the hand-held cymbals.

Music for the Martial Arts

Stemming from *silat* or *pencak silat*, the Malay art of self-defense, some dancelike forms have evolved. Though performed in peninsular Malaysia in a variety of styles as a competitive event among men, the *silat* also occurs as a fight-dance, performed by both men and women in Kelantan. The ensembles that accompany the *silat*, whether in its competitive martial-arts style or as a dance, are the *gendang silat* in the northern states, and the *caklempong* in the southern states.

A small orchestra, the *gendang silat* provides highly dynamic music to accompany the movements of *silat* in north Malaysia. It consists of one hanging knobbed gong, one oboe, and two *gendang*. Two drummers play the latter. They hit the small drumhead with the hand and the large drumhead with an outcurved stick. *Pencak silat*, exhibiting either armed or unarmed movements of self-defense, was brought by Minangkabau peoples, who migrated to peninsular Malaysia before the 1900s. It is accompanied by the *caklempong* ensemble: one *caklempong*, two *rebana* (with a deep frame and no jingles), and one hanging, knobbed gong.

Music for Work, Life-Cycle Events, General Entertainment

Work

Since rice and fish are staple foods throughout the peninsula, the major occupations in villages are agriculture and fishing. Along the coast, fishing and related activities are the predominant kinds of work for most of the year. Typical occupational activities—catching fish, maintaining boats, hauling nets, repairing nets—are sometimes accompanied by songs with rhythms and tempi that match the motions of the work.

In inland communities, the growing of rice and vegetables preoccupies most rural dwellers. Though music and song are usually heard after the harvest of the crops, some communities carry on musical activities to accompany the work of planting and caring for the crops during the growing season. Women in some remote villages of Pahang, as they weed dry rice fields, perform *main pulau*, songs to whose rhythms they step slowly in a circle (Mohd. Taib Osman 1982:58). A leader, who stands in the middle, directs the singing and guides the work from one part of the field to another.

In Negeri Sembilan, the *tumbuk kalang* (or *antan tumbuk kalang*) is played by peoples of Minangkabau descent. Formerly it was one stage of processing rice. It stems from the activity of pounding (*tumbuk*) the rice in a mortar (*lesung*) with a wooden pestle (*antan*). Before industrial methods were used in processing rice, two or three people parched newly harvested grains, put them into the well of the mortar, pounded them, and winnowed the chaff from the edible grains. The ancient activity of pounding rice by two or three people who, sequentially in rhythm, stamped their poles into the well of the mortar, led to the stamping of the pestles on various parts of the mortar to achieve a variety of timbres produced in specific rhythms. Eventually, the stamping became enhanced by clapping and the singing of work-related songs in the form of *pantun,* four-line stanzas that were, and still are, sung responsorially.

Villagers perform the *tumbuk kalang* only as entertainment, and they no longer pound rice during the performance. The performances may be heard after the harvest of rice, during performing-arts festivals, on the occasion of a visit of dignitaries to a village, or at special school festivities. The ensemble features a hardwood mortar with a cup-shaped well in the middle of its top surface. It sits securely on a base (*kalang*); the top surface, shaped in a long, narrow rectangle, may be stamped in the central well, on either side of it, or on the outer walls. The rhythms produced by three or four pestles interlock, as each player produces a specific timbre at a specific time. The instrumental parts accompany the singing of the *pantun*, which a soloist and a chorus may sing responsorially. (Two singers may sing the vocal part, alternating verses.) When dance is added, the resulting performance is a *taridra.* The dancers are men and women, whose gestures and steps reflect the topic of the song being sung. A song about planting rice, for example, would require text and movements suggesting hoeing, sowing, replanting the seedlings, harvesting the mature stalks, and pounding the rice.

Life-Cycle Events

Life-cycle events, including the major rites of passage, are usually associated with *adat* (customary law and practice) ceremonies, some of which are highly elaborate and communal.

silat
Martial arts-derived dance with drum accompaniment
gendang
Two-headed, leather-laced drum with slightly bulging body
rebana
Single-headed, round frame drum, sometimes with spokes
main pulau
Type of song performed by women weeding dry rice fields
tumbuk kalang
Folk song derived from rice-pounding songs

Music, often an integral part, is performed by both skilled and semiskilled members of a community. Life-cycle events that make extensive use of music and religious recitation include weddings and circumcisions.

The circumcision (*berkhatan*) ceremony usually follows the chanting of *berzanji*. Also, in the southern states, the ensembles playing *kompang* music with the chanting of *zikir* accompany processions as part of the ceremony. The drumming is performed on the *kompang*, a hand-beaten frame drum. It has a shallow, hardwood body and a single tacked head, sometimes with metal jingles inserted into the frame. The drummers may chant religious texts, and in some social contexts they chant secular texts, but the emphasis is on the drumming, which is in interlocking style, effected by two or more groups of players.

In the northern peninsular states, *hadrah*, the chanting of religious texts at a circumcision, is accompanied by rhythms played on the *rebana*. An ensemble of *rebana* provides percussive accompaniment, but chanting is the focus. In the regions inhabited by peoples of Minangkabau descent, the *bongai* (also *rentak kuda*) is often performed for a circumcision, a wedding, and entertainment after the harvest. It features repartee between two people who sing *pantun* responsorially. A group of some eight men and women perform this genre. The first performer sings a statement. A second singer answers by composing and singing another *pantun* in response; the first singer (or a third singer) then takes up the singing of another statement; and so on. Typical themes of the *pantun* are love, comedy, teasing, and innuendo. The *bongai* is accompanied by a small *caklempong* ensemble: one gong chime (*gereteh*), one oboe, one *rebana* or *gendang*, and one hanging, knobbed gong. It may also be played during national holidays and is sometimes heard during child-associated life-cycle ceremonies.

Weddings call for the performance of musical genres, including the *kompang* or the *hadrah*, as the bridegroom is escorted to the bride's house. The solemn singing of *zikir* in regional styles and the witty entertainment of *bongai* (in Minangkabau communities) may also be heard. Another genre performed especially for weddings is the *tari inai* (*inai* dance), played during the applying of henna (*berinai*) to the bride's hands and feet (see "Dance," above). Especially in urban areas, weddings also feature the latest hits, played by a Western pop band, or by an *asli* ensemble.

Events involving childhood and the stages of development in a child's life are often marked by musical performance. In some parts of the peninsula, the first cutting of the baby's hair (*potong rambut*) and the first time a child's feet touch the ground while it learns to walk (*jejak tanah*) are occasions for the performance of *maulud*, verses praising Muhammad and statements on exemplary behavior (Mohd. Taib Osman 1974:214–215).

General Entertainment

Music that serves for entertainment occurs in the theatrical genres noted above. After harvests, audiences enjoy listening to *rebana ubi*, *kertok kelapa*, *kacapi*, *seruling*, and *dikir barat*, particularly in the northern states (Figure 12.7). In Kelantan, after the harvest of rice, the men of one village often play sets of *rebana ubi* drums in competition with the men of another. The *rebana ubi* is an extremely large, considerably modified version of the *rebana*. It has a wooden, conical body, with a single drumhead measuring nearly a meter

Figure 12.7
Teams competitively play *rebana ubi* drums. Photo by Patricia Matusky.

in diameter. For the head, makers of drums usually employ water-buffalo hide, which they attach to the body by thick rattan laces sewn into the hide and looped around a large rattan ring at the base of the body. They tighten the skin with wooden wedges, which they hammer into the space between the ring and the body. Drummers, one or two to a single drum, beat the instrument by hand or with a padded beater. They play interlocking rhythms.

Another type of ensemble featuring the interlocking playing technique is known as *kertok kelapa* (or *kertok kayu*; see Figure 12.11). The *kertok kelapa* is made from a hollow coconut shell secured on a wooden base. A slab of bamboo or wood of a specific thickness and length is laid across the opening at the top of the coconut and is struck with a wood stick by a single player. A number of these percussive instruments are struck, with each player beating his instrument at specific times to produce resultant melodic-rhythmic patterns.

For solo entertainment, a single player strikes and plucks a tube zither (*kacapi*), producing a combination of percussive rhythms and short melodies plucked on strings. Imitating music from shadow plays or other theatrical genres, the performer simultaneously plays the parts of two or three different instruments. Another instrument that plays melodies for individual enjoyment in intimate settings is the end-blown flute (*seruling*).

A favorite choral vocal form found in the northeast states is the *dikir barat*, in which men sitting in circle sing verses of popular, nonreligious texts. A soloist begins a piece with an introductory text, sung on a lengthy, improvised melody in free rhythm. A performance in responsorial style follows. Unison choral singing answers the soloist, in strictly duple rhythm. A *rebana kercing* (*rebana* with jingles) usually provides rhythms, and a hanging, knobbed gong marks the end of every two- or four-beat unit. The clapping of hands, gestures of hands and arms, and the swaying of the body enhance the performance.

Traditional Urban Musical-Theatrical Genres

Begun in Penang Island, the *boria* and the *bangsawan* are the products of nineteenth-century urban culture in peninsular Malaysia. Both forms incorporate spoken dialogue, songs, and dances.

The Boria

Formerly in Penang, at fun-filled New Year's celebrations during the first ten days of Muharram, men traditionally performed the *boria*. Troupes of twenty or more gathered under the leadership of a composer-manager, the troupe's lead singer. Each year, the troupe selected a theme (such as Arab warriors, European traders, or Chinese shopkeepers) around which their costumes and comic improvisations revolved. For their performances, troupes expected monetary remuneration. In the early 1900s, they wandered from one neighborhood to another, performing in people's yards, or in the halls of clubs and associations.

A typical performance is in two parts, consisting of a short comic sketch and a song-dance routine. The sketch, acted by four or more men playing rural people, often highlights local events and domestic situations. In the late 1900s, it sometimes served as a vehicle for political propaganda. The song-dance routines usually begin with an orchestral introduction, using popular Western music for dancing. Rumbas and cha-chas have been favorite openers. The accompanying ensemble varies in instrumentation from one troupe to another. The main melodic instrument has consistently been the violin. Players optionally add various Western, Malay, or Indian drums, plus Chinese cymbals. The lead singer and the chorus alternately sing twelve or more verses, featuring a set routine of gestures and steps. The troupe then goes to its next location, where it gives a similar performance.

The Bangsawan

This genre is more formalized in performance and repertory. Brought by performers from Bombay in the late 1800s, it developed as an adaptation of Parsi theater. Plays about romances and situations concerning Malay royalty became locally known as nobility (*bangsawan*). Eclectic, the repertoire features Hindustani and Arabian legends, Chinese romances, English dramas, and Malay legends (Tan 1993). Some troupes have as many as fifty actors, plus musicians and a manager.

In its early days, the *bangsawan* stage was a temporary, roofed platform, raised to ease viewing, with a backdrop near the rear. Later, troupes adopted the Western indoor proscenium stage with elaborate backdrops—a convention still in use. The cast consists of several stereotyped roles: the hero, the heroine, the leading lady, comedians, a king, a queen, and villains (Ghulam-Sarwar 1987:7–17). The costumes are elaborate.

Spoken dialogue alternates with song and dance. At first, the musical pieces came from different sources, including older American pop-dance styles (such as the cakewalk and the Charleston), Spanish dances, and other popular musics from Western Europe and India. The original orchestral instruments were the harmonium and the tabla, instruments of Parsi theater. As the form and its repertoire evolved, the instrumentation changed. The musicians optionally used a piano, a flute, a violin, and a *rebana*. In the

Figure 12.8
The *ronggeng* ensemble for *bangsawan* and other syncretic genres, including (left to right) tambourine, knobbed gong, two *rebana*, violin, and accordion. Photo by Tan Sooi Beng.

late 1900s, in an effort to make the music more Malay, orchestras began featuring a violin, an accordion, a *rebana*, and a knobbed gong (Tan 1988:255) (Figure 12.8). Since the 1970s, the music has featured the rhythms and melodies of the *asli* repertoire—a syncretic musical tradition, emerging from Malay urban and semiurban culture, featuring multiple elements (Western, Arabic, Indian) and incorporating aspects of indigenous Malay music.

Musical Traditions at Court

Royal patronage was once generous, but after World War II it almost completely ceased. The *nobat* remains the only musical tradition still viable at court. The other musical-theatrical genres once performed there—the *wayang kulit melayu*, the *mak yong*, the *tari inai*—survive only as traditions among the folk, and some are nearly extinct. These and other traditional forms are fast losing their significance, for they compete in a society bounded by the strictures of orthodox Islam on the one side and the influence of television, films, and changing values on the other. One traditional dance-drama (*joget gamelan*) has taken on the status of a national art. This has been possible in part because of the support the Terengganu state government has given the genre and the use of the genre in the development of modern dance-drama in urban contexts.

Shadow-Play Music

The *wayang kulit melayu* (also *wayang melayu* or *wayang jawa*) is the shadow theater performed under court patronage in Kelantan and Kedah and formerly in the Patani sultanate. As entertainment for aristocrats, it was performed only in palaces. During the late 1800s and early 1900s, Malay courts sent puppeteers to Java to learn their art, and they returned with manuscripts of stories from the *Mahabharata* and the knowledge of playing techniques in the Javanese style. Malay puppeteers used Hindu stories and cowhide puppets in Javanese design, but told the stories in local Malay dialects. By the 1990s, royal patronage had ceased. Though puppeteers and musicians still live in Kelantan, performances are rare, and the form is nearly extinct. The orchestra that accompanies performances features a set of six or more bronze idiophones: one *canang*, one *mong*, one pair of *kesi*, and two *tetawak*.

Music for Dance and Dance-Drama

Asyek Dance

Two forms of Malay music for dance or dance-drama without speech or song developed in the court tradition. One of these, *tari asyek*, is believed to have originated in the court of the Patani sultanate. It was performed exclusively by female dancers as entertainment for royalty, especially for the sultan. Slow-paced, the dance stresses intricate movement of the arms, hands, and fingers. The dancer may sit or stand. In the 1800s and early 1900s, the dance was accompanied by several *gedumbak* (*gedumbak asyek*) and one boat-shaped xylophone (*gambang*)—all played by women. A rebab, played by a male musician of the court, completed the ensemble (Mohd. Taib Osman 1974:211). In the mid-1990s, however, orchestras were all-male; they included three *canang*, two *gendang*, and one hanging gong (Malm 1974:9).

Joget Gamelan

The second major tradition of dancing at court is *joget gamelan* (also *gamelan tereng-ganu* or *gamelan pahang)*. This style, with roots in the central Javanese traditions of court gamelan and dance, was known at the court of the rulers of Riau-Lingga. Through a marriage between the Pahang and Terengganu royal families, the gamelan and its retinue of musicians and dancers moved to the sultan's palace in Terengganu, where it continued to develop under the patronage and tutorship of the sultan and his wife. The *joget gamelan*, as it became known, was entertainment only for royalty at such court functions as installation ceremonies, birthday celebrations, engagements, and weddings, and for state visits.

Played only by men, the orchestral instruments are one *gendang*, two *saron* (*barung* and *peking*), the *kerumong* "gong chime", one *gambang*, the *kenong* (a set of five large, pot-shaped gongs), and the *gong suwukan* and *agung* (large, hanging gongs, of high and low pitches, respectively). The large gongs and *kenong* mark musical time, while the *gendang* provides rhythms. The nuclear melody of a piece is played on the *saron barung*, while the *peking*, xylophone, and gong chime ornament it (D'Cruz 1979).

Ceremonial Music

Nobat. For several hundred years, the *nobat* and its music have graced the regalia of the Malay sultanates. The concept originated in the Middle East and developed in Islamic societies from southern Spain to India. In about the twelfth century, the sultan of Pasai, Sumatra (who had received the *nobat* from Middle Eastern sources), introduced it to the ruler of Malacca. Subsequently, the *nobat* was used to install the first sultan of Kedah (Ku Zam Zam 1985:177), where it is still used today. The Malay sultanates that own and use this orchestra as part of their regalia are Kedah, Perak, and formerly Selangor on the west coast, and Kelantan on the east.

The *nobat* was a major element in signifying aristocratic rank. In effect, the orchestra validated the sultan and his sultanate: the sound of the music was symbolically equivalent to his presence. The *nobat* still provides music for court ceremonies. The instrumentation of late-twentieth-century *nobat* included one oboe (*serunai*); one trumpet (*nafiri*); two *gendang*, one drumhead, hit with the hand and the other with a stick; one kettledrum (*nehara,* alternately, *nahara* and *nagara*), hit with a pair of rattan sticks; and sometimes one knobbed gong, hit with a padded beater. The instruments of the *nobat* command respect and honor. Legends say they have magical powers, and musicians observe taboos to protect their purity. Wrapped in yellow cloth covers, all stay in a special place in the palace. Musicians learn a repertoire of twenty or more instrumental pieces (*man*). A traditional system of notation (*dai*) records individual pieces (Ku Zam Zam 1985:181). Some pieces, having broad functions, enhance court ceremonies; others, having more specialized functions, highlight festive ceremonies, sensitive or emotional events, and solemn occasions.

musiqa
Arabic word denoting music as distinct from chant
Qur'ān
The Islamic canon of Muhammad's writings, intended to be chanted
azan
The Islamic call to prayer, chanted five times daily from a minaret
zikir
Vocalized religious chants, usually accompanied by drumming

Music and Religion

To speak of music associated with religion among the Malay peoples of peninsular Malaysia is to speak of two different attitudes and paths of development. The first is based on pre-Islamic religious beliefs, rooted in animism and overlaid with precepts from Buddhism and Hinduism. Vestiges of these beliefs survive in the opening rituals of some theatrical forms and in healing rituals and related forms propitiating beings from the world of spirits.

The second main path of development is associated with Islam, a religion many peninsular Malays adopted in the early 1300s. Within its sphere, musical practice was, and still is, bound with orthodox definitions of appropriate musical sound. In Malaysia of the 1990s, the Muslim notion of appropriate musical sound rested to a large degree on sectarian interpretations of context and function. The segment of the population that practices the musical forms found throughout the peninsula takes a less rigidly conservative view. Disregarding context and function, the definition of music used in the West—denoted by the Arabic term *musiqa* (derived from Greek *mousikē*)—does not apply to Islamic religious sounds (al-Faruqi 1985:6).

Consequently, excluding *musiqa*, Malay society considers chanting the Qur'ān the highest form of art involving sound. It may be rendered in a solo or unison choral format, unaccompanied. At the annual Qur'ān-reading competition (held in Kuala Lumpur), crowds listen to highly skilled chanters, both male and female. The chanting mixes syllabic and melismatic styles.

Another form of cantillation that excludes *musiqa* is the call to prayer *(azan, adhan)*, vocalized five times a day from minarets. It is always chanted by a man, the *muezzin,* usually amplified by loudspeakers. To reach a wide audience, government television channels broadcast it nationally.

Other forms of vocalizing religious texts (*zikir*) involve some degree of *musiqa*, including drumming. The most notable drum used to serve this function is a frame drum. Ubiquitous in peninsular Malaysia, it features in many distinct regional styles. Formerly in Kelantan (and possibly still in its remote regions), *rebana besar*, a popular type of *zikir* performance, featured a large *rebana ubi*, hit with the hands (Figure 12.9). The drummers sing Arabic or Malay verses praising Muhammad or commenting on moral behavior. A player opens a verse by singing a rhythmically free phrase in melismatic style; to complete the verse, the chorus sings in unison. The choral style of singing is distinctly syllabic; ornamentation occurs only in the soloist's part. Unison drumming in duple meter and slow tempo provides accompaniment.

Religious genres that include elements of *musiqa* are considered appropriate in the

Figure 12.9
Singing a form of *zikir* accompanied by hand-hit *rebana ubi* drums. Photo by Patricia Matusky.

proper social and religious setting. In a religious context, Muhammad's birthday (Maulud-an-Nabi), fasting at Ramadan (Puasa), leaving on a pilgrimage to Mecca, and celebrating the conclusion of Ramadan or the pilgrimage (Hari Raya Puasa, Hari Raya Haji) are formal Islamic rituals during which people sing *zikir*. These genres also serve in *adat* ceremonies, for they may be performed in celebration of life-cycle events, such as the first cutting of a baby's hair, and rites of passage, such as weddings or circumcisions.

URBAN-BASED FOLK MUSIC

Traditional Malay culture has often been noted for its eclecticism. Many of the world's important cultural and religious influences have passed through this region, so it is no surprise that Malay music and musical instruments reflect diverse influences.

The music that developed among the ordinary people of Malaysia is distinct from that of courtly traditions. It is the music that has interacted with, and been a reflection of, the mainstream culture of the west coast of peninsular Malaysia. These musical genres had a much greater impact on Malaysian music in the twentieth century than any other traditional musical forms. They occur in many geographic variants, depending on the performers' places of origin.

Musical Instruments

Melodic Instruments

The violin is one of the most widely used Western instruments in performances of traditional Malay music. Brought into Malaya by the Portuguese more than four hundred years ago, it is held by Malaysian musicians in the same manner as in the European tradition. The flute is also commonly used as a melodic instrument. Locally constructed bamboo instruments were formerly used, but in the twentieth century, metal European flutes have almost replaced them. In some performances, a plucked, pear-shaped lute (*gambus*) serves as a melodic instrument; the Malay variant of the Arab *'ud*, it closely resembles its Arab ancestor. The guitar is now sometimes used with, or to replace the *gambus* (Figure 12.10) The

Figure 12.10
The *gambus* lute. Photo by Gerald Moore.

Figure 12.11
Three men play the single-keyed *kertok kelapa* coconut xylophones. Photo by Gerald Moore.

harmonium, and more recently, the accordion have also developed roles as melodic instruments; though added only since the 1940s, the accordion is widely used in traditional performances.

Rhythmic Instruments

Two basic types of membranophones are used for rhythmic accompaniment: two-headed, barrel-shaped drums and single-headed, frame drums. These instruments come in many sizes and styles of construction. The most widely used are the *gendang* (lashed two-headed drum, resembling the Javanese *kendang*) and the *rebana* (a single-headed frame drum, resembling the Arab *tar*). The Indian tabla is also used in genres influenced by music from India.

Colotomic Instruments

The main instruments formerly used to mark off points in time were knobbed bronze gongs resembling bronze gongs found in other parts of Southeast Asia. Most of the gongs used in Malaysia today are believed to have been made in either Java or Sumatra. They come in various sizes, between 30 and 60 centimeters in diameter.

Genres of West Malaysian Popular Music

Asli and Dondang Saying

The term *asli* denotes a particular musical genre that dates from the 1600s or 1700s. Though regional variations occur, this genre is widely acknowledged to have developed from *dondang sayang* "melody of love" of the Malaysian Chinese community in Melaka. The texts of *asli* and *dondang sayang* are related to the Malay *pantun* in form, style, and rhyme. This poetic form has greatly influenced the lyrics of most other genres. It is the most widely known and most popular Malay poetic form. In its fundamental form, it has four lines, each eight syllables long, rhyming *abab*: the first line rhymes with the third, and the second line rhymes with the fourth. *Pantun* can be spoken, recited, or sung, for a variety of social occasions. Often they are performed in a competition to determine who can create the best ones. Traditionally, such competitions have played a part in courting among young Malay men and women.

A Malaysian *pantun* commonly begins with a reference to nature or a place within Malaysia. The text is always secular. Its topics are love and personal relationships. The following is a famous Malaysian *pantun*.

> Apa kena padi-ku ini,
> What ails my ricefield so fine,
> Sini sangku, sana pun goyang?

Entangled here, there on the move?
Apa kena hati-ku ini
Whatever ails this heart of mine,
Sini sangku, sana pun sayang.
Entangled here, there in love.

A. W. Hamilton explained this text: "The effect of a fitful breeze on a field of growing rice is likened to the gusts of a conflicting passion of the heart" (1982 [1941]:96).

Joget and Ronggeng

The terms *joget* and *ronggeng* denote the most famous and popular traditional Malaysian dance, often called the unofficial national social dance. The word *joget* has two literal meanings: "dance" and "dancing girl." The instrumental ensemble that accompanied the dance was known as a *joget gamelan*. This ensemble still exists in Pahang and Trengganu but is not related to *the joget* discussed here.

The form of the *joget* was influenced by Portuguese and Malaysian-Portuguese dancers and musicians from the time of the Portuguese occupation of Melaka, four hundred years ago. Until the early twentieth century, it was known by the name *ronggeng*. With the creation of *joget modern*, the term *joget* generally replaced the term *ronggeng* as the name of the genre. The *joget modern*, in its original form, used European (modern) instruments in an outdoor dancehall-like setting. It was considered improper for unmarried women to take part in such affairs, so men paid to dance with professional female dancers (*joget*). It is widely believed that one of the main reasons for the popularity of the *joget* is that it is a social form of dance, in which male and female performers move flirtatiously around each other.

The traditional *joget* was accompanied by an ensemble essentially the same as the *asli* band: a violin, a knobbed gong, a flute (optional), and at least two *rebana* or *gendan*. *Joget* music is fast. It emphasizes duple- and triple-beat divisions, both in alternation and simultaneously. This rhythm resembles that of many European 6/8 dances, like the tarantella and the fandango; however, the *joget* is commonly notated in 2/4 time.

Zapin

The *zapin* is believed to have been an Arabic dance, which en route to Malaysia absorbed influences from Indian dances. Accordingly, the *gambus* and the harmonium are used widely in performing it. The *gambus* part stands out. The rhythm of the melody closely relates to the rhythm played by the drums. Strongly accented rhythms are a feature of *zapin*. This pattern is often associated with specific scalar degrees. Most commonly, it reinforces the tonic and the dominant.

Ghazal

The Malaysian *ghazal*, a new genre of traditional Malay music, originated in the late 1800s in the state of Johore, which is in the southern part of the Malay peninsula. The Malaysian version of the *ghazal* is different from, but related to, the *ghazal* as found in parts of the Middle

East and northern India. It is also believed to have gained some Portuguese influence en route to Malaysia. The main pulse of a Malaysian *ghazal* is about twice as fast as *asli* tempo. A basic accompanimental rhythm, called *ghazal* rhythm, is more a rhythmic framework than a strictly followed accompanimental pattern. The typical instrumental ensemble used in performing *ghazals* includes a violin, a guitar, a *gambus*, a tambourine, maracas, two tablas, and a harmonium. A Malay *rebana* or *gendang* (or both) sometimes supplement(s) or replace(s) the second tabla.

Keroncong

Keroncong is probably the oldest form of popular Malaysian music. It is closely related to, and widely believed to derive from, Indonesian *kroncong*. It is thought to have originated in the music of the sixteenth-century Portuguese colonies in the Moluccas (Maluku) and Batavia (Jakarta). In Malaysia, *keroncong* is mainly associated with the former colony of Malacca (Melaka). It is not so much a musical form as a style of performance.

Dangdut

Dangdut is another example of Hindustani-influenced music in Malaysia. Though the term itself originated in Indonesia, the style of music it denotes originated in Malaysia. Hindustani music has long influenced many types of music in the Malay Peninsula. Perhaps as a result, no single name has been used to denote Hindustani-influenced music in Malaysia; however, when one of these forms traveled to Indonesia, it became known (by the mid-1940s) as *orkes melayu* "Malay orchestra." In common usage, *dangdut* denotes virtually any vocal or instrumental popular music that uses a tabla and electric guitars. The melodies most commonly are a Malay-Indian mixture.

European Music

Muzik klasik "classical music" and *muzik seriosa* "serious music" are the most common Malaysian terms used for Western classical or serious music. *Muzik klasik* has been associated with the largest urban areas of the Malay Peninsula: Ipoh, Kuala Lumpur, Penang, and Singapore, but even rural towns today have piano-oriented private music schools, which follow a British syllabus. The music is by European composers or Malaysian composers, written in Western classical music formats.

Throughout the twentieth century, European brass bands have played important roles in Malaysian society, affecting both traditional and contemporary musics. The Selangor State Band, begun by the British to provide public and private popular entertainment for colonial officials and their families, was the first military-style wind band in Malaya.

Since there were not enough Western-trained musicians in Malaysia in 1894, when the band was founded, the British contracted to import the entire sixty-four-member Manila Band from the Philippines to form this band. Within a few years, similar state bands, also comprised of Filipino musicians, were established in the Malaysian states of Perak and Penang. Though the bands consisted of civilians, they were usually associated with local police regiments. The Malayan Police Band, begun in 1905, included musicians from

India and the Philippines. Many of these musicians settled in Malaya, married, and had children who often became musicians. The musicians and their descendants have had an enormous effect on music in Malaysia. They formed Malaysian dance and cabaret bands in the early 1900s, performed in *bangsawan* theaters, and even played for Malaysian productions of Chinese opera.

Music in Contemporary West Malaysian Society

Throughout Malaysian history, instruments and other aspects of foreign music were often adopted and adapted to local situations. This phenomenon has continued in popular music. As a result, many international trends in popular music have surfaced in Malaysian popular music. Malaysian rock has been conservative. Throughout the 1960s and early 1970s, a modified rock combo accompanied most singers. In the 1970s and early 1980s, most popular albums tried to achieve an orchestral sound for accompaniment—widely assumed to be an influence of the RTM Orchestra. Guitar-dominated bands (*kugiran*, from *kumpulan gitar ran-cak* "lively guitar group") became common in the late 1960s and early 1970s. Most members began as self-taught part-time or totally amateur musicians who played for parties, dances, and nightclubs. Many bands play a mixture of traditional and modern Malay songs, plus Western-style popular songs and rock.

Since the mid-1980s, Malaysian rock bands have developed large, loyal followings. They still play a variety of styles, ranging from heavy metal to middle-of-the-road or easy-listening styles. The most common style can be best described as Malay balladry. Some musicians try to project a Malaysian image by utilizing the rhythms found in traditional genres. As in earlier history (with *keroncong* and *lagu-lagu rakyat*), some styles—and even specific songs and performers—are active participants in both Malaysian and Indonesian musical cultures.

Malaysian popular music is the most important musical genre in Malaysia. The annual national talent time (*Bintang* RTM) features only popular songs, and national popular-song competitions (such as *Pesta Lagu Malaysia*) have occurred since Malaysia became independent. Televised specials to celebrate religious and national holidays use popular songs much more than any other musical genre. Malaysian songs for *Hari Raya* (a Muslim holiday celebrating the end of Ramadan) are performed in conservative popular styles.

As Malaysia has become more prosperous and economically advanced, the commercial-music industry has become locally more important. Malaysian popular music, though based on Western or international pop-music styles, can be seen as representing a true expression of contemporary Malaysian culture. More Malaysians listen to it than to any other musical style and it is the only kind of music composed, arranged, performed, marketed, and followed by all the ethnic groups in Malaysia.

REFERENCES

D'Cruz, Marion Francena. 1979. "Joget Gamdan, a Study of Its Contemporary Practice." M.A. thesis, Universiti Sains Malaysia.
al-Faruqi, Lois Ibsen. 1985. "Music, Musicians and Muslim Law." *Asian Music* 17(1):3–36.

Ghulam-Sarwar Yousof. 1976. "The Kelantan Mak Yong Dance Theater, a Study of Performance Structure." Ph.D. dissertation, University of Hawai'i.

———. 1987. "Bangsawan: The Malay Opera." *Tenggara* 20:3–20.

Ginsberg, Henry D. 1972. "The Manohra Dance-Drama: An Introduction." *Journal of the Siam Society* 60:169–181.

Hamilton, A. W. 1982 [1941]. *Malay Pantuns*. Singapore: Eastern Universities Press.

Ku Zam Zam, Ku Idris. 1983. "Alat-Alat Muzik Dalam Ensembel Wayang Kulit, Mek Mulung dan Gendang Keling di Kedah Utara" (Musical instruments in the shadow play, *mek mulung*, and *gendang keling* ensembles of North Kedah). In *Kajian Budaya dan Masyarakat di Malaysia*, ed. Mohd. Taib Osman and Wan Kadir Yusoff, 1–52. Kuala Lumpur: Dewan Bahasa dan Pustaka.

———. 1985. "Nobat DiRaja Kedah: Warisan Seni Muzik Istana Melayu Melaka" (Nobat of the Kedah Sultan: A Musical Heritage of the Malay Malacca Sultanate). In *Warisan Dunia Melayu, Teras Peradaban Malaysia*, ed. Abdul Latiff Abu Bakar. Kuala Lumpur: Biro Penerbitan GAPENA.

Malm, William. 1974. "Music in Kelantan, Malaysia and Some of Its Cultural Implications." In *Studies in Malaysian Oral and Musical Traditions*, 1–49. Michigan. Papers on South and Southeast Asia, 8. Ann Arbor: University of Michigan Press.

Matusky, Patricia. 1993. *Malaysian Shadow Play and Music: Continuity of an Oral Tradition*. Kuala Lumpur: Oxford University Press.

Mohammad Anis Mohammad Nor. 1986. *Randai Dance of Minangkabau Sumatra, with Labanotation Scores*. Kuala Lumpur: University of Malaysia.

Mohammad Ghouse Nasaruddin. 1979. "The Desa Performing Arts of Malaysia." Ph.D. dissertation, Indiana University.

Mohd. Taib Osman, ed. 1974. *Traditional Drama and Music in Southeast Asia*. Kuala Lumpur: Dewan Bahasa dan Pustaka.

Sweeney, Amin. 1972. *Ramayana and the Malay Shadow Play*. Kuala Lumpur: National University of Malaysia Press.

Tan Sooi Beng. 1988. "The Thai Manora in Malaysia: Adapting to the Penang Chinese Community." *Asian Folklore Studies* 47(1):19–34.

———. 1993. *Bangsawan: A Social and Stylistic History of Popular Malay Opera*. Singapore: Oxford University Press.

Vietnam

Phong T. Nguyễn

The Socialist Republic of Vietnam (Cộng Hòa Xã Hội Chủ Nghiã Việt Nam) occupies the coastal area of mainland Southeast Asia from China in the north to Cambodia in the south, and shares its western border with Laos. These borders were established in the 1600s after a long process of expansion southward. The area of Vietnam—331,689 square kilometers—roughly equals those of Malaysia, New Mexico, or Norway. The country is narrow and elongated: its distance from north to south is some 3,444 kilometers, but at some points it is only 50 kilometers wide. A highway and a railway furnish transportation from one end of the country to the other. Vietnam has fifty provinces, which can be grouped into three cultural regions: the north, the center, and the south. Each is distinct in language or accent, character, attitude, and music.

The population of Vietnam, 85.2 million (estimate, 2007), can be divided into the Việt and fifty-three minorities, the majority of whom live in the uplands. The Việt, who primarily inhabit lowland areas, are called urban (*kinh*), and the minority ethnic groups, tending to occupy highland and mountain areas, are called high (*thượng*). Among the upland groups are the Muòng, the Thái, the Hmông, the Mán, the Bahnar, and the Jarai, speaking languages from three families, Austroasiatic, Austronesian (Malayo-Polynesian), and Tai. The language of the Việt and that of their cousins the Muòng belong to the

Austroasiatic group. In addition to the upland minorities (about 10 percent of the population), Chinese live mainly in the urban areas. Life expectancy is about sixty-five years.

Most Việt are Buddhists, primarily of the Mahayana sect, but notable percentages are Chinese Buddhist-Taoist, Roman Catholic, Muslim, and Cao Đài (an indigenous religion). Vietnamese multiculturalism has resulted in a complex intertwining of musics. To date, however, most musical research has focused on the Việt.

HISTORY

The Văn Lang Period (2879–258 B.C.E.)

Archaeologists have found it difficult to document music in the days of the Thẩmkhuyên *Homo erectus* and the Kéo-làng *Homo sapiens* in northern Vietnam, but discoveries regarding the lithic culture of Hòa Bình and Bắc Son and the bronze culture of Đông Sơn provide evidence of music and dance in prehistoric Vietnam (Phan, Hà, and Hoàng 1989).

Musical instruments found in Vietnam, including bronze drums, bells, and lithophones, and the images depicted on these instruments, provide valuable historical clues. Several sets of lithophones from Ndut Lieng Krak, Khánh Son, and Bác Ái villages—the music of which remains unknown—date back to this era, extending from the third to the first millennium B.C.E. These lithophones were likely played by ancestors of the highlanders who live in the Truòng Son mountains near the border with Laos and Cambodia. The discovery of these lithophones and bronze gong drums confirms a direct connection between Vietnamese music and that of Southeast Asia in general. Vietnamese lithophones may have been precursors of Southeast Asian xylophones, such as the bamboo xylophones called *t'rung* in Vietnam and *ch'lung* in Indonesia. The Đông S10 ptn bronze gong drums are of major significance, as they were distributed throughout Southeast Asia and southern China. Many Vietnamese scholars regard the Đông S10 ptn period (700–100 B.C.E.) as a foundation of their culture, but relating that period to later ones has proved impossible.

After the Văn Lang Period (258 B.C.E.–939 C.E.)

After 258 B.C.E., the dearth of descriptions of music has led some scholars to speculate that indigenous music became an integral part of customary festivals and religious ceremonies and was therefore kept secret. Buddhism and Indian culture were introduced to Giao Châu by ship-borne merchants, who helped establish thriving commercial relations with Western Asia as early as the first century. In the second century, envoys of Roman emperor Marcus Aurelius (reigned 161–180 C.E.) arrived in the coastal city of Vinh. Vietnam then served as the eastern terminus of maritime trade from the West. Indian Buddhism, therefore, was known in Giao Châu, and in the second century became an important religion there. Vietnam won its independence from China in 938. Music, dance, and theatrical genres were major entertainments at Vietnam's royal palace. From 985, annual water-puppet theater performances and boat races were held to celebrate the king's birthday. In the tenth century, Buddhist dynasties, the Ngô, Đinh, and earlier Lê dynasties (939–1009) served as a transition to the more prominent reigns of the Buddhist zealots and kings of the Lý and Trần dynasties (eleventh to thirteenth centuries). Vietnamese consider this a golden age of music and culture. A kind of vocal chamber music began to evolve in the royal court, and an illustrious female singer, Đào Thị, received an award from the king. As a result, many singers thereafter were named in her honor, and the phrase "songs of Lady Đào" (*hát ả đào,* Sino-Vietnamese *đào nuong ca*) became synonymous with the musical genre she performed.

After many years of neglect, water-puppet plays were again treated to full productions, with a full complement of musicians, singers, and dancers. Music from Laos and Champa was regularly performed for Vietnamese kings as a tribute. The song style *ải lao,* still practiced in festivals for Saint Dóng, is believed to be the first foreign music presented to Vietnamese kings during the Lý period. Hundreds of singers and dancers captured during victories over Champa performed, and by all accounts were well treated, in the royal palace.

Foreign elements were also assimilated into theatrical performances at the Trần court. In a thirteenth-century battle with Chinese invaders, the soldier Li Yuan Ki (in Vietnamese, Lý Nguyên Cát) was captured. Until recently it was widely believed that his skills as an actor were so apparent that he was granted a pardon and subsequently treated as a guest artist. Therefore, it was thought that he introduced Chinese stories, costumes, roles, and acrobatics into Vietnamese theater.

Lê and Nguyễn Dynasties

The beginning of the 1400s witnessed a shift in political power to the Lê family (fifteenth to eighteenth centuries). This shift was accompanied by a movement toward a more Confucian society, with heavy Chinese influences at the royal court. As a result, popular forms of music began to break away from the courtly arena, and rigid Confucians insisted that the elegant music (*nhã nhạc*) of the court be clearly distinguished from the vulgar music (*tục nhạc*) of commoners. By decree, the court orchestra adopted the instrumentations of the Ming court of China.

A result of the legal code of 1437 was the collapse of theatrical genres such as *chèo* and *tuồng* and folk dances, all of which had received support from the Đại Việt court during the Lý and Trần Dynasties and flourished through the first quarter of the 1400s. From 1437, all forms of theater were prohibited by King Lê Thái Tông, much influenced by Confucian aesthetics. Musicians and singers, with their offspring, were not permitted to take national civil service examinations.

The Nguyễn, whose court was at Huế in central Vietnam, however, began to restore ritual music to the Confucian temples and temples of the royal family in the later eighteenth century. The Commission on Music permitted the string-and-wind ensemble (*ty bã lệnh*) and the ritual ensemble (*nhạc huyền*), which later came to be known as the small ensemble (*tiểu nhạc*) and the large ensemble (*đại nhạc*), respectively. The string-and-wind ensemble had two three-stringed lutes, two two-stringed fiddles, two two-stringed coconut-shell fiddles,

Figure 13.1
Stone carving of a mythological "bird musician" playing a *đan nguyet* lute with a large plectrum found among apparent rubble at Van Phuc Temple in Bac Ninh province north of Hanoi, from the Lý Dynasty (11th-13th centuries). Photo by Phong Nguyễn, 2004.

two moon-shaped lutes, two pear-shaped lutes, two oboes, two small drums, two one-headed drums, one hourglass-shaped drum, one three-gong set, and one coin clapper. The ritual ensemble had one large drum, one small drum, one large stone chime, twelve small stone chimes, one large bell, twelve small bells, one wooden idiophone (*chúc*), one wooden tiger-shaped idiophone (*ngữ*), two *cầm* zithers, two *sắt* zithers, two small vertical bamboo flutes, two transverse bamboo flutes, two long transverse bamboo flutes, two mouth organs, and two ocarinas. The large ensemble included twenty large drums, eight trumpets, four large gongs, four small gongs, four conch trumpets, and four water-buffalo horns.

The Nguyễn kings favored music and literature. King Tự Đức and various princes and princesses were prominent songwriters and musicians. Their contributions to present-day chamber music (*ca huế*) and songs show how influential this genre was. In the 1800s, the greatest musical honor bestowed by the Nguyễn court and its mandarins was on the theatrical genre called *hát bội* in the south and *tuồng* in the north. Nightly performances of *hát bội*, with highly sophisticated theatrical techniques and long stories, were presented inside the royal palace. Some stories lasted more than one hundred nights and involved hundreds of characters.

Reform Movements in the Twentieth Century

The Nguyễn Dynasty ended in 1945, when Emperor Bảo Đại abdicated. Traditional music was severely affected by World War II and by the ways of life that had developed in urban areas. Since the late 1800s, music of the French colonialists (from sources as varied as the military, the Roman Catholic Church, and nightclubs) and many European instruments had made their way into Vietnam. However, despite the war and the influx of foreign music, traditional music survived. Around 1900, a reform movement spread throughout the country, starting with *cải lương* "reform, innovation," a new form of theater that originated in the south.

In the cities, music students in French colonial and Roman Catholic schools began to embrace the Western system of music. They composed Vietnamese-language songs, first called modernized music (*nhạc cải cách*), then new music (*tân nhạc*), with accompaniment based on tempered scales and Western rules of harmony. Despite many moves toward reform and modernization, the country lapsed into yet another war—first a war of independence against the French, then a civil conflict in which the United States supported the south, which resulted in the loss of many lives and a country divided into north and south for twenty years. Unification occurred in 1975 under a socialist regime with the capital in Hanoi.

Music in Yearly Cycles

To many observers, Vietnam is at its most beautiful in the spring and fall. Spring usually begins in late January or early February. The cycles of the year commence on the first day of the Vietnamese New Year, the beginning of spring. Both spring and fall provide opportunities for relaxation and fun; the most important festivals are held in the countryside during these periods of good weather. Men and women enjoy singing folk songs and ritual music to celebrate these seasons, and temples resound with joyous songs, dances, processions, and games. These events last for several days; in some areas, celebrations may last a whole month (Figure 13.2).

Music is also an integral part of most daily activities, whether rocking a baby, praying at a holy place, attending a wedding or a funeral, honoring the anniversary of a loved one's birth or death, or just enjoying personal entertainment. Some of these events are marked by their own specific cycles: a death is followed by a sequence of rituals starting with the funeral and ending two years later; a local deity may be commemorated once a year on a specific date.

Figure 13.2
A festival in Lim village, Hà Bắc Province. Photo by Phong T. Nguyễn.

Music Theory

Vietnamese scholars have not thoroughly and conclusively addressed questions of music theory. The difficulty lies in the fact that, even though Vietnamese music is nationally and culturally unified to a great extent, regional styles and ensembles exhibit striking differences. A general formality and customary manner of presentation are typical of all Vietnamese music, but no all-embracing theory can be applied to the genres found from north to south.

However, certain conventions—some quite strict—can be observed in Vietnamese musics. Whether oral or written, they make up a music theory. Included are several systems of instruction in music, developed by respected regional masters whose "theories" are based on those of their elders. To validate a student's played version of beats, measures, rhythms, pitches, and ornamentations, a demanding music teacher may well ask a student, "Who is your teacher?" In this way, the prevalent, yet informal, music theories remain relatively uncorrupted. Good teachers must therefore agree on certain conventions to preserve the character of a specific region's music.

Thus, the term *Vietnamese music theory* should properly be pluralized and considered within the contexts of three distinct geographical regions: north, central, and south. In each region, various ensembles and theatrical genres are created according to specific rules. Methods of learning and instrumentation vary greatly from one region to another, and musicians from different regional ensembles do not play together.

Vocal music dominates many musical performances. Since Vietnamese is a tonal language with distinct regional variations, the traditional songs of a particular region are best understood only within their regional contexts. Oral instruction is more the rule than the exception, and the conversion of known musical notations into an orally transmissible form is common. Notation is used primarily by students—for the sake of memorization (Figures 13.3, 13.4).

Vietnamese ethnomusicologists have speculated about whether folk songs adhere to any discernible music theory or theories. In Vietnam, it is difficult to define performances

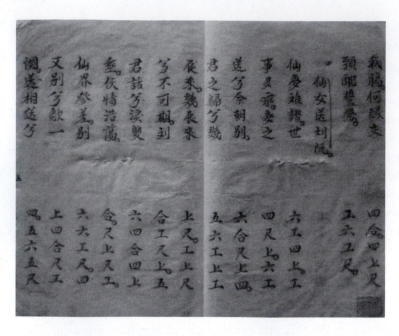

Figure 13.3
Old notation in Chinese characters. The song is "*Tiên Nữ Tống Luu Nguyễn*" ('The Fairies Say Farewell to Luu and Nguyễn'). The lyrics (*above*) and schematic music (*below*) are read from top to bottom, right to left. Each vertical line has five words, which correspond to five musical notes.

as either purely folk or purely artistic, as most performances bear traits of both traditions. Still, even if it is not possible to establish definitely that folk songs reflect one or more theories, observers can at least note theoretical ties between artistic and folkloric musics in Vietnam. This connection may be explained by the fact that peasants who sing folk songs may also be amateur, semiprofessional, or professional musicians, actors, and actresses. Professionalism is manifested when, for example, a village ritualist performs his songs and dances in an organized and reserved manner.

Forms of Presentation

Xuân Tình
(*Spring Love*)

Lớp I
(*Section I*)

Câu
(*Phrase*)

1. ___ Cống cống ___ xù
2. Xừ ___ xê cống xàng
3. Xang xự xê ___ hò
4. Xê ___ hò hò xang
5. Xang xự xê ___ hò
6. Xê ___ hò ___ hò xang
7. Xang cống cống ___ xù
8. Xừ ___ xê ___ cống xàng
9. Xang xự xê hò
10. Xê ___ hò ___ hò xang
11. Xang xự xê xự
12. Xự cống cống xang
13. Xê xề xề liu
14. Liu ___ xê xề liu

Figure 13.4
Notation in romanized characters from the 1950s. The piece, "*Xuân Tình*" ('Love in Spring'), is notated in a skeletal manner. In each four-measure phrase, the weak beats are underlined, and the strong beats are doubly underlined.

Traditionally in many Vietnamese genres, the performance of songs and other music is realized first in speech rhythm, then in meter. This form of presentation embodies the socioaesthetic philosophy that things must be done in a formal order: first nonmetric, then metric; first slow, then fast; first new, then familiar. This results in a gradual, orderly introduction of the soundscape. It is important to involve both kinds of metrical organization in presenting a mode in chamber music; a complete performance must include both of them. The nonmetric introduction is denoted by a variety of terms used in different contexts, more for voice than for instrumental ensemble, depending on musical genres or styles. For instrumental music, *rao* "announcement" or *dạo* (pronounced *zaow*) "promenade," and for voice, an introductory recitative (*nói lối* "speaking the way"), *nói sử* "telling a story," *ngâm* "sung poetry," *văn* "complaint," *vỉa* "edge, side," *bỉ* (derived from *vỉ* or *vỉa*), and other terms, denote this introduction.

In a typical chamber-music ensemble, a song or instrumental piece is performed in one of three forms: (1) a short, improvised, and nonmetrical introduction followed by composed music; (2) an improvised, nonmetrical poetic song accompanied by instruments; (3) an improvised, metrical song accompanied by instruments. For the introduction, a short song is sometimes used instead. This use happens only in *cải lương* or modern *vọng cổ*, songs called *tân cổ giao duyên* in southern Vietnam (Figure 13.5).

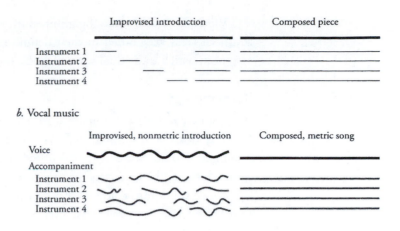

Figure 13.5
Forms of presentation in music.

A feature common to Vietnamese traditions is heterophony, in which several versions of the same melodic lines are superimposed. To create a timbral play, three, five, or eight instruments together display their distinctive timbres, highlighted by syncopated rhythmic cells. This noncomposed character makes room for improvised melodies and rhythms derived from the conventional notes of an instrumental piece, a song, or both. Though the music is monophonically based, musicians in ensembles may hear a kind of polyphony of instrumental improvisation played contrapuntally. This tendency makes Vietnamese music heterophonic.

Scales and Modes

When viewing Vietnamese musical culture, one must focus on two essential elements: the nontempered character of the scales and the transmigration of scalar units. Tones used in folk songs are more localized than those of art music, the latter mostly having been codified nationwide. Finely adjusted intervals, even microtones, are typical of folk songs. Two to twelve tones may be selected from the twelve-tone system of tuning available in Vietnamese music (Figure 13.6).

The Vietnamese concept of mode involves a rich combination of elements constituting the basis for a complete performance. It must therefore cover both the musical rules and the extramusical meanings of a given piece of music. In certain performances, including peasants' songs and folk-ritual music, mode is simplified, but in more sophisticated genres and performance styles, the concept of mode becomes paramount.

There is room to believe that this modal conceptualization, probably nurtured from time immemorial, is based on combined notions of both exact and flexible pitches, melodic patterns, specific ornamentations, timing, quality and type of vocal sound, and particular modal sentiments. The totality does not, however, contradict the idea that performances of modes must comprise all these features individually. For the music to be modally effective, three basic elements must be employed: sentiment, scale, and ornamentation.

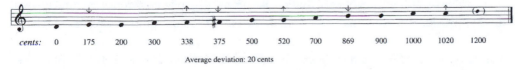

cents: 0   175   200   300   338   375   500   520   700   869   900   1000   1020   1200

Average deviation: 20 cents

Figure 13.6
The tonal material of Vietnamese music.

Vietnamese songs may be grouped into two major musical systems: the central and southern areas are unified in their definition of modes, whereas the northern area has a system in which individual songs define a mode.

Terminology

It is not easy to find a nationally accepted term equivalent to "mode." Some scholars have considered *điệu* (also called *điệu thức* or *thức điệu*)—a term used not only in music, but also in art and literature—equivalent to "mode." Each *điệu* has a distinctive modal expression, which can be understood as a mode or type of song, and each has seemingly endless variations. Ethnomusicologists in Vietnam are still working toward a unified definition of terms to be used at the national level.

Điệu, a term commonly known to musicians and singers in the central region and the south, is somewhat equivalent to "mode" in music; however, because of the generalized meanings of *điệu*, the term *hơi* is locally preferred. *Hơi* "breath, air, nuance" may describe either the meaning of a mode or a specific nuance, distinguishing one mode from another by means of specific ornamentations. A musician playing a wrong ornament may destroy a mode. Therefore, the combined term *hơi-điệu* is used for clarity's sake. The meanings of these terms are also shared by Vietnamese actors and religious singers.

An extensive repertoire of traditional pieces and songs in both chamber and theatrical music requires executing the modes with subtlety and consistency. This process calls for four basic skills: organizing tonal materials in a hierarchical pattern, displaying ornamentation, using specific melodic patterns, and preparing modal sentiments for a given song or piece. For an accomplished musician, the last skill is the most important, in that the musician must shape the sentiment before realizing it through the appropriate expressive mode.

Scales

A scalar system plays a preliminary role in all musical performances. It varies according to the genre, subgenre, or social context in which a song or instrumental piece is constructed. Convention dictates that, in Vietnamese music, there is no such thing as absolute pitch. The fundamental tone of a scale may be chosen to fit the voice of a singer or the acoustic capacity of an instrument; thus, for best results, singers and musicians need to tailor solutions to individual needs. Other scalar tones are then proportionally derived from this fundamental pitch.

The total number of possible tones is considered to be twelve and constitutes a theoretical system of tuning. Vietnamese scales use fewer than twelve tones in virtually all cases. The number of tones used has sociocultural connotations. Many lullabies and ritualistic songs (including Buddhist cantillations and religious chants) have two- or three-tone scales. The scales of chamber music and theatrical pieces have five to seven tones. Having more tones permits the transmigration of scalar units, also known as metabole.

In art music, three categories of tones make up a scale: obligatory tones are fundamental, and they provide the structural framework of the piece or song; additional tones, which may be added to the initial scalar unit, may or may not lead to the transmigration of scalar units; passing tones, heard only a few times during the piece or song, are especially applicable in music built on a clearly established pentatonic or hexatonic scale. Traditional Vietnamese music is thus not restricted to a five-tone system of tuning, but is expanded by additional tones produced by pressing on the strings. Soft, flexible strings ease the creation of passing and additional notes.

Transmigration of Scales

The transmigration of scalar units within a song or instrumental piece creates sentiments appreciated by both singers and listeners. This transmigration, involving a change from one scale to another, with or without

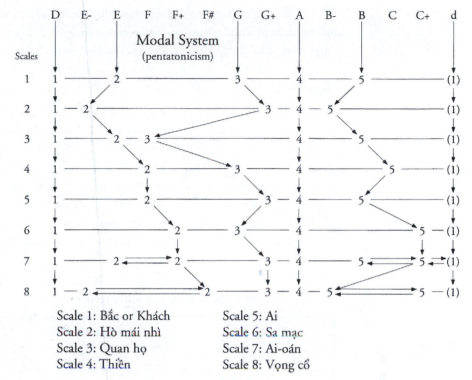

Scale 1: Bắc or Khách
Scale 2: Hồ mái nhì
Scale 3: Quan họ
Scale 4: Thiền

Scale 5: Ai
Scale 6: Sa mạc
Scale 7: Ai-oán
Scale 8: Vọng cổ

Figure 13.7
Chart of scales used in the artistic tradition.

a return to the original, conforms closely to what Constantin Brăiloiu termed *metabole* (1955:63–75). After a scale (pentatonic or not) has been established in a piece, its gravitational center may shift to a tone a fifth higher, establishing the new scale on this tone before returning to the original scale. In other instances, a new scale may be superimposed on the original, using the same fundamental tone. The number of tones in a given song can be classified as main, additional, and passing degrees (Figure 13.7).

Ornamentation

The elaboration of tones occurs frequently in many folk traditions, but ornamentation is far more prevalent in art music and depends on the musical context. That some ornamentations are associated, though not required, with particular scalar tones is a striking aspect of Vietnamese music. The complexity of the ornamentation allows each singer and musician to individualize expression. In vocal music, language naturally plays a major role in this individualization; the three prevalent accents (north, central, and south) also influence ornamentation. Specific terms for ornamental figures, clearly defined in each geographical area, differ greatly from one vocal or instrumental genre to another. It is far more difficult to deal with vocal than instrumental music, because of the myriad linguistic subtleties inherent in the former (see Figure 13.8).

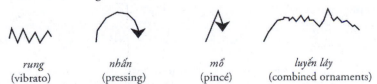

rung
(vibrato)

nhấn
(pressing)

mổ
(pincé)

luyến láy
(combined ornaments)

Figure 13.8
The signs and names of ornaments.

Vibrato can be either sustained or brief, according to the degree of the mode. Besides using conventional patterns, a musician can individualize vibrato to a level of expertise appreciated by the most sensitive of connoisseurs.

Sentiments

Ingrained in Vietnamese musicians' and singers' minds are the types of sentiment through which a performer can establish a presence in the music world and communicate with the audience. An artfully ornamented note or a melodious motive can move listeners. Performers must prepare their minds before playing or singing; only by doing so can they correctly express the desired mode. Conversely, poorly wrought ornamentation may expose the weakness in a musician's talent. The improvised introduction (*rao* or *dạo*) thus becomes necessary for any adjustment, as does the exposition of sentiments through musical notes.

Modal sentiments are felt and described according to generally accepted definitions, which include classification into the modal systems *nam* and *bắc*. These are commonly defined by all genres and traditions in Vietnam: *nam* is sad, and *bắc* is happy; however, regional traditions use and define other terms:

ca trù (north)	*huỳnh*	rhapsodic
	pha	mixture of sad and happy feelings
	nao	bright, delightful, overjoyed
ca huế (central)	*ai*	sorrowful
	thiền	religiously solemn
nhạc tài tử (south)	*xuân*	serene and lively
	ail	amen table
	đảo	serene but straight
	oán	plaintive

Rhythm and Meter

Rhythm in Vietnamese music is complex. Syncopation gives the music a spiciness that distinguishes it from Chinese music, superficially the most closely related music style. In addition to metrical organization, some Vietnamese music is unmeasured or nonmetrical. Instrumental ensembles are not only heterophonic in melody but heterorhythmic, creating an interplay that gives Vietnamese music added drive.

Nonmetrical Organization

Nonmetrical rhythms play an important role in Vietnamese music, particularly in sung poetry and Buddhist hymns. Sung poetry can last for hours without establishing a musical meter. Buddhist hymns may be preceded or followed by metrical cantillation. In songs, sections of free rhythm may occur as a modal preparation in the beginning or as a transition to another section.

Metrical Organization

Nhịp denotes metrical rhythm. Most Vietnamese music is organized metrically according to cycles of beats, with patterns having one, two, three, four, and eight beats. The final beat of each unit is the most emphasized. Three-beat units or ternary meter is rare in Vietnam. What is traditionally called a three-beat measure (*nhịp ba*) is, in fact, a cycle of four beats, of which three are emphasized (Figure 13.9). Cyclical music is most clearly heard in the percussion-dominated ensembles of ritual, festival music (*nhạc lễ*), and theatrical music. A basic pattern can be elaborated and improvised on in various ways.

Theatrical and ceremonial musics emphasize multiple rhythmic patterns by superimposing patterns played on percussion instruments. In theatrical and ritual music, a wooden drum (*mõ*), a clapper (*phách*), and a water-buffalo-horn drum (*mõ sừng trâu*) play interlocking patterns, while other drums and clappers serve as the rhythmic foundation. They assist stage movement and signal on-stage sectional changes. Musicians are trained in standard patterns (*chân phương* "square"), and then they advance to elaborations (*hoa lá* "flourishing, flowers and leaves"). A good musician would use the *hoa lá* pattern for most of a performance.

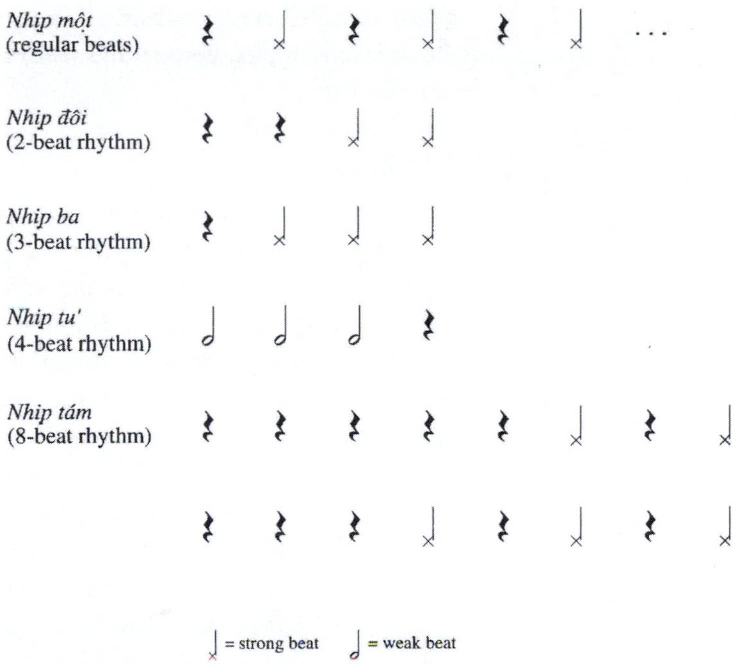

Melodic improvisation is characteristic of Vietnamese music as a whole, but free-metered improvisation by the drummer in introductions and interludes is probably the most appreciated part of any performance. The drummer, as leader of the ensemble, uses special rhythmic formulas to start and end pieces.

Figure 13.9
Rhythmic patterns: *nhịp đôi* (two-beat rhythm), *nhịp ba* (three-beat rhythm), *nhịp tu* (four-beat rhythm), and *nhịp tám* (eight-beat rhythm).

MUSICAL INSTRUMENTS

Vietnamese musical instruments have a wide variety of origins. Besides indigenous creations, many traditional stringed and wind instruments migrated from Central Asia via China. Since colonization (1884–1954), many Western instruments have been assimilated into Vietnamese music. In all, more than fifty instruments are played by the lowland Vietnamese and nearly two hundred by upland minorities. Although there is some overlap, each group plays mostly distinct instruments.

Because the voice is prominent in Vietnamese chamber music and theatrical music, instruments tend to play an accompanying role in those genres; however, since the voice cannot replace instrumental music in certain aspects of rituals, instruments play an essential role in ceremonial musics, such as those of the imperial court and in temples.

Except for court music, no orchestral ensembles in Vietnam have more than five stringed instruments. For instance, ceremonial ensembles (*nhạc lễ*) of southern Vietnam use twelve to twenty instruments, but most are percussive. The northern chamber-music genres *ca trù* and *hát ả đào* have only three instruments, of which *đàn đáy* is the only stringed one. Where several instruments play together, the texture is heterophonic. In ceremonial ensembles, both strings (*văn*) and percussion (*võ*) combine for an entire piece or for a section.

Idiophones

Idiophones may be the earliest and are the most numerous instruments in Vietnam. In many respects, they mark the rhythms of Vietnamese life, announcing, governing, and developing ritual ceremonies and changes in theatrical performances, thus becoming an integral part of them. They are capable of both braying and delicate sonorities. The materials used to make them are wood, bamboo, horn, bronze, and stone. Vietnamese idiophones include prehistoric bronze drums and lithophones, bamboo xylophones, gongs, cymbals, wooden slit drums, bells, and clappers.

The bronze drum (*trống đồng*) is among the oldest of Vietnamese idiophones. It first appeared in the Đong-Son period. The Mường still use it for festivals. Since the 1970s, it has been revived for concert performances, but its modern use likely bears little relationship to its earlier musical contexts .

A *đại hồng chung* (Figure 13.10), a large bronze bell, is played in Buddhist ceremonies. It is the largest Vietnamese bell still played. As a type, it is descended from a bell dated in the Lý Dynasty (eleventh to twelfth centuries) and housed in the National Historical Museum, Hanoi. About 1.25 meters high, it hangs inside a tower. Another tower, on the left side of the hall, holds the drum of wisdom (*trống bát nhã*), which, when struck with a wooden club covered with tissues, produces a long-resounding, low sound.

The small bell (*tiểu chung*) is a smaller version of the *đại hồng chung*. It is also called *chuông báo chúng* because it calls the monks to assemble. It is hung under the roof of the meeting hall of the museum.

The bell of religious perseverance (*chuông gia trì*), a hemispheric bowl chime, is used in Buddhist ceremonies. It ranges from 20 to 75 centimeters in diameter and reposes on a cushioned ring. It is played to punctuate musical sections of Buddhist chant.

Figure 13.10
Đại hồng chung, a Buddhist bell of the Lý Dynasty (eleventh to thirteenth centuries). Photo by Phong T. Nguyễn.

Gongs come in three sizes: a large (*chiêng*, also *cổng*), a middle-sized (*thanh la*, also *tum*), and a small and hand-held (*đẩu*, also *tang*) instrument. The *cổng* is probably the original term for gong; *chiêng* is an onomatopoeic form for the sound made by flat gongs. A set of three small gongs hung on a frame by threads and fixed to a handle is called *tam âm la* "three-sound gongs." Vietnamese gongs date to the Bronze Age. They gradually lost most of their ensemble duties and are presently incorporated into ceremonial and theatrical ensembles with many other instruments.

Mõ is a generic Vietnamese term for slit drums

not made from hide or metal. Materials used to craft *mõ* include wood, bamboo, and wa-ter-buffalo horn. A *mõ* accompanies Buddhist chanting. It has a rounded shape, and bears decorations suggesting features of a fish, as with the Chinese *muyu* and the Japanese *mok-kugyo*, both of which mean "wooden fish." *Mõ đình*, the *mõ* employed for rituals in village shrines (*đình*), is shaped like the trunk of a tree, and is placed horizontally on a wooden stand. A slit along its body is a bit distended in the middle. A bamboo slit drum called *mõ làng* "village slit drum" summons people to meetings and signals when there is a thief, fire, or any other local emergency. The *mõ sùng trâu* "water-buffalo horn," 15 to 20 centimeters long, is played in ceremonial ensembles.

Chimes (*khánh*) are made of bronze (*khánh đồng*) and stone (*khánh đá*). Considered by Vietnamese to have the shape of the petal of a flower, *khánh* have a rounded base and a scalloped top resembling a hat. *Khánh* vary from 37 to 125 centimeters long. They are commonly found in temples.

The *chập chõa* is a pair of cymbals; a smaller version is called *chập bạt*, *não bạt*, and *chũm chọe*. The *chập chõa* (about 50 centimeters in diameter) and *bạt* or *chập bạt* (about 15 to 20 centimeters in diameter) differ in size and musical function: the smaller pair elaborates on the rhythm of the larger. Both instruments are played in theatrical, festival, and ritual music.

The *phách* may be among the oldest types of clappers used in religious ceremonies, dances, chamber music, and theater. A small piece of bamboo or a wooden block is select-ed for its sound. Two or three beaters may be used to beat measures on it and to vary the tempo and rhythmic patterns. Probably because of the importance of clappers in singing, the term *phách* also means "'rhythm" and "tempo" in northern Vietnam.

The *song lang*, like the *phách*, is a clapper, used only in southern chamber music. In-vented early in the twentieth century, it consists of a flat round piece of wood with a slit in the curved side about 30 centimeters in circumference. A small rounded piece of wood is attached to a thin, flat, U-shaped buffalo-horn "spring," which in turn is attached to the main piece. The musician plays it with his or her foot by pressing the small piece against the larger one, creating a sharp, high-pitched sound to articulate important beats while playing a melodic instrument. Though a small and simple instrument, it has both cultural and musical values in *nhạc tài tử* and *cải lương*. The singer of a *vọng cổ*, a thirty-two-beat song, must hear clicks of a *song lang* on the twenty-fourth and thirty-second beats.

Sinh tiền (Figure 13.11) is another kind of clapper. Two long, flat pieces of wood are connected at one end by a leather hinge. The lower side of the lower piece has teeth, along which the play-er scrapes a third piece of wood, also notched, to pro-duce a rasping sound. A few old coins, loosely secured to the topmost piece of wood on a nail, add a jingling sound.

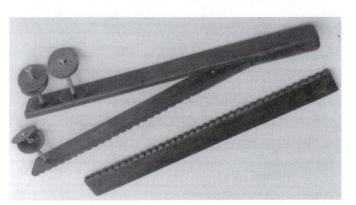

Figure 13.11
Sinh tiền, coin clapper. Photo by Phong T. Nguyễn.

mõ
Slit drums, actually hollowed out of solid material such as wood or bamboo
phách
Piece of wood or bamboo struck by two beaters
song lang
Foot-operated slit drum struck with a wooden beater on a piece of buffalo horn
sinh tiền
Hinged, two-piece clapper with coins on the upper piece and scraped saw teeth on the lower

trống
Generic term for
Vietnamese drums,
most with nailed
head(s)

Membranophones

Trống is a generic term for membranophones that have one or two skin-covered heads and a wooden body. Depending on their use, these drums have different names, sizes, and shapes. More than twenty drums bear different names, and their sizes range from about 20 to 200 centimeters. Each has a unique set of rhythms and a unique teaching method, indigenous to its regional birthplace.

The *bồng*, unusual because its name does not include *trống*, is a southern Vietnamese drum whose name is likely onomatopoeic. It is a small, one-headed drum used in *nhạc lễ* ensembles. With an hourglass-shaped baked-clay body, it has boa-skin heads. Its pitch depends on the tension of the lacing. Both heads are beaten by hand.

The drum of wisdom (*trống bát nhã*), a small drum, announces the beginning and ending of important Buddhist ceremonies. It is placed on a carved wooden stand.

The carrying drum (*trống bưng*, also *trống khẩu* "mouth drum") is a small, two-headed drum with a strap affixed to one side, enabling the player to hold it with one hand while using a wooden stick to beat the drumheads with the other. This drum is played both by Buddhist monks and, in northern villages, to accompany wrestling matches.

The drum of honor (*trống chầu*, also called *trống sấm* "thunder drum," *trống cái*, *trống đại lược*, and *đại cổ* "large drum"), the largest of all Vietnamese drums, is used in court music, village temples, traditional theater, *hát bội*, and *chèo*.

The *trống chầu ca trù* "drum for the *ca trù*" (song with danced accompaniment) or "drum for *hát ả đào*" (song of Lady Đào), is played in northern chamber-music genres (Figure 13.12).

The battle drum (*trống chiến*) is used primarily in on-stage battle scenes in theater.

The rice drum (*trống cơm*) is a portable two-headed drum often tuned (in fifths) by the application of rice paste to the center of each head (Figure 13.13).

Figure 13.12
The drum and clapper used in *ca trù* or *hát ả đào* chamber song. Photo by Phong T. Nguyễn.

The *trống nhạc* or *trống bản* is a pair of drums, each having a different tone, the higher-pitched called female drum (*trống cái*) or civil drum (*trống văn*) and the lower-pitched called male drum (*trống đực*) or military drum (*trống võ*). They are the main instruments of the *nhạc lễ* ensemble.

Chordophones

Vietnamese chordophones include

plucked, bowed, and struck instruments, played both solo and in ensembles. About fifteen stringed instruments are used today, and several others have become obsolete. All of these are identified by the

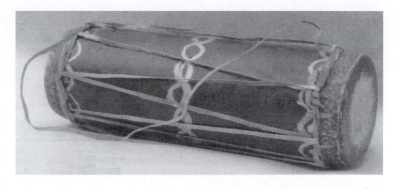

Figure 13.13
A Vietnamese drum (*trống com*) tuned with rice paste. Photo by Phong T. Nguyễn.

classifying word *đàn*. The vibrations of their strings are intended to mimic vocal nuances, both the typical intonations of Vietnamese language and the idiosyncracies of local dialects. A Vietnamese *đàn* (stringed instrument) usually has an alternate name indicating its local or linguistic background.

Zithers

The Vietnamese monochord (*đàn bầu* "gourd instrument," also *đàn độc huyền* "single-stringed instrument") (Figure 13.14) has a wood box resonator, with a flexible vertical stick ("neck"), to which one end of its string is tied. Because it originally had a resonator made of a dried gourd, it was called a gourd (*bầu*)—the name retained in the north and

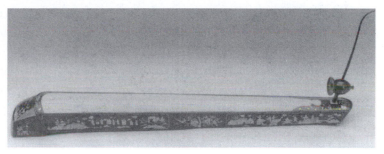

Figure 13.14
A Vietnamese monochord (*đàn bầu*). Photo by Phong T. Nguyễn.

central regions. The vertical stick is made of a thin, flexible piece of water-buffalo horn or bamboo. This monochord is the only Vietnamese instrument that produces harmonics, made with a light pluck and touch of the musician's right hand on any of the five nodes of the string. If the string is tuned to D, its tones are D, A, d, f#, a, and d', all of which may be produced at any of four octaves. The first octave of the string is located in the middle. In addition, the left-hand bending of the stick changes pitches or ornaments them in accordance with the chosen mode. The *đàn bầu* is played solo or to accompany folk songs, tales, and epics. It has had a remarkable history. Discriminated against at times, it has been an instrument of blind street beggars, yet it was also an instrument of choice at the Trần imperial court (1225–1400).

The Vietnamese board zither (*đàn tranh*, also *đàn thập lục*), has sixteen (sometimes seventeen) strings running along a semitubular body of paulownia wood (Figure 13.15). It is thus distantly related to other East Asian board zithers, especially the Chinese *zheng*, the Korean *kayagum*, and the Japanese *koto*. Indeed, the word *tranh* derives from *zheng*, and *đàn thập lục* means "sixteen-

Figure 13.15
A Vietnamese zither (*đàn tranh* or *đàn thập lục*). Photo by Phong T. Nguyễn.

stringed zither." Neither the repertoire nor the theory of this zither, however, resembles those of the East Asian zithers.

Đàn tam thập lục "thirty-six-stringed instrument" is a dulcimer of Chinese origin. It is uncertain whether this dulcimer had been known in Vietnam before it was introduced by Matteo Ricci, an Italian traveler who in the 1600s had journeyed to China's Guangdong Province, where the instrument was a simple dulcimer with thirty-six strings. Today's players, however, usually use one of the large modern Chinese-type models with three or four sets of bridges.

Plucked Lutes

The *đán đáy* is a long-necked, three-stringed lute with a trapezoidal-shaped, backless body (Figure 13.16). Though its neck is 1.2 meters long, the nine frets cover only the lower half, with an additional one fixed to the soundboard. Thick and high, these frets produce seven equidistant notes, but the open strings provide additional, exceptionally low tones. This lute is the only stringed instrument used to accompany *ca trù* singing.

The *đàn nguyệt* or *đàn kìm* is a moon-shaped, long-necked lute with two silk strings (Figure 13.17). Though literary sources suggest that this instrument has an East Asian heritage akin to *the yueqin* (China), *woolkum* (Korea), and *gekkin* (Japan), it may be functionally closer to other Southeast Asian lutes. Its frets are high and fixed on the neck to provide a pentatonic scale. If the fundamental tone is D, the open string and frets produce successively D, E, G, A, B and their octaves. Its strings, the upper one thicker than the lower, are tuned in fourths, fifths, or sevenths. This lute is one of the most frequently played traditional instruments in Vietnam.

The *tỳ bà*, a pear-shaped lute, first appeared in Vietnam in the early 600s, a few centuries after it had been introduced into China, from Kucha in Xinjiang (Central Asia) during the Six Dynasties (386–534). Its shape and four strings resemble those of the early Chinese *pipa* more than those of the Korean *bip'a* or the Japanese *biwa*.

The *đàn xến* is the Vietnamese version of a southern Chinese octagonal lute (*qin-qin*), whose rounded sound box has scallops around the edge. It was introduced into southern Vietnam in the early twentieth century. As with other such instruments, the process of Vietnamization included raising the frets, making adaptations to accommodate a heptatonic scale, and changing the strings to a soft, flexible material.

Lục huyền cầm "six-stringed instrument" and *đàn ghi-ta* are Vietnamese terms for the Western guitar, used in traditional ensembles (Figure 13.18). Originating in the so-called *guitare espagnole* (Spanish *guitarra española*), this instrument was adopted by *tài tử* musicians since 1934. Later, it became a favorite instrument in *tài tử* and *cải lương*. The physical changes it has undergone in Vietnam are noteworthy: its strings, though of metal, are softer than strings used in the West, and the wood between the frets has been scooped out to allow for the deep string bending required to produce typical Vietnamese ornaments (Figure

Figure 13.16
A Vietnamese long lute (*đàn đáy*). Photo by Phong T. Nguyễn.

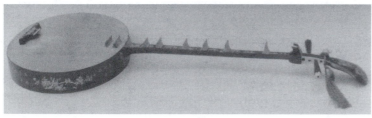

Figure 13.17
A Vietnamese moon-shaped lute (*đàn nguyệt or đàn kìm*). Photo by Phong T. Nguyễn.

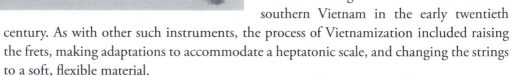

13.19). The number of strings went from four to five and even six. There are three octave-based tunings (*dây*): G–d–g–d'–a'–e" (*dây Rạch-Gía* "Rạch Gía tuning"), G–d–g–d'–g'–d" (*dây Sài-Gòn* "Saigon tuning"), and G–d–g–d'–a'–d ("*dây lai*" acculturated tuning).

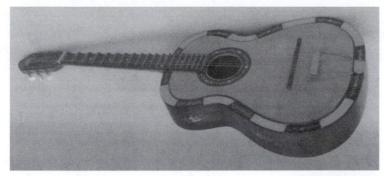

Figure 13.18
A Vietnamese guitar (*lục huyền cầm*, also called *ghi-ta*). Photo by Phong T. Nguyễn.

Bowed Lutes (Fiddles)

The *đàn nhị* or *đàn cò* (Figure 13.20) is a two-stringed fiddle resembling the Chinese *erhu* and related to Southeast Asian fiddles like the Thai *saw duang*. It is one of the primary instruments in court, theatrical, and ritual music. Thought to have been derived from Turkic or Mongol culture, it has a cylindrical wooden sound box, covered at one end with boa skin. At the center of this skin is a tiny bridge supporting two parallel silk strings, one thinner than the other. These strings are wound around pegs piercing a thin neck about 75 centimeters long near its upper curve. A horsetail-hair bow passes over the resonator and between the strings.

Three other bowed lutes have different resonators: *đàn cò phụ* "subordinate fiddle," with its slightly larger resonator; *đàn gáo* or *đàn hồ* "coconut-shell fiddle"; and *đàn cò chi* "little fiddle." For a *nhạc lễ* ritual performance, these instruments are tuned in fifths, from the lowest to the highest instruments as D–A, F–C, G–d, and A–e (using d as the fundamental tone). The G–d tuning is employed for the principal *đàn nhị*.

Figure 13.19
The fingerboard of the Vietnamese guitar, showing scooping. Photo by Phong T. Nguyễn.

Aerophones

The *sáo*, a horizontal bamboo flute, is a favorite wind instrument in Vietnam. Unlike the Chinese *dizi*, it does not have a membrane-covered hole, so its timbre does not include the buzz characteristic of the *di*. The *sáo* has six holes, producing the tones C, D, E, F, G, A, and B. If overblown, it produces octaves. A standard *sáo* is about 50 centimeters long and 1.5 centimeters in diameter.

The *tiêu* is a vertical end-blown notch flute. The bamboo

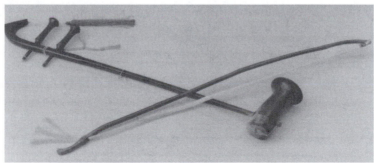

Figure 13.20
A Vietnamese fiddle (*đàn nịh* or *đàn cò*). Photo by Phong T. Nguyễn.

chosen for it must be larger and older than that for a *sáo*, to produce lower tones. The *tiêu* has five holes on top and one underneath.

Kèn is a Vietnamese generic term for all kinds of double-reed aerophones. There is reason to believe that this term originated from terms for free-reed mouth organs known among Tai-speakers, *khèn* and *khaen*. Such instruments may have been used by the Việt during the bronze-drum age, as suggested by engravings on these drums. But the Vietnamese *kèn* is a wooden oboe with a flared bell, resembling many such instruments distributed widely in East, South, West, and Southeast Asia, and even in Africa. It comes in various sizes, differentiated by name. The "presto oboe" (*kèn bóp*) is the smallest; the "gourd oboe" (*kèn bầu*) or "wooden oboe" (*kèn mộc*) is largest. The *kèn thau* has a copper outer ring. The presto oboe and the gourd oboe were used in court, theatrical, and ceremonial music in central Vietnam. The wooden oboe, an equivalent of the gourd oboe, is played in *nhạc lễ* ensembles in southern Vietnam, for weddings, funerals, and village festivals. The *kèn thau* (also called *kèn song hỉ* "double happiness oboe") is a leading instrument of *hát bội* theater.

FOLK SONGS

The Vietnamese term usually glossed as "folk song" denotes songs of common people, especially rice farmers living in villages. Because of their isolation, their music developed distinctive characters according to their individual demographic, historical, and cultural circumstances. Therefore, regional character is a component of Vietnamese folk songs; it is also manifested in regional dialects, tonal systems, metaphors, legends, and poetry. Folk songs include lullabies, work songs, and entertainment songs. Regional accents are a major factor in localizing singing customs. There are five primary linguistic areas among the Việt: North (or northern delta of the Hồng [Red] River), North-Central (Thanh-Nghệ-Tĩnh area), Central (Bình-Trị-Thiên area), South-Central (Quảng-Nam, Quảng Ngãi, Bình-Định, Phú Yên, and Khánh Hòa provinces), and South. Consequently, no single type of folk song represents all of Vietnam.

Folk songs are sung at seasonal festivals, at work, and at private gatherings. The term *lễ hội* denotes festivals involving not only music, songs, and dances, but also ceremonial and ritual activities. Folk songs occur during *lễ hội*, not inside a temple but in its yard or surrounding grounds, because those areas are thought more appropriate for songs that involve games and amorous themes. Occupational songs mirror the work of people sharing the same job who need either encouragement or entertainment; in these cases, rhythm plays an important role, as diversion or competition. At private gatherings, songs are sung for fun, whether as diversion or competition.

Though there are different singing styles in different places in Vietnam, one rule governs all sung performances (*cuộc hát*, or *canh hát* if it lasts all night). The rule is that the singing should occur in three distinct stages: greeting songs, main or contesting songs, and farewell songs. Most Vietnamese folk songs are performed in an alternating or antiphonal pattern (*hát đối*).

Hát

Hát is a general term for "singing" and "acting." In the northern and north-central regions, the first definition commonly applies. Some are sung during special seasons of the lunar year, others at work or on social occasions. *Hát xoan* (the term *xoan* derives from *xuân* "spring") are sung during spring festivals in Vĩnh Phú Province, the heartland of the Việt people. *Xoan* are not solely a singing activity; rather, their performance includes a mix of chanted poetry, drumming, acting, and dancing. Performers, in groups of ten to fifteen, perform songs and dances with themes relating to love, ritual (showing respect to local deities), riddles, and occupations (Figure 13.21).

Figure 13.21
Two men and two women sing *quan họ* on a boat in Bắc Ninh Province. Photo by Phong T. Nguyễn.

Quan Họ

Quan họ (a shortened form of *hát quan họ*) is an antiphonal song heard during the spring and fall, when pairs of men and women sing in alternation. The Lim Village Festival, which begins on the thirteenth day of the first lunar month and lasts for several days, is the most popular time for singing *quan họ*. This festival boasts music, wrestling, cockfighting, rituals, and processions. Competitive songs of love are sung all night between teams from paired villages: usually the women must reply, repartee fashion, to songs sung by the men. *Quan họ* culture involves not only songs of courtship but also songs devoted to social customs practiced in paired villages: friendship (*quan họ nghĩa*), the paired village (*quan họ kết chạ*), worship (*quan họ cầu đảo*), and funerals (*quan họ hiếu*). Today, the *quan họ* is the most pervasive type of folk song in Vietnam.

Hát phường vải

In Nghệ Tĩnh Province, work songs are exemplified by *hát phường vải* "songs of the fabric guild." Making fabric is a second occupation for farmers who have completed the planting of rice and are awaiting the growth of their crops—a process that takes several months. For their literary value, *hát phường vải* are also of interest to lovers of poetry and folklore.

Hò

From Thanh Hóa, Nghệ An, and Hà Tĩnh provinces in the north-central area, the *hò* (pronounced *haw*) is the most popular type of song (Figure 13.22). Mainly sung on the water, *hò* are usually heard during work in the rice fields or on rivers, and only occasionally during work on land. Songs of this kind must include the word *hò*, suggesting coordination between

Figure 13.22
Singers of a *hò* folk song in Bến Tre Province. Photo by Phong T. Nguyễn.

singing and rowing, pulling or pushing a boat, bailing out water, or pounding on the ground. Most *hò* are sung in unmetered rhythms, but some exhibit a rhythmic pulsation. The latter is particularly felt when a song is sung in responsorial style: a soloist is followed by a chorus.

Lý

Lý are rhythmic songs. Distributed over a wide geographical area in both the central and southern regions of Vietnam, they embrace every aspect of Vietnamese life. Using many metaphors, they compare thoughts and sentiments regarding nature to the human condition. Flowers, birds, butterflies, fish, spiders, dragonflies, horses, and many other natural phenomena provide indirect, abstract descriptions of human love, including missing a loved one, waiting, loyalty, and longing for a reunion.

Ru

Ru, a term used nationwide, is a regionally typical lullaby. In nonmetered rhythms or with a slight pulsation, *ru* are sung by mothers, grandfathers, grandmothers, or sisters, who sit beside the infant's hammock and move it gently back and forth in time to the music.

Miscellaneous Songs

The forms and styles of rural traditions are clearly reflected in Vietnamese folk songs. Many songs are performed in antiphonal, responsorial, or repartee forms. Singers learned these songs directly from their families, mostly without written texts. These songs help socialize people, encourage them, and challenge them by requiring responses to each other.

Satirical

Vè are songs that convert various themes into metered humorous or satirical songs. They criticize people who display bad manners and behavior, especially local officials.

Wishing

Wishing songs (*hát sắc bùa*) make wishes on behalf of families on New Year's (Tết). Groups of professional musicians and singers, especially in Nghệ Tĩnh Province and Phú Lễ Village, Bến Tre Province, go from house to house singing *sắc bùa*. In exchange, the performers receive good-luck money from the welcoming families.

Card Game

Card-game songs (*hô bài chòi*) are specific to Bình Định Province. Early in the 1900s, songs developed from the singing of the names of playing cards in the context of actual card games and developed into an independent genre.

Narratives

The longest folk songs are *kể truyện*, narratives in poetry and prose. A poetic story (*truyện*) usually extends a legend to several thousand verses, often in six- and eight-syllable couplets (*lục bát*). In some places, *kể truyện* (also called *nói thơ* "speaking the poetry") are chanted unaccompanied; in others, they are accompanied by rhythmic instruments such as a clapper or a drum.

Children's Songs

Đồng dao are children's songs. Few children's songs consist only of singing; usually they involve a game or an educational activity. Children's games are musically rich. There are simple game songs like counting chopsticks, bouncing a ball, or throwing sticks, and more complicated games like hide and seek, drop the handkerchief, competitive swinging, and others.

CHAMBER MUSIC

The dissemination of chamber songs and instrumental pieces in written form, including a skeletal musical notation, is common. Special vocal and instrumental training is required for chamber music. Chamber music requires the existence of literati who appreciate the role of poetry. The performance of poetry brings together musicians, singers, scholars, and connoisseurs.

A chamber-music performance is aimed at a select group. Dating only from the early twentieth century, these genres have attracted large audiences, particularly in the south. They are characterized by the use of narrative poetry, a specific order of songs or composed pieces, a predetermined combination of instruments, and a music theory unique to chamber music. Today, chamber music is performed primarily in private homes. In northern Vietnam on the anniversaries of the birth and death of a famous singer—one nominated as the patriarch of a music guild—chamber-music singing continues to be associated with ritual ceremonies at certain temples or shrines.

Ca Trù

The oldest surviving form of chamber music is *ca trù*, found in the north. Many esteemed poet-scholars have made contributions to *ca trù*, whose texts are the most refined examples studied in Vietnam's high schools and colleges. The oldest extant text of this kind is a poem by Lê Đức Mao (1462–1529) of the later Lê Dynasty. Traditionally, *ca trù* poetry, delivered more as chant than song, was performed in a sumptuous manner, which, aside from the main part's having a distinct chamber-music character, involved many instruments, singers, dancers, and ceremonial officiants. A complete performance had to include the following selections, presented in order:

1. *Giáo trống* "drumming prologue"
2. *Giáo hương* "introductory song for offering incense"
3. *Dâng hương* "offering of incense"
4. *Thét nhạc* "presentation of music"
5. *Hát giai* "repartee songs by the singer and musician"
6. *Đọc phú* "reading texts in prose-poetry style"
7. *Đọc thơ* "reading poems"
8. *Hát tỳ bà* "singing the song *Tỳ-bà* ("Lute").
9. *Hát đại thực* "song of Đại Thực"
10. *Múa bỏ bộ* "dance of gestures"
11. *Múa bài bông* "dance of flowers"
12. *Tấu nhạc* and *múa tứ linh* "instrumental music and dance of four sacred animals"

Ca trù music is highly improvisatory, with few restrictions as to the encouraged number of beats and the encouraged kind of melodic variations. The singer (*cô đầu*) plays a clapper. Thus, the instrumental ensemble consists of three instruments: a trapezoidal lute (*đàn đáy*), a drum (*trống chầu*), and an idiophone (*phách*) (Figure 11.23).

Ca Huế

In the 1500s, Huế (then called Thuận Hóa) became the second cultural center after Thăng Long (modern Hanoi). It was settled by the Nguyễn Lords, a political faction that defected southward to what is now central Vietnam. Cultural activities were particularly encouraged by the Nguyễns, and Huế therefore attracted artists from the north, including musicians, singers, and literary men who supported music. Huế became a haven for cultured men fleeing the north. These men in the south thus created a culture, politically independent, in opposition to the north, which had imposed restrictions on the arts.

Ca huế is a composed music in which the number of phrases is fixed. The important songs of *ca huế* include a series of ten royal pieces (*mười bài ngự*). Among them are "*Nam Ai*" ("Lamentation in the *Nam*

Figure 13.23
A *ca trù* singer playing a *phách* idiophone and a lutenist playing a *đàn đáy*. Photo by Phong T. Nguyễn.

Mode"), "*Nam Bình*" ("Moderated Mood in the *Nam* Mode"), "*Tú Đại Cảnh*" ("Four Grandiose Landscapes"), "*Cổ Bản*" ("Old Piece"), "*Lưu Thủy*" ("Stream of Water"), and "*Phú Lục*" ("Prose-Poetry Piece"). New lyrics are written with variations and elaborations based on about twenty original songs, which serve as melodic schemata. Some songs are preceded by a non-metric, improvised poem in *hò* style. The equal-measure character of each phrase results in cyclical meter. Songs are organized into two- or four-measure phrases. Syncopation frequently occurs.

Figure 13.24
Ca huế chamber songs sung on a boat in the Perfume River, near Huế. Photo by Terry E. Miller.

The ensemble accompanying *ca huế* is that of the "five excellent instruments" (*ngũ tuyệt*): a board zither, a two-stringed fiddle, a moon-shaped lute, a pear-shaped lute, and a three-stringed lute; a transverse flute can replace a lute. This ensemble plays alone at the beginning of or between songs. *Ca huế* singers, like *ca trù* singers, play a clapper (*phách*), but the clapper used in *ca huế* is smaller than the usual *phách*, consisting of a pair of hard-wood pieces or pairs of handleless teacups (Figure 13.24).

Đờn ca tài tử

Đờn ca tài tử (or simply *tài tử*) may be translated in two ways, both requiring explanation: "music and songs of talented persons" or "amateurs' music." Both terms express something of the nature of this music: it is chamber music performed by artists of great talent (first meaning) and not for profit (second meaning). It was born in southern Vietnam at the beginning of the twentieth century.

Before *tài tử* became an established genre, *nhạc lễ*, a southern instrumental ensemble for ceremonies and celebrations had been created, based on the music of central and south-central Vietnam. *Nhạc lễ* likely began in the 1600s, when the region's temple festivals were founded, and the genre became the foundation of southern music, especially in musical theory and instrumentation.

In *tài tử*, the role of instrumentalists equals that of singers. *Nhạc tài tử* has a larger instrumental ensemble than *ca trù* and *ca huế*. Instrumental pieces can be played either in ensemble or solo; therefore, singers and instrumentalists sometimes compete for dominance. *Ca trù* and *ca huế* singers are normally women, but in *nhạc tài tử*, both men and women sing as social equals. *Tài tử* music has been transmitted through the publication of songs and instrumental pieces in books since 1909. The repertoire of *tài tử* includes both long and short songs. Some were adapted from *nhạc lễ*, *ca huế*, and other southern folk songs, but many new compositions exist. Eventually there were about eighty types of songs for which new lyrics could be provided.

The *tài tử* ensemble (Figure 13.25) is thought a light and flavorful form of music, having clear precedents but changed from them. In contrast to *nhạc lễ*, whose sound is dominated by percussion instruments, *tài tử* consists only of chordophones and one small

Figure 13.25
A performance of *nhạc tài tử* chamber music in Hồ Chí Minh City, 1993. Photo by Terry E. Miller, 1993.

idiophone, the *song lang*. The ensemble normally uses the same instruments as *ca huế*. Some, however, have different names (in the south, the classifier *đàn* is *đờn*). The *tranh*, the *cò*, and the *kìm* are the main instruments of the ensemble.

With continuity of tradition comes the phenomenon of adoption and adaptation. Since 1920, Western instruments have been adopted and successfully modified for use in *tài tử*: the *lục huyền cầm* derives from the acoustic guitar *vĩ cầm* from the violin, and *hạ uy cầm* from the steel guitar. Intellectuals and governmental officials had a special interest in contributing to this genre. They were the amateur connoisseurs who wrote lyrics for songs or simply supported this art financially. Together they formed circles in Saigon and other cities in the south. The most reputed singers and musicians, coming from the Mekong Delta, contributed to the formation of *cải lương*, a southern Vietnamese musical theater that developed soon after *tài tử*.

THEATER

Figure 13.26
Xuan pha masked dance-drama in Tho Xuan, Thanh Hoa Province. Photo by Phong T. Nguyễn, 1994.

Vietnam is particularly rich in the theatrical arts. It is an expressive culture with considerable contributions in literature (both oral and written), singing, dance, mime, music, and the visual arts (painted faces, costumes, props, decorations). The history of the theater parallels the history of the Vietnamese, if the earliest form of the bronze gong drums is considered. Vietnam's recorded history documents theater for at least a thousand years. There are six major theatrical genres and twenty-plus local folk-drama types. Though more may not have been described yet by researchers in Vietnam, currently available materials show that, within a period of thirty years, their efforts at collection have answered the most intriguing questions of these musical arts (Figure 13.26).

Most scholars agree that folk drama provided the fundamental elements in the gestation of dramatic genres. These elements include mime and dance, vocal forms and instrumental techniques, speech, and plots. Props such as a walking cane, a stick, oars, masks, a painted face, and costumes not only decorate the stage, but materially and abstractly guide all related dance movements.

Water-Puppet Theater

Water has been closely associated with the lives of the Việt since antiquity, as recounted in legends and narratives. Farmers of rice, used to working in water, bathe in the ponds in front of their houses, and children play with water and sing while bathing. Water buffalo fight in the fields, keepers of ducks herd their flocks home at dusk, a fisherman catches a large fish, a woman mills rice—these and other scenes are captured in local minds and figure in the stories of water puppetry. Water-puppet theater (*rối nước*, also *múa rối nước*) is probably unique to Vietnam. Its cradle was the Red River delta. It was, in the beginning, an art of peasants. Living persons no longer recall its birth, an event engraved in their minds as "from an old time." As recounted in rare historical books of saints, water-puppet theater came into existence sometime before the sixth century. This art did not remain within village boundaries. In content, it has always been inclined to innovation: new stories and techniques have been added. Not only ponds but rivers could serve for performances. From the tenth century, the genre became a royal entertainment for kings' birthdays (Figure 13.27).

Figure 13.27
A village water-puppet theater with the ensemble and singers seated near "stage left." Photo by Terry E. Miller, 2005.

The puppets (*con rối*) are carved from a light wood, and range from 30 to 60 centimeters high. Depending on the story, puppets are painted with an assortment of colors in the forms of a man, a woman, a child, a fairy, an animal, and many other stock types. Puppeteers standing in water behind a screen manipulate them using an intricate mechanism of underwater rods. One stick may control one or more puppets. A stick can move a simple puppet in and out of the water, but it requires both movable parts of the puppet and a complicated mechanism on the stick to manipulate a swimming fish, a dancing dragon, a phoenix, a lion, or a fairy. Sometimes the puppet is fixed onto a turnable disc with additional mechanisms—smaller rods, ropes, or wheels (Figure 13.28).

Figure 13.28
A water-puppet-theater play: *King Lê Lợi Returns His Sword to the Turtle*. Photo by Phong T. Nguyễn.

Puppeteers remain behind a backdrop, a thin bamboo frame and curtain that prevents the audience from seeing them. Looking through the curtain, they coordinate all movements to make the story come alive. The puppets' dancing, acting, and acrobatics occur with music and songs. The show is not simple. The concept requires considerable training.

Researchers have collected more than two hundred water-puppet plays in Vietnam. A troupe realizes a literary work through a long, musical structure, a codified form of aesthetics in performance, the highly skilled coordination between music and puppeteers, the articulation of meanings, and reflections on contemporary society, be it village, city, or royal palace.

Singers and musicians present the melodies and styles of *chèo* in the context of *rối nước* stories. A small temple on water (*thủy đình*) is built at the side of the pond. The backdrop, representing the front of the temple, has one or two openings, through which the puppets enter and exit as actors and actresses do on a regular stage. The water surface in front of the backdrop serves as a stage. The audience faces the stage from around the lake. Singers and musicians sit inside the temple or on stage right, performing their songs and music, strictly following the movements of the puppets. As many as fifteen puppets may interact on stage at once, making wonderful scenes of battles, fairy dances, boat races, or agriculture. Usually, a performance begins with a flag hoisting and a greeting sung by the happy *tễu*, a smiling little-boy puppet.

Today, the art of water puppetry is included in the curriculum of the School of Dramatic Arts in Hanoi. Professional water-puppet troupes present this art in cities throughout Vietnam and abroad. For foreign visitors to Hanoi, a permanent theater near the Lake of the Restored Sword gives performances nightly; in Hồ Chí Minh City, the Historical Museum within the zoo offers performances daily.

Chèo

The term *hát* also pertains to theater in Vietnam. It has broad meanings: "singing," "song and dance," and "singing, dance, mime, acting, and music," depending on specific applications. Though the human voice is central to Vietnamese music, *hát* links singing with performative aspects that illustrate the song. In other words, *hát* may mean only "singing" or some or all of the above aspects. This is illustrated by the fact that in other performing arts (such as *hát chầu văn* "possession ritual," *hát chèo tàu* "theater on a boat," *hát bá trạo* "paddle dance," *hát ả đào* "chamber songs," and many others) singing is not the only act. Probably because of its religious origin, singing has been conceptually central in *hát* from time immemorial.

Hát chèo, or, as commonly abbreviated, *chèo*, is a form or art born in northern Vietnam. Originating in tradition, *chèo* and *tuồng* were probably the theatrical genres held in highest regard by the Lý and Trần dynasties (eleventh to fourteenth centuries). Because satire was a prominent trait, this genre possibly underwent discrimination and was ousted from the Le court in the 1400s. The term *chèo*, besides its literal meaning as "oar theater," may derive from *trạo* "satire." In the 1700s, with the decline of the Lê Dynasty, *chèo* regained its influence. Now a new generation of actors and actresses who had mingled with the peasants—even peasants themselves—saw social injustices happening in their villages. They created folklore-based plays that explored social conflict and humor. However, the long-term aim of *chèo* is social education (Figure 13.29).

Chèo is traditionally performed on a mat in the courtyard of a village temple, forming a stage having three sides open to the audience and the front wall of the temple serving as the background. This sort of structure allows the audience and musicians to interact with the actors and actresses. The role of each character, whether good or evil, is judged according to its social value, not according to the artistic skill of the actor or actress. The audience directs comments, exclamations, and answers directly to the characters: "Yes," "Can you behave better than that?" "No, you cannot do that!" or just "O!" Such responses are still heard in city theaters. They create a playful ambience and encourage the performers. Makeup, costumes, and props are also necessary. Since *chèo* is an abstract theater, no scenic decoration is needed. The task of the actor or actress is to give the appearance of reality through acting, dancing, miming, and singing.

Figure 13.29
Chèo musical theater, Quan Âm Thị Kính (Thị Kinh Becomes a Bodhisattva Avalokitesvara), performed by Thúy Ngần and Vân Quyền. Photo by Phong T. Nguyễn.

There are more than sixty *làn điệu* (melodic types) in *chèo*. New words are composed for each story. The playwright selects the songs, but the artistic director (*bác hai* "the elder uncle") is in charge of creating the staged version of the play. Below are the main categories expressing specific sentiments. Other songs are classified as "various":

sắp	delight, happiness, or satire
sử	metric (*hát sử*) and nonmetric (*nói sử*) style for various sentiments
hề mồi	buffoonery
vãn	sadness, chagrin
hát cách	stylistic form, subtlety
lão say	drunk old person
sa lệch	love, sentimentality
đường trường	peace, remembrance, melancholy

Most of these songs consist of four parts: introduction, body, repetition, and conclusion. The introduction is often nonmetrical.

Dance in *chèo* is elaborate. It is associated with songs that include movements used to embellish, feature, and symbolize a character. A fan is the central prop for *chèo* dance, but walking canes, oars, and swords may also be used.

The *chèo* instrumental ensemble includes a small fiddle (*nhị*), a large fiddle (*hồ*), a transverse flute (*sáo*), a moon-shaped lute (*nguyệt*), a zither (*thập lục*), a vertical flute (*tiêu*), a three-stringed lute (*tam*), a dulcimer (*tam thập lục*), gongs, drums of various sizes, and cymbals. The drummer coordinates the music with the actors and actresses and leads the ensemble.

Hát Bội, or Tuồng

The "classical" theater of Vietnam is called *tuồng* in the north and *hát bội* in the center and the south. Spectators can easily see that the differences between *tuồng* and *chèo* involve costumes, makeup, props, and instrumentation. The songs and music of *tuồng* are based on principles different from those of *chèo*. *Tuồng* has often been compared with Beijing opera (*jingxi*), especially for the painted faces, costumes, and gestures, but there are important differences between the genres.

New research has questioned the long-held theory that a Chinese-Mongolian actor named Li Yuan Ki introduced Chinese theater to Vietnam in the 1200s. A soldier captured by the Vietnamese army during an invasion by Mongols of the Yuan Dynasty, he used to be considered the founder of *tuồng*. Newer studies of language, music, dance, and the principles of the genre show that no originally Chinese theatrical texts and music were used in Vietnam (Mịch Quang 1963). Rather, old Chinese stories have been adapted. They constituted a part of the *tuồng*, and required painted faces, costumes, and other conventions of Chinese theater that could not be replaced. It is especially in the use of colors, painted faces, and shoes that reveals the concepts that differentiate *tuồng* and *jingxi*. *Tuồng's* use of Chinese materials resembles how Western operatic composers approached Oriental subjects, in that changes express the culture of the borrower (Figure 13.30).

Tuồng has three categories of vocalization: recitative (*nói lối*), modal songs (*điệu hát*), and melodic types (*bài hát, bài bản*). Recitative is a nonmetrical, declamatory style, used as an introduction or passage from one song to another. Aria is a metrical, narrative style describing characters' actions. The main style expressing *tuồng* traits is the modal songs. *Tuồng* vocal music involves instrumental music functioning both as an independent element and as an accompaniment. Instead of being based on melody types (as in *chèo*), songs in *tuồng* are modal, and the instrumental ensemble realizes a musical mode in an asymmetrical form with the vocal element as two independent units.

The modal category consists of eight modes, representing eight modal sentiments (*điệu*):

ngâm "declamation"	leisure
oán "complaint"	chagrin
vịnh "declamation"	solemnity
bạch "exposition"	straightforwardness
thán "lamentation"	regret
xướng "announcement"	invitation, announcing an event
nam "south"	sadness
khách "guest (opposed to host)"	happiness, heroic character

Figure 13.30
Vietnamese classical theater (*tuồng, hát bội*) performed in Nha Trang. Photo by Terry E. Miller.

nói lối
A nonmetrical introductory recitative preceding the sung poetry of Vietnamese theater
láy
Patterned documentation characteristic of *tuồng* theater
trống chầu
In *tuồng* theater, a large drum played by an audience member offering praise or criticism

There are seven types of Vietnamese voice: intestine voice (*hơi ruột*), liver voice (*hơi gan*), cheek voice (*hơi má*), jaw voice (*hơi hờm*), head voice (*hơi óc*), chest voice (*hơi ngực*), and throat voice (*hơi cổ*). To visualize the abstract contents of a story, the actor or actress sometimes uses more than one type of voice.

Though singing occurs in a nonmetrical, pulsating, and improvisatory style, instrumental music is realized in a metrical, repetitive manner. The *tuồng* ensemble is composed of idiophones, membranophones, chordophones, and aerophones, but the primary instruments are an oboe with a wooden or copper outer ring (called *kèn bóp* "urging oboe," *kèn song hỉ* "double happiness oboe," or *kèn thau* "copper oboe") and a drum (*trống chiến* "battle drum"), which leads the ensemble with specific rhythmic patterns at the beginnings and endings of pieces. It coordinates the ensemble with the actors and actresses by supporting their dance movements. There is also a set of drums played by different drummers. The largest one (*trống chầu*) is played by an expert, representing the audience. He praises the artist by playing on the drumhead and he makes unfavorable comments by striking the side of the drum. Originally, this task was assumed by the chief of the village.

Cải Lương

glossary_note
Cải lương developed from *hát bội* and *tài tử*. Until the beginning of the twentieth century, *hát bội* had been the only major form of theater known to people in south, south-central, and central Vietnam. The genre underwent reform by urban artists and cognoscenti around 1900. Because of the adaptability of *tài tử*, musicians and actors of *hát bội* embraced this reform, which, they believed, could respond to the needs of the new social order.

As with other traditional forms of chamber music, *tài tử* singers had performed sitting on a wooden platform; but in the reformed theater, actors and actresses stood to coordinate their actions with the meanings of the songs, creating songs with gestures (*ca ra bộ*). In 1916, the first performance of this kind occurred during an informal meeting at the home of a vice chairman of Vũng Liêm District, Vĩnh Long Province. The first public performance, in 1917, was presented in Sa Đéc Province by André Nguyễn Văn Thận's *Cirque jeune Annam et ca ra bộ Sadec amis* ("Young Annamese Circus and the Friends of *Ca Ra Bộ* of Sadec" [Sa Đéc]). This genre then became popular throughout the prosperous cities of Mỹ Tho, Vĩnh Long, Cần Thơ, and Sa Đéc provinces. Three plays were acted by three performers each.

The landmark of the reform movement was the 1920 presentation of Trương Duy Toản's *Kim Vân Kiều* ("The Story of Kim Trọng, Thúy Vân, and Thúy Kiều"), part I, a long theatrical piece, by the actors and actresses of Châu Văn Tú's troupe. Châu Văn Tú pieced together songs he had composed earlier in Cần Thơ and crafted them into an organized composition based on the famous poetic story of the same title by Nguyễn Du, an eminent eighteenth-century poet. Also in 1920, the term *reform* (*cải lương*) was first applied to this genre.

With repertoire derived from chamber music, *cải lương* was presented as a new form of expression, involving not only singing, but also acting and dancing. Only four years after the birth of *ca ra bộ*, more than twenty *cải lương* troupes were active in major cities of the southern region, supported by wealthy businessmen. Adopting modern techniques of staging and using new songs, this form of theater influenced many aspects of other national

sidebar
cải luong
Genre of popular southern Vietnamese theater that developed around 1920

performances. Several *cải lương* troupes successfully toured the country. Between 1930 and 1945, many businessmen invested their money in *cải lương* troupes. In that period, at least sixty-seven major troupes were performing new theatrical pieces in the south, and three theaters in Hanoi and the northern provinces offered nightly performances (Figure 13.31).

Unlike *chèo* and *hát bội* (*tuồng*), which use primarily Vietnamese and Chinese stories, *cải lương* adapted legends, epics, romances, satires, and histories, both of Vietnam and of many other countries—China, Egypt, France, India, Japan, ancient Rome, and so on. Its sets require decoration, scenery, and other techniques, as in Western opera. A performance features both singing and spoken dialogue, and though it has acting, dancing, speaking, and mime, the foremost interest in it is singing (Figure 13.32).

Songs are based on the *tài tử* tunes, classified into modes and submodes (the latter called *nuances* by Vietnamese scholars). Special songs are composed for *cải lương* at the climax. These are not complete songs, but sections of songs, performed during specific moments as the story develops. With a basic melody and prescribed phrases, new words express the moods of songs.

Figure 13.31
Quốc Thanh *cải luong* theater in Saigon during its heyday, 1970. Photo by Terry. E. Miller.

The intrinsic value of *cải lương* lies in how within a song there is a seamless flow between speech and song. Dialogue may be inserted during a rest, or between the vocal sections. The most important type of this genre is *vọng cổ* "longing for the past," a phenomenon that developed from ordinary Vietnamese music. The first song of this type, "*Dạ Cổ Hoài Lang*" ("Thinking of My Husband on Hearing the Sounds of the Night Drum"), was composed by a *nhạc lễ* musician in 1918. It became popular in traditional private and public performances. The original version consisted of twenty two-measure phrases, each of which eventually increased to four measures. The song was used as a basis for multiple versions and variations. In some cases, each phrase was extended from four to eight measures with a sec-

Figure 13.32
Cải luong performance of a domestic, modern story, *Làm Trai Hai Vợ* ("A Husband with Two Wives"), 1970. Photo by Terry E. Miller.

tion containing sixteen, thirty-two, or sixty-four measures. Later, though rare, *vọng cổ* has been performed with doubled measures; therefore, each section comprises 128 measures, providing a challenge for musicians and singers to create new ways of performing it—creating new texts, inventing new melodic phrases and tunings, and inventing elaborate techniques.

Besides *vọng cổ*, about sixty-seven melodies are available for use in theatrical pieces. As in much Vietnamese theatrical music, a recitative, nonmetric style also exists. The best known are introductory recitative (*nói lối*) and sung poetry (*ngâm*). These terms, used in many regional genres, represent various concepts and definitions. The *nói lối*, most frequently applied in *cải lương* and *tài tử*, is half spoken, half sung, and precedes the *vọng cổ* song; however, singing in *ngâm* style, as a short song, may also occur here.

Cải lương emphasizes singing, and the instrumental accompaniment consists predominantly of stringed instruments. A few percussion instruments are used occasionally in a play. Unlike other traditional theatrical forms, *cải lương* also employs a Western band (guitar, electric bass, saxophone, trumpet, synthesizer, and drums), which plays during the introduction, interludes, intermissions, and/or conclusions of a performance. This band, which does not accompany the traditional songs, plays popular tunes, improvises collectively, or plays loud chords to enhance the drama's climax, taking the place of traditional percussion instruments, rarely used today. A foot clapper (*song lang*) is still used with the strings.

Cải lương came to permeate the country as *tuồng* once did. In the far north, it proved a success into the 1930s. Nevertheless, a Vietnamese proverb states: "prosperity engenders decadence"; therefore, despite its success, *cải lương* appears to have illustrated this maxim. In the 1970s, a saturation of randomly selected topics and themes, with an abuse of modern technology, led to a swift decline for this art; in addition, the war and its consequences played a role in its destruction. Today's *cải lương*, as seen in Hồ Chì Minh City, consists of newly written, fantasylike plays, performed for small audiences in rundown theaters by young and lightly skilled performers.

Hát Bài Chòi

The origin and development of *hát bài chòi* (or *bài chòi*) followed a pattern common to several kinds of Vietnamese theater. The type most similar is *ca ra bộ*, derived from a folk-riddle game (*hô thai*) in which pairs of verses were sung during the spring festival. An elaboration was made with longer poems (*bài chòi câu*), and then a poetic story (*bài chòi truyện*) was created. In 1933 and 1934, this evolved into *hát bài chòi* in Bình Định Province.

Originally *bài chòi* meant "card game in huts." The game is played in nine huts built in a circle. The player in each hut has three cards, each containing different two-word names. Eventually the person who calls the names written on these cards (*anh hiệu*) began to sing them. This game continues, but the singing evolved into a form of theater. The development of *hát bài chòi* likely proceeded in four steps, emerging from performances on the ground to a raised stage (*từ đất lên dàn*): one performer sang and played a pair of wooden sticks to the beat; one performer sang and acted, accompanied by musicians playing one to three fiddles, a drummer, and a player of claves; a small troupe of actors and musicians performed; a professional troupe used stage decoration and lighting, accompanied by an instrumental ensemble. During the fourth stage, *hát bài chòi* was widely performed in Bình Định Province. After the Geneva conference of 1954, many artists in one revolutionary *hát bài chòi* troupe fled to the north. Thereafter, audiences in Hanoi and northern provincial cities had opportunities to watch *hát bài chòi* with stories used for political propaganda.

Kịch nói

In Hanoi and Saigon, French-educated students and literary men created *kịch nói* or *thoại kịch*, a genre derived from Western spoken drama. *Chén Thuốc Độc* (*A Bowl of Poison*), the first piece of spoken theater performed for the public, premiered in 1921 at the French Opera House (Nhà Hát Tây). Other stories, written as poetry meant to be declaimed, were known as *kịch thơ*. Most actors and actresses of this genre had been trained in traditional theatrical genres, which have large repertoires of songs. The performers found *kịch thơ* too restrictive musically and the acting too simplistic. As a result, they soon abandoned it. *Kịch nói* still exists, with a repertoire of several hundred plays.

DANCE

Dance is not usually a part of most public performances in cities today. Consequently, it does not stand out as an independent performance genre. For many centuries, a great number of its techniques, costumes, and metaphoric meanings have been integrated into theater. It is typically associated with instrumental music, songs, storytelling, plays, and rituals. Apart from theatrical stage performances, most dances are performed as part of the yearly cycle of festivals—Buddhist, folk, ritual—and take place in temple yards.

In the first millennium B.C.E., dancing was represented in engravings on Đông Son bronze gong drums and other archaeological artifacts. Dance gestures of peasant and military derivation reflect the life of the Lạc Việt. Occupational dances, sword dances, shield dances, musicians' dances (accompanied by mouth organ, drum, and bells), rowing dances, and dances in a circle were prevalent. The latter two remain in practice today in the region of the delta of the Red River and appear to resemble the original forms. As pictured on bronze gong drums, dancers wearing feather headdresses making a circle around the sun suggest both a circular type of dance and a cult of the sun. The most typical kind of dance is the rowing dance, still preserved in most ritual and theatrical performances.

Court Dances

Dance evolved extensively in contexts among both peasants and courtiers from the tenth century. A masked-dance tradition, *xuân phả*, considered a folk dance, was named after a town (Xuân Phố, Spring Town) near the home of King Đinh Tiên Hoàng and was thus related to his court, in what is now Thanh Hóa Province. To these dances were added the roles of foreigners (ambassadors and soldiers) from five countries: Champa, China, Holland, Laos, and *Lục Hồn Nhung* (also called Tú Huần). The last name is unidentified today. The painted masks used in three of the dances are made of cowhide or wood.

To celebrate the victory over the Yuan Chinese invasion in 1288, Trần Quang Khải and Trần Nhật Duật, generals of the Vietnamese court, created the dance of flowers (*múa bài bông*) for a major three-day festival in Thăng Long. This dance has been handed down to the present and is still performed at local festivals in the northern region, albeit in a modified version.

From the 1400s, the imperial court elaborated on the distinctiveness of its dances by creating theatrical dances that eventually became famous. These dances included *bình ngô phá trận* "victory over the Chinese invasion" and *chư hầu lai triều* "foreign ambassadors visiting our court," created in 1456 under King Lê Nhân Tông. The Nguyễn Dynasty (1802–1945) commissioned works for ceremonial dances at court. Unlike in previous periods, the kings of the later Lê and Nguyễn dynasties replicated the convention of the Chinese emperors, who did not dance.

The Đàn Nam Giao, Vietnam's "Heaven-and-Earth Copulation Esplanade" at Viên Khâu (Round Hill, near Huế), built during King Lý Anh Tông's sovereignty (1138–1175), served for rituals and dances for peace once every three years. After being interrupted for about a century during the Trần Dynasty, this ceremony resumed from about 1403 to 1407. During the Nguyễn Dynasty, 128 dances were performed for it and other important events. They were divided into two groups: civil (*văn*) and military (*võ*). The number of dancers varied. Songs were sung in Sino-Vietnamese, accompanied by an instrumental ensemble. Other dances with folk origins were also used in some thirty court ceremonies; they include the boat dance, the unicorn dance, and the male and female phoenix dances.

Folk Dances

Among the rural populace, agricultural arts and handicrafts stimulated the creation of several kinds of descriptive dances related to planting rice, plowing, fishing, rowing, sewing, making baskets, weaving, raising silkworms, and other activities. These dances are presented in traditional festivals. In the oldest region of the Red River delta, the basic techniques are holding hands in a circle, stretching and waving the arms, lowering the body by bending the legs, and tapping the feet. Other dances show agricultural work and other livelihoods: *mo* and *tùng rí*, which involve animal sounds, have a long history rooted in ancient times.

Because Vietnamese life is traditionally associated with the sea and rivers, many work songs and ritual songs and dances feature the gesture of rowing a boat while traveling or fishing. The most famous dance, the rowing dance, is widespread in Vietnam and is found in various contexts: folk dance, rituals, theatrical genres, and annual ceremonies for gods of the sea at coastal village temples.

The *bá trạo* is a dance related to the worship of gods of the sea. When a whale dies, fishermen move it to the shore for a funeral near a temple, where they perform a rowing dance meant to carry the whale's soul to the other world. Each year afterward, a ceremony is danced to commemorate this event. The dance is composed of thirty-two to thirty-six dancers, led by a captain (*tổng mũi*), who sings alone and plays a small single-headed drum while rowing dancers arranged in two lines respond to him. To entertain the oarsmen, a buffoon (*tổng lái*) plays the role of steersman and cook. This dance, widely known in Bình Định and Khánh Hòa provinces, has a variety of movements, including opposing, circular, and crossing lines of dancers. The main props are red and white oars, which the performers move up, down, and in circles. This dance is often preceded by two other dances: *múa dâng*

Sisters Trung
Two celebrated sisters who led a rebellion against the Chinese about 40 C.E.

chầu văn
Spirit possession ritual of central Vietnam

múa đâng bông
The "flower dance," associated with religious occasions

Figure 13.33
A rowing dance (*múa bá trạo*) in Vạn Ninh Village, Khánh Hòa Province, north of Nha Trang. Photo by Phong T. Nguyễn.

bông "flower-offering dance" and *múa siêu* "broadsword dance." The *bá trạo* is accompanied by an oboe, a two-stringed fiddle, an optional lute, and drums (Figure 13.33).

Many aspects of work are represented in other dances. Farming and handicraft skills are presented in the twelve sequences of the light dance in Đông Anh District, Thanh Hóa Province. Dancers carry candles in their hands or on their heads, dancing in twelve sections, eleven of which are accompanied by songs: lighting a lamp, planting flowers and beans, sowing seeds of rice (two sections), making baskets, uprooting young rice, planting rice, weaving, making clothes, sewing, and harvesting rice. After each dance section, the dancers and the audience interact in a question-and-answer process.

Theatrical Dances

Dance is a part of all musical theater in Vietnam. Accompanied by instrumental music and songs, dances are symbolic, metaphoric, and expressive of the content of the texts. Two characteristic schools are those of *chèo* and *tuồng*.

Chèo dancers use upper-body movement (trunk, arms, hands, eyes), but *tuồng* dancers emphasize steps and balance their limbs in conformity with the martial arts. In each gesture, dancers express the meanings of the texts. *Chèo* dance is believed to imitate everyday actions, to contain certain rudimentary techniques, and to express in pantomime. During the past three centuries, *chèo* dance was formalized into three kinds of movement: presentational, illustrative, and symbolic. Because of an absence of scenery and props, a performer must dance a typical role: a student (*thư sinh*), a sincere, good woman (*nữ chính*), a bad, immoral, or sinful woman (*nữ lệch*), an old woman (*mụ*), and so on. He or she uses multiple gestures to illustrate songs.

Dancers' props include torches, walking canes, sticks, swords, oars, and fans. The fan, central to most *chèo*, symbolizes aspects of the character, such as shyness, subtlety, dignity, flirtatiousness, and lasciviousness. Holding a fan in her hand, an actress moves toward the center of the stage. The audience cannot see the character until the middle of her introductory song, when she shows her face and begins to dance. This procedure has a great deal to do with the artistic planning and socioaesthetic meaning of the art of *chèo*. It includes three traits: avoiding sharp contrasts, which might go against the social and behavioral nature of the traditional audience; having a song begin to tell the story because of the prominent role of voices; and later illustrating with a fan dance more about the traits and function of the role in the plot.

Tuồng dance adds to Vietnamese theatrical arts a rich terminology. Favored at the imperial court, this art is rooted in folk resources, and boasts the greatest repertoire of the danced arts of Vietnam. It was supported by scholars and senior artists, who devised complex training with specific terms and conventions. Numerous terms define dance movements. The main categories of dance are called movements (*bộ*). There are seventeen basic movements for the hands, ten for the legs. Some dances are performed in bare feet, others in shoes.

Dancing in *tuồng* is an expression of human feelings. Movements of the trunk, arms, head (including a hat), legs, and especially the hands and feet, in stationary and moving positions, convey the meanings of the plot. Many kinds of emotions can be expressed using the head and hat, feet and shoes. Anger is represented by the shaking of ornate items on the actor's hat, or by trembling shoes. The shoes are soled with wood and curved up at the toes to ease the making of back-to-front and left-to-right rocking movements.

Hands and feet are coordinated in a choreographic articulation that balances the structural design of the dancer's bodily movements. Therefore, professional instruction in *tuồng* prohibits performers from breaking lines of arm movement toward the left or right. The soft motion of the arms contrasts with the stiff motions made by the legs.

Dance is also associated with instrumental music and songs. Most songs are in poetic (*thơ*) or prose-poetic (*phú*) form. Speaking is also accompanied by strict techniques of acting. Solo pantomime assisted by the ensemble displays the talents of an actor or actress portraying a military man or a madwoman who, for reasons of extreme anxiety, cannot express himself or herself in words (songs).

Figure 13.34
A Buddhist ceremony at Tù Hiếu Temple in Huế. Photo by Phong T. Nguyễn.

RELIGIOUS MUSIC

Among the most interesting of musics in Vietnam are those associated with religious beliefs. Buddhism, Confucianism, and Taoism are traditionally considered the religions that have long influenced the philosophical life of the Vietnamese. However, the earliest rituals probably derived from animism, a system of beliefs later integrated into the present adoration of saints, gods and goddesses, and heroes and heroines who successfully defended the country from foreign invasions. Religions from India, the West, and the Middle East occur to a lesser degree, but Buddhism, with the most organized system of music, is found in more than one thousand temples nationwide.

The Buddhist Liturgy

The basis of ceremonies is the collections of various texts: sutras (*kinh*), the main liturgical texts, translated from Sanskrit to Sino-Vietnamese and Vietnamese; poems of praise (*kệ, tán*); mantras (*chú*), a secret language transliterated from Sanskrit; and short phrases and texts used in particular ceremonies. Sutras and mantras are texts commonly found in

China, Korea, and Japan. More than thirty services and ceremonies are held in Buddhist temples, public places, and private homes. Any of more than three hundred texts may be selected for use on these occasions (Figure 13.34).

Chanting and singing reveal the same organizational trends found in traditional Vietnamese performing arts. Buddhist music uses three vocal styles: cantillating sutras and mantras, singing poetic hymns, and mixing speech and song. Numerous percussion instruments are used in Buddhist temples. These include a slit drum, a bowl bell (*chuông gia trì*), a large bell (*đại hồng chung*), a small bell (*chuông báo chúng*), a large drum (*trống bát nhã*), a small drum (*trống đạo*), a bronze or stone plaque (*khánh*), a wooden plaque (*mộc bảng*), a gong, a hand bell (*linh*), and a pair of conchs (*pháp loa* "the voice of Buddha's teaching"). Teaching these instruments is part of musical training in the temples, and it is more specialized in the temples of the *ứng phú*, the Vietnamese Buddhist school of chants.

Like traditional music, Buddhist chanting varies regionally. No orthodox manner of chanting and singing is consistent throughout the country, though the methods of teaching and the styles of chanting are quite similar. Thus, performances of the Buddhist liturgy conform to the regional and traditional traits of Vietnamese music. Buddhist influence is not limited to the boundaries of temple compounds and to communities of monks and laymen: it has spread to other religious systems, such as local cults and newer sects.

The Chầu Văn Ritual

Music may serve as an intermediary between the living and the dead during ceremonies and rites in which one pays respect and offers thanks to gods and historical figures honored for their good deeds. There is neither one god, nor one kind of music. The *chầu văn* in the northern and central regions and the *rỗi bóng* in the southern areas of Vietnam are two of these practices.

The *chầu văn*, one of the most typical religious sects in Vietnam, has many religious and musical practices. The most important instrument of this ritual is the moon-shaped lute; others are gongs and drums. In this ritual, a medium (*đồng*) is possessed by one or more of twenty-four deities. According to this belief, there is a hidden—but real—world of saints, gods, and spirits living in mountains, highlands, jungles, and elsewhere. Mystical, powerful, miraculous, and always helpful, they are worthy of admiration and honor. Though their bodies are dead, their souls are permanently alive. A child who died at a sacred hour might become a saint of this kind. He or she may come to help villagers when invited through a ritual ceremony. *Chầu văn* has two supreme personalities: Trần Hưng Đạo, a thirteenth-century general of the Trần Dynasty, and Liễu Hạnh, a sixteenth-century figure of the later Lê Dynasty.

CD TRACK 8

Figure 13.35
A *nhạc lễ* ceremonial ensemble in Bến Tre Province. Photo by Phong T. Nguyễn.

Chầu văn temples are dedicated to these gods and goddesses, and to others. The temples are lavishly decorated, inside and out. The world of the gods and saints, centered in the praying hall, is much adorned. A possession ritual is organized on the anniversary days of important gods or on private occasions. A medium may be a female or male, who, when in trance, performs dances in front of the altar. A singer and some musicians, sitting on one side, begin to sing and play songs corresponding to the god in possession. Famous, standard texts are used in the rituals: twenty-four texts in temples for

Figure 13.36
A *chầu văn* possession ritual singer and male accompanist playing the *đàn nguyệt* lute. Photo by Phong T. Nguyễn.

the goddess Liễu Hạnh and nine in temples for the god Trần. Texts of praise continue to be composed.

Chầu văn songs are sung in ten modes. Each is associated with a specific mood, scale, rhythmic structure, tempo, and ornamentation. The following is a general outline:

hát dọc	singing in free rhythm
phú bình	sung poetry: happy mood, metric
phú dựng	sung poetry: accent, rising tones
phú chênh	sung poetry: a moderately sad mood
phú rầu	sung poetry: sad mood
thỏng	additional, short poem: moderate tempo
cờn	energetic: acceleration of tempo
sơn trang	clear, happy mood
thánh thượng ngàn	celebrating: fantasy
xá	Cantonese music style (of the Xá minority)

Because a ritual may last for several hours, the cycle of modes is performed consecutively, and a reprise customarily occurs. The last four modes tend to be expressed as fixed melodies, while the rest are improvised, by both voice and instruments (Figure 13.36).

Vietnam has remarkable religious diversity. Traveling from north to south, one finds distinct faiths active in particular areas. Cao Đài, a newer religion, is peculiar to the southern area. Its liturgical songs, associated with traditional music, have not yet been studied in depth. Roman Catholic and Protestant churches reflect musical traditions derived from the West. Roman Catholic rituals were introduced to Vietnam during the 1500s by missionaries, and the church prospered under French colonization. Though its Latin and French texts were translated into Vietnamese, the foundation of its music was European—with tempered scales, harmony, and instrumental accompaniments. Culturally and musically, this church remains apart from traditional Vietnamese music.

Settings

Before 1900, Vietnam had experienced four centuries of exposure to European culture, first from Roman Catholic missionaries and then through French colonialism. The first attempt to introduce Roman Catholicism into Vietnam began about 1533, with visits by Dominican missionaries (Phan 1961:32). Their efforts were unsuccessful until 1625, when their activities became systematically intensified through their connection with an established base in the Portuguese enclave of Macau. Italian, Portuguese, Spanish, French, and Japanese Jesuit priests visited Vietnam during the north-south division (1500s to 1700s) under the Trịnh and Nguyễn lords, respectively. In collaboration with Vietnamese Roman Catholics, they created the system of romanization still used for Vietnamese.

Soon after Lord Trịnh Tráng (reigned 1623–1657) sent a letter to Pope Urban VIII praising the cooperation of the Roman Catholic Church, political incidents and cultural misunderstandings disrupted Vietnam's relationship with the church. Persecutions began in the 1800s. Some high-ranking Roman Catholic missionaries with a good knowledge of Vietnam collaborated with French colonial forces as intermediaries or political advisers in planning an invasion. The pretext for this act was to be the protection of their religious men. After decades of bloody fighting, during which the Vietnamese goal of independence failed, the treaties of 25 August 1883 and 6 June 1884 were signed, and France forced the Nguyễn Dynasty to accept the status of protectorate of France. This arrangement led to broad social changes that affected all aspects of Vietnamese life, including the country's cultural, educational, and political affairs.

Early European Musical Influence

In the 1500s, Latin masses were likely sung by European priests, and possibly by Vietnamese followers. There is, however, reason to believe that no Roman Catholic chant in the Vietnamese language was performed until about 1648, the year in which a baptismal text was created and approved. The musical rules remained European. From the 1700s, as church-state relations improved, this music expanded among Vietnamese Roman Catholic communities, and more than three hundred thousand Vietnamese converted to Roman Catholicism. In the southern part of the country, there were about three hundred churches (Phan 1961:41–43).

During the colonial period, Western music was taught only in Roman Catholic churches and French schools. This training was offered only for religious usage and to schoolchildren. The general public also heard Western music in military bands, nightclubs, classical-music concerts, and other forms of entertainment for French colonial administrators and their army. The Vietnamese, including those who served the colonial government, remained a passive audience until the 1910s, when a group of them became involved in the movement for reform and modernization, which strove for social and economic changes resembling those sought in other Asian countries at the time. These changes massively and deeply affected Vietnamese music and culture.

Early in the twentieth century, some Vietnamese worried that their traditional music was becoming extinct. With colonial music pervading society, some sought a remedy in reform. From their efforts sprang musically innovative movements. In Haiphong and Hanoi in 1914, *chèo* gave rise to progressive *chèo* (*chèo văn minh*). In the south in 1918, a new musical theatrical genre, *cải lương*, grew from the roots of chamber music (*tài tử*), while classical theater (*hát bội, tuồng*) was also affected by the obsession for reform. These were followed by reformed *chèo* (*chèo cải lương*) in 1923 in the north.

The invention of new instruments and modifications to traditional instruments occurred not only in musical theater, but also in traditional ensembles. Ten new instruments, including zithers, lutes, and fiddles, were derived from extant traditional or Western instruments. Three Western instruments, the acoustic guitar, the violin, and the steel guitar, were adopted into the *tài tử* ensemble. Southern musicians during the 1930s briefly used mandolins to play *vọng cổ* style with the tunings *bạc liêu* (C–F–c–g) and *rạch gía* (C–G–d–a), named after the southernmost provinces (Trần 1962:180). The guitar, however, remains a favorite instrument in *tài tử* and *cải lương*. It shows how a foreign instrument can be adapted to play Vietnamese music. The wood of the neck between the frets is scooped out to ease the deep pressing on the strings necessary for Vietnamese music. The strings are more pliable than regular ones, and they are tuned differently from Western standards in any of several tunings (Bamman 1991). Currently, an electric version of this guitar has become prevalent.

In the early 1930s, Thái Thị Lang, a close friend of the French composer Henri Tomasi (1901–1971), studied and performed music in Paris, and thus became the first known female Vietnamese pianist and composer. In 1936, after returning to Vietnam, she developed esteem for Vietnamese traditional music and pursued the idea that the piano was capable of playing its repertoires. Her attempts to realize these goals met with little success.

As opposed to the skeletal melodies indicated by Chinese character notation, a new musical notation, based on romanized Vietnamese, was invented to help students memorize completely detailed melodies. Teachers of traditional music created new tablatures and notations of pitches, some of which are still used privately or in music schools.

Modernization

The process of modernization began modestly. After only two decades, it was a powerful force. French songs sung in Vietnamese were first heard during the intermission on the *cải lương* stage in 1923. Considerably popular in the cities for about a decade afterward, this type of entertainment gave rise to other urban fads after 1934. People in Hanoi, Saigon, and some provincial cities enjoyed playing Western instruments, listening to the songs of Tino Rossi and Josephine Baker, and singing French songs with Vietnamese lyrics including "*La Marseillaise*," "*Madelon*," "*J'ai Deux Amours*," the "*Chant du Marin*," and others. Accompanying these songs were traditional instruments, though undoubtedly some Western instruments were also used.

A kind of popular music called modernized music (*nhạc cải cách*) formed in Hanoi in 1937 and 1938 with the creation of two groups of amateur musician-composers: Myosotis and Tricéa. A campaign to modernize music was triggered by Nguyễn Văn Tuyên, a famous singer in Saigon, whose 1938 nationwide lecturing tour was sponsored by the

nhạc cải cách
Early form of Vietnamese popular music from the late 1930s
nhạc tiền chiến
Romantic songs of the 1940s, inspired by German lieder

French Governor of Cochin China (southern Vietnam). Though the general public embraced modernization hesitantly, francophile Vietnamese viewed it positively, as a new expression of Vietnamese culture. Most of the latter, who represented the learned class, had been students at the École Française d'Extrême-Orient in Hanoi. They were confident of being able to create a new kind of music, blending European compositional techniques, Vietnamese lyrics, and, where applicable, traditional melodic idioms.

These songs do not depend on the traditional system of scales, modes, and contexts. Traditional music, according to the creators of *nhạc cải cách*, was "dissonant, monotonous, unchanged," and "if the listener does not understand the lyrics, the music alone would cause an incompleteness and boredom" (*Việt Nhạc* 1948:1:2). During the first two years (1937–1938) about ten songs were published, of which three were in French; about ten more appeared in the next year. From 1940 to 1954, more than one hundred new modern songs were composed. These songs were of many types: romantic songs, poetic theater songs, songs adopted from poems, Boy Scout songs, children's songs, revolutionary songs, and religious songs.

Composers tended to follow one of two tendencies: romantic or activist-revolutionary. Romantic songs that flourished between 1938 and 1945, later called prewar music (*nhạc tiền chiến*), are still sung, both in Vietnam and by overseas Vietnamese. They were inspired by Schubert's and Schumann's lieder, the melodic style of Chopin, and other sources. Their composers had little appreciation for Vietnamese traditional instruments and melodies. The acoustic guitar, both portable and inexpensive, became a favorite instrument in many social gatherings and concerts where a piano was unaffordable. A few dozen professional bands were formed in Hanoi, Saigon, and elsewhere.

Activist-composers belonging to various political persuasions began interjecting patriotic themes into their songs. From 1941, many young Vietnamese men joined the Boy Scouts as a reaction against the perceived moral corruption in the cities (nightclubs, drugs, and other matters). They advocated a better and healthier life, and gradually invoked in their songs a sense of patriotism aimed at the youth. Finally, revolutionary songs appeared.

Several of the nation's anthems were composed during this period. The "*Marche des Étudiants*" ("Students' March"), composed in late 1941, which later became "*Tiếng Gọi Sinh Viên* ("Call for the Patriotic Students") and later "*Tiếng Gọi Thanh Niên*" ("Call for the Patriotic Youth"), was eventually used by the former Republic of Vietnam. At the same time, "*Tiến Quân Ca*" ("March to the Front") was, as it remains, the national anthem of the Democratic Republic of Vietnam (1945–1975) and its successor, the Socialist Republic of Vietnam. Both national anthems were composed by revolutionists: Luu Hữu Phuóc ("*Tiếng Gọi Thanh Niên*") and Văn Cao ("*Tiến Quân Ca*").

Before the Vietnamese victory over the French at Điện Biên Phủ in 1954, patriotic music in the revolutionary zone had been under the leadership of the Việt Minh, in which the Communist Party was prominent. The first Communist song of this kind, "*Cùng Nhau Đi Hồng Binh*" ("March of the Red Army"), was composed in 1930 by Đinh Nhu. After 1954, the latter government moved to the south and continued as the Republic of Vietnam, with support from the United States. Meanwhile, revolutionary songs flourished in the north and in rural areas of the south controlled by the National Liberation Front.

Western Classical Music

In 1927, the French administration in Vietnam created the Conservatoire Française d'Extrême-Orient, but this institution could not function and after a short period was forced to close. In the 1940s, a strong interest in classical and modern Western music developed. The first successful formal music school was founded in 1943 by the Association for Music Studies (Hội Khuyến Nhạc). This school was closed after the reestablishment of the French colonial administration in 1946. During its three years of operation, some three thousand students were enrolled. A thirty-musician brass band was formed, followed in 1945 by an orchestra. During this period, Western trained pianist Thái Thị Lang performed regularly on Vietnam's radio system and in concerts with European musicians.

Interest in Western music intensified with the import of instruments and the study of theory, history, musical practice, and the lives of European and American composers. Concerts of modern music and songs were performed on stage and radio. News of music in Europe and the United States was spread by major musical magazines. A government-supported magazine, *Việt Nhạc* (*Music of Vietnam*), an official organ of the Ministry of Information, promoted the modernization of Vietnamese music in every issue after its inception in 1948. Thẩm Oánh, an advocate of this movement and editor of the magazine, composed a wide range of modern songs. The first modern children's songbook was also published by composers trained in Roman Catholic institutions.

Music schools similar to the Association for Music Studies were established in 1956 in Hanoi and Saigon, after the division of the country. Both composition and Western classical music performance were strongly encouraged in the conservatories. In the north, the composition of popular and revolutionary songs served the government's goals of supporting the war and building a socialist régime. Until 1975, the music school in Saigon was not ostensibly required to serve political purposes.

The Hanoi government received generous support from the former socialist countries of eastern Europe (the Union of Soviet Socialist Republics, Hungary, Bulgaria, and Romania), China, and North Korea, allowing it to send many students to study Western music, including conducting, theory, and instrumental and vocal performance. Foreign instructors regularly taught Western music at the Hanoi Conservatory. Today, the current administrators and most instructors in Vietnam's conservatories were trained in these countries, especially in Russia. A smaller number of instructors at the former Saigon National Conservatory of Music and Theatrical Art studied in France and elsewhere in Western Europe.

Since 1956 in Hanoi, there have been a large number of instrumental compositions for symphony and chamber orchestras and for solo performance. Some of these works are purely Western; others combine Western compositional techniques with Vietnamese lyrics or melodic motifs, or use traditional instruments. Some compositions feature a traditional instrument as a solo instrument and attract the interest of traditional musicians and their audiences. Operatic works use Vietnamese historical or political stories.

Modern pedagogical methods and curricula are customarily used by all departments of conservatories, including the Traditional Music Department. Students at the Hanoi and Hồ Chí Minh City Conservatories are expected to study the basic elements of Western music before further study, whether they specialize in Vietnamese or Western music. All portions of the traditional repertoire known to the teachers have been transcribed into staff notation and are consequently studied by Western methods.

The term *modern music* has various meanings in modern Vietnam. First, there are three musical tendencies in Vietnam: traditional Vietnamese music, popular music, and Western classical music. All involve Vietnamese musicians and composers. Western music encompasses both the classical European repertoire and new—primarily instrumental—compositions by Vietnamese composers. Among these categories, the boundaries between *Western* and *popular* are not clearly defined, and the categories share common ground. Symphonies, concertos, sonatas, and operas are understood as *Western classical*, even though new compositions exist, and some of them involve traditional Vietnamese instruments, but without the traditional conceptual and modal structures.

New "Traditional" Music

For several decades, the general governmental directive called "traditional but modern" (*dân tộc hiện đại*) has deeply influenced traditional music performances and transmission. Some genres of traditional chamber music and folk song survive in urban areas, but more common are hybrid compositions, mainly created by conservatory composers with training in Western music. The most prominent response to the directive has been the creation of revised traditional music (*nhạc dân tộc cải biên*, or simply *cải biên*), a new traditional music, which, unlike older types, uses traditional Vietnamese, "ethnic" (minority), and modern instruments. The former two have undergone physical and functional modifications to allow for virtuosity and the use of Western scales. The main purposes of the changes are to provide contrasting timbres and ranges within an ensemble (loud against soft, low against high); to combine instruments of different cultural and regional backgrounds; to explore new instruments previously unknown to the Việt to create a music that better expresses modern society (fast tempos, loud volume); and to perform new compositions that respond to current social and political demands.

Though *cải biên* is actually a modern genre, many official representatives of the cultural establishment represent it as traditional. Numerous foreign recording companies have sent recording teams to Vietnam seeking traditional music, and they have returned with virtually nothing but *cải biên*; consequently, many recordings of this music have appeared in the West labeled traditional. Furthermore, the music is amplified, and the instrumentation somewhat resembles that of rock bands, with drums in the back center and melodic instruments in the front. A bass guitar disguised as a long lute (*đàn đáy*) provides the roots of harmonically functional chords. Most musicians stand to play, unless the instrument requires them to sit. A variety of modified ethnic instruments are featured in new compositions. The music confines itself to dominant-tonic chordal patterns, is usually constructed in an ABA form, is metrical throughout, and allows little or no improvisation (Figure 13.37).

Popular Song

Another kind of modern music is new music (*nhạc mới*), also called modern music (*tân nhạc*), formerly called modernized music (*nhạc cải cách*). This is today's popular music. With roots to the 1940s, it is primarily disseminated in commercial settings (clubs and restaurants), on radio and television, in Christian churches (both Roman Catholic and Protestant), and in Buddhist temples where this music is encouraged by the Gia Đình Phật Tử (Buddhist Families, a kind of Buddhist Boy Scouts). In both form and cultural context, this music defines a rather clear boundary between it and traditional music. Consider its musical instruments,

Figure 13.37
An ensemble plays the modernized instrumental music called *nhạc cải biên*. Photo by Phong T. Nguyễn.

entirely of Western origin: to accompany their songs, *nhạc mới* musicians use piano, electric keyboard, guitar, drums, and harmonica whenever financial circumstances allow. The traditional and ethnic instruments of Vietnam are rarely used except to create a folklike character in songs having indigenous traits. Western harmony and vibrato are commonly used.

Its cultural message, as most makers of popular music put it, is not only "to be like people in advanced Western countries" but also, in this musical and cultural mix, "to bridge the differences between East and West." It closes the gap among the linguistic tonal systems of the various regions by using one linguistic accent, that of the north. With its use of ballroom (tango, waltz, slow, or bolero) rhythms, it can transport listeners' imaginations to the ambience of Europe or North America. With the expression of marchlike rhythms, it links people politically, in powerful revolutionary songs.

The Modern Folk Song

The modern folk song—a genre that no longer belongs only to workers, rural or urban (*dân ca*)—is one of Vietnam's popular musics. It is featured in concerts and is heard on radio and television throughout the country. Both traditional and newly composed but Vietnamese-style melodies have been forced into tempered scales and Western harmony. The potential of improvisation, ornamentation, and syncopation have been greatly reduced. New words have replaced the old.

The modern *dân ca* is roughly the Vietnamese equivalent to the Thai *phleng luk thung* and the Japanese *enka*, newly composed popular songs derived from traditional styles but accompanied by modern instruments playing functional harmonies. In some songs, the instrumentalists accommodate singers by imitating traditional instruments and their way of following the contours of the vocal melody.

In Hồ Chí Minh City and Hanoi, concerts of popular music take place nightly at major modern theaters and in artists' cafes (*quán nghệ sĩ*). These are often integrated into comic skits. A basic instrumental combo must include an electric keyboard, a guitar, a bass guitar, and drums. The acoustic guitar, used as a symbol of modernization, has been replaced by the electric version or by keyboard synthesizer. Electric-organ festivals take place annually in the country's major cities.

Dancing to popular music began in the mid-1970s in Vietnamese communities in the United States and Europe and spread back to Vietnam. During the 1980s, with the new government's policy of reform (đổi mới), private businesses, including dance clubs and artists' cafés grew, and both are as popular now as they were before 1975 in the south. Karaoke is also widespread, from Hanoi to Hồ Chí Minh City and beyond.

As new technology has allowed the production of audiocassettes and videocassettes earlier and compact discs and video compact discs later, the music business in Vietnam has grown. These media feature popular music, cải lương, spoken theater, and traditional music. Much rarer is Western classical music, which, despite its honored place in the conservatories, is popular mainly among faculty, students, and their friends.

The Dynamics Change and the Future of Vietnamese Music

Despite myriad efforts to make nhạc mới a national music, its composers continue to have little knowledge of traditional music—knowledge of the sort that must be gained through experience rather than systematic training in essentials. In contrast, though traditional musicians were interested in some popular and Western-derived compositions, they have maintained reserved attitudes. Though they might be impressed by large Western instrumental ensembles, many traditional musicians—and perhaps many ordinary Vietnamese—have not seen the Western values expressed there as being equivalent with their own. To trained traditional musicians, the incompatibility of these systems is obvious. To them, the style of the modern folk song is of limited interest and provides little satisfaction.

It is difficult to define Vietnamese music in the twenty-first century. Music has become a complex of types that can be viewed from different social, historical, and musical perspectives, and their contents and numerous conflicting conceptions symbolize the difficulties of interfacing tradition and modernity, leaving artists in a dilemma.

Technology does not exist independent of the humans who create and use it. The same traditional musicians who reject Western musical culture may embrace Western technology. The crucial issue today is how Vietnam can modernize without losing its identity. Vietnamese musicians and scholars disagree more about methods and rates than on needs for change and modernization, yet few are willing to abandon the culture's traditions.

REFERENCES

Bamman, Richard Jones. 1991. "The Dan Tranh and the Luc Huyen Cam." In *New Perspectives in Vietnamese Music*, ed. Phong T Nguyễn, 67–78. New Haven, CT: Yale Council on Southeast Asia Studies.

Brăiloiu, Constantin. 1955. "Un problème de tonalité." In *Mélanges d'histoire et d'esthétique musicales offerts à Paul-Marie Masson*, 1: 63–75. Paris: Richard Masse.

Mich Quang. 1963. *Tim hieu nghe thuat Tuong (A Study of the Art of Tuong Classical Theater)*. Hanoi: Van Hoa Nghe Thuat.

Phan Huy Lê, Hà Văn Tấn, and Hoàng Xuân Chinh. 1989. "Những buóc đi cửa lịch sử Việt Nam." In *Văn Hóa Việt Nam*, 34–40. Hànội: Ban Văn Nghệ Trung Uong.

Phan Khoang. 1961. *Việt Nam pháp thuộc sử (History of Colonialism in Vietnam)*. Saigon: Sống Mói.

Trần Văn Khê. 1962. *La musique Vietnamienne traditionelle*. Paris: Presses Universitaires de France.

Việt Nhạc. 1948. Number 1, 16 August.

Singapore

Lee Tong Soon

Musics of Specific Communities
Musical Genres

Founded in 1819 by Sir Stamford Raffles, Singapore served as an important port of call for the British Empire in Southeast Asia. From 1826 to 1946, with Penang and Melaka, it was part of the Straits Settlements. In 1963, Singapore, Malaya, Sabah, and Sarawak formed what is now known as Malaysia. Two years later, on 9 August 1965, Singapore separated from Malaysia and became a sovereign nation.

Singapore is situated just above the equator, between peninsular Malaysia and the islands of Indonesia. Most of its early immigrants, indigenous to Malaysia and Indonesia, included Malay, Javanese, Boyanese, Bugis, and Balinese. The earliest Chinese immigrants came mainly from Malacca and Riau, and later generations migrated primarily from Guangdong and Fujian provinces, southeast China. The first Indian immigrants arrived from Penang and later from India. Other nationalities among immigrant peoples in Singapore include Arabs and Europeans.

Singapore is among the smallest states in the world, with a land area of 692 square kilometers, comparable to Bahrain, St. Lucia, or Tonga. In 2006, with a total population of 4.5 million, the ethnic makeup of Singapore consists mainly of Chinese (76.8 percent), Malays (13.9 percent), and Indians (7.1 percent), with other peoples (such as Eurasians, Armenians, and Jews) making up the remainder. The Singapore population accounts for the diversity of music in the country, which, through the fusion of traditional and modern aspects, has created a distinctly Singaporean lifestyle.

Singapore has four distinct cultures: Chinese, Malay, Indian, and Eurasian. Among the Chinese population is a group known as Peranakans, with a distinctive mixture of Chinese and Malay cultural traits.

The Chinese

The Chinese population in Singapore speaks various dialects, including Fujian, Chaozhou, Guangdong, Hainan, and Kejia. Dialect groups formed clan associations to support their respective forms of opera (*wayang*), making these genres locally prominent. Hand-puppet and string-puppet theaters, traditions popular during the first half of the twentieth century, are now mainly engaged during Taoist ceremonies.

A minstrel-like tradition, *zouchang* "walk-sing," is performed during festive seasons (such as the Chinese Lunar New Year), celebrations of deities' birthdays, and private birthday parties. Walking performers, mostly members of operatic troupes, form ensembles ranging from six to fifteen musicians, accompanied by instruments from the theater (Perris 1978).

During the seventh month of the lunar calendar, the month of hungry ghosts (usually in August), various traditional theatrical genres appear on makeshift stages along the streets. Contemporary urban performances are known as *getai* "song-stage." During these performances, popular Mandarin, Fujian, and occasionally English songs are performed to the accompaniment of electric guitars, keyboards, and drum set. Performances by famous local comedians are also part of *getai*, which often highlight current social and political issues.

A contemporary Mandarin vocal genre, *xinyao* "Singapore ballad," is being revived through the mass media and the openings of cafés and pubs that cater specially to lovers of ballads. *Xinyao* began in the early 1980s among teenage students who sang about unforgettable love affairs, broken dreams, school life, cherished longings, and local topics, usually accompanied by a guitar. The mid-1980s witnessed the rise to fame of several *xinyao* artists, both in Singapore and abroad.

Besides theatrical and vocal performances, the Chinese performing arts scene in Singapore is also marked by orchestral, chamber, and vocal performances, such as *nanguan*, a chamber-music genre from Xiamen in China's Fujian Province. Drumming for the lion dance, a tradition that has always been prevalent in Chinese festive celebrations, is fast becoming a popular musical genre in Singapore. It involves the beating of drums, embellished with the drummer's complex acrobatic movements.

The Malays

Vocal genres accompanied by the frame drums *kompang* and *hadrah* are among the most popular kinds of Malay music in Singapore. They involve single-sided, handheld frame drums, which are said to be of Arabic origin. The *hadrah*, like the tambourine, has cymbal-like discs around its circumference. The frame drums engage in interlocking rhythmic patterns in different rhythmic strains, consistently maintained throughout a performance. Songs accompanied by *kompang* and *hadrah* usually contain religious connotations, sung

Figure 14.1
A performance of *dikir banrat*. Photo by Low Eng Teong, 1995.

in praise of God. Necessary at traditional Malay weddings and official functions, both *kompang* and *hadrah* ensembles are recognized as musical symbols of Malay culture in Singapore.

Dikir barat, a traditional Malay vocal genre, is said to have originated in Kelantan, a state on the east coast of peninsular Malaysia. A usual performance involves two leaders (*juara* and *tukang karat*) and a chorus (*awok*). The vocal ensemble sings catchy lyrics with engaging rhythms, enhanced by lively movements of the hands and upper body (Figure 14.1). The lyrics of *dikir barat* are secular and often suggest patriotism and other themes concerning one's own culture. Often, they are newly composed, tailored to suit the situation, and attached to stock melodies in a verse-refrain form. The *juara* delivers solo renditions of the verses, the *tukang karat* interjects comical remarks, and the *awok* joins in the refrains. The upper-body movements are choreographed to provide visual representations of the words. The ensemble is usually accompanied by Malay instruments such as *kompang*, gong, and *bonang*.

Ghazal is a vocal tradition said to have been introduced to Singapore via peninsular Malaysia by Arab, Persian, and Indian traders. A popular form of Malay music in the 1950s in Singapore, it preserved some of the most famous *pantuns* (Malay poetical forms) and Malay folk songs. Accompanying the voices are instruments such as a lute (*gambus*), a drum (*tabla*), a frame drum, an accordion, and a violin.

Kuda kepang "horse-trance dance" and various traditional *joget* dances may still be seen in Singapore during special events, such as cultural shows. *Bangsawan,* a Malay operatic genre that began in the late 1800s, is performed in Singapore mainly during festivals and for tourists (Figure 14.2).

The Indians

The two main styles of Indian classical music, Hindustani and Karnatic, inform the Indian artistic scene in Singapore. The Singapore Indian Fine Arts Society, founded in 1949,

Figure 14.2
Young players of
angklung in Singapore.
Photo by Low Eng
Teong, 1995.

locally promotes Indian fine arts. With its philosophy (Art Characterizes Civilization), it is apt to say that the society is foremost in preserving Indian culture in Singapore through the performing arts. Its Academy of Fine Arts supports the Singapore Indian Orchestra and Choir and conducts graded courses on instruments such as flute, *mridangam, sarod, sitar, tabla,* and *veena,* with classes on vocal techniques and classical dances such as *bharata natyam.*

Other forms of Indian music prevalent among the Indian population include *bhajanai* (known as *bhajan* in North India), film music, and temple music that features the *nadhaswaran* oboe and the *thavil* drum as its main instruments. Indian temples in Singapore are patrons of Indian performing arts, and by sponsoring concerts have played a crucial role in promoting Indian music

Indian music and dance are prevalent in the Indian festivals celebrated in Singapore, including Pongal (Harvest Festival), Navarathiri (Festivals of Nine Lights), Theemithi (Firewalking), Vaisakhi, and Thaipusam. The *bhangra* (Figure 14.3), a popular Indian dance that originated in the Punjab, is usually associated with the Punjabi Sikhs. It is usually performed during harvest, Sikh weddings, and other joyous occasions.

Figure 14.3
A performance of
bhangra. Photo by Low
Eng Teong, 1995.

REFERENCE

Perris, Arnold. 1978. "Chinese Wayang: The Survival of Chinese Opera in the Streets of Singapore." *Ethnomusicology* 22(2):297–306.

Upland and Minority Peoples of Mainland Southeast Asia: An Introduction

Terry E. Miller

Language Families of Mainland Southeast Asia

Demographically, mainland Southeast Asia can be divided into lowland and upland peoples. In each nation-state (excepting the Republic of Singapore), a significant portion of the population consists of minority groups, most of whom live in the higher elevations. Some groups, like the Karen of Burma and Thailand and the Chăm of Vietnam, have lowland counterparts who have largely adopted lowland, majority life styles. Frank M. Lebar's 1964 publication *Ethnic Groups of Mainland Southeast Asia* names 151 ethnic groups, including the majority peoples. In variety, minority groups vastly outnumber the majority groups, but in population, power, and organization, they remain marginal in most countries.

LANGUAGE FAMILIES OF MAINLAND SOUTHEAST ASIA

It is customary to organize the upland and minority peoples of mainland Southeast Asia according to language family, though the exact classification of some languages remains conjectural. There are four principal language families in mainland Southeast Asia.

The Sino-Tibetan Family

Speakers of Sino-Tibetan languages range from northeastern India to Vietnam and include many groups that straddle national borders. Most are minorities, except those of the Sinitic subclass, which includes more than a billion people in the People's Republic of China and ethnic Chinese in Southeast Asia. The Tibeto-Burman subclass includes twenty groups, all minorities except the Burmese. Most such groups living in Southeast Asia migrated there from China. Among them are such groups as the Nagas, who straddle the border of Burma into India and Bangladesh. There are two other major subclasses, the Karen and the so-called Miao-Yao (so-called because both terms were given by outsiders and are pejorative); the people themselves prefer the terms *Hmong* and *Mian*, respectively.

The Austroasiatic Family

The Austroasiatic family includes three subclasses: Mon-Khmer, Việt-Mường, and Senoi-Semang. Mon-Khmer includes the majority Khmer of Cambodia and the formerly powerful Mon, but the remaining seventy-four named groups, found mainly in the mountains of Cambodia, Laos, and Vietnam, include mostly little-known peoples. A few, however, including the Bahnar of Vietnam, are somewhat better known. The Việt-Mường subclass includes the majority Vietnamese and the Mường (people usually considered to be the ancestors of the Vietnamese, who continue to live in the uplands). The Senoi-Semang group includes only peoples who live in the mountains of Malaysia.

The Tai Family

The Tai classification embraces mainly the Tai family of languages. The Tai include all mainstream, majority people in Thailand and Laos, plus the Shan of Burma, but also upland and nonmainstream groups, like the Black Tai, the White Tai, the Red Tai, the Phuan, and minority Tai-speakers in parts of northern Vietnam and southern China.

The Austronesian (Malayo-Polynesian) Family

This language family is extremely widespread. It extends from the mainland into Indonesia and the Philippines and reaches out through Oceania as far east as Rapanui (Easter Island) and into the Indian Ocean as far west as Madagascar. Mainland speakers of Austronesian languages live mainly in Malaysia and Vietnam. There are two subclasses, Chăm and Malay, the latter primarily the language of the majority lowland Malay. Chăm includes lowland Chăm in Vietnam and Cambodia, plus nine upland groups, among which the Jarai and the Rhade are fairly well known.

REFERENCE

Lebar, Frank M. 1964. *Ethnic Groups of Mainland Southeast Asia.* New Haven, CT: Human Relations Area Files.

Minority Musics of Vietnam

Phong T. Nguyễn

Musical Contexts and Genres
Musical Instruments

The musics of the minority peoples of Vietnam have remained obscure to outsiders. The minorities of the central area of Vietnam were difficult to study during the war years, and the area remained off limits to most foreign researchers until 1994. The minorities in the north remain almost unknown to outsiders. Consequently, this article must be based on limited fieldwork.

Two groups of minority peoples live in Vietnam, one in the uplands and the other in the lowlands. The uplanders live in the cool, mountainous areas bordering Cambodia, Laos, and China, where sources of water are few; the lowlanders live alongside the majority Viet and have easier access to rivers and the sea. Each group has created particular musical expressions. Lowlanders are mainly the Khmer, the Chăm, and the Hoa (Chinese). A small number of Hoa live in the areas bordering China, but larger groups of them settled as businesspeople in the south during the 1800s.

It is convenient to divide upland culture and music according to two geographical regions: the Truòng Son Ranges in the central region (often called the central highlands) and the mountains and plateaus of the north (more exactly, the northeast and the northwest). The peoples living in the central highlands belong to an older layer of population and are probably descended from peoples who settled there about two thousand to four thousand years ago. In the north (except for the Tày, the Muòng, and the Thái), most uplanders migrated from southern China between the 1300s and the 1800s. Living along the Truòng Son Ranges in the central highlands some twenty ethnic groups speak languages belonging to either the Mon-Khmer or Austronesian language families. Although both vocal and instrumental musics exist in the upland areas, the most representative types are bronze gong ensembles and a rich collection of instruments, mostly of bamboo. In contrast, the northern uplanders emphasize vocal music sung in Thai-Lao, Viet-Muong, and Sino-Tibetan languages.

MUSICAL CONTEXTS AND GENRES

Songs of Courtship and Friendship

Many minority-group songs are sung in alternation by male and female singers of all ages. This pattern, which may alternate young boys and girls, married men and women, or widows and widowers, is not limited to a specific population in Vietnam. Young men and women sing while courting on the side of a mountain or hill.

In Thai, *khắp* means "to sing." In a fixed order from the opening of a singing session to the farewell, the Thai sing songs of love (*khắp tua*), including traveling songs, gate-opening songs, introductory songs, greetings, wishing songs, and farewells. The San Diu sing *soọng cô* in a format comparable to that of the *quan họ* of the lowland Việt. Pairs of men and women sing alternately around a campfire (formerly the site of cooking) and thereby invoke an age-old concept of prosperity through its association with cooking, warmth, and community. When singing occurs inside a house, participants give consideration to the relationship between host and guests. If the guests are young men, the host's family must present the young women, led by an experienced female singer from within the family, who sings with them at first. The beginning of the courtship is marked by the serving of betel leaves. These singing sessions may last up to three nights during the spring or fall.

Narratives

Stories, both short and long, are preserved in the minds of many minorities. Among the lowland Chăm of central Vietnam, epics have more than a thousand verses. The most famous stories among the minorities are epics named after heroes. The Jarai and the Ede tell stories of Dam San, Dam Di, and Xinh Nha, while the Muòng story *Tẻ Tất Tẻ Nát* ("The Birth of Life") lasts several nights—a story consisting of more than four thousand lines.

Ritual Songs

Perhaps the most prevalent types of song practiced by minorities concern rituals—for healing, commemorations, weddings, funerals, and other purposes. Among the Tày and the Nùng, the singer-ritualist (usually female) is called *then*, and among the Muòng and the Thái in the north, he or she is called *mo*. Specifically, a *then* should be a handsome and skillful performer who can sing, play instruments, and dance. Whether in trance or not, the *then* performs to heal sick people, to attract rain, and to ensure good crops, successful conceptions, and long lives. People believe the *then* has the power to create a friendship between the god of the sun and the god of rain. The healing songs of the Thai *mo* can have up to 450 verses.

In the central highlands, Ede singer-ritualists (*khoa kam*) conduct a ceremony for the god of winds, including songs wishing for the avoidance of storms and for fertility in farm-

Truòng Son Ranges
Mountain range running through southern Vietnam, home to minorities

khắp
Upland Thai term for repartee song

m'buôt
Free-reed mouth organ with gourd wind chest, found in Truòng Son Ranges

goong
Jarai tube zither with eleven separate strings

ing. The greatest festival in the central highlands is the Sedang water-buffalo sacrifice (*ting ka kpo*), which includes many gong ensembles and songs.

Lullabies and Other Songs

Most minority peoples have lullabies (Xtiêng *niên con,* Khmer *bompê kôn,* Chăm *ru anuk,* Việt *ru con*). These are often forgotten in urban areas, but they continue to flourish in rural areas, among both the Việt and minorities.

MUSICAL INSTRUMENTS

With fifty-three minority groups in Vietnam, a complete survey of musical instruments would require much space. Many groups live in scattered and remote mountainous villages, making generalizations risky. At this point, we can roughly estimate that minorities in both lowlands and uplands have about two hundred kinds of instruments, belonging to all four standard organological categories.

The Trường Son Ranges in the central region offer the most extensive concentration of instruments; in other areas, the variety of instruments is more modest. Among both Mon-Khmer and Austronesians of the central highlands, the gong ensemble is central, though both wooden and bamboo instruments are widely used by individuals. Gong ensembles of some sort are also found among the Mường and the Thái in the north, while the lowland Khmer, living in southern Vietnam, use a set of tuned bossed gongs on a circular rattan rack (*kong thum*) as part of their standard ensemble (*pinn peat*).

The Central Highlands

In the central highlands, gongs play an important role in the villagers' lives. Each ensemble consists of from three to thirteen flat and bossed gongs, some of which may be doubled or tripled, making a full ensemble large and impressive. The gongs, varying from 30 to 86 centimeters in diameter, are named by size, musical role, and hierarchical function. Gongs may be identified as mother, father, older sister, or younger sister. Each set of gongs has a specific use. The *trum* is associated with the planting of the pole to which the buffalo about to be sacrificed is tied; the *m'nhum,* with festivals; the *arap,* with the abandonment of a tomb (*pothi*); the

CD TRACK 10

Figure 16.1
While two men sip rice beer, a gong ensemble plays for a funeral in an upland village. Photo by Paul Langman, about 1968.

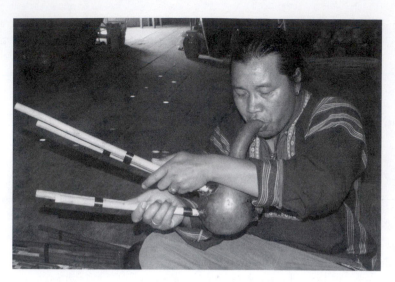

Figure 16.2
Dock Ramah, a Jarai minority musician, plays the *k'ni* mouth-resonated bowed monochord. Photo by Terry E. Miller, 2005.

avong, with gong competitions; the *ho duc,* with a victory celebration; and the *khah,* with a healing ritual. Gongs are held in the players' hands unless they are too heavy, in which case they are supported by a shoulder strap. Drums, having two heads and made in three sizes, are also members of the gong ensembles. The ensembles can play alone or to accompany dance (Figure 16.1).

Other central-highland idiophones include xylophones and bamboo xylophones (*t'rung, khinh khung*), wooden slit drums and bamboo slit drums (*tol mo*), bamboo tubes beaten with a stick (*goong ting leng*), bamboo tubes beaten by hand (*t'pol*), and Jew's

harps. Among the most remarkable of instruments is a hydraulic bamboo xylophone, the Sedang *koangtác,* complex in both construction and musical function. A frame is built over a stream, especially in rapids or a small waterfall, and bamboo tubes are hung from the frame into the water, resting against a lower frame. The currents fill, tilt, and then empty the tubes, letting them fall back against the frame, sounding a pitch. The biggest of these

Figure 16.3
A Xtiêng musician plays a bamboo tube zither (*goong*). Phuóc Long, Vietnam. Photo by Phong T. Nguyễn, 1994.

frames are 60 meters wide and have 120 tubes. Lithophones from prehistoric times have been unearthed in Vietnam, but whether they originated among the ancestors of the present-day minorities is uncertain.

Many aerophones are conceived of as being voices of nature. These include bamboo flutes, single- and double-reed pipes, and free-reed instruments. Among the simplest is the animal horn (*t'diep*), and among the more complex is the polyphonic gourd free-reed mouth organ (*m'buôt*) (Figure 16.2) Seven vertical, open-ended bamboo tubes set in a frame (*klông pút*) are sounded when the player claps his or her hands over the openings. Some believe that this instrument originated with farmers who stored grain in bamboo tubes and clapped their hands over the openings to make the last grains fall out when sowing the fields. In the process, they discovered that sounds were resonated by the tubes, and they later added more tubes until the set was standardized as seven. Single- and double-reed instruments are little known, but the Thái and Yao, among others, have such instruments, which they call *pí pập* and *pí đôi* respectively.

Though less numerous than idiophones and aerophones, chordophones exhibit complex tunings and playing techniques. The most important of these are idiochord tube zithers. The sophisticated Jarai version (*goong*) is played polyphonically to imitate the gong ensembles. Likely the original version is still played by the Xtiêng, who cut the bamboo skin in strips and raise them on tiny pieces of bamboo; the player plucks these strips (Figure 16.3). Others amplify the instrument's sounds with an empty, dried gourd. The Jarai *goong* has eleven metal strings, stretched along the outside of a thick bamboo tube to wooden tuning pegs at the top end. Its tuning is based on that of the gongs.

The Jarai also have a plucked bamboo tube zither (*tol alao*), one of whose strings are beaten with two sticks. Especially unusual is the Jarai one-stringed spike fiddle (*k'ni*). The bowed string, attached to the lower part of the instrument's body, passes over six frets to a tuning peg. A second, resonating string stretches from the bowed string to a piece of wood held in the player's mouth, which serves as a resonator. The main string is set into vibration when bowed with a thin piece of bamboo, 40 centimeters long (Figure 16.4).

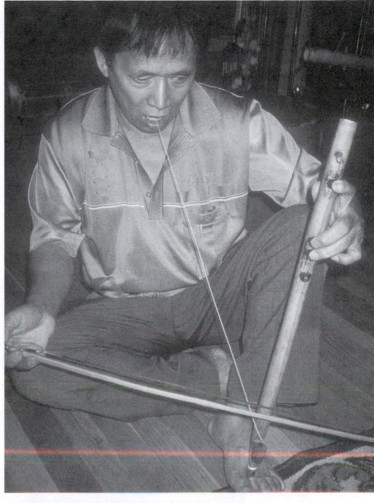

Figure 16.4
A Black Tai ensemble plays the ricepestling trough (*quánh loóng*) with hanging gongs and a drum. Photo by Terry E. Miller, 1994.

The North

Among the cultural groups of northern Vietnam, musical instruments are fewer, though all four categories exist. In Mường villages, bronze instruments are likely among the oldest. Both the Thái and the Mường, particularly in Hoà Bình and Thanh Hóa provinces, retain bronze drum gongs and gongs. A Mường gong ensemble, consisting of both flat and bossed gongs, has from three to twelve gongs. The Mường have a custom of distinguishing gong sizes by giving them ages: the smallest gong, about 20 centimeters in diameter, is "age one," the next larger one "age two," and so forth. According to Mường custom, only the lower-pitched gongs may be played at funerals.

In Thanh Hóa Province, both the Thái and the Mường have an unusual idiophone—a

Figure 16.5
A free-reed mouth organ (*mboat*) of the K'por minority in Dalat, Vietnam. Photo by Terry E. Miller, 2007.

large log, carved into a boat-shaped wooden trough (Thái *loỏng*, Mường *duống*), played by ten or twelve young women, who on both sides of the trough beat sticks rhythmically against the bottom and the inside. This instrument originated as a rice-pestling trough. It is played with a set of four or five hanging bossed gongs and a hanging drum (Figure 16.5).

The Lô Lô still count the rarely used bronze gong drum as their favorite instrument. They store a pair of drums (male and female) in the ground and unearth them for ceremonies. Accompanying the gong drum is a two-stringed fiddle, whose player dances while playing.

Chordophones, both plucked and bowed, are found commonly among northern groups. These instruments include the Thái-Tày gourd lute (*tính tẩu*) (Figure 16.6) and the Hà Nhì three-stringed lute (*ta in*).

The Hmong of Vietnam appear to have the most extensive collection of instruments. These include the following: a musical leaf (*blùng*), a water-buffalo-horn oboe (*cu tủ*), a Jew's harp (*u cha*), an end-blown flute (*trà pua*), a side-blown flute (*trà pùn tủ*), a wooden oboe (*xi u*), a copper oboe (*pua*), a two-stringed fiddle (*lụ phù*), a jingling hollow metal ring (*chia nếnh*), a rattle (*trù nếnh*), small cymbals (*u siề*), a two headed drum (*chua*), a moon-shaped lute (*diển xin,* also *thà chinh*), and a free-reed mouth organ (*kểnh*). The *kểnh* has six bamboo pipes, fixed into a long wooden wind chest. Each pipe has one metal free reed, except the shortest and longest pipes, which have two reeds in each; this arrangement allows the playing of an interval—a second or third—on a single pipe, but a single note can be obtained by opening or covering the respective holes for fingering.

Figure 16.6
A Tày minority woman plays the *tính tẩu* lute in northeastern Vietnam. From *Vietnam: A Multicultural Mosic.* 1991. Hanoi: Vietnam Foreign Languages Publishing House, fig. 65.

Music of Upland Minorities in Burma, Laos, and Thailand

Ruriko Uchida and Amy Catlin

The Sino-Tibetan (Tibeto-Burman) Language Family
The Austroasiatic (Mon-Khmer) Language Family
The Tai-Kadai Language Family
The Miao-Yao Language Family

The peoples who inhabit the high plateau near the Golden Triangle of Burma, Laos, and Thailand live in villages consisting of about twenty households each. As isolated minorities, they have few indigenous social or political groupings larger than villages. Some have accepted the central government of the state in which they live, but most have only a tenuous relationship to it. There are more than a hundred such groups, including the Karen of Thailand and Burma; the Kachin in Burma; the Akha, the Lahu, and the Lisu in Thailand; the Hmong, the Kmhmu, and the Yao in Laos; and the Nùng and the Lati in Vietnam. All practice slash-and-burn agriculture and subsist mainly on rice. Some grow opium poppies. Most are illiterate and animistic and have no formal system of education. Their indigenous dress is highly colorful, often indicative of their subgroup.

Their method of agriculture follows a pattern that affects other aspects of their lives. At the beginning of the dry season, from January to mid-February, the people choose new areas for planting dry rice. In March, they go to the forest and clear a block of land. In April, they burn the cut trees and undergrowth and spread the ashes over the land as fertilizer. After the paddy has been prepared, each family builds a simple bamboo hut in the corner of its field, so members of the family can guard against animals during the growing season. Just before the rainy season (in May and June), the villagers sow the rice: with sticks, the men dig shallow holes into which the women and children place the seeds. During the months of July and August, they weed the paddy. At the beginning of the dry season (November), they harvest the crops. In December, they thresh. While sowing and harvesting, they conduct collective rituals.

At the foot of the mountains, lowland minorities live agricultural lives influenced by social modernization. They have more complex cultures, combining elements from both the mountains and the plains. Most are integrated into their central governments. They include the Mon and the Shan in Burma; the Lawa, the Plains Karen, and the Tai-lue in Thailand; and the Black Tai and the Red Tai in Laos and Vietnam.

The upland minorities prefer simple traditional songs. Life and music are closely related for them, and they have no professional musicians. The structure of the music is mostly monophonic. Five-tone scales predominate, with a nucleus of a fourth. Improvisation appears in the variations of repeated phrases. The upland peoples enjoy dancing to a simple instrumental accompaniment.

THE SINO-TIBETAN (TIBETO-BURMAN) LANGUAGE FAMILY

The Lahu (Mussur)

The Lahu are among the Lolo branch of the Tibeto-Burman family. The Lahu live in villages spread over a wide area: China's Yunnan Province; the Kengtung area of Burma's Shan State; the northern Thai provinces of Chiangmai, Chiengrai, Lamping, Mae Hongson, and Tak; Nam Tha Province in northern Laos; and parts of northwestern Vietnam. Villages are usually located above 1,300 meters, and houses are built on pilings. In 1990, the estimated Lahu population was roughly six hundred thousand, divided by country as follows: China, 411,000; Burma, 150,000; Thailand, 68,000; Laos, 10,000; and Vietnam, 4,000. The Lahu in Thailand and Laos have immigrated within the last century or so.

Most Lahu are animistic, believing in good, neutral, and evil spirits, above which is a supreme creator (*G'ui-Sha Er* "Sky Ghost"). American missionaries, who have been preaching to the Lahu since the beginning of the twentieth century, reinterpret this deity as the Christian God. For the Lahu in Thailand, the annual celebration of the lunar New Year affords traditional opportunities for courtship. Young men visit young women's villages, and boys and girls sing amatory songs to each other. Once a pair chooses to marry, a go-between makes the necessary arrangements. A period of premarital sexual activity invariably precedes the marriage.

The Musical Life of the Lahu

During the New Year celebrations (the most important and joyful time for the Lahu), ancestral spirits return to the village to witness the festivities. An altar is decorated with white paper streamers attached to bamboo sticks. To please the supreme creator, male and female human figures representing human souls are cut from paper. The senior village priest, headman, and elders offer prayers at a rice-cake altar, a symbolic New Year's tree, and an ancestral shrine. Each head of a household prays to the spirits for the prosperity and health of his household during the coming year. Then villagers gather in their most colorful attire to drink, eat, sing New Year's songs, and dance.

The Lahu perform a dance in which men stamp their feet collectively, and women form a closely swaying circle around them. The men continuously play a free-reed mouth organ with a gourd wind chest (*naw*) (Figure 17.1). This is also a period of courtship for young people, who camp out some distance from the village around two big fires, one for the girls and one for the boys. All through the night, songs of love are sung back and forth, as are ballads and improvised prose. In the morning, the boys playfully rush the girls, and each boy tries to take the turban from the head of a girl who appeals to him. Returning this turban initiates negotiation and more serious contacts. Individual courting-song and love-song singing occurs throughout the year, encouraging sexual play.

Figure 17.1
The free-reed gourd mouth organ (*naw*) used in a Lahu-Shehleh bridge (soul-calling) ceremony. Photo by Paul and Elaine Lewis; used with permission.

The harvest celebration is also important to the Lahu. This ceremony is similar to the New Year's celebration. Beating a gong, the senior village priest chants prayers at his house, where a decorated altar has been set up. He gives thanks to the spirit guardian for that year's harvest and asks for a good harvest in the coming year. Then, dressed in their finery, the villagers gather to sing harvest songs and dance passionately, accompanied by a *naw*, a cymbal (*shae*), a gong (*bluck*), and a drum (*chack*).

While sawing, planting, cutting, harvesting, and pounding rice, the Lahu sing, play the *naw*, and dance. Beyond this, they have songs for weddings, funerals, shamanistic activities, curing, narration, and lullabies. At a wedding, the bride and bridegroom sing alternately about their expectations for their future; then guests sing congratulatory songs.

Lahu Musical Instruments

The most characteristic Lahu instruments are free-reed mouth organs, the *naw* and the *nokuma* (also *tolem*). The *naw* is widespread in Yunnan, northern Thailand, Laos, and Vietnam. About 35 centimeters long, it usually has five pipes; in some Lahu regions, it has three, six, or seven. The pipes are of bamboo, with a free reed of metal embedded in each. In bundle form, the pipes pierce a gourd, which serves as a wind chest. The *naw* is known to the Akha as *lachi* and to the Lisu *as fulu*. All Lahu use it for prayer, dancing, and entertainment. The Lahu also have a Jew's harp (*ata*). Other Lahu instruments include a three-stringed lute, a gong, and a goblet-shaped drum.

The Akha (Kaw, Ekaw, Hani)

The Akha language belongs to the southern Lolo branch of Tibeto-Burman. Not having their own writing, they use both Roman-based and Thai-based orthographies, devised for them by Christian missionaries. Akha villages are above 2,000 meters. The houses are built on pilings, with the chief's house in the center. On the path entering the village, a sacred gate is constructed, flanked by figures of male and female fertility. Since many Akha live far from administrative centers, their population is difficult to gauge. The most recent estimated figures are Burma, 180,000; China, 150,000; Laos, 59,000; and Thailand, 34,541.

The economic life of the Akha is based primarily on shifting agriculture and the cultivation of opium poppies. Hunting and fishing are subsidiary activities, and the Akha have retained their skills as gatherers. Pigs and chickens serve as food and sacrifices. Other livestock include cattle, buffaloes, and horses; the Akha in Thailand also eat dogs.

The Akha are animists. They respect ancestral spirits (*ne*), some of which are malevolent and cause illness; others, including the guardian spirits of houses and villages, are associated with familiar but benign objects. Sometimes, the functions of village priest and village shaman are handled by one person. The shaman (*tumo*) can communicate with good and evil spirits alike. He conducts ceremonies and cures sick people.

The Musical Life of the Akha

Akha singing voices are good and so is their breath control. Conscientious about maintaining their traditional festivals, they have many annual ceremonies during which music is performed. The relationship of ceremonial music to farming plays an important role in Akha society. There are nine annual ceremonies, each with special songs about the cultivation of rice.

The Akha are tolerant in raising their children. After coming of age, boys (at fifteen) and girls (at thirteen) can marry at will. Young people of these ages sing courtship songs every evening, often at the holy grounds at the edge of a village, where they set up special swings. Annual festivals and New Year's celebrations are prime occasions for courting: young women and men dress up and strut about, showing off their finery and singing songs to one another.

When someone becomes ill, villagers summon a healer. They offer two chickens, a pig, and three eggs in the patient's house, and outside the house they prepare a dog, a pig, five chickens, and a cup of rice wine as sacrifices. The healer sings magically curative songs and offers up prayers. Elders sing admonitory songs to young people, both to keep village life orderly and to instill tribal identity.

Akha funerals are accompanied by animal sacrifices. The corpse is left for a week in the house. Attaching considerable importance to the souls of the dead, the Akha often offer food to the ancestral spirits who attend the funeral. The ritualist sings a funeral song over and over, including a biography of the deceased and instructions on how to serve the ancestral spirits.

Akha Musical Instruments

The Akha play a three-stringed lute (*döm*), a free-reed mouth organ (*lachi*), and a Jew's harp (*chau*), both during festivals and at leisure. They use the *chau* as a disguiser of the voice to speak songs of love. They also dance. Young girls often sing while dancing in various styles, including skipping or jumping in lines or circles. During some ceremonies

Akha women and girls beat bamboo tubes rhythmically into an overturned pig-feeding trough accompanied by a drum and a gong (Figure 17.2).

The Lisu (Lisaw, Lu-tzu)

The Lisu language belongs to the southern Lolo branch of Tibeto-Burman. The Chinese classify Lisu-speakers according to differences in dress and dialect: Bai Lisu (White Lisu), He Lisu (Black Lisu), and Hua Lisu (Flowery Lisu). The Black Lisu of the Upper Salween River have been independent since the early twentieth century. Today they are concentrated in Yunnan, China; scattered communities live in Shan State (Burma) and northern Thailand. Villages are located on ridges and mountaintops, at elevations ranging from 1,300 to 3,000 meters. Houses are built on piles or directly on the ground. Swidden agriculture and hunting are the most important economic activities. Rice and maize are the staples. Opium poppies are raised by most Lisu, who rank second only to the Hmong as producers of opium.

Figure 17.2
Akha women and girls rhythmically pound bamboo sections on an overturned pig trough to honor village leaders during the swing ceremony. Photo by Paul and Elaine Lewis; used with permission.

The Lisu are animists who practice both the worship of ancestors and exorcism. They believe in a variety of spirits, including spirits of the jungle, the earth, the wind, the field, the crops, and heaven; village guardian spirits; and a lightning demon. Malevolent spirits cause illnesses. In shamanistic rituals (*ne pha*), performers treat illnesses by going into trance, singing, and shaking. The annual spring festival is the high point of the Lisu year. One day during this period is reserved for honoring ancestors with sacrifices of pigs and with visits to graves—a time of drinking and merrymaking, the prime occasion for boys to go courting in neighboring villages.

The Musical Life of the Lisu

All Lisu instrumentalists are men. Young, unmarried men are the most active instrumentalists, and in every village a few are recognized as the most gifted. This reputation depends not so much on technical skill (as long as the musician upholds the community-wide standards of performance) as on the extent of repertoire and ability to play for hours, or even days, during festivals.

Instrumental music has a strict meter and sung music is freely metered. The two repertoires do not mix, though they are sometimes performed side by side at the same functions. Songs are sung by both sexes. Boys and girls sing songs of courtship, not only during New Year's celebrations, but also in everyday life. On these occasions, someone usually plays an instrument nearby. Both dance and music have a religious function to the Lisu. They say that the sounds of instruments and vocalizations please good spirits and prevent disaster.

Figure 17.3
A Lisu male musician plays the lute (*subü*) to accompany his village dance troupe. Photo by Terry E. Miller, 2005.

Lisu
Tibeto-Burman-speaking people living in Thailand, Burma, and China
fulu
Lisu free-reed mouth organ with bamboo pipes and gourd wind chest
subü
Lisu three-stringed, fretted lute

Figure 17.4.
A Lisu instrument maker and musician plays the free-reed mouth organ with gourd windchest (*fulu*). Photo by Terry E. Miller, 2005.

Lisu Musical Instruments

Lisu instruments include a free-reed mouth organ (*fulu*), a flute (*julü*), and a three-stringed long lute (*subü*) (Figures 17.3 and 17.4). The three may play together as an ensemble.

The Karen

Widely distributed throughout the northern parts of Burma, Laos, and Thailand, the Karen number about 3.4 million. They are usually divided into four subgroups, the Sgaw, the P'wo, the Thaungthu (or Pa-o), and the Kayah (Karenni). Linguists accept that the Karen language belongs to the Tibeto-Burman family. Formerly the Karen led a typical tribal life, living in longhouses, cultivating hill rice, and practicing animism. Today, the Karen who live in mountainous districts preserve their traditional customs, but those living in the plains engage in paddy-rice cultivation and have changed their lifestyle from tribal to agricultural. In many areas, the lives of the plains Karen are indistinguishable from those of the Thai peasants with whom they share the plains.

Traditionally the Karen were animists. They believed in a variety of spirits, both good and malevolent. These included spirits of water, earth, rocks, trees, paddies, and swidden fields. Ceremonies of prayer in the paddies and swidden fields were performed several times a year to request spiritual aid in growing rice. Some village leaders acted as shamans, conducting worship and medical treatment and administering the village. Toward the end of the 1800s, missionaries—primarily American Baptists—came from Burma to Karen villages.

After the introduction of Christianity, a group calling itself Christian Karen was organized, and they have renounced animistic worship and the use of opium and alcohol. The missionaries also devised a Karen alphabet, based on Burmese. Buddhism was introduced to the upland Karen from both lowland Karen and the lowland mainstream population. Buddhist Karen are quite devout: they often visit temples and making offerings. On the traditional New Year's festival (*songklan*), they gather at temples and vigorously sing merit-making songs while wearing their best red (adults, boys) or white (girls) clothes.

Figure 17.5
Musical instruments: left, two Karen drums, an Akha drum, bamboo flutes, a Hmong mouth organ; middle, a Lahu Shehleh free-reed gourd mouth organ; right, four similar instruments of the Lahu, the Akha, and the Lisu. Photo by Paul and Elaine Lewis; used with permission.

The Musical Life of the Karen

The Karen have long had a distinctive traditional music, which has played important roles in their lives. At weddings, the elders, invited as guests, sing to newlyweds about how to earn a living and how to preserve Karen traditional culture. During funerals, elders sing laments and walk around the coffin for three days and nights. After that, young boys and girls alternately sing courtship songs—a custom that may have arisen from a wish to regenerate the soul of the deceased. The Karen have an abundance of amatory songs: a young boy sings in the evening underneath his sweetheart's window, or each sings to the other while working in a rice field.

The Karen have an especially large collection of legends, whose performance is accompanied by the traditional harp (*tünak*). Other traditional songs include New Year's songs, cradle songs, children's songs, admonitory songs, house-building songs, and drinking songs. After 1945, American popular music, including jazz and rock, entered Karen villages through Thailand.

> **Karen**
> Tibeto-Burman-speaking people living primarily in upland Burma and northwest

Figure 17.6
Chordophones: top, used by the Karen; bottom, used by the Lisu, the Lahu, and sometimes the Akha. Photo by Paul and Elaine Lewis; used with permission.

Karen Musical Instruments

Besides the harp the Karen play a buffalo horn (*kui*), a bronze drum (*mahoratuk*), a bamboo tube zither (*pap law*), and a three-stringed lute (*tha*). They play the buffalo horn and the bronze drum for religious occasions. Other instruments include a goblet-shaped drum, a gong, and cymbals, all of Thai origin (Figures 17.5 and 17.6). Around 1900, Christian missionaries from Burma

set up schools in Karen villages and taught gospel songs and other Western religious music (which they call chant). The Karen succeeded in playing gospel songs and composing new ones.

THE AUSTROASIATIC (MON-KHMER) LANGUAGE FAMILY

The Kmhmu (Kammu, Khmu, Khamu)

The Kmhmu are the largest of the Mon-Khmer groups in northern Laos; they also dwell in northern Thailand and northern Vietnam. The Kmhmu language belongs to the Kmhmu-ic branch of the northern Mon-Khmer family. Estimates of Kmhmu population in northern Laos are around 400,000, in Thailand between 5,000 and 50,000, and in Vietnam, 32,000. Most Kmhmu living in Thailand have become assimilated into the prevailing national culture. Since Mon-Khmer-speakers preceded the Lao in Laos, the ethnic Lao call the Kmhmu their older brothers.

Kmhmu houses are often built on pilings on mountainsides, at elevations of around 1 kilometer. The Kmhmu engage in slash-and-burn agriculture, and their staple is rice. Permanent wet-rice cultivation techniques, where they are used, are borrowed from the Lao, because many Kmhmu work for Lao farmers as hired laborers. Buffaloes are highly valued both for food and for sacrifices, but few Kmhmu can afford them. The Kmhmu are skilled weavers of baskets and trays, which they trade through Lao merchants.

The traditional Kmhmu system of beliefs is animistic. It deals with spirits of the village, the jungle, mountains, rocks, the sun, and water. When there is an illness, a shaman determines which spirit is causing it, and prescribes the necessary sacrifices; he also takes part in other village ceremonies.

The Musical Life of the Kmhmu

Music has an important role in Kmhmu ceremonies. Shamans ritually call on ancestral spirits and spirits of water, rice, and other items. By chanting and playing the gong, they send off the spirit of a dead person. They sing songs and play musical instruments in ceremonies for weddings, building new houses, harvests, and the New Year. When the Kmhmu entertain guests, they gather in their houses, drink homemade grain alcohol from jars, sing welcoming songs, and play musical instruments. During such times of amusement, young men and women sing long amatory songs in alternation; they usually express affection indirectly, but on such occasions choose their life partners. The Kmhmu also sing lowland-derived popular songs.

Kmhmu Musical Instruments

Kmhmu musical instruments are two bamboo flutes (*pii, tot*), a free-reed raft mouth organ (*khen*), a lute (*saw*), a Jew's harp, a pair of bamboo beaters (*klt*), a clapper (*taaw taaw*), a gong, and a bronze drum. The flutes are of Kmhmu origin, but the *khen* was adapted from the lowland Lao people. The bronze drum is used in ceremonies, especially for summoning rain.

The Shan (Taiyai, Dai [China])

The term *Shan* is Burmese for Tai-speakers in eastern Burma, but related people live in northern Thailand and southern China, where they are called Taiyai and Dai, respectively. The Shan are primarily concentrated in Burma's Shan State, where they are strongly Burmanized, though Tai speech, Buddhist religion, and a unique musical style make the Shan distinctive.

Shan settlements tend to be permanent. Villages are located in valleys or on pockets of level land in the hills. The houses, built almost entirely of bamboo, are raised as high as three meters off the ground. At one end of the village, pagodas, monasteries, shrines, and rest houses, all of which are essential to the religious life of the community, are clustered together. The Shan engage primarily in wet-rice cultivation.

The Shan are predominantly Theravada Buddhists. Between the ages of ten and twelve, boys enter a monastery for a short time, serving the monks and learning from them the precepts of Buddhism. With Buddhism, the Shan believe in the existence of spirits, supernatural forces, omens, and the significance of dreams. At about age fourteen, boys are decorated by a specialist in tattooing. This is regarded as a sign of manhood. Girls ignore as potential spouses any boys who have not been tattooed.

The Musical Life of the Shan

Shan ensemble music is nearly as complex as that of lowland Southeast Asian peoples. There are three major Shan ensembles—for Buddhist ceremonies, dramas, and entertainment.

The Shan perform Buddhist music in Buddhist ceremonies, especially on the traditional New Year (*songklan*). Villagers in the temple often perform Buddhist music. The Shan often sing Buddhist songs accompanied by the ceremonial ensemble, consisting of a large two-headed drum (*khong*), three sizes of pitched gongs (*mong*), and cymbals (*chap*).

The Shan also have a repertoire of artistic dramas (*yikay*), which resemble the Thai *lakhawm* more than they do its namesake, the Thai *li-ke*. These dramas combine dancing, singing, and instrumental music. Sometimes a performance continues throughout a day and a night. The ensemble for the drama consists of a four-stringed lute, a three-stringed lute, a violin, a flute, a two-headed drum, and cymbals.

The ensemble for leisure music performs the most refined music of the Shan. This ensemble consists of a xylophone (*ranat thum*), a violin, a drum (*taphon*), a tuned drum set (*patt waiñ*), cymbals (*chap*), a fiddle (*toro*), and a small, stick-beaten wooden block (*sengkok*). This ensemble has been influenced by the Burmese *hsaiñwaiñ* and the *piphat* and *mahori* of the central Thai.

The Shan also have songs for social occasions, including amatory songs, New Year's songs, rice-planting songs, harvest songs, fishing songs, visiting songs, drinking songs, and cradle songs. There are, however, no customary songs for funerals.

The Yao (Mian, Man)

The widely used linguistic term *Miao-Yao* is problematic, since both designations are pejorative terms assigned by outsiders. Though officially known as *Yao*, a Chinese term (meaning "dog" or "savage"), these people refer to themselves as Mian or Iu Mian (People). In Laos and Vietnam, they are called Man, also meaning "people." The Yao language belongs to the Miao-Yao family. They have no indigenous script, but some Yao use Chinese characters. The Yao prefer to locate along streams, at heights of about 1 kilometer. Their houses are large, built directly on the ground. They engage in slash-and-burn agriculture. They also engage in commercial crafts such as embroidery and silversmithing.

The Yao are animists, who place great importance on reverence for ancestors. A priest (*mo kung*), conducts spirit-related ceremonies. His power lies in his knowledge of incantations taken from books written in adaptations of Chinese characters. The coming-of-age ceremony (*gua deng*), ancestral worship (*on tsau, ho nian*), and the rite of prayer for everlasting life and immortality (*zuddan*) are important Yao rites, some of which have been influenced by Chinese Taoism.

The Musical Life of the Yao

The Yao sometimes play music for entertainment, but most of their music is closely related to important events of human life. Ceremonial music, performed for weddings, funerals, and worship of ancestors, has a particularly important role.

Young guest musicians play congratulatory music on an ensemble of drums, cymbals, gongs, and an oboe (*yat*) during a wedding, and other guests sing nuptial songs. At a funeral, the ritualist plays a free-reed buffalo-horn aerophone before the coffin is carried from the house; then he continues the service by reciting funeral songs and Buddhist sutras.

At harvest ceremonies, ritualists hold shamanistic services. They call ancestral spirits, go into trance, and dance while holding live chickens with both hands, accompanied by drums, gongs, and cymbals. They groan a descending melody. The pace of their dancing accelerates; they become possessed and begin shouting. After sacrificing chickens and offering the blood to spirits, they dance again, carrying the dead chickens and communicating with the spirits. This kind of shamanistic worship appears in many kinds of ancestral ceremonies.

At New Year's festivals, villagers dress up, drink liquor, sing, and dance, and the most important event is the singing of the narrative song "Banko," about the Yao ancestral dog—a story that helps keep the identity of the Yao alive.

The Yao encourage premarital sex. A girl sings amatory songs beside her lover's house at night. When the boy comes out, they go to a hidden place, sing alternately, and if both agree, sleep in the same bed.

The Hmong

Hmong words are spelled here in the Roman Popular Alphabet (RPA). Final consonants indicate the tone of the word and are thus not pronounced the way they look to most

Hmong
Formerly called Miao, a Sino-Tibetan group living in Thailand, Laos, Vietnam, and China
swidden
Shifting cultivated field on land cleared of forest
qeej
Hmong free-reed mouth organ with six bamboo pipes and elongated wind chest
ncas
Hmong Jew's harp, made of metal
raj nplaim
Hmong free-reed pipe with finger holes
animism
Indigenous religion based on belief in spirits
ua neeb
Hmong shaman ceremony accompanied by gong, sistrum, and rattle

readers. Double vowels indicate nasalization. Hence, *qeej* is pronounced something like /kaeŋ/, with a falling tone. A *b* denotes a high-level tone; a *j,* high-falling; a *v,* mid-rising; an N-dash (–), midlevel; an *s,* lower midlevel; a *g,* low-breathy; an *m,* low-glottalized; a *d,* low-rising.

Hmong (Mong, Hmoob, Moob) is the name of certain swidden agriculturalists in the higher elevations (900 to 1,500 meters) of northern Vietnam, Laos, and Thailand. They are also known in Western literature as Meo and Miao, an adaptation from *miao* "sprouts," the pejorative Chinese name for non-Chinese peoples of southern and southwestern China, who number about 6 million. The Chinese distinguish the Hmong-Miao according to the predominant color of their dress: Bai Miao (White), Hei Miao (Black), Hong Miao (Red), Hua Miao (Flowery), and Qing Miao (Blue). The Hmong build their houses on the ground and practice shifting cultivation; some have begun cultivating irrigated paddies. Their staples are rice and maize.

The Hmong of Southeast Asia first came from Guizhou to Vietnam in the mid-1700s, when, in successive waves, they fled Chinese persecution. By 1900, between forty thousand and sixty thousand had emigrated, mainly from Guizhou, Sichuan, Guangxi, and Yunnan provinces, settling in the highlands of Vietnam and Laos, with a few thousand reaching Thailand. After the Pathet Lao victory in 1975, many thousands of these fled to refugee camps along the Thai-Lao border. About one hundred thousand have since resettled in Australia, Canada, France, and the United States.

Figure 17.7
During a New Year's celebration, two men play Hmong mouth organs (*qeej*). The White Hmong village of Long Lan, Luang Prabang District, Laos. Photo by Amy Catlin, 1989.

Hmong Musical Instruments

The *qeej* consists of a wooden wind chest with a long tapering neck ending in a mouth hole. The wooden section is made from two identical pieces of mahogany, bound together with straps. The six bamboo tubes are variously curving or straight; they vary in length about two meters. Each has a single hole for fingering above the wind chest and a metal free reed over a hole in the pipe enclosed within the wind chest. For extra volume, the lowest tube, the thickest and shortest one, often contains two or three reeds. The tubes are inserted vertically through the wind chest. When the player exhales or inhales and covers one or more holes for fingering, eddies at the edge of the vibrating reed create a standing wave in the tube, and a musical tone is heard (Figures 17.7, 17.8).

There are two genres of *qeej* compositions:

Figure 17.8
The named parts of the Hmong mouth organ (*qeej*). Courtesy of John Michael Kohler Arts Center.

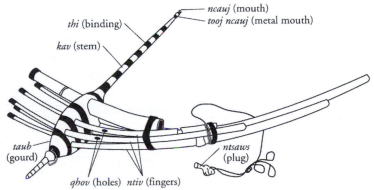

ncauj (mouth)
tooj ncauj (metal mouth)
thi (binding)
kav (stem)
taub (gourd)
ntsaws (plug)
qhov (holes) *ntiv* (fingers)

texted and textless. Both genres are played successively in rituals, including funerals, ancestral rites, offerings to vital spirits, sacrifices to the drum, and marriages. When playing around or under the framework for the drum, the player makes three turns counterclockwise to represent the voyage in search of the vital spirit, three turns in place to disorient the spirit so it does not invade the material world, three turns clockwise for the return voyage, and three turns in place again.

The Hmong maintain a close relationship between speech and music. The instrument most capable of conveying the vowels and consonants of Hmong speech is the Jew's harp (*ncas*) (Figure 17.9). It is also quiet, so the player and any listeners must be close together, and others cannot easily eavesdrop. The *ncas* is made of brass, often protected in a scrimshaw case adorned with beads, coins, and colorful threads. Made of a single sheet of brass, whose thickness varies from handle to tip, the blade often thins to less than a millimeter. The tongue and the frame are separated by a hairline incision, which typically outlines three points (Figure 17.10).

The free-reed pipe (*raj nplaim*) may also be used as an instrument of courting. It is not capable of conveying vowels and consonants, but the player always uses sung poetry for the source of the melody, and frequently both player and listener believe that the text has been understood from the melody alone. The pipe resembles a single *qeej* pipe, but with additional holes for fingering (Figure 17.11). Other secular instruments include a fipple flute (*raj pus li*) and a two-stringed bowed fiddle (*xi xov*), both played for courting.

Hmong Ritual Music

Most Hmong are animists. They revere ancestors and believe that spirits (looking and behaving like human beings) inhabit trees, rocks, and fields. Both male and female shamans cure illnesses, practice divining, and conduct exorcisms. Chinese culture has strongly influenced Hmong material culture and religious beliefs. Consequently, some Hmong ceremonies (such as the Quest of the souls) mix an archaic Hmong character with elements of Chinese Taoism. Some Hmong have converted to Christianity.

A cultural feature is the rite conducted as if the shaman were on horseback, riding

Figure 17.9
May Seha, a Blue Hmong singer, holds a Jew's harp (*ncas*). Chiangmai, Thailand. Photo by Amy Catlin, 1980.

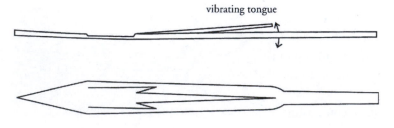

vibrating tongue

Figure 17.10
Front and side views of the Hmong Jew's harp (*ncas*). Courtesy of John Michael Kohler Arts Center.

through the cosmos, accompanied by the sounds of a gong, a sistrum, and a rattle. The shaman sits facing the altar on a flexible four-legged bench, which serves as his horse; the shaman's journey in trance is conducted to cure sickness by fighting with a sword the evil spirits the shaman hunts down in the cosmos. While he shakes his sistrum (held in his right hand like the horse's reins, and sounding the cadence of a gallop), his helper strikes the gong. The ring rattle held on the shaman's left index finger serves as the horse's bell. A blade protruding from the sistrum cuts invisible connections between spirits and pathways to death. All three musical instruments are festooned with strips of red cloth to frighten evil spirits (Figure 17.12). The shaman liberally punctuates his chants with sounds like *brrr-brrr-brrr*, with tongue trilling in imitation of a horse's whinny.

Funerals

At Hmong funerals, the corpse lies on a bier. Facing the body, one musician plays the *qeej* and another beats a drum. A lamenter stands to one side of the body, and the spouse of the dead person (if living) to the other; the singer sings loudly, with a descending melody, while the spouse sobs. A priest prays to the dead soul. After the ceremony, the guests form a procession and, accompanied by solemn music, carry the corpse to a nearby mountain.

Throughout the funeral, the six-tubed free-reed mouth organ portrays liturgical texts in a speech-surrogate system. Four of the pipes represent the eight-word tones. The other two pipes add drones and harmony. The texts, played and danced by the musician-liturgist using circular and spiral movements to confuse evil spirits, instruct the soul in its ascent through the stages of heaven and back again to the body before burial. These texts are sung first by a singer and then reproduced by the player of the *qeej*, who, during some periods, must entertain the soul of the deceased to keep it from wandering away. After guiding the soul for three days and nights, the musicians release it to find its way to heaven.

Figiure 17.11
A Hmong player of the free-reed pipe with finger holes. Photo by Terry E. Miller.

Figure 17.12
While an assistant holds a gong (*doua neeb*), the shaman Ka Pao Her plays a sistrum (*txia neeb*) and a rattle (*tsu neeb*). Khek Noy, Thailand. Photo by Amy Catlin, 1984.

A drum is also used for the funeral and other ritual occasions. One type, destroyed after the ceremony, is also used when a cow is sacrificed. It is placed either at the central column of the house or according to other clan directives. It must be placed high enough for people to pass under; the player uses two drumsticks while standing on a bench. The other, a permanent drum to protect the house, must be nourished every morning. At New Year's, a chicken must be sacrificed to it. Its spirit is usually considered to be masculine, and that of the *qeej*, feminine.

Courtship and Nuptials

Ritual music is designed to communicate with the world of the spirits, but secular music seeks to express thoughts and feelings that transcend the bounds of normal discourse among the living. Like sacred music, Hmong secular music derives largely from speech and conceptual thought, whether sung or played on instruments. Most of its subjects concern love and its manifestations.

The most important context for singing takes place during the courtship games of the New Year's festival. This begins as early as 13 December or as late as 11 January, according to the lunar calendar. During the festival rows of unmarried boys and girls throw courtship balls while singing.

REFERENCE

Lewis, Paul, and Elaine Lewis. 1984. *Peoples of the Golden Triangle: Six Tribes in Thailand*. London: Thames and Hudson.

The Indigenous Peoples (Orang Asli) of the Malay Peninsula

Marina Roseman, partly based on a manuscript
by Hans Oesch as translated by J. O'Connell

Lifestyle and Its Implications for Musical Culture
Animist Religious Philosophy and Shamanistic Practice
Timbre as a Significant Musical Parameter
Acculturated Music of the Orang Melayu Asli

Three tribal groupings on the Malay Peninsula—the Semang, the Senoi, and the Orang Melayu Asli—are known collectively by the generic term *Orang Asli* (Original People). They live in the tropical forest, on the mangrove coast, and in other hinterland and urban areas of the Malayan Peninsula, in western Malaysia.

One way the Orang Asli can be differentiated from one another is by their traditional lifestyles. The Semang are mostly hunters who live in impermanent constructions. The Senoi, as shifting cultivators, are semisedentary and practice some cultivation in addition to gathering fruits, hunting, and fishing. The Orang Melayu Asli intermarried to a greater degree with Austronesian-speaking maritime peoples now known as Malays, who arrived on the peninsula about 2000 B.C.E. They live in permanent housing and are cultivators. The Orang Melayu Asli are also known as Proto-Malays or Aboriginal Malays. These peoples share a close linguistic affiliation with Malays. The Austroasiatic languages of the Semang and the Senoi are incomprehensible to most Malay-speakers. Another way the Orang Asli groups have been distinguished from one another is by their physical attributes. The Semang (also known as Negritos, derived from the word for "small dark person") are often darker-skinned and smaller in stature with thick, curly hair. The Senoi are typified by both curly-haired and straight-haired individuals with darker or lighter brown-toned skin and small stature. The Orang Melayu Asli share more biological attributes with the Malays, given the greater degree of intermarriage among them.

Within the context of the contemporary Malaysian nation, the more than 84,000 Orang Asli make up less than 1 percent of the current national population of about 24.8 million (2007). The Temiar and the Semai, both of the Senoi ethnic division, constitute the two largest Orang Asli linguistic groups.

LIFESTYLE AND ITS IMPLICATIONS FOR MUSICAL CULTURE

Each group's technology and lifestyle has implications in the dimensions of musical form, performance practice, and instrument manufacture. Among the Semang, who traditionally had no stable dwellings, musical instruments are always disposable. When the impulse or necessity for the instrumental making of music arises, a Semang may seek out available bamboo from which she or he fashions an instrument, plays it, and then discards it; instruments are thus designed to be both easily made and expendable. The tube zither (*kərantuŋ*) cannot be played after a short period of use. Its three strings easily become worn and extracted. Cut out of the bamboo's epiderm, the strings pass over a bridge and continue to the tube's end, where they split and pass underneath. These production techniques produce a distinctive, richly overtoned and "noisy" timbre. Bamboo tube stampers, melodic and percussive instruments played in pairs, serve as markers of time in Semang and Senoi rituals. Their lengths, with implications for pitch, are unequal.

The Senoi are semisedentary settlers. They live in raised wood, bamboo, and thatch homes, in which they make and store their musical instruments. Every two to five years Senoi would move their settlements of twenty-five to one hundred people nearer to fertile areas, leaving fallow fields to regenerate from surrounding forest seed and growth.

The Senoi *kərab* is a two-stringed chordophone (Figure 18.1). Its strings are made of gut threads or jungle vines, not (as with Semang idiophones) bamboo bark. The strings are

Figure 18.1
Senoi tube zithers: (*left*), five instruments of the *kərantuŋ*, an idiophone; (*right*), the *kərab*, a chordophone. Photo by Hans Oesch, 1963.

threaded through drilled holes and knotted underneath. On the upper side, they are tied in a loop around a plank that allows the possibility of individual and precise tuning, often in fourths.

Temiar mediums carefully execute the technical design of the Senoi tube zither *kərantuŋ* (Figure 18.2). The cavities at the ends of the bamboo tube contain seven idiochordal strings, held in place by two nodes at each end and further fastened with rattan vines. This instrument, used for shamanistic purposes, may last for longer than a month, on account of its sturdy construction and infrequent use. In the middle of the tube are two rectangular holes; two parallel strings lie over these, wedged in place by iron (visible in Figure 18.2 by the left side of the first finger of the player's left hand). The lower of the tube's two nodes is closed, and four gaps are bored in the upper portion. The seated shaman, keeping the tube stable between his left palm and knees, plucks three of the free strings with the thumb and first finger of his left hand. He hits the upper extremity of the tube in a quick, regular pattern with a cupped right hand. This action causes vibrations in the body of the *kərantuŋ* and the strings, and displaces the column of air within the tubes. The energy of hitting the tube is transmitted through iron wedges holding the strings, resulting in complexly textured, "noisy" vibrations of the four unplucked strings.

The musical instruments of the Orang Melayu Asli, who have maintained consistently closer contact with the Malay and Chinese inhabitants of the Malayan Peninsula, cover a wide variety, from the simpler thigh xylophone (*kongkong*) to the modern violin. Their tube zithers, strung with iron wires, are probably copied from models derived from Sumatra.

More men than women play the ceremonial role of initial singer (medium) in the singing and trance-dancing ceremonies (*gənabag, pəhnɔɔh*) that form the core of the Temiar musical repertoire. Initial singers play this performance role primarily by virtue of having received a song during their dreams from the animated spirits of the Temiar social or physical environment—from trees, birds, riverine rapids, and other human beings of their forest environment, and from more recently arriving peoples and commodities from outside the forest: airplanes, wristwatches, canned sardines. Temiar explain that men receive songs more often than women because of their differential relationship to the environment. As hunters, men have access to the blowpipe. They traverse long distances in smaller, quieter groups, and are thus more inclined to have daily experiences with the forest environment that might lead later to dream encounters with the spirits of that environment. Women, as gatherers working in larger, noisier groups with children in tow, have a smaller geographical range and a less intimate relationship with the forest; they are thus less likely, though not unable, to receive songs from the animated environment (Figure 18.3).

Figure 18.2
Technique of playing a Temiar Senoi *kərantuŋ*, an idiochord tube zither. Photo by Hans Oesch, 1963.

Figure 18.3
During a singing and trance-dancing ceremony, Senoi Temiar women and girls play pairs of short (female) and long (male) bamboo stamping tubes and sing choral responses in interactive overlap with a male shaman, who sings his spirit guide's dream song. Photo by Marina Roseman, 1981.

medium
Tranced ritualist who is possessed by visiting spirits
shaman
Ritualist who, in trance, travels to the land of the spirits to obtain knowledge
hala?
The Semang shaman, called halaa? by the Temiar
cenoi
Temiar term for rays of light that bear spiritual substances throughout the universe
pano'
Temiar ceremonial genre in which spirits are contacted

As indicated in the discussion of the Senoi Temiar dream-song ceremony above, Orang Asli traditionally practice animistic religions based on belief in the potential for animated soul or personhood, not only in humans, but also in animals, plants, and all other entities. Through magical practices, they try to influence, soothe, and engage the spirits of these entities to render them serviceable to humankind. Performing on musical instruments plays an important role in calling spiritual substances from their natural habitat.

A prerequisite for instrumental invocation and entreaty of these spiritual substances among some Orang Asli groups is the perceived existence of living tonalities, with an array of distinct timbral consistencies: the souls of each wild animal, plant, rock, or the earth contain a sound characterized by distinct timbres, tonal rows, melodic contours, vocal ornamentations, rhythms, and other formal musical parameters.

Oesch's research indicates that the function of the instrumental playing differs for Semang and Senoi. Among some Semang groups, the nose flute (*salet, nabad*), usually of three holes, but sometimes of two to seven, is played for its utility in magical invocation (Figure 18.4). In the performance of this flute, the nose emits air derived directly from the human soul and uncontaminated by contact with the mouth. The Senoi Temiar say they obtained their nose flutes from the neighboring Senoi Semai, and use the instrument in courtship.

Figure 18.4
A Senoi Temiar woman. living on the upper Nenggiri River in Kelantan plays a nose flute. Photo by Hans Oesch, 1963.

Built on an anhemitonic scale, the mouth-blown transverse flute may be played when a traveler has to wade through a river or slash through underbrush. Motifs played on the Jew's harp may also influence those entities. Senoi construct melodic motifs on Jew's harp and tube zither that iconically replicate the human and forest soundscape—birdsongs and the sounds of walking in the forest or clearing fields.

The tube zither is usually played by women (Figure 18.5). Its sounds invoke all kinds of actions, environments, and beings, including those that might endanger the forest traveler: if a man works during the day in the jungle or operates fish traps in the rivers, a Senoi woman back home in the village may play it to protect him in his travels. Before some Senoi healers administer medicinal substances, such as roots, leaves, or bark, they may use its sound to invoke and activate the spirit of that vegetation.

Oesch finds that the appropriate timbre must be replicated to enable the medication to work.

Shamanism or mediumship, a linchpin of Orang Asli life, is a ritual technique fostering participatory relationships between humans and other entities. Singing and trance-dancing ceremonies directed toward such purposes are led by a medium and require musical and choreographic participation by community members of both genders. Southeast Asian shamanism joins religious, magical, musical, ecological, and medical components. Trance is differentially experienced by members of various Orang Asli groups and can take shape either as the soul's journey to the spiritual world, the spirit's visitation to the human realm, or a dialectical conjunction of the two. During such a ritual, the shaman gains supernatural knowledge, exorcises malevolent spiritual substances, asks for compassion, and requests assistance for the community and others.

Figure 18.5
A Senoi Temiar woman living upriver on the Berok River in Kelantan plays a tube zither. The song she is playing can be heard on *Dream Songs and Healing Sounds: In the Rainforest of Malaysia* (Roseman 1995, band 5). Photo by Marina Roseman, 1982.

Music is essential to shamanistic activities of all Orang Asli. Imbued with knowledge and power transmitted through a spirit guide's musical gifts, the medium sucks malevolent spiritual substances out of a sick person's body, or returns lost soul components to the patient during rituals of healing (Roseman 1990, 1991, 1996). The medical function of the medium may also involve administering to patients outside the context of singing and trance-dancing rituals. Healing rituals also contain preventive therapeutic functions, as participants join in harmonious, yet paradoxically dangerous, relations with their social and spiritual universe.

Semang Animism and Musical Shamanism

Schebesta (1928) and Oesch (1977) tell us that *cenoi* are small, colorful rays of light—often personified in male or female form—that bear spiritual substances throughout the universe. They connect earth and the human realm with the spiritual world. The shaman initiates ritual contact through contact with personified *cenoi* spirit guides; with their friendly assistance, a Jahai shaman traces the route for the human soul's journey to the spiritual world. The singing medium's soul leaves his body, which lies quivering on the ground, goes on its journeys, and returns to him well after fifteen minutes. By then, the spirit guide will have contacted the upper earthly powers, enabling the shaman to relay to his community the transcendental knowledge gained during the ritual journey. While in a trance, the shaman is a conduit for the *cenoi,* and the force of his religious activities stems from them. Without the *cenoi,* his dialogue with the spiritual realm during the evening ritual would not be possible, for they aid in his ceremonial transformation. In this space of transformation, he can answer questions, heal, and foretell future events.

The predominant *cenoi* among the Semang is the tiger, who arrives in the specially built hut during Semang musical spirit séances. Cross-influences among Orang Asli groups are apparent in the importance the Senoi Temiar, as well, and are placed on the tiger spirit guide and his musico-ceremonial genre, termed *panoh* or *mamug*. The awe in which tiger shamanism is held is exhibited in the practice of extinguishing all sources of light (including fires in hearths, cigarettes, and kerosene lanterns) when a tiger spirit guide sings through Temiar mediums. A small hut (*panoh, paleey*) similar to those constructed by the Semang Jahai may be constructed in the ceremonial space using bertam fronds.

Mediums, given the leeway of individual revelation in this relatively egalitarian society, dream-compose their songs in response to personal and historical experiences. Operating within larger stylistic constraints, mediums innovate musically, choreographically, and in the construction of leaf and flower ornaments associated with particular genres according to the instructions received during dreams from their spirit guides (Roseman 1994). Temiar musico-choreographic genres may thus be associated with specific geographical locations, historical periods, and individual dream-song composers (see Figures 18.4 and 18.5).

Temiar musical genres include those received from tigers (*mamug, panoh*); mountains, rivers, and flowers (*taŋgəəy*); blossoming fruit trees (*pɛnhəəy, noŋ tahun, taŋgəəy*); spirits of deceased humans (*cincɛm*), the sap of the *ipoh* tree (*gamok*), lightning (*?pɛŋkuu?*), and other forest sources. The genres *səlombaŋ* (dragon of the water) and *pəhnɔɔh gɔb* (Malay-style trance ceremony) are associated with Malays and Chinese; other songs and genres have been received from "outforester" peoples and things.

Songs received from spirits during dreams are sung by Senoi Temiar mediums during nighttime, housebound ceremonial events termed *gənabag* "singing" if the session is not intended to invoke the spirits' presence, and *gənabag pəhnɔɔh* "singing and trance-dancing ceremony with leaf and flower ornaments" if it is. Singing and trance-dancing ceremonies may be held to celebrate visitors' arrival or impending departure; to punctuate the agricultural cycle of clearing, planting, and harvesting rice swiddens; to effect healing or prevent illness; for the joy of gathering community members and spirits; to end a period of mourning; or to mark points within the fruiting season (i.e., end of rains, onset of new foliage, blossoms, fruiting, and harvest).

Mediums, who may be male or female, are joined by an interactive choral response usually performed by women, though both genders join in the chorus that initiates the ceremony to conclude a mourning period. Members of the chorus beat pairs of tube stampers against a log (Figure 18.3); their duple rhythms of alternating high and low pitches are accentuated and subdivided by the rhythms of single-headed drums (*batak, bərano?*) played by men or women.

Senoi Temiar Singers and Healers in a Modern World

In dream-song compositions and performances, Temiar situate themselves in relation to the forest around them and increasingly with concepts, commodities, and persons from outside the forest. Orang Asli have long engaged with peoples and things from beyond the forest: Temiar call themselves the people of the forest distinguishing themselves from more recently arriving foreign out-foresters. Temiar dream songs record their interactions with outsiders, among whom are Malays, British colonials, Chinese and Tamil workers brought to work British mines and plantations, Japanese occupying Malaya during World War II, anthropologists of varied descent, and Malays in their postindependence roles as members of the mainstream Islamic population and as governmental administrators.

TIMBRE AS A SIGNIFICANT MUSICAL PARAMETER

Customarily melody and rhythm are the most important musical traits, but in the magical effectiveness of Orang Asli music, others are also decisive. In particular, timbre is a significant parameter, both in the stylistic definition of genres, and in the effectiveness of music upon the world as the Temiar configure it.

According to the Temiar *halaa*? tone color is one of the most important parameters manipulated when a man plays the tube zither (*kərantuŋ*) as an instrument of animistic conjuration. For healing, he plays it to address the soul substances of the medicines and agents of illness and to give voice to his spirit guides. While plucking its strings, he beats its body, creating a sound that contains an especially great amount of noise.

In the role of healer, a shaman plays his *kərantuŋ* for varying amounts of time, knowing how long he has to perform to interact with agents of illness and spiritual helpers. Orang Asli shamans believe they do not play their instruments so much as they enable the instruments to speak; when they manipulate their instruments, they activate spirits' voices.

Spectral analyses of vocal production show the significance of timbre in stylistic differentiation of Temiar spirit-song genres For example, compositions in the genre *cincɛm*, received in dreams from the spirits of people who have died, are noted for their vocal icons of crying—sob breaks, vibrato—incorporated into the vocal delivery and melodic structure. As with shamans' instrumental techniques, a spirit song when performed ceases to be considered the shaman's voice, but becomes the voice of the spirit who bestowed it. Calling up that spirit by envoicing its musical gift to the accompaniment of one-headed wooden drums (*bəranɔ?, batak*) and bamboo tube stampers (*gɔh*), a shaman becomes endowed with the spirit's long-range vision, extensive knowledge, and powers of healing.

timbre
The quality or character of a musical sound

ACCULTURATED MUSIC OF THE ORANG MELAYU ASLI

Before the 1940s, the Semang and Senoi lived in relative isolation from the lowland court, colonial, and national cultures. Traders and missionaries operated at the headwaters of major rivers but rarely entered the mountainous regions at the source of the Nenggiri and Perak rivers. The Orang Melayu Asli, dwelling in villages at the edge of the forest or in mangrove swamps along the coast, historically maintained a greater degree of interactive relations with the village-dwelling and city-dwelling Malays and Chinese.

A feeling of inferiority among the Orang Melayu Asli persists and is stronger than ever, especially since World War II, when police stations and military forts were built in the regions of their settlements. The government in Kuala Lumpur regularly sends administrators from the Jabatan Hal Ehwal Orang Asli (Department of Orang Asli Affairs), schoolteachers, agricultural specialists, medical doctors, veterinary personnel, and Islamic religious specialists into the country. Although some developmental strategies take Orang Asli interests into account, many governmental projects are rhetorical screens for the appropriation of the forest and for religious evangelism. Clearly, indigenous Orang Asli culture and property rights are threatened, and in some places the authority of village leaders and shamans has been weakened by Malay governmental administration. Pan-aboriginal grassroots political organizations and an Orang Asli daily broadcast of news, interviews, and music have helped forge a growing pantribal consciousness and pride among the linguistic and ethnic divisions.

Many Orang Melayu Asli are still dedicated to shamanism and animism, but others have largely been Islamized. The clash of indigenous cultural traditions with those of Malays and Chinese, and the clash between rural and urban cultures generally, have had serious repercussions, even to the extent of having negative effects on the morality and health of the Aboriginal Malay population. In some regions, Orang Asli musical culture has lost its traditional basis, but in more isolated areas, animism and shamanism (and their accompanying musics) continue to be practiced. Musical rituals held in the evening are often directed toward evicting negative spirits and magically healing illnesses.

Many songs of past rituals are but dimly remembered. Among the Temuan, Oesch recorded a song of the *palong* genre, traditionally a shamanistic call-and-response song ceremonially performed for the growing of fruit during the fruit-harvest season. In 1963, however, it was performed by one male singer and two female singers in a social context—as a song of love (Oesch 1977, band 9). That song's transformation from a religious function to the context of courtship illustrates the depth of change in Orang Asli musical culture.

In isolated regions, the Aboriginal Malays still summon spirits using instruments, including the large tube zither *kərantuŋ* strung with metal strings (among the Jakun); the Jew's harp; the horizontal flute *buhbut* (among the Temuan), and the thigh xylophone *kongkong* (among the Temuan). To play the *kongkong,* each of two seated women lays two pieces of hardwood about 61 centimeters long on her thighs so the points of contact correspond to the nodal points of vibration in the wood. The four pieces of wood are cut ideally to produce four tones of the anhemitonic scale when struck with two coarse mallets (*penengkoh*).

The *kongkong* also sometimes accompanies dance-songs performed to encourage abundance while the Temuan plant and harvest rice; this usage may be the result of acculturation, with the *kongkong* replacing tube stampers. In its construction and manner of playing, the *kongkong* harks back to wooden xylophones commonly found in Sumatra and elsewhere in insular and mainland Southeast Asia. An adoption influenced by northern Sumatran musical culture is the small, conical aerophones, the *serunai* (oboe) of the Semelai, which instrumentally performs sorrowful songs (*menangis* "to cry"). Orang Melayu Asli also integrate violins into musical performances, following Malay adaptations of the violin within instrumental ensembles to accompany vocal music and dance in social contexts.

REFERENCES

Oesch, Hans. 1977. *The Protomalayans of Malacca*. Bärenreiter Musicaphon BM 30 L 2563. LP disk.

Roseman, Marina. 1990. "Head, Heart, Odor and Shadow: The Structure of the Self, Ritual Performance and the Emotional World." *Ethos* 18(3):227–250.

———. 1991. *Healing Sounds from the Malaysian Rainforest*. Berkeley: University of California Press.

———. 1994. "Les chants de rêve: des frontièrs mouvantes dans le monde temiar." *Anthropologie et Sociétés* 18(2):121–144.

———. 1995. *Dream Songs and Healing Sounds in the Rainforests of Malaysia*. Smithsonian Folkways SF CD 40417. Compact disc.

———. 1996. "'Pure Products Go Crazy': Rainforest Healing in a Nation-State." In *The Performance of Healing*, ed. Carol Laderman and Marina Roseman, 233–269. New York: Routledge.

Schebesta, Paul. 1928. *Among the Forest Dwarfs of Malaya*, trans. Arthur Chambers. London: Hutchinson.

The Lowland Chăm

Phong T. Nguyễn

The Kingdom of Champa once ruled much of the coast of Vietnam from Da Nang south. The Cham are a Malay people who likely came to coastal Vietnam from Java around 200 C.E., bringing Hinduism (in the form called Shaioita Brahmanism) and Mahayana Buddhism. Over time, the Vietnamese kingdom expanded southward, gradually conquering Champa until its demise in 1471. All that remains of the former glory of Champa are the ruins of great temples. Today, the Cham constitute distinct lowland minorities along the Tonle Sap in Cambodia and in the Chau Doc area of Vietnam. Their total population in 1988 was estimated to be 155,000, including about 80,000 in Vietnam. Most Cham in Vietnam remain Hindu, whereas those in Cambodia are largely Shiite Muslim.

Little is known of Cham music. Most documentation has been done in Phan Rang, where a troupe of musicians and dancers performs for tourists and visiting delegations. A double-reed oboe and various drums predominate, but the Cham retain an unusual turtleshell fiddle. A full ensemble includes a two-headed drum (*kinang*), a one-headed drum (*baranung*), an oboe (*saranai*), a turtleshell-body fiddle (*kanhi*), a gong (*chieng*), and bells (*grung*) (Figure 19.1). Other instruments accompany dancing in which the instrumental styles—including *pidenh, patra,* and *chava*—take their names from the dances. Strokes on the leading drum (*kinang*) have names and can be notated with four special signs. Less commonly seen are the spike fiddle (*koke*), which vaguely resembles spike fiddles of the Thai (*saw sam sai*), the Khmer (*tror Khmer*), and the Arabs; the gourd mouth organ (*rakle*); the bamboo tube zither (*kopin*); the monochord (*kopil*); and cluster bells (*karong*).

The Cham adopted the culture of India early in their history and were later influenced by Islam, so it is not surprising that some Cham instrumentals resemble those of India and Western Asia. Similarly, Cham melodic style is continuously active, based on small intervals within a narrow range, using unarticulated phrases to build longer melodies. The oboist uses circular breathing to maintain a continuous sound, while the drummer plays cyclic patterns of beats. Superficially, the resulting combination is more like music from the Arabic world than from Southeast Asia, but it also resembles Batak music from Sumatra in Indonesia. The music of the upland Cham living in the mountains of southern Vietnam is quite different, both in style and in organology.

Figure 19.1
Cham musicians play an oboe (*saranai*) and a drum (*baranung*) near Phan Rang, Vietnam. Photo by Phong T. Nguyễn, 1993.

Questions for Critical Thinking:

Mainland Southeast Asia

1. Discuss the differences and similarities among the classical ("court") musics of Cambodia, Thailand, and Laos.

2. How do the early influences of Indian civilization on most of mainland Southeast Asia bring about different results from that of Chinese civilization on Vietnam? What are some specific differences?

3. Islam has been a major cultural force on the Malay majority in Malaysia. In what ways is Islam a factor or not a factor in traditional Malaysian music?

4. What role does improvisation, understood both broadly and narrowly, play in the musics of mainland Southeast Asia?

5. Looking across mainland Southeast Asia, what types of instruments are most prominent and distinctive? Do these appear to have been acculturated or are they possibly native to the region?

6. What role does language—and especially tonal language—play in the composition and performance of musics in mainland Southeast Asia?

7. Discuss the terms "heterophony" and "polyphonic stratification" as they apply to musics in mainland Southeast Asia. Are they different or similar in meaning? Specifically, which musical types in which cultures exhibit the traits denoted by these terms?

8. For each nation-state in mainland Southeast Asia, is there a musical type or style which could be described as "national" and representative of the culture as a whole? If so, what is it and how does it express the greater culture?

9. How does courtship, real or feigned, play a significant role in musical genres in Vietnam, Cambodia, Laos, and Thailand? What is "repartee" and what is its significance in music?

10. What are the most significant and compelling historical relationships among the nations of mainland Southeast Asia that have an apparent impact on the nature of music in specific places?

PART III

Island Southeast Asia

Island Southeast Asia: An Introduction

Patricia Matusky

The archipelago that extends southward and eastward from the Indochinese mainland stretches more than 5,000 kilometers in an arc encompassing the island of Borneo and all the islands of Indonesia and the Philippines. A constellation of islands large and small, the region has been home to related peoples since prehistoric times.

Four nations currently recognized among these islands are Malaysia, Brunei, Indonesia, and the Philippines. Malay-Indonesian culture, in its broadest sense, predominates in all but the Philippines, where only the peoples of the extreme southern islands and some interior uplands have retained strong links to cultures farther south [see THE PHILIPPINES]. A fifth nation of the archipelago is Singapore, where Malay culture is a part of the minority.

Most of the islands in this archipelago are geophysically characterized by chains of mountains, active volcanoes, plains, riverine valleys, and coastal swamplands. The mountains, the plains, and the coasts have provided regions for the habitation of peoples who may be broadly distinguished as upland, interior-plains, and lowland groups, each with a distinct kind of sociocultural expression. Most of these peoples are of Malay stock and speak a language of the Austronesian (Malayo-Polynesian) family. A tiny minority living in the extreme highlands of the Malay Peninsula and the Philippines are Negritos, an aboriginal people who live in small communities and maintain traditions separate from those of Malay ancestry [see THE PHILIPPINES].

Most highlanders belong to tribes, some of which include nomadic hunters and gatherers; most are sedentary dwellers, who practice swidden agriculture, fish, and hunt. In contrast, people of the plains and coasts practice the cultivation of wet rice, often supplemented by farming, fishing, and hunting. The coastal peoples, particularly in western Indonesia, are predominantly Muslim Malays, who claim a great trading and seafaring tradition.

swidden
Agricultural practice in which steep hillside fields are cleared and burned

Gong-chimes and rame drum ensemble (*talempong* and *rabano*), Desa Nan XII and Desa Delimo, Padang Lawas, West Sumatra Province. Photo by H. Kartomi, 1985,

They have long been colonizers throughout the islands, and their language (Malay) is the lingua franca of the region. The coastal urban and suburban areas have become home to immigrant minorities, including Arabs, Chinese, Eurasians, Europeans, and Indians.

The great empires of Srivijaya (600s–800s) and Majapahit (1200s–1500s), centered in south Sumatra and central Java, respectively, brought the Hindu and Buddhist religions to the region. These empires, however, eventually gave way to Islam and the supremacy of Brunei, Melaka (Malacca), Sulu, and other Muslim Malay sultanates, established throughout the islands of the archipelago from the 1400s onward. In general, peoples of the plains and coasts have embraced Buddhism, Hinduism, and Islam, mixed in varying degrees with earlier animistic practices. Many highlanders retain traces of animism with their acceptance of Christianity, brought by European missionaries in the 1700s and 1800s.

Among the indigenous peoples of island Southeast Asia, music has traditionally enhanced religious and customary practices and it often reflects aspects of the natural environment. The flora and fauna of a tropical environment, and a mountainous terrain covered with dense rain forests on many islands, have been important determinants of materials used to produce musical instruments. Traditional agricultural, social, and religious practices have established contexts for the use of particular kinds of instruments and the production of specific kinds of musical sounds.

The use of bronze, wood, and bamboo in the manufacture of musical instruments has made musical sounds somewhat homogeneous throughout the islands. The making of bronze was known and practiced on the mainland of Southeast Asia as early as about 3000 B.C.E., as evidenced at Hoabinhian sites, in present-day north Vietnam and northeaast Thailand. Bronze is thought to have been introduced from the mainland in about the third or second century B.C.E. (the time of Đông Son culture); its making and use burgeoned in Java. The use of bronze led to the development of a type of Đông Son bronze kettledrum or gong [see SOUTHEAST ASIA IN PREHISTORY].

During the first or second century before the Common Era, the first bronze bossed gongs may have been created in Java. From there they may have spread to other parts of Southeast Asia. In the islands, bossed gongs, gong chimes, and bronze metallophones consistently exhibit a high level of sophistication in gamelans (the orchestras of Indonesia), though gongs are found throughout most regions of Southeast Asia, particularly in the form of gong chimes. Other aggregations of large, hanging bossed gongs, including the gong-chime ensembles of Borneo, Malaysia, Sumatra, and the southern Philippines, further attest to the importance of the bronze bossed gong in island Southeast Asia.

In addition to bronze, many different woods and bamboo are important materials in making musical instruments throughout the islands. Xylophones—tuned slabs of wood or bamboo—are ubiquitous. They turn up in a variety of forms, including leg, frame, and trough types. Other wood or bamboo instruments include tube and board zithers, mouth organs, flutes, Jew's harps, slit drums, struck and stamped poles and tubes, and several kinds of plucked lutes.

Some musical traits are particularly important in the archipelago. Among cultures using ensembles of bronze gongs and metallophones, musical texture emerges as layer upon layer of distinctive parts. The stratification of sound usually appears as a fixed and repeated

---

gamelan
Stratified gong-chime ensemble
bossed gong
Tuned gong with a raised center for striking
Đông Son
Early period in Southeast Asian history, characterized by bronze drum casting, spreading as far as the Philippines and Borneo
colotomic structure
The organization of music by periodic punctuation

melodic-temporal unit, a slow-moving and repetitive colotomic part (often played on hanging bossed gongs), and one or more densely ornamenting parts (played between the tones of the fixed melody). Gongs, metallophones, xylophones, zithers, lutes, flutes, and vocal parts combine to form the elaborate ensembles of Java and Bali. The phenomenon of interlocking parts (or shared parts) is equally important in other ensembles, including large gong orchestras, the stamped-pole or –tube ensembles of north Borneo, and the *gendèr wayang* of Bali.

In these ensembles, each player contributes specific sounds at specific times, producing composite rhythms and melodies. The rhythmic patterns (or rhythmic modes), most often in duple meters, are focal elements in the playing of gong chimes in Borneo and the Southern Philippines, and a melody accompanied by a drone or an ostinato figure is an important feature of many instrumental and vocal musics heard throughout island Southeast Asia. Vocal music is a rich tradition throughout the region, with many genres. Among these are long narratives of many kinds; songs of love and courting; children's songs; work songs; laments; and sung genealogies and historical accounts. In many regions, vocal pieces have a melodic line accompanied by a drone, or solo lines interspersed with choral passages in a contrapuntal texture.

The geophysical layout of the islands of Southeast Asia and regular contact among islanders have led to the development of musical features that cross provincial and national boundaries. These features include the use of bronze, bamboo, and wood in the construction of instruments; the prevalence of bossed gongs and gong chimes; and the occurrence of layered and interlocking textures. Though contemporary international boundaries separate the island peoples of Southeast Asia, ancient musical culture reveals ties among them—ties that transcend political allegiances.

Indonesia

Margaret J. Kartomi, R. Anderson Sutton,
Endo Suanda, Sean Williams, and David Harnish

Sumatra (Margaret J. Kartomi)
Java (R. Anderson Sutton, Endo Suanda, Sean Williams)
Bali (David Harnish)
Nusa Tenggara Barat (David Harnish)
Sulawesi (Margarat J. Karomi)

Indonesia is an exceptionally diverse island nation, with 250 million citizens drawn from multiple races, ethnicities, and cultural traditions. The people gained independence from the Dutch colonial empire in 1945, and their national language (Bahasa Indonesia) is the fifth most spoken language in the world. Much of the nation's territory includes the ocean; Indonesia comprises over 13,000 islands (only 5% of which are inhabited). This chapter focuses on several major islands renowned for their musical cultures: Sumatra, Java, and Bali, and includes information on the lesser-known islands of Lombok, Sumbawa, and Sulawesi. Many outsiders are already familiar with the sounds of the gamelan, a large gong-chime ensemble, particularly those found in Java and Bali. One reason for this familiarity may be that many North American and European universities own such ensembles, and college radio stations often include gamelan in their world music offerings. Indonesia has much more music to offer, however.

SUMATRA

One of the largest of the Indonesian islands (almost 2,000 kilometers long), Sumatra lies at the westernmost edge of the archipelago, running parallel to the Malay peninsula. Its ecosystems are as diverse as its peoples; from barren, rocky peaks to extensive lowland swamps, the countryside supports a rich variety of flora and fauna. Its natural resources, including oil and rubber, are crucial to the national economy, and it is one of the few remaining areas where Indonesian tigers, elephants, and orangutans live in the wild.

Having attracted foreign traders, religious leaders, conquerors, musicians, and artists for more than two millennia, Sumatra contains many distinct ethnic groups and musical cultures. Moving along the coastal areas and east-west riverine routes, they introduced diverse cultural traditions. The political borders of Sumatra's seven political provinces and the Special Region of Aceh mark approximate borders of some major ethnic groups, but they rarely coincide exactly with cultural areas.

The coastal Malay peoples are distinguishable from the inland peoples as a whole. Each coastal area practices a unique mix of pan-Malay coastal musical styles and repertoires, predominantly vocal, accompanied by frame drum (*rebana*) and pear-shaped lutes of probable West Asian origin (*gambus*) or violins of European origin (*biola*).

Both the inland peoples and the western offshore islanders (on Nias, Mentawai, Enggano, and other islands) have self-contained musical cultures. Even more inward looking and isolated are nomadic or seminomadic gatherers living in the forests, including the Orang Dalem (Kubu) and the Sakai. Inland cultivators typically use gong-and-drum ensembles dating from Buddhist-Hindu times, but isolated forest dwellers favor vocal music accompanied by easily portable instruments, such as flutes and small drums.

Cultural History

The prehistoric musical remains of Sumatra include only iconographical depictions and remnants of bronze kettledrums (*nakara*) of the Đông Sơn culture, which arose in Tonkin about 500 B.C.E. to 100 C.E. [see SOUTHEAST ASIA IN PREHISTORY]. At Basemah, South Sumatra, a megalith in Đông Sơn style (now housed in the Palembang State Museum) depicts an elephant-riding man carrying on his back a Đông Sơn drum, apparently a symbol of power and prestige. Remains of two such drums provisionally dated about 1600 B.C.E. and 600 C.E. (found at Padang Peri and near Curup, respectively) are housed in the Bengkulu State Museum. The frog, the sun, and other designs on their flat circular tympana suggest that they may have been played in rituals to venerate the spirits of nature.

A strong infusion of Buddhist and Hindu elements enriched Sumatra's music, dance, and ritual from the first to the fifteenth centuries, as witnessed by Sanskrit derived names of instruments and titles of musical pieces throughout the island. The names of the boat-shaped lutes which the Batak subgroups variously call *kucapi, kulcapi,* and *hasapi* derive from ancient Indian lutes called in Sanskrit *kāsyapī* or *kaccha-pī-vinā*; the name of the bronze ankle bells (*genta*) worn by Riau-Malay shamans is also of Sanskrit origin.

Music was performed in and around the Buddhist temple complexes built in the great Srivijaya Era, which by the 600s was in full flower, and later included the Malayu Kingdom at Muara Jambi (1050–1250); the kingdom at Muara Takus, on the upper reaches of the river Kampar Kanan (eleventh and twelfth centuries); and the kingdom at Portibi, in Padang Lawas (from the early eleventh century). Only the temples at Padang Lawas have iconographical depictions of scenes of music and dance. These temples belonged to the kingdom of Panei, which in 1024 made obeisance to the South Indian ruler Rajendra-Coladewa and in the 1300s acknowledged the supremacy of the East Javanese kingdom of Majapahit. As Chinese, Arab, and Old Malay records and the iconographical evidence show, Saivite-Mahayana Tantric Buddhist cults were centered at Malayu, Srivijaya, Padang Lawas, and later at Jambi, Muara Takus, and Pagaruyung.

Sets of tuned horizontal gongs with drums are still widely played to accompany ritual and dance throughout Sumatra, and bells are still used in some healing rituals. Ancient music, dance, and ritual based on ancestral and nature-spirit worship tinged with Saivite-Mahayana Tantric beliefs survive in many parts of Sumatra, as do the remains of Buddhist-Hindu inscriptions and statues giving evidence of contact among various parts of Sumatra, Java, India, China, and elsewhere.

Bronze or brass ensembles found throughout Sumatra typically comprise a set of four to twelve small horizontal gongs, a suspended gong or pair of gongs, a set of two to nine drums, and optional wind instrument, vocal part, and cymbals. Flat gongs were once used in Simalungun, but Sumatran gongs normally have a boss, beaten with a soft hammer. Other musical instruments associated with ancient beliefs are (1) solo flutes, oboes, Jew's harps, and bamboo idiochord zithers, used for courting, intimate self-expression, calling a friend in the fields or forest, and magic animal-capturing or honey-collecting rituals; and (2) bowed spiked stringed instruments, usually with covered half-coconut-shell bodies, used to accompany storytelling, rituals of healing, or love magic.

Islam was introduced into Sumatra from India from the end of the 1200s, when two Muslim kingdoms were founded at Pasai and Perlak. A rich array of Sunni and some Shi'a music, dance, and ritual developed around Sumatra's coast, either combined with elements of pre-Muslim belief and ritual or sharply distinguished from it. Shi'a influences were reinforced in the 1700s by sepoys brought to man the British fort at Bengkulu, thereby introducing the Shi'a ceremony *tabut* into Sumatran ports.

With the rise of Muslim harbor kingdoms on both sides of the Malacca Strait in the 1400s, Malay courts were established. Several of them survived into the twentieth century, each a patron of a specific style of music and dance. Coronations (*penobatan*) and royal weddings, funerals, and the breaking of the Muslim fast in the palaces at Bintan, Daik, Indragiri, Melaka, Pagaruyung, Pelalawan, and Siak were marked by music played on the royal *nobat*, an ensemble that originated in Muslim India but developed local styles and became part of the sacred regalia. Basically, *nobat* consist of a pair of two-headed drums and an oboe. Pre-Muslim court dances were accompanied by bronze ensembles. Muslim-influenced songs and dances, such as the male group dance *zapin* (*bedana*), performed in both court and village, were accompanied by two pairs of small two-headed drums (*marwas,* also *rebana*) and by lutes or guitars. Many have survived.

Through migration and extensive maritime contact around Sumatra's coast, many forms of music and dance that had developed in certain areas, such as the inland Minangkabau plate dances and Barus-Sibolga's umbrella dances, were transplanted around Sumatra's coastal areas. Arab-influenced dances such as the *zapin* and song-dances such as *indang* (Minangkabau) and *saman* (Aceh) spread widely.

The European conquest of Sumatra began with the fall of Malacca to the Portuguese in 1511, followed by its capture by the Dutch in 1641. A century of direct Portuguese musical influence on Malay-Sumatran courts and villages resulted in the development of syncretized musical genres accompanied by solo violins and in some cases plucked stringed instruments, with drums or frame drums and optional gongs. In these genres, the cyclic drumming, the playing of gongs, and the texts were Malay components, and the vocal and *biola* melodies were Portuguese components. Each area of coastal Sumatra developed its styles of band music and couple dancing.

In the 1800s and early 1900s, as the Dutch colonial government gained control of parts of Sumatra, Dutch-influenced staged theater (*komedi stambul* and *bangsawan*) accompanied by Portuguese-Malay band music spread along Sumatra's east coast, and brass bands (*tanjidor*) became popular in the Kayu Agung area of South Sumatra, where at weddings such bands still play pre-1939 Malay and international popular songs. As Dutch and German missionaries proselytized in parts of South Sumatra, northern and central Batak lands, Nias, and elsewhere, they introduced the singing of harmonic hymns and the use of Western instruments, notably accordions, which local peoples adapted to accompany traditional pre-Muslim and post-Portuguese Malay songs. The regional musical tradition that developed in Batak coffee shops and wine shops of North Sumatra also adopted Western tonal and harmonic material, producing popular songs with solo and choral response sections.

After 1945, when Indonesia gained independence, and especially after 1965, Sumatran and Indonesian band music for electronic and acoustic instruments became popular and largely replaced traditional bronze orchestral music and associated dances in Sumatra's towns and cities, and even in some villages. *Dangdut*, a music that combines elements of Indian film music with Sumatran, Indonesian, and international popular styles, is one of the most widespread forms of entertainment music; however, *orkes gamat* and other Malay bands still perform local Malay songs, often using electronically amplified instruments, and the old bronze music and associated dances are still performed in many villages.

Regional Music of Sumatra

Sumatra's diversity precludes a universal discussion of its music, so, for clarity, this article divides the island into its major regions. Though certain ensembles and genres are shared among regions, differences in ethnicity (and therefore, musical meaning and context) require separate discussions. The following section starts at Sumatra's northernmost tip and continues along the body of the island, incorporating the small islands within their respective provinces.

The Special Region of Aceh

Aceh, which became a fully Muslim state in the 1500s, is rich in Muslim devotional arts based on solo and choral singing and collective body movement, which developed as missionaries spread Islam throughout the province; however, most of the music, dance, and ritual of Aceh are amalgams of Muslim and pre-Muslim practices. Aceh divides into the coastal Acehnese and the inland Gayo and Alas cultures. Historically, it was one of the most powerful regions in the area. The Acehnese developed elaborate weaponry; they continue to be renowned for their skills in making gold and silver jewelry and for their embroidery using metallic threads. Deeply conservative in their religion, they are recognized across the archipelago for their commitment to Islam, though their cultural practices include harvest rituals and other ceremonies dating from pre-Islamic times.

The frame drum (*rapa'i*) is by far the most important instrument. Good *rapa'i* made by religiously gifted shamans are highly valued as heirlooms because they represent the owner's soul. After an evening of devotional singing (*zikir*), a set of five *rapa'i Pase* may be played until morning in praise of God; in times of war, in praise of heroism. Competitions are held between two villages, with the judges sitting midway between and judging the music according to its clarity and beauty.

Another devotional form is *daboih* (Indonesian *dabus*), in which scores of cross-legged men sing texts about the prophets to their own *rapa'i daboih* accompaniment, rising at times to a pitch of excitement, especially when singing the name of the Prophet Muhammad. On entering a state of religious concentration, its leaders perform spectacular acts of self-mortification, seemingly without damage or pain. *Daboih* has often been performed to raise martial spirits before battle. In competitions, one troupe aims to defeat the other by disrupting its musical beat and thereby the religious concentration and invulnerability of its leader while he is mutilating himself.

The other main instrument is the human body. Choral music is often accompanied by rhythmic stamping, choreographed body movements, slapping, clapping, and finger clicking, as in the *seudati* (from Arabic *sahadati* "Remember God"). The *seudati* features male dancers standing in a row or a circle; they perform extremely vigorous movements accompanied by fast interlocking bodily sounds while two male singers stand apart and sing texts about religion or other topics, ancient or modern. Their leader and his helper sing mainly six-tone melodies in slow and fast tempos between choral responses by the dancers. *Seudati* probably developed in Aceh's golden age, the reign of Sultan Iskandar Muda, who ruled over large areas of northern coastal Sumatra and Malaya in the 1600s. Like *daboih*, it was performed to raise martial spirits before battle or to celebrate a victory. It was therefore subject to the magic power of the enemy's shaman, who sometimes made his foes too sick to dance.

rapa'i
Achenese frame drum
daboih
Achenese Sufi ritual of self-mortification
seudati
Achenese men's martial group dance

North Sumatra Province

The province divides into the Malay coastal areas (east and west), the Batak interior, and the offshore island of Nias. Three main strata of coastal Malay arts coexist: those associated with animist or syncretic animist-Hindu beliefs; those associated with Muslim culture; and the syncretic, Portuguese-influenced Malay. Batak groups include both Christians and Muslims in the northern and southern interior of the province. The island of Nias has developed musical genres unique to the island.

The animist stratum of Malay coastal culture includes narrative and children's songs, which have a narrow melodic range; rice-threshing, honey-collecting, fishing, and fish-trap-invocation songs, which are heptatonic and have a range of an octave or more; xylophone (*gambang*) music, with two women playing interlocking pentatonic structures; spirit-invocation healing songs; instrumental dance music; and art-of-self-defense, plate, candle, and leaf dances, which often combine heptatonic melody with a pentatonic accompaniment on a horizontal five-gong ensemble (*tilempong*). The Muslim stratum consists of the call to prayer, Qur'ānic cantillations, and devotional songs by frame-drum-playing men at Muslim festivals. The only instruments the religious leaders allow are the frame drum (*rebana*), the lute (*gambus*), and drums (*marwas*). Most songs are heptatonic with a range of about an octave, combining metrically free solo introductions with unison main sections in quadruple meter (Goldsworthy 1979).

The Portuguese-Malay stratum combines European, Latin American, and secular West Asian or Indian popular music elements including the *biola* (violin); major and minor scales; melodies focusing on a tonic, a dominant, a subdominant, and a leading note; a tonic triad; harmony; and modulation. The Portuguese-Malay repertoire includes courting dance-songs. Modern forms include Malay pop (*pop Melayu*), in which a Western band and one or two optional Malay instruments accompany a solo singer. In *ronggeng*, couples dance and exchange rhymed couplets to the accompaniment of a violin, one or two frame drums, and a gong. Formerly, professional female entertainers (*ronggeng*) traveled in troupes of dancers and musicians, performing with paying male partners. *Ronggeng* and other Malay dances were included in "nobility" theatrical shows (*bangsawan*) popular in the 1920s and 1930s that combined Malay, Arabic, Indian, and modern Western theatrical and musical qualities. Since the 1970s, Malay pop rhymed couplets accompanied by pop and jazz instruments and West Asian-influenced coastal Malay songs became popular, combining east-coast Malay, West Asian, and Western features. For a fee, bands play them at celebrations, and they are widely disseminated by cassette.

The Batak people, consisting of the predominantly Christian Toba, Simalungun, Karo, and Pakpak or Dairi subgroups in the north and the Muslim Angkola or Mandailing in the south, have an array of animist-Hindu mortuary ceremonies and a varied music-and-dance repertoire for raising warlike spirits before a battle or celebrating a victory. Each group has entire repertoires for honoring ancestors, representing clan relationships, ritually propitiating gods and spirits, curing, and entertainment. The Batak concentrated in the interior of the province for centuries, keeping themselves in isolation until the mid-1800s. Batak houses are raised on stilts; the two roof ends rise higher than the center, somewhat like buffalo horns. Various ceremonies take place in or near the house. At Toba ceremonies, musicians play on a balcony in the roof of a traditional house, with dancing in a square below. In Mandailing, the musicians play a set of nine single-headed drums attached to the wall of a ceremonial pavilion and a gong set suspended from the roof; they hold the gongs, cymbals, and oboes (*sarunei*) by hand as they play.

All Batak subgroups accompany their dances at official ceremonies with sets of drums, gongs, a solo wind instrument, and optional solo voice. In most subgroups the gongs are normally called *ogung* and the oboes *sarunei*. Pieces played by the ensembles are distinguished by their drum rhythms, often named after a spiritual phenomenon, such as Mandailing's *gondang alap-alap tondi* "ancestral-souls-come-down rhythm." Each instrument has a precisely defined musical role. In some cases (such as the Mandailing *gordang sembilan*) drum sets are played in virtuoso interlocking fashion. In Toba, playing is further complicated by the tuning of the drums. The oboist weaves an intricately ornamented, relatively free-rhythmic melody, while the gongs play damped and undamped sounds in cyclic punctuating patterns.

West Sumatra Province

The three musical areas of the province are the highlands or heartland of Minangkabau, the coastal areas, and the Mentawai Islands. The highland Minangkabau are famous throughout the archipelago for their architecture of many-peaked roofs in imitation of curved water-buffalo horns. They are also famous for the spiciness of their food, and Minangkabau restaurants are found in areas outside the heartland. Minangkabau society is matrilineal—one of the few such societies in Indonesia. The stunning scenery of the highlands has made it a target area for tourism, which has in turn led to the packaging of certain forms of the Minangkabau performing arts for tourists. As in other areas within Sumatra, ancient and modern genres exist side by side and may even overlap (Kartomi 1979). Pre-Muslim highland genres include brass or bronze gong ensembles (Figure 21.1); vocal music with flute (and optional fiddle accompaniment); choral singing by dancers as they welcome guests; the art of self-defense; and a theatrical form with circular dances sometimes introduced by or interspersed with gong-chime or flute music between scenes.

The brass or bronze gong-chime ensembles of the highlands are known as *talempong*, *calempong*, or *canang*. The ensembles may be either processional or stationary, depending on the purpose of the performance. *Talempong* normally contain three or four pairs of horizontal gongs or two pairs and a single gong, a pair of two-headed drums (*gandang*), a single-headed drum or frame drum, and in the Sawahlunto-Sijunjung areas, a medium-sized suspended gong or pair of gongs (*aguang*). In processional *talempong*, each player beats one or two *talempong* held on her left hand and arm. Processional *talempong* are played to raise everyone's spirits as they join in a cooperative-work procession to the rice field, and to accompany forms of the plate dance at a wedding or a ceremony to appoint an

Figure 21.1
Gong-chime and frame-drum ensemble (*talempong* and *rabano*), Desa Nan XII and Desa Delimo, Padang Lawas, West Sumatra Province. Photo by H. Kartomi, 1985.

elder. In seated *talempong*, used for indoor ceremonies, five or six small gongs rest in a frame on soft material to improve their resonance. Players of pairs of *talempong* are designated according to their order of entry, which varies from village to village. Tunings, combinations of instruments, and indigenous classifications of bronze ensembles vary from village to village.

The end-blown bamboo flute (*saluang*) is prominent throughout the Minangkabau heartland. Since it is longer than a human arm, the player holds it aslant; continuous sound is produced by circular breathing. It usually accompanies classical songs with a melody that deviates slightly from the vocal line and fills in pauses between vocal phrases. Sometimes the *saluang* produces a countermelody with a high degree of melodic ornamentation and variation in dynamic level, with at least five primary tones in the octave, depending on the area and the genre for which it is used. It accompanies songs about love and nature, or songs with a magic purpose, including, in the Solok area, shamans' tiger-capturing songs.

Minang vocal music consists mainly of slow songs, the texts of which deal with loneliness, unrequited love, and other such topics, especially the traditional practice of young men leaving home to win their fortune in a faraway place. Other genres include laments cried by a professional mourner and songs by a sugar-palm-sap collector, who believes that more sap will flow from the tree if he or she cries.

Randai, theater performed by the light of a full moon after a harvest, a wedding, or other ceremony, combines circular dancing using rising and falling motions (*galombang* "wave"), singing, dramatic scenes, and instrumental music. Audiences are often called together by a coconut-leaf horn, followed by *talempong* music. An introductory dance to greet the audience and a poetic prologue sung by the leader precede the dancing of *galombang,* the main sound effects for which are produced by dancers clapping their hands in front of their bodies or between their legs. Within the circle of dancers, actors perform scenes from a selected traditional or modern story. Between scenes, a pair of singers alternate to comment on the story (Kartomi 1981).

Though the Minangkabau preserve tenets and expressions of pre-Muslim beliefs, they distinguish clearly between instruments and genres of foreign Muslim origin and those of the "authentic" (*asli*) pre-Muslim stratum. In Payakumbuh, *diki Mauluk* focuses on Muhammad's birth in the month of Maulud. All-night performances, sometimes for several nights, celebrate such events as a local man's successful completion of a Qur'ān-reading examination or a local pilgrim's departure for Mecca. Cross-legged men sing religious songs to their own frame-drum accompaniment. Choosing a text from the Qur'ān in front of him, the leader sings two lines for all to join in, repeating it many times, followed by a *pantun* (rhymed couplet) in the vernacular praising Muhammad (Kartomi 1986).

Salawek dulang (from Arabic *sholawat* "to sing"), in which two male singers accompany their singing by rhythmically beating brass trays (*dulang*), are performed at weddings, circumcisions, on the hundredth day after a death, and on national or religious holidays, sometimes in the form of competitions (Figure 21.2). Teenage girls in religious schools sing religious songs (*kasidah*), the poetic texts of which deal with divine and human devotion, and since the 1980s also song-dances (*nasit*), accompanying themselves on frame drums.

As coastal Minangkabau is not a major rice-growing area, *talempong*-playing processions to the rice fields are not widespread along the coast except in Ranah Pasisir, where four players each play a pair of *talempong* with a *gandang* and another plays a wooden oboe (*sarunai kayu*), and in Painan-Salido, where performers play six *talempong*, a frame drum

Figure 21.2
Open end-blown flute (*sempelong*), Kampung Talau, Riau Province. Photo by H. Kartomi, 1984.

(*adok*), and a *sarunai* in processions to clear irrigation channels. Seated ensembles are rare on the coast. Along the northern coast, three-stringed coastal fiddles (*rabab pasisir*) have coconut-shell (and, in the south, wooden) bodies shaped like those of Western violins, with one string that may serve as a drone. Storytellers are employed by hosts to sing long tales, either unaccompanied (except for the storytellers' own *rabab* accompaniment, with extensive double stopping at the octave or fifth) or with a brass tray.

Hunters, gatherers, and fishermen in the Mentawai Islands have a unique non-Muslim culture. Their ensemble of three or four slit drums (Siberut *tuddukat,* Sipora *tuddukan*) serves for making music and signaling. The drums, cut from tree trunks, rest on crossed sticks on the floorboards. Players produce a rhythmic pulse by beating the upper middle edge of the slit with a hammer and create complex improvisatory rhythms by beating the drum with one or two wooden rods. There is no standard tuning. The hammer is used on three drums for signaling; each rhythm and sound has a semantic meaning such as "an old man has died," or "a house is on fire."

Three or four skin drums plus bamboo or metal concussion bars accompany dancers at ceremonies of healing and sacrifice. The *kateobak,* a long, single-headed cylindrical drum, is made from a hollowed-out tree trunk, with a snakeskin, deerskin, or lizardskin head. Mentawai singing tends to use heavy vibrato and make abrupt shifts to and from falsetto voice; performance contexts include both quiet, private moments within the home and shamanic rituals for curing or appeasing spirits. Songs may also accompany ritual dancing.

Riau Province

Many people of Riau believe they are the original Malays from whom sprang the Malay coastal populations of Indonesia and Malaysia. The province divides into halves: the mainland, crossed by four major rivers; and insular Riau, containing more than three thousand offshore islands. Island Riau people practice more Portuguese-Malay and Islamic forms of

music and dance than the people of the mainland area. The most remarkable aspect of mainland performing arts is the rich tradition of pre-Islamic healing ceremonies, practiced to a lesser extent on some of the islands.

Mainland Riau arts linked to animist beliefs include the unaccompanied ritual songs sung by shamans as they perform a dangerous task, such as collecting honey from a hive high in a tree, and music played on the end-blown flute (*sempelong*), which has four or five holes for fingering, each of which is said to have been burned out on the death of a child. The flute is associated with love magic, lullabies, and children (Figure 21.3).

Notable remains of Buddhist-Hindu culture include the string of small bronze bells played by shamans in mainland healing ceremonies,

gambang
Eighteen-key wooden xylophone of Java

Figure 21.3
Bronze trays (*salawek dulang*), Sisawah, Sijunjung, West Sumatra Province. Photo by H. Kartomi, 1985.

the five- or six-key xylophone (*gambang*) ensembles, which occur in three sizes, and the *celempong* ensembles. The latter ensembles have a set of five or six gongs; a pair of suspended thick-rimmed gongs; and a pair of long, two-headed drums, one of which plays the leading rhythmic part and the other the continuous filling-in part. These ensembles, sometimes with an added rice-stalk oboe, accompany plate dances and art-of-self-defense performances.

Malays in Riau and elsewhere in the province are noted for their enjoyment of storytelling, improvised poetry, lullabies, and sad songs sung at funerals. Mainland Riau stories, called long songs, are sung by a storyteller with or without accompaniment.

Another old Malay art in Riau is erotic dancing and exchange of *pantun* with paying male dancers by semiprofessional female dancer-singers (*ronggeng*) accompanied by male musicians, who formerly traveled by boat in itinerant troupes. The slight hops, occasional use of triple meter in a mainly quadruple-meter genre, and the harmonic implications and double stopping of the *biola* part in *ronggeng* are examples of Portuguese influence, though *ronggeng* probably preceded the Portuguese. Partly because of governmental prohibition, a Muslim ban on mixed-sex dancing, and an association of *ronggeng* with love magic, prostitution, and alcohol, traditional Malay *ronggeng* have died out, replaced by modern *ronggeng* performances, in which a singer in a modern band sings popular songs in *pantun* form. The band usually consists of a violin, a flute, a piano-accordion, a double bass, bongos, maracas, and a Western drum kit, or some combination of these. After buying a ticket, men dance with hostesses, facing but not touching them.

Jambi Province

The major groups of people in Jambi are the Jambi Malay lowlanders, living around the Batang Hari River and its tributaries; Kerinci Malays in the highland basin to the west; and nomadic Orang Dalem (Kubu Malays) in the forests of the Sarolangun Bangko, Muarabungo Tebo, and Batang Hari areas. Many other ethnic groups—Chinese, Javanese, Arabs, Malaysians, and Japanese—populate the province, especially its capital city, Jambi.

The pre-Islamic genres of all three groups include ceremonies of healing, other shamanic songs, art-of-self-defense performances, and vocal or instrumental music for intimate emotional expression, courting, and self-entertainment. Brass (*kelintang, kromong*) and xylophone (*kelintang kayu, gambang*) ensembles, with their dances and songs, occur only among the Jambi-Malay lowlanders, whose Muslim genres include *hazrah* (with *rebana* accompaniment) and *sike* (male, female, or mixed singing about Muhammad's life).

Post-Portuguese musical genres in Jambi and among Kerinci Malays include the *orkes Melayu* (violin, gong, *tetawak* "small gong," and a pair of *gendang*) and the songs and dances it accompanies. Vocal and *biola* melodies are punctuated by a gong and *tetawak*, and cyclic rhythms are played on the two-headed drums. This ensemble, with optional Western popular or Latin American instruments added, accompanies dances all over Jambi.

At Jambi-Malay weddings and circumcision ceremonies, the *kelintang* (set of three to six horizontal gongs) or *kromong* (set of five to twelve gongs) are played by one or two women. Others play a suspended large gong, a small *ketawak*, and a pair of *gendang* while a soloist sings. Single or two-part, their interlocking melodic lines accompany art-of-self-

kelintang
Gong chime and ensemble of Sumatra
gendang
Large double-headed drum from Malaysia and Indonesia

defense displays. Sometimes the *kelintang* are played in procession to the fields. Villagers use aged sets of five to twelve horizontal gongs; no two sets tuned alike. Frequent changes of tempo, interlocking and two-part melodic structures, cyclic rhythms, melodies and formulas, and gong and alternating gong or *ketawak* punctuation (mostly every two or four beats) are the operative musical principles. Large and small brass ensembles accompany Malay song-dances.

The most remarkable form of pre-Islamic music and dance in Kerinci (except in the strictly Muslim south) is the weeklong healing ceremony (*asiek*), led by the trance leader, his female assistant, and musicians (a singer and the players of a medium and large frame drum). Once a spirit has been called, the sound of the drums becomes quite penetrating. The assistant believes that in her final spiritual journey she is entering the house of a spirit healer who can help cure the patient. Entranced dancers perform such feats as walking on cups and plates without breaking them. Similar ceremonies, held to celebrate the erection of a new house, to put a man-eating tiger into a trance so it can be caught more easily, to request blessings at planting and harvest times, and to clean gongs and other heirlooms, also feature unaccompanied songs.

The more nomadic of the Orang Dalem, living in Jambi's and Palembang's swampy lowlands, play only portable instruments such as flutes and drums. They sing ornamented descending songs to mourn, to attract and trap a dangerous tiger, and to soothe a child to sleep. The melodic style of their end-blown ring flute resembles their vocal style.

Bengkulu Province

Bengkulu divides into mideastern uplands, coastal areas, and Enggano Island. The province was once a part of South Sumatra, but separated in 1968; it is famous for its megalithic monuments and large national park. Ceremonies based on homage to ancestors and natural spirits are rare except among the Suku Dalem, including the Serawai (in the south) and the Rejang (in the mideastern uplands and midnorthern coastal area), who accompany these ceremonies on brass or bronze ensembles, or on oboe and drums. Lovers still follow the tradition of mouthing responsorial *pantun* rhymed couplets into a Jew's harp in the dead of night at the girl's house. Rituals based on paying homage to natural spirits are also found among the Suku Terasing (Isolated Peoples), whose music, primarily vocal, serves for making love magic, capturing tigers, and performing other mystical rites.

Many traditional Serawai dances are performed around a wooden pole. At Serawai weddings, daytime ritual dances by the bridal chaperone and men or women are performed for the bridal couple around a pole to which a buffalo has been tied, later to be slaughtered for feasting. In the eve-

Figure 21.4
Kelintang ensemble (gong chime and frame drums), Kampung Gelumbang, Bengkulu Province. Photo by H. Kartomi, 1983.

nings, the pole serves the function of separating male and female dancers, who perform supervised courting dances to the accompaniment of a bronze ensemble (*kelintang*; Figure 21.4) comprising a set of six horizontal gongs (*kelintang*) and one or several frame drums (*redap*).

At both upland and coastal Rejang weddings, ritual dancers also dance around a pole to which a sacrificial buffalo has been tied. The nights are occupied by mixed-sex dancing under a chaperone's control. Ancestor-honoring and life-crisis ceremonies are accompanied by the *kromong* ensemble consisting of a set of five, seven, nine, or twelve horizontal gongs (*kromong*), a suspended gong (*gung*), and a long, two-headed drum (*gandang panjang*) or a large frame drum (*dep*).

kromong
Sumatran gong chime and ensemble

Common to all areas of Bengkulu but especially the coastal areas is the unaccompanied Malay or accompanied Portuguese-Malay vocal genre *dendang*, designated the official music of Bengkulu in the Dutch colonial period. Most songs deal with unrequited love or unfortunate fate. Accompanied songs include the responsorial singing of *pantun* between men and women, and the widely known Portuguese-Malay song "*Kaparinyo*," which accompanies the umbrella (*payung*) dance. Songs are usually accompanied by a violin (*biola*) and one or several large, heavy frame drums (*redap*).

The main form of devotional Muslim music in Bengkulu's coastal areas is the *hadrah*. A circle of elders meet in each other's houses or at a ceremony to sing devotional songs to their own frame-drum accompaniment, led by a religious leader. Members of a particular circle of elders, which often contains several violinists, also frequently perform *dendang*.

South Sumatra Province

South Sumatra, especially Palembang, is an important area for the Indonesian economy. Because it has major reserves of oil, it generates a large percentage of the country's export revenue. Palembang, the provincial capital, was once the location of Srivijaya, an important Buddhist-Hindu kingdom that flourished for four centuries from before the 700s. As with Lampung, its proximity to Java and Jakarta, the nation's capital, has made South Sumatra more subject to Javanese and international influences. The main musical areas of South Sumatra are the western uplands and the Musi, Ogan, and Komering river basins. South Sumatra's musical identity is primarily Muslim and Malay, as exemplified by the *dana*, a Muslim dance popular throughout the province. The orchestra and shadow-puppet theater of the former Palembang court are of Javanese origin.

Music that predates the Buddhist-Hindu era is still performed, especially in the uplands of Basemah and Rejang and among the Anak Dalem who inhabit the forest, along the riverbanks and swamps of Musi Banyuasin, Musi Rawas, and Lahat. Honey-collecting singing and other shamanic singing, the music of mourning, courting music played on a Jew's harp, introspective solo or ceremonial singing or playing of flutes after a death or on other sad topics, music for stamping rice, art-of-self-defense displays, and male-female responsorial singing and other vocal music are all based on reverence for natural spirits and ancestors. A Buddhist-Hindu or Muslim attribute may be added to these musical forms in performance, but they primarily express animist beliefs.

In the Basemah uplands, mystical songs to calm the bees while a shaman carries a burning torch up a tall tree and throws it down for the bees to follow while he collects the honey are called songs to defeat the honeybees. Spells sung to praise or censure a tiger are sung by a shaman who has befriended tigers. The Anak Dalem play frame drums and flutes, having healing-dance and vocal-music repertoires. During spiritual journeys, healers dance and shake sets of bronze bells inherited from Buddhist-Hindu times. Rejang shamans express their belief in ancestral spirits' power through singing and ceremonies of divination and healing. Sad music in the highlands is sung by professional mourners and accompanied by a player on the *serdam*, an end-blown ring flute with three front holes and a back hole, which produces elaborate microtonal ornamented passages by circular breathing.

Like most people in Sumatra, the Basemah believe that Jew's harps (*ginggung*), played by lovers to each other, are an ancient kind of instrument. A *ginggung* is a thin, rectangular bamboo strip that has been split to produce a long vibrating tongue. The player holds it with the left hand in his or her half-open mouth; a right-hand finger vibrates the other end by tugging a small cord attached to it. As the player changes the size of the oral cavity, the harmonics change, and a melody is produced.

Vocal music of ancient origins in Baseman includes loud, responsorial jungle-call singing with improvised exchanges of quatrain verses by a mixed couple singing about social issues, such as the good deeds of an elder at his induction ceremony, and sad songs at the loss of a spouse or valuable possessions. Lullabies in Burai have a six-tone palette, with slight melodic ornamentation and frequent changes of tonal center, and sleep- or religion-oriented texts.

The heritage of the golden age of Srivijaya is maintained in South Sumatra by the long-golden-fingernail dances (symbolizing virginity) and other female-welcoming dances, accompanied by a variety of bronze gong-and-drum ensembles, which lend luster to formal occasions in regions—throughout the province and other areas, extending north as far as Thailand—that were once part of greater Srivijaya.

If gongs typify the Buddhist-Hindu stratum, the frame drums and small two-headed drums identify the Muslim stratum. Strict Muslims disassociate themselves from gong ensembles and female or mixed-sex dancing; however, in most areas, Muslim or pre-Muslim conflict has been resolved by the local religious leaders, who respect and allow both traditional and Muslim arts to be practiced.

West Asian music influenced South Sumatra from the early 1500s, when a Muslim sultanate of mixed Javanese and Arabic blood sprang up in Palembang. Many pre-Muslim rural dances are now accompanied by Arabic-influenced instrumental ensembles and local and transplanted Malay songs by an *orkes Melayu*. The most widespread devotional musical form, *zikir*, is performed regularly by male or female groups accompanying themselves on large and small *rebana* and frames with jingles. Devotees repeat the names of God and the prophets to reach an ecstatic state of union with God. In a secular form of this practice (*rodat*) men or women sit, kneel, or stand close together, performing identical or alternating body movements to their own vocal and frame-drum accompaniment. A special form of *zikir* with a solo singer and chorus, or two groups of solo singer and chorus, is *serapal anam* "holy prophet." Besides singing praises of Muhammad, each group takes turns singing texts that pose religious questions to be answered by the other group. Because no instruments are used, *serapal anam* may be performed in mosques.

Another form of West Asian–influenced music is the *orkes gambus*, in which musicians accompany Malay songs with a lute, a gong, drum, and a pair of two-headed small drums (*ketipung*). *Orkes Melayu* ensembles in this area consist of a violin, a harmonica, a guitar, a large bass, a tambourine, a flute (*suling*), and a solo singer performing Malay songs.

Lampung Province

Lampung consists of the Abung (Pepadon) interior, the mainly Javanese transmigrant area around Metro Town, and the Malay coastal areas. The impact of Javanese migration to Lampung cannot be underestimated; the Javanese have had a profound effect on urban and rural social relations, language, and the performing arts.

Bronze ensembles of pre-Muslim origin are still played in the interior and along the coast. However, bronze-ensemble music and other pre-Muslim forms of art are better preserved among the inland people than along the coast. The Abung, who believe they originated in megalithic times around Lake Ranau, spread since the 1700s throughout the north and northeast plains of Lampung. Their royal center at Menggala remains their cultural center. Bronze ensembles around Menggala and the district capital, Kotabumi, usually include nine or twelve horizontal gongs, a pair of large suspended gongs, a small suspended gong, a pair of cymbals, a cylindrical drum, and a frame drum. Similarly, the *kelenongan* ensemble contains a gong and a pair of small gongs. In contrast to the vigor of the music, the dances are slow, with intricate hand-and-finger movements.

Surviving remnants of ancient Abung culture include music for the Jew's harp, played by courting couples, and a large repertoire of ring-flute music to express love or lament a child's death, with ornamented melodies normally moving within the range of up to a fifth. Shamans also sing magic songs to help them capture human-eating tigers and to call for rain in times of drought. Gifted storytellers sing stories for nights on end, interspersing their tales with moral teachings. From the 1940s, these stories were converted into theatrical performances by traveling troupes. Since the 1980s, the Lampung government has encouraged their development. They are now known in Jakarta and elsewhere as the specific form of Lampung theater, accompanied by *kelittang* music.

JAVA

The island of Java has an exceedingly rich musical heritage, representing several major cultural groups and regional traditions. With roughly 100 million people on an island of less than about 130,000 square kilometers, Java is also one of the most densely populated areas of the world. The urban sprawl that characterizes some of Java's largest cities is rapidly encroaching on the countryside, but large portions of Java include expansive areas of rice fields, and the island is home to numerous active volcanoes. Though the term *Java* denotes the entire island, the eastern two-thirds of the island is the culturally Javanese region. The western third, Sunda, is the home of the Sundanese, whose language, music, and culture differ from those of the Javanese (see "Cirebon" and "Sunda," below).

Central and East Java

The Javanese have the longest recorded history of any of the peoples of Indonesia, dating back nearly two thousand years. Major influences have come from India, China, West Asia, Europe, and the Americas. The earliest evidence of musical activity in Java consists of the remnants of several large bronze kettledrums, thought to have been introduced from the Đông Son culture of mainland Southeast Asia and southern China. Indian influence in Java dates back at least to the fifth century. Bas reliefs on Hindu temples and Buddhist structures in Java depict a variety of instruments, mostly derived from India, that were once probably in use, at least within the royal courts. Small Hindu temples on the Dieng plateau in central Java about A.D. 750 depict small bells, small cymbals, a three-stringed lute, and a bar zither (Kunst 1973:107). The reliefs on the Borobudur, the monumental Buddhist stupa built in south-central Java in the 800s, present a vast array of musical instruments, including shell and straight trumpets, side-blown flutes, end-blown flutes (or double-reed aerophones), mouth organs, lutes, bar zithers, arched harps, double-headed drums, a xylophone, bells, and a knobbed kettle-gong (Kunst 1973:107). Similar instruments are also represented in the reliefs of the tenth-century Hindu temple complex Laro Jonggrang, at Prambanan.

During the early Hindu-Javanese period (fifth through eleventh centuries), courtly centers of power were located in central Java, especially in the area of Mataram, south-central Java, near the present-day city of Yogyakarta. Rule then shifted to east Java, with courts located near the present-day cities of Kediri and Singosari. The Hindu-Javanese period culminated with the Majapahit Empire, centered near present-day Mojokerto in east Java, and which lasted from about the 1200s until the end of the 1400s. East Javanese temple reliefs give evidence of additional kinds of instruments, including the banana-shaped *kemanak,* a dumbbell-shaped *réyong* (still occasionally used in Balinese *gamelan angklung*), and a multistringed zither (like the present-day *siter* or *celempung*; see below).

Evidence of musical and theatrical activity in Hindu-Javanese times is found not only in the temple reliefs, but also in literature written in Kawi (Old Javanese), a language whose script and vocabulary are closely related to Sanskrit. From this literature we learn of noisy percussive ensembles used in battles, wind and stringed instruments accompanying female dancers at court, and the existence of masked dance and shadow puppetry—all of which were to undergo substantial transformation, but not eradication, with the rise of Islam and the coming of Western colonials.

Muslim traders introduced Islam to Java over the course of several centuries, primarily along the north coast. By about 1500, the strength of Islam in Java had apparently forced the Hindu courtiers to disperse, mostly to the island of Bali, or to remote areas of east Java. The adoption of Islam does not seem to have radically altered musical practices. The rendering of poetry in song (*tembang*), the playing of ensembles of predominantly percussive instruments (*tetabuhan*), and various combinations of these two seem to have been practiced at all levels, from court to remote hamlet, for many centuries down to the present.

In the early 1500s, visitors from Europe first made their appearance in Java. A century later, they had established what was to be three centuries of colonial rule. Before reaching eastern Indonesia, Portuguese seafarers had arrived, introducing plucked lutes and a vocal style whose influence can still be heard in Indonesian *kroncong*. From the first arrival of the Dutch East-India Company (1596) until the government of the Netherlands took over the company (1800), this private company, with substantial military force at its disposal, took ever greater control of the island of Java. Pitting rival Javanese rulers against one another, it radically transformed the political and cultural map. A dispute over succession between members of the central Javanese royal family, manipulated by the Dutch, resulted in 1755 in the division of Javanese royal power into two rival courts in south-central Java, only 60 kilometers from one another: Surakarta (also called Solo) and Yogyakarta (also called Yogya). Further rivalries a few years later (1757) and again during the period of British rule (1811–1816) produced further divisions with the addition of two lesser courts, the Mangkunegaran in Surakarta and the Pakualaman in Yogyakarta.

Despite the growing presence of European music, from military marching bands to various kinds of entertainment music (see Notosudirdjo 1990), indigenous musical practice appears to have had little European influence, at least with regard to musical instruments, scales, or style of performance. Rather, conceptions about music—even the idea of music as an art, separate from other categories of human expression—seem to have been the most substantial form of Western influence until the 1980s. Nevertheless Javanese rulers came to value Western music with indigenous ensemble music as part of their regalia. And since the early twentieth century, particularly with the advent of mass media (radio and recordings), various forms of Western and Western-influenced music have become widely known by the Javanese, from urban elite to peasant farmers.

The occupation of Java by Japanese troops (1942–1945) was followed by the Indonesian revolution (1945–1949) and the final expulsion of the Dutch. Throughout these upheavals and the subsequent era of independence, indigenous musical traditions of Java have persisted, undergoing varying degrees of change in function, substance, and meaning.

Cultural Geography

Though one can speak of Javanese music in reference to instruments, genres, repertoire, and performance style, many aspects of it are widely acknowledged to have originated in one region or at one court, and to represent the aesthetic sensibilities of one subcultural or social group. The predominant tradition of gamelan music throughout all of Java is the court-derived tradition of Surakarta (or Solonese style), in the province of Central Java. (In the present article, *Central Java,* with uppercase *C,* refers to the province, and *central Java* to the broad cultural region, including Yogyakarta, Surakarta, and other areas culturally central Javanese.) It is sometimes simply called Javanese or central Javanese, but musicians and informed listeners continue to identify it as Solonese style (*gaya Solo*). It consists of a vast repertoire of pieces, most of which emphasize intricate and florid vocal and instrumental lines. It is quintessentially *alus*—a term implying refinement, subtlety, and smoothness.

Within the heartland of south central Java, the Yogyanese cultural tradition contrasts with that of Surakarta. Music in Yogyanese style can be heard throughout much of the Daerah Istimewa Yogyakarta (Special Region of Yogyakarta), a small area with the status of a province within the Republic of Indonesia and governed by the sultan of Yogyakarta. However, this music is nurtured most consistently by the musicians of the Yogyakarta court (*kraton*) and among the elite. Other musicians in the Special Region of Yogyakarta tend to prefer Solonese style or to mix styles and repertoires.

Though based on many of the same principles and drawing on similar repertoire, Yogyanese music tends to be more *gagah* "strong, robust" and *prasaja* "forthright, austere." Yogyanese and Solonese agree that for the most part Yogyanese style represents older practice associated with the Mataram court before the division of Java. Yet whereas Yogyanese argue that their tradition is therefore more legitimate, Solonese argue that Yogyanese music is more archaic and Solonese more progressive. Indeed, certain stylistic elements in Yogyanese practice suggest it is an older tradition; but because the two courts have sought to define themselves in opposition to one another, both traditions have undergone substantial change.

The province of East Java is culturally more complex than either Central Java or the Special Region of Yogyakarta. In cultural orientation, the portion west of the Brantas River—the cultural boundary often called *pinggir-rekso* "guarded edge, guarded border," a line dating back to the eleventh-century rule of King Airlangga—is mostly central Javanese. East of it, in the middle portion of the province (areas around Surabaya, Malang, and Mojokerto) are the east Javanese (*arék* Javanese), including the Tengger. (In the present article this area is called eastern Java, in contrast to the province of East Java.) The island of Madura, part of East Java, is home to the Madurese. Extensive contact with the Javanese over many centuries notwithstanding, the Madurese speak a separate language and maintain arts and culture that differ substantially from any of the Javanese subgroups. Over the past several centuries, Madurese have migrated in large numbers to the eastern portion of the island of Java, where they have maintained a distinctive identity. At the easternmost tip of the island are Osing Javanese of Banyuwangi and rural Blambangan, who speak a dialect of Javanese and practice a range of characteristic performing arts bearing resemblances to several Balinese genres.

Residents of East Java tend to see themselves, and to be judged by others, as more *kasar* "coarse, rough," than central Javanese, the opposite of *alus*; musical traditions throughout the province reflect this contrast. The drumming, for example, in various ensembles among the *arèk* Javanese, the Madurese, and the Osing Javanese, can be loud and syncopated—often complex, seldom subtle. Especially among the *arèk* Javanese (and the central Javanese of this province), the music of the mainstream Solonese tradition has gained increasing prominence, providing a refined alternative to local practice without eradicating it. Nevertheless, strong central Javanese influence has caused concern among some musicians and local officials. To define this province culturally, official governmental directives have encouraged the support of certain genres and practices that contrast most clearly with the Solonese tradition of Central Java, giving greater legitimacy to arts indigenous to East Java and inspiring new combinations of repertoire and style from diverse groups within the province.

kasar
"Crude, rough," Javanese term
alus
"Refined, subtle," applied to Javanese style or to characters in Balinese dance

Through the mass media, in particular among the several star individuals and performing groups most frequently represented on commercial cassettes, borrowing and blending across subcultural boundaries has become increasingly popular. But even as this blending produces a measure of homogenization, it highlights regional differences. Java's cultural geography is in flux but remains diverse, making it necessary to avoid broad generalizations about Javanese music.

Musical Instruments

Javanese culture emphasizes percussive ensembles, usually incorporating one or more knobbed gongs and drums. The larger of these ensembles are usually called gamelans, sets of instruments unified by shared tuning, and often by decorative carvings and paintings. Gamelans exist in multiple configurations at the courts and throughout Java. This section offers, first, a description of the instruments that make up the large, court-derived gamelans of central Java, with comments on differences between Yogyanese and Solonese variants. Coverage of regional variants, instrumental construction, symbolic significance, special ritual ensembles, and other instruments follows.

A large central Javanese gamelan consists mostly of knobbed gongs and metal slab percussive instruments augmented by several drums and other instruments (Figures 21.5 and 21.6). Instruments are tuned either to a version of the *sléndro* scale (five tones with nearly equidistant intervals, usually notated 1-2-3-5-6) or to a version of the *pélog* scale (seven tones with large and small intervals, usually notated 1-2-3-4-5-6-7). Large gamelans (*gamelan seprangkat* or *gamelan sléndro-pélog*) include a complete set of instruments in both scalar systems, but a gamelan can be considered complete with sufficient instruments of one or the other system. Gamelan pieces (*gendhing*) are either in *sléndro* or in *pélog*; the two systems are used together only rarely—in one ritual piece, and in some contemporary experimental works.

The Javanese categorize instruments in several ways—by shape and

Figure 21.5
The knobbed-gong and metal-slab instruments of a central Javanese court gamelan (Surakarta style). Photo by R. Anderson Sutton.

Figure 21.6
Female singers (*pesindhén*) and hanging gongs of a central Javanese gamelan (Yogyakarta style). The writing inside the hanging gongs indicates the degree of pitch and the name of the gamelan (the *pélog* ensemble Kyahi Sirat Madu and the *sléndro* ensemble Kyahi Madu Kéntir). Photo by R. Anderson Sutton.

construction of the sounding part of the instrument, by shape and construction of the resonator or suspending device, by placement in relation to other instruments (front and back), by association with instrumental or vocal music (loud and soft), by performance technique (one-handed or two-handed), and by musical function (melodic, rhythmic, and so on). The definitions below are grouped by the first of these systems, and include gongs and kettle-gongs, keyed metallophones, other melodic instruments, and percussion. Note that precise instrumentation differs according to tuning.

Among the vertical hanging gongs, the *gong ageng* is the largest; the *siyem*, a medium hanging gong, and the *kempul*, small hanging gongs, are all suspended by rope from a wooden rack. The kettle gongs (all of which rest horizontally on string in wooden frames) include *kenong* (large, deep-rimmed kettle-gongs), *kethuk* (a small kettle-gong), *kempy-ang* (a pair of small kettle-gongs), and two pair of *bonang* (*bonang barung*, a set of approximately a dozen kettle gongs in two parallel rows, and *bonang panerus*, a similar set an octave higher). Of the knobbed gong instruments, the *gong ageng*, *siyem*, and *kempul* are struck with a rounded, padded beater; the others with stick beaters padded with wound string.

The category of struck metallophones includes the *saron demung*, largest and lowest-register member of the *saron* family; it features six or seven thick metal keys resting over a trough resonator. It is played with the medium-sized *saron barung*, like the *demung* but one octave higher, and the small *saron peking*, like the *saron barung* but one octave higher. The *gendèr slenthem* has six or seven broad, thin metal keys, each suspended by string over individual bamboo or metal tuned resonators in a wooden frame. An octave higher, the *gendèr barung* has twelve to fourteen narrow, thin metal keys. Still an octave higher is the *gendèr panerus*. The *gambang kayu* is a xylophone with seventeen to twenty-three wooden keys resting over a wooden box resonator. Of the keyed instruments, the *saron* instruments are struck with bare wooden mallets, the *gendèr* instruments and *gambang* with softly padded disc-shaped beaters with handles.

The *celempung* "zither" is supported at about a thirty-degree angle on four legs, with twenty to twenty-six metal strings arranged in ten to thirteen double courses. The *siter*, a small zither, rests on the floor or in a wooden frame, with ten to twenty-six metal strings in single or double courses; the same technique of playing is used as for the *celempung*. The *suling* is an end-blown bamboo notched ring flute. The rebab is a spike fiddle, with one string wrapped around a peg at the lower end, providing two playing filaments, tuned about a fifth apart, and with a small wooden resonator covered by a membrane.

Percussion instruments include the *kendhang gendhing,* which is the largest hand-played drum, having two heads laced onto a barrel shaped shell. The *kendhang ciblon,* a middle-sized hand-played barrel drum, is somewhat smaller. The *kendhang ketipung* is also a hand-played barrel drum, but is the smallest. The *bedhug* is a large stick-beaten barrel drum, with two heads tacked onto a cylindrical shell, suspended in a wooden rack. Other instruments frequently encountered in gamelan performance are the *keprak,* a wooden box used to accompany dancing, and the instruments played by the puppeteer-narrator (*dhalang*) in shadow-puppet performances: metal plaques (*kecrèk*) and the large wooden chest in which puppets are stored, both struck by a wooden knocker. Rarer, but essential for certain pieces, is the pair of banana-shaped metal idiophones known as *kemanak*.

In performance, no ensemble is complete without female solo singers (*pesindhèn*) and a male chorus (*gèrong*); however, some pieces or sections of pieces are strictly instrumental, employing only the instruments of the loud-playing ensemble: *gong ageng, siyem, kempul, kenong, kethuk, kempyang, engkuk-kemong, bonang* family, *saron* family, *gendèr slenthem, kendhang* family, and *bedhug*. Pieces or sections with vocalists feature the soft-playing (*lirihan*) ensemble, though usually with all or most of the loud-playing ensemble being played softly: *gendèr barung, gendèr panerus, gambang kayu, celempung* and/or *siter, suling*, rebab, vocalists (*pesindhèn and gérong*). Soft-playing instruments are usually in the front of the ensemble, nearest to the audience, with the largest gong instruments in the back and the *saron* family in the middle. Instruments are usually arranged either parallel or at right angles to one another, suggesting coordination with cardinal directions; otherwise, the precise arrangement is not standardized.

Other Ensembles and Instruments

The number of combinations of instruments in central and eastern Java is extraordinarily large. Here it will suffice to mention several ensembles prominent within a particular region, with several types of ensembles widespread throughout Java. In central Java, one finds small gamelans. Those consisting mostly of soft-playing instruments, without *bonang* or *saron,* are called *gamelan klenèngan* or *gamelan gadhon*. In place of the *gong ageng*, these often substitute a *gong kemodhong,* consisting of two large keys tuned slightly apart and producing a sound resembling that of the gong. For other knobbed-gong instruments some itinerant gamelans substitute metal-keyed instruments, usually of iron.

In the region of Banyumas, the bamboo-xylophone ensemble *calung* is quite popular. It usually consists of two multioctave bamboo xylophones, two single-octave bamboo xylophones, a blown bamboo gong, and two small *kendhang*. This ensemble accompanies one or more singer-dancers known as *lènggèr* (or sometimes *ronggèng*) (Figure 21.7). Closely related but less common are *angklung* ensembles, in which the two multioctave *gambang* and the *slenthem* are replaced by a single set of fifteen or so shaken bamboo rattles (*angklung*), played by three musicians.

In Banyuwangi, East Java, one finds two distinctive ensembles: one known as *gandrung* (after the female singer-dancer it accompanies), the other as *angklung* (after one of its main instruments, though markedly different from the Banyumas *angklung*). The *gandrung* consists of two Western violins (*biola*), two *kethuk*, a *kempul*, a small gong, a triangle (*kluncing*), and two *kendhang*. It is played mainly at social occasions at which men in the audience are enticed to dance

Figure 21.7
Singer-dancers accompanied by the Banyumas *calung*; on the right, the audience is partly visible. Photo by R. Anderson Sutton.

with one or more *gandrung* (female singer-dancers), the centers of attention. Larger, the *angklung* of Banyuwangi incorporates some of the *gandrung* instruments with others—mostly percussion idiophones. It takes its name from the *angklung*, which here refers not to a shaken bamboo rattle, but to a multioctave bamboo xylophone set in a high frame. The ensemble contains a pair of Banyuwangi *angklung*, with three registers of nine keyed metallophones (all usually of iron), and occasionally adds a bamboo flute (*suling*) or a double-reed oboe (*tètèt*). In addition to accompanying dance and song, Banyuwangi *angklung* ensembles are now used in remarkable and often fiercely competitive musical contests (*angklung caruk*) (Wolbers 1987).

Throughout central and eastern Java, under various local names, one finds hobby-horse-trance dance troupes, usually accompanied by *kendhang* or several single-headed conical drums (*dhog-dhog*), two small gongs, and one or more other melodic instruments: *saron*, double-reed aerophone, *angklung* (the shaken variety), and even *bonang*. Similar ensembles, featuring a double-reed (*slomprèt*), accompany *réyog Ponorogo*, the best-known variant of the processional genres of dance known as *réyog*. And people in certain parts of East Java, especially the Madurese, use small percussion ensembles (*sronèn*) that feature a similar double reed. More purely drum ensembles also exist, such as the *réyog kendhang* of Tulungagung, East Java, with many *dhog-dhog* and just one small kettle gong. Also widespread, particularly in more devout Muslim circles in rural areas, are *terbangan*, ensembles consisting mostly or sometimes entirely of single-headed frame drums. These accompany groups singing in Javanese or Arabic for numerous genres of music related to Islamic themes. In central Java, *terbang* sometimes accompany vocal music in *gérongan* (male-chorus) style, mostly from the standard gamelan repertoire.

Music, Dance, Theater

Musical activity in Java is usually intended in part to entertain its listeners, but this entertainment is often an integral component of ritual ceremony. Other than Western or Western-influenced popular music, the music one is most likely to hear in Java today is that which accompanies dance or theater—many genres of which are themselves most frequently performed for rituals, such as weddings, circumcisions, anniversaries, business openings, and so forth. So-called concerts of music, with an audience intended to listen attentively to a series of musical pieces in the manner of an audience for Western art music, have only recently been staged. One hears gamelan music without dance or drama broadcast on radio and television, on commercial cassette recordings, and live only at events called *uyon-uyon* (Yogya) or *klenèngan* (Solo and eastern Java). Some of the repertoire for these events can be heard also in the accompaniment of dance and theater, and even the patterns of drumming often follow the traditional choreographies of an imagined female dancer, the flirtatious *gambyong*.

Relaxed and informal, an *uyon-uyon* or *klenèngan* permits extensive social interaction among the parties present: the host family, the musicians, the invited guests, and the uninvited guests (neighbors and passersby who wish to stop and listen). These performances are usually sponsored as part of a rite of passage (a wedding, a circumcision) or an anniversary, and are intended both to entertain and to contribute to the maintenance of balance between the supernatural realm and the human realm. Performing the music is therefore important in its own right, independent of the attention and appreciation by any audience, who may be busy conversing and hearing the performance only as background music.

It is not unusual for the musicians at one of these events to perform through most of a night, beginning shortly after dusk and ending only at three or four in the morning. Most of those who attend, whether invited or uninvited, leave long before the event is over. And while they are present, some pay greater attention to the music than do others. Those most interested in the music might offer their praise of a particular player or singer and request a favorite piece. The musicians vary the types of pieces they perform, starting with more subdued and austere pieces and choosing increasingly lively pieces as the evening progresses.

Also widespread until the 1960s were small troupes consisting of several musicians with a reduced set of gamelan instruments (a *saron*, a gong, a *gendèr*, a *kendhang*) and one or more singer-dancers (either female or male in female attire for dancing). Men would pay the singers for the opportunity of joining them in an erotic social dance. Nowadays, the practice of men paying to dance with a singer-dancer survives in hosted *tayuban*, parties in which a group of gamelan musicians and several singer-dancers are hired to perform for a village ceremony, such as the annual village cleansing or a family rite of passage (Figure 21.8). Though casual consumption of alcohol is not typical in Java, the *tayuban* is an occasion at which men are expected to consume generous quantities of it. *Tayuban* often begin in the middle of the day, when children and women flock to watch; they usually last until the early hours before dawn, by which time only the male participants and the professional performers remain. Both the drinking and the erotic social dancing have led many strongly Muslim communities and local and regional governmental officials to frown on *tayuban*, though the government does not ban them (Hefner 1987). Formerly widespread throughout Java, *tayuban* are now found mostly in eastern Java and certain rural areas of central Java.

From the singer-dancer tradition evolved *gambyong*, a more urbane and respectable dance. It stands apart from most other kinds of Javanese dance in the absence of any narrative component; the dancer simply performs a variety of sensuous movements. Many of these occur in other Javanese dances, but usually as the actions of a particular charac-

ter. Somewhat comparable in its essentially nonnarrative quality is *ngrémo*, a popular dance of eastern Java. In its female version, it can be related to the *gambyong*; in its more popular male style, to male bravura and an eastern Javanese stance against colonial oppression during the last years of the Dutch presence in Java.

A Javanese dancer usually represents a particular mythological character—either in a dance-drama or in an excerpt presented as a piece. Though in the dances most closely related to martial arts the individual dancers

tayuban
Musical party with singer-dancers, common in Indonesia and Malaysia

Figure 21.8
Two singer-dancers at the beginning of a *tayuban*, surrounded by women and children. Photo by R. Anderson Sutton.

may not have the names of characters, they present in their dance some kind of martial event (a drill, a challenge, a fight, and so on), and may include dialogue. Highly refined, the female ensemble dances of the Javanese courts—*bedhaya* and *srimpi*—appear rather abstract; but these, too, may present particular Indian-derived or indigenous Javanese stories, albeit by stylized means (Brakel-Papenhuijzen 1992).

Javanese dance movements represent types of characters that can be grouped under three broad headings: female, refined male, and strong male. Many of the named kinetic patterns are used by all three categories of dancer, but with the female version being the most contained and intricate, the refined male version smooth and more open, and the strong male version the most bold and angular. Javanese have developed unique kinetic patterns for numerous major characters representative of these categories, plus certain ogres, clown-servants, and disciples, yielding a rich variety of movements. Javanese audiences widely recognize these movements, with particulars of costuming and style of speaking, as essential markers of a character's identity.

The gamelan accompaniment for Javanese dance, though flexible enough to allow individual interpretation, is highly constrained in several respects. Many dances are set to one piece or a medley of pieces, others to one of several with an identical formal structure (see below). Yet new choreographies abound, often drawing on extant pieces that have not formerly been designated for the character or characters being depicted in the dance. The drumming often specifically relates to the dancers' movements.

Because much of Javanese dance is narrative, it is scarcely possible to mention dance without mentioning theater. Among Java's theatrical genres, the one that Javanese and outsiders consistently single out as the supreme aesthetic achievement of the Javanese is leather-shadow puppetry (*wayang kulit* "leather shadow"), in which two-dimensional leather puppets cast shadows on a screen (Figure 21.9). *Wayang kulit* is accompanied by a gamelan, formerly somewhat reduced in size from the full gamelan described above. This is an ancient tradition in Java, one that has developed over the course of more than one thousand years. Several genres of *wayang kulit* are distinguished by name, based on the source of the stories and characters depicted. By far the most popular is *wayang purwa,* whose stories are episodes based on Javanese versions of the Indian epics *Mahabharata* and *Ramayana*, or interpolated episodes involving the characters from these epics. The repertoire used for the accompaniment of *wayang purwa* is mostly in the *sléndro* system, though since the 1950s pieces in *pélog* have often been used for variety if the ensemble is *sléndro-pélog* (see below).

Performances of *wayang kulit* are nearly always associated with a ritual celebration. They last from early evening (seven-thirty to nine) until around dawn (five to six). Almost as lengthy, but usually performed dur-

wayang kulit
Leather shadow puppetry

Figure 21.9
Dhalang Ki Sugino Siswocarito reaches for a shadow puppet; the puppets at the screen are fixed in a banana trunk. Photo by R. Anderson Sutton.

ing daylight hours, is *ruwatan,* intended to protect against spiritual dangers believed to be unleashed by certain circumstances of life, such as combinations of siblings (for example, the birth of twins or of five boys).

Wayang kulit, whether *ruwatan* or not, is a powerful art. It holds strong symbolic significance for many Javanese, young and old, urban and rural. Many see in its stories a microcosmic representation of divine order, a revelation of archetypal characters and situations lying behind the seeming unpredictability of daily human existence. Javanese frequently interpret current events and everyday human interaction with reference to the plots and characters of the famous wayang stories, and they tend to revere accomplished *dhalang* as spiritually powerful individuals, not merely entertainers. Though cultivated at the royal courts and patronized by wealthy urbanites, *wayang kulit* is widely performed in villages, appreciated by members of all social strata—peasant farmers of rice, urban drivers of pedicabs, and rich businessmen alike.

(CD)TRACK 11

In *wayang kulit,* all narration, dialogue, manipulation of puppets, singing of mood songs, and direction of the musicians is carried out by one individual, the *dhalang.* Though most *dhalang* are male, the profession is not restricted to men. Whether male or female, the *dhalang* must be able to speak in many voices, not only differentiating male and female characters, but between many characters and character types of either sex. So skilled can *dhalang* be at this that *wayang kulit* is widely enjoyed over the radio and on cassette, with audiences able to follow the story and know the characters without even seeing the puppets. Aside from some contemporary experiments, the *dhalang* does not work from a fixed text, being the consummate oral performer, at least after the first scene, and reciting lines from memory. Even if the episode to be presented is a famous one, it will be the *dhalang's* own version, with ample opportunity for interpolation of topical issues, up-to-date humor, and musical choices.

dhalang
Javanese puppeteer

In performance, the *dhalang* sits close to the screen, to the right of a large wooden chest for puppets. By knocking with a wooden beater against the chest, and by knocking, usually with his foot, against metal plaques suspended on its side, the *dhalang* signals the musicians, and accentuates certain movements of the puppets. Most of the puppets needed for a performance will be within reach; many of those not to be used will be arrayed on the left and right sides of the screen, implanted in the extremities of soft banana logs, which also hold the on-stage puppets.

The pieces played for the opening scene in any *wayang kulit* performance in central or east Java are multisectional, some quite lengthy, with sparse gong punctuation. During the scene dominated by clown-servants, the musicians often perform light, humorous pieces often of recent vintage. When tradition does not prescribe the piece, the *dhalang* either requests it by naming its title outright, or by hinting at it through a set phrase or a keyword before the end of his narration or dialogue. At many points during a performance, the *dhalang* sings mood songs that establish a particular emotional atmosphere (calmness, sadness, distress, tension, rage, and so on). The styles of performance used in *wayang kulit* do not differ in fundamental ways from gamelan performance in other contexts. Nevertheless, the music has a distinctive sound to listeners familiar with the range of Javanese music.

Much of the music associated fundamentally with *wayang kulit* is heard also in the accompaniment of the various dance-drama traditions that portray episodes based on the same mythological sources. Most closely related is the dance-drama form known as *wayang wong* "human wayang," in which dancers wear costumes closely imitating the look of the puppets, and often even dance in a quasi-two-dimensional manner resembling the motions of the puppets. With rare exceptions, *wayang wong* presents stories from the repertoire of *purwa*.

Aside from a few roles in the Yogyanese version, *wayang wong* dancer-actors do not wear masks. In the genre known as *wayang topèng* "masked wayang," however, all dancers are masked. Masked dances from this dance-drama are still popular as individual items in a dance concert, but full-length presentation of narrative episodes through masked dance-drama are rather rare.

Tunings, Scalar Systems, Modes

Javanese music employs two scalar systems (*sléndro* and *pélog*), neither of which is standardized with respect to tonal intervals or absolute pitches. The resulting variety is a reflection of keen interest on the part of the Javanese in nuance and subtle variation. Javanese tuners seek not to replicate preexisting tunings, but to create for each ensemble a unique tuning that remains recognizably *sléndro* or *pélog*—and pleasing. Indeed, *laras*, the Javanese term for scale and for tuning, can also mean "harmonious" and "in agreement." Rather than matching the pitch of keys and gongs to those of other ensembles or to some independent standard, tuners work intuitively, often tuning one multioctave instrument first in a painstaking process in which the instrument is played, tuned somewhat, played again, and tuned until a desirable scale is obtained. In former times, it was even forbidden to try to copy the tuning of a royal gamelan.

Javanese gamelan music is essentially pentatonic. *Sléndro* consists of five tones per octave, spaced at nearly equidistant intervals. Though one or two intervals are slightly larger than the others, their sizes (as measured in cents) and their placements within the octave vary from one gamelan to another. Music in *sléndro* may avoid or deemphasize one of these (see the discussion of *pathet* below). The tones are still known by the following names, though reference by numeral is most common now: pitch 1=*barang* "thing"; pitch 2=*gulu* (High Javanese *jangga*) "neck"; pitch 3=*dha-dha* (High Javanese *jaja*) "chest"; pitch 5=*lima* (High Javanese *gangsal*) "five"; pitch 6=*nem* "six."

Pélog is usually described as a seven-tone scalar system with large and small intervals between tones. The names of pitches and the corresponding numerals are: pitch 1=*penunggul* "first" or *bem* (no other meaning); pitch 2=*gulu* (compare *sléndro*); pitch 3=*dhadha* (compare *sléndro*); pitch 4=*pélog* (possibly from *pélo* "unclear pronunciation"); pitch 5 = *lima* (compare *sléndro*); pitch 6=*nem* (compare *sléndro*); pitch 7=*barang* (compare *sléndro*, pitch 1). Though *pélog* is a seven-tone system, no piece of *pélog* music, instrumental or vocal, uses all seven tones in equal or near-equal distribution. Instead, many *pélog* pieces are entirely pentatonic, and the others, using six or even seven tones, are limited within most phrases to five tones at most.

Closely related to the concept of *laras* is the Javanese modal concept *pathet*. It combines elements of tonal hierarchy, range, and intervallic structure with extramusical associations of mood and time of day or night. In each scalar system, Central Javanese identify three main *pathet* (Figure 21.10), which variably emphasize and avoid (or deemphasize by allowing only on weak beats) certain tones. *Pathet* can be understood as something akin to the Western notion of key, with transpositions between *pathet* (and even modula-

	pathet	Tones emphasized	Tone avoided
sléndro	*nem* 'six'	2, 6, 5	1
	sanga 'nine'	5, 1, (2)	3
	manyura 'peacock'	6, 2, (3)	5
pélog	*lima* 'five'	1, 5	7
	nem 'six'	5, 6	7
	barang 'thing'	6, 2, (3, 5)	1

Figure 21.10
Tonal hierarchy and range in central Javanese *pathet*.

tions between *pathet* in some pieces). *Pathet* categories vary slightly within central Java, and extensively between central and eastern Java. Only since the 1970s have *pathet* categories in eastern Java been widely applied to pieces outside the wayang repertoire—apparently in an effort to provide greater legitimacy for local music through emulation of central Javanese theoretical standards.

Repertoires and Formal Structures

No single term in Javanese covers the range of expression identified in English as "music." The term used most widely for the latter is *karawitan,* which includes the instrumental music of gamelans and other ensembles employing Javanese scales, the sung poetry known as *tembang*, and various combinations of instrumental and vocal music. The following section is concerned primarily with gamelan music and *tembang*.

The mainstay of gamelan music is the repertoire of *gendhing*, gamelan pieces with cyclic structures and whose phrases, punctuated by the sound of gongs, repeat until a signal is given to end. The patterns of punctuation are characterized by combinations of interlocking alternation and simultaneities or "coincidences." Each gendhing consists of one or more repeatable *gongan*—phrases marked off by large gongs. After a short solo introduction, each *gendhing* begins with the stroke of a gong; each *gendhing* also ends with the stroke of a gong. Each *gongan* is subdivided into shorter phrases (usually two or four, of equal length) known as *kenongan*, marked off by one of the *kenong*, sounding with the gong stroke and at regular temporal intervals in between. Each *kenongan* is further punctuated by *kethuk*, and longer *kenongan* by *engkuk-kemong* or *kempyang*.

The Javanese differentiate many formal structures by the particular interlocking and coinciding patterns of the gong instruments and their rhythmic fit with the steady beat of the main instrumental melody. This melody (*balungan* "skeleton," "outline") is usually played on the *saron* and the *slenthem* (the two types of metallophones). By Javanese convention, notation of the *balungan* places the strongest beat at the end of a grouping rather than at the beginning. Thus, the even-numbered beats have the greater rhythmic weight. Where Westerners counting four beats would give primary stress to beat one, secondary stress to beat three, and tertiary stress to beats two and four, Javanese would give primary stress to beat four, secondary stress to beat two, and tertiary stress to beats one and three. As a result, the heaviest of all beats, the one coinciding with the gong stroke, is notated at the end of a line, not the beginning. The names of formal structures differ somewhat from one tradition to another. What is presented below is a discussion of formal structures

balungan
The main skeletal "melody" in Central Javanese gamelan music

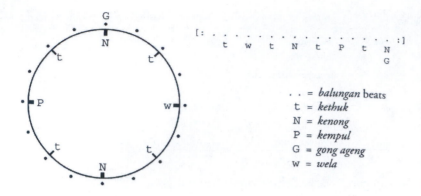

Figure 21.11
The formal structure of a *ketawang*, in circular and linear presentations.

. . = *balungan* beats
t = *kethuk*
N = *kenong*
P = *kempul*
G = *gong ageng*
w = *wela*

in Solonese *karawitan,* with comments on significant differences in other traditions.

Javanese normally represent the schemata for formal structures in linear fashion, as this is the most practical to reproduce. The circular approach developed by J. Becker (1979a, 1979b) and Hoffman (1978), showing the *gongan* as the face of a clock, is a neat visual analog to the cyclic structure of *gendhing*. Figure 21.11 shows the structure of a *gongan* in the form known as *ketawang,* a small form with two *kenongan* per *gongan*.

In performance, a solo introduction leads into the entrance of a full ensemble and the simultaneous sounding of *kenong* and gong, leading without pause into the first *gongan* of a *gendhing*. In some cases, small *gendhing* (such as *ketawang* pieces) are joined directly to other pieces in a medley—in which case no solo introduction would be played.

After a solo introduction, a large *gendhing* proceeds through a calm section consisting of one or more *gongan* with the same formal structure. This section repeats until a signal, usually a change of tempo, cues musicians to make a transition to a second main section, which repeats until a cue is given to end or proceed to a different piece. The category of large *gendhing* incorporates a variety of forms distinguished by the number of *kenongan,* the length of *kenongan* phrases (at least sixteen beats), the number of *kethuk* per *kenongan,* and the density of the playing of the *kethuk*.

Other than by gong structure or *kendhang* pattern, Javanese classifications of *gendhing* draw on several factors, including style and context, predominant instrumentation, and regional association. For instance, the repertoire of *gendhing* Banyumas (a region in west-central Java) is distinguished from *gendhing* Jawa timuran (eastern Javanese). *Gendhing tayub,* pieces are associated with *tayuban,* feature spirited playing and short *gongan*. *Gendhing bonang* (or *gendhing bonangan*) are pieces featuring *bonang* and other loud-playing instruments. The Yogyanese term, in fact, is *gendhing soran* "pieces in loud style." The Solonese sometimes distinguish pieces by the instrument that performs the introduction: *gendhing gendèr* or *gendhing rebab*.

Vocal Music

The Javanese maintain several vocal genres, many of which are combined with instrumental playing. One of the most important criteria in distinguishing among repertorial items within a single regional tradition is the kind of interaction between vocal or vocally oriented melody and instrumental playing. The resulting dichotomy is sometimes expressed as *tembang* ("sung poetry," "vocal") and *gendhing* ("cyclic pieces," "instrumental"). The term *tembang* is also used to denote a subset of songs within the larger category of vocal music.

Musicians usually distinguish three major classes of *tembang*: *tembang gedhé* "large, great," *tembang tengahan* "medium," and *tembang macapat* (etymology unclear, but de-

karawitan
Javanese gamelan-based court music
tembang
Type of metered vocal performance in Indonesia
gendhing
Gamelan-based musical composition of Java
kendhang
Double-headed drum of Java

bated; *maca* "to read," *pat* "four"). In stanzaic patterns, *tembang gedhé* are closely related to patterns of Indian prosody and are distinguishable by number of syllables per line and per segment within a line. All have four lines per stanza. In contrast, *tembang tengahan* and *macapat*—categories that sometimes overlap—are distinguishable by number of lines, number of syllables per line, and ending vowel of each line.

Each *macapat* meter is associated with a limited range of emotions or appropriate subject. For each meter, one or more basic melodies are known. *Tembang* was once quite common in Java, from mothers singing their young ones to sleep, to formal gatherings where readers would take turns reading and singing verses from lengthier works interspersed with discussion of textual meanings and implications (Arps 1992). Since the 1970s, however, the purely vocal rendering of *tembang* has been most evident in occasional government-sponsored *macapat* contests.

Mood songs, sung by *dhalang* in various genres, constitute another major category of vocal repertoire. Usually known as *pathetan*, these set or underscore a calm atmosphere. They are accompanied by soft-playing instruments (rebab, *gendèr*, *gambang*, *suling*), with occasional punctuation by hanging gongs and *kenong* (Brinner 1995). As their name suggests, *pathetan* also serve to establish *pathet* at the beginning of each period of a wayang performance. In purely instrumental renditions, with a rebab serving as the melodic leader, *pathetan* are almost always played before and after a major piece or sequence of pieces in *klenèngan* concerts. Agitated-mood songs indicate anger, danger, impending battle, and other heightened emotions or situations. These are accompanied by *gendèr,* rapid knocking by the *dhalang* on metal plaques and on the chest in which puppets are stored, and occasional punctuation by hanging gongs and *kenong*.

Performance Practice

The rhythmic orientation of Javanese music ranges from steady, even beats in a hierarchy of subdivisions in purely instrumental music to a free-rhythmic, parlando delivery in purely vocal lines. Most of the music combines elements of the two. Binary subdivision characterizes the formal structures discussed above, with the number of beats in full cycles and subsections almost always representing an even multiple of two.

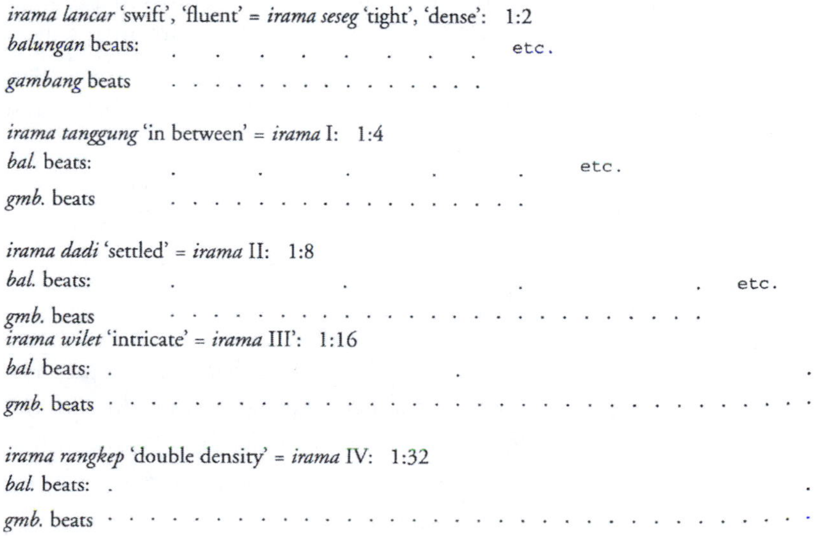

One of the essential elements in the performance of most gamelan pieces, not found in other genres, is the play of *irama*, the level of subdivision of the basic pulse. Javanese currently recognize five levels of subdivision, determined by the ratio between this beat (often represented by the melody played on the *saron barung* and the *saron demung*) and the

Figure 21.12
Five levels of *irama*.

irama lancar 'swift', 'fluent' = *irama seseg* 'tight', 'dense': 1:2
balungan beats: .   .   .   .   .   .   etc.
gambang beats   .   .   .   .

irama tanggung 'in between' = *irama* I: 1:4
bal. beats: .   .   .   .   .   etc.
gmb. beats   .   .   .   .

irama dadi 'settled' = *irama* II: 1:8
bal. beats: .   .   .   .   etc.
gmb. beats   .   .   .   .
irama wilet 'intricate' = *irama* III': 1:16
bal. beats: .   .   .
gmb. beats .   .   .   .

irama rangkep 'double density' = *irama* IV: 1:32
bal. beats: .   .
gmb. beats .   .   .   .

parts that evenly subdivide it (played most consistently on the *saron peking*, the *bonang panerus*, the *gambang*, and the *celempung*). Figure 21.12 portrays the rhythmic relationship between this beat and the fastest pulse, played on the *gambang*.

The term *irama*, sometimes glossed "tempo," is better understood as the temporal "space" between beats, measured by the subdividing instruments. The *irama* level, then, is a result of the *balungan* tempo. As the beat slows down, the tempo reaches a point at which the subdividing instruments can double. At this point, the Javanese speak of a change of *irama* level. Within each level, the tempo can vary without bringing about an *irama* change; but in the performance of many pieces, the tempo of the *balungan* gradually slows to one half, and then to one quarter of its initial rate, yielding a change of *irama* during each transition, as the subdividing instruments double their ratio with the *balungan*. As a result, the tempo of the subdividers remains relatively constant from one settled *irama* level to another. Keeler (1987:225) aptly compares the process of *irama* change to the shifting of gears by the driver of an automobile. In response to changes of tempo, executing smooth changes in *irama* level is one of the skills Javanese musicians must master. Playing with the expansion and compression of time is fundamental to the aesthetics of gamelan music throughout central and eastern Java.

The following is an offering of a description of instrumental conventions in the contemporary performance of central Javanese gamelans, noting some of the most significant divergences among regional traditions.

Fundamental to an understanding of instrumental practice is the relationship between the melodic outline (*balungan*) and the treatment (*garapan*) of this outline in the strands of variations that elaborate or abstract it. The *balungan* is almost always played explicitly on the single-octave *saron barung, saron demung,* and *slenthem*. The *balungan* is the only instrumental part usually played by more than one person simultaneously; it is memorized, though versions of the *balungan* for the same piece vary from region to region, and even from one individual to another within a single locale. Players of the *non-balungan*-carrying instruments are expected to know the *balungan* and to construct their parts in relation to it.

The *balungan* part is often a steady progression of tones, one per *balungan* (four per *gatra,* as 2-3-5-3 2-1-2-1). The instruments that play the *balungan* within their single-octave ranges also perform variations of the *balungan* in certain contexts. In most regional traditions, players insert a single tone between each tone of the *balungan*. In other contexts, particularly in pieces that accompany *wayang kulit* and other dramatic forms, a pair of *saron barung* may perform interlocking variations. The remaining member of the *saron* family, the *saron peking*, plays simple variations of the *balungan* melody, anticipating or echoing the *saron* melody, either tone by tone, or in a simple alternation between two successive tones.

The principal *garapan* instruments of the loud-playing ensemble are the pair of *bonang: barung* and *panerus.* Three basic techniques of variation characterize these instruments. Convention and context determine which of the three is appropriate. The simplest is the anticipation of prominent *balungan* tones with regular offbeat octaves on the *barung,* with something close to triplet subdivision on the *panerus.* This technique is reserved for pieces with short *gongan* phrases, either light or swift in mood. It contrasts to a more contem-

garapan
Formulae for variation and improvisation in Javanese music

plative and subdued technique in which both *bonang barung* and *panerus* vary the *saron* melody, primarily by alternating successive tones, with the *panerus* playing at twice the speed of the *barung*. The third technique is a lively interlocking between *bonang barung* (playing on and between *saron* beats) and *panerus* (playing between *bonang barung* beats). The interlocking on *bonang*—often interspersed with rapid flourishes leading to prominent tones of the *saron* melody—is the flashiest, most playful, and most lighthearted of the three *bonang* techniques.

The *bonang* is often identified as the melodic leader of the loud ensemble. The *bonang's* anticipation of the tones of the melody played on the *saron* can actually spell out the melody well enough that an adept player, with no reference to notation, can perform a piece he has not memorized.

From steady, rapid beats on the *gambang* (wooden xylophone), to florid melodies of *pesindhèn* (singer) to subtle but commanding strains of a rebab, the soft-playing ensemble is the heart of contemporary *garapan*. The soft-playing percussion instruments—*gambang*, *celempung* (and *siter*), *gendèr panerus*, *gendèr barung*—resemble those of the loud-playing ensemble in their adherence to a subdividing rhythmic paradigm, some more strictly than others. Of these, the *gendèr barung* part is rhythmically and melodically the most complex. Playing mostly in a two-part counterpoint, it is the most revered of the soft-playing subdividers. Rhythmically more subtle are the rebab (which may contribute to the subdivision, but often plays in syncopation with the main beat) and the *suling*, many of whose melodic patterns are independent of the predominant instrumental beat.

Players of the soft-playing instruments build their parts mostly by drawing on a vocabulary of melodic elaborations (*cèngkok*), whose precise realizations are closely related, though in small ways distinguishable from those of other players. A flexible but limited relationship exists between the *cèngkok* and the melodic contexts that comprise the *gendhing* in various repertories. A player makes choices based on response to those he or she hears other players using as they perform together, and on his or her own preferences at the moment, including a desire for variation for its own sake.

As is typical in most central Javanese practice, the *gérong* (male chorus) part adheres both to the regular pulse of the percussion instruments and to the melody of the *balungan*, whereas the *pesindhèn* part floats freely over this pulse, exhibiting considerable rhythmic and melodic independence from the *balungan* and other percussive parts. Like the soft-playing instrumental parts, both these vocal parts are built from *cèngkok*, independent of any particular piece.

Many *gendhing* performed in soft-playing style will be stopped in midphrase by a signal from the drum, at which point the *pesindhèn* (or more rarely a solo male vocalist) is expected to perform a florid solo, accompanied only by occasional referential tones supplied by the *gender barung*. At the appropriate moment, the drummer signals the reentry of the other instrumentalists, and the *gendhing* resumes, ending eventually at the sounding of a gong, or proceeding on to another *gendhing*. This stop, known as *andhegan*, provides an opportunity for focus on the skills of the vocalist.

The instruments providing rhythmic direction in gamelan performance are the *kendhang* (drums) and, in dance and dramatic performances, the *keprak* (slit drum) and the

pesindhen
The female vocalist in a Central Javanese gamelan ensemble
suling
End-blown bamboo ring-stop flute, found throughout Indonesia and Philippines
cèngkok
Melodic elaborations based on a central melody

kecrèk (metal plaques). As drumming directs the performative tempo and flow, the drummer's responsibility is usually to signal the ending of a *gendhing*, with a change from the normally repeating pattern (or, in the case of the playing of *ciblon*, repeating paradigm) to a special ending. Usually the drummer does this by gradually slowing the tempo, but on hearing the change in drumstrokes, experienced musicians know to end, even with no change of tempo.

With a limited vocabulary of rhythms, the percussive knocks on the *keprak*, the *kecrèk*, and the chest in which puppets are stored accentuate dancers' or puppets' movements, signal musicians to begin a *gendhing*, change tempos, or end. Initiated by the master of the dance or the *dhalang*, the signals to the gamelan musicians are confirmed by the *kendhang*. The styles of knocking for accompanying puppetry vary from one regional tradition to another, both in the configuration of specific signals and in the basic sound.

Of indigenous instruments other than those heard in gamelans, the most prominent are *terbang* (frame drums), used in various genres throughout central and eastern Java and Madura. Most of these employ several smaller *terbang* playing interlocking polyrhythms, with punctuation provided by one or more large *terbang*. Double-reed instruments (*sronèn*), heard in a variety of ensembles in eastern Java and Madura, perform intricate melodies, alternating sustained tones with rapid figuration, often outside the intervallic structures of either *sléndro* or *pélog* (Kartomi 1976). Rice-block-pounding music, enjoying something of a revival because of government-sponsored contests, involves interlocking patterns of contrasting timbres (and sometimes contrasting pitches), with each of five or six players holding one large pole, pounding one or more surfaces of a large, partially hollowed-out log.

Music and the Mass Media

The mass media, particularly radio and commercial recordings, have played a central role in the dissemination of music in Java. Phonograph recordings have been made in Indonesia since the first decade of the twentieth century, but it was radio, introduced in the 1920s, that had the greater impact on indigenous music until the rise of commercial recordings on cassettes in the 1970s. Cheaper than phonographs, radios could provide aural access to a changing variety of performances.

In the Java of the early 21st century, mass-media technology is widespread. Most urban households have radios and cassette players, many have television sets, and a rapidly increasing minority has DVD players and satellite dishes. Even before villages had lines for electric power, it was not uncommon to find radios, cassette players, and televisions powered by car batteries. Now most Javanese villages have electricity, making such items easier and cheaper to use. Although individuals may tune in to a particular show on radio or television, it is not unusual to find either (or both) turned on and serving as background for socializing, eating, or doing housework. Musicians often listen to the radio to hear new pieces and new renditions of older pieces. For many musicians, radio serves as the primary source for learning new repertoire, as well as current norms and variants in the treatment or interpretation of older pieces. Musicians also learn from cassettes that they purchase themselves or borrow from friends or neighbors.

Some radio broadcasts are live, but there has been a trend toward the use of commercially produced recordings on cassettes or recordings of sessions by professional or amateur musicians in a radio studio, with multiple takes if necessary. At public institutions and in private lessons, recordings on cassettes (commercially available or privately recorded) routinely serve as standard accompaniments for instruction in dancing. In some contexts, public performances of dance are accompanied by cassette rather than live musicians, but this situation is still unusual.

Since the introduction of television (1962), the government-controlled television stations in Indonesia have devoted little attention to traditional performing arts. Gamelan performances are broadcast occasionally, but are usually of amateur groups, rather than the skilled professionals of the radio stations, courts, or puppeteer troupes. Musicians may be entertained by some of these broadcasts, but the forum for important new repertoire and innovative treatment of traditional *gendhing* is widely acknowledged to be radio—and since the early 1970s, the commercial cassette industry.

Having made recorded music accessible to a wide sector of society, the cassette industry has sometimes been regarded as a threat to the continuation of live musical performance. Indeed, Javanese not uncommonly purchase or even rent a recording of an eight-hour *wayang kulit* for playing at a family ritual event (wedding or circumcision). And although live performance does continue, the Javanese strongly prefer to hire star performers (famous puppeteers, gamelan groups, *pesindhèn*) whose fame has been gained largely through their representation on commercial cassettes. The cassette industry has produced a sharp division between performers chosen for recordings, who may earn a substantial living as musicians, and competent but nameless performers, who secure only occasional engagements.

The sheer number of cassette releases—thousands of gamelan music cassettes, hundreds of seven- or eight-hour sets of complete *wayang kulit*, and even close to one hundred cassettes of *calung Banyumas*—is staggering. Because the technology is inexpensive, local genres once thought to be near extinction have enjoyed a resurgence of popularity, as their image has been refurbished by the legitimizing powers of representation on cassettes. The potential for homogenization has been largely blunted by the variety of versions available on cassettes.

Performers and Composers

Until the late twentieth century, making music in Java was fundamentally communal, with little public acclaim for players or composers. In villages, many musicians are farmers or petty tradespeople by day and perform music on an occasional basis. In towns and cities, members of the old nobility and new élites may participate as amateurs in gamelan performances. Yet most gamelan music one encounters, whether in live performances or on radio broadcasts or cassettes, is performed by professionals who earn a substantial portion of their income from their activities as musicians. The profession of music goes back many centuries in Java, with large groups of court musicians fully supported by the royal courts, and itinerant rural musicians hiring themselves out for performances, or even begging from one locale to the next. The status of musician is low in Java, lower than that of dancer or puppeteer. Nevertheless, many musicians earn a meager living from their art, and a few have gained fame and wealth, thanks in large measure to modern mass media.

The division of labor in musical performance remains largely segmented by gender.

Professional instrumentalists are nearly always male. In the past, the main exception was the player of the *gendèr* for *wayang kulit*, often the puppeteer's wife. Otherwise, the only professional female musicians were the singers (*pesindhèn*), who before the twentieth century were usually singer-dancers, often associated with prostitution. Since the 1960s, with the profession of *pesindhèn* not only gaining in respectability but becoming lucrative, interest in studying singing has grown significantly, particularly among rural girls. Professional female players of *gendèr* are now a rarity, but amateur women's gamelan groups have sprung up in great numbers, primarily in the larger towns and cities of central and eastern Java, where they probably outnumber amateur men's groups.

Musical patronage takes several forms in contemporary Java. Each of the four central Javanese courts maintains a corps of musicians with the official status of court musician or court singer at various individual ranks; but none of the courts has the financial means to pay even the musical directors a living wage. Musicians still serve the courts, partly out of reverence for royalty, partly for the stature a courtly rank brings to themselves and their families, and partly for the contacts and exposure it provides for other professional musical activities.

Aside from a few famous gamelan music directors and composers (discussed below), those seeking to make a living as gamelan musicians may accompany popular puppeteers (some of whom work nearly every night during certain months of the year), or they may join the ranks of the Indonesian civil service—as musicians affiliated with particular national radio stations (RRI—Radio Republik Indonesia) or as teachers at one of the educational institutions devoted to Java's performing arts. Though the salary is low, the affiliation with one of the RRI stations can win important prestige and invitations for far more remunerative engagements at private events, such as weddings and circumcisions.

Teaching is increasingly the position of choice for Java's young musicians able to secure the necessary formal credentials. Competition for jobs teaching at the arts institutions mentioned above is especially keen. In addition, Javanese gamelan music is taught formally at other institutions offering a broader or differently focused curriculum. Another means of support, usually insufficient by itself, is the offering of private and group instruction outside the formal educational system. Most often, professional musicians combine the activities mentioned above in an effort to patch together a livelihood.

New Developments

Javanese music has never been static. Like many primarily oral traditions, it has been based on internal dynamism and variability. During the colonial era, the size of the ensemble grew, many new pieces entered the repertoire, and some new styles of playing and vocal-instrumental combinations came into vogue.

In the era of Indonesian independence, particularly from the late 1950s onward, accomplished musicians composed many new pieces, many of them based on the style of Javanese children's game songs. These pieces, with more experimental and unusual pieces by Ki Wasitodiningrat and young composers, are usually called *kreasi baru* "new creations." Many of them emphasize the vocal line, often delivered by male and female singers in unison. In a few instances, two vocal lines move in counterpoint—almost certainly a response to Western musical influence, without precedent in the *karawitan* tradition. Since the early 1980s, the composition of *kreasi baru* has grown tremendously, with an enormous increase in both the number of pieces composed and the number of musicians composing them. Many of these imitate or adopt Indonesian popular tunes in *dangdut* style; others employ the infectious rhythms of the popular Sundanese *jaipongan*.

kreasi baru
New musical composition, pan-Indonesian term

Outside the realm of pop styles, the focal point for the most innovative work in recent years has been the postsecondary institution STSI in Surakarta. Before the early 1980s, students were required to demonstrate mastery of the *karawitan* tradition by composing a *gendhing* in traditional style. Since that time, however, students have been required to compose a modern piece demonstrating creativity and originality. The resulting pieces usually employ standard gamelan instruments, though they may use nongamelan instruments, even newly invented ones.

Some of the experimental compositions incorporate substantial passages from extant traditional pieces and employ standard techniques. Others draw on performance styles from the neighboring traditions of Sunda and Bali, but apply them to Javanese instruments in unusual juxtapositions. Nontraditional uses of extant traditional passages and techniques can be just as surprising as the radical techniques mentioned above. They give the compositions a high degree of unpredictability, requiring different attitudes and responses from an audience than do older pieces. They are presented in concerts lasting only a few hours, with small audiences sitting quietly and listening attentively.

It is too early to predict what wider effects experimental compositions will have in Java, but they are bound to influence the history of *karawitan,* which has always evolved in response to changing social conditions and aesthetic sensibilities. The continued vitality of Javanese music is due not only to its basic internal dynamism and tolerance for individual creativity but also to Javanese openness to change.

Cirebon

The region of Cirebon, located at the approximate cultural boundary between the Sundanese and the Javanese, encompasses aspects of both cultures. Linguistically and in some forms of art (such as shadow plays and woodcarving) it is closer to the Javanese than to the Sundanese; in other cultural aspects (such as music and dance) it is closer to the Sundanese.

In reality, however, the situation is more complicated. Cirebonese influences on the Sundanese in music and dance are actually greater than vice versa. In the 1500s, Cirebon developed into an Islamic kingdom. Before then, its area had been part of both Galuh and Pajajaran, Sundanese Hindu kingdoms. Central Javanese cultural influences during the Mataram Period (in the 1600s and the 1700s) are great, but some Cirebonese cultural aspects are older. Architecture, woodcarving, and musical expression are similar to fourteenth-century east Javanese Hindu culture, as well as to Balinese cultures of today (Wagner 1959; Wright 1978). Even now, the musical practices and terminologies in Cirebonese gamelans have more similarities to those of the east Javanese than to those of the central Javanese.

Since 1677, the Cirebonese kingdom has been divided into two kingdoms, Kasepuhan ("The Old") and Kanoman ("The Young"), each with its court (*kraton*). A third court, that of the Kacirebonan principality, was established in 1807 (Sunardjo and Unang

1983). An even smaller court, Kaprabonan, was established before World War II. These divisions were initially the result of political tension, but the courts also function as religious centers. Even now, when none of the courts has political power, they retain strong religious functions. The kings and their descendants are believed to have spiritual power. Villagers, farmers, merchants, and artists come individually or communally to the king or princes to ask for blessings or to be cured of spiritual and physical illnesses.

Islam and Music

Most Cirebonese are Muslims. Consequently, their culture has strong Islamic elements. As in most parts of Java, however, there is little Arabic musical influence. The scalar, modal, and musical influences reflect the regional culture, rather than West Asian musical culture just as Javanese-Hindu music contains few Indian music elements. In the past, the melody of the call to prayer (*adzan*) and the reciting of the Qur'ān in many villages were in *sléndro* or *pélog* scale, rather than in a West Asian scale, as heard today.

Some Cirebonese musical instruments—like frame drums, variously called *trebang* (or *terbang*), *genjring* (with metal jingles) *gembyung,* and *brai*—are believed to have come from West Asia. Drums, the only musical instruments found in mosques, include a slit drum, a large double-headed drum used to signal the time of prayer, and the possible addition of one or more kinds of frame drums. Few musical ensembles with these frame drums, however, are still associated with the mosque. The acrobatic performance of *sidapurna,* which often includes magical elements and has nothing to do with Islam, is accompanied by an ensemble of *genjring.* The *randu kentir,* a folk-dance group in Indramayu, uses these frame drums to function as *ketuk* and *gong.*

Because Islam came to Indonesia through Sufism, it blended easily with the local religion and culture. Indigenous Javanese (Hindu) artistic traditions were adopted by Islam, and were transformed to include Islamic symbolic teaching. Shadow plays, gamelans, and other forms of art are traditionally believed to be the creation of the nine Islamic saints, who invented them to help spread Islam (Ricklefs 1981). The *gamelan sekati,* which does not sound at all like West Asian music, is considered the most Islamic. This type of gamelan is still played in the court compounds, but only for the celebration of Muhammad's birthday (at Kanoman) and major Islamic holidays, Idul-fitri and Idul-'adha (at Kasepuhan). Even though the shadow-puppet theater (*wayang kulit*) is forbidden by fundamentalist Muslims, some people still believe that by understanding the philosophical symbols found in a box of puppets, one can learn as much of Islam as by reading the Qur'ān. Even the monster play (*berokan*) and the *ronggeng* (professional female dancer-singer, often associated with prostitution) are believed to embody elements of Islamic philosophy (Sutton 1989) [see WAVES OF CULTURAL INFLUENCE: ISLAM].

Islamic fundamentalism, however, has grown since the 1800s, as direct contact with West Asia has become more accessible through pilgrimages, Islamic universities (which include the study of Arabic), publications, and other mass media, such as radio, television, and especially the cassette industry. In most parts of Java, every neighborhood has several mosques, whence, through raised loudspeakers, one can hear Qur'ānic recitation and the call to prayer five times daily—all in a West Asian melodic style.

Contexts Involving Musical Performance

Traditional Cirebonese music is rarely performed in concert halls. Performances are associated with one or more kinds of individual or communal ceremonies. Except for ceremonies in villages and courts, performances occur on a temporary stage built in the yard or on the street in front of the house of the person who commissioned them.

The function of the arts is still closely connected to village rituals involving initiation, rice, the sea, and ancestors. Though most artists are not farmers, they not only know much about farming, but in many ways are responsible for its ritual process. Farming rice, the primary and most spiritualized crop, and initiations are the best examples of how traditional performing arts are intrinsic to the entire cultural, spiritual, and ecological setting. Annual village rituals vary from one village to another. For all these ceremonies, all kinds of groups perform predominantly theatrical genres, such as *wayang kulit* "shadow-puppet theater," *wayang golèk* "rod-puppet theater," and *wayang topèng* "masked-dance theater."

The most frequent events involving music, however, are weddings and circumcisions, making up about 60 percent of all such events. The remainder are for other types of life–cycle ceremonies, such as the seventh month of pregnancy (as in several other areas of Indonesia), exorcism, execution of a vow or oath when one recovers from illness or has good luck (often held with weddings and circumcisions), the artists' *buka panggung* (opening of the stage), *atur-atur* ("esteem" from the artists to ancestors), independence-day celebrations, street performances, and festivals. Therefore, the villages, not the courts or the cities, are the center of traditional Cirebonese performances.

Musical Systems

Like other parts of Java, Cirebon has musical forms that can be categorized into gamelans and other ensembles. Cirebon has several types of gamelan, more in the tradition of the folk than that of the courts. Like shadow-puppet theater, the gamelans' refinement and sophistication have less to do with patronage than with professionalism and the family system. Cirebonese artists are exclusively professionals. All the court gamelans are similar in that all have a one-row gong chime (*bonang*) like the Balinese *réyong* and *trompong*, as opposed to the two-row *bonang* of the modern Javanese gamelan. Furthermore, they are all in *pélog*-like tuning and musically refrain from developing or changing to suit modern tastes. The exclusive court gamelan are the *gamelan sekati* (also *gamelan sukati*) and the *gamelan denggung*. The former is found in both the Kasepuhan and Kanoman courts.

The older *gamelan denggung*—perhaps three centuries old or older, and found in the Kasepuhan court but no longer played—resembles the Sundanese *gamelan degung* of today (see below). This means that it could be originally from Sunda (North 1988) or, conversely, that the Sundanese *degung* ensemble originated in Cirebon. Most widely used, the modern gamelan clearly exhibits not only musical theory, tuning, modal, and compositional systems, but also the relationship between music and cultural settings, both traditional and modern. As in most parts of Java and Bali, music is rooted in two systems of tuning, *pélog* and *sléndro*.

Cirebon has two kinds of modern gamelan: *gamelan prawa* and *gamelan pélog*. *Prawa* is basically a high-pitched *sléndro*. Compared with Sundanese *saléndro* and Javanese *slén-*

Figure 21.13
The *gamelan prawa* ensemble is played as dozens of children look on. Photo by Endo Suanda

Figure 21.14
The extra set of high-pitched *bonang* is one of the features that distinguishes *gamelan pélog* from *gamelan prawa*; the difference in tuning is another. Photo by Endo Suanda.

dro, it may be one or two keys (150 to 400 cents) higher. The two are never combined to create one set having both *pélog* and *prawa,* as in Javanese gamelan. Those that have both sets, as in the courts, are kept separate and their functions differ. The *gamelan prawa* accompanies *wayang topèng* (Figure 21.13), and *gamelan pélog* accompanies *tayuban;* however, the *gamelan pélog* is now more and more widely used for both *wayang* and *topeng,* especially in the southern part of Cirebon (Figure 21.14).

Gamelan pieces are cyclic. A large gong marks the ending of each cycle, and other gongs and kettle pots outline the form in a colotomic or punctuating manner. Form is determined by the colotomic instruments and the drums, and the piece adheres to the form. However, one piece may include one or more gong cycles, and one cycle may be subdivided in a variety of ways. In gamelan, a piece is almost always performed repetitively, though it is never repeated in exactly the same way. The composition might also be a suite consisting of several pieces (*lagu*). Changes in density and tempo are among the important aesthetic elements in the playing of gamelans.

Other ensembles of Cirebon are small groups of six or fewer instruments. The frame-drum ensemble, under a variety of names, is widespread. The *genjring* ensemble includes four or more frame drums, which play interlocking rhythms ornamented by strong strokes on a *bedug. Genjring* drums (Figure 21.15) have three pairs of metal rattles attached to them (*genjring* is onomatopoeic, *jring* being the sound of the drum and the rattle), and play loud, exciting music. The vocal parts are mostly in Arabic, especially when the *genjring* accompanies the *rudat,* a devotional dance performed in a mosque. But in the *sidapurna,* an acrobatic show, the text is mixed with local poems in the Cirebonese dialect.

The other frame drums (*gembyung* and *brai*) are usually larger than the *genjring,* and they lack metal attachments, so they sound softer and lower, and utilize less variation in rhythm. Responsorial singing—a solo leader and a chorus (*jawab* "answer")—is more prominent than the playing drums. Until the 1950s, most mosques had some kind of ensemble. Now only a few retain any instruments, and few of them are playable.

Ketuk telu "three *ketuk,*" another small ensemble, resembles Sundanese *ketuk tilu* (see below), but it incorporates Cirebonese songs. The *ketuk* is a horizontal kettle-gong in a wooden frame; three of them form the centerpiece of a *ketuk tilu* ensemble. In Sunda, the *ketuk tilu* in its traditional setting is practically obsolete; in Cirebon, there are still a few ensembles, often performing at the *kasinoman* or *ngarot* ceremony in Indramayu. Today, however, the ensemble also presents traditional pop (*pop Sunda* or *pop Cirebonan*), including *dangdut* and modern music resembling *tarling*, a light form of pop using guitar and *suling*. The current ensemble includes an electric guitar, violin, a pair of gongs, a pair of *klènang*, three *ketuk*, and a set of *kendang*, all of which accompany dancing female vocalists and male instrumentalist-singers (Figure 21.16).

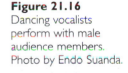

Figure 21.15
The onomatopoeic *genjring* frame drums (background) provide a ringing accompaniment to the *bedug*. Photo by Endo Suanda.

New Developments

The city of Cirebon has only a few Western-style musical bands (such as Indonesian bands that play rock or jazz), for most such groups prefer to live in bigger cities, like Bandung or Jakarta. However, many *dangdut* bands throughout the Cirebon region often combine with modern *tarling* (Wright 1988). Indeed, they are often named *tarling dangdut* and are found even in small towns.

The large groups, popular and therefore wealthy, may also have electric guitars (playing melody and bass), synthesizer, set of drums, tambourine, flute, and violin, along with the traditional *suling, kendang,* gongs, *ketuk-kebluk,* and *kecrèk*. Many have powerful outdoor sound systems, with dozens of microphones and two large walls of speakers. Abdul Ajib's *tarling*, one of the top groups, often comes to the stage with a truck-mounted satellite antenna. The group presents foreign television programs to attract people's attention before the performance, instead of the traditional instrumental introductory section (*talu*).

Figure 21.16
Dancing vocalists perform with male audience members. Photo by Endo Suanda.

The influence of urban (and Western) musical culture on the average Cirebonese village, therefore, comes, not from the city of Cirebon, but from Jakarta and Bandung, both for live performances and especially for radio and television broadcasting and cassettes. *Pop Sunda,* heavily broadcast on Bandung television stations, deeply influences young village artists and results in Cirebonese pop music. The arrangement of Bandung's *gamelan wanda anyar* "fresh-

Figure 21.17
Local drums, a blown bamboo 'gong' (*right*), and *bonang* (*lower left*) blend with a Chinese *sona* (*left*) to create a unique outdoor sound. Photo by Endo Suanda.

breeze gamelan," pioneered by the late Mang Koko Koswara and further developed by Nano Suratno and other Bandung Conservatory graduates, is now being adopted by Cirebonese gamelans.

The most significant Sundanese musical influence on Cirebon is the *jaipongan* style of drumming. Because the old drummers have neither the energy nor the dexterity to perform in its style, they have all now retired from drumming to play other instruments. Therefore, if in earlier times the *wayang kulit* drummers were always the more senior musicians, now all of the groups have young drummers (in their teens or early twenties).

Nevertheless, the influences between modern and traditional music seem to go both ways: traditional groups are adopting urban styles (including Westernization), while urban groups are adopting local and village repertoires. In addition, some musical blending between Chinese and local styles occurs (Figure 21.17). Gamelan groups are incorporating diatonic melodies, notably from *dangdut* (when melodic instruments cannot follow the vocal melodies, they become nonmelodic instruments or simply cease playing), and a few gamelans have started using violin (*biola*). However, it is popular for modern Indonesian bands that play rock to adopt traditional repertoires and instruments.

Sunda

The Sundanese, numbering approximately 30 million people, are Indonesia's second largest ethnic group. They live in the province of West Java, encompassing the interior highlands, the coastal areas, and Cirebon, a culturally distinct region. Most Sundanese are Muslims. Though considered conservative in their faith, they have a broad definition of what constitutes being a Muslim, and they often combine their concepts of Islam with traditional animist beliefs. The Hindu-Buddhist tradition, prevalent in the culture of Central and East Java, is less apparent in Sunda.

Though several small kingdoms rose and fell before the 1300s, none was significant in relation to political powers outside of Sunda. In 1333, the Sundanese kingdom of Pajajaran was founded at Pakuan, near what is now the city of Bogor. The era of Pajajaran represents the Sundanese at their most politically powerful in relation to other Javanese kingdoms. It is considered their most important historical and cultural period. Pajajaran was a pre-Islamic trading kingdom in competition with the East Javanese kingdom of Majagahit (C.E. 1293–1530). In 1579, when the Sultan of Banten had the royal family killed, Pajajaran disappeared. As an important symbol of Sundanese identity, it still features frequently in songs and stories.

After the fall of Pajajaran, the entire area of Sunda was subject to annexation by

Mataram, an Islamic Central Javanese kingdom. By the mid-l600s, Sunda was under the administration of Central Javanese regents, responsible for the importation of Central Javanese cultural traits that continue to influence the upper levels of Sundanese culture: batik, gamelan music, dance, sung poetry, and wayang (Heins 1977). Because of the dispersal of the local population, however, the cultural influence from Central Java among villagers was minimal, and Sundanese musical traditions continued largely unchanged.

In 1677, Mataram relinquished its Sundanese territorial claim to the Dutch East India Company, which then profited from Sundanese cash crops, including coffee and tea. The colonialists expelled the Central Javanese regents from Sunda and replaced them with Sundanese nobles, who, though they answered to Dutch administrators, grew wealthy, and their patronage of the performing arts reached its height during this period. After 1864, the Dutch developed the city of Bandung as the colonial administrative center, and it remains the administrative heart of Sunda.

Structures of Sundanese Music

A large proportion of Sundanese music is performed on gamelans, sets of bronze or iron instruments supported by carved wooden racks. A Sundanese gamelan usually consists of a core group of metallophones, horizontal gong-chime sets, vertically suspended gongs, and a set of barrel drums. Other features, including xylophones, aerophones (flutes or oboes), a bowed lute, and vocalists, are included according to the type of ensemble.

Pieces for gamelan are normally organized in cycles, with the ending of each cycle marked by the low pitch of the *go'ong*. These cycles may be played many times in a single piece. The drummer demarcates the cycle by outlining specific patterns; he also acts as the timekeeper, coordinator, and controller of dynamics. With specific patterns, he outlines dancers' movements. Most cycles include some type of periodic punctuation, performed by the large and small gongs. Each piece derives from a primary structural outline of tones (*patokan*) that determines which pitch of the colotomic instruments is played and the duration of each cycle. A single *patokan* may serve as the structural outline for a large number of melodies; therefore, Sundanese melodies outnumber Sundanese *patokan*. The melodic repertoire in Sundanese music may be shared by a variety of genres; it is not limited to specific types of instruments.

Sundanese music uses three main systems of tuning (*surupan*), called *pélog, sorog* (in gamelan, *madenda*), and *saléndro. Pélog,* in turn, appears in two forms: the five tone *pélog degung* (used for *gamelan degung* and *kacapi*-based genres) and *pélog jawar,* a seven-tone *surupan,* based on Javanese *pélog*. Each Sundanese system of tuning uses five tones, numbered and named in relation to each other. Each system has a unique set of tonal hierarchies that differ from piece to piece.

Because each ensemble differs slightly from the others in tuning, these tunings are always relative. Most ensembles are limited to a single system of tuning (most frequently, *saléndro*) because the pitches of the instruments are fixed, but a few, such as *tembang Sunda,* may change tunings during the course of a performance.

patokan
The structural outline of a piece of Sundanese music

Figure 21.18
The *gamelan saléndro* ensemble of the Festival of Indonesia group from Bandung, West Java; Rina Oesman, Euis Komariah, and Dheniarsah Suratno, vocalists. Photo by Marc Permian.

Sundanese Musical Genres

Gamelans in Sunda encompass a variety of types, from the ubiquitous five-tone *gamelan saléndro* to the rare seven-tone *gamelan pélog, gamelan ajeng,* and others. Gamelans were important to aristocratic households as symbols of power and prestige. The two most common types of gamelans in Sunda today are *gamelan saléndro* and *gamelan degung.* Both are named after their tunings, which in the case of *gamelan degung* refers to *pélog degung,* a special five-tone tuning. *Gamelan saléndro* is used in several different musical contexts: instrumental performance, and as accompaniment for a solo female vocalist, a dance, or the Sundanese three-dimensional rod-puppet theater (*wayang golek*). It sometimes accompanies drama, dance-drama, and martial arts.

Gamelan saléndro includes metallophones, gong chimes, gongs, drums, a bowed spiked lute, and a vocalist (Figure 21.18). The basic rhythmic cycle is demarcated by the gongs—a large gong (*go'ong*), small gongs (*kempul*), and a row of large kettle-gongs (*kenong*). These instruments all play colotomic or punctuating patterns, determined by the *patokan.* This musical structure is tied together with a set of barrel-shaped, double-headed drums (*kendang*). Depending on the style, the drummer is responsible for tempo and dynamic changes, dance accompaniment, and special effects (such as explosive strokes to accompany martial-arts kicks).

The versatility of *gamelan saléndro* has led to its use in many areas of Sunda as the ensemble to be played in nearly any context. It is likely to be heard at important social events—weddings, circumcisions, military or government occasions, store openings, ritual feasts (*hajat*), neighborhood celebrations, and musical rehearsals., The relationship between the drummer and the rest of the ensemble changes when *gamelan saléndro* accompanies dancing. In the performance of instrumental pieces or vocal *kliningan,* the role of the drummer is that of timekeeper, density referent, and follower of the piece's structural outline, but in the accompaniment of dance, the drummer takes a more active role. In general, the drummer is responsible for mirroring the character of the dance by matching the patterns of the drumming to the steps of the dancing.

Performances of rod-puppet theater are accompanied by a small, portable *gamelan saléndro.* A puppet group is frequently hired to perform all night after the formal daytime celebration of a life-cycle ritual (Weintraub 2004). When a performance occurs, loudspeakers, food stalls, and infectious joviality may attract an entire neighborhood or village. Its stories mostly derive from the *Mahabharata* and the *Ramayana,* Hindu epics (in which case the performance is called *wayang golèk purwa*), with occasional Islamic stories (*wayang golèk cepak*). These stories may be supplemented with local tales, anecdotes, songs, comic interludes, and political and social commentary. The puppet master (*dalang*), as leader of the group, is responsible for telling the story, manipulating the puppets, working with the drummer to control the tempo, and determining the overall structure of the performance. Performances are often sponsored in gratitude for good fortune, or simply as one aspect of the ritual celebration of a circumcision or other festive occasion (Figure 21.19).

Gamelan degung is the other primary Sundanese gamelan, formerly an all-male instrumental ensemble, which, in its "classic" version, performs a repertoire of about thirty instrumental pieces. It began as an instrumental ensemble closely associated with the Sundanese aristocracy and was originally performed to welcome visitors to the regents' homes. Its current form developed during the early twentieth century. In the last several decades, these instrumental pieces have been largely supplanted by simple cyclic patterns (*patokan*), which may support any number of melodies. Female vocalists have become a standard feature of *degung* performances. Though the classic repertoire is limited, hundreds of new pieces are now performed regularly on modern *gamelan degung*.

Gamelan degung has far fewer instruments and players than *gamelan saléndro* and is tuned to a type of *pélog* known as *pélog degung*. It performs in a colotomic structure, established by the suspended gong (*go'ong*) and six medium-sized suspended gongs (*jenglong*). The *go'ong* marks the ends of phrases, and the *jenglong* plays the framework of the tune. The main melody in a classic *gamelan degung* is carried by the *bonang*, a single-row gong-chime set placed in a V or U shape. A small, four-hole, end-blown bamboo flute (*suling degung*) plays embellishments of the *bonang* melody. Two metallophones (*saron*) play abstractions of the *suling* and *bonang* melody.

Gamelan degung is most likely to be heard at neighborhood celebrations in Bandung and other towns. Because of its connection to the aristocracy, it is not considered a village ensemble. Competitions among urban districts have led to its local sponsorship. *Gamelan degung* frequently accompanies large numbers of female vocalists (*rampak sekar*) and individuals performing *pop Sunda* songs (Williams 1989).

Ketuk tilu performance is firmly rooted in the villages of Sunda. The ensemble includes three kettle-gongs (*ketuk*) in a single rack; hence the name, *ketuk tilu* "three kettle-gongs." It accompanies traditional Sundanese social dancing. *Ketuk tilu* is performed in the evenings at village celebrations of various types, including harvests and life-cycle ceremonies. In a typical performance, the player of the *ketuk* strikes the instrument in the melodic pattern of low-medium–high-medium, or high-low–medium-low. This pattern is supported by the *go'ong*, struck every eight or sixteen beats; the *kendang*, which outline the rhythmic cycle; and a set of *kecrek*, small percussive metal plates that make a clashing sound. The primary melody is carried by a solo female singer-dancer (*ronggeng*) and a rebab. These instruments are portable, so the ensemble can be taken to whichever village

Figure 21.19
Cepot, a *wayang golek* puppet, represents the Sundanese Everyman. Photo by Cary Black.

ketuk tilu
Sundanese small coastal village ensemble

is having a celebration (Manuel and Baier 1986). The overall texture of a performance is filled in with the interlocking shouts (*senggak*) of male instrumentalists, audience members, and dancers.

Jaipongan was created in the 1970s from the most interesting and compelling elements of *ketuk tilu*, *gamelan salendro*, and dynamic, village-style drumming. It is most often performed on *gamelan salendro*, rather than on *ketuk tilu*. The *kempul* takes a very active role, being played in rapid, syncopated strokes, which often correspond to those of the drum. The patterns of drumming correspond exactly to a repertoire of dance movements, and a good performance usually includes an elegant sequence of improvisational interplay between the drummer and the dancer.

The two main types of Sundanese bamboo ensembles are *angklung* and *calung*. The exact features of each ensemble vary in contexts, related instruments, and relative popularity. *Angklung* is a generic term for sets of tuned, shaken bamboo rattles. Each instrument has two to four bamboo tubes, tuned from one to three octaves apart and suspended loosely from the top of a frame. When the instruments are shaken, two small extensions of each tube strike each side of a slot within the lower part of the frame, creating sounds. *Angklung* are played in interlocking patterns, usually with only one or two instruments played per person (Figure 21.20).

The most common traditional ensemble, *angklung buncis,* uses up to a dozen players of *angklung,* a player of a local oboe, four drummers (playing conical single-headed drums), vocalists, and others, including players of gongs, clowns, and people designated to stimulate audience interaction. The vocalists perform songs in call-and-response, popular styles, interlocking shouts, spontaneous rhymes, and high-pitched melismatic singing. The drummers have polyrhythmic competitions with one another, dodging in and out of the procession and trying to trick one another into making mistakes.

Figure 21.20
College students play bamboo *angklung* in a procession far removed from its ritual origins. Photo by Sean Williams.

Through the performance of *angklung,* the goddess of rice is enticed to the fields to ensure a good harvest. The performance of *angklung* in accordance with the seasonal agricultural calendar ensures the continuity of the cycle of planting, growth, and harvesting. By perpetuating this cycle through joyous, chaotic processions, the performers keep the village in tune with nature. In its most modern incarnation, *angklung* is performed in schools as an aid to learning about music. Tuned diatonically, sets of one hundred or more instruments are played by children. The ease with which these instruments are made (compared with forging a gamelan) and the low cost of a set make *angklung* an Indonesian alternative to other diatonic instruments.

Related ensembles, *calung,* fall into several categories; like those in *angklung,* its instruments are of bamboo, but each consists of several differently tuned tubes that are fixed onto a piece of bamboo instead of being loosely suspended. *Calung* are usually tuned to *saléndro*. The player, usually a man, holds the instrument in his left hand and strikes it with a beater held in his right. The highest-pitched *calung* has the greatest number of tubes and the densest musical activity; the lowest-pitched, with two tubes, has the least. *Calung* is nearly always associated with earthy humor.

The Sundanese zither (*kacapi*) often serves to represent Sundanese culture. It plays as either a solo or an ensemble instrument, associated with both villagers and aristocrats. It may take the form of a boat in *tembang Sunda,* or the form of a board zither in *kacapian.* It is sometimes drastically modified to include more strings, electric and electronic devices, and various styles of playing.

Figure 21.21
The blind singer of *pantun* Ki Subarma of Ciwidey in West Java plays a *kacapi,* accompanied by a rebab. Photo by Andrew Weintraub.

Pantun is a genre of Sundanese epic narrative. It is most often performed by a blind male vocalist, who usually accompanies himself on a *kacapi,* an eighteen-stringed boat-shaped or board zither (Figure 21.21). The performance of *pantun* usually occurs as part of a ritual feast, and dates from before the 1500s—before influences from Central Java or Islam. Because certain stories carry specific ideological, religious, or cultural meanings, stories are selected or rejected according to the type of ceremony being performed. The performer recites Sundanese mythological tales, interspersed with songs, comments, jokes, and allegories. He is believed to have a strong connection to the world of spirits and is respected for his knowledge. His presence is as much a symbolic blessing on the ceremony as the actual blessing he requests from the gods during the performance.

Tembang Sunda is a type of sung poetry developed in the regency of Cianjur in the late 1800s. It began as an entertainment in which aristocrats would sing in poetic meters derived from Central Java or perform songs derived from Sundanese epics, accompanied by local instruments. Its topics include Sundanese history, aspects of nature, mythology, romance, heroic figures, and tragedies. It is currently centered in Bandung, where many descendants of the Sundanese aristocracy and most of the current performers live. In performance, one or more singers are accompanied by an eighteen-stringed zither (*kacapi*), a smaller, fifteen-stringed zither (*rincik*), and a six-hole end-blown bamboo flute (*suling*) (Figure 21.22). For the descendants of the Sundanese aristocracy, *tembang Sunda* functions as a sonic link to the past, not only to the era just before independence (when aristocrats enjoyed certain privileges), but also to precolonial Pajajaran (Williams 2001).

Kacapi-suling is a recent urban offshoot of *tembang Sunda.* It developed during the 1970s as a recorded genre, and is the instrumental performance of the fixed-meter songs of *tembang Sunda.* It includes the usual *tembang Sunda* instrumentation of *kacapi, rincik,* and *suling.* The essential structure of a fixed-meter song resembles the cyclic structure of a *gamelan degung* piece in that a "gong" (bass string) sounds at the end of each cycle, and the internal

Figure 21.22
A *tembang Sunda* ensemble. Left to right: the *kacapi, suling,* and *rincik* are played behind the singers Euis Komariah (holding the microphone) and Neneng Dinar. Photo by Sean Williams..

phrases are separated by colotomic markers of phrases or connective transitional tones, which are also played on the bass strings of the *kacapi*.

In a typical *kacapi-suling* performance, the player of the *kacapi* outlines the cyclic structure, the player of the *rincik* performs elaborate variations of the structural pattern at twice the density of the *kacapi,* and the *suling* flute improvises along the contours of the cyclic structure. Lastly, *kacapian* uses the *kacapi* zither in a virtuosic way to accompany songs called *kawih*, and it is one of the primary sources of Sundanese pop music. *Kawih* lyrics use complicated rhymes, often in the form of rhyming couplets. The first section of a couplet usually describes an aspect of nature, and the second describes the topic of the verse—love, a political situation, religion, or a dispute. Many lyrics are up to date in criticizing current events, and the Sundanese predilection for musical humor allows for subtle plays on words.

Music and Musicians in Sundanese Society

Music is performed in a variety of contexts in Sunda, from department store openings to late-night gatherings among friends. Musical performance does not always involve pay, and performers may be selected as much on the basis of their connection to a patron or their family ties to the primary performers as on their ability to play. Performance is normally a participatory activity; people from the audience are expected to join in (*kaul*) at least once during a performance by singing, playing, or dancing. The concept of *kaul* derives from the sense of fulfilling a vow of participation with one's teacher. When one agrees to *kaul*, the teacher is honored. Guests and government officials are particularly targeted for this type of participation, generally in an atmosphere of gaiety and laughter.

The Sundanese regard music specialists with ambivalence. Strong adherents to Islam often look down on instrumental music. Furthermore, traditional music is sometimes considered ancient and outdated, and performers are sometimes accused of preventing the country from moving forward by persisting in playing music no longer relevant to the needs of a developed society. Musicians are also acknowledged to have a special kind of charismatic power that may be respected and even feared.

Bali, perhaps Indonesia's most famous island, is known worldwide for its art, music, and dance. Visiting writers and scholars have frequently commented on artistic activity in Balinese society since the early 1800s, observing that everyone is both artist and farmer (or nobleman). Though contemporary Balinese society has undergone many changes, this perception remains fairly valid. The local religion, a form of Saivite Hinduism with an integrated pre-Hindu ancestor cult, demands artistic work as a form of religious practice. All Balinese traditional music has roots in religious belief. Music and art are so ingrained into religion and into daily life that until recently they had no equivalent terms in the Balinese language except as components of ritual work (*karya*). Learning and performing the arts are a normal experience of life. Music and dance, like harvesting rice, are believed to be beneficial for the village. They are necessary components of major celebrations, and the performing arts have long functioned as a traditional form of education and enculturation.

The arts, and particularly music, accompany the stages of the human cycle of life. Balinese are greeted with music at birth, and at death are accompanied to the cremation grounds with it. The temples of Bali have a cycle of their own; they must be purified and revived through annual festivals that reconnect the past with the present through prescribed rites, offerings, and performing arts. Among the performing arts of Bali, music has the greatest ritual function.

Most Balinese music is orchestral and is performed on gamelan ensembles (usually bronze, but sometimes made of other materials). Most Balinese orchestral music consists of traditional and ceremonial pieces, theater and dance accompaniment, and a genre developed in the twentieth century, *kebyar* "to flare up," which includes newer recreational compositions based primarily upon traditional forms and styles.

The *gamelan gong kebyar*, a gamelan developed from a ceremonial model, emerged in 1915, and has performed the vast majority of modern compositions. The *kebyar* success led to the later movement *kreasi baru* "new creation," which are virtuoso *kebyar* pieces, still based on traditional forms and structures, but expanding into new musical territory. Two genres initiated in the 1970s reflect globalization but have yet to find general acceptance. They are *musik kontemporer* "contemporary music" (developed primarily in conservatories), which often deviates radically from traditional forms and structures, and *Bali pop* "popular music of Bali," youth-directed songs based on Western popular music with occasional Balinese elements and sung in Balinese and Indonesian languages. In 1986, a *kebyar*-style repertoire, *kreasi baleganjur* "*baleganjur* creation," developed for the processional *gamelan baleganjur*, and has found success. Performed by male youth, *kreasi baleganjur* demonstrates how successive generations of musicians develop new styles from indigenous material in response to social and aesthetic changes.

Traditional music constantly undergoes renewal, change, transformation, and variation, both in the villages and towns and in the influential conservatories. The treatment of traditional material—tempos, figuration, elaboration, dynamics—is repeatedly altered to suit a particular group, or to reflect an emerging aesthetic. Some compositions are known all over the island, and each area has its own preferred style of performance. However, many compositions are known only within certain regions or even within single villages. Bali, an island roughly half the size of Delaware, supports a striking diversity of musical styles, pieces, and orchestral configurations.

There are more than twenty-five different varieties of gamelan in Bali, distinguished by size, musical instruments, tuning, repertoire, context, and function. Among these, six or seven are common throughout the island, whereas others are found in only a few villages. Though some villages own only a single gamelan, others own several of the standard ensembles, with perhaps two or more of certain types. The other gamelans are usually found in remote villages. Each gamelan in a village has its own context, meaning, and function.

The older the ensemble, the greater the closeness to the ancestors and the greater its accumulation of spiritual power; therefore, most older ensembles are considered sacred. These gamelans are thought to possess magical properties, and their performances are believed capable, for example, of creating rainfall or protecting the village. Some of the sacred ensembles are believed to have originated in the East Javanese empire of Majapahit, or to have been bestowed on the village directly by deities. Most gamelans, however, are not held sacred, though they are greatly respected and thought to harbor a spirit presence that normally inhabits the gong(s) of the ensemble. The imagery of Majapahit and other kingdoms in East Java still provides models of refinement and behavior for many Balinese and is the basis for many types of music, theater, and poetry.

Bali is located just to the east of Java. Historically, its culture has experienced several waves of influence from Java, and this has contributed to the development of Balinese ensemble music, as evidenced by a similar music terminology and inventory of instruments. The Javanese also influenced different types of poetry. Poetry in Bali is always sung, and each different type of Balinese poetry has prescribed contexts. The development of context-specific poetry has helped preserve the various poetic forms, and scribes have loyally transcribed the texts for centuries. Bali has retained Javanese poetic forms that have been mostly abandoned by the Javanese. The Balinese rarely adapted Javanese musical traditions, however, but used Javanese concepts to inspire artistic development uniquely their own.

Cultural History

Balinese culture received varying degrees of Javanese influence from the 900s to the 1200s, and was heavily influenced by the East Javanese kingdom of Majapahit during the 1300s and 1400s. In the 1500s, with the encroachment of Islam in Java, artisans, priests, and nobles of this empire fled to Bali, where aspects of Javanese and Balinese culture continued to develop. From this period until Dutch colonization (1908–1942), the courts set the standards for music, dance, and theater, as kings, who invited and supported the finest artists from the villages, and commissioned the development of several types of performing arts, many of which still exist.

Colonization immediately limited court revenues in most districts, which resulted in a sharp decline of patronage for the arts, particularly for the court gamelans and theater genres. Gamelans, like theater, demonstrated the spiritual power of the courts. Following colonization, the court ensembles were sold, pawned, or given outright to the villages. With the decline of the court gamelans, the spiritual power of the courts declined as well. Some ensembles fell into disuse, later to be melted and reforged either into new ensembles or into bullets for the Japanese during their World War II occupation of Indonesia. The courtly theater forms declined and almost vanished after Dutch colonization. The situation worsened during the early period of independence.

The transference of gamelans from the courts to the villages caused greater musical activity in the villages, which in turn led to changes in musical styles and practices, the most important being the development of the *kebyar* instrumental style. This style, which emerged from traditional repertoire and compositional form, resulted in changes of instrumentation, dynamics, and the role of music in general. Derived from the word *byar* "flare," it developed in north Bali in 1915 and quickly spread to south Bali, then more gradually throughout the rest of Bali. A new form of dance was created which expressed the tension and excitement of the music, and the *kebyar* movement gave new recognition to composers and choreographers. Except for sacred forms, this style influenced all forms of music, dance, theater, and even the plastic arts. The *kebyar* movement has since progressed through several phases, and can be seen as an indicator of change within Balinese society.

Music Theory

Form and Structure

Balinese ensemble music is often characterized by the term *stratified polyphony*, though the various melodic lines are usually rooted in the same melodic flow. Certain musical parts and instruments are more important to the music than others, but all are necessary. Musical pieces are normally termed *tabuh* "accent, beat" or *gending* "composition" (referring equally to instrumental and vocal music). The music basically consists of a nuclear melody, the *pokok* "trunk," within a cyclic metric structure. Some instruments perform the *pokok*; some punctuate it; some play an expansion or elaboration of this melody; some perform metrical punctuation; and one or two groups of instruments normally play figurations (*kotekan*) to create multiple layers of musical sound. The higher-pitched instruments, considered the least important to a given composition, usually perform in figuration. These interlocking figurations, in which two musicians play parts of a single line, are found in nearly every type of orchestral music and constitute one of the distinguishing characteristics of Balinese music. Unlike in Java, vocal lines are rare in ensemble music, and there is no concept of an independent vocal melodic line. Similar to Java, however, the drummers set the tempo and signal changes of dynamics, musical sections, and endings.

Because interlocking parts must maintain consistency and many instruments serve metrical functions, little individual improvisation occurs. The term *group improvisation*, sometimes applied to Indonesian ensemble music, may be apt for Balinese music in which a group is led by cues from the drums or from the leaders of particular music sections. The ensemble members as a group treat the material as they see fit, and group precision is the goal. However, the lead drummer has some flexibility in his part as does the melodic leader, who plays a metallophone (*pengugal*) or a gong chime (*trompong*), and both

tabuh
Individual composition in Balinese music
pokok
Central melody and basis for figuration in Balinese music
kotekan
Rapid, interlocking figuration characteristic of Balinese music

practice limited improvisation. Particularly when accompanying theater or narrative dance, where music must follow dance, the group—and especially the drummers—must watch the dancers closely. Pieces may be expanded or contracted to follow the dance or flow of the theater, and transitions may be necessary at any time. Dramatic rhythmic breaks, *angsel*, normally performed by the entire ensemble except for the punctuating instruments and *pokok*, are signaled by the drum to accompany dance movements of particular emphasis. *Angsel* occur in both dance accompaniment and purely orchestral pieces.

Balinese musical form normally includes introductions, one or more sections forming the body of a piece (which may repeat a number of times), and an ending or concluding section. Many pieces have three parts, a configuration that in Bali has extramusical, anthropomorphic, and cosmological significance. The music is cyclic, with large gongs marking the endings of the largest melodic phrases, and other families of instruments punctuating the metric cycle or coinciding at predetermined points within the cycle; the contrasting patterns of punctuation or colotomy define specific forms.

Many scholars argue that the cyclic structure of the music is linked to the conception of the passage of time as cyclic. The ceremonial repertoire of the *gamelan gong*, the orchestra most frequently engaged for ritual events, features compositions with three main sections having anthropomorphic associations—head, body, foot—and constitutes a metaphorical journey from mountain to sea. The head is usually not metered, but the body uses metric gong cycles of from sixty-four to 128 beats for the nuclear melody, and the foot contracts to a form of eight or sixteen beats, and gradually increases in tempo until the final stroke of the gong concludes the piece. One purpose of these pieces, which often require thirty minutes or more for complete realization, is to suspend the normal passage of time.

Melody, colotomic pattern, and number of beats combine to create individual compositions (also called *tabuh*) associated with particular moods, emotions, or characters in dance and theater. Many traditional compositions derive from a single *tabuh* associated with a context or character.

Modes and Systems of Tuning

Most Balinese music is pentatonic. Both instrumental music and vocal music adhere to one of the two tonal systems, known as *pélog* and *sléndro*. *Sléndro* consists of five tones to the octave, spaced at nearly equidistant intervals. *Pélog* is a seven-tone system with large and small intervals (including two intervals close to semitones), from which various pentatonic modes are formed. Most gamelans in Bali, however, are uniquely tuned, with neither a standard beginning pitch nor precise interval distances for the different tunings. Metal smiths use their own collections of bars for tuning, after which the smiths or professional tuners adjust the tuning to suit the musicians or owner. Therefore, there are often major differences between one *sléndro* (or *pélog*) tuning and another. The pitches seem to be placed more within tonal zones than in accordance with a precise intervallic structure.

Not all Balinese musicians use the general terms *sléndro* and *pélog*, which are Javanese in origin. The indigenous concepts of Balinese tonality exist, instead, within the context of the modal system (*patutan*) and scalar system (*saih*) of particular ensembles. *Sléndro*, for example, exists as *saih gendèr wayang* "row of *gendèr wayang* tones" (on the instrument

trompong
Balinese gong chime played by soloist
angsel
Dramatic rhythmic break in Balinese music
patutan
Balinese model system

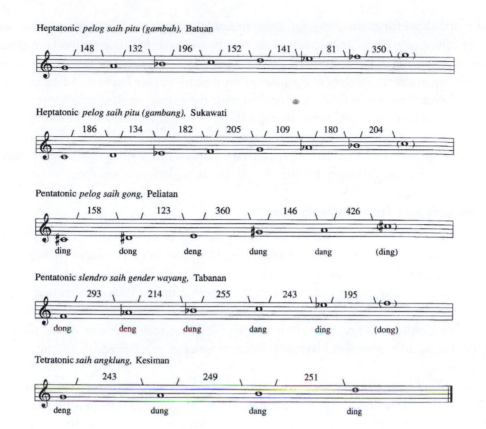

Heptatonic *pelog saih pitu (gambuh)*, Batuan

148   132   196   152   141   81   350

Heptatonic *pelog saih pitu (gambang)*, Sukawati

186   134   182   205   109   180   204

Pentatonic *pelog saih gong*, Peliatan

158   123   360   146   426

ding   dong   deng   dung   dang   (ding)

Pentatonic *slendro saih gender wayang*, Tabanan

293   214   255   243   195

dong   deng   dung   dang   ding   (dong)

Tetratonic *saih angklung*, Kesiman

243   249   251

deng   dung   dang   ding

Figure 21.23
Tunings of various ensembles. The numbers specify the intervals in cents.

used for the shadow-play theater), *pélog* exists as the *saih pitu* "row of seven" tuning used for such ensembles as *gamelan gambuh* and *gamelan gambang*.

The complete seven-tone *saih pitu* system of *gamelan gambuh* incorporates five theorized modal scales, each consisting of five primary and two auxiliary tones; most groups use four or three of these modes. The best known *saih pitu* system consists of pitches named *ding, dong, deng, penyorog, dung, dang, pemero*; and then starts over with *ding* through successive octaves. The terms *penyorog* "inserted tone" and *pemero* "false tone" indicate auxiliary pitches. When these tones are removed, the remaining five tones create the pentatonic modal scales. The pentatonic *saih gendèr wayang* pitches are normally named (from lowest to highest) *dong, deng, dung, dang*, and *ding* (Figure 21.23).

The *saih pitu* scale is not popular but is revered as a mystical scale associated with refined courts and sacred music. The most popular mode derived from it—and the most famous of the Balinese tonal system—is the pentatonic *selisir*, also called *saih gong* "row of gong tones" or *saih lima* "row of five." This scale, the primary realization of *pélog* tuning, is considered an independent system and is used in the *gamelan gong* orchestras; a higher-pitched *selisir* scale is used in the former court *gamelan pelégongan*; and *selisir* is one of the core *gamelan gambuh* and *gamelan Semar pegulingan* modes. This scale has been so influential within Balinese music culture that some bronze heptatonic court orchestras were retuned accordingly. These terms concerning systems of tuning and ensembles are also used in certain types of Balinese vocal music.

Tonality may prescribe function among the ensembles. Gamelans in *saih pitu* tuning

saih pitu
Seven-tone tuning system
saih selisir
Tuning system

have vital ritual functions. However, those in *saih gong, saih gendèr wayang,* and *saih angklung* tunings also have important uses at rituals, and each has its own special qualities. The *saih gong* tonality is considered powerful, able to signal together divine and human worlds and evoke the imagery of the past appropriate for temple festivals and other rituals; the *saih gendèr wayang* tonality is associated with the night, the shadow play, and ancestor spirits to contextualize a rite within the imagery of epic stories; and the *saih angklung* is normally considered to have a sweet but sad quality, appropriate for cremations, other life-cycle rites, and sometimes temple festivals. However, if a village owns only a single gamelan, it will use that ensemble for all vital rituals, regardless of tonality.

Musicians and Their Organization

Musicians organize themselves into collective groups (*seka* or *sekaha*) to perform for particular occasions or to maintain a performing group for village or tourist performances. A *sekaha* generally comprises people who come from a subvillage unit or who are related, though occasionally groups consist of members from different villages. Members include both musicians and dancers, if dance is part of a performance, and the *sekaha* does not acknowledge the modified caste distinctions of Balinese society. Major rituals often include one or more gamelans playing at different times or simultaneously in one or more locations.

The musicians of the *sekaha* are traditionally males from ten to seventy or more years old, with the exception of the growing number of all-female groups (*ibu-ibu*) and some groups in government-sponsored conservatories. Members' ages are sometimes parallel to the ages of repertoires and instruments. Older men usually prefer and are associated with the older and more ceremonial repertoire and ensembles; younger men usually prefer and are associated with faster and more intricate music and *kebyar*. Extensive rehearsals and vigorous musicianship are necessary for a performance of *kebyar*, but are not normally needed for the more static ceremonial repertoire. Though their music is less demanding technically, the maturity of the older musicians is sometimes thought important to the proper realization of the stately or refined ceremonial music, in which lengthy pieces performed only once a year must be recalled.

> **sekaha**
> Communal music-making group in Bali and Lombok

Musical Contexts and Functions

The main contexts for making music are the web of rituals that has sustained Balinese culture over the centuries. These primarily include life-cycle rituals (birthdays, rites of giving names, marriages, the filing of teeth, cremations), and temple festivals, which form parts of the Hindu Balinese theological taxonomy of rituals known as Panca Yadnya (Five Sacrificial Offerings). Other contexts include political affairs, national holidays, village fund-raisers, and performances for tourists.

Temples, numbering more than twenty thousand, are at the center of Balinese ritual activity. Villagers are obligated to attend festivals normally held once every 210 days at these temples, and most individuals participate in festivals at other kinds of temples. Festivals, normally called *odalan*, are held at each of these temples and usually include performances of gamelans and dances. Every Balinese should undergo the life-cycle rites mentioned above, and these usually include music and sometimes dance and theater, if the family involved can afford the expenditure.

Major rituals often include one or more gamelans playing at different times or simultaneously in one or more locations. There are distinctive spatial and temporal orientations to Balinese performing arts, and these orientations relate to the function of the performance and the meaning of the context. Gamelans are held to be able to reference the past or particular imagery, such as evoking the grandeur of the mythic courts or reenacting a local legendary event. The *gamelan gambuh*, for instance, with its combination of flute and bowed lute, is thought to evoke the quality of the fifteenth-century East Javanese Majapahit court. The gamelan is a symbol of that period and can reference it through performance. This type of referencing is beneficial for the successful completion of a ritual context, in which representations of folklore and cosmology are efficacious agents.

All gamelan performances are essentially active ritual offerings. Both the sound structure of the music and the decorated cases of the musical instruments embody codes parallel to those within ritual formulae, food offerings, and cosmology. Gamelan performance in general is believed to embody the second of three elements considered essential to a ritual: thought; sound, word, voice; and action. Prayer and meditation fulfill the thought element; gamelan, the sound; and dance, the action: all can be viewed as extensions of the rites of the high priest. The priests recite mantra invocations (realized as prayer), ring their *genta* bell (whose sound is realized by the gamelan) to reinforce the mantra, and perform hand gestures (*mudra*, realized as dance) to complete the invocations. This establishes the performing arts as elaborate offerings with efficacious qualities necessary to complete a ritual.

Each gamelan represents a particular spiritual value and references a particular past, and when many gamelans perform simultaneously, there is a comprehensive representation of the cosmos and the legendary past. It is not uncommon at a major temple festival to witness two or three different gamelans, two or three dances, theater, or shadow puppetry, and a choir all performing at once. This brings the past into the present and creates the communal spiritual experience intended by the festival.

odalan
Balinese temple festivals
mudra
Ritural hand gestures

Music in Balinese Cosmology

The Balinese view of the world is based on threes. The modified system of castes includes three acknowledged levels and a fourth, outer level; the system of naming children includes three children and a fourth, other child; there are three different levels of requirements within life-cycle rituals; three main village temples with three divisions in their structures and altars; three gods within the Hindu Trinity; and a tripartite structure to both the macrocosm and microcosm. In addition, musical compositions usually include three main sections, the cases of musical instruments have three sections, dance characterization acknowledges three divisions within the body, and most types of painting, statues, dance costumes, and ritual offerings also have three divisions. This links the arts directly to cosmology and worldview.

Balinese gamelan have tripartite dimensions with anthropomorphic and macrocosmic qualities and reflect the village social organization. Gongs, kettle-gongs, and bars of metal-lophones, plus instrument cases, stands, and resonators, all acknowledge three horizontal divisions of head, body, and foot, mirrored in the three divisions of the macrocosm, which in turn are parallel to the geographic configuration (mountain, midworld, sea) related to the layout of temples, home compounds, and whole villages. The instruments also have three vertical divisions, and the resulting three-by-three configuration represents a nine-part mandala, a pictorial display of the cosmos, which is related to the construction of home compounds, pavilions, temples, and the sequence of planting seedlings in the fields. Some scholars have asserted that gamelan music is an aural mandala organized on these same concepts, with metric cycles representing structured mandala and the three-part compositional form representing the tripartite structures of head-body-foot and moun-tain-midworld-sea. Esoteric treatises support this hypothesis and indicate that musical tones are associated with deities, directions, colors, days of the week, and weapons to create a mandala structure.

A gamelan can also be seen to reflect the village order, with the gongs representing the respected elders, low-pitched metallophones as older adults, midrange metallophones as adults, the drums as political leaders, and the high-pitched metallophones, gong chimes, and cymbals as youngsters. A gamelan is thus a self-portrait of the villagers. The instru-ments appear to have additional extramusical associations. For example, the *Prakempa* treatise states that *gong ageng* (largest hanging gong) represent the divine mountain and the Hindu god Siwa, while the *trompong* (gong chime) represents the lotus, the *kempur* (small hanging gong) all that is pure, and so forth.

The concepts underlying Balinese music theory and musical instruments thus have parallels to those that form cosmology and worldview. There is an isomorphic mapping of musical system with cosmology; a similar mapping evident in the plastic arts, dance characterization, temples, home compounds, village positioning, ritual formulae, food of-ferings, macrocosm and microcosm, and so forth. Music is therefore strongly interrelated with other cultural systems that are fed by similar underlying concepts.

Musical Instruments

The Javanese-Indonesian term *gamelan* "things struck together" is applied to every en-semble, and refers to a group of instruments played, or specifically struck, together. Be-cause of variations of tuning, instruments are particular to their ensembles and cannot be played with other gamelans. Gamelans consist primarily of bronze instruments, with a few ensembles featuring bamboo or wood instruments. The original Balinese equivalent for *ensemble* is *gambelan*, from *megambel* "to strike," and the word *gong* is sometimes used to denote entire ensembles. The different types of gamelan are commonly known simply by their name without the word *gamelan* preceding; thus, the ensembles *gamelan gong kebyar* or *gamelan angklung* are usually called *gong kebyar* and *angklung*.

The primary type of instrument in Bali is the bronze idiophone. These include gongs, metallophones, gong chimes, cymbals (made of bronze or iron), rare bell trees, and as-sorted small percussion instruments. Other idiophones include wooden and bamboo xylophones, bamboo tube stampers, bamboo and hollowed-out wooden log idiophones, bamboo or brass cattle bells, palm-rib Jew's harps, bamboo shakers, and several rarer instruments. There is one standard type of membranophone, a double-headed cylindrical drum, which comes in many sizes. Aerophones consist of bamboo, or the rare wooden, straw, and even conch instruments. Chordophones are few, but include one standard bowed lute with limited use; an idiochord one-stringed bamboo tube zither; and only a few rare plucked chordophones. There is no established organological system that separates instruments in terms of the production of sounds. Instruments are regarded in terms of the gamelan to which they belong, and are classified into families of instruments that perform related musical functions within gamelans. Instruments and whole gamelans are highly respected creations and are ritually purified every thirty weeks.

Idiophones

There are clear priorities among the various bronze instruments. Gongs are distinguished from metallophones, which are distinguished from gong chimes. The large hanging gongs are clearly the most important instruments in any ensemble that includes gongs. In fact, the name given to the gong(s) of a gamelan through a name-giving ritual is meant to include the entire ensemble. Gongs also receive offerings and incense before performance on behalf of the ensemble, and the spirit of the gamelan is believed to reside within the gongs.

The largest hanging gongs are the pair of *gong ageng*: the *gong lanang* "male gong" (smaller and pitched slightly higher), and the *gong wadon* "female gong" (larger and pitched slightly lower). These gongs, normally about sixty-five to eighty-five centimeters in diameter, define the colotomic structure as they conclude the largest melodic phrasal lengths and the metric cycles of the music. They are struck in alternation by a large padded mallet. Each produces an acoustical beat (*ombak* "wave"), an amplitude modulation heard as a pulsation.

Other colotomic or structural instruments are the *kempur* and the *kemong*. The former is a much smaller and higher-pitched hanging gong than the *gong ageng*, and it supplies secondary structural punctuation. Some ensembles, such as the *gamelan angklung*, have no large gong and use *kempur* as the main colotomic marker. The smaller hanging gong, the *kemong*, alternates punctuation with *kempur*, except in some ceremonial ensembles where it is replaced by the *kempli*, a horizontally mounted kettle-gong. At other times, the *kempli* acts primarily as a timekeeper, though the *kajar*, a kettle-gong suspended horizontally with a sunken boss, plays syncopated figurations in most ensembles, while the *tawa-tawa* is often a *klentong*-sized gong held on the lap. The *bende* (or *bebende*) is an optional hanging gong with a sunken boss, whose musical role is more related to the cymbals than to the metric cycle.

Metallophones constitute the majority of instruments in most gamelans, and together may cover a range of three to five octaves. Single-octave metallophones normally play the nuclear melody or a reduced abstraction of it, while double-octave metallophones perform figurations or ornamentation. Metallophones, generally called *gangsa*, are of two types: *gangsa jongkok* and *gangsa gantung*. The former are resting-bar instruments of five bronze bars lying over a shallow trough resonator. The latter (also called *gendèr*) are suspended-bar instruments of from four to fifteen bevel-edged bars suspended over individual bamboo resonators in a wooden case.

The *gangsa* are made in identical pairs tuned slightly apart to create an acoustical beat; the closer the tuning, the faster the beat. Different groups have their own preferences, but usually the tunings between the pairs of *gangsa* stay within a range of 25 to 60 cents, with the higher-pitched bars having the smallest intervals and creating beats vibrating at more than seven times per second. This beat, along with those produced on the *gong ageng*, is what gives Balinese gamelan its shimmering effect.

Gong chimes are sets of from four to twelve tuned kettle-gongs resting or suspended in a single row over a long wooden case. The best known are the *trompong*, of ten kettles; and the *réong* (or *reyong*), usually of twelve kettles, but also known with four, six, and eight. The *trompong* is played melodically by a soloist, whereas the *réong* is played by two to (more normally) four players in interlocking figuration.

Cymbals consist primarily of *ceng-ceng* and *rincik* (or *ricik*). *Ceng-ceng* refers generally to cymbals and specifically to a group of hand held cymbals used in large gamelan and in procession. *Rincik* denotes a smaller pair or set of three or five upturned cymbals mounted on a base struck with a pair held by the player.

Membranophones

Most ensembles include two double-headed cylindrical membranophones played together: the *kendang lanang* "male drum" and the *kendang wadon* "female drum." These drums are tuned and come in many different sizes, from the large ones used in *kebyar* to the small ones used in the *gamelan angklung*. In some gamelan traditions, the *kendang wadon* drummer leads; in others, the *kendang lanang* drummer is the leader. For some types of ceremonial music and for accompanying strong male dances, players use a drumstick in the right hand; otherwise, they create a number of open and muted sounds forming an interlocking figuration with the hands alone.

Aerophones

Suling, end-blown bamboo flutes of various sizes, are used in several gamelans. They most frequently perform an expanded version of the nuclear melody. Other aerophones are rare, and include free-reed *padi* pipes (usually called *serunai*), wooden oboes (*preret*), and conchs (*serungu* or *sungu*). The functions of the *serunai* and *preret* are flexible. The latter has been known to accompany the martial-art dance, *pencak silat*, with a small ensemble, and to perform with vocalists at temple festivals—a tradition that may have originated on Lombok. The *serungu* forms part of a rare ensemble of three instruments that calls forth underworld spirits to receive offerings in ritual settings.

Chordophones

Among the chordophones, the rebab is a two-stringed, bowed spike lute, used in a few gamelans, particularly *gamelan gambuh*. With its horsehair bow, it is used to paraphrase or expand the nuclear melody. The *guntang* is a bamboo idiochord zither struck with a small stick. Two of these, a larger one for the main punctuation and a smaller one as timekeeper, are sometimes used in the *gamelan arja*.

Orchestras and Ensembles

Bali has a variety of ensembles: large bronze orchestras consisting of from twenty-five to forty instruments; specific ensembles to accompany theater; processional ensembles; bamboo or palm-rib ensembles; and sacred ensembles. Each has its own orchestration, function, and context.

Gamelan Gong

The Balinese call their largest, most ubiquitous ensembles *gamelan gong* (or, often, simply *gong*). The most common of these is the *gong kebyar*, which developed early in the twentieth century out of the older *gong gedé* and quickly eclipsed it in popularity. The *gamelan gong* in its ceremonial form can perform at virtually any type of ritual, though it is most associated with temple festivals. The orchestra and its repertoire signify ceremony. This gamelan, the loudest of Balinese ensembles, will normally be positioned in a second court-yard at temple festivals, or outside the main home compound at family life-cycle rituals. The positioning is never truly close to the space of the most sacred transformations at such rituals, yet is always in a conspicuous spot between the innermost sacred space and the outer temple or village space. This is because the function of the ensemble is to mark the spatial limits of the event, to signify the transition of normal time to the extranormal or sacred time of the event, and to act as a bridge between inner and outer dimensions—both

Figure 21.24
A *gamelan gong gedé*. To the front are the *gangsa jongkok*; to the left the *trompong*, in the back, the gongs. McPhee Collection, UCLA, 1930s.

in terms of the village and the inner event, and in terms of the world of deities and the world of humans. Like incense, which is believed to ascend to the deity world and entice deities to descend through the smoke, music is often thought to act as a vehicle through which the deities enter the event.

The ceremonial repertoire of the *gamelan gong*, called *gending gong* (or *pegongan*), consists of *gangsaran* "speedy pieces" and *lelambatan* "slow, stately pieces." The performance begins with *gangsaran*, pieces normally consisting of one or two melodic phrases covering short gong cycles (or *gongan*) of sixteen or eight beats per stroke of a gong, repeated many times. This is the explosive start of the ritual. Later, the orchestra will perform the *lelambatan* pieces, which have greater functional importance.

Figure 21.25
Stratification in one complete gong cycle of "Penyuwud," a *gilak* form and concluding composition.

Lelambatan pieces contain *gongan* with from sixty-four to 128 beats. As the event unfolds, the orchestra begins with *lelambatan* pieces in the smaller metric cycles, gradually progressing to those in the largest metric cycles as the ritual approaches its climax.

The *gong gedé*, the elder type of *gamelan gong*, is the largest of Bali's gamelans, with forty or more instruments in its original form (Figure 21.24). Only a few sets remain today. Court gamelans before colonization, most *gong gedé* were reforged as *gong kebyar* to meet the change of Balinese aesthetics during and following colonialism. The orchestras remaining today generally consist of twenty-five to thirty instruments.

Gong kebyar, the more recent type of *gamelan gong*, includes the *gong ageng*, the *kempur*, and the *kendang lanang* and *kendang wadon*; but the *trompong* is replaced by a large ten-bar metallophone (*giying* or *pengugal*), and the *saron* are replaced by four mid-range (*pemade*) and four-octave-higher (*kantilan*) *gendèr* metallophones. A low-octave pair (or two pairs) of single-octave *gendèr* (*jegogan*) punctuate the nuclear melody at regular intervals—at an eight-to-one, a four-to-one, or a two-to-one ratio. Other instruments, such as *suling* and rebab, are often included. The *réong* in *gong kebyar* is greatly expanded from that of the *gong gedé*, and consists of twelve kettles played in changing interlocking parts by four musicians, who sometimes strike the rims or bosses of the kettles together to create brassy or strongly syncopated chordlike clusters of sounds. These syncopated parts, reinforced by cymbals (*rincik*), are also played for *angsel*, which bring the ensemble together for powerful rhythmic breaks. *Gong kebyar* music provides a good example of multilayered sound that can be interpreted as stratified polyphony (Figure 21.25). In many pieces, there is so much embellishment that the nuclear melody can hardly be heard.

The *gong kebyar*, consisting of about twenty-five instruments, often performs in secular contexts; however, it regularly assumes a ritual function and performs the ceremonial repertoire of the *gong gedé*, and many groups and a *trompong* for these pieces. The *gong kebyar* repertoire has also incorporated pieces from bronze court orchestras (*Semar pegulingan*, *pelégongan*) and pieces to accompany masked dances and some types of theater (Figure

21.26). However, the *gong kebyar* is mostly known for its virtuoso repertoire: explosive pieces composed to accentuate the dynamic qualities of the instruments. The term *kebyar*, in fact, refers to the explosive, metrically free unison attack that normally occurs at the beginning of a piece in this style. Because of regular competitions involving the whole island, groups are encouraged to maintain high standards of performance and experiment with new ideas. The repertoire, called *kreasi baru*, is constantly expanding because composers nearly always use the *gong kebyar* for their new works.

Figure 21.26
A *gamelan gong kebyar* in rehearsal. McPhee Collection, UCLA, 1930s.

Smaller Bronze Orchestras

The *gamelan Semar pegulingan* was originally for the private enjoyment of the nobility. It was played when the king was sleeping with the queen in his chambers. The *gamelan Semar pegulingan* "gamelan of the god of love of the bedroom," originally a court orchestra, resembles the *gamelan gong*, but omits *gong ageng, réong*, and large cymbals (Figure 21.27). It is tuned slightly higher than the *gamelan gong* and is played with lighter and more padded hammers; it therefore has a lighter and sweeter sound. The instrumentation includes a fourteen-kettle *trompong* and several pairs of metallophones, often only different sizes of *gendèr*, but sometimes high-pitched *saron*; two *kendang*, a large *kempur*, and a *kajar*; *rebab* and *suling*, one or more small sets of cymbals and other small percussive instruments, sometimes including a bell tree (*gentorak*).

Figure 21.27
A *gamelan Semar pegulingan*: a *gender rawat* and gong. McPhee Collection, UCLA, 1930s.

In its original form, the *Semar pegulingan* was a seven-tone orchestra used to play theater pieces (*gambuh*) instrumentally in the proper modal scales, though the orchestra normally acknowledged only three of the possible five modes. But over the course of the twentieth century, most of these orchestras were retuned or the bars reforged to accommodate solely the pentatonic *selisir* mode. The colotomy, extra percussion, drumming technique, tonality, and much of the repertoire derive from the *gamelan gambuh* (see below). The *trompong*, however, is given the opportunity to freely elaborate and expand upon the original *suling gambuh* melodies. This represents one of the highest levels of improvisation in Balinese music.

The *gamelan pelégongan* is an orchestra

Figure 21.28
A *gamelan angklung*: metallophones in front; the rare *angklung* rattles in back. McPhee Collection, UCLA, 1930s.

closely related to the *Semar pegulingan*. It originally accompanied the *légong* dance in the courts; hence its name. The orchestra uses only the five-tone *selisir* tuning and incorporates *gambuh* pieces and some new pieces into its repertoire of *légong*. The gamelans accompanied a large number of dances and dance-dramas in the courts, but since colonization they have mainly accompanied several *légong* dances, particularly the famous *légong kraton*, featuring two or three girls who take different parts in turn. This orchestra replaces the *trompong* of the *Semar pegulingan* with two pairs of thirteen- to fifteen-bar *gendèr*, but is otherwise almost identical. Sometimes, a reciter will sing narration within the orchestra to accompany the *légong* dances. Today, both the *gamelan pelégongan* and the *Semar pegulingan* borrow repertoire and instruments from each other, and the techniques of both have become so similar that many earlier distinctions have become blurred. The repertoires of both orchestras are often appropriated by the *gong kebyar*.

The *gamelan angklung* is smaller than *gamelan gong* orchestras. It consists of about sixteen instruments, pitched higher and much smaller in size than those of all other gamelans. It has always been a village orchestra, disassociated with the courts. It has a lighter, more intimate sound and carries more emotional associations. It can therefore be placed closer to the inner compound of a home during a family life-cycle ceremony, though the ensemble also performs a repertoire and function similar to the *gamelan gong* when used at temple festivals (Figure 21.28). Today, there are far more *gamelan angklung* than all of the court orchestras mentioned above. This gamelan is tuned to a four-tone scale that probably derives from *sléndro*.

Gamelan angklung uses a small, nonresonant, and often out-of-tune *kempur* as its only gong, and includes several pairs of single-octave (four-key) *gendèr*, a lower-octave pair of *gendèr* to play the nuclear melody, a timekeeping *tawa-tawa*, a *réong* normally of eight kettles, *rincik*, two small *kendang* played with light drumsticks, and often one or more *suling*. The *gamelan angklung* has its own traditional repertoire consisting of pieces of irregular length and whimsical titles, a few pieces from the *gendèr wayang* tradition, and sometimes a special ceremonial repertoire; the orchestra can also play modified *kebyar* pieces with the addition of larger drums and gongs.

Theatrical Ensembles

The *gamelan gambuh* is the former court orchestra that accompanies *gambuh* theater. It was the most important of the ensembles that functioned within the noble houses, and its

Figure 21.29
A gamelan gambuh:
four *suling* on the left;
a rebab on the right;
percussion behind.
McPhee Collection,
UCLA, 1930s.

purpose was to perform for the life-cycle rituals of the nobility. The repertoire, systems of tuning, and hand-drumming technique of its ensemble are credited as the foundations of Balinese music. *Gambuh* is similarly considered a source of Balinese theater and dance. The theater is based mostly on plays of East Javanese court life, and the music and dance are the most refined and solemn in Bali. The function of performances of *gambuh* is to invoke the presence of Indonesian, rather than Indic, legendary figures and heroes. The tradition almost vanished in the twentieth century, and today there are few active groups.

The ensemble contrasts with other Balinese gamelans in that it does not include metallophones or gong chimes (Figure 21.29). Instead, it normally features four *suling* about a meter long, with a range of over two octaves. They perform in unison or slight heterophony a number of melodic compositions connected with a specific character or dramatic situation. A rebab joins the *suling* melody in unison or paraphrase, occasionally breaking off to freely interpret the melody. Main punctuation is supplied by *kempur* and *kajar*, with a few small bronze percussive instruments providing secondary punctuation. Other instruments include the two *kendang, rincik, gentorak* (bell tree), *and gumanak* (a struck metal cylinder similar to the Javanese *kemanak*). The *gumanak* fills in the intervals between the secondary punctuation along with the *kangsi*, two pairs of small cymbals mounted between forked sticks struck against the ground.

The *gamelan arja* (also called *geguntangan* and *pearjaan*) accompanies the popular and relatively secular *arja*, a theatrical genre using many conventions of *gambuh* but placing greater stress on singing and emphases on romance, comedy, ribaldry, and melodrama, combined with contemporary reflection. Described as an operetta, *arja* features actors who sing in a variety of systems of tuning, which better bring out the emotive qualities of the text. *Arja* stories derive from varied sources: Indian epic plots, legends from medieval East Javanese courtly life, similar stories set in Bali, and Chinese tales of passion. Young people flock to performances for opportunities to flirt. The ensemble includes a singer-reciter, and a small group of singers who explain and comment on the dramatic action. The dancer-actors sing in archaic Javanese, with refined characters (nobles) using a high upper voice, and coarse characters (demons, warriors) using a heavy chest voice. The music changes with the entrance of each new character.

Many musicians feel that *arja* is the pinnacle of Balinese performing arts because it demands technique and creative improvisation in music, dance, and drama. The ensemble features a few *suling*, which together can accommodate scales resembling *saih angklung, saih gendèr wayang,* and *saih gong* (*selisir*). The melodies are linked to the melodic formulae and contours of poetic forms called *tembang*, in which the libretti are written.

The other instruments include two *kendang, rincik, guntang, kempli,* and *kelentang*. The *guntang*, a bamboo tube with a thin bamboo strip struck with a small stick, is often called *kempur*, and supplies the main end-marking punctuation. Formerly, a second and smaller *guntang* functioned to keep the beat; it has been replaced by *kempli* and *kelenang*, playing on and off the beat respectively. There are three main types of compositions: short instrumental pieces, acting as an overture and as interludes; pieces that accompany dancers' entrances; and song accompaniment.

The *gendèr wayang* ensemble is used to accompany shadow-puppet plays (*wayang kulit*). It usually consists of a quartet of ten-bar, double-octave *gendèr* metallophones in the five-tone *slèndro* tuning (*saih gendèr wayang*). Stories used in the play are typically derived from the Hindu epic *Mahabharata*. There is a larger pair of instruments (*gedé* or *pemade*), with a second pair (*barangan*) pitched an octave higher. The instruments are played with a padded disk-shaped mallet in each hand, occasionally with unified motions, but usually in a contrapuntal fashion, and the bars must be struck and damped by the same hand. In most of the repertoire, the players' left-hand parts create a nuclear melody in unison in the lower octave, while their right-hand parts normally interlock in figurations in the upper octave (Figure 21.30). The players also frequently perform passages in unison or parallel motion (Figure 21.31).

To accompany shadow plays, there are categories of pieces that are performed differently throughout Bali. Certain pieces are played while the puppeteer (*dalang*) takes his place; some are grouped together into an overture as he readies his puppets; others are reserved for specific parts of the play. There are both refined pieces (often metrically free, normally accompanying the puppeteer's singing) and strong pieces (using ostinatos to accompany action). A few of the pieces are associated with specific characters, especially clowns, and other pieces accompany the drama or specific scenes. For example, "Tetangisan" ("Weeping") accompanies sadness, and *batel* pieces, as in other Balinese music, accompany anger or fighting.

Figure 21.30
Two gendèr wayang with right-hand figuration.

Figure 21.31
Two gendèr wayang in unison style.

Gendèr wayang can also be played outside of *wayang* to accompany life-cycle rites, such as tooth-filing rites and especially cremations. The pieces are normally derived from *wayang*, and the complex theatricality is transmitted through musical association. *Gendèr wayang* are sometimes considered to belong to a family of ensembles associated with cremation ceremonies. The *gendèr wayang* ensemble is considered to be delicate and quite intimate, and may be played in close proximity to the priests as they ritually wash a corpse before a cremation, or placed beside the pavilion used for the filing of teeth. The ordinary evening shadow play maintains ritual importance, but has greater entertainment value, and is performed frequently at life-cycle ceremonies and occasionally at temple festivals.

The *gamelan gong kebyar* can accompany a number of theater genres: *topeng*, traditional masked theater; *prembon*, a popular combination of theater styles; *drama gong*, popular, new theater, based on traditional forms and emphasizing comedy; *sendratari, kebyar-style* theater, first created at the conservatories; sometimes *janger*, flexible youth theater of various styles; and even *arja*.

Processional Ensembles

The main processional gamelans are the *bebonangan* or *baleganjur*, ensembles consisting of two *gong ageng*, a *kempur*, a number of *ceng-ceng kopyak* played in interlocking figuration, a number of kettle-gongs (*réong*) individually held and played in interlocking figuration, a timekeeping *kajar*, and two *kendang*. These ensembles are usually assembled from the instruments of a *gamelan gong*, and only in rare cases are made and kept as independent ensembles. Occasionally, the term *baleganjur* "walking army" is used to denote a larger, more complete ensemble or processional ensembles without kettle-gongs. The pieces played by these processional ensembles consist of an eight-beat metric cycle which is repeated, with the *ceng-ceng* and *réong* providing figuration and often dropping out in alternation. The music has a pronounced martial quality, and often accompanies dancers carrying weapons and ritual objects in procession.

A new style of *baleganjur* music, *kreasi baleganjur*, emerged from the STSI conservatory in 1986 and spread rapidly to urban centers and villages. It features *ceng-ceng kopyak* (usually eight sets), kettle-gongs (*réong*, usually four), a timekeeper (*kempli*), two *kendang*, and gongs, and is virtuosic. Interlocking parts and drum patterns frequently change, and are more complicated than those in traditional pieces. *Kreasi baleganjur* has inspired a whole new repertoire, and has added showmanship and choreography to performance. Heated competitions are common among the growing numbers of groups. Similar to *kreasi baru*, which emerged from traditional *gamelan gong* repertoire, *kreasi baleganjur* arose from traditional *baleganjur* pieces, and has captured the imagination of a new generation of male youth. It has also led to the manufacture and maintenance of *gamelan baleganjur* as complete ensembles disassociated from *gong kebyar*.

Bamboo and Wood Ensembles

The bamboo and wood ensembles include *pejogedan bumbung, genggong, gamelan jegog*, and *gong suling*. The *pejogedan bumbung*, also called *gamelan joged*, accompanies the social dance in which a female dancer (*joged*) selects partners from an audience for short, improvised duets. Originally, bamboo tube stampers accompanied the dance, but today the accompaniment consists of *tingklik* or *rindik* (bamboo xylophones in *sléndro* tuning, occasionally in *pélog*), with *kendang*, *rincik*, *suling*, and *kempur*. The *tingklik* are played with two long mallets in a technique similar to *gendèr wayang*, though the split bamboo bars need not be damped. Frequently, four *tingklik* and one *suling* are invited to play in hotel lobbies, providing atmospheric background music.

Genggong are palm-rib Jew's harps played in an ensemble, often called *gegeng-gongan*, which includes *guntang* (a one-stringed bamboo tube zither functioning as a gong), *kendang*, *suling*, and *rincik*. The ensemble occasionally accompanies small theatrical plays. The *gamelan jegog* is an ensemble of various sizes of bamboo xylophones, the smallest of which include 30.5 centimeter long split-bamboo bars, and the largest of which have bars up to 4 meters long. When entered in regional competitions, there may be twenty or more xylophones, producing a thunderous bamboo sound, and often two groups play at once trying to drown each other out. The *gong suling* is a flexible ensemble found throughout much of Bali, consisting of bamboo flutes at four different sizes, with various percussion, and two *kendang*. The *suling* replicate different *gamelan* parts, the repertoire is derived from the *gamelan gong*, and there is no fixed context for performance.

Sacred Ensembles

There are a variety of sacred ensembles, most of which have seven tones. The *gamelan gambang*, normally consisting of four xylophones of cut bamboo bars and one, two, or four *saron* (*gangsa jongkok*), and the *gamelan selundeng*, consisting of iron metallophones of different sizes, are the best known. The *gambang* instruments are the xylophones with fourteen bars arranged so the player can use a forked mallet in each hand to play octaves in alternation and form a figuration with the other players, while the seven-bar *saron* provides the nuclear melody, nearly always played in a unique, eight-beat rhythm, which can be understood as a meter of 5+3. The ensemble performs primarily at cremation rituals, and it also performs at temple festivals in some old villages of East Bali.

The *gamelan selundeng*, one of the oldest of all Balinese ensembles, consists solely of six to eight iron bar metallophones, some of which replicate the musical functions of colotomic and agogic instruments, while others perform nuclear melody and figuration. This gamelan is especially associated with the Bali Aga, early Balinese who received little or no Javanese influence and are considered descendants of the original inhabitants of Bali. Ensembles exist only within a few villages in East Bali and mountainous Central Bali. The serene and light music of the ensemble includes orchestral pieces and dance accompaniment, which adds a *ceng-ceng*. Some of the pieces are so sacred that their names are secret, and recordings are not permitted. In some villages, nonvillagers, considered impure and polluting, are restricted from even seeing the instruments.

Vocal Music

Unlike Java, Bali has no traditions of vocal music as an integral part of gamelan practice. Vocal music in Bali is sung by individuals, by study groups, and by choirs. The music is normally determined by the length of stanzas, the number of syllables per line, the arrangement of long and short vowels, and the ending vowel of each line. The poetic meter determines the rhythm, number of pitches, melodic patterns, and overall melodic contour. The context of performance, however, governs the musical elements; the same text will be given different musical treatment in different settings. The emotional quality of the poem may inform the selected scalar system, and each type of poetry expresses distinctive historical and cultural values.

There are three broad types of sung Balinese poetry: *kekawin*, *kidung*, and *tembang*. While the structures of these forms originated in Java, most *kidung* and *tembang* and a large portion of *kekawin* were composed in Bali, and the melodies and performance practices of these poetic traditions are purely Balinese today. *Kekawin* are poems in the Old Javanese language based on Indic meters. Parts of major *kekawin* literature, such as the *Ramayana* and the *Bharatayuddha* (the latter derived from the *Mahabharata*), are often "performed" by study groups at life-cycle rites and temple festivals with each line first being sung and then translated and interpreted. *Kekawin* and *kidung* are also performed by individuals at life-cycle rites of prominent villagers and nobility.

Kidung are often romantic, quasi-historical poems mostly in the Middle Javanese language, developed in Bali as a result of Javanese influences, using Indonesian poetic meters and often forming the basis of *gambuh* drama. At temple festivals, *kidung* are usually sung by groups, sometimes organized into *sekaha* and comprising mostly elderly women. The performance accompanies the rites within the inner sanctum of the temple, with one or more leaders singing the text and the others following along, using long sustained tones with little ornamentation. Solo *kidung* performances, however, include extensive ornamentation, embellishment, and melisma and are improvised according to the taste and skill of the singer who usually reads from a palm-leaf manuscript. *Tembang* is the most lyrical form of poetry, derived from the Javanese *macapat* tradition but mostly composed in Balinese. More dramatic and emotional in content, *tembang* are the main vocal idiom in *arja*.

The most famous vocal music is the *kecak* chorus, the group of seventy-five to two hundred men who represent the monkey army from the *Ramayana* and imitate the various instruments of the gamelan with onomatopoeic sounds. *Kecak* (sometimes called *gamelan swara* "voice gamelan"), originally accompanied trance dances and contained sections of interlocking singing of syllables such as *cak*. Around 1931, during experimentation and after a suggestion by Walter Spies, the noted specialist in Balinese arts, the trance group was expanded, and more elaborate parts were added to create a dramatic, quasi-theatrical performance of short story excerpts (normally the "Kidnapping of Sita") from the *Ramayana*. The members of the chorus (clad only in sarongs, and usually wearing a large hibiscus flower behind one ear) follow a leader chanting *cak* and *cok* with a wide range of dynamics. They occasionally sing passages in unison as they perform several choreographed movements while seated. Dancers sing, and a narrator explains the drama. Despite its fame, *kecak* has no ritual and only limited recreational functions within Balinese society, and is primarily a performance designed for foreign audiences, though artists enjoy composing and choreographing new performances. Nevertheless, one can still hear *kecak* in its original trance-accompaniment role in several villages during ritual events.

kekawin
Sung poetry in Old Javanese
kidung
Type of metered sung poetry in Bali and Lombok

Dance

In addition to the purely orchestral pieces of the sacred, ceremonial, and *kebyar* repertoires, a wealth of compositions cannot be separated from dance. Dance ranges from the dynamic expressions of *kebyar*, to the animated faces of stock theater characters, to the serene composure of temple dancers during festivals. There are both narrative and nonnarrative dances, described in an abbreviated fashion here to indicate the relationship of music and dance. The narrative dances include *gambuh, arja, topeng, wayang wong,* and *parwa*. These dances include many stock characters—good kings, princes, bad kings, prime ministers, queens, princesses, clowns, ladies-in-waiting—introduced by the performance of their representative *tabuh*. These *tabuh*, however, are specific to the ensemble; for example, the *tabuh* for a king in *arja* is different from that in *topeng*.

The characters within theater and dance dramas are of two types: *alus* or *manis* "refined, sweet," and *keras* or *kasar* "strong, coarse." Dance characterization acknowledges three components—head and upper body, middle body, and foot and lower body—which mirror the tripartite divisions of compositional form and the macrocosm. The *keras* characters emphasize movements in the lower body, and the *alus* characters in the upper body. Movement vocabulary for the *keras* characters, such as a demon warrior, will stress strong, lower-body movements with legs spread apart and large steps, but *alus* characters, such as a refined prince, move more slowly with limbs closer to the body and more concentrated upper-body movements. Performance contexts are varied: *gambuh* may be performed at life-cycle ceremonies of the nobility; *wayang wong, parwa,* and *arja* are normally attached to performance programs at temple festivals; and *topeng* may occur at both. *Wayang wong, parwa,* and especially *topeng* and *gambuh* have vital ritual functions, while *arja* is less ritualistic and unattached to religious proceedings, but has a greater social function and serves to gather participants to enjoy theater together.

The nonnarrative dances include *kebyar*, social, and temple dances—genres that are totally unrelated. The *kebyar* dances emerged from the technique of *légong* dancing, the narrative dances of girls portraying figures from epic and romantic tales accompanied by the *gamelan pelégongan*. The early *kebyar* dances, made famous by the choreographer and dancer I Mario, mimicked musical expressions and were normally danced in a sitting or squatting position, sometimes with a dancer playing an instrument, such as the spectacular *kebyar trompong* in which the dancer sits or squats in front of the *trompong*, spinning and flourishing his beaters as he plays and dances. *Tari lepas, kebyar* dances invented after World War II, expanded choreographic possibilities and allowed dancers to portray characters with works that embody themes. "*Oleg Tamulilingan*" "Flirtation of Two Bumblebees" and "*Taruna Jaya*" "Victorious Young Man" are examples of this style that are still performed.

The social dances primarily consist of *joged*, a term denoting the female dancer, who selects partners in turn from the audience for spontaneous duets, which are flirtatious or even erotic. Originating in the courts and apparently deriving from *légong, joged* dancers were retained by kings for their own and their guests' entertainment; an introductory dance would mimic *légong*. The most common *joged* form is *joged bumbung*, accompanied by an ensemble of bamboo xylophones, usually in the *sléndro* tuning. Neither *kebyar* nor social dances have contexts of fixed performances.

Among the temple dances are the *rejang*, a dance of either unmarried girls or post-menopausal women of the village, and *baris*, in which male dancers carry either a particular type of weapon or offerings. The *rejang* dances symbolize beauty and humility as offering, while the *baris* dances seek to protect the deities and the temple space. These dances often have their own repertoire; pieces accompanying *rejang* and other dances with offerings are normally lyrical or stately in nature, while those accompanying *baris* dances are martial. A variety of gamelans can supply the accompaniment. Generally, the most refined gamelans accompany offering dances, while *gamelan gong* or processional gamelans accompany *baris* dances. These temple dances, which have the least choreography and demand minimal skill, are among the most sacred dances in Bali. In contrast, the *kebyar* dances, which demand the most skill, are among the most secular dances.

Tourism and Recent Trends

Tourism has had a powerful impact on the arts. Tourists tend to descend on Bali with one of three destinations in mind: the beaches and shops of the coastal areas; the expensive hotel complexes at the southern tip of the island (with their all-inclusive entertainment packages); and the "cultural tourism" village destination of Ubud and its environs, where tourist-oriented performances occur nightly. The success of tourist performances has encouraged the formation of performing groups, supplied much-needed revenues to many villages, and given artists the motivation to seek new material. Artists have frequently sought past material and revived almost obsolete dances and orchestral pieces to present to tourists. Some tourists and foreign scholars have also assisted in preserving threatened performing arts, such as *gambuh,* and supported a revival of these forms. This has led some observers to suggest that tourism has replaced the courts as the primary source of patronage for the arts.

Yet tourism has also encouraged performers to restrict the length of orchestral pieces, pieces for dancing, and theater excerpts to adjust the material to the tastes and limited attention span of tourists. These restrictions have become so standard that the artists themselves are beginning to forget the complete versions of the pieces. Many of the groups performing for tourists are also not well rehearsed and are not doing justice to the material. Tourism has thus encouraged a quantity but not a quality of arts, and has spawned misunderstandings and misinterpretations of material. But what is most threatening about tourism is that farmers are encouraged to sell their fields of rice to businessmen or major corporations who have government support to set up art shops or hotels. If this trend of selling lands continues, it may have an impact on the rice-cultivation practices that are still the backbone of the rituals that sustain the whole culture. This could erode the meaning of both the rituals and the performing arts functioning at those rituals.

NUSA TENGGARA BARAT

Nusa Tenggara Barat (NTB), comprising the islands of Lombok and Sumbawa, lies east of Bali and west of Nusa Tenggara Timur. Sumbawa is far larger than Lombok, but Lombok has far more people. The three main ethnic groups are the Sasak of Lombok and the Samawa and Mbojo of Sumbawa. The Sasak and Samawa are culturally and ethnically related to the Balinese and Javanese; the Mbojo are related to peoples of Flores. Each group has a distinct language and history, but all share Islam, to which 95% of the population adheres, practicing a reformed Sunni version.

Social contexts for making music in NTB include life-cycle rites (marriages and circumcisions), holidays, harvests, and social celebrations. An Islamic reform movement swept over Lombok and Sumbawa in the twentieth century, changing most rituals and their musical traditions; but in Lombok, some musical traditions still function within the contexts of unreformed Islamic rituals. Lombok is enjoying an increase in tourism, and ensembles often play for tourists. Sumbawa is expecting to develop tourism further in the twenty-first century. The performing arts are encouraged throughout NTB to assert regional and national identities.

Before Dutch colonization (1893–1942), Lombok had been colonized by the Balinese, whose influence still marks many Sasak cultural expressions. Music is frequently performed on a variety of gamelans, some consisting primarily of bronze instruments, as in Bali and Java. The instrumentation of this music features a central melody played on a metallophone, a wind instrument, or a gong chime (or any combination of them), punctuated by gongs within specific metrical cycles. Faster-moving ornamentations, often interlocking figurations, are performed on a gong chime or metallophones, and drums have agogic and signaling functions. The aesthetic changes farther east in Lombok: The tonalities, stratified melodic structures, and gong cycles are replaced by quasi-diatonic tunings and heterophonic melodies, accompanied by drumming. Ensembles are smaller. Vocals are more important, and often include Arabic inflections. Instrumentation relies more on winds and strings, with fewer bronze instruments than in the west of the island. These tendencies continue through Sumbawa, with the diversity of instruments decreasing together with the number of tones. Many martial arts dances are performed across Sumbawa, particularly by the Mbojo. Songs are often topical and romantic, and individuals or groups sometimes improvise sung poetry. Samawa and Mbojo musical elements and instruments are similar: double and single reeds are the primary melodic instruments, accompanied by drums and occasionally by a xylophone, cymbals and a gong. Gong chimes and metallophones are not used.

Lombok

Lombok, east of Bali, absorbed extensive cultural influences from Java and Bali, and was colonized and controlled by them. However, other cultural and religious influences, from West Sumatra, and even from West Asia, also inspired the development of several performing-arts traditions on Lombok. These traditions, coupled with those developed internally and others based on Javanese and Balinese models, form a unique and diverse cultural matrix. The music of Lombok has two main cultural strata: one reflects Javanese-Balinese values, and the other reflects Sumatran, pan-Islamic, and Arab-Persian values. The cultural identity of the Sasak has gradually changed orientation from the former to the latter; consequently, the Sasak musical forms associated with the Javanese and Balinese have declined, while those associated with Islam have prospered.

The Sasak have a wealth of musical ensembles and vocal music practices; different districts and villages around the island maintain unique traditions. Music, directly related to cultural orientation, is believed to embody religious values associated with one or the other antecendent (Java-Bali or Sumatran-West Asian). Religious orientation and musical traditions have thus become intertwined. Musical organizations are informal groups drawn from a community. In villages that retain some of the older traditions, most villagers perform artistically at some time during their lives. Within orthodox Sasak villages, musical activity is markedly lower, and few villagers are involved in the performing arts. Groups are normally restricted to males, except for a few dances and theatrical forms that include women. Women who involve themselves in the performing arts are usually ascribed a low social standing.

Most musical traditions involve ensembles usually called gamelans; as in Bali and Java, most instruments belong to a particular gamelan and are not played with other ensembles. There is no island-wide organological system in Lombok, but instruments have ideological associations that classify them as nonbronze and bronze. Nonbronze instruments are mostly free of ideological concern, but bronze instruments are associated with Javanese and Balinese cultural traditions, traditions deemed non-Islamic.

The basic, traditional Sasak ensemble is the *gamelan beleq* or *oncer*, also called by regional names (Figure 21.32). The ensemble can perform at different occasions such as life-cycle rites, ceremonies to invoke rainfall, and national holidays. In addition to a set of four kettle gongs (*réong*), flutes (*suling*), and cymbals (*rincik*), it features two drummers who dramatically confront one another and play interlocking figurations on their large drums. Other ensembles include sacred gamelan (used for accompanying ritual dance), processional gamelan, and a Balinese-influenced gamelan (*gamelan gong Sasak*). The latter is tuned in the *saih gong* or *selisir* pentatonic tonality (see INDONESIA: BALI) and the repertoire includes traditional gamelan pieces, newly created compositions, and Balinese *gong kebyar* compositions. The *gamelan rebana* was reportedly formed in the late 1800s to be a substitute for banned ensembles of bronze. There are normally ten to fifteen *rebana* (drums) in the ensemble,

Figure 21.32
The *gamelan gendang beleq*, a variation of the *gamelan oncer*, the basic Sasak bronze gamelan. Photo by David Harnish, 1988.

Figure 21.33
Different sizes of drums in the *gamelan rebana*. Photo by David Harnish, 1989.

with the various drums tuned to perform the parts of bronze gamelan instruments (Figure 21.33). The ensemble is played primarily for life-cycle rites, especially marriages, and performs both in a stationary position and in procession. Several pieces are considered to have efficacious qualities, such as aiding the fertility of the soil, and performers generally place small offerings around the ensemble to prevent misfortunes during performance. Thus, though the ensemble was developed to replace bronze gamelans in accordance with new religious ideology, it has retained much of the function and repertoire of traditional gamelans.

 The most important ensemble in a theater context is the *gamelan wayang Sasak*, which accompanies the local shadow play. The ensemble features the bamboo flute (*suling pewayangan*) as the sole melodic instrument, with accompaniment by the gong, two drums, and several other tuned percussion instruments. The repertoire of Sasak shadow plays consists of six or seven standard pieces, various sustaining patterns to accompany battles, and special introductory pieces. Shadow plays were used for proselytizing Islam earlier in the 1900s but they have often been forbidden by religious leaders because they depict human forms and retain pre-Islamic ritual processes.

Sasak vocal traditions divide along the same Java-Bali and Sumatra-West Asian lines as the instrumental traditions. The primary vocal music related to Java and Bali is *tembang Sasak*, songs in the Sasak language using Javanese meters, performed in scales related to *pélog* and *sléndro*.

Sumbawa

The contexts for making music are varied in Sumbawa. A number of musical forms are associated with Islam, some with the nobility, a few with romance and courtship, and many with work and recreation. Sumbawa is well known for its horses, and there are frequent horse races in which music is sometimes presented; in addition, buffalo races in West Sumbawa are held before the rice-planting season. There are also dances of mock battles. No theatrical forms of Sumbawa appear to predate the twentieth century, many of the dances are nonnarrative, and there are no masked-dance traditions.

Strings, winds, drums, and other percussion are all found in Sumbawa. The most important stringed instrument is the bowed *biola,* similar to the Western violin but slightly lower in pitch. The *gambo*, an eight-stringed (double course) plucked lute, is sometimes used for songs and dances in various parts of the island and occasionally called *gitar*. Winds consist primarily of double-reed oboes and bamboo flutes. Reed pipes from rice-paddy stalks are sometimes found in small ensembles. Wind instruments are played with a circular breathing technique.

There is a wide variety of drums including the double-headed, slightly conical *kendang*, found everywhere but more concentrated in West Sumbawa; the frame or bowl-shaped *rebana*, found all over the island, and others. Single bronze hanging gongs are common in ensembles, especially in West Sumbawa. Gongs mark melodic cycles of two, four, eight, and (rarely) three beats. Ensembles are small compared to those of islands west, and there are far fewer bronze instruments. Several ensembles consist simply of a single- or double-reed aerophone, a drum, and a gong.

Sulawesi is an island of peninsulas divided into three provinces: North, Central, and South Sulawesi. Most of the population lives in the southern and northern peninsulas, where plains permit large settlements. Four major ethnic groups inhabit Sulawesi: the Makassarese, the Buginese, the Torajans, and the Minahasans. The Buginese and Makassarese (of South Sulawesi) are renowned for their skills as seafarers. Both have seen centuries of foreign trading, and some of their dances and music show Portuguese, Persian-Arabic, and other influences. For both, the most representative musical instruments are a two-stringed spike fiddle (*gesó-gesó*), a boat-shaped two-stringed lute (*Makassarese kacapi, Buginese kacaping*), a reed pipe (*puwi-puwi*), and pairs of two-headed cylindrical drums (*ganrang*). Some Buginese and Makassarese music and dances evoke the sea, as does processional music played on drums (*tunrung ganrang*). Both coastal and inland villagers enjoy listening to storytellers who sing epics or other traditional stories for nights on end, accompanying themselves on a spike fiddle.

After a day spent working at sea or in the fields, some Buginese and the Makassarese like to spend their evenings singing quatrains (*pantun*), sometimes improvising humorously in reply to each other's contributions. These performances are accompanied by a local zither (*kacapi*), which resembles related forms on nearby islands, including the southern Philippines. Buginese and Makassarese conversion to Islam in the 1600s brought about the adoption of some Persian-Arabic musical instruments, including the frame drum (*rebana*) and the *gambus*, a pear-shaped wooden lute with decorated sound holes. Both peoples practice Muslim devotional arts, such as singing songs in Arabic, and the art of self-defense, accompanied by drums.

The Torajan cultures of Central Sulawesi have produced a diverse musical scene; their music may be divided into that which is performed for happy events (harvests, thanksgiving dances, songs to greet the day, etc.), and music performed for sad events (funerals). Funerals are the main musical occasions and the most important artistic, social, religious, and even political events in Toraja. These rituals enact the local religion—animist and based on the worship of ancestors—practiced by about 30 percent of Torajans. Local belief divides the universe and the world of ritual into two halves, marking life and death.

Poetry sung collectively at a Torajan funeral may compare the ancestors of the deceased with the sun, moon, or another natural entity. A massive choir of mourning men, who sing intricately embellished, long-held notes, dances in a slow-moving circle near the house that holds the corpse. The arrival of each party of guests is marked by distinct patterns played on a gong. A pair of flutists and a singer perform almost continuously in the tower house, their laments sounding through loudspeakers over the valley. The bamboo flute, the most common Torajan instrument, is decorated with carvings, and sometimes with a buffalo-horn cone attached to its end. At a different location, professional musicians perform *mámarakka* music in which long bamboo flutes with a carved buffalo-horn flare accompany a female vocalist (Figure 21.34). Aleatoric musical effects result from the arbitrary combination of sounds produced at different parts of the ceremonial site. The lamenting of the male chorus merges with the music of the vocal-flute ensemble, broken up now and

Figure 21.34
A *mámarakka* ensemble: a vocalist and end-blown flutes (*suling lembang* with a buffalo-horn flare and six holes for fingering perform in the tower house at a Toraja funeral. Photo by H. Kartomi, 1974.

then by insistent gong rhythms, while dancers' drumming and whistling contribute an element of gaeity. It is not unusual for hundreds of guests to attend a Torajan funeral, which may last a week.

The Minahasans of North Sulawesi are heavily Christian (mostly Protestant); Spanish missionaries began colonizing North Sulawesi from the 1500s. In the 1600s the Dutch gained control over the area; present-day Minahasan culture shows traces of all these influences. At harvest time, thanksgiving celebrations are held all over Minahasa, featuring indigenous dancing, conch bands, and *kolintang* performances. *Kolintang* is the main musical ensemble of the Minahasans. The modern *kolintang* is a xylophone—not to be confused with the set of bossed kettlegongs known in the Philippines as *kulintang*.

REFERENCES

Arps, Bernard. 1992. *Tembang in Two Traditions: Performance and Interpretation of Javanese Literature.* London: School of Oriental and African Studies.

Becker, Judith. 1979a. "Time and Tune in Java." In *The Imagination of Reality: Essays in Southeast Asian Coherence Systems*, ed. A. L. Becker and Aram Yengovan, 197–210. Norwood, NJ: Ablex.

———. 1979b. "People Who Sing; People Who Dance." In *What is Modern Indonesian Culture?* Ed., Gloria Davis, 3–10. Athens, OH: Ohio University Center for International Studies.

Brakel-Papenhuijzen, Clara. 1992. *The Bedhaya Court Dances of Central Java.* Leiden: E. J. Brill.

Brinner, Benjamin E. 1995. *Knowing Music, Making Music: Javanese Gamelan and the Theory of Musical Competence and Interaction.* Chicago: University of Chicago Press.

Goldsworthy, David K. 1979. "Melayu Music of North Sumatra." Ph.D. Dissertation, Monash University.

Hefner, Robert. 1987. "The Politics of Popular Art: Tayuban Dance and Culture Change in East Java." *Indonesia* 43:75–94.

Heins, Ernst L. 1977. "Goong Renteng: Aspects of Orchestral Music in a Sundanese Village." Ph.D. dissertation, University of Amsterdam.

Hoffman, Stanley B. 1978. "Epistemology and Music: A Javanese Example." *Ethnomusicology* 22(1):69–88.

Kartomi, Margaret. 1976. "Performance, Music and Meaning in Réyog Ponorogo." *Indonesia* 22:85–130.

———. 1979. "Minangkabau Musical Culture: The Contemporary Scene and Recent Attempts at Its Modernization." In *What Is Modern Indonesian Culture?* ed. G. Davis, 19–36. Athens: Ohio University Press.

———. 1981. "Randai Theatre in West Sumatra: Components, Music, Origins, and Recent Change." *Review of Indonesian and Malayan Affairs* 15(l): l–44.

———. 1986. "Muslim Music in West Sumatran Culture." *The World of Music* 3:13–32.

Keeler, Ward. 1987. *Javanese Shadow Plays, Javanese Selves.* Princeton, NJ: Princeton University Press.

Kunst, Jaap. 1973 [1934]. *Music in Java: Its History, Its Theory, and Its Technique.* 3rd ed., rev. and enlarged by Ernst Heins. 2 vols. The Hague: Martinus Nijhoff

Manuel, Peter, and Randal E. Baier. 1986. "Jaipongan: Indigenous Popular Music of West Java." *Asian Music* 18(1):91–110.

North, Richard. 1988. "An Introduction to the Musical Traditions of Cirebon." *Balungan* 3(3):2–6.

Notosudirdjo, R. Frankis. 1990. "European Music in Colonial Life in Nineteenth-Century Java: A Preliminary Study." M.A. thesis, University of Wisconsin–Madison.

Ricklefs, M. C. 1981. *A History of Modern Indonesia: c.1300 to the Present.* Bloomington: Indiana University Press.

Sunardjo, R. H. Unang. 1983. *Meninjau Sepintas Panggung Sejarah Pemerintahan Kerajaan Cerbon 1479-1809.* Bandung: Tarsito.

Sutton, R. Anderson. 1989. "Identity and Individuality in an Ensemble Tradition: The Female Vocalist in Java." In *Women and Music in Cross-Cultural Perspective*, ed. Ellen Koskoff, 111–130. Urbana and Chicago: University of Illinois Press.

Wagner, Frits A. 1959. *Indonesia: The Art of an Island Group.* New York: Crown.

Weintraub, Andrew. 2004. *Power Plays: Wayang Golek Puppet Theater of West Java.* Athens, OH: Center for International Studies, Ohio University.

Williams, Sean. 1989. "Current Developments in Sundanese Popular Music." *Asian Music* 21(1):105–136.

———. 2001. *The Sound of the Ancestral Ship: Highland Music of West Java.* New York, London: Oxford University Press.

Wolbers, Paul Arthur. 1987. "Account of an Angklung Caruk, July 28, 1985." *Indonesia* 43:66–74.

Wright, Michael R. 1978. "The Music Culture of Cirebon." Ph.D. dissertation, University of California, Los Angeles.

———. 1988. Tarling: Modern Music from Cirebon." *Balungan* 3(3):21–25.

Borneo: Sabah, Sarawak, Brunei, Kalimantan

Patricia Matusky

Cultural Geography
Vocal Music
Instrumental Music

The Southeast Asian island commonly known as Borneo is divided into three modern nations. The Malaysian states of Sarawak and Sabah are located in the north and far northeast of the island, respectively. These states joined the Federation of Malaysia in 1963, and are sometimes called East Malaysia. The sultanate of Brunei Darussalam occupies a small area on the north coast between the two Malaysian states, and the three Indonesian provinces of Kalimantan make up the remaining (and largest) part of the island.

The geology of Borneo features mountain ranges and high plateaus. Several navigable rivers drain the island in nearly all directions from its center. Many of the upper reaches of the rivers are interlaced with dangerous, sometimes impassable rapids. Most of the year, the forest covering much of Borneo receives heavy rainfall. The dwellings of most central Borneo peoples are built along waterways, but the difficulty of travel isolates many communities. The distribution of the population is sparse in the interior, but increases toward the coast. Except in the far north, Borneo's coastal areas are swampy, but they remain the sites of its greatest urban development and population density.

CULTURAL GEOGRAPHY

The ethnic groups of Sabah, Sarawak, and Kalimantan are distinguished by culture and language. A long-used term, *Dayak,* once served as an all-encompassing designation for many of the indigenous peoples of the island (excluding Malays and Javanese). It still commonly denotes a much broader group of people in Kalimantan than in Sarawak. In

Kalimantan, it is recognized as a designation that encompasses smaller groups. Along the major rivers, the main groups in Sarawak are the Iban, Bidayuh, Melanau, and Malay. In Sabah, the main groups include the Kadazan, Bajau, Orang Sungei, and Murut. Many minorities also live in these areas. West Kalimantan is home to some of the central Borneo groups, plus the Maloh and Iban; the eastern section finds mainly the Kayan, Kenyah, and related peoples. Javanese people have lived in South Kalimantan since the 1500s. The Malay population, in varying numbers, lives mainly in towns and cities throughout the coastal areas or Borneo, and occasionally in market towns along the major rivers. The coastal towns and cities are the centers of commerce and communication, and most other immigrant groups live in them.

Generations ago, the immigrant peoples brought their own music cultures to Borneo, and their traditions have been perpetuated by their descendants. In the twenty-first century, the Malays still use the frame drum (*rebana*) in making music, and perform musics similar to those of the Peninsular and other Malays. Significant examples include musical genres associated with religious practice—the call to prayer (*azan*) and devotional singing (*zikir*)—and the social dances *zapin* and *joget*, still popular among many young Malays of inland market towns. The early Javanese immigrants brought a form of the gamelan (orchestra of bronze gongs and metallophones), which survives in East and South Kalimantan. The Chinese, who live in great numbers in north and west Borneo, especially in Sarawak and Sabah, excel in Western music. They also continue to perform their traditional instrumental and vocal musics. Their prominence in Sarawak has led to the development of public displays of Chinese culture, including festivals for the deities of various temples, opera troupes in the streets, processions for the Chinese New Year with dragons accompanied by drums and gongs, and clubs for youths. Among the indigenous groups in Sarawak, Sabah, and Kalimantan, the variety of music is a dynamic aspect of traditional life. These indigenous musics appear in both vocal and instrumental forms.

zikir
Chanting of Islamic verse, usually accompanied by drumming; also *dikir*

zapin
West Asian-derived songs and dances of Malaysia and Sumatra

joged/joget
Genre of popular social dance, common to Malaysia and Indonesia

VOCAL MUSIC

The vocal music of the indigenous peoples of Borneo includes epics and other narratives, plus songs for life-cycle events and rituals associated with religion, healing, growing rice, hunting game, and waging war. Songs to welcome visitors to the longhouse or to accompany dancing, and sung narratives to relate genealogies are usually collective endeavors, with both skilled and semiskilled singers taking part. Some vocal genres feature exclusively male or female solo singers; other forms require the effort of an ensemble of either single or mixed genders. No professionalism in musical performance is recognized in traditional Borneo societies, though communities acknowledge expertise in singing a particular genre or playing a given instrument.

The singing voice tends to be small, with moderate resonance and volume. Nasalization varies in intensity from one group to another; most vocalists, exercising the muscles and resonant cavities of the nasal pharynx, use a high proportion of upper partials at all levels of pitch. Consequently, they obtain a strident vocal quality, especially at higher tonal levels; female voices sometimes achieve a shouting quality. In some central Borneo societies, each female singer covers her mouth with one hand as she sings. In Sabah, Sarawak, and Kalimantan, vocal forms reflect various aspects of life. Vocal music—including funeral dirges, epics, and songs of love and courting, war, and general entertainment—remains one of the principal means of preserving and disseminating the oral literature and customary practices of Borneo.

Songs for Dancing

Vocal music is a major form of dance accompaniment. Collective line dances (or long dances), performed in a row or a circle, are accompanied by the dancers' singing, with percussive rhythms created by the dancers' stamping and other footfalls. For example, the Murut peoples of the interior regions of Sabah still perform the *lansaran*, formerly sung to celebrate the taking of heads, but now a form of general community entertainment. It features poetic verses sung by male and female dancers as they dance in circular formations on a specially sprung floor. In community centers, this floor (*lansaran*) is built of elastic planks and logs, which, whenever the dancers shift their weight in tandem with shuffling footsteps, enable the floor to bounce and hit against beams beneath it. As the steps set up a regular, percussive beat and a resulting crash of the floor against the beams beneath it, the male and female dancers alternately sing the poetic verses, each group in unison. A given tune, within the melodic range of a fourth, is repeated for each verse, as the singers focus on a reciting pitch, and finally descend to a lower tone in each line of text.

In Kenyah longhouses of central Borneo and Sarawak, adults perform line dances and a traditional dance of war (*lekupa*). In the latter dances of Kenyah-Badang, one male dancer is a solo singer, and everyone else sings in chorus. The style, predominantly unison, contrasts with some passages in rudimentary singing in parts, stressing the harmonic intervals of octave, unison, and third. The melodic range may be as wide as an octave, using a pentatonic scale. Essentially strophic, this form is accompanied by a repeated percussive rhythm, stamped by the dancers. Kenyah song lyrics tend to outline some of the most fundamental social codes and appropriate standards of behavior (Gorlinski 1995).

Songs for Narration

A notable vocal genre mainly of several Kajang groups of the interior of Sarawak is the sung narrative known as *wa* and *mu'a* "the singing of the *wa*" (Strickland 1988:67). It is usually a lengthy work, performed to welcome a guest to the longhouse, to open or close a specific event, or to relate a genealogy. It is usually sung by several female singers: each in turn serves as a soloist, while the others sing a choral refrain. The narrative is structured in stanzas consisting of lines of text governed by set rhymes and bounded by certain textual markers. A soloist sings the textlines in a strictly syllabic style, and the chorus punctuates the narrative at periodic intervals with a refrainlike, descending melodic line (sung on the vocable *é*), sometimes in unison, but usually in heterophony.

lansaran
Murut headhunting song and dance form
lekupa
Kenyah-Badang songs and dances
wa
Kajang sung narrative form
timang
Iban ritual chanting

Songs for Religion

In the traditional religions of Borneo, the spiritual world is an important and powerful force which always requires attention, and which sometimes requires communication and propitiation. Iban peoples of Sarawak and West Kalimantan perform a form of ritual chanting known as *timang* to communicate with the spiritual world. The chanting is performed by a bard who intones texts to invite spirits to join in a given feast. He is assisted by another bard, who sings or chants in alternation with him. The genre can ensure community welfare, good fortune, requests of fruitful seed and bountiful harvests, and requests of the spirits' presence at any ritual of high significance in the longhouse community.

The *timang* is usually structured in the form of a stanza (sung by the bard), followed by a short refrain (sung by an all-male chorus). The assistant bard responds with a complementary stanza, followed by the refrain. The pattern of statement and response, with the interjected choral refrain, may continue all night, until the intended objective is achieved (Masing 1981). Since many of the indigenous peoples of Sabah, Sarawak, and Kalimantan have accepted Christianity, another type of communication with the spiritual world takes the form of hymns. Robust hymn singing occurs in unison or sometimes in parts, with the accompaniment of a piano or a guitar, using diatonic scales in major and minor modes.

INSTRUMENTAL MUSIC

A rich variety of instruments—for accompanying dance or for personal enjoyment—characterizes the instrumental music of Borneo, including gongs, flutes, zithers, and Jew's harps. People of Malaysian Borneo and Kalimantan consider the bronze bossed gong an object of high value, in both musical and nonmusical contexts. As an item of economic wealth, the gong carries a high price in barter and trade, and its use in rituals and in communication with the spiritual world is important. In musical contexts, it is found in small ensembles that play music to welcome visitors, accompany dances, and enhance rituals. Formerly, gongs were used to transmit messages from one longhouse to another as players beat out rhythmic patterns.

Gongs and Gong Chimes

In Sabah, Sarawak, and parts of Kalimantan, large bossed gongs—in diameters ranging from 30 centimeters to more than 70 centimeters—are heard in ensembles that have from five to nine or more hanging gongs. In Sabah, large gongs are beaten in interlocking rhythms in the music known as *magagung*, which accompanies a traditional dance of the Kadazan. Other musical forms played by orchestras of large gongs occur throughout the northwest and central parts of Borneo, and accompany dances and ceremonies. These ensembles provide the repetitive interlocking rhythmic patterns at thunderous levels of intensity, which signal and welcome the arrival of special guests to longhouses and villages. Among central Borneo peoples, the large gongs are usually beaten by men; the smaller ones, by women. The Iban of Sarawak and West Kalimantan often call this ensemble

Figure 22.1
A typical ensemble of large gongs: one small *canang* (or *gan*, left), one *bandai* (background), two deep-rimmed *tawak*, and one *agung* (middle right). Photo by Patricia Matusky.

gendan raya "celebration drums"; other groups use the phrase *main gong* "playing the gongs." Kenyah gongs tend to be "untuned," relying on overall contrast of pitch rather than the creation of specific tonal contours (Gorlinski 1994).

In these ensembles, players beat repeated rhythmic patterns on the gongs, using either sustained, resonant tones or short, staccato tones. The practice of playing interlocking or shared parts is important in the ensembles of large gongs of Borneo. In a typical ensemble, one or more large, deep-rimmed gongs (*tawak*) are struck with padded beaters (one player per gong) in a set rhythmic pattern (Figure 22.1). One or more large, shallow-rimmed gongs are struck on the boss with a wooden stick in a repeated rhythmic pattern complementing that of large *tawak*. Next, medium- and small-sized hanging gongs of various names are struck on the boss or the rim with wooden sticks. Last, an ostinato of two pitches that alternately signify the downbeat (low pitch or timbre) and the upbeat (high pitch or timbre) of each main pulse is played on a pair of small bossed gongs (Figure 22.2). The rhythmic patterns played by these ensembles are structured in duple meter in repetitive four-beat or eight-beat units.

In addition to hanging gongs, most orchestras of this type include one or more drums, usually hit with a pair of wooden sticks. Drummed rhythmic patterns support those of the deep-voiced gongs. In these orchestras, timbre or tone color is as important as pitch, and specific pitches themselves are insignificant. With the use of the stick-hit drums and the striking of wooden sticks or padded beaters on the gongs, the totality of sound emerges as a multipart interlocking of distinct timbres, with staccato and resonant pitches, producing composite and repetitive rhythms.

The gong-chime ensembles of the Iban peoples of west and northwest Borneo are related to the *gulintangan, kulintangan,* and *kulintang* traditions of Brunei, Sabah, and the southern Philippines, respectively [see THE PHILIPPINES: ISLAMIC COMMUNITIES OF THE SOUTHERN PHILIPPINES). The Iban often call this ensemble long drum (*gendang panjai*) or

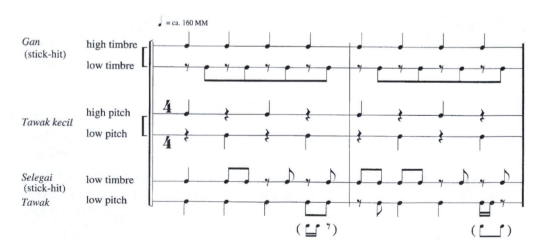

Figure 22.2
Orchestral gong music of the Kajang.

engkeromung, for it consists of one gong chime (*engkeromung,* eight or more small bossed gongs, suspended in a long wooden rack), two or more large-sized and medium-sized hanging bossed gongs (*tawak*), and one or more long, single-headed, cylindrical drums (*gendang panjai,*). Iban women traditionally play the gong chime and the hanging gongs; the men play the hand-hit drums. The drum begins, and the gong chime and then the hanging gongs enter at staggered temporal intervals.

In a typical piece, the long drum sets up a rhythmic pattern (usually four beats long), played and varied by both the gong chime and the low-pitched hanging gong. The basic pattern is sustained throughout a given piece, every other beat punctuated by the player of the smaller hanging gong in unison with another player beating out a drone on the highest-pitched gong of the gong chime. Rhythms are usually in duple meter; the tempo begins at a medium pace and gradually increases in speed. This ensemble provides music to accompany the dance formerly danced by Iban warriors, but today performed as entertainment by a solo male. For celebrations, to entertain guests visiting the longhouse, or for any other festive occasion, the *gendang panjai* is a popular form of music.

Bamboo, Wooden Poles, and Xylophones

Throughout Malaysian Borneo and Kalimantan, large hardwood poles and a wooden mortar are used to pound new rice to separate the chaff from the grain, and bamboo tubes are sometimes used to cook the rice. As an extension of work, the implements used for the physical motions of sowing, harvesting, and pounding the grains of rice and the wooden and bamboo implements used in these events have become music-making instruments in daily activities and ritual contexts.

Several groups living in the central Borneo region stamp poles made of bamboo or wood. Players stamp the poles to chase away unwanted or undesirable elements, originating in both the seen and unseen worlds. For example, in an event called *huduk apa* "chasing away whatever," some Kayan male groups use wooden poles (about 1.4 meters long), one to a player. With poles, they stamp out the pulse of their footsteps as they parade around the veranda of their longhouse. Accompanying them are gongs which provide an interlocking rhythmic pattern in duple meter. Eventually, in a climactic fury of shouts and hisses, the participants gather around a central place on the veranda, waving their poles in the air in a symbolic gesture.

The poles used to pound rice in the traditional method utilizing the mortar (*lesung*) and pestle (*antan*) also serve as stampers in musical contexts. In many parts of Borneo, teams of three to four women pound rice. With precise timing and rhythm, they lift the pestle and pound or stamp the grains of rice in the well of the mortar. This activity finds its musical parallel as entertainment after work, when women, usually in teams of three, stamp the pestles at select locations on the top surface of the mortar. The tradition in Sarawak of striking tuned bamboo tubes in interlocking patterns strongly resembles some of the music traditions of the Sulu Archipelago and the southern Philippines [see THE PHILIPPINES: ISLAMIC COMMUNITIES OF THE SOUTHERN PHILIPPINES].

Sets of bamboo tubes called *togunggak* are carried, one tube to a player, and are struck with a wooden stick to beat out interlocking rhythmic patterns, resulting in repeated

tawak
Deep-rimmed gongs
huduk apa
Kayan pest-dispersal ceremony

Figure 22.3
The ensemble of plucked lute (*sapeh*) and xylophone (*jatung utang*) plays music for dance among the Kayan and Kenyah peoples in Borneo. Photo by Patricia Matusky.

composite melodic and rhythmic phrases. The *togunggak* were formerly played in headhunting ceremonies of the Murut peoples of north Borneo. Imitating music for gong orchestras, the Bidayuh peoples of northwest Sarawak play similar sets of tuned, stick-hit bamboo tubes (*peruncung*) while walking back to the longhouses after work in the paddies. In these ensembles, the two highest-pitched tubes play an ostinato, while the low-pitched tubes play rhythmic patterns imitating those of the large gongs.

The music played on the xylophones of Borneo usually accompanies dancing, but it may also be heard in the performance of sung epics in Sabah, and perhaps in parts of Kalimantan. The xylophone of Sarawak and East Kalimantan (*jatung utang*) is a small raft of slats suspended over a wooden, boxlike frame, or separate, tuned slats laid across the top of the frame. In both cases, the slats are struck with a pair of short wooden beaters as the player sits on the floor before the instrument.

The xylophone in East Kalimantan was formerly a large raft of beams, suspended and played in fields of rice (Gorlinski 1989:286). Among the Kenyah peoples of central Borneo, the *jatung utang* is usually found in ensemble with a plucked lute (*sampi'*, Kayan *sapeh* and *sapi'*), or with a mouth organ and a guitar, to perform music that accompanies dance (Figure 22.3). The dances of war performed today by both male and female dancers are typically accompanied by two plucked lutes and the *jatung utang*. The melodies of music for dancing are played heterophonically on a lute and a xylophone while a second lute provides an ostinato. The xylophonist provides a movable drone in the form of a repeated pitch, changing as required to support the central tone of melodic phrases as they shift from one range of the scale to another.

The Jew's harp is found throughout the island, known by local names, including *ruding, geruding, bungkau, junggotan,* and *tong*. The player taps its base or pulls a string to create short rhythms. It usually played solo, but in parts of central Borneo, it is played with a tube zither (*satong*). In the *tong* and *satong* ensemble of the Kajang, a short, iterative melody on the *satong* is played simultaneously with a dronelike short rhythmic figure plucked on the Jew's harp. It is sometimes played solo during courting; as a solo instrument and in ensembles, it provides music for general entertainment.

jatung utang
Kenyah wooden xylophone
ruding
Jew's harp of Borneo
sapeh/sapi'
Kenyah/Kayan plucked lute

Stringed Instruments

A famous plucked lute in Sarawak and East Kalimantan is the *sapeh* (and related names) of the Kayan, the Kenyan, and more recently the Kajang of the interior of Sarawak. It is usually made in pairs, ideally carved from the same tree trunk (Koizumi 1976:39–47). The body is a meter or more long, in a narrow rectangular shape, with a hollow, open backside and a short homogeneous neck. Usually three or four wire strings, attached near the base of the body, run over small bridges and movable frets to lateral pegs at the top of the neck. The lowermost string, using the greatest number of frets, plays the melody, and the other strings play a dronelike ostinato.

Sapeh tunes may be played for general entertainment, but more frequently they accompany dancing. The melody of a *sapeh* is usually sectionalized, with variations and specific ornaments featured in successive repetitions (Gorlinski 1988). An integral part of *sapeh* pieces is a melodic and rhythmic drone or ostinato, played every four beats throughout a piece by the player of the melody or a second player. Traits of *sapeh* pieces include an abundance of ornaments, the shifting of melodic phrases to and from the high register of the instrument, strict duple meter, and a continuous ostinato.

Another important stringed instrument in Borneo is the bamboo idiochord tube zither called *satong* or *lutong* (in Sarawak and Kalimantan) and *tongkungon* (in Sabah). It consists of a section of bamboo, closed at each end by the natural node, but opened along its length by a carved slit. It has four to eight strings (depending on where it is found) cut from the cortex of the bamboo and tightened and tuned by wooden bridges inserted beneath the strings. The strings are plucked by the fingers as the tube is cradled in the hands and supported against the player's body. Solo, repeated melodies played on the *satong* may be three, four, or five beats in length. Some feature triplet or dotted rhythms, and the harmonic intervals frequently heard are thirds and fifths. The *satong* is usually played alone for personal entertainment, though it may also be heard in ensemble with a Jew's harp.

satong
Kajang bamboo tube zither
suling
End-blown bamboo ring-stop flute, found throughout Indonesia and Philippines

Wind Instruments

The end-blown bamboo flute, ubiquitous in Malaysian Borneo and Kalimantan, is known by many names, including *suling, seruling, kesuling, ensuling,* and *nabat.* Most local flutes have four or more equidistant holes near the distal end of the instrument, and are blown by positioning the tube vertically or somewhat obliquely to the mouth. Some *suling* are capable of playing an octave or more, and their soft melodic phrases are spun out in an improvisatory style, sometimes with little repetition, and descend the interval of a fourth or fifth at the end of each phrase. The rhythm is usually free (Figure 22.4). Flute music is sometimes heard at funerals, but is more commonly played for entertainment in intimate settings.

Mouth organs of Borneo are known by a variety of local names. The number of pipes and the size of the wind chamber vary from one region to another. Most mouth organs of Borneo consist of six to eight single-reed bamboo pipes, tied in a bundle or a raft, with the section of the pipe containing the reed secured by beeswax (or a similar material) in

Figure 22.4
Excerpt from a flute (*seruling*) melody of Borneo, in free rhythm.

a dried, hollowed gourd. The natural stem of the gourd serves as the mouthpiece, into which a player blows air, while covering the holes (at the base of the pipes) or the ends of the pipes themselves, producing specific pitches. One of the pipes always sounds as a drone. The music played on a mouth organ may serve for general entertainment, but also accompanies dance.

REFERENCES

Gorlinski, Virginia K. 1988. "Some Insights into the Art of *Sape* Playing." *Sarawak Museum Journal* 39, 60 (new series):77–104.

———. 1989. "Pangpagaq: Religious and Social Significance of a Traditional Kenyah Music-Dance Form." *Sarawak Museum Journal* 40, 61 (new series), part 3:280–301.

———. 1994. "Gongs among the Kenyah Uma' Jalan: Past and Present Position of an Instrumental Tradition." *Yearbook for Traditional Music* 26:81–99.

———. 1995. "Songs of Honor, Words of Respect: Social Contours of Kenyah Lepo' Tau Versification, Sarawak, Malaysia." Ph.D. dissertation, University of Wisconsin.

Koizumi, Fumio, ed. 1976. *Asian Musics in an Asian Perspective, Report of Asian Traditional Performing Arts.* Tokyo: Heibonsha.

Masing, James Jemut. 1981. "The Coming of the Gods: A Study of the Invocatory Chant (Timang Gawai Amat) of the Iban of the Baleh Region of Sarawak." Ph.D. dissertation, Australian National University.

Strickland, S. S. 1988. "Preliminary Notes on a Kejaman-Sekapan Oral Narrative Form." *Sarawak Museum Journal* 39, 60 (new series):67–75.

The Philippines

Corazon Canave-Dioquino, Ramón P. Santos, and José Maceda

The Lowland Christian Philippines (Corazon Conave-Dioquino)
Art Music of the Philippines in the Twentieth Century (Ramón P. Santos)
Popular Music in the Philippines (Ramón P. Santos)
Islamic Communities of the Southern Philippines (Ramón P. Santos)
Upland Peoples of the Philippines (José Maceda)

The Philippines is an archipelago of 7,100 islands, bounded in the west by the South China Sea, in the south by the Celebes Sea, in the east by the Philippine Sea (which opens into the Pacific Ocean), and in the north by the East China Sea. It consists of seventy-seven provinces grouped in fifteen regions. By religion, the population divides into three broad categories: Christians, Muslims, and followers of indigenous religions. Christians, the most numerous, are concentrated in the lowlands of Luzon and the Visayan Islands. Muslims are concentrated in Mindanao, the Sulu Islands, and southern Palawan. Followers of indigenous religions mostly inhabit upland northern Luzon, Mindanao, and Palawan.

THE LOWLAND CHRISTIAN PHILIPPINES

Pre-Christian Musical Traditions

When the Spaniards landed on Philippine soil, the indigenous Filipinos had a thriving musical culture of their own. Reports made by friars, civil servants, and travelers describe instrumental and vocal music, sometimes mentioned in passing, sometimes in detail. These reports cite various types of vocal genres, including epics relating genealogies and exploits of heroes and gods; work songs related to planting, harvesting, and fishing; ritual songs to drive away evil spirits, or to invoke blessings from good spirits; songs to celebrate festive occasions, particularly marriage, birth, victory at war, and the settling of tribal disputes; songs for mourning the dead; songs of courting; and children's game-playing songs. Musical instruments included those of bronze, wood, or bamboo—gongs, drums, flutes, zithers, lutes, clappers, and buzzers.

Traditional musics still exist among indigenous tribes scattered throughout the archipelago, but the bulk of Filipino music was changed with the influx of Western influences, particularly Spanish-European culture, prevalent from the 1500s to the 1800s. During the period of Spanish colonization, a transformation of the people's musical thinking occurred, and a hybrid form of musical expression, heavily tinged with a Hispanic taste, sprouted and took root. Hispanization was inextricably linked to religious conversion. The Spanish regime made the Filipinos construct parish churches, and missionaries taught the people to live in towns surrounding the churches. To attract the populace, the missionaries enhanced their liturgical rituals—the Mass and offices—with pomp and grandeur. Roman Catholic holy days and civil fiestas were celebrated with elaborate prayers and processions, accompanied by feasting and games.

Early Christian Influences

Friars in religious orders were directly responsible for introducing a new musical language when they taught the *indios* (a term the Spaniards used for the natives) to perform Gregorian chant (*canto llano*) and polyphony (*canto de órgano*). The dispersal of religious orders all over the islands resulted in the widespread establishment of schools, where boys were taught the liturgy and its accompanying music. The Franciscans, Jesuits, Augustinians, and others established primary schools and developed musical training among their pupils with choirs and orchestras by the seventeenth century. The impact of the friars' musical indoctrination of indigenous Filipinos was immeasurable. It gave rise to a new form of Spanish-influenced paraliturgical and secular folkloric music. It also created a new breed of Filipino musicians.

Liturgical and Paraliturgical Musical Genres

As Filipinos embraced the new religion, they grafted indigenous traditions and practices onto Roman Catholic rituals and celebrations, many of which survive. Alongside liturgical music (including the Mass, hymns, psalm verses) many extraliturgical musical genres arose, in conformity with opportunities presented in the Christian liturgical calendar. During Advent, which marks the beginning of the Christian ritual year, it became customary for carolers to roam through streets serenading households with their shepherds' songs. An elaborate outdoor drama, called *panuluyan*, occurs on Christmas Eve. Performed in the streets, this tradition reenacts Mary and Joseph's search for lodging. The Virgin and St. Joseph stop at designated houses, seeking shelter in song. The owner of the house turns them away, also in song. Eventually the holy couple end their search at the courtyard of the church, or inside the church, where a simulated stable has been erected. The pageant ends with the birth of Jesus at midnight, climaxing with the midnight mass, replete with sung alleluias and Christmas carols.

The Lenten season is the occasion for many extraliturgical ceremonies. Foremost is the *pabasa*, the intoning of a passion (*pasyon*), a versified story of Jesus' death. Sponsored as part of a vow of thanksgiving for special favors received, the *pasyon* is sung in homes, in makeshift sheds built along streets, or in barrio chapels. Its singing became nationwide during the Spanish period, but the date of its first public performance is unknown. The *pasyon* text is sung to basic or skeletal melodic formulas (*punto*), based on widely different tunes, ranging from old, traditional, chantlike melodies to those based on Westernized folk songs, operatic airs, and (more recently) popular hits.

May is the month in the Christian calendar dedicated to Mary, and the month when feasts of patron saints are celebrated. Devotion to Mary took the form of several rituals, which (though not part of official texts) are celebrated inside the church. During the whole month of May, it became customary to offer flowers to Mary every afternoon. The offering is called *flores de Mayo*. The practice is said to have started around 1865. The rosary is recited, and between the mysteries, hymns in a nineteenth-century Western idiom, known to adults and children, are sung.

Santacrusan is a widespread folkloric tradition. Processions honoring the holy cross, these are held in the town streets during May. Participants holding lighted candles sing "*Dios te salve, Maria*" ("God save you, Mary") and "*Kruz na Mahal*" ("Beloved Holy Cross"). Sometimes flowers are strewn along the way. The procession is more elaborate and is often accompanied by a band; expenses are borne by a sponsor. The procession follows black-painted children, who represent the pagans before the Spaniards' arrival. At the head of the procession are the holy cross and bearers of candles followed by a flag bearer carrying the Philippine flag and St. Macarius representing the monks. The principal personages are the Empress Helena with her escort Prince Constantine and the Queen of the Flowers.

Secular Music

Lowland rural Christian Filipinos continue to celebrate life-cycle, occupational, and social events with the making of music. The music exhibits a blend of Asian and Western styles. Life-cycle songs include lullabies, songs of love, nuptial songs, songs of death, and burial songs. Lullabies have improvised texts addressed to the child, explaining why the mother is away, exhorting him to be good, or promising a reward on waking up. The melodies have a narrow range—three neighboring notes, ornamented with turns. Comprising a large repertoire, *harana* (Spanish *jarana* "serenade") is the umbrella term for serenades. The *pananapatan* is sung beside a young woman's window. The woman usually waits until after a second song has been sung before opening the window. She then invites the serenaders into the house, and they sing a *pasasalamat* to thank her for the invitation. What ensues is an exchange of songs between the young woman and the serenaders. When the serenaders leave, they sing a *pamamaalam* (Yraola 1977).

A tradition among lowland Christian Filipinos is *pamanhikan*, asking for a prospective bride's hand. In the proposal, the suitor's representatives visit the young woman's parents, subtly expressing their purpose with sung verses. After the proposal, the suitor must render service (cutting firewood, fetching water, helping plant and harvest) to his loved one's family. The agreement takes place after weeks of service. During the last stage of the *pamanhikan*, the date and time for the wedding is set. This stage is accompanied by feasting, merrymaking, singing, and dancing.

pasyon
Versified story of Jesus' death on the cross, a "passion"
pabasa
Another term for the Passion story, or the *pasyon*
punto
Skeletal melodic formula used in singing the *pasyon*
flores de Mayo
Unofficial ritual of presenting flowers to the Virgin each day in May

The Filipinos show love and respect for the dead in different rituals. Wakes are the occasion for friends and relatives to join the grieving family in prayer. Visitors stay up all night, keeping awake by guessing riddles and playing games of pledges. They intone improvised verses, all of which the archbishop of Manila pronounced illegal and irreligious in 1741 (Castro y Amadeo 1790). Farmers in rural areas sing different types of work songs. In Batangas, the *pandanggo* is a song-dance accompanied by a guitar. Participants sing while dancing with stamping steps accentuated by clapping hands. The text of their songs may be based on passages from the Bible or a passion. Sometimes the text is based on metrical romances. When the text is on the subject of love, courtship, or marriage, it is called *pabula*. Singing may be done as in a debate between two participants, or like a narration by one singer.

As most lowland Filipinos converted to Roman Catholicism, pagan rites gave way to folkloric Christianity. Practices involving offerings of food and sacrifices to spirits became intertwined with invocations to Jesus as God, and to his mother and other saints. Among the Christian communities, the most famous epics are the Ilocano *Lam-ang* and the Bicolano *Ibalon*. In the 1800s, the popularity of these epics waned, and in their place metrical romances, introduced by Spanish colonizers, took over. These were stories of dashing knights, of princes and princesses, of biblical heroes, and of Greek and Roman gods. A favorite topic was conflicts between Christians and Muslims. Known as *awit* and *corrido*, the stories were recited on set melodic formulas. The two forms differ in poetic structure and style of rendition. The *awit* as cited in several travelogues bears different connotations. *Awit* is an umbrella term for song; however, it may refer more specifically to the intonation of metrical romances, and to melodic formulas used to improvise texts in accompaniment to dancing. In some hispanized areas, ballads about heroes or historical events, or commentaries on social and political events, are still sung.

Musical Life in the 1800s

In the mid-1800s, exposure to more forms of Western music occurred in urban areas. There was an increased interest in music other than that used in the church or to accompany daily activities. Piano lessons were given to young girls at the Beaterio de Santa Catalina (established in 1696). At the Colegio Español de Educación de Señoritas, music was part of a curriculum that included French, drawing, and sewing. In boys' schools, vocal and instrumental music was taught alongside physics, metaphysics, and philosophy. Eventually the products of such an education formed an elite group that cultivated Western arts, facilitating the further dissemination of Western concepts. The members of this educated elite, called *ilustrados*, patronized concerts and operas, or hosted informal gatherings (*tertulias*), evening entertainments that included renditions of music and poetry. Favorite compositions included light classical works, and piano transcriptions of operatic airs by Rossini and Verdi.

Dances from Mexico, Spain, and other European cities were performed at balls or soirées. Before long, foreign dances like the habanera, the tango, the fandango, the *seguidilla*, the *jota*, the *curacha*, the polka, the mazurka, the *danza*, and the rigadoon were adopted. Today, they form the bulk of popular dances of lowland Christians. The Castilian and

Andalusian fandango became the local *pandanggo*. It retained the triple time and the moderately fast tempo of its model (the waltz), but as it spread, each locality developed its own typical movements and accessories.

The *rondalla* is an ensemble consisting of plucked instruments: the *bandurria*, the *laud*, the *octavina*, the six-stringed *gitara*, and the bass guitar. The *bandurria* is a pear-shaped lute with a flat back, fourteen strings, a round hole, and a fretted neck. It serves as the melodic instrument of the ensemble. The *laud* and the *octavina* are tuned like the *bandurria*, but pitched an octave lower. They supply the inner harmonies of the ensemble, but may furnish contrapuntal elaborations to the *bandurria's* melodic lines. The *gitara* may be six-stringed or five-stringed, the former being more common. Its main function is to supply the arpeggiated or chordal underpinnings of the melody. The four-stringed bass guitar is tuned like the contrabass.

The size of a *rondalla* ensemble ranges from about eight to thirty or more instruments. The percussion group may include a bass drum, a snare drum, cymbals, a marimba, tambourines, castanets, triangles, and a tom-tom. The repertoire of these ensembles ranges from simple folk songs to arrangements of Baroque music for lute and guitar, classical overtures and operatic arias. *Rondallas* were in the early 1900s. Resurgences of *rondalla* groups occurred in the 1940s, the 1950s, and again in the 1970s. Many schools and companies have their own *rondallas*. *Sarswelas* (dramas with musical accompaniment) revolved around idealized Filipino characters and situations in a romantic love story. A prevailing theme was the Filipino family: the love of a poor boy and a rich girl, the quarrel between a jealous wife and a tired husband.

As early as 1788, Juan de la Concepción, an Augustinian friar assigned to the archbishopric of Manila, wrote in his *Historia General de las Islas Filipinos* that "the Filipinos were inclined to play instruments and performed rather well, especially the violin" (1788–92:313). In 1838, Adolfo Puya y Ruiz noted that it was rare to run across moderately educated women who did not know how to play the piano, the harp, or the guitar. In 1856, Henry T. Ellis, an English naval officer, marveled at "how quickly they (the musicians) pick up tunes by ear…. They go through most of the airs of any opera they have once heard with great taste and spirit, without being able to read a note of music" (1856:233).

From these and similar accounts, it can be gathered that in the 1800s, the homes of most wealthy families in Manila and other urban areas had a piano or a harp. Young women were taught to play these instruments, and the head of the household customarily asked his daughter to perform for visitors. The guitar, the violin, the accordion, and the flute were also favored instruments. Every town had its band or orchestra; some towns had two or more. These bands participated in civic festival celebrations. A major function was to play at religious processions in which statues of saints in elaborately decorated carriages were drawn through the major streets.

ART MUSIC OF THE PHILIPPINES IN THE TWENTIETH CENTURY

Since initial missionary contact in the 1500s and subsequent widespread Christianization, the Philippines has been profoundly influenced by composers, compositions, and trends

rondalla
Plucked stringed instrument ensemble of Philippines

imported from Europe and the Americas. These influences have occurred on two major fronts: artistic traditions of the classical, romantic, and modern eras, and popular traditions. On both fronts, the Philippines has produced composers whose creations span all the major genres of the twentieth century.

Philippine Music around 1900

By 1900, European musical traditions had already taken root in most Christianized Filipino communities. In rural areas, the proliferation of Western music and dances, like the *cachucha*, the fandango, and the *zapateado*, had reached remarkable proportions, despite the stylistic retention of pre-Christian musical traits and functions. Western instruments, like the *vihuela*, violins, guitars, flutes, and other instruments had long been assimilated or adopted in the local making of music (Blair and Robertson 1973 [1903]:45:271–278).

Musical life in urban centers and capitals, however, was dominated by a Western repertoire consisting of ecclesiastical choral music, *sarswelas* (from the Spanish *zarzuela*), operas, and performances by various orchestras, bands, and plucked string ensembles called *rondallas*. The training of Filipino natives in singing European vocal music and playing Western instruments started in convents (San Nicolás 1973 [1605]1:21:152) and military regiments as early as the 1500s (De León 1977:2213). By the twentieth century, practically every church had a Filipino maestro and a choir of trained singers. In prominent churches and cathedrals, religious orders, including Recollects (a religious order affiliated with the Augustinians), Franciscans, and Jesuits, conducted semiformal instruction in singing and playing.

Individual musicians became known countrywide for their talents, either as performers or as composers. Musical societies consisted mainly of orchestras and chamber groups, organized by prominent musicians, performing in concerts and assisting opera and *sarswela* productions. Each major city and town had at least one band, usually owned and managed by prominent musicians and their families. The bands performed in processions, parades, and concerts in connection with important feasts and holy days. Another band function was, and still is, playing for funerals and other civic gatherings.

The Anglo-American Period: Institutions and Ensembles

In the Treaty of Paris (1898), Spain ceded the Philippines to the United States. A significant change that then occurred was the establishment of a system of public education in which music was part of the curriculum. On the tertiary level, music academies and conservatories replaced centers for training young musicians, previously run by religious orders. These institutions produced professional musicians who not only were trained in performance, but also were taught theory, music history, and composition. After 1945, Filipino musicians continued to gain national and international prominence as concert artists and winners in highly prestigious competitions in Western countries. In the meantime, regular concerts were presented by various orchestral ensembles.

After more than three hundred years of Spanish rule, resistance to yet another colonial power was articulated in the works and activities of artists, political and civic leaders, and

rondalla
Ensemble of plucked, guitarlike instruments
moro-moro
Of Spanish origin, a drama with music depicting conflicts between Christians and Muslims
sarswela
Philippine form of light opera derived from the Spanish *zarzuela*

other members of the local intelligentsia. In music, a big part of the creative output of local composers consisted of patriotic hymns and marches, carryovers from the Philippine Revolution against Spain. Another musical genre used to express turn-of-the-century nationalist sentiments is the *kundiman*, a song of love in moderate 3/4 time, which evolved from pre-Christian courtship songs (*komintang*) of the Tagalog, later developed into cultivated songs (Molina 1977).

During the twentieth century, modern forms, styles, and techniques offered Filipino writers, painters, and musicians new challenges and artistic goals. Early contact with twentieth-century music worldwide was made through local musicians who trained in the West, plus foreign teachers and artists who came to settle or work in the Philippines during the American regime. Composer Nicanor Abelardo, on returning from his studies at the Chicago Musical College in the United States in 1931, was the first to break away from traditional musical idioms. His style of composing shows the influence of Viennese Expressionism, characterized by ambiguous tonalities, long drawn-out and disjunct melodic lines, multimeter, and polyrhythmic structures. His death, in 1934, delayed the spread of modernism in Philippine art music. Being a highly respected pedagogue, he could easily have influenced his peers and pupils with the new musical vocabulary.

Philippine Music during the Japanese Occupation

Musical life during the Japanese occupation (1942–1945) veered in a different direction. The Japanese imperial government implemented a nationalist program in Philippine music, basically promoting Filipino performing artists and encouraging the composition of works (mostly short hymns and marches) that extolled the virtues of the "Co-Prosperity Sphere" and "Pan-Asianism." The program also promoted the exchange of artists between Japan and the Philippines, and the learning of Japanese songs in schools.

Most of the musical products that came out of this period were propagandist. All forms of Anglo-American music, both classical and popular, were banned. Since Hollywood films were also prohibited, many movie houses were available for concerts and staged performances. Some Spanish and local *sarswelas* were revived, and short musical skits were composed by Felipe Padilla de León and aired over the radio. No major musical work written during the period may be considered significant to the development of modernism or art music in the country (Santos 1992).

The Postwar Period

In the 1950s, composers fresh from studies abroad espoused the cause of modern music. Eliseo Pájaro developed a neoclassic style based on counterpoint and fugal devices, pandiatonic harmonization, chromatic sequences of melodic fragments, and syncopation. Another neoclassicist is Lucrecia R. Kasilag, who studied theory and composition in the United States. In her involvement in the folkloric program of the Philippine Women's University as Music Director of the world-famous Bayanihan Dance Troupe, she collected and studied indigenous and other Asian instruments and music that she encountered during her travels. Her concept of East-West fusion became the underlying principle in her works, where she would combine timbres of Western and non-Western musical instruments and the scales of different musical systems.

New Music

The 1960s saw dramatic changes. With the spread of avant-gardism in the West and the discovery of new sources of musical thought through the study of non-Western musics, a new path was opened to modern music in the Philippines. As in other countries, composers in the Philippines realized that extensive exposure to non-Western musics suggested the use of alternative compositional materials and processes. A leading figure in this development, José Maceda (b. 1917–d. 2005), abandoned a notable career as a concert pianist and piano pedagogue in favor of ethnomusicology and composition. He engaged in extensive fieldwork on the musics of non-Christian communities and rural villages in Luzon and Mindanao, and in other parts of Southeast Asia. From these studies, he gained insights into the philosophies of village cultures. In addition, his familiarity with *musique concrète* while training in France provided a contemporary perspective in translating non-Western concepts of music into modern compositions.

What may be regarded as Maceda's style consists of musical and extramusical concepts, like mass structures of timbres (the sonic colors of non-Western instruments) and durations, drone and melody, slow permutation of events in time, rituals, the use of physical space, and a technology made up of human energies as opposed to machine power. Maceda's compositions in the 1960s and 1970s used exclusively native Philippine and Asian instruments, but in the 1980s, he expanded his tonal palette and included Western instruments in his scores. His later works emphasized the aesthetic parameters of non-Western musical systems in opposition to existing tonal and structural functions of the sounds of Western instruments and standard ensembles.

New awareness of the kinship and physical proximity of Filipinos to various forms of music has given rise to the recognition that native musics are an important part of the dynamics of contemporary life. Regional festivals have been either revived or enhanced, partly motivated by governmental tourism programs. In addition to newly composed works, scholars and other creative artists have collaborated to produce modern replicas—stylized or adapted versions—of native folklore, such as epics and dances. Viewed collectively, the musical development in contemporary Philippine society appears to draw resources from older traditions. While it shows various directions and aesthetic orientations, it may be perceived as representing a unique expression of a people seeking alternative musical thought and contributing toward the liberation of music from exclusively Western artistic concepts.

POPULAR MUSIC IN THE PHILIPPINES

A local concept of popular music germinated in the Philippines during the Anglo-American period, catering to a mass-based audience in the field of social entertainment. Beginning in the early decades of the twentieth century, Philippine popular music developed into a varied repertoire of folk songs in dance rhythms, songs of love, Broadway-inspired music, ballads, and rock and its offshoots—disco, jazz fusion, rap, and punk. As in other countries, popular music has thrived extensively among young people and has been widely disseminated through the electronic media of radio, cinema, and television. Live performances are presented as fund-raisers during fiestas, and attractions at political rallies and other forms of public demonstrations. In the last decades of the century, piped-in music—consisting mainly of popular tunes—came into vogue in restaurants and public conveyances.

The Era of Big Bands

Before World War II, various genres of popular music were played in dance halls and vaudeville shows. A potpourri of numbers in these shows included slapstick comedy, skits, tap dancing, song medleys, and *kundiman*. The dance halls, however, featured orchestras and bands that played foxtrot, swing, Charleston, tango, and waltz. American jazz and popular music for dancing were banned during the Japanese occupation, but the postwar period saw a resurgence of popular music. In addition to the previous repertoire of dances originating in the United States, new styles of dancing were introduced, mostly of Latin American origin: *samba, rumba, guaracha, mambo,* and *appalachicola* (a variant of the *mambo,* first popular in the 1950s).

The Era of Rock and Roll

In the 1960s, rock and roll made a strong impact on Filipino musicians and the local mass media. The electrifying performances of its exponents, especially Bill Haley, Elvis Presley, Chubby Checker, and Little Richard reached and captivated Filipino audiences via jukebox, radio, cinema, and records. The Filipino popular-music community absorbed the new currents, and responded by finding local counterparts of American musical idols. To discover the best imitators of the American originals, radio and television sponsored amateur contests for singers.

Despite the widespread appetite for foreign songs and the idolization of foreign artists, original compositions were being written and performed by singers who chose to develop their own styles. In the early 1970s, songs of love in the vernacular began to capture the local market, drawing influences from the *kundiman* and Broadway songs. Movie-music composers had tremendous success, which in turn encouraged a younger generation of composers to contribute to the proliferation of modern songs of love. In the meantime, styles popularized by the Rolling Stones, Led Zeppelin, and the Jefferson Airplane inspired the music of the Juan de la Cruz Band, which in response created "Balong Malalim" ("Deep Well"), "Project," and "Laki Sa Layaw" ("Spoiled Brat"). Other popular rock performers of the period include the Maria Cafra Band, Sampaguita, and Frictions, which entertained the growing local discothèque clientele.

In the 1980s, the Filipinization of popular music gained further headway with the emergence of the Manila sound, which was characterized by schmaltzy lyrics and the use of a form of urban jargon called Taglish, a contraction of Tagalog and English. Manila-sound songs easily spread among young audiences, mostly composed of students from exclusive sectarian schools.

Balladic Styles of Popular Music

The music of Bob Dylan, Joan Baez, and Peter, Paul, and Mary made a strong impact on Filipino folk balladeers, whose poetry covered a broad range of contemporary issues—the tyranny of the Marcos government, corruption, American economic imperialism, gender issues, environmental pollution, and the emulation of Filipino values and patriotism. On the lighter side, Yoyoy Villame, a former driver of a jeepney, caters to a more plebeian audience with his witty narratives. His subjects include folksy interpretations of such historical events as the Spanish discovery of the Philippines and commentaries about everyday experiences such as traffic congestion. He sings his poetry to medleys of preexisting tunes, some of which include nursery songs.

The folk-ballad style was furthered by such late-1980s groups as Asin ("Salt"), Edru Abraham's Kontra-Gapi (a contraction of Kontamporaryong Gamelang Pilipino) ("Contemporary Filipino Gamelan"), and Bagong Lumad ("New Tradition"), led by Joey Ayala. These groups included in their ensembles traditional ethnic instruments such as the Jew's harp (*kubing*), bossed gongs laid in a row (*kulintang*), tube stampers (*tongatong*), deep-rimmed bossed gong (*agung*), and two-stringed lute (*faglong*).

Contemporary Filipino Popular Music

The adoption of the latest trends in the world of American pop remains a strong component in the local youth culture. Rap artists who have created Filipino lyrics have also covered a gamut of topics from positive Filipino values and a sense of patriotism to sex and highly mundane subjects. Pop in the Philippines has branched out into several directions from its initial function as music for dancing and entertainment. It now appears in a variety of forms that represent the multifaceted and complex needs of a highly acculturated society. In spite of the sustained influence of a global pop-music industry, Filipino songwriters have sought to use the medium to express contemporary views and sentiments regarding their own life as a people with a unique history and culture. At the same time, performers have begun to develop styles and mediums with elements related to native Filipino musics.

Contemporary Filipino pop music has developed along two main lines—one in which show bands play covers of international (but especially British and American) hits in bars and hotel lounges, and a thriving do-it-yourself scene in which underground bands take an active role in composing, arranging, and recording their own music. The show bands, at least partly an outgrowth of the vestiges of colonialism, cater to upper middle-class Filipinos, tourists, and American military personnel. In style, instrumentation (singer plus rhythm section) and audience, show bands have not changed since the 1960s; their repertoire relies heavily on standard lounge hits—songs by Barry Manilow, Neil Diamond, and other late-twentieth-century crooners.

The strongest new growth in Filipino popular music has been in the alternative-music scene. The typical band's setup may include a singer, drummer, guitarist, bassist, keyboardist, and any other instruments deemed necessary to the style, or any other instruments that the members happen to play. The alternative-music scene in the Philippines encompasses a variety of styles (some of them blended), including grunge, heavy metal, reggae, ska, folk, and punk, in addition to more standard styles of rock and pop. No matter what the style, however, these bands perform in small clubs for dedicated audiences and are generally not financed by big business; nor do they have the luxury of extended contracts with a hotel or nightclub.

Most of the significant alternative bands tend to model their style after one or more famous foreign bands, but original compositions are the norm. In addition, the vocalists may sing in either English or Filipino. The possibility for one of these alternative bands to produce a hit is fairly limited, because the major record labels do not financially support alternative music as much as they support the kind of mainstream pop that will establish a steady income. The styles of grunge, reggae, ska, and punk have each spawned Filipino practitioners since the mid-1990s. Many of the most important hits from these bands are sung in Filipino, though English is also used. As each new wave of musical influence reached the Philippines in the twentieth century, certain styles and bands caught on with the public. However, a foreign band's popularity does not guarantee the creation of an indigenous response. In addition, any local response may not occur for years, sometimes decades. The rich array of Filipino and foreign popular musics, and the varied settings in which they may occur, have contributed to the availability of virtually any type of popular music that an eager listener desires.

ISLAMIC COMMUNITIES OF THE SOUTHERN PHILIPPINES

Musical practices of the Islamic communities in the southern Philippine islands of Mindanao and the Sulu Archipelago reflect separate pre-Islamic cultural traditions. Histories of relations, contacts, and alliances with peoples outside these communities contributed to the distinctiveness of their characters—the Tausug with peoples from North Borneo and the Samal with communities from Johore. The Maguindanao had a lesser degree of contact with neighboring peoples, and the Maranao were long isolated from the outside world (Cadar 1975), but both eventually became recipients of foreign cultural influences during centuries of dynamic commercial activity.

The Islamic community in the Philippines consists of five major ethnolinguistic groups: the Maguindanao of Cotabato; the Maranao of Lanao and Cotabato; the Samal and Jama Mapun of the Sulu Islands of Sibutu and Cagayan de Sulu; the Tausug of the Sulu islands of Jolo, Siasi, and Tawi Tawi; and the Yakan of Basilan and Zamboanga, on the westernmost tip of Mindanao.

Animistic beliefs and forms of worship pervaded the cultural practices of the early Filipinos before the first traces of contact with other religious civilizations (at the start of the first millennium). Though pre-Islamic faiths drew some influences from Hinduism, they remained essentially characterized by the worship of local divinities and spirits of dead ancestors—worship that called for the services of mediums and shamans. Even today, ritual practices have survived. From the 800s to the 1400s, trade flourished in the region, bringing into close contact peoples from the Middle East, China, the Malay Peninsula, the Philippines, Borneo, the Indonesian Archipelago, and as far south as New Guinea. Participating for centuries in commercial activities, the Philippines not only acquired artifacts but also absorbed cultural influences from overseas.

Islam came to the southern Philippines at different stages. Its presence is attributed to the activities of Muslim traders and Sufi missionaries, and the arrival of Muslim political figures (Abubakar 1983). Its initial presence resulted from international trade controlled by Arabs and other Muslims from West Asia. Many Muslim traders, settling in Borneo and the Sulu Islands, married into the local populations, which consisted of sultanates and extended families. In the 1300s, Islam was formally introduced with the arrival of holy men whose principal mission was to attend to the spiritual needs of the Muslim residents.

In the eastern and northern portions of Mindanao, the proliferation of Muslim traders and teachers eased the founding of Islamic political institutions by Muhamad Kabungsuan, a highly influential Arab-Malay. Marital alliances between foreign Muslims and local converts resulted in the Islamic ancestries of Maguindanao, Buayan, and Butig, and the principle of politics by marriage later spread among the Maranao. In 1521, with the coming of the Spanish, the Philippines became the final frontier of the missionary odyssey of Islam in Southeast Asia. The imposition of Christianity checked the growth of Islam, and through a series of armed conquests and eventual conversions, diminished its influence. However, the Filipino Muslims in Mindanao, who successfully resisted the Spanish conquest of the islands, preserved both a common religious heritage and their ethnic independence.

It is within a larger historic and cultural perspective that the artistic traditions of the Islamic communities can be perceived: the culture combines indigenous practices related to animist worship, a semicourt tradition (emanating from cultural contacts with other Southeast Asian peoples and civilizations), traditional arts from older Islamic countries, Islamic forms of worship, and views on the social distinction between religious and secular forms of art. Through different levels of adaptation and accommodation, most pre-Islamic practices have become cultural icons of the Filipino Muslim communities.

Diversity in Islamic Musical Traditions

The distinctiveness of the cultures that make up the larger Islamic society in Mindanao and Sulu precludes the possibility of viewing their musical practices as belonging to one single tradition. Similarities do exist in the musical inventories, as in some vocal styles within the larger society, but theoretical concepts, functions, aesthetics, and repertoires differ from culture to culture, and even from village to village belonging to one language group.

The musical practices of these societies reflect the fusion of disparate traditional traits. Despite the prominence of Islamic institutional precepts in popular social life, local religious interpretations have allowed pre-Islamic artistic practices to flourish. Ancient rites and beliefs have remained principal sources of communication with a metaphysical world. Instead of setting canonic restrictions on artistic expression, the forms of art of these Is-

Figure 23.1
Horizontal bossed gongs. The wooden frame is 160 centimeters long; the gongs are 18–22 centimeters wide. Courtesy University of the Philippines Archive.

lamic cultures have enhanced the stylistic breadth of existing repertoires, especially vocal ones. This kind of artistic freedom may reflect each local society's sense of independence from any one dominant political or religious ideology.

Instrumental Music

The bossed-gong cultures with horizontal gongs laid in a row (Figure 23.1) are the most visible and familiar symbols of the musical traditions of Filipinos in western Mindanao and the Sulu Archipelago. They are related to other bossed gongs in Southeast Asia—Borneo, Indonesia, Thailand, and some village peoples in the Guangxi, Hubei, and Yunnan provinces of southern China. The principal instrument, called *kulintang* by the Maguindanao and Maranao, is a set of graduated gongs laid in a row in a wooden frame. The set usually consists of seven to eight gongs, with as many as eleven or thirteen in some groups or as few as five. Each of the following groups—the Maguindanao and Maranao of western Mindanao, and the Tausug, the Yakan, and the Sama-Bajao of the Sulu Archipelago—uses some form of bossed-gong ensemble; a discussion of other instruments follows.

The Maguindanao

Maguindanao Province is dominated by the Mindanao River, which runs about 300 kilometers before it spills into Illana Bay. The river's floodplain is responsible for the fertility of the soil. The river serves as an important link among people in the province, and through ease of transport and communication has contributed to a relative consistency in musical ensembles and genres. Most of the Maguindanao people are farmers of rice, and rice is one of the primary exports of the province. Among the Maguindanao of Datu Piang of the upper Mindanao River, the *kulintang* is the primary musical instrument. Other gong instruments of this group include one, two, or three vertically suspended gongs: the *agung* (a large, deep-rimmed gong, with a higher boss), two pairs of *gandingan* (gongs with narrower rim and lower boss), and one *babandil* (smaller than an *agung*, with a narrower, turned-in rim and a low boss). The ensemble is complemented by a drum called *dabakan*.

agung
Suspended bossed gong of Sumatra and the Philippines
dabakan
Goblet-shaped drum of Philippines

Kulintang tones are not tuned to a fixed temperament. Researchers have observed a loose sequential pattern of large and small intervals in extant eight-gong sets, but the arrangements of the tones vary from one set to another. In the construction of *kulintang* gongs, the lowest and the highest are the first to be cast. The tones of the other gongs are then adjusted to each other in relation to the two extremes (Maceda 1963).

The *kulintang* is important social property. Being closely identified with individual families, the instruments of the ensemble are highly valued, priceless heirlooms that can command a high price as dowries. The ownership of these instruments indicates high social status and cultivated taste (Butocan 1987). One primary function of *kulintang* music

Figure 23.2
Aga Mayo-Butocan, professor of Maguindanao music in the College of Music, University of the Philippines, plays a *kulintang*. Visible in the background are one *babandil*, four *gandingan*, and parts of two *agung*. Photo by Ramón P. Santos.

palabunibunyan
Maguindanao traditional ensemble

is to entertain guests at public occasions, including weddings, baptisms, and other formal rites, providing a unique medium of interaction within the community. This interaction may be in the form of a competition, in which players pit their musical and creative skills against each other, or in a dialogue between individual men and women, which could later develop into courtship.

The Maguindanao *palabunibunyan* consists of five performers playing an eight-gong *kulintang*, two *agung*, two pairs of *gandingan*, a *babandil,* and a goblet-shaped drum (*dabakan*). The *kulintang* is played with two mallets of light wood (*basal*) (Figure 23.2).

The two *agung* facing each other, are played with one rubber-padded mallet. Some playing techniques that produce different tones and durations include muffling the boss with the left hand and alternately striking the boss with the padded end of the mallet, followed by striking the surface with the unpadded part. The two pairs of *gandingan* are played by one musician using two padded mallets, with each hand striking two gongs that face each other. The older *gandingan* are larger in size, with a longer resonance (ringing for a longer period of time). The smaller *gandingan,* about 40 centimeters in diameter produce higher tones. The *babandil* is usually struck on the rim with a pair of thin bamboo sticks, producing bright, metallic sounds.

The instruments have different roles in the musical fabric. The *kulintang* serves as a melodic instrument, determining the shape of each piece. The *agung* provides a rhythmic line, while the *gandingan,* with their overlapping sonorities, create a continuum of sound. The *dabakan* maintains the rhythmic motion, while the *babandil* serves as a principal ostinato instrument. In most cases, the *babandil* introduces each piece by playing the appropriate rhythmic mode, followed by the *dabakan*. The function of the *babandil* as an ostinato instrument may be taken by a separate musician on the *pamantikan* (the highest gong of the *kulintang*). The transcription in Figure 23.3 illustrates the arrangement of a typical piece.

Though *kulintang* music is usually regarded as a secular social activity, it has been integrated into religion-sanctioned activities such as weddings and baptisms. In the curing rite called *kapagipat* and its variants, the *tagunggo* rhythm is played to accompany the dance of exorcism by a medium in the patient's house. The *tagunggo* is played by the *kulintang* ensemble to accompany the *sagayan,* a dance of communication with the world of spirits. The dancer-medium is often garbed as a warrior, armed with a *kris* and a shield.

Most of the instruments of the *palabunibunyan* are played singly for various social and religious functions. Young men can play the *gandingan* to communicate their love to young women. Because the four distinct tones of the *gandingan* duplicate different tones in the Maguindanao language, basic phrases can be communicated to people listening for

Figure 23.3
Excerpt from a Maguindanao *kulintang* performance. Transcription by Aga Mayo Butocan and Ramón P Santos.

them. The *agung,* traditionally considered a male instrument, is played to call people to assemble or mark important hours of the day during Ramadan (particularly prior to the beginning and end of fasting), or to announce the death of a parent. The sound of the *agung,* when properly transmitted, is considered to possess supernatural powers. The large drum called *dabu-dabu* is sounded each Friday to mark noontime prayers (Butocan 1987).

Figure 23.4
Four Maguindanao *kulintang* rhythmic modes as played on the goblet-shaped drum (*dabakan*). Transcription by Aga Mayo Butocan.

In a work on the Maguindanao *kulintang* tradition in Datu Piang, José Maceda wrote that the repertoire is based on three rhythmic modes, usually played as a suite of pieces: *duyug, sinulug,* and *tidtu.* A fourth mode, *tagunggo,* is usually reserved for rituals and ceremonies. According to Butocan (1987), the modes relate to different shades of moods and emotions, such as strong feelings, anger, sentimentality, and excitement (Figure 23.4). A series of pieces based on the modes and their variations could be grouped as a suite and played as an extended descriptive composition related to a common theme. The individual pieces in the Simuay *kulintang* repertoire usually consist of five sectional types: an introduction, repeated sections, an ascending transition, a descending transition, and a conclusion. The repeated sections can be extended in length at the player's pleasure.

The Maranao

Most Maranao people live in the province of Lanao del Sur, an area dominated by Lake Lanao, partly bordered by mountains. Like the Maguindanao, the Maranao grow rice as a primary crop. One of the most conservative of the Filipino Muslim groups, the Maranao tend to isolate themselves from outside cultural and political influences. As with the Mindanao River, Lake Lanao's presence in the Maranao heartland has led to greater musical consistency than if the population had been widely dispersed.

Another major bossed-gong tradition exists among the Maranao. The Maranao *kulintang* ensemble consists of an eight-piece *kulintang,* a *dubakan,* a *bubundir,* and two deep-rimmed gongs, played separately by two musicians. Maranao *kulintang* music has been described as a medium for expressing Maranao traditional culture and etiquette, and as a form of communication, especially among the players. Musicians' formal and artistic conduct during a performance is particularly emphasized, including the manner of approaching and moving away from the instruments, and the appropriate position for handling and playing each instrument. Other ceremonial activities, such as short vocal exhortations, could occur before the actual making of music begins. Seniority and deference to the more seasoned masters are also observed whenever many performers are present on a given occasion. The playing of the *kulintang* usually occurs in private homes or ancestral houses (Cadar 1975).

The two principal instruments of the Maranao *kulintangan* are the *kulintang* (usually played by a young woman) and the *dubakan* (traditionally reserved for men). Their musical renditions are likened to a dialogue, sometimes developing into courtship, moderated by the *bubundir* (Cadar 1975). As the *kulintang* sets the musical idea and elaborates on it, the *dubakan* responds according to the musical nuances and permutations, in the manner of a poetic interlocution between a young man and a woman. The two *agung* lend their support to this interaction, with one providing the basic pulse and the other providing elaboration.

Each *kulintang* piece is made up of melodic segments or phrases consisting of eight strokes, called *tukimug*—a term directly related to poetry, song, or proverb (Cadar 1980). Each *tukimug may* be repeated, varied, or extended by one or two more segments. Among the collection of the Maranao *kulintang* repertoire are signature pieces, which usually provide the high point in important public performances. They are highly regarded, not only for their structural complexity and demands on the artist's skills, but also for the depth of their emotional and intellectual content. Some of the instruments can also be played singly. The *agung* is usually sounded to announce the enthronement or crowning of a sultan, or to formally greet distinguished guests in a social gathering. A patriarchal leader can summon his subjects by having the summons sounded on the *agung,* the same instrument that plays the *kabalok* to announce the death of a member of a family.

The Sulu Archipelago

The Sulu Archipelago encompasses at least nine hundred islands (including the large islands of Basilan, Jolo, and Tawi-Tawi) in two provinces: Sulu in the northeast, and Tawi-Tawi in the southwest, close to Borneo. Because of its proximity to northeastern Borneo, the Sulu Archipelago is included in the continuum of horizontal gong-chime music cultures extending from Borneo through Mindanao. *Kulintang* and instruments resembling *kulintang* are used by the Tausug, the Yakan, and the Sama-Bajao.

The *kulintangan* ensemble of the Tausug of Jolo includes a *kulintangan* consisting of eight or eleven gongs laid in a row, and a pair of hanging gongs called *duwahan.* This pair of gongs consists of a medium-sized, deep-rimmed gong; and a large, narrow-rimmed gong that people in Jolo believe was brought by Chinese traders at the turn of the 1300s. In addition to the *kulintangan* and *duwahan,* the basic rhythmic structure is articulated on a large, deep-rimmed gong called *tunggalan* or *aalakan,* and a pair of two-headed drums, the *gandang.* A sixth musician plays the rhythmic ostinato *tung-tung* on *tutuntungan,* one of the upper gongs of the *kulintang. Kulintangan* music is usually heard during weddings and other social functions and serves for general entertainment.

Quite related to the *kulintang* music of the Tausug is the repertoire of the *tagunggu* ensemble of the Yakan of the island of Basilan. The two Yakan types of composition, usually played one after the other, are the preparation (*te-ed*) and the composition proper (*kuriri*), which has a faster tempo. Each composition may be extended indefinitely. The music is highly improvised, revolving around the *lebad,* a musical unit that represents a shade of emotion or extramusical idea. Each piece contains various *lebad,* which the player of the *kwintangan* expands by repetition, juxtaposition, and permutation. A musician's artistic skill is measured by the number of *lebad* he or she can recreate in a performance, and on the manner of putting them together in logical sequence. The basic Yakan scale consists of five tones, roughly corresponding to the intervallic sequence of C–E–G–A–C.

duwahan
Tausug and Sama pair of hanging gongs
tunggalan
Tausug large *agung*

Figure 23.5
The Yakan *kwintang,*
a five-gong melody
instrument. Photo by
Ranón P. Santos.

A principal instrument of the *tagunggu* ensemble is the horizontal five-gong *kwintang* (Figure 23.5). Other instruments are a cracked bamboo tube (*gandang*) and a set of three hanging *agung*. Optional instruments include a five-key xylophone (*gabbang*) and percussion beams (*kwintangan kayu*). A separate player plays a rhythmic ostinato on the highest gong of the *kwintangan*. The number of players varies, because the *agung* may be performed by one, two, or three musicians. The three *agung* may be played independently of the *kwintangan* and the *gandang* (Nicolas 1977).

An even closer association between *kulintang* music and dance is practiced by the Sama, also known as the Bajao, whose main source of livelihood and existence is the seas around the Sulu Archipelago. The orchestra (*pangongka'an*) of the Sama from Sitangkai has a *kulintangan* of seven to nine gongs, played by two performers. The *kulintangan* melodies consist of three to eight tones, normally played by the right hand. The left hand sounds the lower gongs at a slower rhythm. The second *kulintang* musician plays an ostinato pattern on one of the highest gongs. The rest of the ensemble includes the *tamuk*, a large hanging gong played by one musician; the *bua*, a narrow-rimmed gong; and the *pulakan*, a smaller *agung*. The drum (*tambul*) is a long bronze cylinder with a goatskin head.

The entire ensemble is closely associated with dance, and performances occur on special occasions, including circumcision, marriage, and dances of possession. The metaphysical aspect of the musical performance is part of its total effect, since it is believed that the spirits and the powers of dead ancestors reside in the instruments, whose sounds channel communications between the world of spirits and the human community. In the gong music of the Sama, distinctions of gender in instrumental assignment are more strictly observed than in other areas. Women play the *kulintangan*, and men play the hanging gongs. The drum may be handled by either men or women.

Other Instruments

Aside from the bossed-gong traditions, Islamic communities in Mindanao and Sulu have a wide collection of other instruments, ranging from bamboo and wooden idiophones to a variety of strings and winds. Among the Maguindanao of Dinaig, Maguindanao Province, a wooden version of the *kulintang* is made of hardwood slats cut in graduated sizes, each slat tuned by the removal of a sliced curve in its middle. Because the tones on the instrument sound for only a short period of time, the instrument is suited to pieces in the modern or fast style of playing. The modern music of the *agung* is also played on two to four pieces of small bamboo half tubes of varying sizes, called *tamlang agung*. These instruments are usually played for entertainment, especially on occasions that call for the competitive exhibition of musical skills by youths.

The *gabbang*, a bamboo xylophone, is common among several groups, especially in the

Sulu communities. This instrument consists of blades graduated by size and resting on a trapezoidal wooden resonator with cloth padding between the blades and the sides of the box (Figure 23.6). The number of blades varies. It also has the variable function of either solo or accompanying instrument.

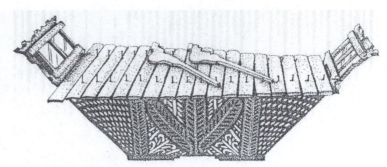

Figure 23.6
The *gabbang*, a bamboo xylophone, with its mallets shown resting on the keys. The longest slat is 50 centimeters long; the shortest, 31 centimeters. Courtesy University of the Philippines Archives.

The agricultural seasons call for several important instruments. The percussion beam set (*luntang*) of the Maguindanao comprises five to eight logs, sharpened on one end and suspended horizontally, one below the other, from a tree or outside a house. One musician plays on the sharpened portion while another beats a rhythmic ostinato on the middle part of one log (Figure 23.7). Farmers play *luntang* to keep birds out of the fields, or simply to while away the time. At the start of the Islamic fasting month of Ramadan, the *luntang* is also sounded to wake up the community so that people can eat their meals before the fast begins (Maceda 1963).

The Maranao scraper (*garakot*) is another instrument used to drive away unwanted scavengers of the field—birds, rats, and insects. Sometimes, however, young men play it to attract the attention of passing women, or to show off their musical skills in friendly competitions. The scraper is a hard-dried bamboo tube, closed on both ends by the nodes. One portion of the body is etched with notches, and a slit hole runs from one end to the other. The scraper is usually tucked on both ends between the performer's legs (Figure 23.8). The left-hand stick plays a steady rhythm on the chipped surface of the tube, while the right-hand stick taps different parts of the body, producing a variety not only of rhythmic patterns, but also of attacks and timbres.

Also popular are two flutes: the ring flute (Maguindanao and Yakan *suling*, Maranao *insi*, Sama *pulao*) and the lip-valley flute (Maguindanao *palendag*). The former, similar to the Javanese *suling*, is identified by a ring made of a rattan strip that is wrapped around the hole for the mouth. The lip-valley flute has an open mouthpiece cut in a curve, supporting the player's lower lip.

The Jew's harp (Maguindanao and Maranao *kubing*, Yakan *kulaing*) is also widespread, not only in the Islamic communities, but also in highland cultures, and even in some rural Christian communities in Luzon and Visayas. Differences in it among the various language communities may lie in make and design (from the simplest to the most elaborately carved, sometimes with tassels) and in their repertoires. A favorite instrument of courtship and recreational

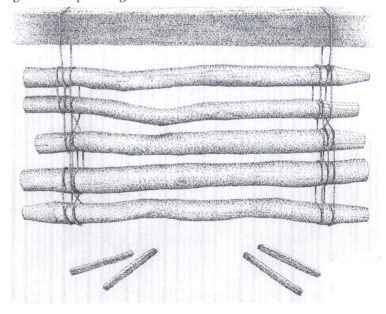

Figure 23.7
A Maguindanao *luntang*, show with sticks. Each log is about 140 centimeters long. Courtesy University of the Philippines Archives.

Figure 23.8
A Maranao musician plays a bamboo scraper (*garakot*). Photo courtesy NAMCYA Foundation.

repartee, the Jew's harp simulates the sounds of speech, including prosody. A nonspeaker of the local language has difficulty understanding renditions in that language, but can appreciate the sounds from a purely aural point of view. Moreover, in courtship, the phrases are based on metaphorical language and local poetic expressions. Because of its portability, almost every young Yakan has a *kulaing* tucked in his headband everywhere he goes (Nicolas 1977).

Another instrument for intimate and familiar listening is the lute, a two-stringed solo instrument, whose body is shaped like a boat with a long neck and an intricately curved pegboard. The thin wire strings, tuned a perfect fourth apart, are plucked with a rattan plectrum. The lute (Maguindanao *kutyapi* or *kutyapiq*, Maranao *kotyapi*) is usually played in a sitting position. A solo instrument, it never accompanies the voice. In the Mindanao lute, the twelve movable pyramid-shaped frets made of beeswax may be arranged according to two pentatonic modes. The repertoire may be classified by these modes. Among the Maranao, the *kotyapi*, besides being a solo instrument, can also be part of a serenade ensemble. The pieces either express abstract feelings and ideas, or derive from existing songs and ballads (Otto 1985). The Tausug *biola* is believed to have been adapted from the Western family of bowed stringed instruments by way of the Portuguese influence in Indonesia. The *biola* can be played as a solo instrument, or used to accompany the voice and the *gabbang*.

Vocal Music

Vocal musical expression in the Islamic communities in Mindanao and Sulu covers a broad spectrum of forms—ancient epics and religious songs, ceremonial exhortations, entertainment ballads, songs of love, lullabies, and songs for various occasions. Stylistic differences exist in rendering these forms, most often indicative of influence from other cultures, like the florid style of singing in West Asia. The vocal styles may well be represented in varying degrees by the two styles of singing among the Tausug from Luuk: *tayil* style, slow, religion-oriented, metrically free, melismatic, with high tessitura and optional accompaniment; and *paggabbang* style, suited to secular songs, in fast tempo, metered, syllabic, and with medium tessitura and instrumental accompaniment.

Locally the most prestigious form of vocal expression is reading the Qur'ān. Qur'ān-reading competitions are held annually to select the Philippine representative to the international meet, held in different Islamic countries. Filipino readers have won major prizes in the International Qur'ān Reading Contest.

Religious songs are closely related to Qur'ānic recitation. They can be heard during the Friday noon service, before and after Ramadan during Maulud, and in commemorating the anniversaries of deaths. The Friday noon service is one of the prayers observed on specific hours of the day, from morning until midnight. It opens with a responsorial invocation sung on melismatic melodies by the imam and the deacon.

Aside from religious musical forms, epics and classical narrative forms have remained an important cultural facet of the vocal repertoires, not only among the Islamic communities, but in almost all major language groups in the Philippines. In most cases, the epics serve as a repository of oral history containing not only the lives and legendary deeds of hero-ancestors, but also genealogies, stories of the origin of the world, and the people's relationship to the major deities, and in the case of the Islamic people, to the Prophet Muhammad. Though some groups might have a collection of epics, one or two of these tales can be considered the primary literary symbols of each group's cultural heritage.

Epics are known only to a select few who have either undergone a semiformal process of learning or have been informally trained by an elderly sage. The epic poems of the Sama and Yakan are recited only by mediums and other important persons who have the authority to conduct rituals. Among the Sama, the singing of an epic story is performed in private, sometimes only by the narrator, or in the company of chosen apprentice. The recitation is usually staged to coincide with a full moon, and the narrator intones the verses while lying on his back (Maceda and Martenot 1976). The singing of the epic, which normally lasts for several nights, serves as the main highlight of an important public gathering (Nicolas 1977).

Short narrative songs are also performed during important gatherings. Tausug traditional ballads are a strong component of contemporary oral literature: they chronicle recent events, ranging from the historic burning of a town in Jolo to humorous accidents in the life of an ordinary person. Singers are often hired to entertain guests, and each narration can run from ten minutes to several hours. The singing is usually accompanied by a *gabbang* or a *biola* (Kiefer 1970).

Expressions of love among the Maguindanao are in either of two styles of song: the *sindil*, replete with vocal devices and requiring subtle changes in vocal timbres, and the *bayok* (also the general term for song), more syllabic, with a limited vocal range and a quality free of special vocal techniques. The former is more difficult to execute, and only a few can master its technique. The *bayok* is used in sung debates; despite the simplicity of its musical elements, it can effectively convey the metaphorical and figurative language of the poetry (Maceda 1963).

In some communities, occupational songs comprise an important segment of local literature. Among the Sama, whose existence is closely associated with marine life, various strophic songs are sung on fishing expeditions. The texts of these songs are usually improvised, alluding to the kinds of fish the mariners intend to catch, and to the manner of catching them. The texts are sung on preexisting musical patterns, representing a vocal range of about an octave.

Highly emotional and personalized vocal exhortations can be heard in connection with the death of a loved one. The Tausug *hadis* tradition has a strong religious orientation in that *hadis* songs (accompanied by the *biola*) usually cover sacred topics, and are sung in a melismatic style. The texts usually express general thoughts on life and death, and memories that the dead person has bequeathed to the community. Before the day of burial, the Qur'ān is recited by a group of young women for seven days in the house of the deceased. The Sama perform a lamentation to relieve the emotional and psychological stress brought about by a death. The song, which consists of somewhat wailed descending vocal phrases, provides a channel for expressing good memories and reproaches the deceased for having abandoned the living.

UPLAND PEOPLES OF THE PHILIPPINES

The languages of the Philippines and the aborigines of Taiwan form the northern group of Austronesian languages of insular Southeast Asia. Philippine languages may be divided into three geographical areas: north, middle, and south (McFarland 1983). Together, they number some 65 million speakers. Musically, what remains of aboriginal traditions is confined to peoples in Northern Luzon, Mindanao, the Sulu archipelago, Palawan, and Mindoro. Accordingly, this article is divided into two segments: the North (covering the traditions of the Cordillera) and the South (dealing mostly with the musics of non-Muslim peoples of Mindanao, Sulu, Palawan, and Mindoro). Filipinos living on Luzon and the Visayan islands created a new music based on Western idioms but with a genuine Philippine character; in the process, however, it lost most of its Asian identity.

The aborigines of the Philippines are a small Negrito group, living in small communities in parts of Luzon, with some in the South. Their language, culture, and music retain some aboriginal qualities, but are much influenced by their Southeast Asian-type neighbors. There are two plants, bamboo and rice, which have a direct relationship with both lowland and upland Philippine music. Bamboo is important not only for shelter, food, weapons, traps, and receptacles, but also for musical instruments: flutes, buzzers, clappers, scrapers, reeds, lutes, zithers, Jew's harps, and slit drums. Though root crops are a staple of mountain peoples, rice has the greatest cultural and ritual value, and is the focus of agricultural feasts, held during planting and especially after the harvest.

The North

The Cordillera of Northern Luzon is home to more than one million people speaking related languages. Each group of languages, with distinct geographical boundaries, has its own political and social structures, divisions of land, agricultural rites, feasts, and music. A wet-rice system of agriculture prevails. The mountainsides are leveled off to form parcels of land or terraces to hold the water necessary for growing rice. They are constructed in many-shaped tiers, one higher than another, along gorges sometimes 600 meters deep. The terraces cover a wide area, creating spectacular panoramic views.

Flat gongs, the principal musical instruments in the Cordillera, are played especially in rice-harvesting ceremonies, weddings, and pacts of peace. The playing of gongs is also associated with headhunting, as indicated by the boasting songs, punctuated with screams and shouts, describing headhunting raids, which heroes declaimed in formal ceremonies after a gong performance. Using percussion sticks to play music similar to the gong music honoring a beheaded person's body, and playing gongs to welcome warriors returning from a raid, are other indications that headhunting had religious significance apart from the mere act of war (Nicolas 1987).

The Bontok of Sadanga, Mountain Province

Among the Bontok, several stages in the cultivation of rice involve rituals: preparation of the field, care of seedlings, planting, weeding, and harvesting. A simple but common ritual is abstinence from work, lasting a few days. Its occurrence is loudly proclaimed in the central part of the village by an elderly ritualist, early in the morning; prayers and the sacrifice of a chicken follow. During the evenings, especially during this abstinence from work, boys court girls in their sleeping quarters. This time is an occasion to play the nose flute (*kalaleng*), whose descending pentatonic melodies sound pleasing in the silence of the night, almost as inaudible as the Jew's harp (*awedeng*) that some boys play instead. The girls sing responsorial songs or choral songs in which they prod the boys, hiding in the darkness, to identify themselves.

Unlike women's sleeping quarters, the men's dwelling is a center for recreation and a formal site for meetings to discuss local issues and wedding plans, or to settle disputes. In preparation for the harvest, elderly members of a men's dwelling may decide to hold a feast, at which choral songs and long solo songs are sung, and flat gongs (*gangsa*) are brought out of their hiding places, each contributing to at least one complete ensemble of six gongs, for rarely does one family have all six (Yraola 1977).

Among the Bontok, nuptial rituals are the most elaborate occasions for feasting and making music. The Bontok have two styles of performance on gongs, *falliwes* and *takik*. In *falliwes*, two groups of players among the six musicians play with soft wooden sticks, hitting the face or outer surface of the gongs in alternating beats. Only men, principally belonging to the same men's dwelling, play these gongs (Figure 23.9). They dance around in circles and spirals, vigorously swaying their hips and stepping high. The gongs are suspended from a wooden handle held waist-high by the left hand, but during the dancing,

Figure 23.9
With sticks, the Bontok of Sadanga, Luzon, play flat gongs (*gangsa*) as they move in circular formations. Photo by José Maceda, 1970s.

the men may lower them near the ground, and in crouching positions, hit them softly. Then, suddenly springing upright, they may hold the gongs head-high and hit them loudly, creating brilliantly exuberant rings, enjoyed by the audience. During the dancing, women gradually join in, making a group of their own, eventually encircling the men, ending the dance.

In the city of Bontok, *takik* is played and danced by one or two men, or a girl and a boy, in freer, faster rhythms and movements than those of *falliwes*. The dancers move independently of each other, quickly changing postures, turning in pirouettes as they hit the gong up in the air, first on one side, and then on the other. One dancer brings the gong near the ground, and quickly raises it back in the air.

The Kalinga of Kalinga-Apayao Province

The Kalinga live just north of Mountain Province. This area, which includes the Isneg, is one of the more isolated of the mountain provinces, but trade and the influx of settlers are influencing traditional culture. More than the other Cordillera groups, the Kalinga have preserved a bamboo-and-gong musical tradition, played in everyday life and festivities, showing the preservation of materials belonging to an earlier bamboo age and a later bronze age. They have more types of bamboo instruments and more varied manners of playing gongs than most other upland groups.

The Southern Kalinga favor two types of playing gongs: *topayya* and *palook*, both reserved for men. In *topayya*, six players tap and slap the gongs with their hands. First they pick up their favorite instruments, which are lying on the ground with rims up, and walk toward a corner of the arena for dancing, where they form a line. As they hang their gongs from their belts, they kneel and let the gongs lie on their laps, face up and rims down. Each instrumentalist taps his instrument with either his left or his right palm, listens to the sound and reverberation, and if dissatisfied, exchanges it for another.

In *gangsa topayya* (Figure 23.10), the player of the lead instrument starts with the traditional beat, consisting of an alternation of a left-hand slap and a slide by the right palm on the face of his gong. The second instrumentalist follows with the same motions, one beat behind. Then the third and fourth do likewise, each behind the other by one beat. The musical result is a rising melody of four tones. After the four gongs are heard, the fifth gong plays an ostinato, a simple ringing left-hand slap toward the edge of the gong, quickly damped by the right hand. The sixth gong first plays a more elaborate improvisatory rhythm before settling into a steady beat, with both hands tapping one side of the gong.

Dance is an integral part of this music. An elderly couple, usually prominent members of the community, move in a circular fashion. In time with the music, the man chases his partner, rushing forward with heavy steps, like a rooster chasing a hen, as she scampers away in small steps to the other side of the circle. She remains in place, dancing light steps with arms held high, bent at the elbows, until she is pursued again to an-

Figure 23.10
A Kalinga *gangsa topayya*, about 1910. Courtesy of Father Francisco Billiet.

other sector of the circle. This dance excites the audience, which laughs and shouts in good-natured fun until the dance ends with the couple shaking hands.

The Ifugao of Ifugao Province

The Ifugao, like the other peoples of the Cordillera, are partly cultivators of a wet system of agriculture. Their old rice terraces, carved out of sharp-edged ridges, are oriented toward the movement of the sun, and their systems of farming are associated with strong religious beliefs. Gong music, songs, and epics are performed within the context of rituals. The Ifugao use three flat gongs (*gangha*) to produce repeating musical patterns as ostinati. One gong lies on the lap of a kneeling performer, who plays it with both hands. The left hand taps the face of the gong to produce a brilliant ring, while the right, clenched into a fist, strikes and slides on the gong to dampen the ring. Alternate strokes between right and left hands create alternately ringing and sliding sounds. The other gongs are beaten with sticks in distinct rhythms.

The Northern Kalinga-Tinggian of Kalinga-Apayao Province

More varied gong musics are found among the Northern Kalinga-Tinggian. The *inila-ud* ensemble consists of three gongs and one drum. Three male performers in a kneeling position lay the gongs on their laps. Each plays his own rhythm, using a stick in the left hand to hit the gong and an open right palm to dampen and tap another beat. The *pinalaiyan* ensemble consists of four gongs and one drum. The first gongs and the third are laid on the ground, rims facing down, and are each struck with a stick, producing a hollow sound with the earth as resonator. The second gong, held by the left hand, is made to stand upright on its rim touching the ground, as the player strikes its ventral side, as opposed to its dorsal side, with a stick. The third gong hangs freely from the left hand, as the right hand strikes its side. The drum provides a steady beat, which holds together the rhythms of these gongs.

Bamboo and Other Instrumental Traditions

The foregoing examples of flat gongs define a music of colors, indefinite pitches, and repeating musical phrases. Similarly, bamboo percussion instruments express themselves with indefinite pitches. The existence of two such similar musics: the older, bamboo; the newer, bronze, shows how the two musical cultures have interrelated over time, particularly in Northern Luzon.

Among the Kalinga, a popular bamboo musical instrument is the buzzer (*balingbing*), with a split dividing its thin bamboo tube in two. When the tube is struck against the ulnar side of the open palm of the left hand, the halves vibrate. Whether the buzz is fast or slow depends on whether the halves are held tightly or loosely against each other. A rattan ring around the base of the tube may be adjusted to tighten the halves, thus tuning the rise or descent in pitch or change in color of the instrument's sound. The *balingbing* is now played as an ensemble of six, but the Ibaloy also know it as a solo instrument.

gangha
Ifugao flat gongs
inila-ud
Kalinga-Tinggian ensemble of three gongs

Idiochord tube zithers (*kolitong*) have as many as ten strings lifted from the bamboo tube itself, carefully tuned to the tones of a pentatonic scale and their upper octaves. The ten tones of the strings are distributed around the tube to ease plucking. The tube is held at its midsection. The thumb and second and third fingers of both hands pluck strings, successively or alternately. The nose flute is played by several groups of people, but among the Kalinga other flutes—a whistle flute and a notched flute—are more often played.

Vocal Music

Vocal music in the Cordillera is known for its epics, chanted songs in verse praising famous heroes. Bontok responsorial vocal music is a powerful means of expression. To emphasize the importance of the song, groups of men and women reiterate the ends of verses. At Bontok wakes, men and women take turns on successive nights sitting before the deceased, who is seated upright and tied to a chair—a ritual practice to honor important personalities before their burial. Responsorial songs praise the dead person and recall his contributions to the community and his help to his family. At Ibaloy political rallies, a leader honors a candidate for office with short poetic lines, the ends of which are repeated by a whole group of followers. In Kalinga pacts of peace, solo forms of song are a means of polite expression; they are sung by representatives of contracting parties in simple melodic formulas, filled in with improvised texts, to greet and welcome guests. At weddings, the bride's party sings in verse its contribution to the nuptial feast, and the groom's side responds with its contribution in the same spirit of gentility.

The South

In the southern Philippines, about 1.5 million people living in the mountains of Mindanao and other islands have kept alive an indigenous music culture related to the music of the Maranao, the Magindanao clustered along the banks of the Mindanao River, and the Tausug, the Sama, the Bajao, and the Yakan of the Sulu islands—all of whom acquired a Muslim culture in the 1300s and 1400s. These people live in dense forests, in small settlements far apart from each other, and are governed by customary law. Especially during harvest, festivities are, as in Palawan, occasions for sipping rice beer from precious jars, followed by gong playing, dancing, and chanting. Mediums cure the sick and perform ablutions in rivers. The exchange of betel is still a practice between bride and bridegroom; blowguns may still be seen in Palawan. A dry-rice system of agriculture is accomplished in stages—slashing, burning, planting, tending, and harvesting—accompanied by rituals, prayers, chanting, and playing musical instruments. Rice is planted in holes dug by a line of men equipped with sharpened dibbles. The men are followed closely by women, who drop seeds of rice into the holes, which boys and girls walking behind the women then fill with soil. Singing, joking, and teasing lessen the burden of the work.

Several ensembles of hanging gongs distinguish the music of the South, where bossed gongs mark the main differentiation from the flat-gong culture of the North. In turn, bossed gongs are related to hanging gongs in Indonesia and Malaysia. Suspended gongs are played mostly by mountain people, practitioners of swidden agriculture, in thanksgiving festivals after harvest. These festivals involve consuming vast quantities of rice, sacrificing animals, drinking rice beer, dancing, and singing. Hanging gongs have a wider geographical distribution than the *kulintang*.

The Tiboli of Western Mindanao

The Tiboli live in the Tiruray highlands of South Cotabato Province. One of their major rituals includes a thanksgiving feast, also a renewal of marriage vows; it is a ritual accomplished in stages lasting several years. Hanging gongs are played during lavish feasts. Tiboli gongs are big, heavy instruments, with a prominent boss and wide turned-in rims.

A Tiboli gong-ensemble performance consists of two musical parts: a repeating sound played by one gong and a melody played by three other suspended gongs. The heaviest gong (*tang*) slowly repeats the lowest sound, interspersed with melodic parts played on three smaller gongs (*semagi*). There may be one player for the two musical parts, or two players—one for the *tang*, and another for the three *semagi*. The players may be men, women, or children. All gongs are damped by assistants who hold the bosses, rims, or faces of the instruments during performance. The *semagi* (melodic) gongs may so interchange that when they are played, their sequence of tones changes. The melody becomes a permutation of the three tones.

The Kalagan of Davao Province

The Kalagan, a group of people living near Davao Gulf, use the *tagunggo*, a set of six large gongs, each as heavy as those of the Tiboli. They are suspended from a sturdy branch, with the lighter gongs on top and the larger ones below, their bosses facing two players of either sex. One plays a regular beat on the largest gong and the other plays pentatonic melodies on the five other gongs (Figure 23.11). After a while, the performer of the melody gongs stops playing. With small steps, he dances away from the gongs, following the drone beats of the largest gong; his steps take the place of the gong melody. Then he winds his way back to the gongs and resumes playing the melodic part.

Figure 23.11
The Takakaolo *tagunggo* is played like a Bagobo *tagunggo*. The player on the left holds the boss to dampen the sound of the gong; the other player holds the rim of her gong, also to dampen the sound. Courtesy of University of Pennsylvania Ethnomusicology Archives.

The Subanun of Zamboanga del Sur Province

The Subanun are the primary tribal group of the far end of Southwest Mindanao. Subanun ensembles use two hanging gongs and other percussion. The variation in their instrumentation and their use in different social functions demonstrate an interest in colors of sound, rather than in pitch.

The *megayep* ensemble is played exclusively by men for healing rituals and to ask the spirits for a good harvest. These rituals are held in the medium's house, where one

sacred gong (*gandingan*) is kept. A medium-sized instrument with a narrow rim and a shallow boss, it is played by two performers. One hits the boss with a mallet, producing a long, rhythmic beat. The other uses two sticks: he holds one in his left hand to strike the back of the boss, and he holds the other in his right hand to strike the rim of the gong. A second gong (*gagung pon*) is a heavier instrument, struck by a mallet on its boss to sound another beat with a lower sound; another player hits the rim of this gong with a pair of sticks. The third instrument, a pair of porcelain bowls, is struck with two sticks, producing two tones.

Palawan Island

Palawan was once a part of a land bridge connecting Borneo to parts of the Philippines. Its inhabitants, like those of the Sulu Islands, bear some relationship to the peoples of North Borneo. The Palawan, Tagbanwa, and Batak are the remaining peoples least influenced by Western culture. The Palawan have another version of a hanging-gong ensemble (*basal*), played in harvest ceremonies, held in large houses especially built for festivities. Drinking rice beer, dancing, singing, and storytelling are integral parts of the celebration. The gong ensemble is led by a drum (*gimbal*), which plays ostinati. A pair of small gongs (*sanang*) played by two men produces brightly metallic sounds when struck with a pair of sticks on the rim and boss. As one *sanang* plays a sequence of loud tinkling sounds, the other attenuates its volume. The loud and soft sounds which alternate between the two *sanang* ebb and flow in contrast to a steady drumbeat. Another pair of heavy gongs (*agung*) supplies yet another layer of low, opaque sounds, playing against each other. If there are three *agung*, the third instrument plays a regular beat, to which the two other *agung* adjust. Sometimes there is only one *agung*, which plays a uniformly booming sound.

The Tiruray of Southern Mindanao, Maguindanao Province

All the foregoing ensembles use large, heavy gongs with wide, turned-in rims. Among the Tiruray, five smaller and lighter gongs (*agung*) are played by men, women, or girls as entertainment during weddings and festivals (Figure 23.12). They produce a gentle music of repeating melodies. Each instrument hangs from a string held by the left hand as the right strikes the boss with a padded stick. The musicians line up following the ascending or descending pitches of their gongs and play standing, walking, or seated. Each gong is assigned a rhythm, and together they produce a melody.

Bamboo and Other Instrumental Traditions

In Mindanao, many musical instruments are not made of bronze. Those made of bamboo include flutes (*palendag, suling, lantoy*), slit drums (*agung a bentong*), scrapers (*tagutok*), paired-string zithers (*takumbo, katimbok*),

megayep
Subanen healing gong ensemble
basal
Palawan gong ensemble

Figure 23.12
Tiruray *agung* are the smallest hanging bossed gongs in Mindanao. Photo by José Maceda.

polychordal zithers (*sluday, tangkol*), and Jew's harps (*kubing, kumbing, aruding*). Those made of other materials are log drums (*edel*), hanging percussion beams (*kagul*), one-stringed fiddles (*duwagey, dayuray*), three-stringed fiddles (*gitgit*), two-stringed lutes (*kudyapiq, kusyapiq, hagelung, faglung*), conch trumpets (*budyung*), and drums (*gimbal*). All these instruments arc widely distributed across the South. In some cases, only the term for the instrument and the repertoire differ from place to place.

Lutes come in different sizes and shapes—long, short, narrow, wide, rectangular, bulbous, and with or without designs, decorations, or tassels. Two-stringed plucked lutes are played by several groups of people: one string plays the melody, while the other twangs a drone. Such lutes may be played with a bamboo polychordal zither, as among the Palawan and the Ata, or as solo instruments practically embraced while danced with, as among the Tiboli.

There are at least four kinds of flutes in the southern Philippines. These are the lip-valley or notched flute, the ring flute, the whistle flute, and the chip-on-tube flute. Lip-valley flutes and ring flutes are longer instruments; in the hands of accomplished musicians, they make long, winding melodies, which can easily change from one octave range to the next by overblowing (Figure 23.13).

Xylophones are used by the Tiruray and Magindanao groups in the South. One type of xylophone uses horizontally suspended logs (*luntang*). The musical principle at work in playing the *luntang* resembles that of playing the *tagunggo*: one musician (or sometimes two) plays a dronelike ostinato while another plays a melody on the remaining logs (Figure 23.14).

Vocal Music

In the South, epics or stories of famous heroes are sung by soloists at special gatherings, when the audience may spend the

Figure 23.13
Among the Tiruray and other linguistic groups, the lip-valley or notched flute (*palendag*) is tuned to a pentatonic anhemitonic scale to play music representing nature and the environment.

ⓒⒹ ᵀᴿᴬᶜᴷ15

Figure 23.14
On Mindanao, suspended logs (*luntang*) are a form of Tiruray and Magindanao xylophone. Here, two players produce a repeating drone while a third plays a melody on the five remaining logs, striking them on their pointed edges. Courtesy of the University of Pennsylvania Ethnomusicology Archives.

night listening to singing. Epic singers are frequently mediums, respected for their ability to communicate with spirits; through the epics they sing, they are the keepers of their people's cultural and historical traditions. Other songs focus on love, drinking, or lullabies.

Musical Styles

The indigenous music of the Philippines is represented by gongs and bamboo instruments played by people living in the Cordillera of Northern Luzon, the mountains and coastal regions of Mindanao, and other islands of the South. Within each area, certain musical constants can be observed. Counting in units of two or four is the basis of the music of gongs and some bamboo instruments. Repetition, ostinato, or drone, with or without melody, makes up the musical structure of most instrumental ensembles in the Philippines (Maceda 1974).

Flat gongs and bossed gongs belong to different geographical areas. In all of Southeast Asia, flat gongs are concentrated in Northern Luzon and the central highlands of Vietnam. Bossed gongs in the southern Philippines are hanging gongs, or gongs laid in a row. Hanging gongs are played by upland peoples for rituals related to a swidden type of agriculture. They are older instruments to which gongs in a row were added and played by riverine peoples in Mindanao and island peoples in Sulu. Cultural groups that use hanging gongs play a music of punctuation and permutation—a musical process different from "melodic" processes, induced by two-handed techniques employed in smaller gongs in a row. The term *gong-chime* does not distinguish between punctuational and melodic gongs, formed by a historical and perhaps an evolutionary process. Neither does it show the difference between flat gongs and bossed gongs belonging to separate cultures and historical periods.

REFERENCES

Abubakar, Carmen. 1983. "Islamization of Southern Philippines: An Overview." In *Filipino Muslims: Their Social Institutions and Cultural Achievements,* ed. F. Landa Jocano, 6–13. Diliman: Asian Center, University of the Philippines.

Blair, Emma Helen, and James Alexander Robertson, eds. 1973 [1903]. *The Philippine Islands 1493–1898.* 55 vols. Mandaluyong: Cachos Hermanosted.

Butocan, Aga Mayo. 1987. *Palabunibunyan: A Repertoire of Musical Pieces for the Maguindanaon Kulintangan.* Manila: Philippine Women's University.

Cadar, Usopay Hamdag. 1975. "The Role of Kulintang Music in Maranao Society." *Selected Reports in Ethnomusicology* 2:2:49–62.

———. 1980. "Context and Style in the Vocal Music of the Muranao in Mindanao, Philippines." Ph.D. dissertation, University of Washington.

Castro y Amadeo, Pedro de. 1790. "Historia de la Provincia de Batangas por Don Pedro Andrés de Castro y Amadeo en sus viajes y contraviajes en toda esta Provincia año de 1790." Madrid: MS Archivo Nacional, Códice 931,7.

de la Concepción, Juan. 1788–92. *Historia general de las islas Filipinos.* Manila: Agustín de la Rosa y Balagtas.

De León, Felipe Padilla. 1977. "Banda Uno, Banda Dos." *Filipino Heritage* 8.

Ellis, Henry T. 1856. *Hongkong to Manila and the Lakes of Luzon in the Philippine Islands in the Year 1856.* London: Smith, Elder.

Kiefer, Thomas. 1970. *Music from the Tausug of Sulu.* Bloomington: Indiana University. LP disk.

Maceda, José. 1963. "The Music of the Maguindanao in the Philippines." Ph.D. dissertation, University of California at Los Angeles.

———. 1974. "Drone and Melody in Philippine Musical Instruments." In *Traditional Drama and Music of Southeast Asia,* ed. Mohd. Taib Osman, 246–273. Kuala Lumpur: Kementerian Pelajaran Malaysia.

Maceda, José, and Alain Martenot. 1976. *Sama de Sitangkai.* Office de la Recherche Scientifique et Technique Outre-Mer, Société de la Recherche Linguistiques et Anthropologiques de France. LP disk.

McFarland, Curtis D. 1983. *A Linguistic Atlas of the Philippines.* Manila: Linguistic Society of the Philippines.

Molina, Antonio J. 1977. "The Sentiments of Kundiman." *Filipino Heritage* 8:2026–29.

Nicolas, Arsenio. 1977. "Ang Musika ng mga Yakan sa Pulo ng Basilan" (The Music of the Yakan on the Island of Basilan). *Musika Jornal* 1:79–10.

———. 1987. "Ritual Transformations and Musical Parameters, a Study of Selected Headhunting Rites on Southern Cordillera, Northern Luzon." M.A. thesis, University of the Philippines.

Otto, Steven, W. 1985. *The Muranao Kakolintang: An Approach to the Repertoire.* Marawi City: Mindanao State University.

Puya y Ruiz, Adolfo. 1838. *Filipinos: Descripción General de la Provincia de Bulacan.* Manila: R. Mercantil de Diaz Puertas.

San Nicolás, Fray Andrés de. 1973 [1605]. "General History of the Discalced Augustinian Fathers." In *The Philippine Islands 1493–1898*, ed. Emma Helen Blair and James Alexander Robertson, 21:111–317. Mandaluyong: Cachos Hermanos.

Santos, Ramón P. 1992. "Nationalism in Philippine Music during the Japanese Occupation: Art or Propaganda." *Panahon ng Hapon* (Japanese Time) 2:93–106.

Tiongson, Nicanor, ed. 1991. *The Cultural Traditional Media of the Philippines.* Manila: ASEAN and the Cultural Center of the Philippines.

Yraola, Marialita T. 1977. "Ang Mga Awiting Tagalog." *Musika Jornal* 1:42–78.

Questions for Critical Thinking:

Island Southeast Asia

1. How would you compare and contrast the impact of Islam and Hinduism on Indonesian gamelan-playing traditions in particular?
2. Catholic and animist traditions coexist in certain parts of the Philippines; how do these multireligious traditions show up in musical performance?
3. Many island musical instruments share similar names and stylistic features across ethnic and national boundaries; what does that tell you about issues of musical transmission?
4. Why is the natural world an important feature of the musics of Borneo?
5. How are the gamelans and gamelan musical styles of Java, Sunda, and Bali both similar and different?
6. What are some essential characteristics of the musics of Sumatra, and how does one attempt to understand such diverse musical features?
7. How and why have the gong-playing traditions of the Southern Philippines developed differently from those of the Northern Philippines?
8. What role have the contemporary media (radio, television, CDs, and cassettes) had in the dissemination and popularization (or lack thereof) of island musics?
9. All of these islands are the home to people who play quiet, solo, intimate musical instruments; what purpose do these instruments serve to those who play them?
10. How do the popular musics of the islands serve to represent local musical cultures both to local people and internationally?

Glossary

See page xvi for a guide to pronunciation.

aalakan
  Tausug deep-rimmed bossed gong

adok
  Minangkabau frame drum

agung
  Suspended bossed gong of Sumatra and the Philippines

agung a bentong
  Maguindanao bamboo slit drum

alus
  "Refined, subtle," applied to Javanese style or to character in Balinese dance

angklung
  Tuned, shaken bamboo rattles from Indonesia

Angkor Vat
  Temple complex in Cambodia, center of ancient Khmer civilization

angkuoch
  Khmer Jew's harp of bamboo or iron

angsel
  Dramatic rhythmic break in Balinese music

animism
  Religion that personifies natural elements

antan
  Pestle used for pounding rice in Borneo

anyeiñ
  Burmese entertainment theater of music, women vocalists, and clowns

apsara
  Khmer heavenly maiden

arakk
  Khmer ceremony for worshipping spirits

arja
  Balinese operetta about romance, comedy

aruding
  Palawan Jew's harp

asli
  Malay song genre using fixed texts

Austroasiatic
  Language family including Khmer, Vietnamese, and Senoi

awedeng
Bontok Jew's harp

awit
Metrical romances of Christians and Muslims, recited on melodic formulas

ayaye
Cambodian village vocal repartee with instrumental ensemble

Ayuthaya
Capital of Siam from 1350 to 1767

azan/adzan
Islamic call to prayer, elsewhere *adban*

babandil
(1) Maguindanao medium-size bossed gong; (2) Subanen suspended gong

bắc
One of two modal systems in Vietnam

balingbing
Kalinga bamboo buzzer

bandurria
European pear-shaped plucked lute, found in Philippines

bangsawan
Theater shows of the Malay nobility, derived from Persia

barang
Javanese pitch name

baris
Men's temple dance of Bali

basakk
Khmer village theater genre of Chinese origin

basal
Palawan gong ensemble

batel
Repetitive pattern accompanying fight scenes in Bali

batil
Malay overturned brass bowl hit with sticks

bayok
Maguindanao syllabic style of singing

bebonangan
Processional ensemble of Bali

bedhaya
Refined women's court dance of Java

bedug
Large double-headed barrel drum of Cirebon and Lombok

bem
Javanese pitch name

berokan
Monster play of Cirebon

bey choan
Long rhythmic cycle, "third level" in Khmer music

bhajanai/bhajan
Lay-sung Hindu devotional songs

bhangra
Popular Indian-derived dance-song

biola
(1) European violin; (2) Low-pitched violin in Sumbawa

boeng mang kawk
Thai set of seven tuned drums, of Mon origin

bonang
Gong-chime, found throughout Java

bonang barung
Larger of two gong-chimes in Java

bonang panerus
Smaller of two gong-chimes in Java

bongai
Malay repartee singing for weddings, circumcisions, etc.

bonn chaul chhnaim
Khmer New Year festival

bonn kathinn
Khmer festival of offerings to Buddhist monks

bonn omm touk
Khmer water festival with boat races

bonn phka
Khmer flower festival to raise money

boria
Theatrical genre from Penang area

boũncì
Large, double-headed barrel drum of Burma

brai
(1) Cirebonese large frame drum without jingles; (2) Muslim ensemble

bua
Tausug and Sama large hanging gong

budyung
Hanunoo shell trumpet

buka panggung
Ritual opening for shadow theater, in Malaysia and Cirebon

byau'
Burmese struck wooden block with stick

byò
Pair of large, stick-beaten drums from Burma

ca huế
Vocal chamber music of central Vietnam and Huế area

ca trù
Northern Vietnamese chamber music

cài lưởng
Genre of popular southern Vietnamese theater that developed around 1920

calung
Struck bamboo xylophone ensemble of Java and Sunda

canang
(1) Pair of small knobbed gongs in rack in Malaysia; (2) Sumatran gong chime and ensemble

celempong
Riau gong-chime and ensemble (615)

celempung
Four-legged metal-stringed box zither of Java

ceng-ceng
Small hand cymbals of Bali and Lombok

cenoi
Temiar term for rays of light that bear spiritual substances throughout the universe

chan dio
Shortest of three rhythmic cycles in Thai music

chant
Musical recitation of a sacred text

chap
Thai medium-size cymbals connected by a cord, flatter and thinner than the ching

chập chỏa
Pair of medium-size cymbals, found in Vietnam

chapei/chapey/chapey dang veng
Cambodian long-necked lute with two to four strings

chầu văn
Vietnamese spirit possession ritual

chèo
Traditional theater of northern Vietnam

chhap
Medium Khmer cymbals, thinner than chhing

chhing
Cambodian pair of small, thick metal cymbals connected by a cord

Chin
Ethnic group from Burma

ching
Pair of Thai small cymbals connected by cord

chordophone
Stringed instrument

chrieng chapey
Khmer narrative accompanied by long-necked lute (chapey)

chuida
Outdoor ensemble from China

ciwaíñ
Burmese set of twenty-one graduated bossed gongs mounted horizontally in a circle

colotomic structure
The organization of music by periodic punctuation

corrido
Story about Christians and Muslims, recited on melodic formulas

counterpoint
Simultaneous multiple lines of music with different rhythms

dabakan
Goblet-shaped drum of Philippines

daboih
Acehnese Sufi ritual of self–mortification

dabu-dabu
Maranaon large religious drum

dabus
(1) Sufi ritual of self–mortification; (2) Sufi–derived dance with iron awl

đại hồng chung
Large bell for Buddhist ceremonies in Vietnam

đại nhạc
The oboe-dominated ritual ensemble of Vietnam's court

dalang
Puppeteer in shadow-puppet theater; also dhalang

daluogu
Percussion ensemble from China

đàn bầu
Monochord with box resonator from Vietnam

dân ca
Modernized Vietnamese folk song

đàn cò
Vietnamese two-stringed fiddle with narrow, waisted body

đàn đáy
Vietnamese long-necked, trapezoidal lure with three strings

đàn độc huyền
Vietnamese monochord with box resonator

đàn gáo
Vietnamese two-stringed fiddle with coconut shell body

đàn nguyệt/đàn kìm
Vietnamese long-necked, moon-shaped lute

đàn nhị
Vietnamese two-stringed fiddle with narrow, waisted body

đàn tam thập lục
Vietnamese hammered zither with thirty–six strings, of Chinese origin

đàn tranh/đàn thập lục
Vietnamese semi–tubular board zither with sixteen or seventeen strings

đàn tỳ-bà
Vietnamese pear-shaped lute, from Chinese pipa

đàn xến
Vietnamese lute with petal-shaped body

dangdut
Hindi-film-influenced popular music, common to Malaysia and Indonesia

dayuray
Bukidnon one-stringed fiddle

degung
Sundanese gong-chime

dendang
(1) West Sumatra songs with *saluang*; (2) Bengkulu songs with *biola* and *redap*

dhadha
Javanese pitch name

dhalang
Puppeteer in shadow puppet theater; also dalang

điệu
Vietnamese system of modes

dikir barat
Malay men's choral singing of secular texts

đông dao
Children's songs of Vietnam

Đông Son
Early period in Southeast Asian history, characterized by bronze drum casting, spreading as far as the Philippines and Borneo

doùpá
Burmese small, double-headed barrel drum

drone
Continuous sound

dubakan
Goblet-shaped drum of Philippines

Dusun
Ethnic group from Kalimantan

duwagey
Manobo one-stringed fiddle

duwahan
Tausug and Sama pair of hanging gongs

duyug
Maguindanao rhythmic mode

edel
Tagakaolu log drum

engkuk-kemong
Pair of kettle gongs in sléndro tuning, Java

ensuling
Bamboo ring-stop flute of Borneo

er hu
Chinese two-stringed fiddle

ethnocentrism
Valuing a particular culture over others

faglung
Bilaan two-stringed lute

falliwes
Bontok dance music with sticks

fawn
Various kinds of northern Thai dance, e.g., *fawn thian*

fixed-pitch instruments
Instruments, such as xylophones and gong circles, whose pitch cannot be changed during performance

flores de Mayo
May rite with flowers and song, in Philippines

free-reed pipe
Aerophone with a free-standing reed

fulu
Upland Thai (Lisu) gourd mouth organ with bamboo pipes and gourd wind chest

gabbang
Bamboo xylophone, common to Borneo and Philippines

gagah
"Strong, robust," in Javanese

gagong pon
Subanen heavy gong

galombang
West Sumatra circular dance form

gambang/gambang kayu
Eighteen-key wooden xylophone of Java

gambo
Eight-stringed plucked lute of Sumbawa

gambub
Theatrical genre of Bali

gambus
Plucked, pear-shaped lute, related to 'ud, common to Malaysia and Indonesia

gambyong
Javanese nonnarrative women's dance

gamelan
Indonesian stratified gong-chime ensemble

gamelan angklung
Four-tone village ensemble of Bali and Lombok

gamelan arja
Balinese suling and percussion ensemble

gamelan baleganjur
Processional ensemble of Bali and Lombok

gamelan degung
Sundanese pélog gong-chime ensemble

gamelan gadhon
Small, soft-sounding ensemble of Java

gamelan gambang
Sacred xylophone and metallophone ensemble of Bali

gamelan gambuh
Suling, rebab, and percussion ensemble of Bali

gamelan gong
Large, older ceremonial ensemble of Bali

gamelan gong kebyar
Balinese dynamic modern gamelan style

gamelan gong Sasak
Modern Sasak ensemble

gamelan jegog
West Bali bamboo xylophone ensemble

gamelan prawa
A sléndro ensemble used to accompany wayang topèng in Cirebon

gamelan rebana
Drums tuned to gamelan pitches in Lombok

gamelan saléndro
Sundanese saléndro gong-chime ensemble

gamelan selundeng
Sacred iron-bar metallophone ensemble of Bali

gamelan wayang Sasak
Ensemble to accompany *wayang* puppetry in Lombok

gandang
(1) Sumatran two-headed drum; (2) Samawan topical sung poetry; (3) Tausug two-headed drum; (4) Yakan cracked bamboo instrument

gandingan
(1) Maguindanao bossed gong; (2) Subanen sacred medium-size gong

gandrung
(1) Java female singer-dancer; (2) Banyuwangi percussion ensemble

gangha
Ifugao flat gongs

gangsa
(1) Kalinga and Bontok flat gongs; (2) Metallophone of Bali and Lombok

gangsaran
Balinese up-tempo piece

ganrang
Buginese/Makassarese two-headed cylindrical drums

garapan
Formulae for variation and improvisation in Javanese music

garokot
Maranao bamboo scraper

gata bera
Drum from Sri Lanka

geduk
Malay double-headed barrel drum hit with stick

gedumbak
Malay single-headed goblet-shaped drum

gembyung
Cirebonese large frame drum without jingles

gendang
Large double-headed drum from Malaysia and Indonesia

gendang panjai
Iban gong-chime ensemble

gendang raya
Iban gong ensemble

gendèr
Indonesian metallophone with tube-resonated keys

gendèr barung
Javanese lower-pitched metallophone with tube-resonated keys

gendèr panerus
Javanese higher-pitched metallophone with tube-resonated keys

gendèr slenthem
Javanese deepest metallophone with tube-resonated keys

gendèr wayang
Balinese metallophone quartet for wayang kulit

gendhing
Gamelan-based musical composition of Java

gendhing bonang
Formal arrangement of Javanese gamelan piece

gending
Gamelan-based musical composition of Bali

genggong
Balinese Jew's harp

genjring
(1) Cirebonese frame drum with jingles; (2) Cirebonese ensemble

genta
Buddhist-Hindu bronze ankle bells, worn in Sumatra

geruding
Jew's harp of Borneo

getai
Contemporary Singaporean stage performance of Chinese origin

ghazal
Genre of Malaysian folk music derived from India and Middle East

gimba
Palawan cylindrical drum

gitara
Six-stringed guitar of Philippines

gitgit
Hanunoo three-stringed fiddle

giying
Balinese metallophone used in gong kebyar

goh
Temiar tube stampers, used in healing rituals

go'ong
Large hanging gong of Sunda

gondang
Toba Batak tuned drum ensemble

gong ageng
Large hanging gong of Indonesia

gong kebyar
Balinese dynamic modern gamelan style

gong lanang
Smaller "male" hanging gong of Lombok

gong suling
Suling used to replicate gamelan in Bali

gong wadon
Larger "female" hanging gong in Lombok

goong
Jatai bamboo tube zither of Vietnam

goong teng leng
Beaten bamboo tubes, upland Vietnam

gordang
(1) Large bass drum in Toba Batak *gondang*; (2) Mandailing Batak drum and gong ensemble

gordang sembilan
Mandailing Batak nine-drum ensemble

gulu
Javanese pitch name

gung
Large vertical gong of Sumatra

guntang
Balinese one-stringed bamboo tube zither

guru
Indian teacher

hadis
Tausug songs about death

hadra/hadrah
(1) Malaysian theatrical genre derived from Islamic singing; (2) Arabic praise songs about Muhammad; (3) Single-headed frame drum of Arabic origin

hagelung
Tiboli two-stringed lute

hajat
Ritual feast or celebration in Sunda

hajji
Muslim who has been to Mecca

hala?
The Semang shaman, called halaa? by the Temiar

harana
Serenade in Philippines

hát
Vietnamese term for "singing"; prefix for theater genres

hát ả đào
Alternate name for *ca trù* chamber song in Vietnam

hát bá trạo
Vietnamese "paddle dance" folk theater of central Vietnam

hát bài chòi
Traditional theater of central Vietnam

hát bội
Central Vietnamese theater

hát chầu văn
Spirit possession ceremony in Vietnam

hát chèo tàu
Ancient folk drama of Gối near Hanoi

hát sắc bùa
Vietnamese wishing songs for New Year (Tết)

Hmong
Sino-Tibetan upland group living in Laos, Thailand, Vietnam, and China

hnè
Burmese conical aerophone with six-piece reed and detached bell

hnyìñ
Extinct Burmese free-reed mouth organ

hò
Vietnamese work songs in rice fields and on rivers

hô bài chòi
Vietnamese songs associated with playing cards

hoho
Nias solo and choral singing

hỏi quảng
Cantonese tune adopted by Vietnamese musicians

hơi
Vietnamese ornamentation specific to a mode

homrong
Thai ceremonial suites and overtures in classical music

hsaìñwaìñ
Burmese classical ensemble

hudhud
Ifugao epic

huduk apa
Kayan pest-dispersal ceremony

hun
Northeast Thai Jew's harp

hün krabawk
Classical-based rod puppet theater of Thailand

Iban
Ethnic group from Borneo

iconography
The visual representation of a subject

ideograph
Graphic depiction of meaning, as in Chinese characters

idiophone
An instrument that itself vibrates to produce sound

inang
Genre of folk dance in Malaysia

indang
(1) West Sumatra religious/political performance; (2) West Sumatra frame drum

inila-ud
Kalinga-Tinggian ensemble of three gongs

insi
Maranao ring-stop flute

irama
Tempo and subdivision levels in Javanese music

ja-khe
Thai three-stringed floor zither in crocodile shape

jaipongan
Sundanese indigenous popular dance form

jataka
Story of a past life of the Buddha

jatung utang
Kenyah wooden xylophone

jenglong
(1) Cirebonese low-pitch horizontal kettle gongs; (2) Sundanese set of six hanging gongs

jikay
Comic theatrical genre of Malaysia and southern Thailand

joged/joget
Genre of popular social dance, common to Malaysia and Indonesia

joi
Northern Thai courtship singing

jata
Triple-time Spanish-derived dance

kaba
(1) Malay storytelling accompanied by *biola* (violin); (2) West Sumatra narratives with two-stringed fiddles

kacapi
(1) Large eighteen-stringed zither from Sunda; (2) Malay tube zither played solo; (3) Makassarese boat-shaped two-stringed lute

kacapi-suling
Instrumental version of tem bang Sunda

kacapian
Modern *kacapi*-accompanied vocal music

kagul
(1) Maguindanao scraper-type instrument; (2) Tiruray suspended percussion beams

kajar
Horizontal kettle gong of Lombok

kalaleng
Bontok nose flute of te-er ritual

kanhi
Lowland Chăm turtle-shell-body fiddle

kantrüm
Khmer village ensemble in northeast Thailand

kar
Khmer wedding ceremony

karawitan
Javanese gamelan-based court music

Karen
Upland ethnic group from northern Thailand and Burma

kasar
"Crude, rough," Javanese term

kasinoman
Ritual party for youth in Cirebon

katimbok
Tagakaolu paired-string zither

kaul
Sundanese casual participation in a musical event

kawih
Fixed-meter songs of Sunda

kbach
Khmer system of dance gestures

kêtruyện
Narratives of poetry and prose of Vietnam

kebluk
Large kettle gong of Cirebon

kecak
Balinese male chorus representing monkey army

kecimol
Wind, string, and drum ensemble of Lombok

kecrèk
Javanese and Sundanese idiophone made of hanging metal plates

kekawin
Sung poetry in Old Javanese

keledi
Kajang mouth organ

kelenongan
Gong-chime and ensemble of Sumatra

kemanak
Banana-shaped metal idiophone of Java and Cirebon

kemong
Balinese small hanging gong

kempli
Balinese horizontally mounted gong

kempul
Small hanging gong of Indonesia

kempur
(1) South Sumatra large horizontal gong; (2) Small hanging gong of Bali

kempyang
Javanese small kettle gong, *pélog* tuning only

ken
Free-reed mouth organ in raft form, found in Cambodia, Laos, and Thailand

kèn
Family of double-reed aerophones of Vietnam

kendang
Double-headed drum from Indonesia

kendhang
Double-headed drum of Java

kendhang ciblon
Medium double-headed barrel drum of Java

kendhang gendhing
Large double-headed barrel drum of Java

kendhang ketipung
Small double-headed barrel drum of Java

kenong
(1) South Sumatra large horizontal gong; (2) Large, deep-rimmed kettle gong of Indonesia

keprak
Javanese wooden box used to accompany dance

keras
"Strong, coarse"; applied to characters in Balinese dance

keroncong
Portuguese-derived folk music from Melaka

kertok kelapa
Series of slabs over coconut resonators, found in Malaysia

kesuling
Bamboo ring-stop flute of Borneo

ketawang
Formal arrangement of Javanese gamelan piece

kethuk
Javanese small kettle gong

ketipung
Cirebonese small double-headed barrel drum

ketuk
Small kettle gong of Cirebon

ketuk telu
Small village ensemble of Cirebon

ketuk tilu
Sundanese small coastal village ensemble

khaen
Free-reed mouth organ from northeast Thailand and Laos

khao
Northern Thai narrative genre, sometimes accompanied

khap/khǎp
Vocal genres common to northeast Thailand and central and northern Laos

khap ngeum
Repartee song genre of Vientiane area

khap phuan
Repartee song genre of Phuan minority, northern Laos

khap sam neua
Repartee song genre of Houaphanh province

khap thai dam
Vocal genre of Thai Dam minority, northern Laos

khap thum
Repartee song genre of Luang Phrabang

khawng
Single, bossed gongs of Thailand

khawng khu
Southern Thai pair of bossed gongs

khawng mawn
Thai vertical, U-shaped set of bossed gongs

khawng wong lek
Smaller circle of eighteen bossed gongs from Thailand

khawng wong yai
Larger circle of sixteen bossed gongs from Thailand

khene
Lao free-reed mouth organ, also khaen (Thailand)

khim
Small hammered zither of Chaozhou, Chinese origin

khimm
Hammered zither of Chinese origin

khloy
Khmer end-blown duct flute of bamboo

khlui
Thai bamboo or wood fipple flutes, in three sizes

Khmer
The mainstream culture of Cambodia

Khmer Rouge
Communist political organization of Cambodia

khan
Classical masked theater, based on the Ramayana; found in Thailand and Laos

khong vong
Lao series of bossed gongs on circular rattan frame

khru
Thai teacher

khrüang sai
Thai court entertainment ensemble of strings and flute

khse muoy
Half-gourd resonated monochord from Cambodia

khui
Lao bamboo fipple flute

khwan
Spirit essence of a human being

kịch nói
Western-inspired spoken theater of Vietnam

kidung
Type of metered sung poetry in Bali and Lombok

kinang
Lowland Chăm two-headed drum

kinh
The mainstream, lowland Vietnamese population

kiwul
Small gong of Cirebon

klang chhnakk
Khmer ensemble used for funerals

klawng ae
Long Northern Thai single-headed drum

klawng khaek
(1) Thai two-headed harrel drums; (2) Ensemble for boxing and theater

klawng that
Pair of Thai large barrel drums played with sticks

klawng yao
Long Central Thai single-headed drum

klentong
Balinese small hanging gong

kolintang
Minahasan xylophone

kolitong
Kalinga polychordal zither

komintang
Tagalog courtship song

kompang
Malay single-headed frame drum of Arab origin

kopak-kopak
Long bamboo pole to disperse birds in Philippines

korng mong
Khmer single, suspended bossed gong

korng vung
Khmer gong circle

korng vung tauch
Khmer higher-pitched gong circle, sixteen to eighteen gongs

korng vung thomm
Khmer lower-pitched gong circle, with sixteen gongs

kotekan
Rapid, interlocking figuration characteristic of Balinese music

kotyapi
Maranao two-stringed plucked lute

krajappi
Central Thai long-necked lute with four strings

krap
Several kinds of Thai concussion idiophones

krapeu
Three-stringed floor zither of Cambodia

krapp
Khmer pair of bamboo or wood clappers

kraton
One of the Central Javanese courts

kreasi baru
New musical composition, pan-Indonesian term

kroeung damm
Khmer classification term for percussion instruments

kroeung khse
Khmer classification term for stringed instruments

kroeung phlomm
Khmer classification term for wind instruments

kromong/kromongan
  Sumatran gong-chime and ensemble
kroncong
  Eurasian colonial-based popular music of Indonesia
kubing
  Mindanao Jew's harp
kuda kepang
  Malay hobby-horse trance dance, preceded by *barongan*
kudyapi/kudyapiq
  Maguindanao two-stringed lute
kugiran
  Guitar-dominated popular song genre of Malaysia
kulaing
  Yakan Jew's harp
kulintang/kulintangan
  Horizontal bronze gong-chime and ensemble of Indonesia and Philippines
kumbing
  Subanen Jew's harp
kundiman
  Lyrical love song of Philippines
kuriri
  Tausug and Yakan single-part piece
kusyapiq
  Palawan two-stringed lute
kutyapiq
  Maguindanao two-stringed plucked lute
kwintangan
  Yakan set of bossed gongs
kwintangan kayu
  Yakan hanging log beams
lagu
  Musical piece from Cirebon and Sunda
lai
  Modal system used for performance on the Thai khaen
lakhon/lakhawn
  Various types of Thai dance-drama
lam
  Vocal performance common to northeast Thailand
lam ban xok
  Repartee song genre of central-southern Laos
lam khon savan
  Repartee song genre of Savannakhet area, central-south Laos
lam klawn
  Northeast Thai repartee song with *khaen*
lam mahaxay
  Repartee song genre of central-southern Laos
lam mu
  Theatrical genre in northeast Thailand
lam phanya yoi
  Regional type of repartee song with *khaen* in northeast Thailand
lam phi fa
  Northeast Thai spirit-healing ceremony

lam phlün
  Local theater from northeast Thailand
lam phu thai
  Vocal genre of the Phu Thai minority of southern Laos
lam phün
  Northeast Thai narrative song accompanied by khaen
lam ploen
  Theatrical genre in northeast Thailand
lam salavane
  Vocal genre of Salavane province, Laos
lam sing
  Modern form of lam in northeast Thailand
lam sithandone
  Repartee vocal genre from Champassak area
lam som
  Nearly extinct vocal genre of southern Laos
lam tang vay
  Repartee song genre of central-southern Laos
lanat
  Laotian suspended horizontal xylophone
lansaran
  Murut headhunting song and dance form
lantoy
  Manobo chip-on-ledge flute
laras
  Tuning, scale, in Javanese
laud
  Pear-shaped plucked lute from Philippines
lày
  Patterned ornamentation characteristic of tuồng theater, Vietnam
lebad
  Yakan musical unit in instrumental music
lekupa
  Kenyah-Badang songs and dances
lelambatan
  Slow, stately piece of Balinese music
lesung
  Rice-pounding block from Java and Borneo
li-ke
  Thai urban street theater
lima
  Javanese pitch name
liriban
  Javanese soft-playing ensemble
Lisu
  Tibeto-Burman-speaking people living in Thailand, Burma, and China
lithophone
  Stone xylophone
lkhaon
  Khmer generic term referring primarily to theater or play
lkhaon khaol
  Masked play of the Khmer court

lục huyền cầm
Modified Spanish guitar found in Vietnam

luk mot
A coda affixed to a Thai classical composition

luk thung
Thai popular music genre

luntang
Maguindanao and Timray suspended xylophone

ly
Class of Vietnamese folk song comparing human actions to nature

macapa
Metered sung poetry of Java

magagung
Kadazan music in which gongs are beaten in interlocking rhythms

Maha Gitá
Printed anthology of Burmese classical songs

Mahabharata
Indian epic

Mahanikai
The older, typical sect of Buddhism

Mahayana
Buddhist sect from China

maholi
String and flute classical ensemble in Vientiane

mahori
Court ensemble blending idiophones and chordophones

main pulau
Type of song performed by Malaysian women weeding dry rice fields

main puteri
Malay healing ceremony

mak yong
Dance-drama of Kelantan province, Malaysia

mak yong laut
Malay theater from southern Thailand, similar *jikay*

Malayo-Polynesian
Language family including Malay, Chăm, and Jarai

manora
Type of southern Thai theater named for the leading character, also performed in Malaysia

maùñ
Hanging, bossed gong of Burma

maùñsaìñ
Burmese set of eighteen or nineteen bossed gongs on wooden frames in five rows

m'buôt
Free-reed mouth organ with gourd wind chest, found in Trường Sơn Ranges

medium
Tranced ritualist who is possessed by visiting spirits

megayep
Subanen healing gong ensemble

mek mulung
Traditional theater of Kedah state, Malaysia

metabole
Transmigration of pitches allowing modal modulation

metallophone
Metal xylophone

mi jaùñ
Mon crocodile-shaped floor zither

microtonal
Interval less than a semitone

Minangkabau
Ethnic group of Sumatra

mõ
Vietnamese wooden slit drum in fish shape for Buddhist rituals

mode
Fundamental guidelines for composition and improvisation

mohlam
Lao singer from northeast Thailand

mohori
Khmer court ensemble for entertainment music

molam
Traditional singer of Laos

mosque
Building designated for Islamic public worship

mridanga
Barrel-shaped drum from India

múa đăng bông
The Vietnamese "flower dance," associated with religious occasions

múa rối nước
Water-puppet theater found in northern Vietnam

muoy choan
Khmer short rhythmic cycle, "first level"

musiqa
Arabic word denoting music as distinct from chant

muzik klasik
Western classical music in Malaysia

muzik seriosa
Western classical music in Malaysia

Myanmar
Current official name of Burma

na'
Burmese spirit

nam
One of two Vietnamese modal systems

nang talung
Southern Thai shadow-puppet theater, also found in Malaysia

nang yai
Large shadow-puppet theater of Thailand

naphat
Classical music genre from Thailand

na'pwè
Spirit propitiation rite of Burma

nathap
Thai cycle of drum strokes

nathap propkai
Thai longer set of three drum-cycle patterns

nathap sawngmai
Thai shorter set of three drum-cycle patterns

naw
Upland Thai (Lahu) gourd mouth organ

ncas
Hmong Jew's harp made of metal

nehara
Kettle drum of nobat ensemble, Malaysia

nem
Javanese pitch name

nhạc cải cách
Early form of Vietnamese popular music from the late 1930s

nhạc dân tộc cải biên
Modernized "traditional" Vietnamese music mixing lowland and upland genres

nhạc huyền
Nguyễn-dynasty court ensemble

nhạc lễ
Ritual ensemble of southern Vietnam

nhạc mới
Modern popular songs of Vietnam

nhạc tài tử
Vocal/instrumental chamber music of southern Vietnam

nhạc tiền chiến
Romantic Vietnamese songs of the 1940s, inspired by German lieder

nhịp
Metrical organization of rhythm in Vietnamese music

nobat
Malay-based Muslim drum and oboe ensemble

node
Vibration-free point

nói lối
Metrically free, introductory phrases for Vietnamese songs

nora
Alternate name for manora theater in Thailand

nose flute
Small, soft-sounding flute activated by air from the player's nostrils

octavina
Guitar-shaped plucked lute of Philippines

ogung
Large vertical gong of Sumatra

Orang Asli
Upland peoples of peninsular Malaysia

orkes gambus
South Sumatra Arab-influenced music

orkes Melayu
Malay songs with stringed instruments

ostinato
Continuously repeated pattern

òzi
Long, single-headed goblet-shaped drum of Burma

pabasa
Chanting of Christ's Passion in Philippines

paggabbang
Tausug secular singing style

paghiling
Sung by serenaders in harana ritual, Philippines

palabunibunyan
Maguindanao traditional ensemble

palendag
Maguindanao notched flute

Pali
Sacred language of Theravada Buddhism

palwei
Bamboo, end-blown fipple flute of Burma

pamamaalam
Serenade at end of harana ritual, Philippines

pamanhikan
Tradition followed during marriage proposal, Philippines

pananapatan
(1) First songs of harana ritual, Philippines; (2) Tagalog outdoor Christmas drama

pandanggo
Batangas song-dance

panerus
Low-pitched metallophone of Sunda

pangongka'an
Sama gong ensemble

pantun
(1) Malay form of four-line poetry verses; (2) rhymed couplets, pan-Indonesian; (3) Buginese/Makassarese sung quatrains, also found in Maluku; (4) Sundanese narrative epic performances with kacapi

panunuluyan
Outdoor Christmas drama in Philippines

parwa
Balinese human theater derived from wayang wong

pasasalamat
Songs sung during harana ritual, Philippines

pasyon
Vernacular text about Christ's Passion, sung in Philippines

pa'talà
Burmese suspended bamboo xylophone with twenty-four keys

pathet
Javanese modal classification system

patokan
The structural outline of a piece of Sundanese music

patut
Cirebonese modal classification system

patutan
Balinese modal classification system

pa'waìñ
Burmese circle of twenty-one tuned drums in a wood frame

pedagogy
Methods of teaching

pejogedan bumbung
Xylophone ensemble for joged dance, Bali

peking
Sundanese high-pitched metallophone

pélog
Gapped-scale pentatonic tuning system, found throughout Indonesia

penca/pencak silat
Indonesian martial arts performance

penunggul
Javanese pitch name

peruncung
Bidayuh bamboo tubes

pey pork
Khmer free-reed pipe with finger holes

pey prabauh
Khmer cylindrical double-reed aerophone

phách
Piece of wood or bamboo struck by two beaters, Vietnam

phanya
Courtship poetry in northeast Thailand

phin
Plucked lute of northeast Thailand

phin hai
Northeast Thai ceramic jars with plucked rubber bands

phin phia
Multi-stringed stick zither from northern Thailand

phleng dio
Solo instrumental classical Thai compositions

phleng hang khrüang
Short "coda" pieces attached to longer compositions in Thailand

phleng kar
Cambodian village wedding song

phleng khorat
Repartee songs of Nakhon Ratchasima (Khorat) city, Thailand

phleng kret
Classification term for "miscellaneous" compositions in Thai music

phleng la
Thai compositions for ending a concert

phleng laim
Class of Khmer court compositions for dance

phleng lamtat
Repartee village song of central Thailand

phleng luk krung
Thai popular song accompanied by Western instruments

phleng luk thung
Popular music genre from Thailand

phleng naphat
Thai instrumental compositions for ceremony and theater

phleng phua chiwit
Thai popular music incorporating social criticism

phleng phuang malai
Thai village song genre sung in a circle

phleng phün ban
Village folk song genres of Thailand

phleng rüa
Antiphonal songs for men and women, sung on boats in Thailand

phleng rüang
Ceremonial suites and overtures in Thai classical music

phleng skor
Class of classical compositions for Khmer drumming

phleng tap
Short suites of melodious compositions in Thailand

phleng thai düm
The classical repertoire of Thailand

phleng thai sakon
Thai popular music genre

phleng thao
Thai composition in three chan tempo levels

phleng yai
Long, texturally complex classical Thai compositions

pi
Thai family of double or quadruple reeds of various shapes

pi aw
Thai short, cylindrical quadruple reed, rare

pi chanai
Double-reed aerophone from Thailand

pi chawa
Thai conical wooden quadruple reed, of Javanese origin

pi choan
Khmer medium rhythmic cycle, "second level"

pi chum
Northern Thai free-reed pipes with finger holes

pi kaeo
Quadruple reed with bulbous-shaped body from Laos

pi mawn
Large, conical quadruple reed of the Man ensemble

pi nai
Double-reed aerophone from Thailand

pinalaiyan
Kalinga-Tinggian gong and drum ensemble

pinn
Extinct angular harp from Angkor carvings

pinn peat
Khmer classical court ensemble

pipa
Chinese pear-shaped lute

piphat
Classical ensemble of Thailand

piphat mai khaeng
Thai piphat ensemble with hard mallets

piphat mai nuam
Thai piphat ensemble with padded mallets

pokok
Central melody and basis for figuration in Balinese music

pong Lang
Northeast Thai vertical xylophone of logs

pop Melayu
Western pop band with solo singer in Sumatra

pop Sunda
Indigenous popular music of Sunda

portamento
Melodic slide between two pitches

Prambanan
Hindu temple in Central Java

prasaja
"Forthright, austere," in Javanese

prawa
Cirebonese five-tone tuning system

preret
Wooden double-reed aerophone of Bali and Lombok

pulakan
Tausug/Sama deep-rimmed bossed gong

pulao
Sama bamboo ring-stop flute

punto
Standard melodic formula in Philippines

qeej
Hmong free-reed mouth organ with bamboo pipes and elongated wind chest

quan họ
Northern Vietnamese antiphonal song performed in boats

Qur'ān
The Islamic canon of Muhammad's writings, intended to be chanted

raj nplaim
Hmong free-reed pipe with finger holes

raj pus li
Hmong fipple flute

Ramakian
Thai version of the Indian Ramayana epic

Ramayana
Indian epic

rammana
Thai wooden frame drum with single head

ramwong
Western-influenced social dance from Thailand

ranat
Thai xylophones

ranat ek
Lead xylophone in a Thai classical ensemble

ranat thum
Thai lower-pitched xylophone, with seventeen or eighteen keys

randai
(1) Type of Minangkabau theater including self-defense (pencak silat); (2) West Sumatra danced theatrical form; (3) South Sumatra welcoming dance

randu kentir
Folk dance of Indramayu

rapa'i
Acehnese frame drum

Reamker
Cambodian version of Indian Ramayana

rebab
(1) Two-stringed bowed spike lute found throughout Southeast Asia; (2) Malay three-stringed, long-necked fiddle

rebana
(1) Malay single-headed, round frame drum, sometimes found with spokes; (2) Frame and bowl-shaped drums of Indonesia

redap
Bengkulu frame drum

rejang
Balinese women's temple dance

repartee
Sung debate pitting men against women; often a courtship ritual

rincik
(1) Sundanese small fifteen-stringed zither; (2) High-pitched gong-chime of Sunda; (3) Balinese small set of upturned cymbals

roam vung
Khmer popular social dance in circular form

rodat
(1) Malaysian theatrical genre of Islamic origin; (2) South Sumatra secularized zikir performance

rôi nuóc
Water-puppet theater found in northern Vietnam

rondalla
Plucked stringed instrument ensemble of Philippines

rondo
Musical form based on a recurring phrase

roneat
Khmer xylophone

roneat dek
Khmer higher-pitched metallophone, with twenty-one keys

roneat ek
Khmer higher-pitched xylophone, with twenty-one keys

roneat thung
Khmer lower-pitched xylophone, with sixteen keys

ronggeng
(1) Professional female singer-dancer of Indonesia; (2) Genre of popular social dance in Malaysia; (3) Couple dancing and singing

ru
Class of Vietnamese lullaby songs

ruan
Chinese moon-shaped lute

rudat
Performance held inside mosques in Cirebon

ruding
Jew's harp of Borneo

rumanea
Khmer frame drum with single head

ruwatan
Type of protective wayang ceremony in Java and Cirebon

sagayan
Maguindanao spirit communication dance

saih
Tuning, scale in Balinese music

saih angklung
Tuning system for Balinese gamelan angklung

saih gendèr wayang
Five-tone tuning system in Balinese music

saih gong
Tuning system for Balinese gamelan gong

saih pitu
Seven-tone tuning system in Balinese music

saing
Khmer conch shell trumpet

salawek dulang
West Sumatra vocal and brass-tray music

saléndro
Nearly equidistant pentatonic tuning system in Sundanese music

saluang
West Sumatra end-blown bamboo flute

sam chan
Longest of three rhythmic cycles in Thai music

saman
Acehnese men's percussive religious dance

Samawa
West Sumbawan culture area

sampho
Khmer horizontal barrel drum with two heads

sampi'/sampeq
Kenyah/Kayan plucked lute

sanang
Palawan pair of suspended gongs

Sanskrit
Classical language of India

santacrusan
Christian Maytime processions in Philippines

sàñdeyà
Old Burmese term now applied to piano

sáo
Horizontal bamboo flute without membrane

sapeh/sapi'
Kenyah/Kayan plucked lute

saron
Indonesian metallophone with trough resonator

saron barung
Javanese medium metallophone with trough resonator

saron demung
Javanese large metallophone with trough resonator

saron peking
Javanese small metallophone with trough resonator

sarswela
Spanish-derived music-drama of Philippines

sarunel sarunei
Reed aerophone of Sumatra

satong
Kajang bamboo tube zither

saúñ
Burmese arched harp, the last surviving harp in Southeast Asia

saw
Northern Thai repartee song accompanied by *pi chum* ensemble

saw duang
Two-stringed fiddle from Thailand

saw lakhawn
Northern Thai theater

saw pip
Northeast Thai bowed lute with metal can body

saw sam sai
Thai three-stringed spike fiddle with coconut body

saw u
Thai two-stringed fiddle with coconut body

sawng chan
Medium-length rhythmic cycle in Thai music

say diev
Half-gourd, chest-resonated monochord of Cambodia

sbek tauch
Khmer small-size shadow-puppet theater

sbek thomm
Khmer large-shadow-puppet theater

seka
Communal music-making group in Bali and Lombok

selampit
Malay narrative genre accompanied by rebab

selengut/selingut
North Borneo nose flute

selisir
Tuning system for Balinese gamelan pelégongan

semagi
Tiboli set of melody gongs

sendratari
Modern Indonesian dance-drama with music, created in the midtwentieth century

sep noi
Laotian string and flute ensemble of Luang Phrabang, called *maholi* in Vientiane

sep nyai
Laotian classical ensemble of Luang Phrabang, called *piphat* in Vientiane

sepha
Thai narrative genre accompanied by pair of krup

serdam
South Sumatra end-blown ring flute

serunai
Malay multiple-reed wooden aerophone

seudati
Acehnese men's martial group dance

shaman
Animistic tranced medium dealing with spirits

shenai
Conical double-reed aerophone from India

sheng
Free-reed mouth organ from China

Shiva
Hindu deity

sì
Pair of small, bell-shaped cymbals from Burma

Siamese
Former name for peoples of Thailand

sidapurna
Acrobatic performance of Cirebon

silat
Malaysian martial-arts-derived dance with drum accompaniment

sindil
Maguindanaon love songs

sing
Pair of Lao small cymbals connected with cord

sinh tiên
Vietnamese scraped wooden clapper with jingling coins

Sino-Tibetan
Language family including Burmese, Hmong, and Yao

sinulug
Maguindanao rhythmic mode

Sisters Trung
Two celebrated Vietnamese sisters who led a rebellion against the Chinese about A. D. 40

sitār
Long-necked plucked Indian lute

Sita
Female lead character from the Indian epic Ramayana

sito
Large, double-headed "royal" drum of Burma

siyem
Medium hanging gong of Java

skor arakk
Khmer single-headed goblet-shaped drum of clay or wood

skor chey
Khmer two-headed cylindrical drum

skor chhaiyaim
Long, vase-shaped single-headed Khmer drum

skor khek
Pair of long drums from Cambodia

skor klang khek
Khmer long, cylindrical, two-headed drums

skor thomm
Pair of large barrel drums from Cambodia

skor yike
Large frame drum in yike theater, Cambodia

slekk
Tree-leaf mirliton of Cambodia

sléndro
Nearly equidistant tuning system, found throughout Indonesia; *saléndro* in Sunda

sluday
Bilaan polychordal tube zither

sneng
Khmer animal horn with free reed

so i
Lao two-stringed fiddle with cylindrical body

so on
Lao two-stringed fiddle with coconut body

song lang
Vietnamese foot-operated wooden drum with clapper attached

soran
Loud-playing ensemble of Java

sorog
Gapped scale pentatonic tuning system in Sundanese music

sralai
Khmer multiple-reed aerophone with bulging shape

sralai klang khek
Khmer small wood or ivory double reed with flared bell

srimpi
Refined women's court dance of Java

stambul
Jakarta-based theatrical form

string
Thai rock and roll music

suat
Ordinary style of chanting Buddhist texts

sukhwan
Spirit ritual common to Thailand, Laos, and Burma

suling
End-blown bamboo ring-stop flute, found throughout Indonesia and Philippines

süng
Northern Thai plucked lute

suona
Chinese oboe

swidden
Agricultural practice in which steep hillside fields are cleared and burned

tabuh
Individual composition in Balinese music

tabuhan
Gong chime and ensemble of Sumatra

tabut
West Sumatra religious theatrical work

tagunggo
(1) Rhythmic mode in Philippines: (2) Yakan *kulintang* ensemble; (3) Kalagan set of heavy suspended gongs

tagutok
Maranao scraper

Tai
Language family common to mainland Southeast Asia

Tai-Kadai
Language family including Thai, Lao, and Shan

takik
Bontok men's dance

taklempong
Malay ensemble for *randai,* consisting of three gong chimes

tala
(1) Rhythmic modal system used in Indian classical performance; (2) Bronze or iron gong, Weyewa language

talempong/tilempong
West/North Sumatra gong-chime and ensemble

tambul
(1) Sama long bronze cylindrical drum; (2) Kalinga-Tinggian cylindrical drum

tamlang agung
Maguindanao small bamboo half-tubes

tamuk
Sama large hanging gong

tân nhạc
Modern popular songs of Vietnam

tang
Tiboli lowest-sounding gong

tanjidor
Brass bands in Sumatra

taphon
Thai asymmetrical, two-headed barrel drum mounted horizontally

tari
Dance, pan-Indonesian term

tari asyek
Court-derived dance and dance-drama of Malaysia

tari inai
Northern Malay dance genre

tarling
Guitar-and-flute-based popular music of Cirebon

tawag/tawak
Large, deep-rimmed gongs of Borneo

tawak-tawak
Medium-size suspended gong of Sumatra

tayil
Tausug slow singing style

tayò
Violin-shaped Mon fiddle, obsolete

tayuban
Musical party with singer-dancers, common in Indonesia and Malaysia

te-ed
Yakan introductory instrumental piece

te-er
Bontok ritual of abstinence from work

tembang
Type of metered vocal performance in Indonesia

tembang Sunda
Aristocratic sung poetry of Sunda

Temiar
Subgroup of the Senoi people of upland Malaysia

teng thing
Northern Thai barrel drum, similar to taphon

terbang
Indonesian single-headed Muslim frame drum

tetawak
(1) Single hanging bossed gong of Malaysia; (2) Hanging gong of Sumatra

tham khwan
Thai ceremony to restore a person's spiritual essence

thang
(1) Thai melodic idiom of a particular instrument; (2) Thai style of a teacher or "school"; (3) Thai pitch level of a composition, mode

thañ hmañ
Tonic pitch based on lowest note of *hnè*, Burma

thaun
Goblet-shaped drum with single head, Cambodia

Theravada
Buddhist sect originating in Sri Lanka

thet
Thai Buddhist preaching, in Pali or vernacular

thet mahachat
Thai preaching/chanting the story of Prince Wetsandon, the Buddha-to-be

thon
Thai wood or clay single-headed, goblet-shaped drum

tidtu
Maguindanao rhythmic mode

tiêu
End-blown notch flute of Vietnam

tiêu nhạc
Vietnam's court ensemble of strings

timang
Iban ritual chanting

timbre
The quality or character of a musical sound

tingklik
Bamboo xylophone of Bali

togunggak/togunggu
Murut interlocking bamboo tubes

tong
Kajang Jew's harp

tongkungon
Sabah bamboo tube zither

Tonle Sap
The "Great Lake" in western Cambodia

topayya
Kalinga gong ensemble of six men

topeng
Indonesian mask or masked dance performance

touxian
Chinese two-stringed fiddle of Chaozhou province, China

trebang
Frame drum of Cirebon

trebang randu kentir
Drumming ensemble of Indramayu

trompong
Balinese gong–chime played by soloist

trông
Generic term for Vietnamese drums, most with nailed head(s)

trông chầu
In tuồng theater of Vietnam, a large drum played by an audience member offering praise or criticism

trông com
Vietnamese two-headed drum with rice paste on heads

trông đồng
Bronze drum idiophone of Vietnam

tror
Generic Khmer term for bowed lutes

tror chhe
Khmer two-stringed cylindrical fiddle, tuned D–A

tror Khmer
Khmer three-stringed spike fiddle with a coconut body

tror ou
Khmer two-stringed fiddle with coconut resonator

tror so tauch
Khmer two-stringed cylindrical fiddle, tuned G–D

tror so thomm
Khmer lower-pitched two-stringed fiddle, tuned D–A

t'rung
Upland Vietnamese vertical bamboo xylophone

Truòng Son Ranges
Mountain range running through southern Vietnam

tukimug
Maranao poetic segment in music

tumbuk kalang
Malaysian folk performance derived from rice-pounding songs

tung-tung
Tausug rhythmic ostinato in kulintangan

tunggalan
Tausug large agung

tunrung ganrang
Makassarese processional drum music for sailors

tuntungan
(1) Tausug upper *kulintang* gong; (2) Yakan log drum

tuồng
Vietnamese theater genre

ty bā lệnh
Nguyễn-dynasty ritual court ensemble

uyon-uyon
Social events accompanying ceremonies in Java

variable-pitch instruments
Instruments, such as fiddles and flutes, whose pitch is infinitely controllable during performance

vè
Class of satirical songs of Vietnam

Vishnu
Hindu deity

vong cổ
Expandable song structure used in cải luong theater, Vietnam

vung phleng pey keo
Khmer court ensemble for ancestral worship

wa
Kajang sung narrative form

wà
Small clapper of split bamboo, from Burma

wai khru
Thai ritual ceremony to honor one's teacher

wat
A Buddhist temple complex in Thailand

wayang
Shadow puppetry of Indonesia

wayang golèk
Three-dimensional rod puppetry in Java, Cirebon, and Sunda

wayang kulit
General term for leather shadow-puppet theater, Throughout Indonesia and Malaysia

wayang purwa
Shadow puppetry based on Hindu epics, found in Java and Sumatra

wayang Sasak
Shadow puppetry about Amir Hamza, found in Lombok

wayang Siam
Indigenous shadow-puppet theater in northern Malaysia

wayang wong
Masked human theater of Bali and Java

wot
Circular bamboo panpipes of northeast Thailand

xi xov
Hmong two-stringed fiddle

xinyao
Contemporary Singaporean songs in Mandarin Chinese

xuân phả
Ancient genre of masked plays from Thanh Hóa province

ya kwìñ
Pair of Burmese large cymbals

yaigho
All-night singing ceremony in Sumba

yikay
Shan (Burma) dance drama

yike
Village theater genre of *Chăm* origin

yoùdayà
Burmese genre of classical songs said to be derived from the Siamese at Ayuthaya

yue qin
Chinese moon-shaped lute

yue she
Chinese music clubs, found in Vietnam

zapin
West Asian-derived songs and dances of Malaysia and Sumatra

za'pwè
Burmese classical theater accompanied by *hsaiñ*

zarzuela
Spanish-language play with music and dance

zheng
Chinese sixteen-stringed zither

zikir
Chanting of Islamic verse, usually accompanied by drumming; also *dikir*

zither
Chordophone with parallel strings

zouchang
Singaporean narrative tradition of Chinese origin

A Guide to Publications

SOUTHEAST ASIAN MUSICS: AN OVERVIEW

Cadar, Usopay Hamdag. 1971. "The Maranao Kolintang Music: An Analysis of the Instruments, Musical Organization, Etymologies, and Historical Documents." M.A. thesis, University of Washington.

———. 1980. "Context and Style in the Vocal Music of the Muranao in Mindanao, Philippines." Ph.D. dissertation, University of Washington.

Gironcourt, Georges de. 1943. "Recherches de geographic musicale en Indochine." *Bulletin de la Société des études indochinoises* 17:3–174.

Kunst, Jaap. 1973 [1934]. *Music in Java: Its History, Its Theory, and Its Technique.* 3rd ed. rev. and enlarged by Ernst Heins. 2 vols. The Hague: Martinus Nijhoff.

McPhee, Colin. 1966. *Music in Bali: A Study in Form and Instrumental Organization in Balinese Orchestral Music.* New Haven, CT, London: Yale University Press.

Osman, Mohd. Taib, ed. 1974. *Traditional Music and Drama of Southeast Asia.* Kuala Lumpur: Dewan Bahasa dan Pustaka.

Sutton, R. Anderson. 1991. *Traditions of Gamelan Music in Java: Musical Pluralism and Regional Identity.* Cambridge Studies in Ethnomusicology. Cambridge: Cambridge University Press.

Tenzer, Michael. 1991. *Balinese Music.* Singapore: Periplus Editions.

Trần văn Khê. 1962. *La musique vietnamienne traditionelle.* Paris: Presses Universitaires de France.

van Zanten, Wim. 1989. *Sundanese Music in the Cianjuran Style: Anthropological and Musicological Aspects of Tembang Sunda.* Providence, RI: Foris Publications.

WAVES OF CULTURAL INFLUENCE

Condominas, Georges. 1952. "Le lithophone préhistorique de Ndut Lieng Krak." *Bulletin de l'École Française d'Extrême-Orient* 45:359–392.

Miller, Terry E., and Jarernchai Chonpairot. 1994. "A History of Siamese Music Reconstructed from Western Documents, 1505–1932." *Crossroads: An Interdisciplinary Journal of Southeast Asian Studies* 8(2):1–192.

Rodrigue, Yves. 1992. *Nat-Pwe.* Garthmore, Scotland: Paul Strachan-Kiscadale.

Roseman, Marina. 1991. *Healing Sounds from the Malaysian Rainforest: Temiar Music and Medicine.* Berkeley: University of California Press.

Stalberg, Roberta Helmer. 1984. *China's Puppets.* San Francisco: China Books.

Yampolsky, Philip. 1991. *Music of Indonesia 3: Music from the Outskirts of Jakarta: Gambang Kromong.* Washington, D.C.: Smithsonian/Folkways SFCD 40057. Liner notes.

CULTURE, POLITICS, AND WAR

Brandon, James R. 1967. *Theatre in Southeast Asia*. Cambridge, MA: Harvard University Press.

Osman, Mohd. Taib, ed. 1974. *Traditional Music and Drama of Southeast Asia*. Kuala Lumpur: Dewan Bahasa dan Pustaka.

Sutton, R. Anderson. 1991. *Traditions of Gamelan Music in Java: Musical Pluralism and Regional Identity*. Cambridge Studies in Ethnomusicology. Cambridge: Cambridge University Press.

Tan Sooi Beng. 1993. *Bangsawan: A Social and Stylistic History of Popular Malay Opera*. Singapore: Oxford University Press.

Tenzer, Michael. 1991. *Balinese Music*. Singapore: Periplus Editions.

Trần văn Khê. 1962. *La musique vietnamienne traditionelle*. Paris: Presses Universitaires de France.

van Zanten, Wim. 1989. *Sundanese Music in the Cianjuran Style: Anthropological and Musicological Aspects of Tembang Sunda*. Providence, RI: Foris Publications.

THE IMPACT OF MODERNIZATION ON TRADITIONAL MUSICS

Ryker, Harrison, ed. 1991. *New Music in the Orient*. Buren, Netherlands: Frits Knuf.

Sanger, Annette. 1988. "Blessing or Blight? The Effects of Touristic Dance-Drama on Village-Life in Singapadu, Bali." In *Come Mek Me Hol' Yu Han': The Impact of Tourism on Traditional Music*, ed. Adrienne L. Kaeppler, 89–104. Kingston: Jamaica Memory Bank.

Sarkissian, Margaret. 1994. "'Whose Tradition?' Tourism as a Catalyst in the Creation of a Modern Malaysian 'Tradition'." *Nhac Viet* 3(1–2):31–46.

Tenzer, Michael. 1991. *Balinese Music*. Singapore: Periplus Editions.

THE KHMER PEOPLE OF CAMBODIA

Chonpairot, Jarernchai. 1981. "The Diffusion of the Vina in Southeast Asia." In *Proceedings of the Saint Thyagaraja Music Festivals: Cleveland, Ohio, 1978-81*, ed. T. Temple Tuttle. 98–108.

His Royal Highness Prince Damrong (Rajanubhap). 1931. *Siamese Musical Instruments*. 2nd ed. Bangkok: The Royal Institute.

Groslier, Bernard-Philippe. 1965. "Danse et musique sous les rois d'Angkor." *Felicitation Volumes of Southeast Asian Studies* 2:283–292.

Hood, Mantle. 1982. *The Ethnomusicologist*. 2nd ed. Kent, OH: Kent State University Press.

Jacq-Hergoualc'h, Michel. 1982. "Le Roman source d'inscription de la peinture khmère à la fin du XIXe et au debut du XXe siècle." *Bulletin de l'École Française d'Extrême-Orient* 126:3–10.

Morton, David. 1974. "Vocal Tones in Traditional Thai Music" *Selected Reports in Ethnomusicology* 2(l):89–99.

———. 1976. *The Traditional Music of Thailand*. Berkeley: University of California Press.

Musique Khmère. 1969. Phnom Penh: Imprimerie Sangkum Reastr Niyum.

Pich, Sal. 1970. *Lumnoam Sangkhep ney Phleng Khmer* (A Brief Survey on Khmer Music). Phnom Penh: Éditions de l'Institut Bouddhique.

Sachs, Curt. 1940. *The History of Musical Instruments*. New York: Norton.

Smithies, Michael. 1971. "*Likay*: A Note on the Origin, Form, and Future of Siamese Folk Opera." *Journal of the Siam Society* 59:33–64.

Thiounn, Samdech Chaufea. 1930. *Danses cambodgiennes*. Phnom Penh: Bibliothèque Royale Cambodge.

Zhou Daguan. 1967. *Notes on the Customs of Cambodia*. Trans. from French of Paul Pelliot by J. Gillman D'arcy Paul. Bangkok: Social Science Association Press.

THAILAND

Bowring, John. 1969 [1857]. *The Kingdom and People of Siam.* Kuala Lumpur: Oxford University Press.

Dhanit Yupho. 1987. *Nangsü khrüang dontri thai/Book of Thai Musical Instruments,* combination reprint of Dhanit Yupho 1957 and 1971, with new illustrations. Bangkok: Fine Arts Department.

Ellis, Alexander J. 1885. "On the Musical Scales of Various Nations." *Journal of the Society of Arts* 33:485–527.

Glanius, Mr. 1682. *A New Voyage to the East-Indies,* 2nd ed. London: H. Rodes.

Graham, W[alter]. A[rmstrong]. 1912. *Siam: A Handbook of Practical, Commercial, and Political Information.* London: Alexander Moring.

Hipkins, A.J. 1945 [1888]. *Musical Instruments Historic, Rare, and Unique.* London: A. and C. Black.

La Loubere, Simon de. 1691. *Du Royaume de Siam.* Paris: Jean-Baptiste Coignard.

———. 1969 [1693]. *A New Historical Relation of the Kingdom of Siam.* Kuala Lumpur: Oxford University Press.

Landon, Margaret. 1944. *Anna and the King of Siam.* New York: John Day.

Léonowens, Anna Harriette. 1870. *The English Governess at the Siamese Court.* Boston: Fields, Osgood.

Mendes Pinto, Fernão. 1663 [1558]. *The Voyages and Adventures of Ferdinand Mendez Pinto [Peregrinação].* Translated by H. C. Gent. London: J. Macock.

Miller, Terry E., and Jarernchai Chonpairot. 1994. "A History of Siamese Music Reconstructed from Western Documents, 1505–1932." *Crossroads* 8:1–192.

Morton, David. 1976. *The Traditional Music of Thailand.* Berkeley: University of California Press.

Verney, Frederick. 1885. *Notes on Siamese Musical Instruments.* London: William Clowes and Sons.

Vincent, Frank, Jr. 1874. *The Land of the White Elephant.* New York: Harper and Brothers.

LAOS

Brunet, Jacques. 1992 [1973]. *Laos: Traditional Music of the South.* Auvidis/UNESCO D 8042. Compact disc and commentary.

BURMA (MYANMAR)

Becker, Judith. 1969. "Anatomy of a Mode." *Ethnomusicology* 13(2):267–279.

———. 1980. "Burma: Instrumental Ensembles." *The New Grove Dictionary of Music and Musicians,* ed. Stanley Sadie. London: Macmillan.

Garfias, Robert. 1975. "Preliminary Thoughts on Burmese Modes." *Asian Music* 7(1):39–49.

———. 1980a. "Burma: Classical Vocal Music." *The New Grove Dictionary of Music and Musicians,* ed. Stanley Sadie. London: Macmillan.

———. 1980b. "Burma: Theory." *The New Grove Dictionary of Music and Musicians,* ed. Stanley Sadie. London: Macmillan.

———. 1985. "The Development of the Modern Burmese Hsaing Ensemble." *Asian Music* 16:1–28.

K [Khin Zaw]. 1981. *Burmese Culture: General and Particular.* Rangoon: Sarpay Beikman.

Khin Zaw. 1940. "Burmese Music: a Preliminary Enquiry." *Journal of the Burma Research Society* 30(3):387–460.

Marano, P A. 1900. "A Note on Burmese Music." In *Burma,* ed. Max Ferrar and Bertha Ferrar, appendix C. London: Sampson Low, Marston.

Okell, John. 1964. "Learning Music from a Burmese Master." *Man* 64:183.

Powers, Harold S. 1980. "Mode." *The New Grove Dictionary of Music and Musicians,* ed. Stanley Sadie. London: Macmillan.

Williamson, Muriel, ed. 1968. "The Construction and Decoration of One Burmese Harp." *Selected Reports in Ethnomusicology* 1(2):45–72.

———. 1979. "The Basic Tune of a Late Eighteenth-Century Burmese Classical Song." *Musica Asiatica* 2:155–195.

———. 1980. "Burma: Harp." *The New Grove Dictionary of Music and Musicians*, ed. Stanley Sadie. London: Macmillan.

PENINSULAR MALAYSIA

D'Cruz, Marion Francena. 1979. "Joget Gamdan, a Study of Its Contemporary Practice." M.A. thesis, Universiti Sains Malaysia.

al-Faruqi, Lois Ibsen. 1985. "Music, Musicians and Muslim Law." *Asian Music* 17(l):3–36.

Ghulam-Sarwar Yousof. 1976. "The Kelantan Mak Yong Dance Theater, a Study of Performance Structure." Ph.D. dissertation, University of Hawai'i.

———. 1987. "Bangsawan: The Malay Opera." *Tenggara* 20:3–20.

Ginsberg, Henry D. 1972. "The Manohra Dance-Drama: An Introduction." *Journal of the Siam Society* 60:169–181.

Hamilton, A. W. 1982 [1941]. *Malay Pantuns.* Singapore: Eastern Universities Press.

Ku Zam Zam, Ku Idris. 1983. "Alat-Alat Muzik Dalam Ensembel Wayang Kulit, Mek Mulung dan Gendang Keling di Kedah Utara" (Musical Instruments in the Shadow Play, *mek mulung*, and *gendang keling* Ensembles of North Kedah). In *Kajian Budaya dan Masyarakat di Malaysia*, ed. Mohd. Taib Osman and Wan Kadir Yusoff, 1–52. Kuala Lumpur: Dewan Bahasa dan Pustaka.

———. 1985. "Nobat DiRaja Kedah: Warisan Seni Muzik Istana Melayu Melaka" (Nobat of the Kedah Sultan: A Musical Heritage of the Malay Malacca Sultanate). In *Warisan Dunia Melayu, Teras Peradaban Malaysia,* ed. Abdul Latiff Abu Bakar. Kuala Lumpur: Biro Penerbitan GAPENA.

Malm, William. 1974. "Music in Kelantan, Malaysia and Some of Its Cultural Implications." In *Studies in Malaysian Oral and Musical Traditions*, 1–49. Michigan. Papers on South and Southeast Asia, 8. Ann Arbor: University of Michigan Press.

Matusky, Patricia. 1993. *Malaysian Shadow Play and Music: Continuity of an Oral Tradition.* Kuala Lumpur: Oxford University Press.

Mohammad Anis Mohammad Nor. 1986. *Randai Dance of Minangkabau Sumatra, with Labanotation Scores.* Kuala Lumpur: University of Malaysia.

Mohammad Ghouse Nasaruddin. 1979. "The Desa Performing Arts of Malaysia." Ph.D. dissertation, Indiana University.

Mohd. Taib Osman, ed. 1974. *Traditional Drama and Music in Southeast Asia.* Kuala Lumpur: Dewan Bahasa dan Pustaka.

Sweeney, Amin. 1972. *Ramayana and the Malay Shadow Play.* Kuala Lumpur: National University of Malaysia Press.

Tan Sooi Beng. 1988. "The Thai Manora in Malaysia: Adapting to the Penang Chinese Community." *Asian Folklore Studies* 47(1):19–34.

———. 1993. *Bangsawan: A Social and Stylistic History of Popular Malay Opera.* Singapore: Oxford University Press.

VIETNAM

Brăiloiu, Constantin. 1955. "Un problème de tonalité." In *Mélanges d'histoire et d'esthétique musicales offerts à Paul-Marie Masson*, 1: 63–75. Paris: Richard Masse.

Phan Huy Lê, Hà Văn Tấn, and Hoàng Xuân Chinh. 1989. "Những buóc đi cửa lịch sử Việt Nam." In *Văn Hóa Việt Nam*, 34–40. Hànội: Ban Văn Nghệ Trung Uong.

Phan Khoang. 1961. *Việt Nam pháp thuộc sử* (History of Colonialism in Vietnam). Saigon: Sống Mói.

Trần Văn Khê. 1962. *La musique Vietnamienne traditionelle.* Paris: Presses Universitaires de France.

Việt Nhạc. 1948. Number 1, 16 August.

SINGAPORE

Perris, Arnold. 1978. "Chinese Wayang: The Survival of Chinese Opera in the Streets of Singapore." *Ethnomusicology* 22(2):297–306.

UPLAND AND MINORITY PEOPLES OF MAINLAND SOUTHEAST ASIA

Lebar, Frank M. 1964. *Ethnic Groups of Mainland Southeast Asia.* New Haven, CT: Human Relations Area Files.

MUSIC OF UPLAND MINORITIES IN BURMA, LAOS, AND THAILAND

Lewis, Paul, and Elaine Lewis. 1984. *Peoples of the Golden Triangle: Six Tribes in Thailand.* London: Thames and Hudson.

THE INDIGENOUS PEOPLES (ORANG ASLI) OF THE MALAY PENINSULA

Oesch, Hans. 1977 *The Protomalayans of Malacca.* Bärenreiter Musicaphon BM 30 L 2563. LP disk.
Roseman, Marina. 1990. "Head, Heart, Odor and Shadow: The Structure of the Self, Ritual Performance and the Emotional World." *Ethos* 18(3):227–250.
———. 1991. *Healing Sounds from the Malaysian Rainforest.* Berkeley: University of California Press.
———. 1994. "Les chants de rêve: des frontièrs mouvantes dans le monde temiar." *Anthropologie et Sociétés* 18(2):121–144.
———. 1995. *Dream Songs and Healing Sounds in the Rainforests of Malaysia.* Smithsonian Folkways SF CD 40417. Compact disc.
———. 1996. "'Pure Products Go Crazy': Rainforest Healing in a Nation-State." In *The Performance of Healing,* ed. Carol Laderman and Marina Roseman, 233–269. New York: Routledge.
Schebesta, Paul. 1928. *Among the Forest Dwarfs of Malaya,* trans. Arthur Chambers. London: Hutchinson.

INDONESIA

Arps, Bernard. 1992. *Tembang in Two Traditions: Performance and Interpretation of Javanese Literature.* London: School of Oriental and African Studies.
Baier, Randal E. 1986. "Si Duriat Keueung: The Sundanese Angklung Ensemble of West Java, Indonesia." MA thesis, Wesleyan University.
Bakan, Michael B. 1999. *Music of Death and New Creation: Experiences in the World of Balinese Gamelan Beleganjur.* Chicago: University of Chicago Press.
Brakel-Papenhuijzen, Clara. 1992. *The Bedhaya Court Dances of Central Java.* Leiden: E. J. Brill.
Brinner, Benjamin E. 1995. *Knowing Music, Making Music: Javanese Gamelan and the Theory of Musical Competence and Interaction.* Chicago: University of Chicago Press.
———. 2007. *The Music of Central Java: Experiencing Music, Expressing Culture.* New York: Oxford University Press.
Gold, Lisa. 2004. *Music in Bali: Experiencing Music, Expressing Culture.* New York: Oxford University Press.
Hefner, Robert. 1987. "The Politics of Popular Art: Tayuban Dance and Culture Change in East Java." *Indonesia* 43:75–94.
Heimarck, Brita. 2004. *Balinese Discourses on Music and Modernization: Village Voices and Urban Views.* New York: Routledge.

Heins, Ernst L. 1977. "Goong Renteng: Aspects of Orchestral Music in a Sundanese Village." Ph.D. dissertation, University of Amsterdam.

Herbert, Mimi. 2002. *Voices of the Puppet Masters: The Wayang Golek Theater of Indonesia*. Honolulu: University of Hawaii Press.

Hoffman, Stanley B. 1978. "Epistemology and Music: A Javanese Example." *Ethnomusicology* 22(1):69–88.

Kartomi, Margaret. 1976. "Performance, Music and Meaning in Réyog Ponorogo." *Indonesia* 22:85–130.

———. 1979. "Minangkabau Musical Culture: The Contemporary Scene and Recent Attempts at its Modernization." In *What Is Modern Indonesian Culture?* ed. G. Davis, 19–36. Athens: Ohio University Press.

———. 1981. "Randai Theatre in West Sumatra: Components, Music, Origins, and Recent Change." *Review of Indonesian and Malayan Affairs* 15(l):l–44.

———. 1986. "Muslim Music in West Sumatran Culture." *The World of Music* 3:13–32.

Keeler, Ward. 1987. *Javanese Shadow Plays, Javanese Selves*. Princeton, NJ: Princeton University Press.

Kunst, Jaap. 1973 [1934]. *Music in Java: Its History, Its Theory, and Its Technique*. 3rd ed., rev. and enlarged by Ernst Heins. 2 vols. The Hague: Martinus Nijhoff

Manuel, Peter, and Randal E. Baier. 1986. "Jaipongan: Indigenous Popular Music of West Java." *Asian Music* 18(1):91–110.

North, Richard. 1988. "An Introduction to the Musical Traditions of Cirebon." *Balungan* 3(3):2–6.

Notosudirdjo, R Franki S. 1990. "European Music in Colonial Life in Nineteenth-Century Java: A Preliminary Study." M.A. thesis, University of Wisconsin-Madison.

Ricklefs, M. C. 1981. *A History of Modern Indonesia: c.1300 to the Present*. Bloomington: Indiana University Press.

Pauka, Kirstin. 1998. *Theater and Martial Arts in West Sumatra: Randai and Silek of the Minangkabau*. Athens, OH: Ohio University Center for International Studies.

Perlman, Marc. 2003. *Unplayed Melodies: Javanese Gamelan and the Genesis of Music Theory*. Berkeley: University of California Press.

Spiller, Henry. 2004. *Gamelan: The Traditional Sounds of Indonesia*. New York: ABC-CLIO.

Sunardjo, R. H. Unang. 1983. *Meninjau Sepintas Panggung Sejarah Pemerintahan Kerajaan Cerbon 1479-1809*. Bandung: Tarsito.

Sutton, R. Anderson. 1989. "Identity and Individuality in an Ensemble Tradition: The Female Vocalist in Java." In *Women and Music in Cross-Cultural Perspective*, ed. Ellen Koskoff, 111–130. Urbana and Chicago: University of Illinois Press.

———. 2002. *Calling Back the Spirit: Music, Dance, and Cultural Politics in Lowland South Sulawesi*. New York: Oxford University Press.

Tenzer, Michael. 1999. *Gamelan Gong Kebyar: The Art of Twentieth-Century Balinese* Music. Chicago: University of Chicago Press.

Wagner, Frits A. 1959. *Indonesia: The Art of an Island Group*. New York: Crown.

Weintraub, Andrew. 2004. *Power Plays: Wayang Golek Puppet Theater of West Java*. Athens, OH: Center for International Studies, Ohio University.

Williams, Sean. 1989. "Current Developments in Sundanese Popular Music." *Asian Music* 21(1):105–136.

———. 2001. *The Sound of the Ancestral Ship: Highland Music of West Java*. New York, London: Oxford University Press.

Wolbers, Paul Arthur. 1987. "Account of an Angklung Caruk, July 28, 1985." *Indonesia* 43:66–74.

Wright, Michael R. 1978. "The Music Culture of Cirebon." Ph.D. dissertation, University of California, Los Angeles.

———. 1988. "Tarling Modern Music from Cirebon." *Balungan* 3(3):21–25.

BORNEO

Gorlinski, Virginia K. 1988. "Some Insights into the Art of *Sape* Playing." *Sarawak Museum Journal* 39, 60 (new series):77–104.

———. 1989. "Pangpagaq: Religious and Social Significance of a Traditional Kenyah Music-Dance Form." *Sarawak Museum Journal* 40, 61 (new series), part 3:280–301.

———. 1994 "Gongs among the Kenyah Uma' Jalan: Past and Present Position of an Instrumental Tradition." *Yearbook for Traditional Music* 26:81–99.

———. 1995. "Songs of Honor, Words of Respect: Social Contours of Kenyah Lepo' Tau Versification, Sarawak, Malaysia." Ph.D. dissertation, University of Wisconsin.

Koizumi, Fumio, ed. 1976. *Asian Musics in an Asian Perspective, Report of Asian Traditional Performing Arts.* Tokyo: Heibonsha.

Masing, James Jemut. 1981. "The Coming of the Gods: A Study of the Invocatory Chant (Timang Gawai Amat) of the Iban of the Baleh Region of Sarawak." Ph.D. dissertation, Australian National University.

Strickland, S. S. 1988. "Preliminary Notes on a Kejaman-Sekapan Oral Narrative Form." *Sarawak Museum Journal* 39, 60 (new series):67–75.

THE PHILIPPINES

Abubakar, Carmen. 1983. "Islamization of Southern Philippines: An Overview." In *Filipino Muslims: Their Social Institutions and Cultural Achievements,* ed. F. Landa Jocano, 6–13. Diliman: Asian Center, University of the Philippines.

Blair, Emma Helen, and James Alexander Robertson, eds. 1973 [1903]. *The Philippine Islands 1493–1898.* 55 vols. Mandaluyong: Cachos Hermanosted.

Buenconsejo, Jos. 2004. *Songs and Gifts at the Frontier* (Current Research in Ethnomusicology, Vol. 4). New York: Routledge.

Butocan, Aga Mayo. 1987. *Palabunibunyan: A Repertoire of Musical Pieces for the Maguindanaon Kulintangan.* Manila: Philippine Women's University.

Cadar, Usopay Hamdag. 1975. "The Role of Kulintang Music in Maranao Society." *Selected Reports in Ethnomusicology* 2:2:49–62.

———. 1980. "Context and Style in the Vocal Music of the Muranao in Mindanao, Philippines." Ph.D. dissertation, University of Washington.

Castro y Amadeo, Pedro de. 1790. "Historia de la Provincia de Batangas por Don Pedro Andrés de Castro y Amadeo en sus viajes y contraviajes en toda esta Provincia año de 1790." Madrid: MS Archivo Nacional, Códice 931,7.

de la Concepción, Juan. 1788–92. *Historia general de las islas Filipinos.* Manila: Agustín de la Rosa y Balagtas.

De León, Felipe Padilla. 1977. "Banda Uno, Banda Dos." *Filipino Heritage* 8.

Ellis, Henry T. 1856. Hongkong to Manila and the Lakes of Luzon in the Philippine Islands in the Year 1856. London: Smith, Elder.

Kiefer, Thomas. 1970. *Music from the Tausug of Sulu.* Bloomington: Indiana University. LP disk.

Maceda, Jose. 1963. "The Music of the Maguindanao in the Philippines." Ph.D. dissertation, University of California at Los Angeles.

———. 1974. "Drone and Melody in Philippine Musical Instruments." In *Traditional Drama and Music of Southeast Asia,* ed. Mohd. Taib Osman, 246–273. Kuala Lumpur: Kementerian Pelajaran Malaysia.

———. 1999. *Gongs and Bamboo: A Panorama of Philippine Music Instruments.* Manila: University of Philippines Press.

Maceda, José, and Alain Martenot. 1976. *Sama de Sitangkai.* Office de la Recherche Scientifique et Technique Outre-Mer, Société de la Recherche Linguistiques et Anthropologiques de France. LP disk.

McFarland, Curtis D. 1983. *A Linguistic Atlas of the Philippines.* Manila: Linguistic Society of the Philippines.

Molina, Antonio J. 1977. "The Sentiments of Kundiman." *Filipino Heritage* 8:2026–29.

Nicolas, Arsenio. 1977. "Ang Musika ng mga Yakan sa Pulo ng Basilan" (The Music of the Yakan on the Island of Basilan). *Musika Jornal* 1:79–10.

———. 1987. "Ritual Transformations and Musical Parameters, a Study of Selected Headhunting Rites on Southern Cordillera, Northern Luzon." M.A. thesis, University of the Philippines.

Puya y Ruiz, Adolfo. 1838. *Filipinos: Descripón General de la Provincia de Bulacan.* Manila: R. Mercantil de Diaz Puertas.

San Nicolás, Fray Andrés de. 1973 [1605]. "General History of the Discalced Augustinian Fathers." In *The*

Philippine Islands 1493–1898, ed. Emma Helen Blair and James Alexander Robertson, 21:111–317. Mandaluyong: Cachos Hermanos.

Santos, Ramón P. 1992. "Nationalism in Philippine Music during the Japanese Occupation: Art or Propaganda." *Panahon ng Hapon* (Japanese Time) 2:93–106.

Tiongson, Nicanor, ed. 1991. *The Cultural Traditional Media of the Philippines*. Manila: ASEAN and the Cultural Center of the Philippines.

Yraola, Marialita T. 1977. "Ang Mga Awiting Tagalog." *Musika Jornal* 1:42–78.

A Guide to Recordings of Southeast Asian Music

MAINLAND SOUTHEAST ASIA

Cambodia

Angkor Journey. 2001. Commentary by Um Mongkol. Les Artisans d'Angkor. Compact disc.

Cambodge: Musique classique khmère, théâtre d'ombres et chants de mariage, 1995. Recording and commentary by Loch Chhanchhai and Pierre Bois. Paris: Inedit, Maison des Cultures du Monde W 260002. Compact disc.

Cambodia. 1990. Commentary in French by Catherine Basset, based on remarks by Jacques Brunet. Translated into English by Jeffrey Grice. Translated into Italian by Marie-Christine Reverte. Translated into German by Brigittc Nelles. Music of the Ramayana, 2. Ocora Radio France C 560015. Compact disc.

Cambodia: Folk and Ceremonial Music. 1996. Musical Atlas. Recording and commentary by Jacques Brunet. Auvidis-Unesco D-8068. Compact disc.

Cambodia: Music of the Exile. 1992. The Orchestra of the Khmer Classical Dance Troupe. Recording by Jean-Daniel Bloesch and Khao-I-Dang. Commentary by Giovanni Giurate with Jean-Daniel Bloesch. VDE-Gallo 698. Compact disc.

Cambodia: Music of the Royal Palace (The 1960s). 1994. Commentary in French by Jacques Brunet. Translated into English by Peter Lee. Translated into German by Volker Haller. Ocora Radio France C 560034. Compact disc.

Cambodia: Royal Music. 1971–1989. Recording and commentary by Jacques Brunet. Musics and Musicians of the World. International Music Council. Auvidis/Unesco D 8011. Compact disc.

Classical Music From Cambodia: Homrong Chum Ngek. 2004. Commentary by Chum Ngek and Joanna Pecore. Celestial Harmonies 13237-2. Compact disc.

Court Dance of Cambodia. 1994. Recording by Teodor Octavio Graca. Commentary by Sam-Ang Sam. AVL 95001. Compact disc.

Echoes from the Palace: Court Music of Cambodia: Sam-Ang Sam Ensemble. 1996. Recording and commentary by Sam-Ang Sam. Music of the World CDT–140. Compact disc.

Khmer Passages: Songs for Cycles of Cambodian Life. 2006. Commentary by Elizabeth Chey et al. Cambodian Living Arts. Compact disc.

Les musiques du Ramayana, vol. 2. 1990. Commentary by Pierre Toureille. Ocora C 560015 HM 78. Compact disc.

Light From Heaven: Classical Cambodian Music. 2001. Commentary by Dick Hensold. Private, Minneapolis, MN. Compact disc.

Mohori: Sam Ang Sam Ensemble. 1997. World Music Institute and Music of the World. Latitudes I.AT50609. Compact disc.

Musicians of the National Dance Company of Cambodia: Homrong. 1991. Recording by Richard Blair. Lyrics transcribed by students of the Fine Arts University of Phnom Penh. Lyrics translated by Sam Phany and Bill Labban. Real World Records 2–91734. Compact disc.

9 Gong Gamelan Recorded inside Angkor Wat. 1993. Recording by David and Kay Parsons. Commentary by John Schaefer. *The Music of Cambodia*, vol. 1. Celestial Harmonies 13074–2. Compact disc.

Royal Court Music Recorded in Phnom Penh. 1992. Recording by David and Kay Parsons. Commentary by John Schaefer. *The Music of Cambodia*, vol. 2. Celestial Harmonies 13075–2. Compact disc.

Solo Instrumental Music Recorded in Phnom Penh. 1994. Recording by David and Kay Parsons. Commentary by John Schaefer. *The Music of Cambodia*, vol. 3. Celestial Harmonies. 13076–2. Compact disc.

Thailand

Ceremonial Music of Thailand: Music for Sacred Rituals and Theatre. 1989. Siamese Music Ensemble. Pacific Music Co. 8.260581. Compact disc.

Chang Saw: Ensemble Si Nuan Thung Pong/Village Music of Northern Thailand. 2000. Commentary by Fred Gales. Pan 2075CD. Compact disc.

Classical Music of Thailand. 1991. World Music Library, King Record Co. KICC 5125. Compact disc.

Dontri Chao Sayam—Traditional Folk Music of Siam. 1993. Produced by Saeng Arun Arts Centre. SAACI CD 001-006. 6 compact discs.

The Flower of Isan: Songs and Music from North East Thailand. 1989. Commentary by Ginny Landgraf. Acc Records CDORBD 051. Compact disc.

Fong Naam: Ancient-Contemporary Music from Thailand. 1995. Commentary by Bruce Gaston. Celestial Harmonies 14098-2. Compact disc.

Instrumental Music of Northeast Thailand. 1991. World Music Library. King Record Co. KICC 5124. Compact disc.

Karenni: Music from the Border areas of Thailand and Burma. 1994. Recording and commentary by Fred Gales. Paradox Records. PAN 2040CD. Compact disc.

Lanna Thai: Instrumental Music of North-West Thailand. 1997. Commentary by Fred Gales. Pan 2045CD. Compact disc.

Maan Mongkhon: an Auspicious Piece in the Burmese Style. 1997. Thai Music Circle (London). Pan Records 2049. Compact disc.

The Mahori Orchestra. 1994. Fong Naam. Commentary by Prasarn Wongwirojruk and Bruce Gaston. Siamese Classical Music, 5. HNH International. Marco Polo 8.223493. Compact disc.

Mo Lam Singing of Northeast Thailand. 1991. Chawiwan Damnoen and Thongkham Thaikla. World Music Library. King Record Co. KICC 5123. Compact disc.

Music of Northeast Thailand. 1992. Chagkachan. Commentary in Japanese by Sentoku Miho. Translated by Larry Richards. World Music Library. King Record Co. KICC 5159. Compact disc.

Music from Thailand: Field Recordings by Master Ethnomusicologist Deben Bhattacharya. 1999. Commentary by Deben Bhattacharya. ARC Music, EUCD 1557. Compact disc.

Music of Thailand. 1959. Recording and commentary by Howard K. Kaufman. Folkways FE 4463. LP disk and Compact disc.

The Nang Hong Suite: Siamese Funeral Music. 1992. Fong Naam. Commentary by Neil Sorrell and Bruce Gaston. Nimbus Records NI 5332. Compact disc.

The Piphat Ensemble before 1400 A.D. 1990. Fong Naam. Commentary by Bruce Gaston. Siamese Classical Music, 1. HNH International. Marco Polo 8.223197. Compact disc.

The Piphat Ensemble 1351–1767 A.D. (The Afternoon Overture). 1990. Fong Naam. Commentary by Montri Tramoj. Siamese Classical Music, 2. HNH International. Marco Polo 8.223198. Compact disc.

The Piphat Sepha. 1992. Fong Naam. Commentary by Prasarn Wongwirojruk and Bruce Gaston. Siamese Classical Music, 4. HNH International, Marco Polo 8.223200. Compact disc.

Royal Court Music of Thailand. 1994. Recording and commentary by M. R. Chakrarot Chitrabongs. Smithsonian/Folkways Recordings. SF 40413. Compact disc.

Shiva's Drum: Spiritual Music from the Beginning of Time. 1989. Siamese Music Ensemble. Commentary by Bruce Gaston. Pacific Music Co. 8.260582. Compact disc.

Siamese Classical Music, Vol.5: The Mahori Orchestra, Fong Naam. 1994. Commentary by Prasarn Wongwirojruk and Bruce Gaston. Marco Polo 8.223493. Compact disc.

Silk, Spirits & Song: Music from North Thailand. 2006. Commentary by Andrew C. Shahriari. Lyrichord LYRCD 7451. Compact disc.

The Sleeping Angel Thai Classical Music. 1991. Fong Naam. Commentary by Neil Sorrell and Bruce Gaston. Nimbus Records NI 5319. Compact disc.

The String Ensemble. 1992. Fong Naam. Siamese Classical Music, 3. HNH Interational. Marco Polo 8.223199. Compact disc.

Thai Classical Music. 1994. The Prasit Thawon Ensemble. Commentary by Somsak Ketukaenchan and Donald Mitchell. Nimbus Records. NI 5412. Compact disc.

Thailand: Ceremonial and Court Music from Central Thailand. 1997. Commentary by James Upton. Multicultural Media MCM 3014. Compact disc.

Thailand: Classical Instrumental Traditions. 1993. JVC World Sounds (recorded in 1976). JVC Musical Industries. VICG 5262–2. Compact disc.

Thailand: Music and Songs from the Golden Triangle. n.d. Commentary by François Jouffa. Buda 92754-2. Compact disc.

Thailand: The Music of Chieng Mai. 1988 [1975]. Recording and commentary by Jacques Brunet. Musics and Musicians of the World. International Music Council, Auvidis/Unesco D 8007. Compact disc.

Thailande: Danses. 1994. Commentary by Gerard Kremer. Arion ARN 64284. Compact disc.

Thailande: The Music of the Mons. 1988. Commentary by Hubert de Fraysseix. Playa Sound PS 65019. Compact disc.

Laos

Bamboo Voices: Folk Music from Laos. 1997. World Music Institute and Music of the World. Latitudes LAT50601. Compact disc.

Boua Xou Mua: The Music of the Hmong People of Laos. 1995. Produced by Alan Govenar for Documentary Arts. Arhoolie CD 446. Compact disc.

Lam lao sut phiset: Phouvieng & Malavanh. 1995. Huntington Beach, CA: JKB Productions. Compact disc.

Laos. Recorded by Jacques Brunet. 1989. Ocora C 559 058. Compact disc.

Laos: Musique pour le khène/Lam Saravane. 1989. Recording and commentary by Jacques Brunet. Translation by David Stevens. Ocora C 559 058. Compact disc.

Laos: Traditional Music of the South. 1992 [1973]. Recording and commentary by Jacques Brunet. International Music Council. Musics and Musicians of the World. Auvidis/Unesco D 8042. Compact disc.

Mohlan of Siiphandon/Wannaa Keaopidom. 1997. King Record Co. KICC 5225. Compact disc.

Music of Laos: The Buddhist Tradition. 2003. Commentary by John Schaefer. Celestial Harmonies 13218-2. Compact disc.

Music from Southern Laos. 1994. Molam Lao. Recording by Robin Broadbank. Commentary in French by Jacques Brunet. Translated by Atlas Translations, Cambridge, England. Nimbus Records NI 5401. Compact disc.

Music from Thailand and Laos. 1997. Commentary by David Fanshawe. ARC Music EUCD 1425. Compact disc.

The Songs of the Lao. 1997. Musicians of the National Music School, Vientiane. King Record Co. KICC 5226. Compact disc.

Visions of the Orient: Nouthong Phimvilayphone: Music from Laos. 1995. Amiata Records ARNR 0195. Compact disc.

Burma (Myanmar)

Asian Percussions: Bali, Burma, China, India, Sri Lanka, Thailand. 1988. Commentary by Gerard Kremer. Playasound PS 65026. Compact disc.

Birmanie: Musique d'art. 1989. Recording and commentary by Jacques Brunet. Translation into English by Derek Yeld. Ocora 559019/20. 2 compact discs.

Burmese Folk and Traditional Music. 1953. Commentary by Maung Than Myint. Folkways FE 4436. Compact disc.

Green Tea Leaf Salad: Flavors of Burmese Music. 2000. Commentary by Rick Heizman. Pan 2083. Compact disc.

La Harpe Birmane. 1980 Commentary by Jacques Brunet. Musiques de l'Asie Traditionnelle, 22. Playasound PS 33528. LP disk.

Harp Birmane/Burmese Harp. 1994. Commentary by Moe Moe Yee. Playa Sound PS 65135. Compact disc.

Hsaing Waing of Myanmar. 1992. World Music Library. King Record Co. KICC 5162. Compact disc.

Mahagita: Harp and Vocal Music of Burma. 2003. Commentary by Ward Keeler. Smithsonian Folkways Recordings LC 9628. Compact disc.

The Moken: Sea Gypsies of the Andaman Sea. 2001. Commentary by Tom Vater. Topic Records TSCD 919. Compact disc.

Music of Myanmar. 1988. World Music Library. King Record Co. KICC 5132. Compact disc.

Myanmar: Music by the Hsaing Waing Orchestra/The Burmese Harp. 1977/2001. Commentary by Jacques Brunet. UNESCO D8261. Compact disc.

Pat Waing: The Magic Drum Circle of Burma. 1998. Commentary by Rick Heizman. Shanachie 66005. Compact disc.

Piano Birman/Burmese Piano: U Ko Ko. 1995. UM MUS, SRC Radio (Canada) UMM 203. Compact disc.

Sandaya: The Spellbinding Piano of Burma. 1998. Commentary by Rick Heizman. Shanachie 66005. Compact disc.

White Elephants and Golden Ducks: Enchanting Musical Treasures from Burma. 1997. Newton, NJ: Shanachie 64087. Compact disc.

Malaysia

Dream Songs and Healing Sounds in the Rainforests of Malaysia. 1995. Recordings and commentary by Marina Roseman. Smithsonian/Folkways SF CD 40417. Compact disc.

Singapore

New Music Compositions. 1993. Second ASEAN Composers Forum on Traditional Music, 1. ASEAN Committee on Culture and Information. Compact disc.

Traditional Music of Singapore. 1993. Second ASEAN Composers Forum on Traditional Music, 2. ASEAN Committee on Culture and Information. Compact disc.

Vietnam

The Art of Kim Sinh. 1992. Kim Sinh. Commentary in Japanese by Hoshikawa Kyoji. Translated by Larry Richards. World Music Library. King Record Co. KICC 5161. Compact disc.

The Art of the Khen [Hmong mouth organ]. 1995. Commentary by Patrick Kersale. Arion ARN 60367. Compact disc.

The Art of the Vietnamese Fiddle. 1998. Commentary by Patrick Kersale. Arion ARN 60417. Compact disc.

Ca Tru: The Music of North Vietnam. The Hanoi Ca Tru Thai Ha Ensemble. 2001. Commentary by anonymous. Nimbus NI 5626. Compact disc.

The City of Huế. 1995. Commentary by Sten Sandahl. Music from Vietnam, 2. Caprice Records CAP 21463. Compact disc.

Dân Ca Cổ Truyền V. N. 1993. Hoàng Oanh. Hoàng Oanh Music Center HOCD 08. Compact disc.

Escale au Vietnam/A Journey to Vietnam. 1995. Commentary and recording by Gerard Kremer. Playasound PS 66509. Compact disc.

Eternal Voices: Traditional Vietnamese Music in the United States. 1993. Commentary by Phong Nguyễn and Terry E. Miller. New Alliance Records NAR CD 053. Compact disc.

Ethnic Minorities. 1995. Commentary by Sten Sandahl. Music from Vietnam, 3. Caprice Records CAP 21479. Compact disc.

From Saigon to Hanoi: Traditional Songs and Music of Vietnam. Tieng Hat Que Huong Ensemble. 2001. Milan 73138 35934-2. Compact disc.

Imperial Court Music Recorded in Huế. 1994. *The Music of Vietnam,* Vol. 2 2. 13084–2. Celestial Harmonies Compact disc.

Instrumental Music of Vietnam, 1992. Commentary in Japanese by Hoshikawa Kyoji. Translated by Larry Richards. World Music Library. King Record Co. KICC 5160. Compact disc.

Landscape of the Highlands. 1997. Tran Quang Hai. Chapel Hill, NC: Music of the World. Latitudes LAT50612. Compact disc.

Mekong River: Traditional Music of Vietnam. 1992. Ngoc Lam and Que Lam. Recording by Oliver DiCicco. 1 LCD. Compact disc.

Music from Vietnam. 1991. Commentary by Nguyen Thuy Loan and Sten Sandahl. Caprice Records CAP 21406. Compact disc.

Music from Vietnam 2: The City of Hue. 1995. Commentary by Sten Sandahl. Caprice CAP 21463. Compact disc.

Music from the Lost Kingdom: Hue. 1995. Commentary by Phong T. Nguyen and Terry E. Miller. Lyrichord LYRCD 7440. Compact disc.

The Music of Vietnam, vol. 1.1. 1994. Recording by David and Kay Parsons. Commentary by John Schaefer. Celestial Harmonies 13082-2. Compact disc.

The Music of Vietnam, vol. 1.2. 1994. Recording by David and Kay Parsons. Commentary by John Schaefer. Celestial Harmonies 13083-2. Compact disc.

The Music of Vietnam: vol. 2, Imperial Court Music Recorded in Hue. 1995. Commentary by La Thi Cam Van and Nguyen Xuan Hoa. Celestial Harmonies 13084-2. Compact disc.

Nhạc Lễ, Ritual Music of Vietnam. 1997. King Record Co. KICC 5224. Compact disc.

Northern Viet-nam: Music and Songs of the Minorities. n.d. Commentary by Patrick Kersale. Buda 92669-2. Compact disc.

Northern Viet-nam: Possession Songs. n.d. Commentary by Dam Quang Minh and Patrick Kersale. Buda 92657-2. Compact disc.

Song of the Banyan: Folk Music of Vietnam. 1997. Phong Nguyen Ensemble. World Music Institute and Music of the World. Latitudes LAT 50607. Compact disc.

Stilling Time: Người Ngời Ru Thời Gian. 1994. Recording by Philip Blackburn and Miranda Arana. Innova 112. Compact disc.

String Instruments of Vietnam. 1991. World Music Library. King Record Co. KICC 5121. Compact disc.

Tai Tu Nam Bo: Saigon: Masters of Traditional Music. 2000. Commentary by Gisa Jahnichen. Wergo SM 1533-2. Compact disc.

The Traditional Songs of Huế. 1997. King Record Co. KICC 5223. Compact disc.

Viet-Nam: Anthology of Ede Music. n.d. Commentary by Patrick Kersale. Buda 92726-2. Compact disc.

Viet Nam: Buddhist Music from Hue/Ceremony of the Opening of the Sacred Texts. 1998. Commentary by Tran Van Khe. Inedit W 260082. Compact disc.

Viet Nam: Court Theatre Music: Hat Boi. 1994. Commentary by Tran Van Khe. UNESCO Collection Auvidis D 8058. Compact disc.

Viet-nam: Le dan tranh, musiques d'hier et d'aujourd'hui. 1994. Commentary by Tran van Khe. Ocora C 560055. Compact disc.

Vietnam: Mother Mountain and Father Sea. 6 CDs. 2003. Commentary by Phong Nguyễn and Terry Miller. White Cliffs Media WCM 9991. Compact disc.

Vietnam: Music of the Montagnards. 1997. Commentary by Tran Quang Hai and Pribislav Pitoeff. Harmonia Mundi CNR 2741085.86. Compact disc.

Viet-Nam: Musique funeraire du Nord. 1997. Commentary by Patrick Kersale. Arion ARN 58456. Compact disc.

Viet-Nam: Popular Songs and Music from Hanoi/Royal Music from Hue. 1999. Anonymous commentary. Playa Sound PS 65214. Compact disc.

Viet-Nam: Theatre populaire du Nord (Hat cheo). 1995. Commentary by Patrick Kersale. Arion ARN 64368.

Viet-Nam: The voice of the "song houses." 2001. Commentary by Ngo Linh Ngoc, Dam Quang Minh, and Patrick Kersale. Buda 1987282. Compact disc.

Việt Nam Ca Trù: Tradition du Nord. Ensemble Ca Trù Thài Hà de Hanội. 1996. Paris: Inedit, Maison des Cultures du Monde W 260070. Compact disc.

Vietnam Hat Cheo: Traditional Folk Theatre. 1989 [1978]. Recording and commentary by Trần Vān Khê. Anthology of Traditional Musics. International Music Council. Auvidis/Unesco D 8022. Compact disc.

Viêt-Nam: Instruments et ensembles de musique traditionnelle. 1995 [1984]. Recorded by Maison des Cultures du Monde, Paris. Arion ARN 64603. Compact disc.

Viet Nam: Musiques de Huế. 1996. Paris: Inedit W 260073. Compact disc.

Viet-Nam: Musiques et chants des minorités du nord. 1997. Buda 92669-2. Compact disc.

Viet-Nam: Poéies et Chants. 1994. Trăn Văn Khê and Trân Thi Thuy Ngoc. Commentary in French by Professor Trần Văn Khê. Translated into English by Jeffrey Grice. Translated into German by Volker Haller. Ocora C 560054. Compact disc.

Vietnam: Reviving a Tradition. 1993. Bibliographic References by Trần Văn Khê. Commentary in French by Bach Thai Hao and Patrick Kersale. Translated into English by Mary Pardoe. Auvidis Playasound PS 65116. Compact disc.

Viet Nam: Tradition of the South. 1993 [1975]. Recording by Hubert de Fraysseix. Commentary by Trần Văn Khê. Anthology of Traditional Musics. International Music Council. Auvidis/Unesco D 8070. Compact disc.

Vietnamese Folk Theatre: Hat Cheo. 1991. World Music Library. King Record Co. KICC 5122. Compact disc.

Vietnamese Zither: The Water and the Wind. 1993. Trân Quang Hai. Commentary in French by Tran Quang Hai. Translated into English by Mary Pardoe. Auvidis Playasound PS 65103. Compact disc.

ISLAND SOUTHEAST ASIA

Indonesia

The Angkola People of Sumatra: An Anthology of Southeast Asian Music. 1983. Bärenreiter Musicaphon SL 2568. LP disk.

Asmat Dream; New Music Indonesia, vol. 1. 1992. Lyrichord LYRCD 7415. Compact disc.

Baleganjur of Pande and Angklung of Sidan, Bali. 1995. World Music Library KICC-5197. Compact disc.

Bali: Barong—The Dance Drama of Singapudu Village. 1992. JVC World Sounds. JVC VICG-5217. Compact disc.

Bali: The Celebrated Gamelans. 1976. Musical Heritage Society MHS 3505. LP disk.

Bali: Divertissements Musicaux et Danses de Transe.1973. Ocora OCR 72. LP disk.

Bali: Gamelan and Kecak. 1989. Nonesuch 9-79204. LP disk.

Bali: Joged Bumbung. 1987. Ocora 558 501. LP disk.

Bali: Le Gong Gedé de Batur. 1975. Ocora 558 510. LP disk,

Bali: Musique de Danse. 1976. Playa Sound PS 33503. LP disk.

Bali: Musique et Théâtre. 1971. Ocora OCR 60. LP disk,

Bali: Musique pour le Gong Gedé/Gong Gedé de Batur. 1987. Ocora C559002. Compact disc.

Bali: Musique Sacrée. 1972. CBS 65173. LP. disk.

Bali: Musiques du Nord-Ouest. 1992. Ethnic/Auvidis B 6769. Compact disc.

Bali: Stage and Dance Music. 1973. Philips 6586 015. LP disk.

Barong, Drame Musical Balinais. 1971. Vogue LD 763. LP disk.

Batak of North Sumatra. 1992. New Albion Records NA 046. Compact disc. Bärenreiter Musicaphon BM 30 SL 2567. LP disk.

Bédhaya Duradasih—Court Music of Kraton Surakarta, vol. 1. 1995. World Music Library KICC-5193. Compact disc.

Betawi and Sundanese Music of the North Coast of Java: Topeng Betawi, Tanjidor, Ajeng. 1994. Music of Indonesia, 5. Smithsonian/Folkways SF 40421. Compact disc.

Between Heaven and Earth: Traditional Gamelan Music of Bali. 1999. Music Club B00000K53F. Compact disc.

Chamber Music of Central Java. 1992. World Music Library KICC-5152. Compact disc.

Cilokaq Music of Lombok. 1994. World Music Library KICC-5178. Compact disc.

Court Music of Kraton Surakarta. 1992. World Music Library KICC-5151. Compact disc.

Dancers of Bali. 1952. Columbia ML 4618. LP disk.

Detty Kurnia: Coyor Panon. 1993. Timbuktu Records FLTRCD519. Compact disc.

The Exotic Sounds of Bali. 1963. Columbia ML 5845. LP disk.

Fantastic and Meditative Gamelan: "Tirta Sari" Semar Pegulingan of Peliatan Village. 1988. JVC Ethnic Sound, 7. JVC VID 25024. Compact disc.

Fantastic Sound Art "Mababbarata"/"Wayang Krit": A Virtuoso Shadow Play in Bali. 1987. JVC Ethnic Sound, 14. JVC VID 25028. Compact disc.

Folk and Pop Sounds of Sumatra, vol.1. 2003. Sublime Frequencies B0000ZH0BM. Compact disc.

Gamelan Batel Wayang Ramayana. 1990. Creative Music Productions CMP CD 3003, Compact disc.

Gamelan Degung: Classical Music of Sunda, West Java. 1996. Pan Records Pan 2053 CD. Compact disc.

Gamelan Gong Gedé of Batur Temple. 1992. World Music Library KICC-5153. Compact disc.

Gamelan Gong Kebyar of "Eka Cita," Abian Kapas Kaja. 1992. World Music Library. KICC-5154. Compact disc.

Gamelan Joged Bumbung "Suar Agung," Negara. 1994. World Music Library KTCC-5181. Compact disc.

Gamelan Music of Bali. 1960s. Lyrichord LLST 7179. LP disk.

The Gamelan Music of Bali. 1991. World Music Library KICC-5126. Compact disc.

Gamelan Music from Java. 1963. Philips 831 209. LP disk.

The Gamelan of Bali. 1975. Arion. FARN 91009. LP disk.

The Gamelan of Cirebon. 1991. World Music Library KICC-5130. Compact disc.

*Gamelan Selondtng "Guna Winangun." Teganan.*1994. World Music Library KICC-5182. Compact disc.

Gamelan Semar Pegulingan: Gamelan of the Love God. 1972. Nonesuch H-72046. LP disk.

Gamelan Semar Pegulingan "Gunung Jati," Br. Teges Kanginan. 1994. World Music Library KICC-5180. Compact disc.

Gamelan Semar Pegulingan of Binoh Village. 1992. World Music Library KICC-5155. Compact disc.

Gamelan Semar Pegulingan Saih Pitu: The Heavenly Orchestra of Bali. 1991. Creative Music Productions CMP CD 3008. Compact disc.

Geguntangan Arja "Arja Bon Bali." 1994. World Music Library KICC-5183. Compact disc.

Gendèr Wayang of Sukawati Village. 1992. World Music Library KICC-5156. Compact disc.

Golden Rain: Balinese Gamelan Music. 1969. Nonesuch H-72028. LP disk.

Golden Rain/Gong Kebyar of Gunung Sari, Bali. 1995. World Music Library KICC-5195. Compact disc.

Gondang Tuba/Northern Sumatra. 1985. Museum Collection Berlin, ISBN 3 88 609 5126. LP disk.

Indonesia I: Java Court Music. 1970s. Bärenreicet Musicaphon BM SL 2031. LP disk.

Indonesia-Jegog: The Rhythmic Power of Bamboo. 1997. Music Earth B000005BMO. Compact disc.

Indonesia-Madura: Musique Savante. 1996. Ocora B000003IFH. Compact disc.

Indonesia, Toraja: Funerals and Fertility Feasts. 1995. Recordings by Dana Rappoport. Collection du Centre National de la Recherche Scientifique et du Musée de l'Homme, CNR 2741004. Harmonia Mundi HM 91.

Indonesia-Wayang Golek: The Sound and Celebration of Sundanese Puppet Theater. 2002. Music Earth Multic B00005YQRD. Compact disc.

Indonesian Music: from New Guinea, the Moluccas, Borneo, Bali, and Java. 1954. Columbia SL 210. LP disk.

Indonesian Popular Music: Kroncong, Dangdut, and Langgam Jawa. 1991. Music of Indonesia, 2. Smithsonian/Folkways SF 40056. Compact disc.

Jaipongan Java; Euis Komariah with Jugala Orchestra. 1990. Globestyle CDORB 057. Compact disc.

The Jasmine Isle: Javanese Gamelan Music. 1969. Nonesuch H-72031. LP disk.

Java: Gamelans from the Sultan's Palace in Jogjakarta. 1973. Music Traditions in Asia Series. Archive 2723 017. LP disk.

Java: Historic Gamelans. 1972. UNESCO Collection, Musical Sources, Art Music from Southeast Asia Series, 9, 2. Philips 6586 004. LP disk.

Java: "Langen Mandra Wanara," Opèra de Danuredjo VII. 1987. Musiques Traditionelles Vivantes, vol. 3. Ocora C559 014/15. Compact disc.

Java: Royal Palace of Yogyakarta, vol. 4. 2000. Ocora B0000021FL. Compact disc.

Java: Une Nuit de Wayang Kulit; Légende de Wahju Tjakraningrat. 1973. CDS 65,440. Compact disc.

Javanese Court Gamelan from the Pura Paku Alaman, Jogyakarta. 1971. Nonesuch H-72044. LP disk.

Javanese Court Gamelan vol, 2, Recorded at the Istana Mangkunegaran, Surakarta. 1977. Nonesuch H-72074. LP disk.

Javanese Court Gamelan, vol. 3, Recorded at the Kraton, Yogyakarta. 1979. Nonesuch H-72083. LP disk.

The Javanese Gamelan. 1987. World Music Library KICC-5129. Compact disc.

Javanese Music from Surinam. 1977. Lyrichord. LLST 7317. LP disk.

Java-Sunda Country: Musique Savante: vol. 2, The Art of the Gamelan Degung. 1996. Ocora B000003IFT. Compact disc.

Jegog: Dynamic Sound of the Earth: A Percussion Ensemble of Gigantic Bamboo in Sangkar Agung, Bali. 1987. JVC Ethnic Sound, 12. JVC VID 25026. Compact disc.

Jegog [II]; "Suar Agung," The Bamboo Ensemble of Sangkar Agung Village. 1992. JVC World Sounds. JVC VICG-5218. Compact disc.

Jegog of Negara. 1992. World Music Library KICC-5157. Compact disc.

Kartomi, Margaret J. 1979. *The Mandailing People of Sumatra: An Anthology of Southeast Asian Music.* Bärenreiter Musicaphon BM 30 SL 2567. LP disk.

Kecak: A Balinese Music Drama. 1990. Bridge BCD 9019. Compact disc.

Kecak and Sanghyang of Bali. 1991. World Music Library KICC-5128. Compact disc.

Kecak in the Forest of Anima: The Choral Spectacle of Singapadu Village in Bali. 1987. JVC Ethnic Sound, 13. JVC VID 25027. Compact disc.

Klênêngan Session of Solonese Gamelan,, vol. 1. 1994. World Music Library KICC-5185. Compact disc.

Langêndriyan—Music of Mangkunêgaran Solo, vol. 2. 1995. World Music Library KICC-5194, Compact disc.

Lolongkrang: Gamelan Degung Music of West Java. 1994. Sakti Records Sakti 33. Compact disc.

Melayu Music of Sumatra and the Riau Islands: Zapin, Mak Yong, Mendu, Ronggeng. 1996. Music of Indonesia, 11, Smithsonian/Folkways SF 40427. Compact disc.

Music for the Balinese Shadow Play: Gendèr Wayang from Teges Kanyinan, Pliatan, Bali. 1970. Nonesuch H-72037. LP disk.

Music for the Gods: The Fahnestock South Sea Expedition: Indonesia. 1994. Rykodisc RCD 10315. Compact disc.

Music from the Forests of Riau and Mentawai. 1995. Music of Indonesia, 7. Smithsonian/Folkways SF 40423. Compact disc.

Music from the Morning of the World: The Balinese Gamelan. 1967. Nonesuch H-22015. LP disk.

Music from West Java. 1992. Ethnic/Auvidis Series D8041. Compact disc.

Music in Bali. 1991. World Music Library KICC-5127. Compact disc.

Music of Indonesia: Flores. 2000. Celestial Harmonies B00003W8BX. Compact disc.

Music of Indonesia: Maluku and North Maluku. 2004. Celestial Harmonies 0000DKFZ7. Compact disc.

Music of Indonesia, vol. 10: Music of Biak, Irian Jaya: Wor, Church Songs, Yospan. 1996. SFW CD 40426. Compact disc.

Music of Indonesia, vol. 15: South Sulawesi Strings. 1997. SFW CD 40442. Compact disc.

Music of Indonesia, vol. 16: Music from the Southeast: Sumba, Sumbawa, Timor. 1998. SFW CD 40443. Compact disc.

Music of Indonesia, vol. 17: Kalimantan: Dayak Ritual and Festival Music. 1998. SFW CD 40444. Compact disc.

Music of Indonesia, vol. 18: Sulawesi—Festivals, Funerals, Work. 1999. SFW CD 40445. Compact disc.

Music of Indonesia, vol. 19: Music of Maluku: Halmahera, Bura, Kei. 1999. SFW CD 40446. Compact disc.

Music of Indonesia, vol. 20: Indonesian Guitars. 1999. SFW CD 40447. Compact disc.

Music of Islam, vol. 15: Muslim Music of Indonesia. 1998. Celestial Harmonies B000000805. Compact disc.

The Music of Lombok. 1995. World Music Library KICC-5198. Compact disc.

The Music of Madura. 1991. ODE Recording ODE CD 1381. Compact disc.

Music of Mangkunêgaran Solo, vol. 1. 1994. World Music Library KICC-5184. Compact disc.

Music of Nias and North Sumatra: Hoho, Gendang Kara, Gondang Toba. 1992. Music of Indonesia, 4. Smithsonian/Folkways SF 40420. Compact disc.

Music of Sasandu. 1994. World Music Library KICC-5179. Compact disc.

Music of Sulawesi. 1973. Ethnic Folkways FE 4351. LP disk.

Music of the Gambuh Theater. 1999. Vital B00000K4JY. Compact disc.

Music of Timor. 2000. Celestial Harmonies B00003W8BY. Compact disc.

Music of the Venerable Dark Cloud: The Javanese Gamelan Khjai Mendung. 1967. Institute of Ethnomusicology (University of California at Los Angeles) IER-7501. LP disk.

The Music of K. R. T. Wasitodiningrat: Performed by Gamelan Sekar Tunjung. 1991. Creative Music Productions CMP CD 3007. Compact disc.

Music from the Outskirts of Jakarta: Gambang Kromong. 1991. *Music of Indonesia,* vol. 3. Smithsonian/Folkways SF 40057. Compact disc.

Musiques du Ramayana, vol. 3: Bali-Sunda. 1990. Ocora C560016. Compact disc.

Musiques Populaires d'Indonesie: Folk Music from West Java. 1968. Ocora OCR 46. LP disk.

Nasida Ria: Qasidah Music from Java. 1991. Piranha Music PIR 26-2. Compact disc.

Nias: Epic Songs and Instrumental Music. 1994. Pan Records PAN 2014CD. Compact disc.

Night Music of West Sumatra: Saluang, Rabab Pariaman, Dendang Pauah. 1994. Music of Indonesia, 6. Smithsonian/Folkways SF 40422. Compact disc.

Night Recordings from Bali. 2003. Sublime Frequencies B0000ZH0C6. Compact disc.

Palais Royal de Yogyakarta, Musique de Concert. 1995. Ocora C560087. Compact disc.

Panji in Bali I. 1972. Bärenreiter Musicaphon BM 30 SL 2565. LP disk.

Panji in Lombok I, 1972. Bärenreiter Musicaphon BM 30 SL 2560. LP disk.

Panji in Lombok II. 1970s. Bärenreiter Musicaphon BM 30 SL 2564. LP disk.

The Polyphony of South-East Asia; Court Music and Banjar Music. 1971. Philips 6586 008. LP disk.

Radio Java. 2003. Sublime Frequencies B0000ZH0BW. Compact disc.

Rahwana's Cry (Sambasunda). 2005. Network Germany B000BGUUQM. Compact disc.

The Rough Guide to the Music of Indonesia. 2001. World Music Network B00004YNCQ. Compact disc.

Sangkala. 1985. Icon Records 5501. LP disk.

Saron of Singapadu. 1995. World Music Library KICC-5196. Compact disc.

Scintillating Sounds of Bali. 1976. Lyrichord LLST 7305. LP disk.

Simon, Artur, 1984–1985. *Gondang Toba/Northern Sumatra.* Museum Collection Berlin (West) 12. 2 LP disks.

———. 1987. *Gendang Kara/Northern Sumatra, Indonesia—Trance and Dance Music of the Karo Batak.* Museum Collection, Berlin (West) 13. LP disk.

Songs Before Dawn: Gandrung Banyuwangi. Music of Indonesia, vol. 1. 1991. Smithsonian/Folkways SF 40055. Compact disc.

The Sound of Sunda. 1990. Globestyle CDORB 060. Compact disc.

Street Music of Central Java. 1976. Lyrichord LLST 7310. Compact disc.

Street Music of Java. 1989. Original Music OMCD 006. Compact disc.

The Sultan's Pleasure, Javanese Gamelan and Vocal Music. 1994. Music of the World CDT-116. Compact disc.

Sumatra: Gongs and Vocal Music. 1996. Music of Indonesia, 12. Smithsonian/Folkways SF 40428. Compact disc.

Sunda: Musique et chants traditionnels. 1985. Ocora 558 502. LP disk.

The Sunda Music (Sambasunda). 2004. Rice B0006333OQ. Compact disc.

Sundanese Classical Music. 1991. World Music Library KICC-5131. Compact disc.

Sundanese Music from Java. 1976. Philips 6586 031. LP disk.

Tektekan: The Dance Drama "Calonarang" of Krambitan Village. 1991. JVC World Sounds JVC VICG-5226. Compact disc.

Tembang Sunda: Sundanese Classical Songs. 1993. Nimbus Records NI 5378. Compact disc.

Tonggeret. 1987. Electra/Nonesuch 79173-2. Compact disc.

Vocal and Instrumental Music from East and Central Flores. 1995. *Music of Indonesia,* vol. 8. Smithsonian/Folkways SF 40424. Compact disc.

Vocal Art from Java. 1979. Philips 6586 041. Compact disc.

Vocal Music from Central and West Flores. 1995. *Music of Indonesia,* vol. 9. Smithsonian/Folkways SF 40425. Compact disc.

Borneo

Borneo: Music of the Dayak and Punan. 1999. Buda Musique B00000HY47. Compact disc.

Borneo; Musique Traditionelles. 1979. Playa P533506. Compact disc.

Dayak Festival and Ritual Music. 1997. Music of Indonesia, 14. Smithsonian/Folkways. Compact disc.

Dayak Lutes. 1997. Music of Indonesia, 13. Smithsonian/Folkways. Compact disc.

Murut Music of North Borneo. 1961. Folkways FE 4459. LP disk.

The Music of the Kenyah and Modang in Bast Kalimantan, Indonesia. 1979, UNESCO: University of Philippines. LP disk.

Musique Dayak. 1972. Collection Musée de L'Homme. Disques Vogue LDM 30108. LP disk.

A Visit to Borneo. 1961. Capitol T 10271. LP disk.

The Philippines

Gifts from the Past: Philippine Music of the Kalinga, Maranao, and Yakan People. 1996. Notes by Ramon Santos. P&C Ode Records CD MANU 1518. Compact disc.

Hanunoo Music from the Philippines. 1956. Folkways FE 4466. LP disk.

Kulintang: Ancient Gong/Drum Music from the Southern Philippines. 1994. World Kulintang Institute WKCD 72551. Compact disc.

Kulintang and Kudyapiq: Gong Ensemble and Two-String Lute among the Maguinanaon in Mindanao Philippines. 1989. College of Music, University of the Philippines UPCM-LP UP. Compact disc.

Muranao Kakolintang: Philippine Gong Music from Lanao; vol 1, The Villages of Romayas and Buribid. 1978. Lytichord LLST 7322. LP disk.

Muranao Kakvlintang: Philippine Gong Music from Lanao; vol 2. The Villages of Taraka, Molondo and Bagoaingud. 1970s. Lyrichord LLST 7326. LP disk.

Music from the Tausug of Sulu. 1970. Ethnosound EST 8000–8001. LP disk.

Music of the Philippines: Fiesta Filipina. 2002. Arc Music B00008J2RQ. Compact disc.

Pangkat Kawayan: The Singing Bamboos. 2006. Villar Music Philippines B000MTD6C8. Compact disc.

Revel, Nicole. 1987. *Philippines, Musique des Hautes Terres Palawan.* CNRS, Le Chant du Monde LDX 74 865. Compact disc.

Utom: Summoning the Spirit: Music in the T'boli Heartland. 1997. Rykodisc B0000009R8. Compact disc.

Notes on the Audio Examples

1. Frogs (4:45). Although these sounds might seem merely curious, frogs in fact have great significance to Southeast Asian farmers. Frog sounds are welcome as an indication that generous rains have fallen, that the rice crop will be successful, and that the flooded fields are full of delicious fish, shrimp, insects, and frogs. Prosperity will follow, at least for that year. Recorded by Terry E. Miller on 14 September 1988 in Mahasarakham, Thailand.

2. Chinese-Thai *xianshi* ensemble piece "*Chung we meng*" ("Moon Shining Brightly in the Spring") (4:55). The majority of Chinese-Thai trace their lineage to the Chaozhou area of Guangdong province. The amateur "silk and bamboo" ensemble heard here is distinguished by its lead fiddle (the nasal and piercing *tou xian)* and its stereotyped rhythmic variation patterns, some of which are heard in this piece. Amateur musicians, primarily local businessmen, play this music for recreation in a music room attached to one of the local Chinese temples. They use a variety of instruments, including—in this case—certain modern "bass" versions of traditional plucked and bowed lutes. Recorded by Terry E. Miller on 27 January 1974 at a Chinese temple in Roi-et, Thailand.

3. Khmer classical *pinn peat* ensemble dance piece "*Thep monorom*" (4:48). Performed by musicians from the Royal University of Fine Arts, Phnom Penh. During the years of the Khmer Rouge reign of terror (1975–1979), the city of Phnom Penh was emptied and thousands died or were exiled, including most musicians and dancers. After being liberated in 1979, the few surviving musicians and dancers began rebuilding Cambodia's classical traditions. The ensemble heard here consists of survivors—and young musicians trained by them—accompanying the great dance *thep monorom.* Instrumental sections alternate with vocal interludes. Recorded by Terry E. Miller on 13 December 1988 at the Royal Palace Dance Pavilion, Phnom Penh, Cambodia.

4. Thai *salaw seung pi* ensemble music (4:20). Performed by musicians led by Sanit A-phai. Northern Thai instrumental music is often called *salaw seung pi* after its three most important instruments (*salaw* being a family of bowed lutes, *seung* a plucked lute, and *pi* a free-reed pipe with finger holes). In this recording, a fipple flute *(khlui)* is substituted for the free-reed pipe. In addition, there is a pair of

small cymbals *(ching)* and a drum *(klawng)*. Playing in a tuning system distinct from those in both central and northeast Thailand, the instruments repeat a relatively short melody with continuous variations, producing heterophonic texture. Recorded by Terry E. Miller on 2 July 1994 at Mae San Pakham village, Lamphun Province, Thailand.

5. Thai *lam sing* repartee song (4:25). Sung by Mawlam Vgatri Si-wilai. Although *lam sing* is a northeastern Thai repartee genre created in 1989 by Mawlam Rattri and her brother, it has become the rage throughout Thailand. It combines the traditional accompaniment of free-reed mouth organ *(khaen)* with modern pop instruments such as electric lute *(phin)* and drum set to give it a driving, modern sound. Recorded by Terry E. Miller on 20 June 1991 in Khon Kaen, Thailand.

6. Laotian *lam salavane* repartee song ("Song of Salavane") (4:29). Sung by Bounta Duang-panya, accompanied by *khene* "free-reed mouth organ" (Mr. Bountem), *ka-japi* "lute" (Mr. Bountawee), *so i kang* "fiddle" (Mr. Bounta Duang-panya), and *kong* "drum" (Mr. Surat). This vocal genre of southern Laos, performed by acculturated Lao of upland Mon-Khmer origin, is typically accompanied by a small ensemble or by *khene* alone. This recording includes only the male singer, but a full performance would consist of male-female repartee in which the singers test each other's wits with questions of knowledge and a feigned love affair. Recorded by Terry E. Miller on 2 July 1991 in Salavane, Laos.

7. Burmese *kyo* classical song (3:36). Sung by Daw Yi Yi Thant, accompanied by *saùñ* "harp" (played by Ù Myint Mauñ) and *siwa* "cymbals and clapper" (played by Ù Mauñ Then). Recorded during a government radio station recording session as part of the preparation for a national contest, this song is performed by two of the country's most senior artists. While the vocal melody and harp accompaniment sound somewhat free and are quite flexible, they fit into a regular metric pattern articulated by the cymbals and castanet-like hinged clapper. Recorded by Terry E. Miller on 16 July 1994 at the National Theater, Rangoon, Burma.

8. Vietnamese *nhạc lễ* ritual ensemble (5:45). Musicians led by Nguyen Van Tam. *Nhạc lễ* music is associated with many kinds of rituals, both Buddhist and family centered, and is played by double reeds, fiddles, drum, gong, and a struck water buffalo horn. This recording is in the style typical of southern Vietnam, especially the delta area of the Mekong. Recorded by Terry E. Miller on 23 June 1993 in Vinh Xuan, Vinh Long Province, Vietnam.

9. Thai Dam *khắp* repartee singing (3:20). Sung by Ha Long and Ngan Thi Quang. The Thai Dam (Black Thai) minority in northern Vietnam is closely related to upland Tai minorities in Laos. This special performance was given in a large stilted wooden house for a group of visiting ethnomusicologists, surrounded by a crowd of curious onlookers. Heard first is an excerpt of the male singer's part, followed by the opening of his female partner's song. Such unaccompanied singing consists of stanzas of poetry, with the melody being generated in part by the lexical tones of the words. Recorded by Terry E. Miller on 23 June 1994 in Binh Son Village, Thanh Hoa Province, Vietnam.

10. Jarai gong ensemble with song *"Yong Thoach"* ("Brother Thoach, Please Come Back") (3:28). Sung by Y Yon. Accompanied by an ensemble consisting of individually held gongs played by members of the Jarai upland ethnic group, Y Yon sings: "Brother Thoach, please come home/The village is waiting for you/The rice fields are beautiful/Please come home to a safe place." While he is singing, female dancers encircle him and the instrumental ensemble. Recorded by Phong T. Nguyễn in February 1996 in Ae H'leo district, Dak Lak Province, in central Vietnam.

11. East Javanese *"Srempeg, pelog patet wolu"* (4:30). Gamelan ensemble directed by Pak Kasdu (drummer), managed by Pak Taslan Harsono. An example of East Javanese gamelan music used to accompany *wayang topèng* (masked dance drama) and *wayang kulit* (shadow puppetry) in the Malang region, *"Srempeg"* is similar to a Central Javanese piece of the same name used to accompany entrances, exits, and moderate levels of fighting in the theater. However, the structures are different, and East Javanese playing emphasizes crisp, highly syncopated drumming. Recorded by R. Anderson Sutton on 10 July 1986 in Karang Tengah, Java.

12. Accompanied *cakepung* song *"Pemungkah"* ("Opening") (3:41). Sekaha Cakepung "Taat," codirected by Ida Bagus Gede and Ida Bagus Djelantik. A recreational music-dance form that originated in Lombok, *cakepung* employs a group of male singers who imitate the sounds and functions of gamelan instruments. An unmetered introduction based on Hindu East Javanese romantic poems is followed by a metered section involving both instruments (flutes and bowed lute) and voices. Although such performances may accompany ritual, they can also be recreational, with much drinking of palm wine and a progressive lowering of players' inhibitions. Recorded by David Harnish on 9 July 1983 in Amlapura, Bali.

13. Sasak shadow play music *"Telaga dundan"* ("Eternal Pond") (3:30). Musicians directed by I Gede Budiarta. The theatrical tales portrayed in the shadow-puppet theater of the Sasak people of Lombok derive from the Menak cycle concerning the hero Amir Hamzah and the early Islamic world. "Telaga dundan" accompanies both the removal of the puppets from their box and the introduction of the main puppet, the gunungan (symbolizing the cosmic mountain), with two smaller puppets behind it representing Adam and Eve. The ensemble, tuned in pelog, is led by a flute (suling). Recorded by David Harnish on 23 July 1989 in Cakranegara, West Lombok.

14. Filipino ensemble pieces *"Te-ed"* and *"Kuriri"* (2:37). Performed by members of the Ajijil family. These are two examples of instrumental music performed during a festival by members of the Yakan minority from Lamitan in the southern Philippines. The instruments used are the *kwintang* (set of five small bossed gongs in a rack), *agung* (set of three deep-rimmed hanging gongs), *gabbang* (five-key xylophone), and *gandang* (bamboo slit drum). Recorded by Ramón P. Santos in 1994 in Davao City, Basilan Province, Philippines.

15. Song *"Kulilal ni puguq"* ("Kulilal of the Quail") (3:50). Performed by Bunjag (vocal) and Lamuna O (tube zither). The *kulilal* love song is of recent origin and stems from contact with peoples of the Sulu Sea. The poetry, which mixes several

languages, is made exceptionally intimate through severe simplification, allowing lovers to exchange messages in subtle and secret ways. The text is: "Oh, yes, I know it/ A weir of stones, a stony weir/ Tagperara is beyond/ I only have to walk/ And I went there/For a graceful maiden." Recorded by Nicole Revel-Macdonald, Charles Macdonald, and José Maceda in March 1972 in Kangrian, Palawan Highlands, Philippines.

INDEX

Page numbers in italics refer to figures.